THE ANIMALS READER

THE ANIMALS READER

The Essential Classic and Contemporary Writings

Edited by

Linda Kalof

and

Amy Fitzgerald

Oxford • New York

First published in 2007 by
Berg

Editorial offices:
1st Floor, Angel Court, 81 St Clements Street, Oxford, OX4 1AW, UK
175 Fifth Avenue, New York, NY 10010, USA

Berg is the imprint of Oxford International Publishers Ltd.

Library of Congress Cataloging-in-Publication Data

The animals reader : the essential classic and contemporary writings / Edited by Linda Kalof and
Amy Fitzgerald.
   p. cm.
   Includes bibliographical references and index.
   ISBN-13: 978-1-84520-469-3 (cloth)
   ISBN-10: 1-84520-469-7 (cloth)
   ISBN-13: 978-1-84520-470-9 (pbk.)
   ISBN-10: 1-84520-470-0 (pbk.)
   1. Animal welfare. 2. Animal welfare—Moral and ethical aspects. 3. Animals—Social
aspects. 4. Human-animal relationships. 5. Animal rights. I. Kalof, Linda. II. Fitzgerald, Amy J.

   HV4703.A65 2007
   179'.3—dc22

                                                                              2006037869

British Library Cataloguing-in-Publication Data

A catalogue record for this book is available from the British Library.

ISBN 978 1 84520 469 3 (Cloth)

ISBN 978 1 84520 470 9 (Paper)

Typeset by JS Typesetting, Porthcawl, Mid Glamorgan
Printed in the United Kingdom by Biddles Ltd, King's Lynn

www.bergpublishers.com

CONTENTS

3. ANIMALS AS DOMESTICATES, "PETS" AND FOOD

4. ANIMALS AS SPECTACLE AND SPORT

5. ANIMALS AS SYMBOLS

6. ANIMALS AS SCIENTIFIC OBJECTS

LIST OF ILLUSTRATIONS

Cover. Black macaques behind scratched glass, reproduced with permission of Britta Jaschinski, © Britta Jaschinski

RANDY MALAMUD

Prologue: Animals

Britta Jaschinski, whose images are reproduced at the front of each section throughout this book, is one of the premier contemporary photographers engaged in the work of representing animals. German-born and based in London, she works throughout Europe and globally. Her first collection, *Zoo* (Phaidon 1996), depicts animals in captivity from zoos around the world; her more recent *Wild Things* (powerHouse 2003) offers an ecological meditation on animals and habitats.

Jaschinski's photography is profound, and profoundly troubling. It features individual animals in settings that are often disorienting – caged, for example, or against a blank backdrop – because they are unnatural: many of the animals we see are starkly alienated from their natural habitat. The aesthetic of her photography exacerbates viewers' sense of disorientation as we look at images that are dark, or grainy, or blurry, or silhouetted, or otherwise weirdly lit and brusquely cropped.

In some ways, Jaschinski's photographs are portraits of animals: they resonate with a sense of connection to the subject; an insightful expression of the animal's identity and individuality; and an almost devout fascination with the animal's spirit. But at other times these pictures resemble mugshots: images of trapped and unhappy creatures at their worst moments of suffering, caught and fixed in the harsh frame of the image (which metaphorically evokes all the other sorts of frames people create for nonhuman animals). Paradoxically, sometimes a single picture may evoke these seemingly disparate sensibilities at the same time: both a homage to the animal's nobility and an angry protest at its constraints.

These images of animals vividly open up a panoply of questions and responses: they make us think of animals in all sorts of ways relating to their natural, active lives. What are they doing as we look at the sliver of their existence that is frozen and framed in the moment of each photograph? How are the creatures living? What movements, what instinctual urges, what behavioral patterns are suggested in the picture? And what sorts of movements, instincts, and behaviors are suppressed in these images? A large "negative text" pervades Jaschinski's photography: we are asked to see many things – habitat, activities – that are *not there*; we are forced to contemplate their absence.

What are the animals thinking at the moment we "see" them? Are the black macaques on the cover of this book sad and confused? Are they, as one might imagine, stoic, still, but with a barely suppressed fear at where they find themselves? (In this photograph they are at Chessington World of Adventure, a cheesy amusement park on the outskirts of London, of all places; they belong, of course, in a tropical rainforest. Probably they are thinking about that, too: the trees and sounds of where they aren't.) Is the Asian elephant shown at the head of Section 1 thinking, "What the hell am I doing in Hamburg? How can I get out of here?!" The killer whale, shown at the head of the volume introduction (in a tank at Sea World instead of in the ocean), seems (to me) to be thinking: steady; onward; around and around . . . can't swim straight ahead. And the gorilla, at the head of Section 6: well, I can't even venture a guess at what he's thinking – some thoughts do lie too deep.

Certainly all these conjectures are wrong. We can't know what they are thinking. It's troubling for human beings not to be able to exercise our epistemological powers, our imperial intellectual consciousness, over these creatures who are, according to the human fantasy expressed in the Book of Genesis, under our dominion. I look and look at Jaschinski's photograph of a gorilla, a lion (at the beginning of this essay), a llama (Section 3), and wonder, ceaselessly, what are they thinking? Who are they? And the answers are unresolvable, unknowable . . . and *this* is an insight.

As viewers, we must confront our own relationship to nonhuman animals – both our individual relationship and our larger implication, as a species, in a culture that exploits and oppresses animals on a vast scale – in ways that invoke the Foucauldian dynamics of power and visualization. Where are we positioned as we look at these animals (both literally – physically, spatially – and politically, in terms of our power over them)?

What are we looking at? Real animals, or culturally framed and tamed diminutions of real animals? Why are we looking at them – what do we hope to see? Something about *them*? Something "authentic"? (Would we recognize this if we saw it? Or would the experience confirm Wittgenstein's remark: "If a lion could speak, we would not understand him"?)

Or, are we looking at them to see something about ourselves? Our power over them? Our guilt? Our abrogation of their wildness as we have squandered our own wildness? Our fantasies, our fetishes, our fear/shame/insecurities about our own bodies, our selves, our presence, that we hope to salve, somehow, by looking at them? The human animal is always absent from Jaschinski's images, though we are there in spirit, and it is not a comforting spirit, but rather, a force of intrusive and blundering hubris; it is a spirit inimical to the well-being, and the natural prosperity, of the animals who are in the frame.

In this volume, Linda Kalof and Amy Fitzgerald broach the historically complex range of human cultural relations with animals. The editors have presented a rich account of this relationship from the perspective (of course) of our own species. What about the animals: who speaks for them? Jaschinski, I think, would not presume to do so, nor could she: none of us can. But her images (if we extrapolate their ethical implications) at least point us along the way toward imagining what the animals might think about their relationship with us. The essays in this book represent an accumulation of human documents, an intellectual paper trail that informs thousands of years in many cultures of human thought about animals. On their side, the animals, presumably, have no such cultural memory, no comparable cognitive archive. They must, I think, figure it out anew, each animal, in each generation, each moment in time: who *are* these creatures, clothed and intrusive, staring, menacing, possessive? Why are they looking at me? How can I live with them? Or, how can I escape from them?

Perhaps all this is self-flattery, and the animals don't spend as much time thinking about me, wondering about me, as I imagine. We cannot – despite the overarching claim of animal behaviorists – know what is in their minds. We can train them to salivate at bells and play with language blocks, but we should not delude ourselves that this is the same as knowing what they are thinking. We cannot know who they are; but this does not stop us from wondering. Jaschinski's photography brims with her own sense of wonder at animals, and inspires us to share in it. It taunts us, at times, with our lack of total power over their minds and lives. But also, it inspires us to grapple with the force that draws us, over and over, however clumsily, to these animals.

LINDA KALOF and AMY FITZGERALD

Editorial Introduction

This volume is a collection of essential readings in animal studies and was inspired by the stunning explosion in recent research and theory on the relationship between humans and other animals in both contemporary and historical contexts. The anthology addresses one of the most fiercely debated topics in contemporary science and culture: How shall we (and, some would ask, should we) rethink, rebuild and recast our relationships with other animals? Contemporary struggles with the "animal question" began to take hold in the 1970s, and over the last four decades the relationship between humans and other animals has undergone a sweeping reevaluation. It is now widely acknowledged that, in addition to human-driven habitat loss and species extinction, untold numbers of animals are commodified for consumption, exhibition, labor, science, and recreation, only to be discarded when they have outlived their usefulness – when indeed they are allowed to live at all. In addition, many now recognize the close link between our relationships with other animals and some of the most pernicious human social problems, such as slavery, sexism, and environmental degradation.

Unique in its coverage of both historical and contemporary material, *The Animals Reader* brings together 35 key writings in animal studies from a wide arena of scholarship, including philosophy, cultural studies, anthropology, environmental studies, history, geography, sociology, law, ethology, and science. Choosing material for this anthology was no easy task. For each exemplary piece included, dozens had to be passed over because of the lack of space (and, truth be told, in some cases inclusion was compromised by inordinately high permission fees). Our major criteria for selection were interdisciplinarity, influence and intrigue. We sought out those special pieces that would appeal to a broad interdisciplinary audience, that have had a major influence in how the Western world thinks about animals, and that would pique the interest of readers. Spanning thousands of years and a wide array of theoretical perspectives (including positivism, feminism, Marxism, structuralism, poststructuralism, postmodernism, and posthumanism) the readings in this anthology will provide a solid framework for understanding the current state of the multidisciplinary field of animal studies.

We have organized the material into six thematic sections. While many readings resisted easy categorization into a single section, preferring instead to span across several thematic groups (particularly the postmodern/posthumanist scholarship), we believe these six groupings are good representations of how one might collapse the voluminous historical and contemporary writings in animal studies. Each section begins with a general introduction, includes 5–7 readings and concludes with a list of further reading. Individual readings are preceded by an editorial commentary that provides a contextual background for the authors and their work and a brief preview of the reading.

We begin with a section on *Animals as Philosophical and Ethical Subjects*. Our goal here is to introduce the reader to the central philosophical and ethical underpinnings regarding the role of animals in human society and in some cases the role of humans in animal society. While the human treatment of other animals has become an increasingly hard-to-ignore contemporary social justice issue, numerous classical writers have also addressed the "animal question" and we have included this important historical perspective. Aristotle's *History of Animals* and an essay from Jeremy Bentham provide the grounding material for discussions of the hierarchical human-animal natural order that appears again and again throughout the centuries and throughout this volume. We end Section 1 with the hugely influential essay by Gilles Deleuze and Félix Guattari on *becoming-animal*, a theoretical breakthrough in thinking about the human-animal relationship and one which has centered much of the work that appears in other sections in this volume.

Animals as Reflexive Thinkers contains readings that address animal cognition, emotion, and culture. We include letters written in the mid-1600s by Réne Descartes in which he claims that animals, because they have no language, have no "thoughts." Descartes considers his opinion "not so much cruel to animals as indulgent to men" since his position allows for the guiltless killing and eating of animals. Other writings in this section provide a very different view of animals' cognitive abilities – such as Marc Bekoff's essay on cooperation and forgiveness in animals and Jeffrey Moussaieff Masson and Susan McCarthy on the evidence that many animals experience emotions such as depression, nostalgia, loneliness, disappointment, and grief.

The third section, *Animals as Domesticates, "Pets" and Food*, examines the thorny issues of pet-keeping and eating animals. These two apparently disparate themes are actually more similar in terms of the domestication of animals than they are different (although it is usually only in extreme circumstances that contemporary humans eat their pets). Steven Mithen sets the stage for thinking about animals as sources of food and affection with his essay on the archeological evidence of the prehistoric evolution of our relationship with other animals. Mithen argues that while our ancestors had a predator–prey relationship with other animals for most of prehistory, in the last 30,000 years or so animals were brought into the human social group as objects of affection. (Dogs, for example, were buried with humans in the Near East around 12,000 BC.) Harriet Ritvo discusses hunting animals to extinction, the overexploitation of animals for commercial gain, and the practices of pet-keeping that exacerbate contagious diseases including epizootic diseases that afflict factory farmed animals. Yi-Fu Tuan examines the making of pets and the "petrification" of nature and animals as aesthetically-driven practices that are at the same time both cruel and affectionate. The rest of the section is devoted to two of the most hotly contested human-animal relationship issues in contemporary society – factory farming and meat-eating.

The use of animals in sport hunting and animal-fighting activities is also a fiercely debated topic and one that we examine in Section 4 on *Animals as Spectacle and Sport*. This group of readings includes essays on the use of animals in entertainment spectacles in ancient Rome and in the contemporary world of zoos, dogfighting, and bullfighting. The section ends with an article by Matt Cartmill on sport hunting and the rise of anti-hunting sentiment with the decreasing acceptance of the arbitrary nature of the human-animal boundary.

Animals as Symbols is the theme of Section 5, and here we include some of the most cited works in the field of animal studies. First is John Berger's "Why Look at Animals?" – a very influential essay that from its inception in 1980 has probably done more to set us rethinking our relationship with animals than has any other modern piece. Written in a simple and straightforward manner, Berger despairs that animals are always the observed and never the observers, and that they have been "co-opted" into spectacles and into the family (primarily as pets or "human puppets"). We also reproduce an extract from Claude Lévi-Strauss's classic book on *Totemism* in which he argues that animals are chosen as totems not because they are good to eat but rather because they are "good to think." Boria Sax expands on this notion in an essay on "Animals as Tradition," and the last two pieces focus on animal bodies – Steve Baker writes about the body-focused postmodern animal art and Jonathan Burt takes us back to the late nineteenth century in an examination of the connection between technology and animal visibility and invisibility.

Our last theme is *Animals as Scientific Objects* – yet another highly controversial topic. The readings in Section 6 pick up on prior themes (particularly philosophy, ethics, and symbolism) in an examination of animals in science and technology. We begin with a chapter from Coral Lansbury's *The Old Brown Dog*, in which she chronicles the anti-vivisection movement of the early twenthieth century in the UK, and we end with an essay by Donna Haraway that also focuses on dogs, but in terms of biological diversity and technoscience. While a feminist critique of scientific objectivity figures prominently in many of the readings in this section, the most compelling theme is a rethinking of the boundaries between humans and animals and culture and nature – a theme that is pervasive throughout this anthology. Such a rethinking is, in our minds, an essential part of the intellectual struggle with the animal question, and we leave you with a quotation that typifies much of that endeavor:

> When your views on the world
> and your intellect are being challenged
> and you begin to feel uncomfortable
> because of a contradiction you've detected
> that is threatening your current model
> of the world or some aspect of it,
> pay attention.
> You are about to learn something.
>
> (William H. Drury, Jr., College of the
> Atlantic, Bar Harbor, Maine)

NOTE

The Editors and the Publishers have attempted to contact all copyright holders. If any omission has occurred the Publisher will be pleased to make full acknowledgement in any future edition of *The Animals Reader*.

SECTION 1

*A*nimals as Philosophical and Ethical Subjects

INTRODUCTION

Humans have been debating the philosophical and ethical dimension of our relationship with other animals since the time of the early Greeks. Pythagoras, Aristotle, Theophrastus, and later Plutarch and Porphyry have all had something to say about the ways in which humans relate to other animals, with the issues swirling around such concepts as intelligence, rationality, kinship, morality, justice and flesh-eating. Now, thousands of years later, these very same issues are part of an ongoing contentious and compelling debate surrounding the animal question: What are the similarities and differences between humans and other animals? On what grounds should we extend consideration and compassion to animals? To be treated justly, must an animal first have the capacity for language and rational thought? Is there a connection between our treatment of animals and our treatment of marginalized human groups?

We begin with readings from Aristotle's *History of Animals*. In these essays on zoology, Aristotle describes the psychological characteristics of animals, noting that some attributes such as intelligence differ only in quantity with those possessed by humans. He is well known for his description of nature as a procession from lifeless things to plants which have a progressive natural order and then to animals who have their own natural graduated differentiation. Aristotle is also known for his denial of reason to animals, a proposition that has been recast over the centuries as a denial of human kinship with animals and eventually transformed into a rigid hierarchical natural system known as the "Great Chain of Being," a ladder-type ordering system with God at the top, humans below God, other animals below humans, and the rocky earth at the very bottom. The belief that humans have dominion over "lower" animals is a pernicious consequence of this conceptualization, exaggerating the distance between humans and other animals and thus minimizing our ethical obligations to them.

Over the ensuing centuries, scholars have contested the rigid hierarchical view of nature, humans and animals, with the link between the oppression of animals and the oppression of certain human groups becoming a major theme in the philosophical and ethical discourse on the animal question. In the eighteenth century, Jeremy Bentham [whose work is reproduced in this section] contended that abuse based on species, like abuse based on race, is unjust and that moral consideration should be extended to animals because, like humans, they are capable of suffering.

Also in the eighteenth century, German philosopher Immanuel Kant argued that our ethical duties to animals are simply indirect duties to other humans, since the maltreatment of animals may make us more inclined to mistreat our fellow humans. And in the nineteenth century, Henry S. Salt wrote that the condition of domestic animals in his time was no different than the condition of slaves 100 years earlier. More recently, Marjorie Spiegel [whose work is reproduced in this section] makes the explicit link between the enslavement of animals and human slavery. She argues that the tools, structures and ideologies that make the enslavement and oppression of other species possible are similarly employed in the enslavement of humans.

Jeremy Bentham's extension of consideration to animals was part of his concept of "utilitarianism," in which he advocated the "greatest happiness principle" that that which brings the greatest happiness is good. The moral principle of "equal consideration of interests" (derived from Bentham's "each to count for one, and none for more than one") is egalitarian and proposes that no interests should be excluded or treated differently – that all interests have equal weight. Peter Singer, perhaps the world's most influential living philosopher, also promotes a utilitarian approach to animal ethics, adopting Bentham's equal-consideration-of-interests principle as the foundation of his own ethical theory. Singer argues that we should treat other animals at least as well as we would treat cognitively similar humans. As outlined in his reading reproduced in this section, Singer's ethical argument is not based on the claim that animals are entitled to rights. A rights-based position is presented by Tom Regan, who argues that animals possess moral rights, as humans do – animals, like humans, are "subjects-of-a-life," and all subjects-of-a-life have inherent value and thus moral rights. In this reading, Regan argues that rights are conceptually and realistically important to the lives of animals – "Rights being the trump card in the moral game, it is not larger cages [as might satisfy animal welfarists], but empty cages" that are needed.

Martha Nussbaum has yet another ethical view on the animal question – we should not focus on animal interests or rights, but rather on animal capabilities. She draws on the confinement of circus animals to argue that preventing animals from actualizing their capabilities and living with dignity is unjust. Nussbaum perceives her approach as different from Kantian philosophy (which accords respect and moral concern only to rational beings) and utilitarian approaches (which are concerned with the maximization of happiness or pleasure and the reduction of pain). Nussbaum's approach is therefore similar to Regan's in that her focus is more on individual-level functioning. She also contends that the capabilities of some types of animals (such as primates) are greater than the capabilities of other types of animals (such as mice) so that the level of treatment that might be considered unjust for one might not be considered unjust for another.

We end the section with a reading by Gilles Deleuze and Félix Guattari that takes the philosophy of our relationship with other animals in a different direction altogether. In their essay on *becoming-animal*, Deleuze and Guattari argue that the focus should be on affinity relations, or an alliance with animals. They reject the importance of pointing to similarities between humans and animals (such as rationality and sentience); instead they emphasize *differences*. Thus, becoming-animal is not about family, nor about imitating or regressing or progressing toward something, but rather is about a *multiplicity* of differences, with beings always expanding and in transition. Developed in opposition to Hegelian dialectics which perceives the world in terms of polarities, the notions of becoming-animal and multiplicity capture the importance of celebrating difference and diversity over sameness, similarity, and kinship, issues which have dominated our ethical stance toward other animals for centuries.

1

ARISTOTLE

The History of Animals*

Aristotle lived in the fourth century BC, studied philosophy with Plato and was Alexander the Great's teacher. A devout materialist who emphasized biology and matter, Aristotle wrote about physics, zoology, ethics and politics, and his expansive work on animal physiology was considered authoritative many centuries after his death. We reproduce extracts from two of Aristotle's essays from The History of Animals, in which he proposes the existence of fixed categories of beings, or "species." He conceptualizes these categories as being hierarchically ordered, with humans at the top and insects at the bottom – a system later known as "scala naturae" or the "Great Chain of Being." Aristotle's hierarchical view of species has a strong legacy, and many scholars have engaged in a dialogue against it, as will be seen in numerous readings in this volume. While arguing that the life of animals is entirely concentrated into two activities (procreating and feeding), Aristotle also maintains that animals are cunning and have intelligence, characteristics that differ only quantitatively in humans, a notion that will be taken up in Section 2.

BOOK VIII, 1

In the great majority of animals there are traces of psychical qualities or attitudes, which qualities are more markedly differentiated in the case of human beings. For just as we pointed out resemblances in the physical organs, so in a number of animals we observe gentleness or fierceness, mildness or cross temper, courage, or timidity, fear or confidence, high spirit or low cunning, and, with regard to intelligence, something equivalent to sagacity. Some of these qualities in man, as compared with the corresponding qualities in animals, differ only quantitatively: that is to say, a man has more or less of this quality, and an animal has more or less of some other; other qualities in man are represented by analogous and not identical qualities: for instance, just as in man we find knowledge, wisdom, and sagacity, so in certain animals there exists some other natural potentiality akin to these. The truth of this statement will be the more clearly apprehended if we have regard to the phenomena of childhood: for in children may be observed the traces and seeds of what will one day be settled psychological habits,

* These extracts are in the public domain and were reprinted from Aristotle's *The History of Animals*, obtained from eBooks@Adelaide, University of Adelaide Library, at the following website: http://etext.library.adelaide.edu.au/a/aristotle/history/index.html. The text is based on the translation of *The History of Animals* by D'Arcy Wentworth Thompson.

though psychologically a child hardly differs for the time being from an animal; so that one is quite justified in saying that, as regards man and animals, certain psychical qualities are identical with one another, while others resemble, and others are analogous to, each other.

Nature proceeds little by little from things lifeless to animal life in such a way that it is impossible to determine the exact line of demarcation, nor on which side thereof an intermediate form should lie. Thus, next after lifeless things in the upward scale comes the plant, and of plants one will differ from another as to its amount of apparent vitality; and, in a word, the whole genus of plants, while it is devoid of life as compared with an animal, is endowed with life as compared with other corporeal entities. Indeed, as we just remarked, there is observed in plants a continuous scale of ascent toward the animal. So, in the sea, there are certain objects concerning which one would be at a loss to determine whether they be animal or vegetable. For instance, certain of these objects are fairly rooted, and in several cases perish if detached; thus the pinna is rooted to a particular spot, and the solen (or razor-shell) cannot survive withdrawal from its burrow. Indeed, broadly speaking, the entire genus of testaceans have a resemblance to vegetables, if they be contrasted with such animals as are capable of progression.

In regard to sensibility, some animals give no indication whatsoever of it, while others indicate it but indistinctly. Further, the substance of some of these intermediate creatures is fleshlike, as is the case with the so-called tethya (or ascidians) and the acalephae (or sea-anemones); but the sponge is in every respect like a vegetable. And so throughout the entire animal scale there is a graduated differentiation in amount of vitality and in capacity for motion.

A similar statement holds good with regard to habits of life. Thus of plants that spring from seed the one function seems to be the reproduction of their own particular species, and the sphere of action with certain animals is similarly limited. The faculty of reproduction, then, is common to

all alike. If sensibility be superadded, then their lives will differ from one another in respect to sexual intercourse through the varying amount of pleasure derived therefrom, and also in regard to modes of parturition and ways of rearing their young. Some animals, like plants, simply procreate their own species at definite seasons; other animals busy themselves also in procuring food for their young, and after they are reared quit them and have no further dealings with them; other animals are more intelligent and endowed with memory, and they live with their offspring for a longer period and on a more social footing.

The life of animals, then, may be divided into two acts – procreation and feeding; for on these two acts all their interests and life concentrate. Their food depends chiefly on the substance of which they are severally constituted; for the source of their growth in all cases will be this substance. And whatsoever is in conformity with nature is pleasant, and all animals pursue pleasure in keeping with their nature.

BOOK IX, 7

[…] In a general way in the lives of animals many resemblances to human life may be observed. Preeminent intelligence will be seen more in small creatures than in large ones, as is exemplified in the case of birds by the nest building of the swallow. In the same way as men do, the bird mixes mud and chaff together; if it runs short of mud, it souses its body in water and rolls about in the dry dust with wet feathers; furthermore, just as man does, it makes a bed of straw, putting hard material below for a foundation, and adapting all to suit its own size. Both parents cooperate in the rearing of the young; each of the parents will detect, with practised eye, the young one that has had a helping, and will take care it is not helped twice over; at first the parents will rid the nest of excrement, but, when the young are grown, they will teach their young to shift their position and let their excrement fall over the side of the nest.

Pigeons exhibit other phenomena with a similar likeness to the ways of humankind. In pairing the same male and the same female keep together; and the union is only broken by the death of one of the two parties. At the time of parturition in the female the sympathetic attentions of the male are extraordinary; if the female is afraid on account of the impending parturition to enter the nest, the male will beat her and force her to come in. When the young are born, he will take and masticate pieces of suitable food, will open the beaks of the fledglings, and inject these pieces, thus preparing them betimes to take food. (When the male bird is about to expel the the young ones from the nest he cohabits with them all.) As a general rule these birds show this conjugal fidelity, but occasionally a female will cohabit with other than her mate. These birds are combative, and quarrel with one another, and enter each other's nests, though this occurs but seldom; at a distance from their nests this quarrelsomeness is less marked, but in the close neighbourhood of their nests they will fight desperately. [...]

2

JEREMY BENTHAM

Principles of Morals and Legislation*

Jeremy Bentham was an eighteenth-century English philosopher, jurist, legal critic and social reformer [he supported animal rights, equal rights for women, the abolition of slavery and the abolition of physical punishment]. Bentham is known for his engineering marvel the panopticon, or "inspection house," an octagonal design used to keep persons under constant inspection [later called surveillance by Foucault] – such as prisons, mental institutions and zoos – an architectural design that was first used in the construction of the famous menagerie at Versailles in the seventeenth century. But Bentham is best known for his groundbreaking work in utilitarian philosophy (a proposition that the greatest good comes from that which brings the greatest happiness). In his maxim that "each to count for one, and none for more than one" (called the moral principle of "equal consideration of interests"), all interests have equal weight, and Bentham included the interests of animals in that calculation. We reproduce an extract from Bentham's *Principles of Morals and Legislation* (1789) in which he reflects upon the plight of animals and draws a comparison between their treatment and that of human slaves, a link that was taken up again in the late 1800s by Henry S. Salt and also by numerous contemporary scholars such as Marjorie Spiegel [whose work is represented later in this section]. Bentham raises a question that is still being debated today: On what grounds should humans extend consideration and compassion to animals? Bentham's response to his own question is widely quoted: "the question is not, Can they reason? Nor Can they talk? But, Can they suffer?"

CHAPTER XVII

Under the Gentoo and Mahometan religions, the interests of the rest of the animal creation seem to have met with some attention. Why have they not universally, with as much as those of human creatures, allowance made for the difference in point of sensibility? Because the laws that are have been the work of mutual fear; a sentiment which the less rational animals have not had the same means as man has of turning to account. Why *ought* they not? No reason can be given. If the being eaten were all, there is very good reason why we should be suffered to eat

* This extract was reprinted from Jeremy Bentham's *Principles of Morals and Legislation*, obtained from the following website maintained by the University of Texas at Austin: http://www.la.utexas.edu/research/poltheory/bentham/ipml/ ipml.c17.s01.n02.html

such of them as we like to eat: we are the better for it, and they are never the worse. They have none of those long-protracted anticipations of future misery which we have. The death they suffer in our hands commonly is, and always may be, a speedier, and by that means a less painful one, than that which would await them in the inevitable course of nature. If the being killed were all, there is very good reason why we should be suffered to kill such as molest us: we should be the worse for their living, and they are never the worse for being dead. But is there any reason why we should be suffered to torment them? Not any that I can see. Are there any why we should *not* be suffered to torment them? Yes, several.

[...]

The day has been, I grieve to say in many places it is not yet past, in which the greater part of the species, under the denomination of slaves, have been treated by the law exactly upon the same footing as, in England for example, the inferior races of animals are still. The day *may* come, when the rest of the animal creation may acquire those rights which never could have been withholden from them but by the hand of tyranny. The French have already discovered that the blackness of the skin is no reason why a human being should be abandoned without redress to the caprice of a tormentor (see Lewis XIV's Code Noir). It may come one day to be recognized, that the number of the legs, the villosity of the skin, or the termination of the *os sacrum*, are reasons equally insufficient for abandoning a sensitive being to the same fate. What else is it that should trace the insuperable line? Is it the faculty of reason, or, perhaps, the faculty of discourse? But a full-grown horse or dog is beyond comparison a more rational, as well as a more conversable animal, than an infant of a day, or a week, or even a month, old. But suppose the case were otherwise, what would it avail? the question is not, Can they *reason*? nor, Can they *talk*? but, Can they *suffer*?

3

MARJORIE SPIEGEL

In Defense of Slavery*

Marjorie Spiegel is the co-founder and executive director of the Institute for the Development of Earth Awareness (IDEA). We reproduce a chapter from her thought-provoking book, *The Dreaded Comparison: Human and Animal Slavery* [originally published in 1988 and revised in 1997] in which she examines the similarities between the enslavement of oppressed humans and the enslavement of other animals, such as the brandings and auctions of human slaves and animals, transportation of humans and animals within both "slave trades," and the ideological rationalizations used to justify both forms of slavery. In this extract, Spiegel focuses on the justification of both human and animal slavery based on the specious notion that enslavement is in the best interests of the slaves, through the assertion that they are incapable of providing for themselves. She cites the writings of Aristotle [who wrote that animals and some groups of humans actually benefit from enslavement], a pro-slavery novel, and sentiments among workers in factory farms as evidence of a common rationalization for the enslavement of others, and she argues that the oppression of one group can be mobilized to justify the oppression of another. Spiegel's book title, *The Dreaded Comparison*, purposefully confronts the difficulty of acknowledging the connection between the oppression of humans and the oppression of other animals. Some would be more comfortable not making such comparisons. However, Spiegel demonstrates that the connection between the oppression of human groups and that of other animals has serious implications, and that failure to address the ideologies, values and beliefs which make oppression possible places both humans and other animals at risk.

[The abolition of the slave trade] would be extreme cruelty to the African savages, a portion of whom it saves from massacre, or intolerable bondage in their own country, and introduces into a much happier state of life. (James Boswell, 1740–1795)

In the eighteenth century it was widely urged that domestication was good for animals; it civilized them and increased their numbers: "we multiply life, sensation and enjoyment." (Keith Thomas, *Man and the Natural World*, quoting Benjamin Rush, M.D., 1746–1813)

[It was] best for the beasts that they should be under man. (*The Theological, Philosophical, Miscellaneous Works of the Reverend William Jones*, 1801)

* Reprinted with permission from Marjorie Spiegel and Mirror Books/IDEA (1997) *The Dreaded Comparison*. New York: Mirror Books/IDEA.

It has long been contended that, for some – and of course, never *us*, but always them – life as a slave proves more beneficial than detrimental. In fact, two thousand years before any of the above sentiments were expressed, Aristotle had used this same approach in his attempt to justify the subjugation and domestication of animals and some humans. For this rationalization to be effective, the victims need to be transformed – in the mind of the captor/master – from oppressed beings to thankful underlings; grateful for being used, appreciated, and protected, while fulfilling the needs of their superiors. Wrote Aristotle:

> For all tame animals there is an advantage in being under human control, as this secures their survival. And as regards the relationship between male and female, the former is naturally superior, the latter inferior, the former rules and the latter is subject.
>
> By analogy, the same must necessarily apply to mankind as a whole. Therefore all men who differ from one another by as much as the soul differs from the body or man from a wild beast (and that is the state of those who can work by using their bodies, and for whom that is the best they can do) – these people are slaves by nature, and it is better for them to be subject to this kind of control, and it is better for the other creatures I have mentioned. For a man who is able to belong to another person is by nature a slave (for that IS why he belongs to someone else) ... Assistance regarding the necessities of life is provided by both groups, by slaves and by domestic animals. Nature must therefore have intended to make the bodies of free men and of slaves different also; slaves' bodies strong for the services they have to do, those of free men upright and not much use for that kind of work, but instead useful for community life.[1]

In 1832, John P. Kennedy published a widely read novel, *Swallow Barn*, whose narrator was supposed to be from the liberal North. The narrator visits a plantation in Virginia expecting to see all manner of horrors perpetrated upon those whom he presupposes are the miserable victims of slavery. But, (and what an enlightening experience!) he finds only, in the words of Sterling Brown, "a kindly patriarchy and grateful, happy slaves." [2] Kennedy's narrator croons,

> I am sure they could never become a happier people than I find here ... No tribe of people has ever passed from barbarism to civilization whose progress has been more secure from harm, more genial to their character, or better supplied with mild and beneficent guardianship, adapted to the actual state of their intellectual feebleness, than the Negroes of Swallow Barn. And from what I can gather, it is pretty much the same on the other estates in this region.[3]

Similarly, a worker in an egg "factory" revealed parallel attitudes to me in the course of an interview I conducted with her. The conditions in the area where the chickens were housed were so abhorrent that I had to go outside every few minutes to breathe. Dust and ammonia filled the air, as the excrement pit beneath the rows and rows of cages holding the "laying-hens" was emptied only once every two years. The chickens were living four-to-a-cage a little larger than the size of a record album cover, and had been de-beaked, a process in which part of their upper mandibles are cut off. They lived in these conditions for two years until they were moved into trucks – their first and only experience of the outdoors – and driven to a slaughter-house. Below is a portion of my conversation with the worker:

Q: Do you think about the chickens much?
A: Usually I don't ... The chickens here ... know where their next meal is coming from, and they don't have to worry about predators ...
Q: It seems like a lot of their natural tendencies are inhibited, though, in terms of expression, a pecking order, being able to mate ...
A: Well, no, they don't mate. They do, oh ... they stretch; and they're happy. We see them, when we're walking through the place removing the dead and they stretch. The pecking order: I think they have it in their individual cages.

Q: Well, not being able to walk, or turn around, or scratch ...

A: Well on the other hand, if we were to put them out on the floor, it would take a lot more labor to gather the eggs. And eggs would cost a great deal more.

Q: But in terms of the chickens who are doing the actual work, producing the eggs. What would they be happier with?

A: On the other hand, what's the alternative? Do we quit eating eggs?

Q: Why do you have to de-beak them?

A: The chickens will, in their pecking order, pick on the weakest chicken ... Once they draw blood, then they just keep ongoing. They're quite cannibalistic.

Q: But when they're in a barnyard that usually doesn't happen.

A: No, but then the one who's being picked on can get away.

Swallow Barn was intentionally written as a pro-slavery propaganda piece, whereas the comments of the egg-worker show how thoroughly a person is able to *internalize* propaganda. While the novel hoped to convince those who had *never visited* a plantation of the idyllic life led by plantation slaves, the interview reveals how it is possible to be daily confronted with reality, yet cease to see it.

What is at work here in both these instances is an attempt to brush over a potentially unsettling reality; to cease to hear the cries of our slaves, to believe that their spilt blood means something different from our own, and, finally, to believe that not only is the bondage we impose upon our slaves not a hindrance to them, but that it is a benefit.

In his book *The Pursuit of Loneliness: American Culture at the Breaking Point*, sociologist Philip Slater describes a pattern of thought which he terms "The Toilet Assumption,"

the notion that unwanted matter, unwanted difficulties, unwanted complexities and obstacles will disappear if they're removed from our immediate field of vision ...

He continues:

Our approach to social problems is to decrease their visibility. This is the real foundation of racial segregation, especially in its most extreme case, the Indian "reservation." The result of our social efforts has been to remove the underlying problems of our society farther and farther from daily experiences and daily consciousness, and hence to decrease in the mass of the population, the knowledge, skill, and motivation necessary to deal with them.[4]

Whether we defend the violation of another's life through our denial of a reality which makes us uncomfortable, or through outright enthusiasm for oppressive power relations, the results are devastating. Such dynamics allow us to perpetuate and escalate actions which prevent others from pursuing their own destinies. Thus it is that we can happily bring our children to the zoo, to see the animals permanently displayed there, and believe that their comparatively barren, uni-dimensional existences might mimic the wild, that their dearly-gained "security" might compensate for their almost fathomless lost freedom – a freedom doubly, irretrievably, lost because beyond the walls and cages of the zoo we are permitting the irrevocable destruction of their natural habitats. It is noteworthy that even as recently as 1906, the New York Zoological Society displayed an African Pygmy, named Ota Benga, in a cage with chimpanzees.[5]

The pattern of thought described so insightfully by Slater and which is so necessary for those who wish to simply ignore the myriad problems and suffering inherent to oppression is also an integral requirement for the maintenance and perpetuation of the secrecy which surrounds the machinery of oppression. [...]

If you do not see the victims of cruelty and can explain cruelty away and live with the destruction comfortably, you are adrift ...

Philip P. Hallie, *Cruelty*

NOTES

1. Aristotle, *Politics,* 1.5.
2. Sterling A. Brown, "Negro Character as Seen by White Authors," in *Dark Symphony: Negro Literature in America* (New York: The Free Press, 1968), 155–156.
3. John P. Kennedy, *Swallow Barn* (Carey and Lea, 1832), cited in Brown, "Negro Character," 142.
4. Philip Slater, *The Pursuit of Loneliness: American Culture at the Breaking Point* (Boston: Beacon, 1970), 21–22.
5. Phillips Verner Bradford and Harvey Blume, *Ota Benga* (New York: St. Martin's, 1992), 168–190. Ten years after his release from the zoo, and unable to afford passage back to Africa, Ota Benga committed suicide.

4

PETER SINGER

Animal Liberation or Animal Rights?*

Peter Singer is an Australian philosopher and author of *Animal Liberation*, an enormously influential book about our ethical obligations to animals. In addition to writing about the ethical treatment of animals, Singer is the author of books on topics as varied as reproductive ethics, issues related to disability, and the ethics of US President George W. Bush. He is also one of the founding members of the Great Ape Project, an international group dedicated to changing the classification of great apes from property to sentient beings protected by rights. In his writings Singer embraces Bentham's utilitarian approach to ethics, and the principle of "equal consideration of interests" serves as the foundation of his theory of ethics. Singer argues that the interests of animals should not be considered less than those of humans at a similar cognitive level, and in calculating whether the benefits of an action outweigh the harms it would bring, the interests of animals must be given equal consideration to those of humans. The implication of this reasoning is that most of the ways in which animals are currently treated must be deemed unethical; however, in some instances, such as certain types of animal experimentation, the use of animals could be considered ethical if the benefits outweigh the harms, taking both human and animal interests into consideration. Singer's writings have had a profound influence on what has come to be known as the animal-rights movement, and on articulations of demands for animal rights. However, Singer does not invoke a rights-based discourse per se, and in the piece reproduced below he is engaged in an exchange with Tom Regan [whose work appears after Singer's extract] over the use of the term "animal rights." On the surface, this may appear to be a trivial matter of linguistic preference, but as Singer and Regan demonstrate, what may appear to some as little more than a choice of terminology actually obscures the larger philosophical debate between utilitarian and rights-based positions.

In replying to my review of *The Case for Animal Rights* in *The New York Review of Books*, Tom Regan notes that whereas I use the term "the animal liberation movement" to refer to the many people and organizations around the world advocating a complete change in the moral status of animals, he prefers the label "animal rights movement."[1] There is, he says, "more than a verbal difference here." For immediate practical purposes the difference may not matter very much – Regan and I are plainly at one in our attempts to eliminate the atrocities now inflicted on animals in factory farms, laboratories and in the wild. I am even prepared to speak of "animal rights" – just as I am prepared to speak of "human rights" – as a shorthand reference to the way in which the needs and desires of animals give rise to moral obligations on our part. But the philosophical difference between those who, like Regan, ground their case for animals on claims about rights, and those who, like me, do not, is fundamental. In the long run it may also have practical implications. This essay explains why I do not, philosophically, accept the animal rights approach.

I

In *Animals' Rights*, first published in 1892, Henry Salt asked: "Have the lower animals 'rights'?" He answered his own question: "Undoubtedly – if men have."[2] I agree entirely. If there are any rights possessed by all human beings, those rights are also possessed by nonhuman animals. For any rights possessed by all human beings cannot be possessed in virtue of such special human characteristics as rationality, autonomy, self-consciousness, the ability to enter into contracts, or to reciprocate, or anything of this sort. Such a basis for rights would leave out those humans who, through infancy or congenital disability, never have had – and in some cases never will have – these special characteristics.

Some philosophers have suggested that even though infant and brain-damaged humans may not be strictly entitled to the same moral status as more mature normal humans, they should be granted "courtesy status" as humans. Otherwise, it may be argued, the borderline between those who have moral rights and those who do not will become blurred; and there is the possibility of a dangerous slide which could threaten the rights of those who *are* fully entitled to moral rights.[3] This looks suspiciously like an *ad hoc* proposal

designed to protect our conventional attitudes from change; but if it is to be taken seriously, some evidence for the likelihood of such a dangerous slide would need to be provided. Such evidence as is available seems to count against such a slide. Many human societies have denied the right to life to newborn infants, especially those born handicapped. They appear to be no more prone than our own society to violate the rights of adult humans – indeed, if anything, less prone to do so.[4] Moreover if the decision to grant such courtesy status is to be decided by weighing up the consequences of granting or denying it, we must include in the calculation the way in which this enables us to put a fictitious gulf between ourselves and other animals, to the great detriment of the latter.

Nor can we say that all human beings have rights just because they are members of the species *homo sapiens* – that is speciesism, a form of favouritism for our own that is as unjustifiable as racism. Thus if *all* humans have rights, it would have to be because of some much more minimal characteristics, such as being living creatures. Any such minimal characteristics would, of course, be possessed by nonhuman as well as by human animals.

I shall not here consider the view that some more restricted class of human beings has rights not possessed by other humans or by nonhuman animals. This is, for obvious reasons, much easier to defend. If we see rights as arising from tacit acceptance of a social contract, or from an ability to understand a concept of justice and act in accordance with it, then we may limit rights to those beings who satisfy this requirement. Such a limitation cannot explain why – to give just one example – we see fit to poison animals to death in order to test food additives, when we would not contemplate using human infants for the same purpose (not even orphaned or abandoned infants who have been born with severe brain damage). Hence this approach to human rights is not relevant to the aims of the animal liberation/animal rights movement, which seeks to raise the moral status of animals so that they too are not subjected to such treatment.

Thus my rejection of animal rights has nothing to do with the fact that they are the rights of *animals*: it has everything to do with the fact that they are *rights*. The problem is not with the extension to animals of rights possessed by human beings, including those humans who have no relevant characteristics not also possessed by some animals. It is, rather, with the kind of right that could be possessed both by those human beings and by other animals.

II

Attributing rights to animals is not, of course, the only way of changing their moral status. One can also ground the case for change on the fact that animals have interests. Interests are central to many moral theories. Utilitarian theories, in particular, tend to be based on interests or something closely related to interests, such as preferences, or the experience of pleasure and pain. Not all interest-based theories, however, are utilitarian. It is possible to combine a concern with interests and a non-utilitarian principle of distribution, for instance Rawls's maximin principle. Thus one does not have to be a utilitarian to take interests as the basis upon which moral judgments are to be made.

Given a moral theory based on interests, it is easy enough to argue that we are not justified in ignoring or discounting the interests of any human being on the grounds that he or she is not a member of the race or sex to which we belong. This principle of equal consideration of interests is widely accepted in so far as it applies to human beings. Once so accepted, however, it is very difficult to find any logical basis for resisting its extension to *all* beings with interests. This means that nonhuman animals, or at least all nonhuman animals capable of conscious experiences such as pain or pleasure, enter the sphere of moral concern. Moreover they enter it with a fundamentally equal moral status: their interests are to be given the same consideration as the like interests of any other being.[5]

Once nonhuman animals are recognized as coming within the sphere of equal consideration of interests, it is immediately clear that we must stop treating hens as machines for turning grain into eggs, rats as living toxicology testing kits, and whales as floating reservoirs of oil and blubber. All these practices – and the list could be continued for a long time – are based on treating animals as things to be used for our advantage, without any thought being given to the interests of the animals themselves. The inclusion of animals within the sphere of equal consideration could not leave such practices intact.

Other aspects of our treatment of animals require more detailed discussion. Since the interests of nonhuman animals are not always the same as those of normal non-infant human beings, it does not follow from the principle of equal consideration of interests that we must treat nonhuman animals in the same way as we treat humans. Would it, for instance, be morally acceptable to rear animals in conditions which satisfied all their needs, and then kill them painlessly for food? Are *any* experiments on animals justified? These are not easy questions and they do not have simple answers. I shall not attempt to answer them here, beyond saying that one obviously relevant issue is whether nonhuman animals have the same interest in continued life as normal humans do.[6] The point is that we must try in each case to work out what will be best for all those involved. In this way a view based on interests includes nonhuman animals within the moral sphere, on the basis of full equality of consideration. It also remains sensitive to the particular circumstances of the question at issue.

III

So what reason can there be for asserting that animals are entitled not merely to equal consideration of their interests, but to moral *rights*? For an answer we can look at Regan's *The Case for Animal Rights*. Since this is easily the most careful and thorough defense of the claim that animals have rights, we can be sure that in considering its arguments, we are taking the case for rights in its strongest form.

Regan begins by assembling evidence for the belief that some nonhuman animals – in particular, mammals beyond the stage of infancy – are what he calls "subjects-of-a-life." By this expression Regan means that these animals are individuals with beliefs, desires, perception, memory, a sense of the future, an emotional life, preferences, the ability to initiate action in pursuit of goals, psychophysical identity over time, and an individual welfare in the sense that things can go well or badly for them. Regan then asserts that all subjects-of-a-life have inherent value.

To this point there is nothing with which a utilitarian need disagree. Whether nonhuman animals do in fact have beliefs, desires, preferences and so on is, of course, a factual question, not a moral one. Without pursuing the complex philosophical issues it raises, or going into the finer details of the kind of beliefs which creatures without language may have, I shall simply say that I think Regan is, on the whole, right about this factual question.

Moreover, the utilitarian can also accept the substantive moral claim that subjects-of-a-life have inherent value. The meaning a utilitarian would give to this claim is as follows. Subjects-of-a-life are not *things*. They are not like lumps of coal, which have instrumental value because they keep us warm, but have no intrinsic value of their own. On the contrary, subjects-of-a-life have inherent value in precisely the same way as we do. They have preferences, and they have a welfare. Their welfare matters, and no defensible moral judgments can ignore or discount their interests.

Utilitarianism, therefore, does recognize the inherent value of those beings which Regan calls subjects-of-a-life. But Regan does not think that this recognition goes far enough. Let us look at what he says proper recognition would require:

> …we may say that we fail to treat individuals who have inherent value with the respect they are due, as a matter of strict justice, whenever we treat them *as if they lacked* inherent value, and we treat them in this way whenever we treat them *as if they were mere receptacles* of valuable experiences (e.g., pleasure or preference satisfaction) or *as if their value depended upon their utility* relative to the interests of others. In particular, therefore, we fail to display proper respect for those who have inherent value whenever we harm them so that we may bring about the best aggregate consequences for everyone affected by the outcome of such treatment.[7]

This passage needs to be dissected with some care, for it lumps together, under the heading of "treating individuals as if they lacked inherent value," three quite separate forms of treatment. These three forms of treatment are:

i.   Treating individuals as if they were mere receptacles of valuable experiences;

ii. Treating individuals as if their value depended upon their utility relative to the interests of others; and

iii. Harming individuals so that we may bring about the best aggregate consequences for everyone affected by the outcome of such treatment.

It is obvious that the first two are not equivalent. Nor is it apparent how, as Regan's words suggest, the third can in some way be a particular application of the first two. We must therefore ask separately in each case whether the form of treatment described is genuinely a case of treating individuals as if they lacked inherent value.

Let us begin with (ii), since this is the least controversial. It is, in fact, a description of treating individuals as if they possessed only instrumental value. To use my earlier example, it is the way we treat lumps of coal, and Regan is clearly right to say that it is incompatible with a recognition of the inherent value of the individuals so treated. As we have already seen, no utilitarian would accept such treatment of subjects-of-a-life.

What about (i)? This is more difficult. It may seem that to treat individuals as "mere receptacles" must fail to recognize their inherent value. After all, when we think of receptacles such as boxes or bottles – considering them *qua* receptacle, and not as objects of artistic or commercial value in their own right – we think of their instrumental value in holding something else, and it is the contents which really matter. So, if utilitarians think of pigs, for instance, as valuable only because of the capacity of pigs to experience pleasure or preference satisfaction, aren't they necessarily denying inherent value to pigs?

The analogy is misleading. Sentient creatures are not receptacles for valuable experiences in the way that bottles, for instance, are receptacles for wine. If I have a bottle of wine in my hand, I can pour the wine out of the bottle; but there is no way in which I can separate the valuable experiences of pigs from the pigs themselves. We cannot even make sense of the idea of an experience – whether of pleasure, or preference satisfaction, or anything else – floating around detached from all sentient creatures. Hence the distinction between treating individuals as if they possessed inherent value, and treating them as if their experiences possessed inherent value, is much more problematic than we might at first glance suspect.

I can think of only two ways in which such a distinction might make sense. First, one might distinguish between those who hold that individuals possess inherent value only as long as they are capable of having certain experiences, and those who hold that individuals possess inherent value as long as they are alive. On the first view, an individual who falls into a total and irreversible coma ceases to have inherent value; on the second view such an individual continues to have inherent value. Utilitarians would take the first view. It might be said that this shows that they treat individuals as if they were mere receptacles of valuable experiences, for as soon as individuals cease to be capable of having these experiences, utilitarians cease to value them. But I do not think this could be what Regan means

when he refers to treating individuals as if they were mere receptacles of valuable experiences. After all, individuals in total and irreversible comas have ceased to be subjects-of-a-life, and so presumably Regan would agree with the utilitarian that they have lost the inherent value they once possessed.

The key to the second way in which one might distinguish between recognizing the inherent value of individuals, and recognizing the inherent value of their experiences, lies in our attitude to the continued existence of particular individuals over time. Suppose that we have a group of individuals enjoying pleasurable experiences, and we are faced with two options: the same group of individuals will continue to enjoy pleasurable experiences; or, they will all be painlessly killed, and replaced with another group of individuals enjoying equally pleasurable experiences. Utilitarians appear to be committed to saying that, other things being equal, there is no difference between these options. This may be taken as proof that they treat the individuals in question as lacking inherent value.

There are two points to be made about this example. First, it is essential to appreciate that the example does not allow us to drive a wedge between the inherent value of the individuals and the inherent value of their experiences, *while the individuals are having those experiences*. Even if utilitarians are committed to saying that there is no difference between the options, they will still hold that the individuals have inherent value during every instant of their existence. Thus the example has application only to the specific point of whether we attribute inherent value to the *continued* – rather than the moment-by-moment – existence of particular individuals.

Second, not all utilitarians are committed to treating subjects-of-a-life as if they were replaceable in this manner. Hedonistic utilitarians may be, but preference utilitarians are not. In *Practical Ethics* I wrote:

Rational, self-conscious beings are individuals, leading lives of their own, not mere receptacles for containing a certain quantity of happiness. Beings that are conscious, but not self-conscious, on the other hand, can properly be regarded as receptacles for experiences of pleasure and pain, rather than as individuals leading lives of their own.8

With the benefit of hindsight, I can see that the use of the term "receptacles" was liable to mislead; but I still hold that a preference utilitarian must take into account the preferences for continued life which some individuals have. This means that preference utilitarians will not be indifferent to the choice between the two options described above, except in those cases in which the individuals have no preferences for continued existence. Note, incidentally, that at least so far as my own version of preference utilitarianism is concerned, Regan is wrong to describe "preference satisfaction" as some kind of "experience." What the preference utilitarian seeks to maximize is not an experience of satisfaction, but the bringing about of what is preferred, whether or not this produces "satisfaction" in the individual who has the preference. That is why killing an individual who prefers to go on living is not justified by creating a new individual with a preference to go on living. Even if the preference of this new individual will be satisfied, the negative aspect of the unsatisfied preference of the previous individual has not been made up by the creation of the new preference plus its satisfaction.9

Apart from individuals whose lives are so miserable that they do not wish to continue living, the only individuals likely to have no preferences for continued life will be those incapable of having such preferences because they are not self-conscious and hence are incapable of conceiving of their own life as either continuing or coming to an end. Since Regan includes memory and a sense of the future, including one's own future, in his list of the characteristics which subjects-of-a-life must possess, it is clear that the individuals which a preference utilitarian may regard as replaceable are not subjects-of-a-life.

We have been considering the suggestion that utilitarians fail to recognize the inherent value of individuals when they treat them as if they were mere receptacles of valuable experiences. We have now seen that utilitarians do not regard sentient creatures as "mere receptacles," if by this is meant that they value the experiences of these creatures and not the creatures themselves. Considered on an instant-by-instant basis, this distinction cannot intelligibly be drawn. If, on the other hand, we transform the question into one which hinges on whether utilitarians attribute value to the *continued* existence of particular individuals, we find that preference utilitarians, at least, *will* attribute value to the continued existence of all those beings whom Regan calls subjects-of-a-life. So even if we allow the issue to be re-stated in this manner, we still find that preference utilitarians deny inherent value only to beings who are not subjects-of-a-life. Since Regan attributes inherent value only to beings who are subjects-of-a-life, on this point he and the preference utilitarians do not disagree.

We come now to the third and most crucial of the ways in which Regan seeks to characterize treating individuals as if they lacked inherent value: harming individuals so that we may bring about the best aggregate consequences for everyone affected by the outcome of such treatment. We have seen that Regan writes as if the assertion that such treatment indicates a lack of proper respect for inherent value has somehow been deduced from the more general descriptions of treatment which preceded it. Even if we had unquestioningly accepted that the forms of treatment I have labeled (i) and (ii) were indicative of lack of respect for inherent value, however, it isn't easy to see how we could validly infer that this was also true of (iii). Regan gives a hint as to what he has in mind in the following passage:

The grounds for claiming that such treatment is disrespectful and unjust should be apparent. It can hardly be just or respectful to harm individuals who have inherent value merely in order to secure the best aggregate consequences for everyone affected by the outcome. This cannot be respectful of inherent value because it is to view the individual who is harmed *merely* as a receptacle of what has value (e.g. pleasure), so that the losses of such value credited to the harmed individual can be made up for, or more than compensated, by the sum of the gains in such values by others, *without any wrong having been done to the loser*. Individuals who have inherent value, however, have a kind of value that is distinct from, is not reducible to, and is incommensurate with such values as pleasure or preference satisfaction, either their own or those of others. To harm such individuals *merely* in order to produce the best consequences for all involved is to do what is wrong – is to treat them unjustly – because it fails to respect their inherent value. To borrow part of a phrase from Kant, individuals who have inherent value must never be treated *merely as means* to securing the best aggregate consequences.[10]

The first part of this passage attempts to link (iii) with (i) by claiming that (iii) involves treating individuals as if they were *merely* receptacles for valuable experiences. We have already seen that such references to receptacles can be misleading, and that to treat individuals as valuable only because of their capacity for certain experiences is not to deny them inherent value. So even if (iii) could be linked with (i), this would not show that (iii) involved a denial of inherent value. But this is by no means the only gap in the argument. It is simply not true that to harm an individual in order to secure the best aggregate consequences for everyone "is to view the individual who is harmed *merely* as a receptacle of what has value …" After all, utilitarians and others who are prepared to harm individuals for this end will view those they are harming, along with those they are benefiting, as equally possessing inherent value. They differ with Regan only in that they prefer to maximize benefits to individuals, rather than to restrict such benefits by a requirement that no individual may be harmed.

Those who incline towards Regan's view of this matter might consider the following. Suppose you had to choose to live in one of two societies, call them R and S. All you know is that in R, no individual is ever harmed to secure the best aggregate consequences for everyone, while in S individuals are harmed if careful scrutiny shows beyond any doubt that such harm is the only possible way to secure the best aggregate outcome for everyone. (Such harm is, of course, kept to the minimum necessary to secure the beneficial outcome, and the harm is included in the calculation as to whether the consequences really are the best aggregate outcome for everyone.) Assume that there are no differences between R and S, other than those traceable to this difference of moral principle. Let us also assume that the worst off in R and the worst off in S are at the same level; though there might, of course, be different reasons in the two societies for why they were at this level. Remember that you have no way of knowing whether, if you choose S, you will yourself be harmed; but you know from the description already given that, if there is any difference in the overall welfare of the two societies, it must favour S. How would you choose? I would certainly choose S, and so would anyone seeking to maximize her or his expected welfare. Is it plausible to say that a moral principle which would be chosen under such conditions is a principle which views those harmed merely as receptacles? Since we do not know if we will be harmed, to say this would imply that people who are rationally seeking to maximize their own welfare must view *themselves* merely as receptacles. This strikes me as absurd; and at the very least, it makes it clear that to maintain such a view is to empty all the critical impact from the charge of viewing individuals as receptacles.

We have now considered the first part of the passage in which Regan offers reasons for his view that (iii) involves a denial of the inherent value of individuals. In this first part, Regan attempted to link (iii) with (i). This attempt fails. Regan goes on, however, to make two additional claims about (iii), claims which go beyond (i) and (ii) and could thus be seen as giving support to (iii) as an independent assertion.

The first of these additional claims is that "individuals who have inherent value … have a kind of value that is distinct from, is not reducible to, and is incommensurate with such values as pleasure or preference satisfaction, either their own or those of others." The second claim is the Kantian assertion that "Individuals who have inherent value must never be treated *merely as means* to securing the best aggregate consequences."

The first claim looks like the point about receptacles again, but it adds to that a point about incommensurability. The difficulty of weighing up incommensurable values is a familiar one in normative ethics. Regan's invocation of incommensurability, however, is unusual in that he is not referring to the incommensurability of, say, justice and welfare, or knowledge and beauty. The incommensurability to which he refers is that between the inherent value of individuals, and values such as pleasure or preference satisfaction. For reasons already given in our discussion of receptacles, it is not easy to see how the individuals and the valued experiences are to be separated; but in any case, more crucial to the present discussion is the absence of any explanation why (iii) requires that these values be commensurable. Suppose, for example, that we inflict a specified harm on one individual in order to prevent ten other individuals from suffering exactly the same harm. Here there is no problem of comparing incommensurable values. All that is needed is the recognition that ten harms are worse than one harm, when all the harms to be considered are exactly the same. If, therefore, harming one person in order to secure the best aggregate consequences for everyone involves denying inherent value, this cannot be shown by reference to incommensurability.[11]

What of the second claim? Taken literally, the second claim is merely a re-statement of (ii). It amounts to a rejection of treating beings with inherent value as if they possessed only instrumental value. It is obvious that to harm an individual in order to produce the best aggregate outcome for everyone is not necessarily to treat that individual *merely as a means*. It is compatible with giving as much consideration to the interests of that individual as one gives to any other individual, including oneself.

Perhaps Regan means to assert more than this; Kant, no doubt, did mean much more. But there are notorious difficulties in Kant's own attempt to defend his categorical imperative. Moreover, as Regan himself acknowledges, he is borrowing only "part of a phrase" from Kant. To borrow Kant's argument in full, and apply it to all subjects-of-a-life, Regan would have to find an alternative to Kant's reliance on rationality and autonomy. It is not obvious what this would be. Regan certainly offers no further account.

We have now completed our discussion of the three ways of treating individuals which Regan says indicate a lack of respect for their inherent value. We have found that only the second is a clear-cut case, and this, of course, is the one that utilitarians reject as emphatically as Regan does. The third is not indicative of treating individuals as if they lacked inherent value; and the first is also not indicative of such treatment, unless we consider the attitude to continued, rather than instant-by-instant, existence. Even then, preference utilitarians will value the continued existence of subjects-of-a-life who wish to go on living, just as Regan will. We can conclude that respect for the inherent value of subjects-of-a-life is not a reason for embracing the rights view rather than the utilitarian view. The principle of equal consideration of interests, which is the foundation of utilitarianism as well as of many other ethical views, fully satisfies the demand that we recognize the inherent value of subjects-of-a-life.

IV

It is not my aim, in this essay, to indicate all the difficulties which face defenders of rights. I have elsewhere indicated some of the problems Regan has in applying his moral views to two apparently similar situations: the experimental use of animals, and his own hypothetical case of the dog in the overcrowded lifeboat.[12] These problems are characteristic of the difficulties faced by all adherents of rights-based ethical theories, because such theories are too inflexible to respond to the various real and imaginary circumstances in which we want to make moral judgments. That is, however, another issue. My aim here has been to show how a position based on equal consideration of interests recognizes the inherent value of individuals, including nonhuman animals. The most impressive case for animal rights published so far is unable to provide adequate grounds for moving beyond the equal consideration stance, to a view based on rights. In the absence of any such grounds, there is no case for attributing rights, rather than equal consideration, to animals.

NOTES

1. The review was part of "Ten Years of Animal Liberation," *New York Review of Books* (January 17, 1985), pp. 46–52; Regan's response is in "The Dog in the Lifeboat: An Exchange," *New York Review of Books* (April 25, 1985), pp. 57–58.
2. Henry S. Salt, *Animals' Rights Considered in Relation to Social Progress*, London, 1892.
3. See, for instance, A. V. Townsend, "Radical Vegetarians," *Australasian Journal of Philosophy*, vol. 57, no. 1 (1979), p. 93.
4. For further discussion of this point, see Helga Kuhse and Peter Singer, *Should the Baby Live?* (Oxford: Oxford University Press, 1985), ch. 5.
5. For a more detailed exposition of this point, see the first chapter of my *Animal Liberation* (New York, 1975).
6. See my *Practical Ethics* (Cambridge, 1979) chs. 4 and 5.
7. T. Regan, *The Case for Animal Rights* (Berkeley, CA: University of California Press, 1983), pp. 248–49; italics in original.
8. *Practical Ethics*, p. 102.
9. For further details see *Practical Ethics*, ch. 4; and also my reply to H. L. A. Hart's review of that book, in *The New York Review of Books* (August 14, 1980), pp. 53–54. I develop these ideas further in "Life's Uncertain Voyage," forthcoming in P. Pettit and R. Sylvan (eds), *Mind, Morality and Metaphysics: Essays* in *Honour of J. J. C. Smart* (Blackwell, Oxford, 1987).
10. *The Case for Animal Rights*, p. 249; italics in original.
11. Frank Jackson has pointed out to me that Regan's assertion of the incommensurability of the inherent value of the individuals, and values such as pleasure or preference satisfaction, should in any case be rejected because it has absurd consequences. Consider, for instance, what taking such a view seriously would do to perfectly ordinary projects, like your next car trip to the movies. There is a finite, though very slight, probability that you will hit and kill a pedestrian. Are you nevertheless justified in making the trip? We all agree that the death of a pedestrian is a *very* much greater evil than your enjoyment of the movie is a good; but the risk of killing a pedestrian is so extremely slight that we think it outweighed by a strong probability of achieving the lesser value. What if, however, the value of the pedestrian's life and of your enjoyment of the movie are truly *incommensurable*? If this means anything, it must mean that *no* finite probability of your causing the death of the pedestrian could be outweighed by *any* amount of enjoyment. You would never be justified in furthering your own, or anyone else's, pleasure or preference satisfaction by any activity which carried any finite risk of causing an individual's death. So long, movies – and most other recreational activities as well.
12. See my comments in "Ten Years of Animal Liberation," *New York Review of Books* (January 17, 1985), pp. 46-52; and Regan's response, with my rejoinder, in "The Dog in the Lifeboat: An Exchange," *New York Review of Books* (April 25, 1985), pp. 57–58.

5

TOM REGAN

The Rights of Humans and Other Animals*

Tom Regan, an American philosopher, is frequently credited with being the philosophical leader of the animal-rights movement in the United States. He is cofounder of the Culture and Animals Foundation, an organization dedicated to facilitating intellectual and artistic activities related to animal concerns. While he has addressed both environmental and medical ethics in his writings, Regan is best known for his scholarship on animal issues, such as his highly influential book, *The Case for Animal Rights*. The position Regan articulates in his writings is that animals, like humans, have moral rights, and treating them as if they do not possess such rights is a form of prejudice and is unjust. In the extract below, Regan is engaged in a dialogue with other philosophers regarding human and animal rights. He articulates his philosophical position by juxtaposing it with the utilitarian perspectivo - a position articulated in the previous reading by Peter Singer. Regan also discusses what characteristics might make the attribution of rights to animals appropriate. Using the case of animal experimentation he highlights the differences between his position and that of utilitarian philosophers: whereas philosophers of a utilitarian bent would concede that the use of some animals in some medical experiments could be warranted in the interests of the greater good, those who grant moral rights to animals [as Regan does] would contend that using animals in such experiments violates their individual rights and is therefore unjust under all conditions.

Human moral rights place justified limits on what people are free to do to one another. Animals also have moral rights, and arguments to support the use of animals in scientific research based on the benefits allegedly derived from animal model research are thus invalid. Animals do not belong in laboratories because placing them there, in the hope of benefits for others, violates their rights.

Because the theme of this issue [of the journal *Ethics and Behavior*] lends itself to emphasizing the differences that exist between the participating philosophers, it seems especially important to make a few observations about some fundamental points on which we are all agreed. As will be clear momentarily, our unanimity concerns what we all think is false rather than what we think is true.

* Reprinted from Regan, T. (1997). "The rights of humans and other animals." *Ethics and Behavior*, 7, 103–111, with permission from Lawrence Erlbaum Associates.

POINTS OF AGREEMENT

We all agree that moral judgments – judgments about what is right and wrong, good and bad, just and unjust – are not simply and solely expressions of individual feeling or attitude. Some of the things we say are simply and solely of this sort. For example, if I say "I like coffee," and you say "I like tea," each of us has expressed our personal preference regarding what we like to drink. And about such matters there is, of course, no right or wrong, no true or false, and no thought of justifying or supporting or validating what is said. About matters of taste, things just are the way they are, with different people liking different things.

Moral judgments are not like this. When two people make conflicting judgments about a controversial moral issue – about the morality of abortion, for example – they are not simply and solely saying what they like or dislike, as a matter of personal preference. They are saying something *about abortion*, not something *about their individual response* to abortion. And the person who says that abortion is always wrong is saying something about abortion that contradicts what is said by someone who says that abortion is sometimes morally permissible. As such, and unlike the situation in which different people simply and solely express their feelings or preferences, moral judgments do need to be defended, do need to be justified, do need to be validated. *How* to do this is a question whose possible answer divides the philosophers taking part in this discussion. But *that* this needs to be done – that moral judgments need to be justified, defended, validated – is common ground among all of us.

A second important agreement concerns a second falsehood. Just as some people think (mistakenly, in our view) that moral judgments are simply and solely expressions of personal feelings or attitudes, others think they are statements about a culture's mores. On this view, moral right and wrong are defined by the dominant customs of a culture, at any given period of its history; and because different cultures have different customs, this view, which usually is referred to as *cultural relativism*, concludes that there is no universal right and wrong; rather, there are as many rights and wrongs as there are different cultures with different customs.

The philosophers here, without exception, reject cultural relativism. When Frey [*Ethics and Behavior* 7(2)] denies that human beings have moral rights, he does not think he can be shown to be mistaken if we point out that most Americans disagree with him, any more than the rest of us are inclined to agree that slavery was not wrong among White citizens of the antebellum South, given the prevailing customs of that time and place. Even if it is an exaggeration to say, as Henrik Ibsen is said to have observed, that "the minority is always right," it is too obvious to need argument that the majority sometimes is wrong. We do not defend, justify, or validate a moral judgment by doing cultural anthropology.

Neither do we do this – and here I come to the third and final point of agreement among all of us – by consulting some holy book or by taking instruction from God's will. In saying this, I am not saying that no books are holy or that there is no God. I am only saying that, among the philosophers writing here, we all agree that judgments about moral right and wrong, good or bad, the just and the unjust must be defended, justified, or validated independently of what any God says or wills.

THE NATURE AND IMPORTANCE OF HUMAN RIGHTS

As for our disagreements, it is important to realize that it is not only our respective views about animal rights that divide us. We also are divided when it comes to human rights. Cohen [*Ethics and Behavior* 7(2)], Beauchamp [*Ethics and Behavior* 7(2)], and I seem to be of one mind concerning the nature of human rights. (Let me add parenthetically that when I speak of human rights this is shorthand for human *moral* rights; and the same is true when I speak of animal rights: I am referring to their moral rights. Questions involving human or animal legal rights are an entirely separate matter.) Here, briefly, are those points on which I think the three of us agree.

Human rights place justified limits on what people are free to do to one another. For example, the right to bodily integrity disallows physically assaulting another person's body simply on the grounds that others might benefit as a result. To use Cohen's example, one cannot justify the Nazi hypothermia research because what was learned might help other people who suffer from exposure. Or take what I call the Mickey Mantle case. Mickey has a good heart, good kidneys, and, recently, a good liver.[1] Suppose that Cal Ripken, Bobby Bonds, and Kirby Puckett each needs one of these vital organs. Would it be permissible to transplant Mickey's organs, against his will, in these other ball players? After all, other things being equal, the world would be a better place with three healthy ball players in it than it is with just one aging former player.

Well, this is not something that is permissible, given that Mickey has a right to bodily integrity. There are some things that *morally cannot be done* to the individual even if others stand to benefit as a result of doing it. As Ronald Dworkin (1984) said, the rights of the individual "trump" (153) the collective interest. In the moral game, the rights card is the trump card.

Even with these very few comments about rights on the table, I think we should be able to see why Cohen is correct when he says that the idea of animal rights is a very important idea, one fraught with massive potential practical significance. Because if animals have rights – including, for example, the right to bodily integrity and the right not to be made to suffer gratuitously – it is difficult to see how anything less than the total abolition of animal model research could be morally acceptable. In particular, if animals have rights, certain familiar ways of defending animal model research will be silenced. No longer will we want to listen to the long list of benefits attributed to research of this kind. If animals have rights, and if rights are the trump card in the moral game, their rights

override any benefits, real or imagined, we have gained, or stand to gain, from using them in biomedical research. So, yes, Cohen is on the money when he states that animal rights is an important idea.

Now, Cohen, Beauchamp, and I agree that humans have rights. And Beauchamp and I agree that animals have rights (although we disagree over what rights they have). It is Frey who disagrees with all of us, maintaining, as he does, that neither animals nor humans have rights. Before going on to state my views concerning animal rights, I want to say something about his views concerning human rights.

FREY'S UTILITARIANISM

Frey is a utilitarian, and a utilitarian of a certain stripe. All utilitarians think that the morality of what we do – whether our acts are morally right or wrong – depends on what happens as a result of the choices we make. Utilitarianism is a forward-looking view. The consequences, results, or effects of our actions determine their morality. And by our actions we should be trying to make the world better, to bring about the best possible consequences or results, in any given situation.

What is best all considered, however, is not necessarily what is best for each individual. Utilitarians are committed to aggregating – to adding and subtracting – the positive and negative consequences experienced by different individuals. This means that one person might lose a lot so that another might gain. The Mickey Mantle case illustrates this general point. Mickey (literally) loses everything, but the three other ball players each gets back a healthy life. From the point of view of Frey's utilitarianism, it is an open moral question whether anything wrong would be done if Mickey were treated in this way.

Now, Frey has two choices. He could try to tell some story or another that is supposed to show why the consequences really would be better if Mickey's organs were not transplanted in the way we have imagined. This maneuver is known as *the utilitarian shuffle*. Or Frey could say, "Look, sometimes you just have to bite the bullet. If the world really would be a better place without Mickey, but with Mickey's organs redistributed, then that *is* the right thing to do."

Whichever option Frey chooses, the essential point is that his utilitarianism is, in my view, a fundamentally mistaken way to think about morality. Here is a simple test case that I think makes my point. Some time back four teenage boys raped and in other ways sexually abused a seriously retarded teenage girl. Among other things, as I recall, the boys took special pleasure in invading her body with a broom handle and a Coke bottle.

I assume that no one will question that the abuse this poor girl suffered was wrong. But I hope you will notice that Frey's theory cannot easily explain why it is wrong. After all, there were four boys and just the one girl, and the boys evidently had a very good time. Shuffling along, Frey might suggest that there are other consequences that need to be taken into account – for example, the insecurity experienced by other young girls as a result of what happened to this one, and so on.

But this is not the central point. The central point is that, *before* Frey can pass a moral judgment in this case, his theory requires that we take the pleasures the four boys experienced into account – that we count *their* equal interests equally. By my lights, however, the pleasures experienced by these four boys are *totally irrelevant* to assessing the morality of their actions. More generally, the interests of those who do what is morally wrong have no bearing on the determination of the wrong they do. It is because Frey's view requires that we count these interests, *and weigh them equally with those of the victims of wrongdoing*, that I think his way of thinking is fundamentally mistaken.

Thus, the importance of human rights, in my view. Because if we suppose that this young girl has rights, then the good time had by the boys – the benefits they derived from abusing her – emerge as beside the moral point. Her rights trump their good time; indeed, their good time has no bearing whatsoever on assessing the morality of what they did. If there is a valid way of defending or justifying our moral judgments, I believe that it involves thinking along the lines I have just sketched, crude as that sketch is.

ANIMAL WELFARE AND ANIMAL RIGHTS

I turn now to the topic of animal rights, beginning with some comments on the distinction between animal welfarists and animal rightists. As the name suggests, animal welfarists are in theory committed to taking the welfare of animals seriously. Animals should not be caused gratuitous physical pain; their psychological well-being should not be diminished unnecessarily. These are among the principles that guide a conscientious welfarist.

As such, welfarists can, and some of them sometimes do, call for important reforms, in the name of humane improvements, regarding how humans utilize nonhuman animals. Provided, however, that the welfare interests of these animals are taken into account and counted fairly, we do nothing wrong in principle by utilizing them to advance human interests. In particular, the use of nonhuman animals in biomedical research is in principle morally right, from a welfarist perspective, even if this human endeavor occasionally goes wrong in practice, as when a particular researcher neglects or otherwise mistreats animals in his laboratory.

Animal welfarism, therefore, can be seen to embody the utilitarianism championed by someone like Frey. The many benefits allegedly derived from animal model research outweigh the many harms experienced by the animals. Indeed, if the biomedical community is looking for a coherent spokesperson to defend their activities philosophically, it could well be true that they will not be able to find anyone better than Frey and his utilitarianism.

Animal rightists differ from animal welfarists. Although animal welfarists can have reformist aspirations, animal rightists are necessarily abolitionists. From their perspective, the use of nonhuman animals in scientific research is wrong in principle, not simply occasionally wrong in practice. These animals do not belong in laboratories in the first place: They do not belong there because placing them there, in the hope of gaining benefits for others, violates their rights. Rights being the trump card in the moral game, it is not larger cages, but empty cages, that animal rightists call for.

Whatever we might think of the animal rights-animal welfare debate, it is important to realize that it represents a type of debate that has many logical cousins. The ongoing debate over the justice of the death penalty is an example. Some people believe there is nothing wrong with capital punishment in principle, even as they acknowledge there certainly have been some things wrong with it in practice. It was not too long ago that convicted criminals were hanged in public, burnt to death, or drowned for offenses that included such crimes as (here I cite North Carolina law) breaking a fish pond, stealing apples, dueling if death ensued, and (most remarkable of all) growing tobacco plants. Over the years, reformers of the death penalty sought to make the setting of the punishment more dignified and the method of execution more humane. Death by lethal injection, carried out in a sterile, hospital-like setting, would seem to represent as far as we might be able to go in the direction of such reforms.

This is not far enough for death-penalty abolitionists. Think what one might of their arguments, these critics of capital punishment believe that it is wrong in principle, not merely sometimes grotesquely immoral in practice, and they therefore call for its complete abolition, not merely various "humane" reforms.

Thus does the logic of the animal rights-animal welfare debate mirror the logic of other important, divisive, and enduring social controversies. Other examples include the debates over reforming or abolishing slavery, child labor, and legal access to abortion. That all these controversies differ in important ways from the animal rights-animal welfare debate is too obvious to

be denied. My point is not that this debate is like these other controversies in each and every way; mine is the far more modest point that they share a common logic.

ANIMAL RIGHTS

But *do* animals have rights? And if they do, what rights do they have? My answers to these questions are explained in my book, *The Case for Animal Rights* (1983), and it is this work that I recommend to anyone who is interested seriously in what my answers are and why I answer as I do. Concerning the latter point, let me remind you that all the philosophers writing in this issue [of *Ethics and Behavior*] agree that we do not offer answers to moral questions just by saying how we happen to feel or what we happen to like, or by making reference to the dominant customs in America today, or by citing selected passages in the Bible or some other sacred book. Our moral thinking needs to move in a different direction than those these paths open up to us.

But if not in these ways, how? No easy question, this; certainly not for the philosophically faint of heart. But here is a way, although certainly not the only way, to proceed.

Suppose we begin by assuming that humans have rights and ask how we might be able to illuminate or explain why we do. Of course, Frey will protest. You will recall that he denies *both* animal *and* human rights. But you also will recall where, in my opinion, his utilitarianism-without-rights lands him. So, although beginning with the assumption that humans have rights is certainly not noncontroversial, it is a place we can defend using on this occasion – one that, by the way, Beauchamp and Cohen can be counted on as approving, given their agreement that humans do indeed have rights.

If humans have rights, there must be something about being human that helps explain or illuminates why we have them. Put another way, there must be some characteristic or set of characteristics (for brevity's sake, I refer to these possibilities as C) that makes the attribution of rights plausible in our case and implausible in the case of, for example, clouds, negative afterimages, and microfungi. The question is: What could this C be?

Possible answers are many. Some, although possibly widely believed, will not pass muster with my fellow philosophers. The idea that C is the soul, and that God endowed us with rights when he endowed us with a soul, rests on a religious basis that we agree is unsatisfactory. A more promising, nonreligious candidate is rational autonomy. It is because humans are rational autonomous agents, and because clouds, negative afterimages, and microfungi are not, that we have rights and they do not.

Suppose we grant this candidate for C for the moment; then we can ask how nonhuman animals would fare. In other words, we can ask, Are any nonhuman animals rational and autonomous? Because if some are, it would smack of prejudice to deny that they have rights but to affirm that we do.

Whether any nonhuman animals are rational and autonomous is a very difficult empirical question, one that we are unlikely to settle on this occasion. My own view, for what it is worth, is that there are many species of animals whose members satisfy these conditions. Nonhuman primates are the most obvious example. Next are the great whales and other mammals. Obviously where we draw the line that separates those animals who are rational and autonomous from those who are not will be neither easy nor free of controversy. Indeed, it may be that there is no clearly defined line we can draw with confidence, given the abundance of our individual and collective ignorance. However, it is enough for our purposes to recognize that *some* nonhuman animals are like humans in being rational and autonomous. So if rational autonomy explains or illuminates why we have rights, consistency requires that we make the same judgment in the case of these other animals: They, too, would have rights.

There is, however, a problem. Not all human beings are rational, autonomous agents. Infants are not, although most of them some day will be,

and older people who suffer from serious mental deterioration are not, although most of them once were. Plus there are those many thousands of humans who, like the young woman raped by the four teenage boys, are seriously mentally retarded throughout their entire lives. In any or all of these cases we have individuals who *are* human beings but who are *not* rational and autonomous. So if C is rational autonomy, it appears that billions of human beings lack rights and, in lacking them, lack the most important card in the moral game. In their case, we cannot say that it would be wrong to harm them in the hope of benefiting others because their rights trump the collective interest. In the nature of the case, they have no rights.

This problem can be avoided by putting forth a different candidate for C. Instead of using what Beauchamp refers to as "cognitive criteria" (*Ethics and Behavior* 7(2), 115), criteria such as rationality, we might instead rely on noncognitive criteria, criteria such as sentience (the capacity to be able to experience pain and pleasure) or emotion. And this does seem to be a more promising way to think about C, especially because all those humans who were denied rights, given the criterion of rational autonomy, seem to satisfy these noncognitive criteria.

Noncognitive criteria do more than increase the number of human beings who qualify as rights holders. These same criteria also increase the number of nonhuman animals who qualify. Line-drawing problems doubtless will persist, but, wherever one reasonably draws the line, it seems evident that there are many more nonhuman animals who are sentient or who feel emotions than there are nonhuman animals who are rational and autonomous.

Although much more needs to be said to complete the argument for animal rights, some features of the central plot emerge from the little that has been said here. We face a choice: *Either* we can set the criteria of rights-possession (C) rather high, so to speak, requiring capacities such as rationality and autonomy, *or* we can set the criteria of rights-possession lower, requiring noncognitive capacities such as sentience. If we choose the former, some (but not a great many) nonhuman animals arguably will qualify as possessors of rights; but many human beings also will fail to qualify. If we choose the latter alternative, these humans will be enfranchised within the class of rights holders; but so will many nonhuman animals. Rationally, we cannot have it both ways – cannot, that is, rationally defend the view that all and only human beings have rights. Cohen may think he can do this. But for reasons I hope to explain in the future, I believe he is seriously confused and mistaken.

Which choice should we make? Informed people of goodwill can answer this question differently. I favor a view of rights that enfranchises the most vulnerable humans among us. Infants and young children, the elderly who suffer from degenerative diseases of the brain, the seriously mentally retarded of all ages are the most obvious examples. I do not think those of us who are more fortunate should be free to utilize these human beings – in biomedical research, for example – in the hope that we might learn something that will benefit us or others. Frey's utilitarianism certainly could allow this, which in my opinion is all the more reason not to accept his moral philosophy. If we recognize the rights of these humans, however, we recognize that they hold trump cards that have greater ethical force than what is in the general interest. And that certainly is the position I hold and recommend in their case.

I also recognize, however, that any plausible criterion that would enfranchise these humans within the class of rights holders will spill over the species boundary, so to speak, and enfranchise many hundreds, possibly many thousands of species of animals. That being the case, these animals also must be viewed as holding the trump card in the moral game. And because the rights they have should not be overridden in the name of seeking benefits for ourselves or others, it follows that none of these animals should be in any laboratory for that purpose. From an animal-rights perspective, as noted earlier, it is not larger cages, it is empty cages that recognition of animal rights requires.

NOTE

1. This article was written before Mickey Mantle's death.

REFERENCES

Dworkin, R. (1984). Rights as trumps. In J. Waldron (ed.), *Theories of rights*, Oxford: Oxford University Press.

Regan, T. (1983). *The case for animal rights*, Berkeley: University of California Press.

6

MARTHA NUSSBAUM

The Moral Status of Animals*

Martha Nussbaum is an American philosopher whose areas of interest include law and ethics. She has written several books on topics as varied as education, development, and the law. She advocates a "capabilities" approach to theorizing difficult-to-reconcile issues of justice, with a focus on the ability of individuals to develop to the point where they can fulfill their potential capabilities. Nussbaum uses this ethical approach to build upon the notion of "justice as fairness" (from John Rawls's *Theory of Justice*) to address issues of disability, nationality and the treatment of animals. The extract reproduced here is an article adapted from her book, *Frontiers of Justice*, in which she concentrates on the moral status of animals. She argues that preventing animals from reaching their capabilities is a justice issue, and she suggests that countries include in their constitutions a commitment to treating animals in ways congruent with their dignity. Nussbaum argues that her capabilities approach is able to ameliorate some of the shortcomings of the Utilitarian approach [addressed in the previous readings by Bentham and Singer] and the Kantian approach (which considers our obligations to animals to be merely in the form of indirect duties to humans, asserting that cruelty to animals is problematic because it makes people more inclined to be cruel to each other). Nussbaum's approach is an excellent philosophical precursor to the material in Section 2 on the cognitive and emotional abilities of other animals.

In 55 BC, the Roman leader Pompey staged a combat between humans and elephants. Surrounded in the arena, the animals perceived that they had no hope of escape. According to Pliny, they then "entreated the crowd, trying to win its compassion with indescribable gestures, bewailing their plight with a sort of lamentation." The audience, moved to pity and anger by their plight, rose to curse Pompey – feeling, wrote Cicero, that the elephants had a relation of commonality (societas) with the human race.

In AD 2000, the High Court of Kerala, in India, addressed the plight of circus animals "housed in cramped cages, subjected to fear, hunger, pain, not to mention the undignified way of life they have to live." It found those

* "The Moral Status of Animals" is adapted from *Frontiers of Justice: Disability, Nationality, Species Membership* by Martha C. Nussbaum, Cambridge, Mass.: The Belknap Press of Harvard University Press, Copyright ©2006 by the President and Fellows of Harvard College. Reprinted by permission of the publisher. This article appeared in the *Chronicle of Higher Education* 52(22), February 2006.

animals "beings entitled to dignified existence" within the meaning of Article 21 of the Indian Constitution, which protects the right to life with dignity. "If humans are entitled to fundamental rights, why not animals?" the court asked.

We humans share a world and its scarce resources with other intelligent creatures. As the court said, those creatures are capable of dignified existence. It is difficult to know precisely what that means, but it is rather clear what it does not mean: the conditions of the circus animals beaten and housed in filthy cramped cages, the even more horrific conditions endured by chickens, calves, and pigs raised for food in factory farming, and many other comparable conditions of deprivation, suffering, and indignity. The fact that humans act in ways that deny other animals a dignified existence appears to be an issue of justice, and an urgent one.

Indeed, there is no obvious reason why notions of basic justice, entitlement, and law cannot be extended across the species barrier, as the Indian court boldly did.

In some ways, our imaginative sympathy with the suffering of nonhuman animals must be our guide as we try to define a just relation between humans and animals. Sympathy, however, is malleable. It can all too easily be corrupted by our interest in protecting the comforts of a way of life that includes the use of other animals as objects for our own gain and pleasure. That is why we typically need philosophy and its theories of justice. Theories help us to get the best out of our own ethical intuitions, preventing self-serving distortions of our thought. They also help us extend our ethical commitments to new, less familiar cases. It seems plausible to think that we will not approach the question of justice for nonhuman animals well if we do not ask, first, what theory or theories might give us the best guidance.

In my new book, *Frontiers of Justice: Disability, Nationality, Species Membership* [Harvard University Press 2006], I consider three urgent problems of justice involving large asymmetries of power: justice for people with disabilities, justice across national boundaries, and justice

for nonhuman animals. During the past 35 years, theories of justice have been elaborated and refined with great subtlety and insight, stimulated by John Rawls's great books, which built, in turn, on the classical doctrine of the social contract in Locke, Kant, and Rousseau. The social-contract tradition has enormous strength in thinking about justice. Devised in the first instance to help us reflect on the irrelevance of class, inherited wealth, and religion to just social arrangements, its theories have been successfully extended, in recent years, to deal with inequalities based on race and gender. The three issues that are my theme, however, have not been successfully addressed by such theories, for reasons inherent in their very structure – or so I argue.

In each case, a "capabilities approach" [which] I have developed provides theoretical guidance. It begins from the question, "What are people actually able to do and to be?" It holds that each person is entitled to a decent level of opportunity in 10 areas of particular centrality, such as life, health, bodily integrity, affiliation, and practical reason.

On the question of animal entitlements, the approach gives better results than existing Kantian theories – which hold that respect should be given to rational beings – or Utilitarian approaches – which hold that the best choice is to maximize the pleasure or satisfaction of preferences. A capabilities approach can recognize a wide range of types of animal dignity, and of what animals need in order to flourish, restoring to Western debate some of the complexity the issue had in the time of Cicero, which it has subsequently lost.

As Richard Sorabji argues in his excellent book *Animal Minds and Human Morals: The Origins of the Western Debate* (Cornell University Press 1993), the ancient Greek and Roman world contained a wide range of views that held promise for thinking about the moral status of animals. However, Stoicism, with its emphasis on the capacity of humans for virtue and ethical choice, exercised far more widespread influence than any other philosophical school in a world of war and uncertainty – but it had a very unappealing view of animals, denying them all capacity for intelligent reaction to the world, and denying, in consequence, that we could have any moral duties to them. Because of the attractiveness of Stoicism's view of human virtue and choice, that picture of animals became widespread. I think we need to add to Sorabji's account the fact that Stoic views of animals fit better than others with the Judeo-Christian idea that human beings have been given dominion over animals. Although that idea has been interpreted in a variety of ways, it has standardly been understood to give humans license to do whatever they like to nonhuman species and to use them for human purposes.

Kant argues that all duties to animals are merely indirect duties to human beings: Cruel or kind treatment of animals strengthens tendencies to behave in similar fashion to our fellow humans. So animals matter only because of us. Kant cannot imagine that beings who (as he believes) lack self-consciousness and the capacity for ethical choice can possibly have dignity, or be objects of direct ethical duties. The fact that all Kantian views ground moral concern in our rational and moral capacities makes it difficult to treat animals as beings to whom justice is due.

Classical Utilitarianism has no such problem. It begins, admirably, with a focus on suffering. Its great theoretical pioneers, Jeremy Bentham and John Stuart Mill, had intense concern for the well-being of animals. Bentham famously argued that the species to which a creature belongs is as irrelevant, for ethical purposes, as race: it does not supply a valid reason to deprive a sentient being of a decent life. If, as Utilitarianism holds, the best choice is the one that maximizes total (or, in some versions, average) utility, understood as pleasure and/or the absence of pain, good choice would lead to radical change in our treatment of animals. Peter Singer's courageous work on animal suffering today follows the Utilitarian paradigm. Singer argues that the right question to ask, when we think about our conduct toward animals, is, What choice will maximize the satisfaction of the preferences of all sentient beings? That calculation, he believes, would put most

of our current pain-inflicting use of animals off limits.

Nevertheless, valuable though Utilitarian work on animal suffering has been, it has some serious difficulties. One notorious problem concerns the Utilitarian commitment to aggregation: that is, to summing together all pleasures and pains. The choice-maker is instructed to produce the largest total (or average) pleasure. That can allow results in which a small number of creatures have very miserable lives, so long as their miseries are compensated for by a great deal of pleasure elsewhere. Even slavery is ruled out – if it is – only by fragile empirical calculations urging its ultimate inefficiency. It remains unclear whether such a view can really rule out the cruel treatment of at least some animals, which undoubtedly causes great pleasure to a very large number of meat-eaters, or the infliction of pain on small numbers of animals in laboratory testing in order to provide benefits for many humans. (Here Kantian views about humans offer a good corrective, insisting that even the well-being of society as a whole does not justify egregious harms and indignities to any individual.)

Another sort of aggregation also causes difficulty: Utilitarians consider together diverse aspects of lives, reducing them all to experienced pain and pleasure. But we might think that a good life, for an animal as for a human, has many different aspects: movement, affection, health, community, dignity, bodily integrity, as well as the avoidance of pain. Some valuable aspects of animal lives might not even lead to pain when withheld. Animals, like humans, often don't miss what they don't know, and it is hard to believe that animals cramped in small cages all their lives can dream of the free movement that is denied them. Nonetheless, it remains valuable as a part of their flourishing, and not just because its absence is fraught with pain. Even a comfortable immobility would be wrong for a horse, an elephant, or a gorilla. Those creatures characteristically live a life full of movement, space, and complex social interaction. To deprive them of those things is to give them a distorted and impoverished existence.

Finally, all Utilitarian views are highly vulnerable on the question of numbers. The meat industry brings countless animals into the world who would never have existed otherwise. For Utilitarians, that is not a bad thing. Indeed, we can expect new births to add to the total of social utility, from which we could then subtract the pain the animals suffer. Wherever that calculation might come out, such a view would countenance the production of large numbers of creatures with lives only marginally worth living. So Utilitarianism has great merits, but also significant problems.

My capabilities approach, as so far developed, starts from the notion of human dignity and a life worthy of it. But it can be extended to provide a more adequate basis for animal entitlements than the other two theories under consideration. It seems wrong to think that only human life has dignity. As the Indian court said, the idea of a life commensurate with a creature's dignity has clear implications for assessing the lives we all too often make animals live.

The basic moral intuition behind my approach concerns the dignity of a form of life that possesses both deep needs and abilities. Its basic goal is to take into account the rich plurality of activities that sentient beings need – all those that are required for a life with dignity. With Aristotle and the young Marx, I argue that it is a waste and a tragedy when a living creature has an innate capability for some functions that are evaluated as important and good, but never gets the opportunity to perform those functions. Failures to educate women, failures to promote adequate health care, failures to extend the freedoms of speech and conscience to all citizens – all those are treated as causing a kind of premature death, the death of a form of flourishing that has been judged to be essential for a life with dignity. Political principles concerning basic entitlements are to be framed with those ideas in view.

The species standard is evaluative. It does not simply read off norms from the way nature actually is. Once we have judged, however, that a central human power is one of the good ones, one of the ones whose flourishing is essential for the creature to have a life with dignity, we have a very strong moral reason for promoting it and removing obstacles to its development.

The same attitude to natural powers that guides the approach in the case of human beings guides it in the case of nonhuman animals: Each form of life is worthy of respect, and it is a problem of justice when a creature does not have the opportunity to unfold its (valuable) power, to flourish in its own way, and to lead a life with dignity. The fact that so many animals never get to move around, enjoy the air, exchange affection with other members of their kind – all that is a waste and a tragedy, and it is not a life in keeping with the dignity of such creatures.

So the capabilities approach is well placed, intuitively, to go beyond both Kantian and Utilitarian views. It goes beyond Kant in seeing our ethical duties to animals as direct, not indirect, and also in its starting point, a basic concern for sentient life, not just rational life (though there is surely far more rationality in animal lives than Kant would have acknowledged). It goes beyond the intuitive starting point of Utilitarianism because it takes an interest not just in pleasure and pain, but in complex forms of life. It wants to see each living thing flourish as the sort of thing it is, and wants political principles to protect, for all sentient beings, a set of basic opportunities for flourishing.

Does justice focus on the individual, or on the species? It seems that here, as in the human case, the focus should be the individual creature. The capabilities approach attaches no ethical importance to increased numbers as such; its focus is on the well-being of existing creatures, and the harm that is done to them when their powers are blighted. Consequently the survival of a species may have weight as a scientific or aesthetic issue, but it is not an ethical issue, and certainly not an issue of justice – apart from the harms to existing creatures that are usually involved in the extinction of a species. When elephants are deprived of a congenial habitat and hunted for their tusks, harm is done to individual creatures, and it is that harm that should be our primary focus when justice is our concern, even while we may for other reasons seek the preservation of elephant species.

Almost all ethical views of animal entitlements hold that there are morally relevant distinctions among forms of life. Killing a mouse seems to be different from killing a chimpanzee. But what sort of difference is relevant for basic justice? Singer, following Bentham, puts the issue in terms of sentience. Animals of many kinds can suffer bodily pain, and it is always bad to cause pain to a sentient being. If there are animals that do not feel pain – and it appears that crustaceans and mollusks, as well as sponges and the other creatures Aristotle called "stationary animals," fall in that category – there is either no harm or only a trivial harm done in killing them. Among the sentient creatures, moreover, some can suffer additional harms through their cognitive capacity: A few animals can foresee and mind their own death, and others will have conscious interest in continuing to live. The painless killing of an animal that does not foresee its own death or take a conscious interest in the continuation of its life is, for Singer and Bentham, not bad, for all badness consists in the frustration of interests, understood as forms of conscious awareness. Singer is not, then, saying that some animals are inherently more worthy of esteem than others; he is simply saying that, if we agree with him that all harms reside in sentience, the creature's form of life limits the conditions under which it can actually suffer harm.

Similarly, James Rachels, whose view does not focus on sentience alone, holds that the level of complexity of a creature affects what can be a harm for it. What is relevant to the harm of pain is sentience; what is relevant to the harm of a specific type of pain is a specific type of sentience (for example, the ability to imagine one's own death). What is relevant to the harm of diminishing freedom, Rachels goes on, is a being's capacity for freedom or autonomy. It would make no sense to complain that a worm is being deprived of autonomy, or a rabbit of the right to vote. My capabilities view follows Rachels, denying that there is a natural ranking of forms of life, but holding that the level of

complexity of a creature affects what can be considered to be a harm to it.

Like Bentham, however, I do think of sentience as a minimum necessary condition for moral status. Does species membership matter when we consider the form of life that is good for a creature? For Utilitarians, and for Rachels, the species to which a creature belongs has no moral relevance. What matters are the capacities of the individual creature: in Rachels's words, "moral individualism." Utilitarian writers are fond of comparing apes to young children and to mentally disabled humans, suggesting that the ethical questions we should consider are the same in all those cases. The capabilities approach, by contrast, with its talk of characteristic functioning and forms of life, seems to attach some significance to species membership as such.

What type of significance is that? There is much to be learned from reflection on the continuum of life. Capacities do crisscross and overlap: A chimpanzee may have more capacity for empathy and perspectival thinking than a very young child, or than an older child with autism. And capacities that humans sometimes arrogantly claim for themselves alone are found very widely in nature. But it seems wrong to conclude from such facts that species membership is morally and politically irrelevant. A child with mental disabilities is actually very different from a chimpanzee, though in certain respects some of her capacities may be comparable. Such a child's life is difficult in a way that the life of a chimpanzee is not difficult: She is cut off from forms of flourishing that, but for the disability, she might have had. There is something blighted and disharmonious in her life, whereas the life of a chimpanzee may be perfectly flourishing. Her social and political functioning, her friendships, her ability to have a family all may be threatened by her disabilities, in a way that the normal functioning of a chimpanzee in the community of chimpanzees is not threatened by its cognitive endowment.

That is relevant when we consider issues of basic justice. For children born with Down syndrome, it is crucial that the political culture in which they live make a big effort to extend to them the fullest benefits of citizenship they can attain, through health benefits, education, and reeducation of public culture. That is so because they can flourish only as human beings. They have no option of flourishing as happy chimpanzees. For a chimpanzee, on the other hand, it seems to me that expensive efforts to teach language, while interesting and revealing for human scientists, are not matters of basic justice. A chimpanzee flourishes in its own way, communicating with its own community in a perfectly adequate manner that has gone on for ages.

In short, the species norm (duly evaluated) tells us what the appropriate benchmark is for judging whether a given creature has decent opportunities for flourishing.

There is a danger in any theory that alludes to the characteristic flourishing and form of life of a species: the danger of romanticizing "Nature," or seeing nature as a direct source of ethical norms. Nature is not particularly ethical or good. It should not be used as a direct source of norms. In the human case, therefore, my capabilities view does not attempt to extract norms directly from some facts about human nature. We must begin by evaluating the innate powers of human beings, asking which ones are central to the notion of a life with dignity. Thus not only evaluation but also ethical evaluation is put into the approach from the start. Many things that are found in human life, like the capacities for cruelty, despair, or self-destruction, are not on the capabilities list.

In the case of nonhuman animals, however, we need to remember that we are relatively ignorant of what a good life for each sort of animal is and strongly biased in favor of our own power interests. Thus our attempts to evaluate the capacities of animals, saying that some are good and others not so good, may easily go wrong. Moreover, while we can expect a potentially violent human (as all humans are) to learn to restrain her or his capacity for violence, we cannot expect so much learning and control from many

animal species. Thus to deny a tiger the exercise of its predatory capacities may inflict significant suffering, whereas we require a human to learn to live at peace with others (or we should!).

Here the capabilities view may, however, distinguish two aspects of the capability in question. A tiger's capability to kill small animals, defined as such, does not have intrinsic ethical value, and political principles can omit it (and even inhibit it in some cases). But a tiger's capability to exercise its predatory nature so as to avoid the pain of frustration may well have value, if the pain of frustration is considerable. Zoos have learned how to make that distinction. Noticing that they were giving predatory animals insufficient exercise for their predatory capacities, they have had to face the question of the harm done to smaller animals by allowing such capabilities to be exercised. Should they give a tiger a tender gazelle to crunch on? The Bronx Zoo has found that it can give the tiger a large ball on a rope, whose resistance and weight symbolize the gazelle. The tiger seems satisfied. Wherever predatory animals are living under direct human support and control, such solutions seem the most ethically sound.

Much more remains to be done to ground this approach philosophically and to articulate its results, which I try to do in *Frontiers*. What, however, should the practical upshot be?

In general the capabilities approach suggests that it is appropriate for each nation to include in its constitution or other founding statement of principle a commitment to regarding nonhuman animals as subjects of political justice and to treating them in accordance with their dignity. The constitution might also spell out some of the very general principles suggested by the capabilities approach, and judicial interpretation can make the ideas more concrete. The High Court of Kerala made a good beginning, thinking about what the idea of "life with dignity" implies for the circus animals in the case. The rest of the work of protecting animal entitlements might be done by suitable legislation and by court cases demanding the enforcement of laws, where they are not enforced. At the same time, many of the issues covered by this approach cannot be dealt with by nations taken in isolation, but can be treated only through international cooperation. So we also need international accords committing the world community to the protection of animal habitats and the eradication of cruel practices.

It has been obvious for a long time that the pursuit of global justice requires the inclusion of many people and groups not previously included as fully equal subjects of justice: the poor; members of religious, ethnic, and racial minorities; and more recently women, the disabled, and inhabitants of poor nations distant from one's own. But a truly global justice requires not simply looking across the world for fellow species members who are entitled to a decent life.

It also requires looking around the world at the other sentient beings with whose lives our own are inextricably and complexly intertwined. Kant's approach does not confront these questions as questions of justice. Probably a strict Kantian could not so confront them, not without considerably modifying Kant's own view about rationality as the basis of moral respect. Utilitarian approaches boldly confront the wrongs animals suffer, and they deserve high praise. But in the end, I have argued, Utilitarianism is too homogenizing – both across lives and with respect to the heterogeneous constituents of each life – to provide us with a fully adequate theory of animal justice. The capabilities approach, which begins from an ethically attuned concern for each form of animal life, offers a model that does justice to the complexity of animal lives and their strivings for flourishing. Such a model seems an important part of a fully global theory of justice.

7

GILLES DELEUZE and FÉLIX GUATTARI

Becoming-Animal*

Gilles Deleuze and **Félix Guattari**, both now deceased, were French intellectuals whose collaborative work is considered classic in the development of critical theory. Deleuze, one of the most influential postmodern philosophers of the twentieth century, was politically active in France and had a close friendship with Michel Foucault, with whom he advocated prison reform in the 1970s. With Félix Guattari, a psychotherapist, Deleuze wrote *A Thousand Plateaus* in 1980, borrowing the concept of "plateau" from Gregory Bateson's essay on the Balinese libidinal "plateau." [However, for Deleuze and Guattari, a plateau constitutes a heightening of an intense state of thought, rather than sex] *A Thousand Plateaus* is a collection of essays each of which represents a "plateau" and begins with a date in human history corresponding to a dynamic point of reference for the article. The extract reproduced here on "becoming-animal" has been central to the contemporary animal-studies landscape, and is taken from their chapter entitled "1730: Becoming-Intense, Becoming-Animal, Becoming-Imperceptible . . ." The date, 1730, refers to a time when "all we hear about are vampires." Using this point of reference, Deleuze and Guattari develop the concept "becoming-animal" to capture the notion of human-animal relationships based on affinity rather than identity or imitation – with a heavy emphasis on difference. First discussed by Deleuze in an earlier work on Nietzsche, becoming and multiplicity [which mean the same thing] refer to an ever expanding set of differences that are always in transition and in continuous creation. Developed in reaction to Hegelian dialectics and its thesis-antithesis-synthesis framework, the concept of becoming-multiple is related to the notion that there is a politics of becomings-animal that is expressed in assemblages or groups that are "oppressed, prohibited, in revolt, or always on the fringe." One enters into becoming alliances with anomalous beings, such as Captain Ahab who entered into a "monstrous alliance" with Moby Dick, his becoming-whale. Deleuze and Guattari's focus on affinity, alliances and multiple differences provides a new way to think about our ethical relations with other animals – relations that cannot be defined in terms of kinship, or sameness, or capacities, or identities, or progression – "becoming produces nothing other than itself."

* Reprinted from chapter 10 ("1730: Becoming-Intense, Becoming-Animal, Becoming-Imperceptible . . .") of Gilles Deleuze and Félix Guattari (1987) *A Thousand Plateaus: Capitalism and Schizophrenia*, translation and foreword by Brian Massumi. Minneapolis: University of Minnesota Press and Continuum International Publishing Group. Copyright 1987 by the University of Minnesota Press. Originally published as *Mille Plateaux*, volume 2 of *Capitalisme et schizophrénie* © 1980 by Les Editions de Minuit, Paris. Reprinted with permission of the publisher, University of Minnesota Press and with permission of the publisher, The Continuum International Publishing Group.

MEMORIES OF A MOVIEGOER

I recall the fine film *Willard* (1972, Daniel Mann). A "B" movie perhaps, but a fine unpopular film: unpopular because the heroes are rats. My memory of it is not necessarily accurate. I will recount the story in broad outline. Willard lives with his authoritarian mother in the old family house. Dreadful Oedipal atmosphere. His mother orders him to destroy a litter of rats. He spares one (or two or several). After a violent argument, the mother, who "resembles" a dog, dies. The house is coveted by a businessman, and Willard is in danger of losing it. He likes the principal rat he saved, Ben, who proves to be of prodigious intelligence. There is also a white female rat, Ben's companion. Willard spends all his free time with them. They multiply. Willard takes the rat pack, led by Ben, to the home of the businessman, who is put to a terrible death. But he foolishly takes his two favorites to the office with him and has no choice but to let the employees kill the white rat. Ben escapes, after throwing Willard a long, hard glare. Willard then experiences a pause in his destiny, in his *becoming-rat*. He tries with all his might to remain among humans. He even responds to the advances of a young woman in the office who bears a strong "resemblance" to a rat – but it is only a resemblance. One day when he has invited the young woman over, all set to be conjugalized, reoedipalized, Ben suddenly reappears, full of hate. Willard tries to drive him away, but succeeds only in driving away the young woman: he then is lured to the basement by Ben, where a pack of countless rats is waiting to tear him to shreds. It is like a tale; it is never disturbing.

It is all there: there is a becoming-animal not content to proceed by resemblance and for which resemblance, on the contrary, would represent an obstacle or stoppage; the proliferation of rats, the pack, brings a becoming-molecular that undermines the great molar powers of family, career, and conjugality; there is a sinister choice since there is a "favorite" in the pack with which a kind of contract of alliance, a hideous pact, is made; there is the institution of an assemblage, a war machine or criminal machine, which can reach the point of self-destruction; there is a circulation of impersonal affects, an alternate current that disrupts signifying projects as well as subjective feelings, and constitutes a nonhuman sexuality; and there is an irresistible deterritorialization that forestalls attempts at professional, conjugal, or Oedipal reterritorialization. (Are there Oedipal animals with which one can "play Oedipus," play family, my little dog, my little cat, and then other animals that by contrast draw us into an irresistible becoming? Or another hypothesis: Can the same animal be taken up by two opposing functions and movements, depending on the case?)

[...]

A becoming is not a correspondence between relations. But neither is it a resemblance, an imitation, or, at the limit, an identification. The whole structuralist critique of the series seems irrefutable. To become is not to progress or regress along a series. Above all, becoming does not occur in the imagination, even when the imagination reaches the highest cosmic or dynamic level, as in Jung or Bachelard. Becomings-animal are neither dreams nor phantasies. They are perfectly real. But which reality is at issue here? For if becoming animal does not consist in playing animal or imitating an animal, it is clear that the human being does not "really" become an animal any more than the animal "really" becomes something else. Becoming produces nothing other than itself. We fall into a false alternative if we say that you either imitate or you are. What is real is the becoming itself, the block of becoming, not the supposedly fixed terms through which that which becomes passes. Becoming can and should be qualified as becoming-animal even in the absence of a term that would be the animal become. The becoming-animal of the human being is real, even if the animal [which] the human being becomes is not; and the becoming-other of the animal is real, even if that something other [which] it becomes is not. This is the point to clarify: that a becoming lacks a subject distinct from itself; but also that it has no term, since its term in turn exists only as taken up in another becoming of which it is the subject, and which coexists, forms a block, with the first. This is the principle according to which there is a reality specific to becoming (the Bergsonian idea of a coexistence of very different "durations," superior or inferior to "ours," all of them in communication).

Finally, becoming is not an evolution, at least not an evolution by descent and filiation. Becoming produces nothing by filiation; all filiation is imaginary. Becoming is always of a different order than filiation. It concerns alliance. If evolution includes any veritable becomings, it is in the domain of *symbioses* that bring into play beings of totally different scales and kingdoms, with no possible filiation. There is a block of becoming that snaps up the wasp and the orchid, but from which no wasp-orchid can ever descend. There is a block of becoming that takes hold of the cat and baboon, the alliance between which is effected by a C virus. There is a block of becoming between young roots and certain microorganisms, the alliance between which is effected by the materials synthesized in the leaves (rhizosphere). If there is originality in neoevolutionism, it is attributable part to phenomena of this kind in which evolution does not go from something less differentiated to something more differentiated, in which it ceases to be a hereditary filiative evolution, becoming communicative or contagious. Accordingly, the term we would prefer for this form of evolution between heterogeneous terms is "involution," on the condition that involution is in no way confused with regression. Becoming is involutionary, involution is creative. To regress is to move in the direction of something less differentiated. But to involve is to form a block that runs its own line "between" the terms in play and beneath assignable relations.

Neoevolutionism seems important for two reasons: the animal is defined not by characteristics (specific, generic, etc.) but by populations that vary from milieu to milieu or within the same milieu; movement occurs not only, or not primarily, by filiative productions but also by transversal communications between heterogeneous populations. Becoming is a rhizome, not a classificatory or genealogical tree. Becoming is certainly not imitating, or identifying with something; neither is it regressing-progressing; neither is it corresponding, establishing corresponding relations; neither is it producing, producing a filiation or producing through filiation. Becoming is a verb with a consistency all its own; it does not reduce to, or lead back to, "appearing," "being," "equaling," or "producing."

MEMORIES OF A SORCERER, I

A becoming-animal always involves a pack, a band, a population, a peopling, in short, a multiplicity. We sorcerers have always known that. It may very well be that other agencies, moreover very different from one another, have a different appraisal of the animal. One may retain or extract from the animal certain characteristics: species and genera, forms and functions, etc. Society and the State need animal characteristics to use for classifying people; natural history and science need characteristics in order to classify the animals themselves. Serialism and structuralism either graduate characteristics according to their resemblances, or order them according to their differences. Animal characteristics can be mythic or scientific. But we are not interested in characteristics; what interests us are modes of expansion, propagation, occupation, contagion, peopling. I am legion. The Wolf-Man fascinated by several wolves watching him. What would a lone wolf be? Or a whale, a louse, a rat, a fly? Beelzebub is the Devil, but the Devil as lord of the flies. The wolf is not fundamentally a characteristic or a certain number of characteristics; it is a wolfing. The louse is a lousing, and so on. What is a cry independent of the population it appeals to or takes as its witness? Virginia Woolf experiences herself not as a monkey or a fish but as a troop of monkeys, a school of fish, according to her variable relations of becoming with the people she approaches. We do not wish to say that certain animals live in packs. We want nothing to do with ridiculous evolutionary classifications à la Lorenz, according to which there are inferior packs and superior societies. What we are saying is that every animal is fundamentally a band, a pack. That it has pack modes, rather than characteristics, even if further distinctions within these modes are called for. It is at this point that the human being encounters the animal. We do not become animal without a fascination for the pack, for multiplicity. A fascination for the outside? Or is the multiplicity that fascinates us already related to a multiplicity dwelling within us? In one of his masterpieces, H. P. Lovecraft recounts the story of Randolph Carter, who feels his "self" reel and who experiences a fear worse than that of annihilation: "Carters of forms both human and nonhuman, vertebrate and invertebrate, conscious and mindless, animal and vegetable. And, more, there were Carters having nothing in common with earthly life, but moving outrageously amidst backgrounds of other planets and systems and galaxies and cosmic continua ... Merging with nothingness is peaceful oblivion; but to be aware of existence and yet to know that one is no longer a definite being distinguished from other beings," nor from all of the becomings running through us, "that is the nameless summit of agony and dread."[1] Hofmannsthal, or rather Lord Chandos, becomes fascinated with a "people" of dying rats, and it is in him, through him, in the interstices of his disrupted self that the "soul of the animal bares its teeth at monsterous fate":[2] not pity, but *unnatural participation*. Then a strange imperative wells up in him: either stop writing, or write like a rat ... If the writer is a sorcerer, it is because writing is a becoming, writing is traversed by strange becomings that are not becomings-writer, but becomings-rat, becomings-insect, becomings-wolf, etc. We will have to explain why. Many suicides by writers are explained by these unnatural participations, these unnatural nuptials. Writers are sorcerers because they experience the animal as the only population before which they are responsible in principle. The German preromantic Karl Philipp Moritz feels responsible not for the calves that die but before the calves that die and give him the incredible feeling of an unknown Nature – *affect*.[3] For the affect is

not a personal feeling, nor is it a characteristic; it is the effectuation of a power of the pack that throws the self into upheaval and makes it reel. Who has not known the violence of these animal sequences, which uproot one from humanity, if only for an instant, making one scrape at one's bread like a rodent or giving one the yellow eyes of a feline? A fearsome involution calling us toward unheard-of becomings. These are not regressions, although fragments of regression, sequences of regression may enter in.

We must distinguish three kinds of animals. First, individuated animals, family pets, sentimental, Oedipal animals each with its own petty history, "my" cat, "my" dog. These animals invite us to regress, draw us into a narcissistic contemplation, and they are the only kind of animal psychoanalysis understands, the better to discover a daddy, a mommy, a little brother behind them (when psychoanalysis talks about animals, animals learn to laugh): *anyone who likes cats or dogs is a fool*. And then there is a second kind: animals with characteristics or attributes; genus, classification, or State animals; animals as they are treated in the great divine myths, in such a way as to extract from them series or structures, archetypes or models. (Jung is in any event profounder than Freud.) Finally, there are more demonic animals, pack or affect animals that form a multiplicity, a becoming, a population, a tale ... Or once again, cannot any animal be treated in all three ways? There is always the possibility that a given animal, a louse, a cheetah or an elephant, will be treated as a pet, my little beast. And at the other extreme, it is also possible for any animal to be treated in the mode of the pack or swarm; that is our way, fellow sorcerers. Even the cat, even the dog. And the shepherd, the animal trainer, the Devil, may have a favorite animal in the pack, although not at all in the way we were just discussing. Yes, any animal is or can be a pack, but to varying degrees of vocation that make it easier or harder to discover the multiplicity, or multiplicity-grade, an animal contains (actually or virtually according to the case). Schools, bands, herds, populations are not inferior social forms; they are affects and powers, involutions that grip every animal in a becoming just as powerful as that of the human being with the animal.

Jorge Luis Borges, an author renowned for his excess of culture, botched at least two books, only the titles of which are nice: first, A *Universal History of Infamy*, because he did not see the sorcerer's fundamental distinction between deception and treason (becomings-animal are there from the start, on the treason side); second, his *Manual de zoología fantástica*, where he not only adopts a composite and bland image of myth but also eliminates all of the problems of the pack and the corresponding becoming-animal of the human being: "We have deliberately excluded from this manual legends of transformations of the human being, the *lobizon*, the werewolf, etc."[4] Borges is interested only in characteristics, even the most fantastic ones, whereas sorcerers know that werewolves are bands, and vampires too, and that bands transform themselves into one another. But what exactly does that mean, the animal as band or pack? Does a band not imply a filiation, bringing us back to the re-production of given characteristics? How can we conceive of a peopling, a propagation, a becoming that is without filiation or hereditary production? A multiplicity without the unity of an ancestor? It is quite simple; everybody knows it, but it is discussed only in secret. We oppose epidemic to filiation, contagion to heredity, peopling by contagion to sexual reproduction, sexual production. Bands, human or animal, proliferate by contagion, epidemics, battlefields, and catastrophes. Like hybrids, which are in themselves sterile, born of a sexual union that will not reproduce itself, but which begins over again every time, gaining that much more ground. Unnatural participations or nuptials are the true Nature spanning the kingdoms of nature. Propagation by epidemic, by contagion, has nothing to do with filiation by heredity, even if the two themes intermingle and require each other. The vampire does not filiate, it infects. The difference is that contagion, epidemic, involves terms that are entirely heterogeneous: for example, a human being, an animal, and a

bacterium, a virus, a molecule, a microorganism. Or in the case of the truffle, a tree, a fly, and a pig. These combinations are neither genetic nor structural; they are inter-kingdoms, unnatural participations. That is the only way Nature operates – against itself. This is a far cry from filiative production or hereditary reproduction, in which the only differences retained are a simple duality between sexes within the same species, and small modifications across genera-tions. For us, on the other hand, there are as many sexes as there are terms in symbiosis, as many differences as elements contributing to a process of contagion. We know that many beings pass between a man and a woman; they come from different worlds, are borne on the wind, form rhizomes around roots; they cannot be understood in terms of production, only in terms of becoming. The Universe does not function by filiation. All we are saying is that animals are packs, and that packs form, develop, and are transformed by contagion.

These multiplicities with heterogeneous terms, cofunctioning by contagion, enter certain *assemblages*; it is there that human beings effect their becomings-animal. But we should not con-fuse these dark assemblages, which stir what is deepest within us, with organizations such as the institution of the family and the State apparatus. We could cite hunting societies, war societies, secret societies, crime societies, etc. Becomings-animal are proper to them. We will not expect to find filiative regimes of the family type or modes of classification and attribution of the State or pre-State type or even serial organizations of the religious type. Despite appearances and possible confusions, this is not the site of origin or point of application for myths. These are tales, or narratives and statements of becoming. It is therefore absurd to establish a hierarchy even of animal collectivities from the standpoint of a whimsical evolutionism according to which packs are lower on the scale and are superseded by State or familial societies. On the contrary, there is a difference in nature. The origin of packs is entirely different from that of families and States; they continually work them from within and trouble them from without, with other forms of content, other forms of expression. The pack is simultaneously an animal reality, and the reality of the becoming-animal of the human being; contagion is simultaneously an animal peopling, and the propagation of the animal peopling of the human being. The hunting machine, the war machine, the crime machine entail all kinds of becomings-animal that are not articulated in myth, *still less in totemism*. Dumézil showed that becomings of this kind pertain essentially to the man of war, but only insofar as he is external to families and States, insofar as he upsets filiations and classifications. The war machine is always exterior to the State, even when the State uses it, appropriates it. The man of war has an entire becoming that implies multiplicity, celerity, ubiquity, metamorphosis and treason, the power of affect. Wolf-men, bear-men, wildcat-men, men of every animality, secret brotherhoods, animate the battlefields. But so do the animal packs used by men in battle, or which trail the battles and take advantage of them. And together they spread contagion.[5] There is a complex aggregate: the becoming-animal of men, packs of animals, elephants and rats, winds and tempests, bacteria sowing contagion. A single *Furor*. War contained zoological sequences before it became bacteriological. It is in war, famine, and epidemic that werewolves and vampires proliferate. Any animal can be swept up in these packs and the corresponding becomings; cats have been seen on the battlefield, and even in armies. That is why the distinction we must make is less between kinds of animals than between the different states according to which they are integrated into family institutions, State apparatuses, war machines, etc. (and what is the relation of the writing machine and the musical machine to becomings-animal?)

MEMORIES OF A SORCERER, II

Our first principle was: pack and contagion, the contagion of the pack, such is the path becoming-animal takes. But a second principle seemed

to tell us the opposite: wherever there is multiplicity, you will also find an exceptional individual, and it is with that individual that an alliance must be made in order to become-animal. There may be no such thing as a lone wolf, but there is a leader of the pack, a master of the pack, or else the old deposed head of the pack now living alone, there is the Loner, and there is the Demon. Willard has his favorite, the rat Ben, and only becomes-rat through his relation with him, in a kind of alliance of love, then of hate. *Moby-Dick* in its entirety is one of the greatest masterpieces of becoming; Captain Ahab has an irresistible becoming-whale, but one that bypasses the pack or the school, operating directly through a monstrous alliance with the Unique, the Leviathan, Moby-Dick. There is always a pact with a demon; the demon sometimes appears as the head of the band, sometimes as the Loner on the sidelines of the pack, and sometimes as the higher Power (*Puissance*) of the band. The exceptional individual has many possible positions. Kafka, another great author of real becomings-animal, sings of mouse society; but Josephine, the mouse singer, sometimes holds a privileged position in the pack, sometimes a position outside the pack, and sometimes slips into and is lost in the anonymity of the collective statements of the pack.[6] In short, every Animal has its Anomalous. Let us clarify that: every animal swept up in its pack or multiplicity has its anomalous. It has been noted that the origin of the word *anomal* ("anomalous"), an adjective that has fallen into disuse in French, is very different from that of *anormal* ("abnormal"): *a-normal*, a Latin adjective lacking a noun in French, refers to that which is outside rules or goes against the rules, whereas *an-omalie*, a Greek noun that has lost its adjective, designates the unequal, the coarse, the rough, the cutting edge of deterritorialization.[7] The abnormal can be defined only in terms of characteristics, specific or generic; but the anomalous is a position or set of positions in relation to a multiplicity. Sorcerers therefore use the old adjective "anomalous" to situate the positions of the exceptional individual in the pack. It is always with the Anomalous, Moby-Dick or

Josephine, that one enters into alliance to become-animal.

It does seem as though there is a contradiction: between the pack and the loner; between mass contagion and preferential alliance; between pure multiplicity and the exceptional individual; between the aleatory aggregate and a predestined choice. And the contradiction is real: Ahab chooses Moby-Dick, in a choosing that exceeds him and comes from elsewhere, and in so doing breaks with the law of the whalers according to which one should first pursue the pack. Penthesilea shatters the law of the pack, the pack of women, the pack of she-dogs, by choosing Achilles as her favorite enemy. Yet it is by means of this anomalous choice that each enters into his or her becoming-animal, the becoming-dog of Penthesilea, the becoming-whale of Captain Ahab. We sorcerers know quite well that the contradictions are real but that real contradictions are not just for laughs. For the whole question is this: What exactly is the nature of the anomalous? What function does it have in relation to the band, to the pack? It is clear that the anomalous is not simply an exceptional individual; that would be to equate it with the family animal or pet, the Oedipalized animal as psychoanalysis sees it, as the image of the father, etc. Ahab's Moby-Dick is not like the little cat or dog owned by an elderly woman who honors and cherishes it. Lawrence's becoming-tortoise has nothing to do with a sentimental or domestic relation. Lawrence is another of the writers who leave us troubled and filled with admiration because they were able to tie their writing to real and unheard-of becomings. But the objection is raised against Lawrence: "Your tortoises aren't real!" And he answers: Possibly, but my becoming is, my becoming is real, even and especially if you have no way of judging it, because you're just little house dogs … [8] The anomalous, the preferential element in the pack, has nothing to do with the preferred, domestic, and psychoanalytic individual. Nor is the anomalous the bearer of a species presenting specific or generic characteristics in their purest state; nor is it a model or unique specimen; nor is it the perfection of a type incarnate; nor is it the eminent term of a series; nor is it the basis of an absolutely harmonious correspondence. The anomalous is neither an individual nor a species; it has only affects, it has neither familiar or subjectified feelings, nor specific or significant characteristics. Human tenderness is as foreign to it as human classifications. Lovecraft applies the term "Outsider" to this thing or entity, the Thing, which arrives and passes at the edge, which is linear yet multiple, "teeming, seething, swelling, foaming, spreading like an infectious disease, this nameless horror."

If the anomalous is neither an individual nor a species, then what is it? It is a phenomenon, but a phenomenon of bordering. This is our hypothesis: a multiplicity is defined not by the elements that compose it in extension, not by the characteristics that compose it in comprehension, but by the lines and dimensions it encompasses in "intension." If you change dimensions, if you add or subtract one, you change multiplicity. Thus there is a borderline for each multiplicity; it is in no way a center but rather the enveloping line or farthest dimension, as a function of which it is possible to count the others, all those lines or dimensions constitute the pack at a given moment (beyond the borderline, the multiplicity changes nature). That is what Captain Ahab says to his first mate: I have no personal history with Moby-Dick, no revenge to take, any more than I have a myth to play out; but I do have a becoming! Moby-Dick is neither an individual nor a genus; he is the borderline, and I have to strike him to get at the pack as a whole, to reach the pack as a whole and pass beyond it. The elements of the pack are only imaginary "dummies," the characteristics of the pack are only symbolic entities; all that counts is the borderline-the anomalous. "To me, the white whale is that wall, shoved near to me." The white wall. "Sometimes I think there is naught beyond. But 'tis enough."[9] That the anomalous is the borderline makes it easier for us to understand the various positions it occupies in relation to the pack or the multiplicity it borders, and the various positions occupied by a fascinated Self (*Moi*). It is now even possible to establish a classification system for packs while avoiding the pitfalls of an evolutionism that sees them only as an inferior collective stage (instead of taking into consideration the particular assemblages they bring into play). In any event, the pack has a borderline, and an anomalous position, whenever in a given space an animal is on the line or in the act of drawing the line in relation to which all the other members of the pack will fall into one of two halves, left or right: a peripheral position, such that it is impossible to tell if the anomalous is still in the band, already outside the band, or at the shifting boundary of the band. Sometimes each and every animal reaches this line or occupies this dynamic position, as in a swarm of mosquitoes, where "each individual moves randomly unless it sees the rest of [the swarm] in the same half-space; then it hurries to re-enter the group. Thus stability is assured in catastrophe by a *barrier*."[10] Sometimes it is a specific animal that draws and occupies the borderline, as leader of the pack. Sometimes the borderline is defined or doubled by a being of another nature that no longer belongs to the pack, or never belonged to it, and that represents a power of another order, potentially acting as a threat as well as a trainer, outsider, etc. In any case, no band is without this phenomenon of bordering, or the anomalous. It is true that bands are also undermined by extremely varied forces that establish in them interior centers of the conjugal, familial, or State type, and that make them pass into an entirely different form of sociability, replacing pack affects with family feelings or State intelligibilities. The center, or internal black holes, assumes the principal role. This is what evolutionism sees as progress, this adventure also befalls bands of humans when they reconstitute group familialism, or even authoritarianism or pack fascism.

Sorcerers have always held the anomalous position, at the edge of the fields or woods. They haunt the fringes. They are at the borderline of the village, or *between* villages. The important thing is their affinity with alliance, with the pact, which gives them a status opposed to that of filiation. The relation with the anomalous is one of alliance. The sorcerer has a relation of alliance with the demon as the power of the anomalous. The old-time theologians drew a clear distinction between two kinds of curses against sexuality. The first concerns sexuality as a process of filiation transmitting the original sin. But the second concerns it as a power of alliance inspiring illicit unions or abominable loves. This differs significantly from the first in that it tends to prevent procreation; since the demon does not himself have the ability to procreate, he must adopt indirect means (for example, being the female succubus of a man and then becoming the male incubus of a woman, to whom he transmits the man's semen). It is true that the relations between alliance and filiation come to be regulated by laws of marriage, but even then alliance retains a dangerous and contagious power. Leach was able to demonstrate that despite all the exceptions that seemingly disprove the rule, the sorcerer belongs first of all to a group united to the group over which he or she exercises influence only by alliance: thus in a matrilineal group we look to the father's side for the sorcerer or witch. And there is an entire evolution of sorcery depending on whether the relation of alliance acquires permanence or assumes political weight.[11] In order to produce werewolves in your own family it is not enough to resemble a wolf, or to live like a wolf: the pact with the Devil must be coupled with an alliance with another family, and it is the return of this alliance to the first family, the reaction of this alliance on the first family, that produces werewolves by feedback effect. A fine tale by Erckmann and Chatrian, *Hugues-le-loup,* assembles the traditions concerning this complex situation.[12]

The contradiction between the two themes, "contagion through the animal as pack," and "pact with the anomalous as exceptional being," is progressively fading. It is with good reason that Leach links the two concepts of alliance and contagion, pact and epidemic. Analyzing Kachin sorcery, he writes: "Witch influence was thought to be transmitted in the food that the women prepared ... Kachin witchcraft is contagious rather than hereditary ... it is associated with affinity, not filiation."[13] Alliance or the pact is the form of expression for an infection or epidemic constituting the form of content. In sorcery, blood is of the order of contagion and alliance. It can be said that becoming-animal is an affair of sorcery because (1) it implies an initial relation of alliance with a demon; (2) the demon functions as the borderline of an animal pack, into which the human being passes or in which his or her becoming takes place, by contagion; (3) this becoming itself implies a second alliance, with another human group; (4) this new borderline between the two groups guides the contagion of animal and human being within the pack. There is an entire politics of becomings-animal, as well as a politics of sorcery, which is elaborated in assemblages that are neither those of the family nor of religion nor of the State. Instead, they express minoritarian groups, or groups that are oppressed, prohibited, in revolt, or always on the fringe of recognized institutions, groups all the more secret for being extrinsic, in other words, anomic. If becoming-animal takes the form of a Temptation, and of monsters aroused in the imagination by the demon, it is because it is accompanied, at its origin as in its undertaking, by a rupture with the central institutions that have established themselves or seek to become established.

Let us cite pell-mell, not as mixes to be made, but as different cases to be studied: becomings-animal in the war machine, wildmen of all kinds (the war machine indeed comes from without, it is extrinsic to the State, which treats the warrior as an anomalous power); becomings-animal in crime societies, leopard-men, crocodile-men (when the State prohibits tribal and local wars); becomings-animal in riot groups (when the Church and State are faced with peasant movements containing a sorcery component, which they repress by setting up a whole trial and legal system designed to expose pacts with the Devil); becomings-animal in asceticism groups, the grazing anchorite or wild-beast anchorite (the asceticism machine is in an anomalous position, on a line of flight, off to the side of the Church, and disputes the Church's pretension to set itself up as an imperial institution);[14] becomings-animal in societies practicing sexual initiation of the "sacred deflowerer" type, wolf-men, goat-men, etc. (who claim an Alliance superior and exterior to the order of families; families have to win from them the right to regulate their own alliances, to determine them according to relations of complementary lines of descent, and to domesticate this unbridled power of alliance).[15]

The politics of becomings-animal remains, of course, extremely ambiguous. For societies, even primitive societies, have always appropriated these becomings in order to break them, reduce them to relations of totemic or symbolic correspondence. States have always appropriated the war machine in the form of national armies that strictly limit the becomings of the warrior. The Church has always burned sorcerers, or reintegrated anchorites into the toned-down image of a series of saints whose only remaining relation to animals is strangely familiar, domestic. Families have always warded off the demonic Alliance gnawing at them, in order to regulate alliances among themselves as they see fit. We have seen sorcerers serve as leaders, rally to the cause of despotism, create the countersorcery of exorcism, pass over to the side of the family and descent. But this spells the death of the sorcerer, and also the death of becoming. We have seen becoming spawn nothing more than a big domestic dog, as in Henry Miller's damnation ("it would be better to feign, to pretend to be an animal, a dog for example, and catch the bone thrown to me from time to time") or Fitzgerald's ("I will try to be a correct animal though, and if you throw me a bone with enough meat on it I may even lick your hand."). Invert Faust's formula: So that is what it was, the form of the traveling scholar? A mere poodle?[16]

MEMORIES OF A SORCERER, III

Exclusive importance should not be attached to becomings-animal. Rather, they are segments occupying a median region. On the near side, we encounter becomings-woman, becomings-child.

(Becoming-woman, more than any other becoming, possesses a special introductory power; it is not so much that women are witches, but that sorcery proceeds by way of this becoming-woman.) On the far side, we find becomings-elementary, -cellular, -molecular, and even becomings-imperceptible. Toward what void does the witch's broom lead? And where is Moby-Dick leading Ahab so silently? Lovecraft's hero encounters strange animals, but he finally reaches the ultimate regions of a Continuum inhabited by unnameable waves and unfindable particles. Science fiction has gone through a whole evolution taking it from animal, vegetable, and mineral becomings to becomings of bacteria, viruses, molecules, and things imperceptible.[17] The properly musical content of music is plied by becomings-woman, becomings-child, becomings-animal; however, it tends, under all sorts of influences, having to do also with the instruments, to become progressively more molecular in a kind of cosmic lapping through which the inaudible makes itself heard and the imperceptible appears as such: no longer the songbird, but the sound molecule.

If the experimentation with drugs has left its mark on everyone, even nonusers, it is because it changed the perceptive coordinates of space-time and introduced us to a universe of microperceptions in which becomings-molecular take over where becomings-animal leave off. Carlos Castaneda's books clearly illustrate this evolution, or rather this involution, in which the affects of a becoming-dog, for example, are succeeded by those of a becoming-molecular, microperceptions of water, air, etc. A man totters from one door to the next and disappears into thin air: "All I can tell you is that we are fluid, luminous beings made of fibers."[18] All so-called initiatory journeys include these thresholds and doors where becoming itself becomes, and where one changes becoming depending on the "hour" of the world, the circles of hell, or the stages of a journey that sets scales, forms, and cries in variation. From the howling of animals to the wailing of elements and particles.

Thus packs, or multiplicities, continually transform themselves into each other, cross over into each other. Werewolves become vampires when they die. This is not surprising, since becoming and multiplicity are the same thing. A multiplicity is defined not by its elements, nor by a center of unification or comprehension. It is defined by the number of dimensions it has; it is not divisible, it cannot lose or gain a dimension *without changing its nature*. Since its variations and dimensions are immanent to it, *it amounts to the same thing to say that each multiplicity is already composed of heterogeneous terms in symbiosis, and that a multiplicity is continually transforming itself into a string of other multiplicities, according to its thresholds and doors.* For example, the Wolf-Man's pack of wolves also becomes a swarm of bees, and a field of anuses, and a collection of small holes and tiny ulcerations (the theme of contagion): all these heterogeneous elements compose "the" multiplicity of symbiosis and becoming. If we imagined the position of a fascinated Self, it was because the multiplicity toward which it leans, stretching to the breaking point, is the continuation of another multiplicity that works it and strains it from the inside. In fact, the self is only a threshold, a door, a becoming between two multiplicities. Each multiplicity is defined by a borderline functioning as Anomalous, but there is a string of borderlines, a continuous line of borderlines (*fiber*) following which the multiplicity changes. And at each threshold or door, a new pact? A fiber stretches from a human to an animal, from a human or an animal to molecules, from molecules to particles, and so on to the imperceptible. Every fiber is a Universe fiber. A fiber strung across borderlines constitutes a line of flight or of deterritorialization. It is evident that the Anomalous, the Outsider, has several functions: not only does it border each multiplicity, of which it determines the temporary or local stability (with the highest number of dimensions possible under the circumstances), not only is it the precondition for the alliance necessary to becoming, but it also carries the transformations of becoming or crossings of multiplicities always farther down the line of flight. Moby-Dick is the *White Wall* bordering the pack; he is also the demonic *Term of the Alliance*; finally, he is the terrible *Fishing Line* with nothing on the other end, the line that crosses the wall and drags the captain... where? Into the void ...

The error we must guard against is to believe that there is a kind of logical order to this string, these crossings or transformations. It is already going too far to postulate an order descending from the animal to the vegetable, then to molecules, to particles. "Each multiplicity is symbiotic; its becoming ties together animals, plants, microorganisms, mad particles, a whole galaxy. Nor is there a preformed logical order to these heterogeneities, the Wolf-Man's wolves, bees, anuses, little scars. Of course, sorcery always codifies certain transformations of becomings. Take a novel steeped in the traditions of sorcery, Alexandre Dumas's *Meneur de loups*; in a first pact, the man of the fringes gets the Devil to agree to make his wishes come true, with the stipulation that a lock of his hair turn red each time he gets a wish. We are in the hair multiplicity, hair is the borderline. The man himself takes a position on the wolves' borderline, as leader of the pack. Then when he no longer has a single human hair left, a second pact makes him become-wolf himself; it is an endless becoming since he is only vulnerable one day in the year. We are aware that between the hair-multiplicity and the wolf-multiplicity it is always possible to induce an order of resemblance (red like the fur of a wolf); but the resemblance remains quite secondary (the wolf of the transformation is black, with one white hair). In fact, there is a first multiplicity, of hair, taken up in a becoming-red fur; and a second multiplicity, of wolves, which in turn takes up the becoming-animal of the man. Between the two, there is threshold and fiber, symbiosis of or passage between heterogeneities. That is how we sorcerers operate. Not following a logical order, but following alogical consistencies or compatibilities. The reason is simple. It is because no one, not even God, can say in advance whether two borderlines will string together or form a fiber, whether a given multiplicity will or will not cross over into another given multiplicity, or even if given heterogeneous elements will enter symbiosis, will form a consistent, or cofunctioning, multiplicity susceptible to transformation. No one can say where the line of flight will pass: Will it let itself get bogged down and fall back to the Oedipal family animal, a mere poodle? Or will it succumb to another danger, for example, turning into a line of abolition, annihilation, self-destruction, Ahab, Ahab...? We are all too familiar with the dangers of the line of flight, and with its ambiguities. The risks are ever-present, but it is always possible to have the good fortune of avoiding them. Case by case, we can tell whether the line is consistent, in other words, whether the heterogeneities effectively function in a multiplicity of symbiosis, whether the multiplicities are effectively transformed through the becomings of passage. Let us take an example as simple as: x starts practicing piano again. Is it an Oedipal return to childhood? Is it a way of dying, in a kind of sonorous abolition? Is it a new borderline, an active line that will bring other becomings entirely different from becoming or rebecoming a pianist, that will induce a transformation of all of the preceding assemblages to which x was prisoner? Is it a way out? Is it a pact with the Devil? Schizoanalysis, or pragmatics, has no other meaning: Make a rhizome. But you don't know what you can make a rhizome with, you don't know which subterranean stem is effectively going to make a rhizome, or enter a becoming, people your desert. So experiment.

That's easy to say? Although there is no preformed logical order to becomings and multiplicities, there are *criteria*, and the important thing is that they not be used after the fact, that they be applied in the course of events, that they be sufficient to guide us through the dangers. If multiplicities are defined and transformed by the borderline that determines in each instance their number of dimensions, we can conceive of the possibility of laying them out on a plane, the borderlines succeeding one another, forming a broken line. It is only in appearance that a plane of this kind "reduces" the number of dimensions; for it gathers in all the dimensions to the extent that *flat multiplicities* – which nonetheless have *an increasing or decreasing number of dimensions* – are inscribed upon it. It is in grandiose and simplified terms that Lovecraft attempted to pronounce sorcery's final word: "Then the waves increased in strength and sought to improve his understanding, reconciling him to the multiform entity of which his present fragment was an infinitesimal part. They told him that every figure of space is but the result of the intersection by a plane of some corresponding figure of one more dimension – as a square is cut from a cube, or a circle from a sphere. The cube and sphere, of three dimensions, are thus cut from corresponding forms of four dimensions, which men know only through guesses and dreams; and these in turn are cut from forms of five dimensions, and so on up to the dizzy and reachless heights of archetypal infinity."[19] Far from reducing the multiplicities' number of dimensions to two, the *plane of consistency* cuts across them all, intersects them in order to bring into coexistence any number of multiplicities, with any number of dimensions. The plane of consistency is the intersection of all concrete forms. Therefore all becomings are written like sorcerers' drawings on this plane of consistency, which is the ultimate Door providing a way out for them. This is the only criterion to prevent them from bogging down, or veering into the void. The only question is: Does a given becoming reach that point? Can a given multiplicity flatten and conserve all its dimensions in this way, like a pressed flower that remains just as alive dry? Lawrence, in his becoming-tortoise, moves from the most obstinate animal dynamism to the abstract, pure geometry of scales and "cleavages of division," without, however, losing any of the dynamism: he pushes becoming-tortoise all the way to the plane of consistency.[20] Everything becomes imperceptible, everything is becoming imperceptible on the plane of consistency, which is nevertheless precisely where the imperceptible is seen and heard. It is the Planomenon, or the Rhizosphere, the Criterium (and still other names, as the number of dimensions increases). At *n* dimensions, it is called the Hypersphere,

the Mechanosphere. It is the abstract Figure, or rather, since it has no form itself, the abstract Machine of which each concrete assemblage is a multiplicity, a becoming, a segment, a vibration. And the abstract machine is the intersection of them all.

Waves are vibrations, shifting borderlines inscribed on the plane of consistency as so many abstractions. The abstract machine of the waves. In *The Waves*, Virginia Woolf – who made all of her life and work a passage, a becoming, all kinds of be comings between ages, sexes, elements, and kingdoms – intermingles seven characters, Bernard, Neville, Louis, Jinny, Rhoda, Suzanne, and Percival. But each of these characters, with his or her name, its individuality, designates a multiplicity (for example, Bernard and the school of fish). Each is simultaneously in this multiplicity and at its edge, and crosses over into the others. Percival is like the ultimate multiplicity enveloping the greatest number of dimensions. But he is not yet the plane of consistency. Although Rhoda thinks she sees him rising out of the sea, no, it is not he. "When the white arm rests upon the knee it is a triangle; now it is upright – a column; now a fountain ... Behind it roars the sea. It is beyond our reach."[21] Each advances like a wave, but on the plane of consistency they are a single abstract Wave whose vibration propagates following a line of flight or deterritorialization traversing the entire plane (each chapter of Woolf's novel is preceded by a meditation on an aspect of the waves, on one of their hours, on one of their becomings).

NOTES

1. Trans: H. P. Lovecraft, "Through the Gates of the Silver Key," in *The Dream-Quest of Unknown Kadath* (New York: Ballantine, 1970), pp. 191–192.

2. Hugo von Hofmannsthal, *Lettres du voyageur à son retour,* trans. Jean-Claude Schneider (Paris: Mercure de France, 1969), letter of May 9, 1901.

3. Anton Reiser (extracts) in *La légende dispersée: Anthologie du romantisme allemand*(Paris: Union Générale d'Editions, 1976), pp. 36-43.

4. Trans: *A Universal History of Infamy,* trans. Norman Thomas di Giovanni (New York: Dutton, 1972); Jorge Luis Borges and Margarita Guerrero, *Manual de zoología fantástica* (Mexico City: Fondo de Cultura Economica, 1957), p. 9. The *lobizón* is a fantastic creature of Uruguayan folklore to which many shapes are attributed.

5. On the man of war, his extrinsic position in relation to the State, the family, and religion, and on the becomings-animal, becomings-wild animal he enters into, see Dumezil, in particular, *Mythes et dieux des Germains* (Paris: E. Leroux, 1939); *Horace et les Curiaces* (Paris: Gallimard, 1942); *The Destiny of the Warrior,* trans. Alf Hiltebeital (Chicago: University of Chicago Press, 1970); *Mythe et épopée* (Paris: Gallimard, 1968–1973), vol. 2. One may also refer to the studies on leopard-man societies, etc., in Black Africa; it is probable that these societies derive from brotherhoods of warriors. But after the colonial State prohibited tribal wars, they turned into crime associations, while still retaining their territorial and political importance. One of the best studies on this subject is Paul Ernest Joset, *Les sociétés secrètes des hommes-léopards en Afrique noire* (Paris: Payot, 1955). The becomings-animal proper to these groups seem to us to be very different from the symbolic relations between human and animal as they appear in State apparatuses, but also in pre-State institutions of the totemism type. Lévi-Strauss clearly demonstrates that totemism already implies a kind of embryonic State, to the extent that it exceeds tribal boundaries (*The Savage Mind,* pp. 157ff.).

6. Trans: Kafka, "Josephine the Singer, or the Mouse Folk," in *The Complete Stories of Franz Kafka,* ed. Nahum N. Glazer (New York: Schocken, 1983).

7. Georges Canguilhem, *On the Normal and the Pathological,* trans. Carolyn R. Fawcett, intro. Michel Foucault (Boston: Reidel, 1978), pp. 73–74.

8. D. H. Lawrence: "I am tired of being told there is no such animal … If I am a giraffe, and the ordinary Englishmen who write about me and say they know me are nice well-behaved dogs, there it is, the animals are different … You don't love me. The animal that I am you instinctively dislike;" *The Collected Letters of D. H. Lawrence,* vol. 2, ed. Harry T. Moore (New York: Viking, 1962), letter to J. M. Murry, May 20, 1929, p. 1154.

9. Trans: Herman Melville, *Moby Dick,* chapter 36, "The Quarter-Deck."

10. Rene Thom, *Structural Stability and Morphogenesis,* trans. D. H. Fowler (Reading, Mass.: Benjamin Fowler/Cummings, 1975), p. 319.

11. Edward Leach, *Rethinking Anthropology* (New York: Humanities Press, 1971), pp. 18–25.

12. Trans: Emile Erckmann and Alexandre Chatrian, *Hugues-le-loup* (Paris: J. Bonaventure, n.d.).

13. Trans: Leach, *Rethinking Anthropology,* p. 18.

14. See Jacques Lacarrière, *Les hommes ivres de dieu* (Paris: Fayard, 1975).

15. Pierre Gordon, in *Sex and Religion,* trans. Renée and Hilda Spodheim (New York: Social Science Publishers, 1949), studied the role of animal-men in rites of "sacred defloration." These animal-men impose a ritual alliance upon filiative groups, themselves belong to brotherhoods that are on the outside or on the fringes, and are masters of contagion and epidemic. Gordon analyzes the reaction of the villages and cities when they begin to fight the animal-men in order to win the right to perform their own initiations and order their alliances according to their respective filiations (for example, the fight against the dragon). We find the same theme, for example, in Geneviève Calame-Griaule and Z. Ligers, "L'homme-hyène dans la tradition soudanaise," *L'Homme,* 1,2 (May–August 1961), pp. 89–118: the hyena-man lives on the fringes of the village, or between two villages, and can keep a lookout in both directions. A hero, or even two heroes with a fiancee in each other's village, triumphs over the man-animal. It is as though it were necessary to distinguish two very different states of alliance: a demonic alliance that imposes itself from without, and imposes its law upon all of the filiations (a forced alliance with the monster, with the man-animal), and a consensual alliance, which is on the contrary in conformity with the law of filiations and is established after the men of the villages have defeated the monster and have organized their own relations. This sheds new light on the question of incest. For it is not enough to say that the prohibition against incest results from the positive requirements of alliance in general. There is instead a kind of alliance that is so foreign and hostile to filiation that it necessarily takes the position of incest (the man-animal always has a relation to incest). The second kind of alliance prohibits incest because it can

subordinate itself to the rights of filiation only by lodging itself, precisely, between two distinct filiations. Incest appears twice, once as a monstrous power of alliance when alliance overturns filiation, and again as a prohibited power of filiation when filiation subordinates alliance and must distribute it among distinct lineages.

16. Trans: See Fitzgerald, "The Crack-up," in *The Crack-up. With Other Uncollected Pieces,* ed. Edmund Wilson (New York: New Directions, 1956). The allusion to Faust is to Goethe, *Faust,* Part I, lines 1323–1324.

17. Richard Matheson and Isaac Asimov are of particular importance in this evolution (Asimov extensively develops the theme of symbiosis).

18. Carlos Castaneda, *Tales of Power* (New York: Simon and Schuster, 1974), p. 159.

19. Trans: H. P. Lovecraft, "Through the Gates of the Silver Key," in *The Dream-Quest of Unknown Kadath* (New York: Ballantine, 1970), p. 197.

20. See D. H. Lawrence, the first and second poems of *Tortoises* (New York: T. Selzer, 1921).

21. Trans: Virginia Woolf, *The Waves* (New York: Harcourt Brace Jovanovich, 1931), p. 139.

FURTHER READING IN ANIMALS AS PHILOSOPHICAL AND ETHICAL SUBJECTS

Acampora, Christa Davis and Ralph R. Acampora (eds.). 2003. *A Nietzschean Bestiary:Becoming Animal Beyond Docile and Brutal.* Lanham, MD: Rowman and Littlefield.

Armstrong, Susan J. and Richard G. Botzler (eds.). 2003. *The Animal Ethics Reader.* New York: Routledge.

Atterton, Peter and Matthew Calarco (eds.). 2005. *Animal Philosophy: Ethics and Identity.* London and New York: Continuum.

Benton, Ted. 1993. *Natural Relations: Ecology, Animal Rights and Social Justice.* London: Verso.

Creager, Angela N. H. and William Chester Jordan (eds.). 2002. *The Animal/Human Boundary: Historical Perspectives.* Rochester, NY: University of Rochester Press.

Dunayer, Joan. 2001. *Animal Equality: Language and Liberation.* Derwood, MD: Ryce.

Gaard, Greta (ed.). 1993. *Ecofeminism: Women, Animals, Nature.* Philadelphia: Temple University Press.

Garner, Robert. 2005. *Animal Ethics.* Cambridge: Polity.

Kean, H. 1998. *Animal Rights: Political and Social Change in Britain Since 1800.* London: Reaktion.

Midgley, Mary. 1993. *Animals and Why They Matter.* Athens, GA: University of Georgia Press.

Newmyer, Stephen T. 2005. *Animals, Rights and Reason in Plutarch and Modern Ethics.* London: Routledge.

Patterson, Charles. 2002. *Eternal Treblinka: Our Treatment of Animals and the Holocaust.* New York: Lantern Books.

Porphyry. 1965. The Life of Pythagoras, in *Heroes and Gods*, Moses Hadas and Morton Smith (eds.), New York: Harper and Row, 105–28.

Preece, Rod. 2002. *Awe for the Tiger, Love for the Lamb: A Chronicle of Sensibility to Animals.* Vancouver: University of British Columbia Press.

Rachels, J. 1990. *Created From Animals: The Moral Implications of Darwinism.* New York: Oxford University Press.

Rollin, Bernard. 1981. *Animal Rights and Human Morality.* New York: Prometheus.

Salt, Henry S. 1892. *Animals' Rights Considered in Relation to Social Progress.* London and New York: G. Bell.

Sorabji, Richard. 1993. *Animal Minds and Human Morals: The Origins of the Western Debate.* Ithaca: Cornell University Press.

Taylor, Angus. 2003. *Animals and Ethics: An Overview of the Philosophical Debate.* Broadview.

Varner, Gary. E. 2002. *In Nature's Interests?: Interests, Animal Rights, and Environmental Ethics.* New York: Oxford University Press.

Wise, Steven M. 2000. *Rattling the Cage: Toward Legal Rights for Animals.* Cambridge, MA: Perseus.

Wolfe, Cary. 2003. *Animal Rites: American Culture, the Discourse of Species and Posthumanist Theory.* Chicago: University of Chicago Press.

SECTION 2
*A*nimals as Reflexive Thinkers

INTRODUCTION

While some early Greeks struggled with the ethics of our relationship with other animals and the permeability of the human-animal boundary, others were busy writing that animals were capable of human-like emotions such as happiness and heartbreak. In his poem *On the Nature of Things* (49 BCE), Lucretius describes the sorrow of an "orphaned mother" whose yearling calf has been snatched away for sacrifice, and nothing "can lure her mind and turn the sudden pain." The conviction implied by Lucretius – that animals are thinking, reflexive, emotional beings – has persisted for centuries, even after Descartes's influential assertion in the seventeenth century that animals are mere unthinking, unfeeling machines. This section discusses animal capabilities – cognitive, emotional and cultural – and the recent research that documents that animals are capable of compassion, morality and a range of emotions from joy to extreme sadness.

We begin this section with an extract from the sixteenth-century essays of Michel de Montaigne. In this short piece, Montaigne argues that animals and humans have similar attributes, such as communication, cunning and playfulness. In the next reading, René Descartes disagrees with Montaigne's contention that animals are thinking beings capable of communication and concludes that since animals lack language they also lack consciousness. According to Descartes, animals do not behave as if they can think, but rather act naturally and mechanically like clocks or machines (although he does not deny that they feel sensations).

Today, the assertion that animals lack consciousness is widely disputed by both scientists and the general public. The linguistic ability of animals, however, is still controversial, despite evidence that primates can learn to communicate their thoughts and feelings in captive environments. Dr. Francine "Penny" Patterson has taught Koko, a gorilla, to use sign language to communicate using more than 1,000 signs, and research led by Dr. E. Sue Savage-Rumbaugh has documented the use of lexigrams (symbols that represents words) by Kanzi, a male bonobo, to communicate more than 200 words. Thus, it is argued that some animals possess a theory of mind – they are not only capable of thoughts and self-awareness, but they also attribute these qualities to others. Alas, remnants of the Cartesian view of animal cognitive capacities remain in the world of science and in the popular culture, and the lack of verbal speech among animals is often used as a pretext for assuming that animals do not have other characteristics that mark what is considered "human," such as morality, emotions and culture.

The rest of the readings in this section provide compelling evidence that animals are reflexive thinkers. Clinton Sanders and Arnold Arluke argue that a spoken language between humans and their animal companions is not even necessary for successful interaction. Humans in relationships with "virtual persons" (such as their dogs) have ongoing interactional experiences in which they "read" the animals' gazes, vocalizations and body expressions. Sanders and Arluke conclude that "language is overrated as the primary vehicle of cognition and coordinated social interaction," animal coactors are often regarded as minded, emotional, and intentional by their human companions and that anthropomorphism (attributing human characteristics to nonhuman beings or objects) is useful in understanding animal behavior.

The other three readings in this section demonstrate that animals possess numerous capabilities usually considered to be the exclusive province of humans. Marc Bekoff examines the play behavior of animals for evidence of social morality (behaving fairly). Bekoff celebrates the use of a biocentrically anthropomorphic approach in understanding animal social behavior, arguing that "we are humans and we have by necessity a human view of the world." He concludes that animals have moral social relationships that are necessary to the maintenance of the group and that those relationships include cooperation, forgiveness, justice, fairness and trust.

The reading from Jeffrey Moussaieff Masson and Susan McCarthy provides insight into the emotional lives of animals. They argue that animals exhibit emotions, such as grief and sadness, in contexts that would elucidate the same emotions in people. Masson and McCarthy tell compelling stories of animals caring for ill companions, mourning the loss of mates, and displaying learned helplessness and a concept of death.

As the evidence amasses that animals have a wide range of cognitive and emotional capacities, humans have turned to yet another quality to emphasize their distinction from other animals – culture. As a last resort, it is argued that only humans have the capacity for socially transmitted behavior. We close this section with an article by Carel van Schaik and colleagues that provides evidence that at least some animals other than humans possess material culture. Their research team studied six populations of orangutans in the wild and found notable variations in their behavior that could not be accounted for by environmental or biological variables. The authors argue that these behavioral differences are the result of cultural transmission and conclude that "great-ape cultures exist, and may have done so for at least 14 million years."

8

MICHEL DE MONTAIGNE

An Apology for Raymond Sebond*

Michel de Montaigne was a Renaissance scholar born in France in 1533. A skeptic, a humanist, and a student of law, Montaigne introduced the essay as a format of literary prose. [He is known for his query, "What Do I Know?"] He was skeptical of humanity's perceived superiority over other life forms, denounced cruelty to animals, and argued that animals with life and sense deserved justice as do humans. We reproduce a short extract from one of his longest and most famous essays, "An Apology for Raymond Sebond," in which Montaigne directly challenges the notion that animals cannot communicate thoughts and emotions. Raymond Sebond was a Spanish theologian who wrote Natural Theology or The Book of Creatures in the early fifteenth century, and Montaigne later translated the book into French at the request of his father. The word "apology" actually means "defense" [Sebond was criticized for arguing that Christians should ground their beliefs in reason as opposed to faith], and Montaigne crafts his essay under the pretense of defending Sebond but actually attacks rational explanations in favor of a skeptical Christianity based on faith not reason – and he uses animal communication to do so. Montaigne argues that drawing rigid distinctions between the abilities of humans and other animals has no rational justification, and that animals are capable of cross-species communication and acts of kindness.

Of all creatures man is the most miserable and fraile, and therewithall the proudest and disdainfullest. Who perceiveth and seeth himself placed here amidst the filth and mire of the world, fast-tied and nailed to the worst, most senselesse, and drooping part of the world, in the vilest corner of the house, and farthest from heavens coape, with those creatures that are the worst of the three conditions ... he selecteth and separateth himselfe from out the ranke of other creatures ... How knoweth he by the vertue of his understanding the inward and secret motions of beasts? By what comparison from them to us doth he conclude the brutishnesse he ascribeth unto them? When I am playing with my cat, who knowes whether she have more sport in dallying with me than I have in gaming with her? We entertain one another with mutuall apish trickes. If I have my houre to begin or to refuse, so hath she hers ... The defect which

* "Apologie de Raimond Sebond" (original title) is reprinted from Michel de Montaigne's *Essays: Book II*, is in the public domain and was obtained from the following website operated by the University of Oregon: http://www.uoregon.edu/%7Erbear/montaigne/2xii.htm. It is based on the translation by John Florio.

hindreth the communication betweene them and us, why may it not as well be in us as in them? It is a matter of divination to guesse in whom the fault is that we understand not one another. For we understand them no more than they us. By the same reason, may they as well esteeme us beasts as we them. It is no great marvell if we understand them not: no more doe we the Cornish, the Welch, or Irish … We have some meane understanding of their senses, so have beasts of ours, about the same measure. They flatter and faune upon us, they threat and entreat us, so doe we them. Touching other matters, we manifestly perceive that there is a full and perfect communication amongst them, and that not only those of one same kinde understand one another, but even such as are of different kindes … By one kinde of barking of a dogge, the horse knoweth he is angrie; by another voice of his, he is nothing dismaid. Even in beasts that have no voice at all, by the reciprocall kindnesse which we see in them, we easily inferre there is some other meane of entercommunication: their jestures treat, and their motions discourse …

Silence also hath a way,
Words and prayers to convay.

9

RENÉ DESCARTES

From the Letters of 1646 and 1649*

René Descartes, who lived from 1596 to 1650, was a French philosopher, scientist, and mathematician. Known as the father of modern science, he rejected all ideas that could not be verified through direct observation, thus establishing the backbone of the scientific method. Also considered the founder of modern philosophy, Descartes wrote on topics related to the natural sciences, mind, body and the nature of reality. [He was the author of the famous dictum, "I think, therefore I am."] His contributions have been varied and numerous, but the most central to the animal question is his distinction between humans and other animals based on the possession of a mind and a capacity for conscious thought. In the extracts presented here from his letters to the Marquess of Newcastle (William Cavendish, Royalist general, patron of science and literature) and Henry More (a Cambridge philosopher), Descartes discusses what he considers to be the prejudicial belief held by Montaigne and Pythagoras that animals are thinking beings. He cites lack of speech by animals as evidence of his claim that animals do not think, reasoning that since animals have the organs necessary for speech their lack thereof must be the result of a paucity of the thoughts necessary to motivate speech. He therefore concludes that animal actions are not inspired by thought, but instead are instinctual or mechanical, and as mechanical entities animals lack souls. This kind of "Cartesian" thinking has had far-reaching impacts on Western philosophy and science, with substantial implications for the moral and ethical issues surrounding the animal question.

FROM THE LETTER TO THE MARQUESS OF NEWCASTLE, 23 NOVEMBER 1646

I cannot share the opinion of Montaigne and others who attribute understanding or thought to animals. I am not worried that people say that men have an absolute empire over all the other animals; because I agree that some of them are stronger than us, and believe that there may also be some who have an instinctive cunning capable of deceiving the shrewdest human beings. But I observe that they only imitate or surpass us in those of our actions which are not guided by our thoughts. It often happens that we walk or eat without thinking at all about what we are

* Reprinted from *Descartes: Philosophical Letters*, translated and edited by Anthony Kenny (1970). Oxford: Clarendon.

doing; and similarly, without using our reason, we reject things which are harmful for us, and parry the blows aimed at us. Indeed, even if we expressly willed not to put our hands in front of our head when we fall, we could not prevent ourselves. I think also that if we had no thought we would eat, as the animals do, without having to learn to; and it is said that those who walk in their sleep sometimes swim across streams in which they would drown if they were awake. As for the movements of our passions, even though in us they are accompanied with thought because we have the faculty of thinking, it is none the less very clear that they do not depend on thought, because they often occur in spite of us. Consequently they can also occur in animals, even more violently than they do in human beings, without our being able to conclude from that that they have thoughts.

In fact, none of our external actions can show anyone who examines them that our body is not just a self-moving machine but contains a soul with thoughts, with the exception of words, or other signs that are relevant to particular topics without expressing any passion. I say words or other signs, because deaf-mutes use signs as we use spoken words; and I say that these signs must be relevant, to exclude the speech of parrots, without excluding the speech of madmen, which is relevant to particular topics even though it does not follow reason. I add also that these words or signs must not express any passion, to rule out not only cries of joy or sadness and the like, but also whatever can be taught by training to animals. If you teach a magpie to say good-day to its mistress, when it sees her approach, this can only be by making the utterance of this word the expression of one of its passions. For instance it will be an expression of the hope of eating, if it has always been given a titbit when it says it. Similarly, all the things which dogs, horses, and monkeys are taught to perform are only expressions of their fear, their hope, or their joy; and consequently they can be performed without any thought. Now it seems to me very striking that the use of words, so defined, is something peculiar to human beings. Montaigne and Charron may have said that there is more difference between one human being and another than between a human being and an animal; but there has never been known an animal so perfect as to use a sign to make other animals understand something which expressed no passion; and there is no human being so imperfect as not to do so, since even deaf-mutes invent special signs to express their thoughts. This seems to me a very strong argument to prove that the reason why animals do not speak as we do is not that they lack the organs but that they have no thoughts. It cannot be said that they speak to each other and that we cannot understand them; because since dogs and some other animals express their passions to us, they would express their thoughts also if they had any.

I know that animals do many things better than we do, but this does not surprise me. It can even be used to prove they act naturally and mechanically, like a clock which tells the time better than our judgment does. Doubtless when the swallows come in spring, they operate like clocks. The actions of honeybees are of the same nature, and the discipline of cranes in flight, and of apes in fighting, if it is true that they keep discipline. Their instinct to bury their dead is no stranger than that of dogs and cats who scratch the earth for the purpose of burying their excrement; they hardly ever actually bury it, which shows that they act only by instinct and without thinking. The most that one can say is that though the animals do not perform any action which shows us that they think, still, since the organs of their body are not very different from ours, it may be conjectured that there is attached to those organs some thoughts such as we experience in ourselves, but of a very much less perfect kind. To which I have nothing to reply except that if they thought as we do, they would have an immortal soul like us. This is unlikely, because there is no reason to believe it of some animals without believing it of all, and many of them such as oysters and sponges are too imperfect for this to be credible. But I am afraid of boring you with this discussion, and my only desire is to show you that I am, etc.

FROM LETTER TO MORE, 5 FEBRUARY 1649

But there is no prejudice to which we are all more accustomed from our earliest years than the belief that dumb animals think. Our only reason for this belief is the fact that we see that many of the organs of animals are not very different from ours in shape and movement. Since we believe that there is a single principle within us which causes these motions – namely the soul, which both moves the body and thinks – we do not doubt that some such soul is to be found in animals also. I came to realize, however, that there are two different principles causing our motions: one is purely mechanical and corporeal and depends solely on the force of the spirits and the construction of our organs, and can be called the corporeal soul; the other is the incorporeal mind, the soul which I have defined as a thinking substance. Thereupon I investigated more carefully whether the motions of animals originated from both these principles or from one only. I soon saw clearly that they could all originate from the corporeal and mechanical principle, and I thenceforward regarded it as certain and established that we cannot at all prove the presence of a thinking soul in animals. I am not disturbed by the astuteness and cunning of dogs and foxes, or all the things which animals do for the sake of food, sex, and fear; I claim that I can easily explain the origin of all of them from the constitution of their organs.

But though I regard it as established that we cannot prove there is any thought in animals, I do not think it is thereby proved that there is not, since the human mind does not reach into their hearts. But when I investigate what is most probable in this matter, I see no argument for animals having thoughts except the fact that since they have eyes, ears, tongues, and other sense-organs like ours, it seems likely that they have sensation like us; and since thought is included in our mode of sensation, similar thought seems to be attributable to them. This argument, which is very obvious, has taken possession of the minds of all men from their earliest age. But there are other arguments, stronger and more numerous, but not so obvious to everyone, which strongly urge the opposite. One is that it is more probable that worms and flies and caterpillars move mechanically than that they all have immortal souls.

It is certain that in the bodies of animals, as in ours, there are bones, nerves, muscles, animal spirits, and other organs so disposed that they can by themselves, without any thought, give rise to all the animal motions we observe. This is very clear in convulsive movements when the machine of the body moves despite the soul, and sometimes more violently and in a more varied manner than when it is moved by the will.

Second, it seems reasonable, since art copies nature, and men can make various automata which move without thought, that nature should produce its own automata, much more splendid than artificial ones. These natural automata are the animals. This is especially likely since we have no reason to believe that thought always accompanies the disposition of organs which we find in animals. It is much more wonderful that a mind should be found in every human body than that one should be lacking in every animal.

But in my opinion the main reason which suggests that the beasts lack thought is the following. Within a single species some of them are more perfect than others, as men are too. This can be seen in horses and dogs, some of whom learn what they are taught much better than others. Yet, although all animals easily communicate to us, by voice or bodily movement, their natural impulses of anger, fear, hunger, and so on, it has never yet been observed that any brute animal reached the stage of using real speech, that is to say, of indicating by word or sign something pertaining to pure thought and not to natural impulse. Such speech is the only certain sign of thought hidden in a body. All men use it, however stupid and insane they may be, and though they may lack tongue and organs of voice; but no animals do. Consequently it can be taken as a real specific difference between men and dumb animals.

For brevity's sake I here omit the other reasons for denying thought to animals. Please note that I am speaking of thought, and not of life or sensation. I do not deny life to animals, since I regard it as consisting simply in the heat of the heart; and I do not deny sensation, in so far as it depends on a bodily organ. Thus my opinion is not so much cruel to animals as indulgent to men – at least to those who are not given to the superstitions of Pythagoras – since it absolves them from the suspicion of crime when they eat or kill animals.

Perhaps I have written at too great length for the sharpness of your intelligence; but I wished to show you that very few people have yet sent me objections which were as agreeable as yours. Your kindness and candour has made you a friend of that most respectful admirer of all who seek true wisdom,

René Descartes

10

CLINTON R. SANDERS and ARNOLD ARLUKE

Speaking for Dogs*

Clinton Sanders and **Arnold Arluke** are sociologists who have published extensively in the field of animal studies. Sanders studies human-animal interactions, notably the relationship between people and dogs in contexts such as veterinary clinics and guide-dog programs, and Arluke has studied animal-shelter workers, humane law-enforcement officers, scientists who experiment on animals, animal hoarders and animal abuse. In the extract reproduced here from their book, *Regarding Animals*, Sanders and Arluke discuss how companion animals are perceived as minded coactors by their human companions [reminiscent of Montaigne's contention earlier in this section that communication between humans and animals can occur even in the absence of verbal communication]. They describe how people generally "speak for" or articulate the perceived perspective of companion animals, noting that through our interactions with animals we construct an understanding of their minds. The implication is that language is not a requirement for social interactions: humans are able to empathize with animals, or speak for them, without the benefit of verbally communicating with them. Sanders and Arluke argue that, while largely out of favor among scientists, anthropomorphism is "a useful heuristic device" that helps humans understand other animals, coordinating social behavior and anticipating the future acts of our animal cointeractants.

Typically, those who live with companion animals routinely define them as minded coactors, as virtual persons whose abilities are quantitatively different, but not qualitatively different, from those of humans (Rasmussen et al. 1993). Instead of employing what Bernard Rollin (1990) refers to as the "common-sense of science," animal caretakers, as practical actors, regard their animals as conscious, purposive, and as engaging in minded behavior (Sanders 1993). In particular, companion dogs (the focus of this discussion) are seen as eminently social creatures with distinct personalities with whom one may develop close and rewarding relationships (Bulcroft et al. 1986; Shapiro 1989). As virtual persons dogs typically are socially incorporated as members of the

* "Speaking for Dogs" from *Regarding Animals* by Arnold Arluke and Clinton R. Sanders. Used by permission of Temple University Press. ©1996 by Temple University. All Rights Reserved.

family (Katcher and Beck 1991) who regularly engage in communicative activities similar to those of the other family members. It is through ongoing interactional experience with the dog that the owner learns to "read" gaze, vocalizations, bodily expressions, and other communicative acts (Baer 1989; McConnell 1991; Ross and McKinney 1992; Serpell 1986; Shapiro 1990b) and, in turn, speaks with the dog in ways that presume that the animal understands what the owner means. As described by Aaron Katcher and Alan Beck (1991, 268), the owner's communicative behavior displays distinct characteristics much like those used in interactions with a child. The owner typically places his or her head close to the animal's and speaks in a quiet voice with a somewhat raised pitch. The rate of speech is slowed and vocalizations tend to be short with phrases rising at the end in a conventional questioning mode.

The animal-person is, however, unable to employ language to respond to the owner's talk or effectively express the content of his or her mind. Like those who have intimate relationships with retarded, ill, or immature humans, owners commonly find themselves in situations in which they feel obliged to translate the dog's point of view, desires, thoughts, or experiences. As the competent language-user, the owner commonly speaks for the animal companion. We turn now to various forms this interlocution takes and some specific settings in which it is practiced.

This discussion is drawn from data collected in two major settings. Sanders spent fourteen months doing participant observation in a large veterinary hospital in the northeast. Some material is drawn from observations of clinical interactions that occurred in this setting. Following the work in the clinic, Sanders was involved in a field study of a guide-dog breeding, training, and placement program. In this setting he became particularly interested in the trainers' interactions with the dogs and their (often ambivalent) understandings of the animals in their charge. Parts of this discussion are based on observations and field conversations recorded in the course of this study.

MODES OF "SPEAKING FOR"

No matter what the setting in which it occurs, as the "word-user" the human coactor typically gives voice to what he or she understands to be the thoughts or perspective of the dog. In some circumstances, this verbalization is for the speaker's own benefit in that it is central to constructing a dialogue-like exchange with the animal. In other circumstances, for example, in the veterinary setting discussed in the following section, interpreting for the dog or explaining his or her experiences and feelings is intended to promote the interests of the animal. Most basically, then, through empathically determining the feelings, preferences, and thoughts of their dogs and subsequently speaking for their animals, owners actively incorporate their mute companions into the "language community."

In speaking for the dog, the owner demonstrates the intimacy of his or her relationship – the animal other is known so well that the owner can effectively discern what is "on his or her mind." Furthermore, the empathic and verbalizing process is intrinsically pleasurable. It is an integral part of and promotes the intimate relationship between, dog and owner.

It is also through the process of speaking for the dog that the owner actively constructs – both for him- or herself and for others – the identity of the animal (cf. Goode and Waksler 1990). The verbalizations help define the dog and ground its behavior in an understandable context, thereby aiding in constructing the practical interaction chains that constitute collective action.

The interaction of caretakers with their canine companions is commonly quite verbal. Beck and Katcher (1983), for example, found that 80 percent of the veterinary clients they studied talked to their pets "in the same way they talked to people." This communicative activity is typically defined as an authentic conversational exchange in that human caretakers believe that the animal understands what they say and responds appropriately (Beck and Katcher 1983, 44; Cain 1985, 7). Usually the owner speaks slowly and quietly, using short phrases while stretching out words and accenting certain syllables. Katcher and Beck (1991, 268) refer to this "baby-talk" style as "motherese," while Jean Veevers (1985, 20) calls it "doggeral" (cf. Tannen and Wallat 1983).

When speaking to or about a dog or other animal companion owners commonly employ conventional familial labels to incorporate the animal into an everyday, intimate relational context. Veterinary clients routinely presented their relationship with their dogs as familial – they referred to themselves as "Mommy" or "Dad," spoke of their dogs as "the children," and so forth. This convention is so socially powerful that some owners interviewed in the course of the veterinary study – primarily younger couples without children – cited examples in which their own parents spoke of themselves as the dogs' "grandparents." Similarly, veterinarians and support staff often referred to clients as "mommy" and "daddy" when speaking to animal patients in the presence of the owners.

A questioning mode is very common in the verbalizations directed at dogs and other companion animals. The owner's vocal inflection rises at the end of the phrase and then he or she typically pauses to allow the animal to "respond." Owners frequently use this postquestion pause as a "speaking for" opportunity. They "fill in" an appropriate response for the animal, just as humans do for their children. These "priming moves" (Goffman 1971) were observed by Spencer Cahill (1987) in public situations where parents direct "elicitation" questions such as, "What do you say to the nice man?" to their children as part of the socializing process (see also Kaye 1982; West and Zimmerman 1977). In Sanders's observations in the veterinary clinic, he noted that this questioning mode was especially common when owners spoke to their animals. Dogs were frequently asked such direct questions as, "What do you see?" or "Do you want to leave now?" by their human companions.

The question-constructed response style is an example of how owners directly give voice to what they believe their dogs would say if they could use words. In general, this direct, first-person form is common in speaking for. An entry from Sanders's field notes provides an example:

A young male shepherd with long hair is brought into the exam room by an older couple. The woman does all the talking and even tells us all about what her husband (Frank) does for a living. The husband is generally treated as a nonperson, though he does chime in at times with additions to the information his wife provides. The woman goes on at some length about the dog's long hair and how they hadn't anticipated this when the dog was a puppy. As the talker, the woman does a lot of speaking for the dog (as she does for her husband). The dog lies down with his head on the woman's feet and she says, "Oh, I'm so tired. I just have to lie down here." Later, as the dog is having his nails trimmed, she speaks for the dog in observing, "Oh, I have such nice nails." During much of the time she holds the dog's head tenderly and stares into his eyes.

Veterinarians are accustomed to clients speaking for their animals in the first person and typically find it amusing. As one related, "I come into the exam room and I say, 'Well, how are you doing?' and the woman says, 'Oh Doctor, I'm not feeling all that well.' Later when I'm getting the hypo out, she says, 'Oh Doctor, are you going to give me that shot?' I say, 'No, lady, it's not for you. I don't work on humans.'"

Frequently, in employing the direct manner of speaking for, owners will use the collective "we" convention, as in "We aren't feeling well today." In so doing, the owner clearly demonstrates that he or she, together with the dog, constitute what Erving Goffman (1971) refers to as a "with." The dog-person dyad should be perceived by others as a single acting unit.

Owners also routinely use a somewhat less direct mode of speaking for the animal, typically opening with such statements as, "He doesn't want," or "She feels that." For example:

A chubby middle-aged man has brought in an old black mix-breed dog for her rabies shot. The owner holds the dog on the exam table and constantly strokes her. He tells us about her subjective experience. "She's not in the best of moods. We have a new litter of kittens at home, and they are upsetting her. She hasn't eaten today and she also hasn't peed." [The vet] says, "Well, we'll get this over with fast so that you can get her home and get her filled and emptied." Later we talk about the dog's age and the owner reports on her personal interests. He says, "She still loves to chase sticks. She's just like a puppy."

A subcategory of this type of second-level speaking for is seen when owners employ what Sanders has referred to elsewhere (1990a) as "excusing tactics." When socially more competent actors act in concert with less competent ones, they often feel obliged to provide justifying "accounts" (Hewitt and Stokes 1975; Scott and Lyman 1968) for the others' infractions of social rules. In constructing and offering these "vocabularies of motive" (Mills 1940) for the other, the ostensibly more responsible (i.e., powerful) member of the dyad works to repair the damage the violation may have done to the normal flow of social intercourse and the resulting degradation of the responsible member's identity. In human-with-human dyads, these types of surrogate explanation are found when adults are linked with children (Cahill 1987), mentally competent persons are linked with Alzheimer's patients (Fontana and Smith 1989; Gubrium 1986), and psychologically "normal" individuals present the perspectives of associates whose behavior could be interpreted as symptomatic of mental disorder (Lynch 1983).

A final and especially interesting form of speaking for is seen when caretakers engage in what Ann Cain (1983, 79–80) has referred to as "triangling." Essentially, turning the speaking for process around, the speaker presents the virtual voice of the animal to express his or her own orientation, desires, or concerns. The caretaker often uses this mode, like excusing, as a means of protecting social identity in situations where more direct expression could cause embarrassment or discomfort. For example, in the fieldnote excerpt below, a veterinary client uses the dog to "give orders" to her husband (notice the use of parental references), just as triangling has been observed between people and dogs in public parks (Robbins et al. 1991).

> The owners – a middle-aged married couple – had apparently been involved in some form of argument prior to entering the examination room and the lingering bad feelings between them are fairly obvious. Following the examination and treatment of their dog, the wife asks me where she should go to pay. I tell her where the discharge desk is located. She bends over the dog, turning her back to her husband who is standing at the door, and says, "Why doesn't Daddy take me out to the car while Mommy pays the bill?"

Exchanges between people and animals are central to the ongoing flow of contemporary social life. As is the case of interactions with other alingual actors (Goode 1990; Gubrium 1986; Pollner and McDonald-Wikler 1985), the understandings we derive in our encounters with companion animals are found largely in our connections to them built up over the course of the routine, practical, and empathetic interactions that make up our shared biographies (Shapiro 1989). In other words, through understanding the bodies and behaviors of companion animals we actively construct a view of their minds. This is especially so with canine companions in that, of all pet animals, dogs are most likely to be defined by their human coactors as possessing minds that operate in many ways like our own (Eddy et al. 1993; Rasmussen et al. 1993). A natural and useful consequence of our socially constructed understanding of the dog's mind is that we regularly find ourselves in situations that make it necessary, convenient, or intrinsically rewarding for us to give voice to what we "know" to be the dog's subjective experience.

Whether this construction of the dog's mind is "true" in some objective sense – that is, whether the animal is "actually" thinking planning, intending, or feeling in the ways we present – is not the central issue. It may be, of course, that in speaking for the dogs with whom we share our daily lives we are simply, as Eugene

Rochberg-Halton (1985) presumes, constructing "dialogues with the self." But, as Alfred Schutz (1970) and other phenomenologists emphasize, this may also be true of our interactions with human cointeractants. Even for language-users, intersubjectivity is a notoriously presumptive endeavor. The accuracy of our understandings of the other – human or nonhuman – is grounded primarily on our *sense* of his or her body and behavior. The validity of this understanding is confirmed or denied by its practical outcomes. The "truth" of our perceptions and expressions of the other's orientation derives from whether these understandings work to establish communication (Bright 1990) and sustain a viable and mutually rewarding flow of interaction.

Social scientists tend to take a linguacentric stance in their attempts to understand social interaction and the presumed "inner dialogue" that constitutes "mind." This privileging of language frequently is used to deny that nonhuman animals engage in minded behavior. We would maintain, as do the cognitive ethologists and many other analysts of animal behavior, that language is overrated as the primary vehicle of cognition and coordinated social interaction. As human mental and physical "disabilities" are matters of social construction rather than determinations of the actual abilities of the other (Higgins 1992), so the view of dogs and other animal companions as mindless and uncommunicative is a social construction. The presumption that language is essential for an actor to experience empathy with others, construct viable lines of collective action, and engage in cognitive activities is, at best, debatable. As Donald Ellis (1991, 217) observes in his critique of poststructuralism's focus on language:

> Thought and cognition exist in the absence of natural language ... Thought exists in the absence of oral language and it is even possible to make the argument that language and thought are independent. Experiments that compare the problem solving of deaf children who have no verbal symbol system to that of hearing children with sophisticated language conclude that both groups solve problems with equal effectiveness and use identical strategies ... Deaf children with no language (including no sign language) still possess and represent information in some mode other than a linguistic one ... *Interaction* is *more necessary for thinking and cognition than language.* (Emphasis added; see also Tester 1991, 1–16)

Conventionally, those enamored of "objective" science have denigrated owners' understandings and articulations of their animals' subjectivities as grounded in "folk psychology," the simplistic and unscientific view that our own behaviors and those of our cointeractants are shaped by such commonsense constructs as "desire" or "belief" (see Beer 1991). When these folk psychological concepts are applied specifically to the subjective experience and behavior of nonhuman animals, this point of view is further derogated as representing anthropomorphism. Around this issue a vigorous and often rancorous debate revolves (see, for example, Eddy et al. 1993; Fisher 1991; Kennedy 1992; Stebbins 1993). Behaviorists and many ethologists roundly condemn anthropomorphic descriptions while everyday pet owners and most members of the animal-rights community routinely make use of anthropomorphism as a dominant vehicle *for* making sense of animal behavior.

The middle ground in this debate is mapped out by those who identify with what has come to be known as "cognitive ethology" (Griffin 1992; Ristau 1991; Wilder 1990). This orientation, in essence, views anthropomorphism as a useful heuristic device. In advocating what he calls "critical anthropomorphism," Gordon Burghardt (1991) maintains that building a systematic understanding of animal behavior is the prime goal. In achieving this goal, such tools as introspection, reasoning by analogy, interpretive analysis, and intuition should not be discarded simply because they are not currently in favor in certain scientific circles. In this regard, Timothy Eddy and his associates (1993) as well as James Serpell (1986) emphasize the evolutionary roots of anthropomorphism in the necessity of coordinating social behavior and the practical utility of employing an understanding of one's own perspectives, emotions, thoughts, and intentions as a basis for understanding the situational definitions and plans of action constructed by cointeractants, be they human or nonhuman. The Cartesian construction of nonhuman animals as behavioristic machines (the dominant view that Hearne [1987] derogatorily refers to as "mechanomorphism"), in contrast, yields an impoverished and impractical view of animal behavior. As Hearne notes:

> To the extent that the behaviorist manages to deny any belief in the dog's potential for believing, intending, meaning, etc., there will be no flow of intention, meaning, believing, hoping going on. The dog may try to respond to the behaviorist, but the behaviorist won't respond to the dog's response … The behaviorist's dog will not only seem stupid, she will be stupid (p 58).

At the same time, the behaviorist perspective allows humans to maintain the psychological distance necessary to exploit animals ruthlessly, untroubled by feelings of guilt while still retaining a view of humans as a qualitatively unique category of being.

On the other hand, the natural attitude in which companion animals and other nonhuman actors are regarded as minded, emotional, and intentional – and whose orientations and interests can be spoken for with some degree of validity – has the practical utility of allowing the construction of effective and mutually rewarding patterns of social interaction. Additionally, this perspective casts nonhuman animals as worthy of moral concern (Rowan 1991).

Human exchanges with nonhuman animals involve knowing, relating to, shaping interactions with, and responding to the interactional moves of the animal-other. Systematically studying these social exchanges provides us with what Donald Griffin (1976) refers to as a major "window to animal mind." The usual stance of empathetic pet caretakers and practical dog trainers, as demonstrated in their experientially acquired ability to comprehend and give voice to the mind and experience of their animal companions, offers a worthy model to social scientists devoted to examining and understanding interspecies interactions.

REFERENCES

Baer, Ted. 1989. *Communicating with Your Dog.* Hauppauge, NY: Barrons.

Beck, Alan and Aaron Katcher. 1983. *Between Pets and People.* New York: Putnam.

Beer, Colin. 1991. "From Folk Psychology to Cognitive Ethology." In Carolyn Ristau, ed., *Cognitive Ethology: The Minds of Other Animals,* 19–33. Hillsdale, NJ: Lawrence Erlbaum.

Bekoff, Marc. 1994. "Cognitive Ethology and the Treatment of Non-Human Animals: How Matters of Mind Inform Matters of Welfare." *Animal Welfare* 3: 75–96.

Belk, Russell. 1988. "Possessions and the Extended Self." *Journal of Consumer Research* 15: 139–168.

Berger, Peter and Thomas Luckmann. 1966. *The Social Construction of Reality.* New York: Doubleday.

Bogdan, Robert and Steven Taylor. 1989. "Relationships with Severely Disabled People: The Social Construction of Humanness." *Social Problems* 36: 135–148.

Brazelton, T. Berry. 1984. "Four Stages in the Development of Mother-Infant Interaction." In Noboru Kobayashi and T. B. Brazelton, eds., *The Growing Child in Family and Society,* Tokyo: University of Tokyo Press.

Bright, Michael. 1990. *Barks, Roars, and Siren Songs.* New York: Carol.

Buchanan, Allen, and Dan Brock. 1989. *Deciding for Others: The Ethics of Surrogate Decision Making.* New York: Cambridge University Press.

Bulcroft, Kris, George Helling, and Alexa Albert. 1986. "Pets as Intimate Others." Paper presented at the Midwest Sociological Society meeting, May.

Burghardt, Gordon. 1991. "Cognitive Ethology and Critical Anthropomorphism: A Snake with Two Heads and Hog-Nosed Snakes that Play Dead." In Carolyn Ristau, Ed., *Cognitive Ethology: The Minds of Other Animals*, 53–90. Hillsdale, NJ: Lawrence Erlbaum.

Cahill, Spencer. 1987. "Children and Civility: Ceremonial Deviance and the Acquisition of Ritual

Competence." *Social Psychology Quarterly* 50: 312–321.

Cain, Ann. 1983. "A Study of Pets in the Family System." In Aaron Katcher and Alan Beck, eds., *New Perspectives on Our Lives with Companion Animals*, 72–81. Philadelphia: University of Pennsylvania Press.

Cain, Ann. 1985. "Pets as Family Members." In Marvin Sussman, ed., *Pets and the Family*, 5–10. New York: Haworth.

Coe, Rodney and Christopher Prendergast. 1985. "The Formation of Coalitions: Interactive Strategies in Triads." *Sociology of Health and Illness* 7: 236–247.

Coren, Stanley. 1994. *The Intelligence of Dogs*. New York: Free Press.

Crist, Eileen and Michael Lynch. 1990. "The Analyzability of Human-Animal Interaction: The Case of Dog Training." Paper presented at the International Sociological Association meeting, Madrid, July.

Dupre, John. 1990. "The Mental Lives of Nonhuman Animals." In Marc Bekoff and Dale Jamieson, eds., *Interpretation and Explanation in the Study of Animal Behavior* 1: 428–448. Boulder: Westview.

Edelman, Murray. 1981. "The Political Language of the Helping Professions." In Oscar Grusky and Melvin Pollner, eds., *The Sociology of Mental Illness*, 329–334. New York: Holt, Rinehart, and Winston.

Eddy, Timothy, Gordon Gallup, Jr., and Daniel Povinelli. 1993. "Attribution of Cognitive States to Animals: Anthropomorphism in Comparative Perspective." *Journal of Social Issues* 49: 87–101.

Ellis, Donald. 1991. "Post-Structuralism and Language: Non-Sense." *Communication Monographs* 58: 213–223.

Fisher, John. 1991. "Disambiguating Anthropomorphism: An Interdisciplinary Review." In P. P. G. Bateson and Peter Klopfer, eds., *Perspectives on Ethology* 9: 49–85, New York: Plenum.

Fogle, Bruce. 1990. *The Dog's Mind: Understanding Your Dog's Behavior*. New York: Howell.

Fontana, Andrea and Ronald Smith. 1989. "Alzheimer's Disease Victims: The 'Unbecoming' of Self and the Normalization of Competence." *Sociological Perspectives* 32: 35–46.

Goffman, Erving. 1971. *Relations in Public*. New York: Basic.

Goode, David. 1990. "On Understanding Without Words: Communication Between a Deaf-Blind Child and Her Parents." *Human Studies* 13: 1–27.

Goode, David. 1992. "Who Is Bobby? Ideology and Method in the Discovery of a Down Syndrome Person's Competence." In Philip Ferguson, Dianne Ferguson, and Steven Taylor, eds., *Interpreting Disability: A Qualitative Reader*, 197–213. New York: Teachers College Press.

Goode, David. 1994. *A World Without Words: The Social Construction of Children Born Deaf and Blind*. Philadelphia: Temple University Press.

Goode, David and Frances Waksler. 1990. "The Missing 'Who': Situational Identity and Fault-Finding with an Alingual Blind-Deaf Child." *Sociological Studies of Child Development* 3: 203–223.

Gregory, Stanford and Stephen Keto. 1991. "Creation of the 'Virtual Patient' in Medical Interaction: A Comparison of Doctor/Patient and Veterinarian/ Client Relationships." Paper presented at the annual meeting of the American Sociological Association, Cincinnati, August.

Griffin, Donald. 1976. *The Question of Animal Awareness*. New York: Rockefeller University Press.

Griffin, Donald. 1992. *Animal Minds*. Chicago: University of Chicago Press.

Gubrium, Jaber. 1986. "The Social Preservation of Mind: The Alzheimer's Disease Experience." *Symbolic Interaction* 9: 37–51.

Hearne, Vicki. 1987. *Adam's Task*. New York: Knopf.

Hewitt, John and Randall Stokes. 1975. "Disclaimers." *American Sociological Review* 40: 1–11.

Higgins, Paul. 1992. *Making Disabilities: Exploring the Social Transformation of Human Variation*. Springfield: Charles C. Thomas.

Katcher, Aaron and Alan Beck. 1991. "Animal Companions: More Companion than Animal." In Michael Robinson and Lionel Tiger, eds., *Man and Beast Revisited*, 265–278. Washington, D.C.: Smithsonian Institute Press.

Kaye, Kenneth. 1982. *The Mental and Social Life of Babies*. Chicago: University of Chicago Press.

Kennedy, John S. 1992. *The New Anthropomorphism*. Cambridge: Cambridge University Press.

Kielhofner, Gary. 1983. "'Teaching' Retarded Adults: Paradoxical Effects of a Pedagogical Enterprise." *Urban Life* 12: 307–326.

Koehler, William. 1962. *The Koehler Method of Dog Training*. New York: Howell.

Lenehan, Michael. 1986. "Four Ways to Walk a Dog." *The Atlantic Monthly* 257(April): 35–48, 89–99.

Lynch, Michael. 1983. "Accommodation Practices: Vernacular Treatment of Madness." *Social Problems* 31: 152–164.

McConnell, Patricia. 1991. "Lessons from Animal Trainers: The Effect of Acoustic Structure on an Animal's Response." In P .P. G. Bateson and Peter Klopfer, eds., *Perspectives on Ethology* 9: 165–187. New York: Plenum.

Mills, C. Wright. 1940. "Situated Actions and Vocabularies of Motive." *American Sociological Review* 5: 904–913.

Pollner, Melvin and David Goode. 1990. "Ethnomethodology and Person-Centering Practices." *Person-Centered Review* 5: 203–220.

Pollner, Melvin and Lynn McDonald-Wikler. 1985. "The Social Construction of Unreality: A Case of a Family's Attribution of Competence to a Severely Retarded Child." *Family Process* 24: 241–254.

Rasmussen, Jeffrey, D. W. Rajecki, and H. D. Craft. 1993. "Human Perceptions of Animal Mentality: Ascription of Thinking." *Journal of Comparative Psychology* 107: 283–290.

Ristau, Carolyn, ed. 1991. *Cognitive Ethology: The Minds of Other Animals.* Hillsdale, NJ: Lawrence Erlbaum.

Robbins, Douglas, Clinton Sanders, and Spencer Cahill. 1991. "Dogs and Their People: Pet Facilitated Interaction in a Public Setting." *Journal of Contemporary Ethnography* 20: 3–25.

Rochberg-Halton, Eugene. 1985. "Life in the Treehouse: Pet Therapy as Family Metaphor and Self-Dialogue." In Marvin Sussman, ed., *Pets and the Family*, 175–190. New Haven: Haworth.

Rollin, Bernard. 1990. *The Unheeded Cry: Animal Consciousness, Animal Pain, and Science.* New York: Oxford University Press.

Ross, John and Barbara McKinney. 1992. *Dog Talk.* New York: St. Martin's.

Rowan, Andrew. 1991. "The Human-Animal Interface: Chasm or Continuum?" In Michael Robinson and Lionel Tiger, eds., *Man and Beast Revisited*, 279–290. Washington, DC: Smithsonian Institute Press.

Sacks, Harvey, Emmanuel Schegloff, and Gail Jefferson. 1974. "A Simplest Systematics for the Organization of Turn-Taking for Conversation." *Language* 50: 696–735.

Sanders, Clinton. 1990a. Excusing Tactics: Social Responses to the Public Misbehavior of Companion Animals." *Anthrozoös* 4: 82–90.

Sanders, Clinton. 1990b. "The Animal Other: Self Definition, Social Identity, and the Companion Animals." In Gerald Gorn, Richard Pollay, and Marvin Goldberg, eds., *Advances in Consumer Research* 17: 662–668. Provo, Utah: Association for Consumer Research.

Sanders, Clinton. 1993. "Understanding Dogs: Caretakers' Attributions of Mindedness in Canine-Human Relationships." *Journal of Contemporary Ethnography* 22: 205–226.

Schutz, Alfred. 1962. *Collected Papers.* Vol. I, *The Problem of Social Reality.* The Hague: Nijhoff.

Schutz, Alfred. 1970. *On Phenomenology and Social Relations.* Chicago: University of Chicago Press.

Scott, Marvin and Stanford Lyman. 1968. "Accounts." *American Sociological Review* 33: 46–62.

Serpell, James. 1986. *In the Company of Animals.* Oxford: Basil Blackwell.

Shapiro, Kenneth. 1989. "The Death of the Animal: Ontological Vulnerability." *Between the Species* 5: 183–193.

Shapiro, Kenneth. 1990a. "Animal Rights Versus Humanism: The Charge of Speciesism." *Journal of Humanistic Psychology* 30: 9–37.

Shapiro, Kenneth. 1990b. "Understanding Dogs Through Kinesthetic Empathy, Social Construction, and History." *Anthrozoös* 3: 184–195.

Sheets-Johnstone, Maxine. 1992. "The Possibility of an Evolutionary Semantics." *Between the Species* 8: 88–94.

Stebbins, Sarah. 1993. "Anthropomorphism." *Philosophical Studies* 69: 113–122.

Tannen, Deborah and Cynthia Wallat. 1983. "Doctor/Mother/Child Communication: Linguistic Analysis of a Pediatric Interaction." In Sue Fisher and Alexandra D. Todd, eds., *The Social Organization of Doctor-Patient Communication*, 203–219. Washington, D.C.: Center for Applied Linguistics.

Tester, Keith. 1991. *Animals and Society.* London: Routledge.

Veevers, Jean. 1985. "The Social Meaning of Pets: Alternative Roles for Companion Animals." In Marvin Sussman, ed., *Pets and the Family*, 11–30. New York: Haworth.

Wemelsfelder, Françoise. 1993. *Animal Boredom: Towards an Empirical Approach to Animal Subjectivity.* Utrecht, Netherlands: Elinkwijk.

West, Candace and Don Zimmerman. 1977. "Women's Place in Everyday Talk: Reflections on

Parent-Child Interaction." *Social Problems* 24: 521–529.

Wieder, D. Lawrence. 1980. "Behavioristic Operationalism and the Life-World: Chimpanzees and Chimpanzee Researchers in Face-to-Face Interaction." *Sociological Inquiry* 50: 75–103.

Wilder, Hugh. 1990. "Interpretative Cognitive Ethology." In Marc Bekoff and Dale Jamieson, eds., *Interpretation and Explanation in the Study of Animal Behavior* 1: 344–368. Boulder: Westview.

11

MARC BEKOFF

Wild Justice and Fair Play: Cooperation, Forgiveness, and Morality in Animals*

Marc Bekoff is an internationally known biologist who specializes in cognitive ethology, animal behavior and behavioral ecology. Author of hundreds of articles and almost two dozen books on animal issues, Bekoff is the recipient of the Exemplar Award from the Animal Behavior Society, a member of the Ethics Committee for the Jane Goodall Institute, and cofounder (with Jane Goodall) of the Ethologists for the Ethical Treatment of Animals: Citizens for Responsible Animal Behavior Studies, an organization that promotes ethical and responsible ethological research. He is on the board of numerous organizations that promote the ethical treatment of animals, including the Fauna Sanctuary, Prairie Preservation Alliance, Animal Defenders, The Cougar Fund and The Great Ape Trust. In the extract reproduced here, Bekoff argues that examining the play behavior of other animals using a "biocentrically anthropomorphic" approach (acknowledging our unavoidable human view of the world while at the same time keeping the animal's point of view) provides important insights into the minds of animals and the origins of social morality. He contends that cooperation and fairness are critical in the formation and maintenance of social relationships, and that morality evolves in humans and other animals because it is adaptive (contrary to the argument that cooperation and fairness in animals are the byproducts of a need to temper aggressiveness). Bekoff concludes that cooperative fair play is a kind of social contract that is mutually beneficial to individuals and to the group, and that animal play is moral because it includes cooperation, justice, fairness, and trust.

In this paper I argue that we can learn much about "wild justice" and the evolutionary origins of social morality – behaving fairly – by studying social play behavior in group-living animals, and that interdisciplinary cooperation will help immensely. In our efforts to learn more about the evolution of morality we need to broaden our comparative research to include animals other than nonhuman primates. If one is a good Darwinian, it is premature to claim that only humans can be empathic and moral beings. By asking the question "What is it like to be another animal?" we can discover rules of engagement that guide animals in their social encounters.

* Reprinted from Bekoff, M. (2004) "Wild Justice and Fair Play: Cooperation, Forgiveness, and Morality in Animals," *Biology and Philosophy* 19, 489–520, with permission of Kluwer Academic Publishers.

When I study dogs, for example, I try to be a "dogocentrist" and practice "dogomorphism." My major arguments center on the following "big" questions: Can animals be moral beings or do they merely act as if they are? What are the evolutionary roots of cooperation, fairness, trust, forgiveness, and morality? What do animals do when they engage in social play? How do animals negotiate agreements to cooperate, to forgive, to behave fairly, to develop trust? Can animals forgive? Why cooperate and play fairly? Why did play evolve as it has? Does "being fair" mean being more fit – do individual variations in play influence an individual's reproductive fitness, are more virtuous individuals more fit than less virtuous individuals? What is the taxonomic distribution of cognitive skills and emotional capacities necessary for individuals to be able to behave fairly, to empathize, to behave morally? Can we use information about moral behavior in animals to help us understand ourselves? I conclude that there is strong selection for co-operative fair play in which individuals establish and maintain a social contract to play because there are mutual benefits when individuals adopt this strategy and group stability may be also be fostered. Numerous mechanisms have evolved to facilitate the initiation and maintenance of social play to keep others engaged, so that agreeing to play fairly and the resulting benefits of doing so can be readily achieved. I also claim that the ability to make accurate predictions about what an individual is likely to do in a given social situation is a useful litmus test for explaining what might be happening in an individual's brain during social encounters, and that intentional or representational explanations are often important for making these predictions.

[...]

CLASSICAL ETHOLOGY AND COGNITIVE ETHOLOGY: WHAT IS IT LIKE TO BE A ____?

Nobel Laureate Niko Tinbergen (1963) identified four overlapping areas with which ethological investigations should be concerned, namely, evolution (phylogeny), adaptation (function), causation, and development (ontogeny). Tinbergen's framework is also useful for those interested in animal cognition (Jamieson and Bekoff 1993; Allen and Bekoff 1997; Smuts 2001). Burghardt (1997) suggested adding a fifth area, private experience. He (276) noted that "[t]he fifth aim is nothing less than a deliberate attempt to understand the private experience, including the perceptual world and mental states, of other organisms. The term private experience is advanced as a preferred label that is most inclusive of the full range of phenomena that have been identified without prejudging any particular theoretical or methodological approach."

Burghardt's suggestion invites what he calls "critical anthropomorphism," carefully used anthropomorphism, an approach with which many agree. I have suggested that we be "bio-centrically anthropomorphic" and that by doing so we do not necessarily lose the animal's point of view. We are humans and we have by neces-sity a human view of the world (Bekoff 2000b; see also Keeley's and Allen's essays in *Biology and Philosophy* 19).

The way we describe and explain the behavior of other animals is influenced and limited by the language we use to talk about things in general. By engaging in anthropomorphism we make the world of other animals accessible to ourselves and to other human beings. By being anthropomorphic we can more readily understand and explain the emotions or feel-ings of other animals. But this is not to say that other animals are happy or sad in the same ways in which humans (or even other members of the same species) are happy or sad. Of course, I cannot be absolutely certain that my late dog, Jethro, was happy, sad, angry, upset, or in love, but these words serve to explain what he might have been feeling. Merely referring to the firing of different neurons or to the activity of different muscles in the absence of behavioral information and context is insufficiently in-formative because we do not know about the specific situation in which the animal finds [him- or] herself.

BEING A DOG-O-CENTRIST

My research and that of others begins with the question "What is it like to be a specific animal?" So, when I study dogs, for example, I try to be a dog-o-centrist and practice dogomorphism. Thus, when I claim that a dog is happy, for example when playing, I am saying it is dog-joy, and that dog-joy may be different from chimpanzee-joy. While I will not go into it any further, this is a very important stance for it stresses that there are important species and individual differences in behavior, cognitive capacities, and emotions, and that it is wrong and simplistic to claim that if animal joy is not like our joy then they do not have it.

What it basically comes down to is that as humans studying other animals, we cannot totally lose our anthropocentric perspective. But we can try as hard as possible to combine the animals' viewpoints to the ways in which we study, describe, interpret, and explain their behavior.

THE EVOLUTION OF SOCIAL MORALITY: CONTINUITY, PROTO-MORALITY, AND QUESTIONS OF HUMAN UNIQUENESS

Evolutionary reconstructions of social behavior often depend on educated guesses (some better than others) about the past social (and other) environments in which ancestral beings lived. In the same sense that other's minds are private, so is evolution (Bekoff 2002a). Often it is difficult to know with a great deal of certainty very much about these variables and how they may have figured into evolutionary scenarios. It is an understatement to note that is extremely difficult to study the evolution of morality in any animal species, and the very notion of animal morality itself often makes

for heated discussions. Bernstein (2000) claims that "morality in animals might lie outside of the realm of measurement techniques available to science" (34). Nonetheless, it seems clear that detailed comparative analyses of social behavior in animals can indeed provide insights into the evolution of social morality. Certainly, these sorts of study are extremely challenging, but the knowledge gained is essential in our efforts to learn more about the evolution of sociality and social morality and to learn more about human nature and perhaps human uniqueness.

Many discussions of the evolution of morality center on the development of various sorts of models (e.g. Axelrod 1984; Ridley 1996, 2001; Skyrms 1996; Dugatkin 1997; Sober and Wilson 1998, 2000; essays in *Journal of Consciousness Studies* 2000, volume 7, No. 1/2). While these models are very useful for stimulating discussion and further research, they do not substitute for available data (however few) that may bear on animal morality (see, for example, some essays in Aureli and de Waal (2000) for additional comparative information and also Dugatkin and Bekoff (2003)).

The study of the evolution of morality, specifically cooperation and fairness, is closely linked to science, religion, theology, spirituality and perhaps even different notions of God, in that ideas about continuity and discontinuity (the possible uniqueness of humans and other species), individuality, and freedom need to be considered in detail. Furthermore, it is important to discuss relationships among science, religion, and God because spirituality and the notion of one form of God or another had strong influences on the evolution of our ancestors, their cognitive, emotional, and moral lives.

Peterson (2000; see also Peterson 1999) has discussed the evolutionary roots of morality (stages that he refers to as "quasi-morality" and "proto-morality" in animals) and religion in relation to the roles played by cognition and culture. He also stresses the importance of recognizing continuities and discontinuities with other animals, arguing ultimately (and speciesistically) that while some animals might possess proto-morality (they are able "to rationally deliberate actions and their consequences," 475) none other than humans is "genuinely moral" because to be able to be genuinely moral requires higher emergent levels of cognition as well as culture and the worldview that culture provides, namely, religion. Peterson (2000, 478) claims that "Quasi-moral and protomoral systems do not require a global framework that guides decision making. They are always proximate and pragmatic. In these systems, there is no long-term goal or ideal state to be achieved. Yet, genuine morality is virtually inconceivable without such conceptions."

Peterson also claims that any sociobiological account (based on selfishness or combativeness) of human morality is incomplete. I agree and also argue that this is so for some nonhuman animals as well. When animals are studied in their own worlds they may indeed have their own form of genuine morality, there might indeed be long-term goals and ideal states to be achieved. Our anthropocentric view of other animals, in which humans are so taken with themselves, is far too narrow. The worlds and lives of other animals are not identical to those of humans and may vary from species to species and even within species. The same problems arise in the study of emotions (Bekoff 2000a; 2002a; 2004) if we believe that emotions in animals are going to be identical to or even recognizably similar [to those] among different species. There is also variability among humans in what some might view as long-term goals and ideal states, and it would be premature to conclude that there is one set of long-term goals and ideal states that characterize, or are essential to, the capacity to be genuinely moral. To cash out stages of moral evolution as does Peterson, it looks like quasi-morality and proto-morality are less than genuine morality.

COOPERATION AND FAIRNESS ARE NOT BY-PRODUCTS OF AGGRESSION AND SELFISHNESS

[M]y thesis is that justice is first of all a natural sentiment, an inborn sense of our connectedness with others and our shared interests and concerns. (Solomon 1995, 153)

My arguments center on the view that cooperation is not merely always a byproduct of tempering aggressive and selfish tendencies (combating Richard Dawkins' (1976) selfish genes) and attempts at reconciliation. Rather, cooperation and fairness can evolve on their own because they are important in the formation and maintenance of social relationships. (Solomon 1995 also forcefully argues this point.) This view contrasts with those who see aggression, cheating, selfishness, and perhaps amorality as driving the evolution of sociality, fairness, and justice. The combative Hobbesian world in which individuals are constantly at one another's throat is not the natural state of affairs. Nature is not always red in tooth and claw. Dawkins (2001) himself has been quoted as saying "A pretty good definition of the kind of society in which I don't want to live is a society founded on the principles of Darwinism."

DOES IT FEEL GOOD TO BE FAIR?

It will be only after we have established the facts of mutual aid in different classes of animals and their importance for evolution, that we shall be able to study what belongs in the evolution of sociable feelings, to parental feelings, and what to sociability proper . . . Mutual Aid [is] an argument in favor of a pre-human origin of moral instincts, but also as a law of Nature and a factor of evolution (Petr Kropotkin 1902, x–xii).

Justice begins with our emotional engagement in the world, not in philosophical detachment or in any merely hypothetical situation (Solomon 1995, 199).

Studies of the evolution of social morality need to pay close attention to the rich cognitive, intellectual, and deep emotional lives of animals (Bekoff 2000a,b; 2002a,b) and how these capacities figure into moral sensibility and the ability to make moral judgments. Truth be told, we really do not know much about these capacities even in our primate relatives despite claims that we do (Bekoff 2002c; 2003a; in press). We know that animals and humans share many of the same emotions and same chemicals that play a role in the experience and expressions of emotions such as joy and pleasure. If being nice feels good then that is a good reason for being nice. It is also a good reason for a pattern of behavior to evolve and to remain in an animal's arsenal.

Are some animals capable of the emotions and empathy that might underlie morality? We know that in humans the amygdala and hypothalamus are important in emotional experiences and that they are mediated by neurotransmitters such as dopamine, serotonin, and oxytocin. We also know that many animals, especially mammals, share with humans the same neurological structures and chemicals (Panksepp 1998; Bekoff 2002a). Of course, this does not necessarily mean animals share our feelings, but careful observation of individuals during social encounters suggests that at least some of them do. While their feelings are not necessarily identical to ours this is of little or no concern because it is unlikely that they should be the same as ours.

Empathy is also important to consider. Preston and de Waal (2002) argue that empathy is more widespread among animals than has previously been recognized (see also Kuczaj et al. 2001). In a classic study, Wechlin et al. (1964) showed that a hungry rhesus monkey would not take food if doing so subjected another monkey to an electric shock. In similar situations rats will also restrain themselves when they know their actions would cause pain to another individual (Church 1959). In another study, Diana monkeys were trained to insert a token into a slot to obtain food (Markowitz 1982). A male was observed helping the oldest female who had failed to learn the task. On three occasions he picked up the tokens she had dropped, put them into the machine, and allowed her to have the food. His behavior seemed to have no benefits for him at all; there did not seem to be any hidden agenda.

Along these lines, de Waal observed Kuni, a captive female bonobo, capture a starling and take the bird outside and place it on its feet (Preston and de Waal 2002). When the bird did not move Kuni tossed it in the air. When the starling did not fly Kuni took it to the highest point in her enclosure, carefully unfolded its wings and threw it in the air. The starling still did not fly and Kuni then guarded and protected it from a curious juvenile.

Elephants also may show concern for others. Poole (1998), who has studied African elephants for decades, was told a story about a teenage female who was suffering from a withered leg on which she could put no weight. When a young male from another group began attacking the injured female, a large adult female chased the attacking male, returned to the young female, and touched her crippled leg with her trunk. Poole argues that the adult female was showing empathy and sympathy.

While good stories alone are not enough to make a compelling argument, when there are many such anecdotes they can be used to provide a solid basis for further detailed empirical research. Ignoring them is to ignore a rich data base. I have argued elsewhere that "the plural of anecdote is data" (Bekoff 2002a).

We will probably never know whether these rats, monkeys, and elephants were feeling empathy as we do. But there are ways in which we can begin comparing what is going on in animal brains to what happens in our own. Neuroimaging techniques are shedding new light on human emotions, and it likely will not be long before we begin doing similar studies with other animals.

It is important to consider the possibility that it feels good to be fair to others, to cooperate with them and to treat them fairly, to forgive them for their mistakes and shortcomings. Recent neural imaging research on humans by Rilling and his colleagues (Rilling et al. 2002) has shown that the brain's pleasure centers are strongly activated when people cooperate with one another, that we might be wired to be fair or nice to one another. (I do not want to argue here that "being fair" always means "being nice.") This is extremely significant research for it posits that there is a strong neural basis for human cooperation and that it feels good to cooperate, that being nice is rewarding in social interactions and might be a stimulus for fostering cooperation and fairness. Despite challenging technical difficulties, this sort of non-invasive research is just what is needed on other animals.

ANIMAL PLAY AND SOCIAL CONTRACTS: LESSONS IN COOPERATION, JUSTICE, FAIRNESS, AND TRUST

What is justice? Justice is fairness, so they say. But, what is fair? (Bradie 1999, 607)

"Happiness is never better exhibited than by young animals, such as puppies, kittens, lambs, & c., when playing together, like our own children." So wrote Charles Darwin in *The Descent of Man and Selection in Relation to Sex* (Darwin 1871/1936, 448).

Animal play is obvious and few if any people would argue that play is not an important category of behavior. (For definitions of social play see Bekoff and Byers 1981, 1998; Fagen 1981; Power 2000; Burghardt 2005.) Animal social morality, however, is a more slippery concept. Cognitive ethological approaches are useful for gaining an understanding of social play for various reasons including (Allen and Bekoff 1997): (1) it exemplifies many of the theoretical issues faced by cognitive ethologists; (2) empirical research on social play has [benefited] and will benefit from a cognitive approach, because play involves communication, intention, role-playing, and cooperation; (3) detailed analyses of social play may provide more promising evidence of animal minds than research in many other areas, for it may yield clues about the ability of animals to understand one another's intentions; and (4) play occurs in a wide range of mammalian species and in a number of avian species, and thus it affords the opportunity for a comparative investigation of cognitive abilities extending beyond the narrow focus on primates that often dominates discussions of nonhuman cognition. For example, during social play, many animals engage in self-handicapping and role-reversals, two behavior patterns that are often used to make inferences about intentionality (and consciousness and self-consciousness).

Social play in animals is an exhilarating activity in which to engage and to observe. The rhythm, dance, and spirit of animals at play is incredibly contagious. Not only do their animal friends want to join in or find others with whom to romp, but I also want to play when I see animals chasing one another, playing hide-and-seek, and wresting with reckless abandon. My body once tingled with delight as I watched a young elk in Rocky Mountain National Park, Colorado, running across a snow field, jumping in the air and twisting his body while in flight, stopping to catch his breath, and then jumping and twisting over and over and again. There was plenty of grassy terrain around but he chose the more challenging snow field in which to romp (supporting Byers' (1977, 1998) idea that play may be very important in physical training). Buffaloes will also follow one another and playfully run onto and slide across ice, excitedly bellowing "Gwaaa" as they do so. And, of course, we all know that dogs and cats love to play, as do many other mammals. I and many others have observed birds also playfully soar across the sky chasing, diving here and there, and frolicking with one another.

Consider also some of my field notes of two dogs at play:

Jethro bounds towards Zeke, stops immediately in front of him, crouches on his forelimbs, wags his tail, barks, and immediately lunges at him, bites his scruff and shakes his head rapidly from side-to-side, works his way around to his backside and mounts him, jumps off, does a rapid bow, lunges at his side and slams him with his hips, leaps up and bites his neck, and runs away. Zeke takes wild pursuit of Jethro and leaps on his back and bites his muzzle and then his scruff, and shakes his head rapidly from side to side. Suki bounds in and chases Jethro and Zeke and they all wrestle with one another. They part for a few minutes, sniffing here and there and resting. Then, Jethro walks slowly over to Zeke, extends his paw toward Zeke's head, and nips at his ears. Zeke gets up and jumps on Jethro's back, bites him, and grasps him around his waist. They then fall to the ground and mouth wrestle. Then they chase one another and roll over and play. Suki decides to jump in and the three of them frolic until they're exhausted. Never did their play escalate into aggression.

The unmistakable emotions associated with play – joy and happiness – drive animals into becoming at one with the activity. One way to get animals (including humans) to do something is to make it fun, and there is no doubt that animals enjoy playing. Studies of the chemistry of play support the claim that play is fun. Dopamine (and perhaps serotonin and norepinephrine) are important in the regulation of play. Rats show an increase in dopamine activity when anticipating the opportunity to play (Siviy 1998) and enjoy being playfully tickled (Panksepp 1998; 2000). There is also a close association between opiates and play (Panksepp 1998).

Neurobiological data are essential for learning more about whether play truly is a subjectively pleasurable activity for animals as it seems to be for humans. Siviy's and Panksepp's findings suggest that it is. In light of these neurobiological ("hard") data concerning possible neurochemical bases for various moods, in this case joy and pleasure, skeptics who claim that animals do not feel emotions might be more likely to accept the idea that enjoyment could well be a motivator for play behavior.

IT BEGINS WITH A "BOW": "I WANT TO PLAY WITH YOU"

To learn about the dynamics of play it is essential to pay attention to subtle details that are otherwise lost in superficial analyses. During play there are continuous rapid exchanges of information "on the run." Dogs and other animals keep track of what is happening when they play so we also need to pay attention to details. My studies of play are based on careful observation and analyses – some might say obsessive analyses – of video-tape. I watch tapes of play one frame at a time to see what the animals are doing and how they exchange information about their intentions and desires to play. This is tedious work and some of my students who were excited about studying dog play had second thoughts after watching the same video frames over and over again. But when they then were able to go out and watch dogs play and understand what was happening they came to appreciate that while studying play can be hard work it's well-worth the effort.

So, a typical scene might go as follows. "Would you care to play" asks one wolf of another? "Yes, I would" says the other. After each individual agrees to play and not to fight, prey on, or mate with the other, there are on-going rapid and subtle exchanges of information so that their cooperative agreement can be fine-tuned and negotiated on the run, so that the activity remains playful. Incorporated into many explanations of social play are such notions as making a deal, trusting, behaving fairly, forgiving, apologizing, and perhaps justice, behavioral attributes that underlie social morality and moral agency (Bekoff 2002a). Recent research by Okamoto and Matsumara (2000) suggests that punishment and apology play a role in maintaining cooperation between individual nonhuman primates.

When individuals play they typically use action patterns that are also used in other contexts, such as predatory behavior, antipredatory behavior, and mating activities. Behavior patterns that are observed in mating may be intermixed in flexible kaleidoscopic sequences with actions that are used during fighting, looking for prey, and avoiding being eaten. These actions may not vary much across different contexts, or they may be hard to discriminate even for the participants. So, how do animals know that they are playing? How do they communicate their desires or intentions to play or to continue to play? How is the play mood maintained?

Because there is a chance that various behavior patterns that are performed during on-going social play can be misinterpreted, individuals need to tell others "I want to play," "this is still play no matter what I am going to do to you," or "this is still play regardless of what I just did to you." An agreement to play, rather than to fight, mate, or engage in predatory activities can be negotiated in various ways. Individuals may use various behavior patterns – play markers – to initiate play or to maintain (prevent termination of) a play mood (Bekoff 1975; 1977a; 1995; Bekoff and Allen 1992, 1998; Allen and Bekoff 1997; Flack, Jeannotte, and de Waal 2004) by punctuating play sequences with these actions when it is likely that a particular behavior may have been, or will be, misinterpreted (it is also possible that there are auditory, olfactory, and tactile play markers (Bekoff and Byers 1981; Fagen 1981).

One action that is very common in play among canids (members of the dog family) is the "bow." Bows occur almost exclusively in the context of social play. The "bow," a highly ritualized and stereotyped movement that seems to function to stimulate recipients to engage (or to continue to engage) in social play, has been extensively studied in various canids in this context. Bows (the animal crouches on her forelimbs and elevates her hindlimbs) occur throughout play sequences, but most commonly at the beginning or toward the middle of playful encounters. In a detailed analysis of the form and duration of play bows (Bekoff 1977a) I discovered that duration was more variable than form, and that play bows were always less variable when performed at the beginning, rather than in the middle of, ongoing play sequences. Three possible explanations for this change in variability include: (1) fatigue, (2) the fact that animals are performing them from a wide variety of preceding postures, and (3) there is less of a need to communicate that "this is still play" than there is when trying to initiate a new interaction. These explanations are not exclusive alternatives.

In a long-term and continuing study of social play I also found that play signals in infant canids (domestic dogs, wolves, and coyotes) were used nonrandomly, especially when biting accompanied by rapid side-to-side shaking of

the head was performed (Bekoff 1995). Biting accompanied by rapid side-to-side shaking of the head is performed during serious aggressive and predatory encounters and can easily be misinterpreted if its meaning is not modified by a play signal. Following the work of Bateson (2000); Neuman (2003, 1) argues that in certain situations such as play "meaning is a form of coordination between interacting agents, and that this form of coordination is orchestrated through context markers …" He refers to this process as "meaning-in-context."

Play signals are an example of what ethologists call "honest signals." There is little evidence that social play is a manipulative or "Machiavellian" activity. Play signals are rarely used to deceive others in canids or other species. There are no studies of which I am aware that actually look at the relative frequencies of occurrence of honest and deceptive play signaling, but my own long-term observations indicate that deceptive signaling is so rare that I cannot remember more than a few occurrences in thousands of play sequences. Cheaters are unlikely to be chosen as play partners because others can simply refuse to play with them and choose others. Limited data on infant coyotes show that cheaters have difficulty getting other young coyotes to play (personal observations). It is not known if individuals select play partners based on what they have observed during play by others.

In domestic dogs there is little tolerance for non-cooperative cheaters. Cheaters may be avoided or chased from play groups. There seems to be a sense of what is right, wrong, and fair. While studying dog play on a beach in San Diego, California, Horowitz (2002) observed a dog she called Up-ears enter into a play group and interrupt the play of two other dogs, Blackie and Roxy. Up-ears was chased out of the group and when she returned Blackie and Roxy stopped playing and looked off toward a distant sound. Roxy began moving in the direction of the sound and Up-ears ran off following their line of sight. Roxy and Blackie immediately began playing once again. Even in rats fairness and trust are important in the dynamics of playful interactions. Pellis (2002), a psychologist at the University of Lethbridge in Canada, discovered that sequences of rat play consist of individuals assessing and monitoring one another and then fine-tuning and changing their own behavior to maintain the play mood. When the rules of play are violated, when fairness breaks down, so does play.

Detailed analyses show that individual actions may change their form and duration during play. Individuals might also know that they are playing because the actions that are performed differ when they are performed during play when compared to other contexts (Hill and Bekoff 1977), or the order in which motor patterns are performed differs from, and might be more variable than, the order in which they are performed during the performance of, for example, serious aggressive, predatory, or reproductive activities (Bekoff and Byers 1981).

Individuals also engage in role-reversing and self-handicapping (Bekoff and Allen 1998; Bauer and Smuts 2002; Horowitz 2002) to maintain social play. Each can serve to reduce asymmetries between the interacting animals and foster the reciprocity that is needed for play to occur. Self-handicapping happens when an individual performs a behavior pattern that might compromise herself. For example, a coyote might not bite her play partner as hard as she can, or she might not play as vigorously as she can. Watson and Croft (1996) found that red-neck wallabies adjusted their play to the age of their partner. When a partner was younger, the older animal adopted a defensive, flat-footed posture, and pawing rather than sparring occurred. In addition, the older player was more tolerant of its partner's tactics and took the initiative in prolonging interactions.

Role-reversing occurs when a dominant animal performs an action during play that would not normally occur during real aggression. For example, a dominant animal might voluntarily not roll-over on his back during fighting, but would do so while playing. In some instances role-reversing and self-handicapping might oc-

cur together. For example, a dominant individual might roll over while playing with a subordinate animal and inhibit the intensity of a bite.

From a functional perspective, self-handicapping and role-reversing, similar to using specific play invitation signals and gestures, or altering behavioral sequences, might serve to signal an individual's intention to continue to play. In this way there can be mutual benefits to each individual player because of their agreeing to play and not fight or mate. This might differentiate cooperative play from the situation described above in which a male Diana's monkey helped a female get food when she could not learn the task that would bring her food. There seemed to be no benefit to the male to do so. (I thank Jan Nystrom for marking this distinction.)

CAN ANIMALS FORGIVE?

Even for the behavior of forgiving, which is often attributed solely to humans, the renowned evolutionary biologist David Sloan Wilson (2002) shows that forgiveness is a complex biological adaptation. In his book *Darwin's Cathedral: Evolution, Religion, and the Nature of Society*, Wilson concludes that "… forgiveness has a biological foundation that extends throughout the animal kingdom" (195). And further, "… Forgiveness has many faces – and needs to – in order to function adaptively in so many different contexts" (212). While Wilson concentrates mainly on human societies his views can easily be extended – and responsibly so – to non-human animals. Indeed, Wilson points out that adaptive traits such as forgiveness might not require as much brain power as once thought. This is not to say that animals aren't smart but rather that forgiveness might be a trait that is basic to many animals even if they don't have especially big and active brains. Perhaps if we try to learn more about forgiveness in animals and how it functions in play we will also learn to live more compassionately and cooperatively with one another.

FINE-TUNING PLAY: WHY COOPERATE AND PLAY FAIRLY?

Why do animals carefully use play signals to tell others that they really want to play and not try to dominate them, why do they engage in self-handicapping and role-reversing? Why do they plan play? During social play, while individuals are having fun in a relatively safe environment, they learn ground rules that are acceptable to others – how hard they can bite, how roughly they can interact – and how to resolve conflicts. There is a premium on playing fairly and trusting others to do so as well. There are codes of social conduct that regulate actions that are and are not permissible, and the existence of these codes likely speak to the evolution of social morality. What could be a better atmosphere in which to learn social skills than during social play, where there are few penalties for transgressions? Individuals might also generalize codes of conduct learned in playing with specific individuals to other group members and to other situations such as sharing food, defending resources, grooming, and giving care. (Social morality does not mean other animals are behaving unfairly when they kill for food, for example, for they have evolved to do this.)

Playtime generally is safe time. Transgressions and mistakes are forgiven and apologies are accepted by others especially when one player is a youngster who is not yet a competitor for social status, food, or mates. There is a certain innocence or ingenuousness in play. Individuals must cooperate with one another when they play – they must negotiate agreements to play (Bekoff 1995). Fagen (1993, 192) noted that "Levels of cooperation in play of juvenile primates may exceed those predicted by simple evolutionary arguments…" The highly cooperative nature of play has evolved in many other species (Fagen 1981; Bekoff 1995; Bekoff and Allen 1998; Power 2000; Drea and Frank 2003; Burghardt 2005). Detailed studies of play in various species indicate that individuals trust others to maintain the rules of the game (Bekoff and Byers 1998). While there have been numerous discussions of cooperative behavior in animals (e.g. Axelrod 1984; de Waal 1996; Ridley 1996; Dugatkin 1997; Hauser 2000; essays in *Journal of Consciousness Studies*, Volume 7, No. 1/2, 2000 and references therein), none has considered the details of social play, the requirement for cooperation and reciprocity and its possible role in the evolution of social morality, namely behaving fairly.

Individuals of different species seem to fine-tune on-going play sequences to maintain a play mood and to prevent play from escalating into real aggression. Detailed analyses of film show that in canids there are subtle and fleeting movements and rapid exchanges of eye contact that suggest that players are exchanging information on the run, from moment-to-moment, to make certain everything is all right, that this is still play. Aldis (1975) suggested that in play, there is a 50:50 rule so that each player "wins" about 50% of their play bouts by adjusting their behavior to accomplish this (for further discussion and details on rodent play, see Pellis 2002).

Why might animals fine-tune play? Why might they try hard to share one another's intentions? While play in most species does not take up much time and energy (Bekoff and Byers 1998; Power 2000), and in some species only minimal amounts of social play during short windows of time early in development are necessary to produce socialized individuals (two [20-minute] play sessions with another dog, twice a week, are sufficient for domestic dogs from 3 to 7 weeks of age (Scott and Fuller 1965)), researchers agree that play is very important in social, cognitive, and/or physical development, and may also be important for training youngsters for unexpected circumstances (Spinka, Newberry, and Bekoff 2001). While there are few data concerning the actual benefits of social play in terms of survival and reproductive success, it generally is assumed that short-term and long-terms functions (benefits) vary from species-to-species and among different age groups and between the sexes within a species. No matter what the functions of play may be, there seems to be little doubt that play has some benefits and that the absence of play can have devastating effects on social development (Power 2000; Spinka Newberry, and Bekoff, 2000; Burghardt 2005).

During early development there is a small time window when individuals can play without being responsible for their own well-being. This time period is generally referred to as the "socialization period" for this is when species-typical social skills are learned most rapidly. It is important for individuals to engage in at least some play. All individuals need to play and there is a premium for playing fairly if one is to be able to play at all. If individuals do not play fairly they may not be able to find willing play partners. In coyotes, for example, youngsters are hesitant to play with an individual who does not play fairly or with an individual whom they fear (Bekoff 1977b). In many species individuals also show play-partner preferences and it is possible that these preferences are based on the trust that individuals place in one another.

FAIRNESS AND FITNESS: COYOTES, PLAY, AND DISPERSAL

One big question of interest to biologists is how differences in the performance of a given behavior influence an individual's reproductive success. It is extremely difficult to show with great certainty that the performance of a specific behavior is directly and causally coupled to reproductive success, especially under field conditions, so in many instances we have to rely on guesswork.

With respect to the topic at hand the question is "Do differences in play and variations in fair play influence an individual's reproductive fitness?" I am not arguing that there is a gene for social morality but I am claiming that it is reasonable to ask if there are differences among individuals and that perhaps more virtuous individuals are more fit and have more offspring than less virtuous individuals. A sense of fairness is common to many animals, and without it social play would be difficult to maintain. And without social play I and others have argued individual animals and entire groups would

be at a disadvantage (Bekoff 2002a). If I am correct, morality evolved because it is adaptive in its own right, not because it is merely an antidote to competition or aggression. Behaving fairly helps many animals, including humans, to survive and flourish in their particular social environment. I fully realize that this may sound like a radical idea, particularly if one views morality as uniquely human (and a sort of puzzling capacity) that sets us apart from other animals. But if you accept my argument that play and fairness may be linked then we need to demonstrate that individual animals might benefit from these behaviors.

Dogs, coyotes, and wolves are fast learners when it comes to fair play and I bet that other animals are as well. There are serious sanctions when they breach the trust of their friends and these penalties might indeed become public information if others see an individual cheating his companions. Biologists call these penalties "costs," which means that an individual might suffer some decline in his or her reproductive fitness if they do not play by the expected and accepted rules of the game.

My fieldwork on coyotes has revealed one direct cost paid by animals who fail to engage in fair play or who do not play much at all. I found that coyote pups who do not play as much as others because they are avoided by others or because they themselves avoid others are less tightly bonded to other members of their group and more likely to strike out on their own (Bekoff 1977b). But life outside the group is much more risky than within it. In a seven-year study of coyotes living in the Grand Teton National Park outside Moose, Wyoming, we found that more than 55% of yearlings who drifted away from their social group died, whereas fewer than 20% of their stay-at-home peers did (Bekoff and Wells 1986). Was it because of play? We are not sure, but information that we collected on captive coyotes suggested that the lack of play was a major factor in individuals spending more time alone, away from their littermates and other group members.

[. . .]

THERE IS WILD JUSTICE, FAIRNESS, AND SOCIAL COOPERATION: DOING WHAT COMES NATURALLY

Justice presumes a personal concern for others. It is first of all a sense, not a rational or social construction, and I want to argue that this sense is, in an important sense, natural. (Solomon 1995, 102)

It is not difficult to imagine the emergence of justice and honor out of the practices of cooperation. (Damasio 2003, 162)

More than any other species, we are beneficiaries and victims of a wealth of emotional experience. (Dolan 2002, 1191)

Our evaluative conceptions from the nature and ideals of right-living are drawn from vast networks of social activities that have transpired over enormous reaches of time: models of conduct and character have been established, assayed, rejected, confirmed, revised, redrawn, shown unfit. (Hudson 1986, 121)

To learn more about the evolution of cognitive capacities and morality we need to broaden our taxonomic studies to include species other than nonhuman primates. We need to go beyond primatocentrism which usually is "great ape-o-centrism" [...]. Some authors have been more resistant to this idea than others. Consider the following claims by Richard Byrne (1995, my emphases added) from his book *The Thinking Ape*.

It *seems* that the great apes, especially the common chimpanzee, can attribute mental states to other individuals; but no other group of animals can do so – apart from ourselves, and perhaps cetaceans (146). This contrasts with the findings on understanding of beliefs, attribution of intentions, and how things work – where a sharp discontinuity is *implied* between great apes and all other animals. (154)

Of course, until similar painstaking work is done with monkeys, we *cannot* argue that only apes

have such abilities ... and no-one has yet risked the huge expenditure of time and money to find out. (172)

We simply do not have enough data to make hard and fast claims about the taxonomic distribution among different species of the cognitive skills and emotional capacities necessary for being able to empathize with others, to behave fairly, or to be moral agents. Marler (1996, 22) concluded a review of social cognition in nonhuman primates and birds as follows: "I am driven to conclude, at least provisionally, that there are more similarities than differences between birds and primates. Each taxon has significant advantages that the other lacks." Tomasello and Call (1997, 399–400) summarized their comprehensive review of primate cognition by noting that "The experimental foundation for claims that apes are 'more intelligent' than monkeys is not a solid one, and there are few if any naturalistic observations that would substantiate such broad-based, species-general claims." While Flack and de Waal's (2000) and others' focus is on nonhuman primates as the most likely animals to show precursors to human morality, others have argued that we might learn as much or more about the evolution of human social behavior by studying social carnivores (Schaller and Lowther 1969; Tinbergen 1972; Thompson 1975; Drea and Frank 2003), species whose social behavior and organization resemble that of early hominids in a number of ways (divisions of labor, food sharing, care of young, and inter- and intrasexual dominance hierarchies).

What we really need are long-term field studies of social animals for which it would be reasonable to hypothesize that emotions and morality have played a role in the evolution of sociality, that emotions and morality are important in the development and maintenance of social bonds that allow individuals to work together for the benefit of all group members (see also Gruen 2002).

To stimulate further comparative research (and the development of models) on a wider array of species than has previously been studied,

I offer the hypothesis that social morality, in this case behaving fairly, is an adaptation that is shared by many mammals, not only by non-human and human primates. Behaving fairly evolved because it helped young animals acquire social (and other) skills needed as they mature into adults. A focus on social cooperation is needed to balance the plethora of research that is devoted to social competition and selfishness. (For further discussion, see Boehm 1999; Singer 1999; Wilson 2002.)

I also wonder if our view of the world would have been different had Charles Darwin been a female, if some or many of the instances in which competition is invoked were viewed as coopera-tion. Women tend to "see" more cooperation in nature than do men. Adams and Burnett (1991) discovered that female ethologists working in East Africa use a substantially different descrip-tive vocabulary than do male ethologists. Of the nine variables they studied, those concerning co-operation and female gender were the most im-portant discriminating women's and men's word use. They concluded (558) that "The variable COOPERATION demonstrates the appropri-ateness of feminist claims to connection and co-operation as women's models for behavior, as di-vergent from the traditional competitive model." Why women and men approach the same sub-ject from a different perspective remains largely unanswered. Perhaps there is more cooperation than meets the eye.

Group-living animals in which there is a variety of complex social interactions among individuals and in which individuals assess social relationships may provide many insights into animal morality (Bekoff 2002a,b; 2003b; Drea and Frank 2003). In many social groups individuals establish social hierarchies and develop and maintain tight social bonds that help to regulate social behavior. Individuals coordinate their behavior – some mate, some hunt, some defend resources, some accept subordinate status – to achieve common goals and to maintain social stability. Consider briefly pack-living wolves, exemplars of highly developed cooperative and coordinated behavior. Solomon (1995, 139ff) also considers

the importance of learning more about wolves in his discussion of justice, emotions, and the origins of social contracts.

For a long time researchers thought pack size was regulated by available food resources. Wolves typically feed on such prey as elk and moose, each of which is larger than an individual wolf. Hunting such large ungulates successfully takes more than one wolf, so it made sense to postulate that wolf packs evolved because of the size of wolves' prey. Defending food might also be associated with pack-living. However, long-term research by Mech (1970) showed that pack size in wolves was regulated by social and not food-related factors. Mech discovered that the number of wolves who could live together in a coordinated pack was governed by the number of wolves with whom individuals could closely bond ("social attraction factor") balanced against the number of individuals from whom an individual could tolerate competition ("social competition factor"). Codes of conduct and packs broke down when there were too many wolves. (Colin Allen, personal communication, notes that it is possible that social factors might be proximate influences after long periods of selection for hunting prey of a certain size favoring packs of a certain size.) Whether or not the dissolution of packs was due to individuals behaving unfairly is unknown, but this would be a valuable topic for future research in wolves and other social animals. Solomon (1995, 143) contends that "A wolf who is generous can expect generosity in return. A wolf who violates another's ownership zone can expect to be punished, perhaps fero-ciously, by others." These claims can easily be studied empirically. (For interesting studies of the "social complexity hypothesis" that claims "that animals living in large social groups should display enhanced cognitive abilities" when compared to those who do not, see Bond et al. (2003, 479) and Drea and Frank (2003).)

In social groups, individuals often learn what they can and cannot do, and the group's integrity depends upon individuals agreeing that certain rules regulate their behavior. At any given mo-ment individuals know their place or role and that of other group members. As a result of lessons in social cognition and empathy that are offered in social play, individuals learn what is "right" or "wrong" – what is acceptable to others – the result of which is the development and maintenance of a social group that operates efficiently. The absence of social structure and boundaries can produce gaps in morality that lead to the dissolution of a group (Bruce Gottlieb, personal communication).

In summary, I argue that mammalian social play is a useful behavioral phenotype on which to concentrate in order to learn more about the evolution of fairness and social morality. (While birds and individuals of other species engage in social play, there are too few data from which to draw detailed conclusions about the nature of their play.) There is strong selection for playing fairly because most if not all individuals benefit from adopting this behavioral strategy (and group stability may be also be fostered). Numerous mechanisms (play invitation signals, variations in the sequencing of actions performed during play when compared to other contexts, self-handicapping, role-reversing) have evolved to facilitate the initiation and maintenance of social play in numerous mammals – to keep others engaged – so that agreeing to play fairly and the resulting benefits of doing so can be readily achieved.

Ridley (1996) points out that humans seem to be inordinately upset about unfairness, but we do not know much about others animals' reaction to unfairness. He suggests that perhaps behaving fairly pays off in the long run. Brosnan and de Waal (2003) have recently shown that captive brown capuchin monkeys who were trained to exchange a token for cucumber would no longer do so when they saw another monkey receive a grape, a more favored reward. The monkeys' response to unequal reward distribution was interpreted as their having a sense of fairness. Dugatkin's and my model of the development and evolution of cooperation and fairness (Dugatkin and Bekoff 2003) suggests it might. Hauser (2000) concluded that there is no evidence that animals can evaluate whether an

act of reciprocation is fair. However, he did not consider social play in his discussion of animal morality and moral agency. de Waal (1996) remains skeptical about the widespread taxonomic distribution of cognitive empathy after briefly considering social play, but he remains open to the possibility that cognitive empathy might be found in animals other than the great apes (see Preston and de Waal 2002). It is premature to dismiss the possibility that social play plays some role in the evolution of fairness and social morality or that animals other than primates are unable intentionally to choose to behave fairly because they lack the necessary cognitive skills or emotional capacities. We really have very little information that bears on these questions.

Let me emphasize again that I am not arguing that there is a gene for fair or moral behavior. As with any behavioral trait, the underlying genetics is bound to be complex, and environmental influences may be large and difficult to pin down. Nonetheless, provided there is variation in levels of morality among individuals and the trait is highly heritable, and provided virtue is rewarded by a greater number of offspring, then genes associated with good behavior are likely to accumulate in subsequent generations. The observation that play is rarely unfair or uncooperative is surely an indication that natural selection acts to weed out those individuals who do not play by the rules.

Future comparative research that considers the nature and details of the social exchanges that are needed for animals to engage in play – reciprocity and cooperation – will undoubtedly produce data that bear on the questions that I raise in this brief essay and also help to "operationalize" the notion of behaving fairly by informing us about what sorts of evidence confirm that animals are behaving with some sense of fairness. In the absence of this information it is premature to dismiss the possibility that social play plays some role in the evolution of fairness and social morality or that animals other than primates are unable intentionally to choose to behave fairly because they lack the necessary cognitive skills or emotional capacities. These are empirical questions for which the comparative data base is scant.

Gruen (2002) also correctly points out that we still need to come to terms with what it means to be moral. She also suggests that we need to find out what cognitive and emotional capacities operate when humans perform various moral actions, and to study animals to determine if they share these capacities or some variation of them. Even if it were the case that available data suggested that nonhuman primates do not seem to behave in a specific way, for example, playing fairly, in the absence of comparative data this does not justify the claim that individuals of other taxa cannot play fairly. (At a meeting in Chicago, Illinois in August 2000 dealing with social organization and social complexity (see de Waal and Tyack 2003), it was hinted to me that while my ideas about social morality are interesting, there really is no way that social carnivores could be said to be so decent – to behave (play) fairly – because it was unlikely that even nonhuman primates were this virtuous.)

Learning about the taxonomic distribution of animal morality involves answering numerous and often difficult questions. Perhaps it will turn out that the best explanation for existing data in some taxa is that some individuals do indeed on some occasions modify their behavior to play fairly.

Play may be a unique category of behavior in that asymmetries are tolerated more so than in other social contexts. Play cannot occur if the individuals choose not to engage in the activity, and the equality (or symmetry and kindness) needed for play to continue makes it different from other forms of seemingly cooperative behavior (e.g. hunting, care-giving). This sort of egalitarianism is thought to be a precondition for the evolution of social morality in humans. From whence did it arise? Truth be told, we really do not know much about the origins of egalitarianism. Arm-chair discussions, while important, will do little in comparison to our having direct experiences with other animals.

In my view, studies of the evolution of social morality are among the most exciting and challenging projects that behavioral scientists (ethologists, geneticists, evolutionary biologists, neurobiologists, psychologists, anthropologists), theologians, and religious scholars face. We need to rise to the extremely challenging (and frustrating) task before us rather than dismissing summarily and unfairly, in a speciesistic manner, the moral lives of other animals. *Fair is fair.*

[. . .]

ACKNOWLEDGMENTS

Much of this discussion appeared in two of my previous papers (Bekoff 2001a, b) and has been updated where possible. Some of this material is reprinted from *The Origins and Nature of Sociality*, R. Sussman and A. Chapman, eds., pp. 53–80, Copyright © 2004 Walter de Gruyter, Inc. Published by Aldine de Gruyter, Hawthorne, NY. I thank Jan Nystrom, Bob Sussman, and especially Colin Allen and Rob Skipper for comments on an earlier draft of this paper.

REFERENCES

Adams,E.R. and Burnett G.W. 1991. Scientific vocabulary divergence among female primatologists working in East Africa. *Soc. Stud. Sci.* 21: 547–560.

Aldis O. 1975. *Play Fighting*. Academic Press, New York.

Allen C. 2004. Is Anyone a Cognitive Ethologist? *Biology and Philosophy* 19: 589–607.

Allen C. and Bekoff M. 1997. *Species of Mind: The Philosophy and Biology of Cognitive Ethology*. MIT Press, Cambridge, Massachusetts.

Aureli F. and de Waal F.B.M. (ed.) 2000. *Natural Conflict Resolution*. University of California Press, Berkeley.

Aviles L. 1999. Cooperation and non-linear dynamics: an ecological perspective on the evolution of sociality. *Evol. Ecol. Res.* 1: 459–477.

Axelrod R. 1984. *The Evolution of Cooperation*. Basic Books, New York.

Bateson G. 2000. *Steps to an Ecology of Mind*. University of Chicago Press, Chicago.

Bauer E.B. and Smuts B.B. 2002. Role reversal and self-handicapping during playfighting in domestic dogs, Canis familiaris. Paper presented at the meetings of the Animal Behavior Society. University of Indiana.

Bekoff M. 1975. The communication of play intention: are play signals functional? *Semiotica* 15: 231–239.

Bekoff M. 1977a. Social communication in canids: evidence for the evolution of a stereotyped mammalian display. *Science* 197: 1097–1099.

Bekoff M. 1977b. Mammalian dispersal and the ontogeny of individual behavioral phenotypes. *Am. Nat.* 111: 715–732.

Bekoff M. 1995. Play signals as punctuation: the structure of social play in canids. *Behaviour*132: 419–429.

Bekoff M. 1996. Cognitive ethology, vigilance, information gathering, and representation: who might know what and why? *Behav. Process.* 35: 225–237.

Bekoff M. (ed.) 2000a. *The Smile of a Dolphin: Remarkable Accounts of Animal Emotions.*

Discovery Books/Random House, New York.

Bekoff M. 2000b. Animal emotions: exploring passionate natures. *BioScience* 50: 861–870.

Bekoff M. 2001a. Social play behaviour, cooperation, fairness, trust and the evolution of morality. *J. Conscious. Stud.* 8(2): 81–90.

Bekoff M. 2001b. The evolution of animal play, emotions, and social morality: on science, theology, spirituality, personhood, and love. *Zygon (J. Reli. Sci.)* 36: 615–655. 516.

Bekoff M. 2002a. *Minding Animals: Awareness, Emotions, and Heart.* Oxford University Press, New York.

Bekoff M. 2002b. Virtuous nature. *New Scientist* 13 July, pp. 34–37.

Bekoff M. 2002c. Self-awareness. *Nature* 419: 255.

Bekoff M. 2003a. Consciousness and self in animals: some reflections. *Zygon (J. Reli. Sci.)* 38: 229–245.

Bekoff M. 2003b. Empathy: common sense, science sense, wolves, and well-being. *Behav. Brain Sci.* 25: 26–27.

Bekoff M. 2004. The question of animal emotions: an ethological perspective. In McMillan, F. (ed.), *Mental Health and Well-being in Animals.* Iowa State University Press, Ames, Iowa.

Bekoff M. (in press). *Wild Justice and Fair Play: Cooperation, Forgiveness and Morality in Animals.* University of Chicago Press, Chicago.

Bekoff M. and Allen C. 1992. Intentional icons: towards an evolutionary cognitive ethology. *Ethology* 91: 1–16.

Bekoff M. and Allen C. 1997. Cognitive ethology: slayers, skeptics, and proponents. In: Mitchell R.W., Thompson N. and Miles L. (eds), *Anthropomorphism, Anecdote, and Animals: The Emperor's New Clothes?* State University of New York Press, Albany, New York, pp 313–334.

Bekoff M. and Allen C. 1998. Intentional communication and social play: how and why animals negotiate and agree to play. In: Bekoff, M. and Byers, J.A. (ed.), *Animal Play: Evolutionary, Comparative, and Ecological Perspectives.* Cambridge University Press, Cambridge and New York, pp. 97–114.

Bekoff M., Allen C. and Burghardt G.M. (eds), 2002. *The Cognitive Animal.* MIT Press, Cambridge, Massachusetts.

Bekoff M. and Byers J.A. 1981. A critical reanalysis of the ontogeny of mammalian social and locomotor play: an ethological hornet's nest. In: Immelmann K., Barlow G.W., Petrinovich L. and Main M. (eds), *Behavioral Development: The Bielefeld Interdisciplinary Project.* Cambridge University Press, New York, pp. 296–337.

Bekoff M. and Byers J.A. (eds), 1998. *Animal Play: Evolutionary, Comparative, and Ecological Approaches.* Cambridge University Press, New York.

Bekoff M. and Wells M.C. 1986. Social behavior and ecology of coyotes. *Adv. Study Behav.* 16: 251–338.

Bernstein I.S. 2000. The law of parsimony prevails: missing premises allow any conclusion. *J. Conscious. Stud.* 7: 31–34.

Bewley T. 2003. Fair's fair. *Nature* 422: 125–126.

Boehm C. 1999. *Hierarchy in the Forest: The Evolution of Egalitarian Behavior.* Harvard University Press, Cambridge, Massachusetts.

Bond A., Kamil A.C. and Balda R.P. 2003. Social complexity and transitive inference in corvids. *Animal Behav.* 65: 479–487.

Bowles S. and Gintis H. 2002. Home reciprocans. *Nature* 415: 125–128.

Bradie M. 1999. Evolutionary game theory meets the social contract. *Biol. Philos.* 14: 607–613.

Bradley B.J. 1999. Levels of selection, altruism, and primate behavior. *Quart. Rev. Biol.* 74: 171–194.

Brosnan S.F. and de Waal F.B.M. 2003. Monkeys reject unequal pay. *Nature* 425: 297–299.

Burghardt G.M. 1997. Amending Tinbergen: A fifth aim for ethology. In: Thomson Mitchell R.W.N. and Miles L. (eds), *Anthropomorphism, Anecdote,* and Animals: The Emperor's New clothes? State University of New York Press, Albany, New York, pp. 254–276.

Burghardt G.M. 2005. The Genesis of Play. MIT Press, Cambridge, Massachusetts.

Byers J.A. 1977. Terrain preferences in the play of Siberian ibex kids (Capra ibex sibirica). *Zeitschrift fur Tierpsychologie* 45: 199–209.

Byers J.A. 1998. Biological effects of locomotor play: getting into shape or something else. In: Bekoff M. and Byers J.A. (eds), *Animal Play: Evolutionary, Comparative, and Ecological Perspectives.* Cambridge University Press, New York, pp. 205–220.

Byrne R. 1995. *Thinking Primates.* Oxford: Oxford University Press.

Church F. 1959. Emotional reactions of rats to the pain of others. *J. Compar. Physiol. Psychol.* 52: 132–134.

Dalai Lama 2002. Understanding our fundamental nature. In: Davidson R.J. and Harrington A. (eds), *Visions of Compassion: Western Scientists and Tibetan Buddhists Examine Human Nature.* Oxford University Press, New York, pp. 66–80.

Damasio A. 2003. *Looking for Spinoza: Joy, Sorrow, and the Feeling Brain.* Harcourt, New York.

Darwin C. 1859. *On the Origin of Species By Means of Natural Selection.* Murray, London.

Darwin C. 1871/1936. *The Descent of Man and Selection in Relation to Sex.* Random House, New York.

Darwin C. 1872/1998. *The Expression of the Emotions in Man and Animals,* 3rd edn. Oxford University Press, New York (with an Introduction, Afterword, and Commentaries by Paul Ekman).

Dawkins R. 1976. *The Selfish Gene.* Oxford University Press, New York.

Dawkins R. 2001. Sustainability doesn't come naturally: a Darwinian perspective on values. www.environmentfoundation.net/richard-dawkins.htm.

de Waal F. 1991. Complementary methods and convergent evidence in the study of primate social cognition. *Behaviour* 18: 297–320.

de Waal F. 1996. *Good-natured: The Origins of Right and Wrong in Humans and other Animals.* Harvard University Press, Cambridge, Massachusetts.

de Waal F. 2001. *The Ape and the Sushi Master: Cultural Reflections of a Primatologist.* Basic Books, New York.

de Waal F. and Tyack P.L. (eds), 2003. *Animal Social Complexity: Intelligence, Culture, and Individualized Societies.* Harvard University Press, Cambridge, Massachusetts.

Dolan R.J. Emotion, cognition, and behavior. 2002. *Science* 298: 1191–1194.

Douglas K. 2001. Playing fair. *New Scientist* 10 March (No. 2281). pp. 38–42.

Drea C.M. and Frank L.G. 2003. The social complexity of spotted hyenas. In: de Waal F. and Tyack P.L. (eds), *Animal Social Complexity: Intelligence, Culture, and Individualized Societies.* Harvard University Press, Cambridge, Massachusetts, pp. 121–148.

Dugatkin L.A. 1997. *Cooperation Among Animals: An Evolutionary Perspective.* Oxford University Press, New York.

Dugatkin L.A. and Bekoff M. 2003. Play and the evolution of fairness: a game theory model. *Behav. Proc.* 60: 209–214.

Dylan B. 1983. *Infidels.* CBS Inc.

Fagen R. 1981. *Animal Play Behavior.* Oxford University Press, New York.

Fagen R. 1993. Primate juveniles and primate play. In: Pereira M.E. and Fairbanks L.A. (eds), *Juvenile Primates: Life History, Development, and Behavior.* Oxford University Press, New York, pp. 183–196.

Fehr E. and Gächter S. 2002. Altruistic punishment in humans. *Nature* 415: 137–140.

Fehr E. and Rockenbach B. 2003. Detrimental effect of sanctions on human altruism. *Nature* 422: 137–140.

Field A. 2001. *Altruistically Inclined? The Behavioral Sciences, Evolutionary Theory, and the Origins of Reciprocity.* University of Michigan Press, Ann Arbor.

Flack J.C. and de Waal F. 2000. Any animal whatever: Darwinian building blocks of morality in monkeys and apes. *J. Conscious. Stud.* 7: 1–29.

Flack J.C., Jeannotte L.A. and de Waal F. 2004. Play signaling and the perception of social rules by juvenile chimpanzees. *J. Compar. Psychol*, 118: 149–159.

Frith C.D. and Frith U. 1999. Interacting minds - a biological basis. *Science* 286: 1692–1695.

Gallese V. 1998. Mirror neurons, from grasping to language. *Conscious. Bull.* Fall 3–4.

Gallese V. and Goldman A. 1998. Mirror neurons and the simulation theory of mind-reading. *Trends Cogn. Sci.* 2: 493–501.

Gould S.J. and Lloyd E.A. 1999. Individuality and adaptation across levels of selection: how shall we name and generalize the unit of Darwinism. *Proc. Natl. Acad. Sci.* 96: 11904–11909.

Griffin D.R. 2001. *Animal Minds.* University of Chicago Press, Chicago.

Gruen L. 2002. The morals of animal minds. In: Bekoff, Allen and Burghardt (eds), *The Cognitive Animal*, MIT Press, Cambridge, Massachusetts, pp. 437–442.

Guzeldere G. and Nahmias E. 2002. Darwin's continuum and the building blocks of deception. In: Bekoff , Allen and Burghardt (eds), *The Cognitive Animal*, MIT Press, Cambridge, Massachusetts, pp. 353–362.

Hauser M. 2000. *Wild Minds.* Henry Holt, New York.

Hill H.L. and Bekoff M. 1977. The variability of some motor components of social play and agonistic behaviour in infant eastern coyotes, Canis latrans var. *Animal Behav.* 25: 907–909.

Hinde R.A. 2002. *Why Good is Good: The Sources of Morality.* Routledge, New York.

Horowitz A.C. 2002. The behaviors of theories of mind, and a case study of dogs at play. Ph.D. dissertation, University of California, San Diego.

Hudson S.D. 1986. *Human Character and Morality: Reflections from the History of Ideas.* Routledge & Kegan Paul, Boston.

Hurd J.P. 1996. (ed) *Investigating the Biological Foundations of Human Morality.* Edwin Mellen Press, Lewiston, New York.

Jamieson D. 2002. Sober and Wilson on psychological altruism. *Philos. Phenomenol. Res.* LXV: 702–710.

Jamieson D. and Bekoff M. 1993. On aims and methods of cognitive ethology. *Philosophy of Science Association* 2: 110–124.

Keeley B.L. 2004. Anthropomorphism, Primatomorphism, Mammalomorphism: Understanding Cross-Species Comparisons. *Biology and Philosophy* 19: 521–540.

Kitchen D.M. and Packer C. 1999. Complexity in vertebrate societies. In: Keller L. (ed.), *Levels of Selection in Evolution.* Princeton University Press, Princeton, New Jersey, pp. 176–196.

Kropotkin P. 1902. *Mutual Aid: a Factor of Evolution.* Philips & Co, McClure, New York.

Kuczaj S., Tranel K., Trone M. and Hill H. 2001. Are animals capable of deception or empathy? Implications for animal consciousness and animal welfare. *Animal Welfare* 10: S161–173.

Leigh E.G. Jr. 1999. Levels of selection, potential conflicts, and their resolution: Role of the 'Common good'. In: Keller L. (ed.), *Levels of Selection in Evolution.* Princeton University Press, Princeton, New Jersey, pp. 15–30.

Macintyre A. 1999. *Dependent Rational Animals: Why Human Beings Need the Virtues.* Open Court, Chicago.

Markowitz H. 1982. *Behavioral Enrichment in the Zoo.* Van Reinhold Company, New York.

Marler P. 1996. Social cognition: are primates smarter than birds? In: Nolan V. Jr. and Ketterson E.D. (eds), *Current Ornithology*, Vol. 13. Plenum Press, New York, pp. 1–32.

Mayr E. 2000. Darwin's influence on modern thought. *Sci. Am.* 283: 67–71.

Mech L.D. 1970. *The Wolf.* Doubleday, Garden City, New York.

Mitchell L.E. 1998. *Stacked Deck: A Story of Selfishness in America.* Temple University Press, Philadelphia, Pennsylvania.

Motluk A. 2001. Read my mind. *New Sci.* 169: 22–26.

Neuman Y. 2003. The logic of meaning-in-context. *Am. J. Semiotics* (special issue: Gregory Bateson).

Okamoto K. and Matsumara S. 2000. The evolution of punishment and apology: an iterated prisoner's dilemma model. *Evol. Ecol.* 14: 703–720.

Poole J. 1998. An exploration of a commonality between ourselves and elephants. *Etica Animali* 9/98: 85–110.

Panksepp J. 1998. *Affective Neuroscience.* Oxford University Press, New York.

Panksepp J. 2000. The rat will play. In: Bekoff M. (ed.), *The Smile of a Dolphin: Remarkable Accounts of Animal Emotions.* Random House/Discovery Books, New York, pp. 146–147.

Pellis S. 2002. Keeping in touch: play fighting and social knowledge. In: Bekoff, Allen and Burghardt (eds), *The Cognitive Animal*, MIT Press, Cambridge, Massachusetts, pp. 421–427.

Peterson G.R. 1999. The evolution of consciousness and the theology of nature. *Zygon* 34: 283–306.

Peterson G.R. 2000. God, genes, and cognizing agents. *Zygon* 35: 469–480.

Pigliucci M. 2002. Are ecology and evolutionary biology "soft" sciences? *Ann. Zool. Fenn.* 39: 87–98.

Poole J. 1998. An Exploration of a Commonality Between Ourselves and Elephants. *Etica Animali* 9/98: 85–110.

Power T.G. 2000. *Play and Exploration in Children and Animals.* Lawrence Erlbaum Associates, Hillsdale, New Jersey.

Preston S.D. and de Waal F.B.M. 2002. Empathy: its ultimate and proximate bases. *Behav. Brain Sci.* 25: 1–72.

Ridley M. 1996. *The Origins of Virtue: Human Instincts and the Evolution of Cooperation.* Viking, New York.

Ridley M. 2001. *The Cooperative Gene.* The Free Press, New York.

Rilling J.K., Gutman D.A., Zeh T.R., Pagnoni G., Berns G.S. and Kitts C.D. 2002. A neural basis for cooperation. *Neuron* 36: 395–405.

Riolo R.L., Cohen M.D. and Zelrod R. 2001. Evolution of cooperation without reciprocity. *Nature* 414: 441–443.

Schaller G.B. and Lowther G.R. 1969. The relevance of carnivore behavior to the study of early hominids. *Southwestern J. Anthropol.* 25: 307–341.

Scott J.P. and Fuller J.L. 1965. *Genetics and the Social Behavior of the Dog.* University of Chicago Press, Chicago.

Sigmund K., Fehr E. and Nowak M.A. 2002. The economics of fair play. *Sci. Am.* 286(1): 83–87.

Sigmund K. and Nowak M.A. 2001. Evolution: tides of tolerance. *Nature* 414: 403–405.

Singer P. 1999. *A Darwinian Left: Politics, Evolution, and Cooperation.* Yale University Press, New Haven.

Siviy S. 1998. Neurobiological substrates of play behavior: Glimpses into the structure and function of mammalian playfulness. In: Bekoff M. and Byers J.A. (eds), *Animal Play: Evolutionary, Comparative, and Ecological Perspectives.* Cambridge University Press, New York, 221–242.

Skyrms B. 1996. *Evolution of the Social Contract.* Cambridge University Press, New York.

Smuts B.B. 2001. Encounters with animal minds. *J. Conscious. Stud.* 8: 293–309.

Sober E. and Wilson D.S. 1998. *Unto Others: The Evolution and Psychology of Unselfish Behavior.* Harvard University Press, Cambridge, Massachusetts.

Sober E. and Wilson D.S. 2000. Summary of: unto others: the evolution and psychology of unselfish behavior. *J. Conscious. Stud.* 7: 185–206.

Solomon R. 1995. *A passion for justice: Emotions and the origins of the social contract.* Rowman & Littlefield, Lanham, Maryland.

Spinka M., Newberry R.C. and Bekoff M. 2000. Mammalian play: training for the unexpected. *Quart. Rev. Biol.* 76: 141–168.

Thompson P.R. 1975. A cross-species analysis of carnivore, primate, and hominid behavior. *J. Human Evol.* 4: 113–124.

Tinbergen N. 1963. On Aims and Methods of Ethology. *Zeitschrift für Tierpsychologie* 20: 410–433.

Tinbergen N. 1972. Introduction. In Hans Kruuk, *The Spotted Hyena.* University of Chicago Press, Chicago.

Tomasello M. and Call J. 1997. *Primate Cognition.* Oxford University Press, New York.

Watson D.M. and Croft D.B. 1996. Age-related differences in playfighting strategies of captive male red-necked wallabies (Macropus rufogriseus banksianus). *Ethology* 102: 33–346.

Wechlin S., Masserman J.H. and Terris W. Jr. 1964. Shock to a conspecific as an aversive stimulus. *Psychon. Sci.* 1: 17–18.

Wilson D.S. 2002. *Darwin's Cathedral: Evolution, Religion, and the Nature of Society.* University of Chicago Press, Chicago.

Wrangham R. and Conklin-Brittain N. 2003. Cooking as a biological trait. *Compar. Biochem. Physiol.,* Part A, 136: 35–46.

12

JEFFREY MOUSSAIEFF MASSON and SUSAN McCARTHY

Grief, Sadness, and the Bones of Elephants*

Jeffrey Moussaieff Masson has a background in Sanskrit and Indian studies, Freudian psycho-analysis and journalism. He has written several books about animal emotions, including the emotional worlds of dogs, cats, and farm animals. **Susan McCarthy** has a background in biology and journalism and has published a book about how young animals learn in which she concludes that many skills and pieces of knowledge must be learned for animals to survive in their natural environments (Baby chicks, for example, must learn to recognize water.) The extract reproduced here is from *When Elephants Weep: The Emotional Lives of Animals*, a best-seller that has been translated into twenty languages and argues that animals display a wide variety of emotions, including fear, hope, love, joy, compassion, shame, grief, and sadness. In this chapter on grief and sadness, the authors recount stories of animal sorrow (such as the male dolphin who died three days after the death of his companion because he refused to eat) that produce emotions as profound in animals as in the lives of humans. The level of emotional development described in this extract might also provide evidence for the contention that at least some animals possess a theory of mind. A major implication of the complex reality of animal emotions is that the confinement of animals, such as in zoos, can produce very negative emotional consequences for captive animals. Masson and McCarthy show us that animals "feel" in a myriad of ways – they love, suffer, cry, laugh and they look back with nostalgia and anticipate future happiness – as subjects of a life, animals "feel" just as humans do, adding yet another layer to the complex ethical conundrum of the animal question.

In the Rocky Mountains, biologist Marcy Cottrell Houle was observing the eyrie of two peregrine falcons, Arthur and Jenny, as both parents busily fed their five nestlings. One morning only the male falcon visited the nest. Jenny did not appear at all, and Arthur's behavior changed markedly. When he arrived with food, he waited by the eyrie for as much as an hour before flying off to hunt again, something he had never done before. He called out again and again and listened for his mate's answer, or looked into the nest uttering an enquiring "echup." Houle

* Reproduced with permission from Jeffrey Moussaieff Masson and Susan McCarthy (1995), *When Elephants Weep: The Emotional Lives of Animals*. New York: Delta.

struggled not to interpret his behavior as expectation and disappointment. Jenny did not appear the next day or the next. Late on the third day, perched by the eyrie, Arthur uttered an unfamiliar sound, "a cry like the screeching moan of a wounded animal, the cry of a creature in suffering." The shocked Houle wrote, "The sadness in the outcry was unmistakable; having heard it, I will never doubt that an animal can suffer emotions that we humans think belong to our species alone."[1]

After the cry, Arthur sat motionless on the rock and did not stir for a whole day. On the fifth day after Jenny's disappearance, Arthur went on a frenzy of hunting, bringing food to his nestlings from dawn to dusk, without pausing to rest. Before Jenny's disappearance, his efforts had been less frenetic; Houle notes that she never again saw a falcon work so incessantly. When biologists climbed to the nest a week after Jenny's disappearance, they found that three of the nestlings had starved to death, but two had survived and were thriving under their father's care. Houle later learned that Jenny had probably been shot. The two surviving nestlings fledged successfully.

It is impossible to predict how deeply affected we will be when somebody close to us dies. Sometimes people show no external reaction, but their lives are shattered. They may feel nothing consciously, or even feel relief, when they are inwardly devastated and may never recover. The external signs of grief tell something, but they may not tell everything. Introspection may tell something, too, but may be misleading. Faced with human sadness in its depths, scientific curiosity should be tempered with humility: no one, certainly not the somatically oriented psychiatrist (offering pills for misery), can speak with any authority about its source, duration, or pathology. Even greater humility is required before the permutations of nonhuman grief and sadness.

When nonscientists speak of animal sadness, the most common evidence they give is the behavior of one of a pair when its mate dies, or the behavior of a pet when its owner dies or leaves. This kind of grief receives notice and respect,

yet there are many other griefs that pass unremarked – the cow separated from its calf or the dog deliberately abandoned. Then there are all the griefs humans never see: unheard cries in the forest, herds in the remote hills whose losses are unknown.

MOURNING LOST LOVE

Wild animals have been observed mourning for a mate. According to naturalist Georg Steller,[2] the now-extinct sea cow named after him was a monogamous species, with families consisting usually of a female, a male, and two young of different ages: "one grown offspring, and a little, tender one." Steller, a ship's naturalist, saw that when the crew of the ship killed a female whose body washed up on the beach, the male returned to her body for two consecutive days, "as if he were inquiring about her."

As the fate of the three dead peregrine nestlings shows, it can be disastrous for a wild animal to display grief. There is no survival value in not eating, or moping and grieving. While love can be readily reduced to evolutionary function (for those so inclined), grief over the loss of a loved one – another expression of love – often threatens survival. Grief thus calls for explanation on its own terms.

The sorrow of bereavement is easily observed in captive or pet animals. Elizabeth Marshall Thomas gives a moving account of Maria and Misha, two huskies who had formed a pair bond, when Misha's owners gave him away.

Both he and Maria knew that something was terribly wrong when his owners came for him the last time, so that Maria struggled to follow him out the door. When she was prevented, she rushed to the window seat and, with her back to the room, watched Misha get into the car. She stayed in the window for weeks thereafter, sitting backward on the seat with her face to the window and her tail to the room, watching and waiting for Misha. At last she must have realized that he wasn't going to come. Something happened to her at that point.

She lost her radiance and became depressed. She moved more slowly, was less responsive, and got angry rather easily at things that before she would have overlooked … Maria never recovered from her loss, and although she never forfeited her place as alpha female, she showed no interest in forming a permanent bond with another male …[3]

Maria knew that Misha was gone from her. Her behavior is reminiscent of human grief at permanent separation and loss of a loved one. Wolves and coyotes, to whom dogs are very closely related, do form pairs. The conditions in which dogs are kept are very different from those in which wild canids live. Probably dog behavior is more flexible than has been realized, more strongly dictated by the conditions humans provide for them. While both female and male dogs have come to symbolize promiscuity to many humans, this behavior has been created by the way humans breed and maintain dogs; it is not intrinsic to their nature. One has to wonder how much so-called "natural" human sexuality is equally produced by social arrangements and expectations.

Some animals who do not form pairs in the wild are housed in pairs in captivity and grow deeply attached to one another. Often the mate is the only companion the animal has. Ackman and Alle, two circus horses, were stabled together.[4] No particular attachment between them was noticed until Ackman's unexpected death. Alle "whinnied continually." She scarcely ate or slept. In an effort to distract her, she was moved, given new companions, and offered special foods. She was examined and medicated, in case she was ill. Within two months she had wasted to death.

Two Pacific "kiko" dolphins in a marine park in Hawaii, Kiko and Hoku, were devoted to each other for years, often making a point to touch one another with a fin while swimming around in their tank. When Kiko suddenly died, Hoku refused to eat. He swam slowly in circles, with his eyes clenched shut "as if he did not want to look on a world that did not contain Kiko," as trainer Karen Pryor wrote.[5] He was given a new companion, Kolohi, who swam beside him and

caressed him. Eventually he opened his eyes and ate once more. Although he became attached to Kolohi, observers felt that he never became as fond of her as he had been of Kiko. While the interpretation that Hoku did not want to see a world without Kiko remains speculative, it is clear that Hoku was grieving.

Researchers who had caught a dolphin on a fishhook and put her in a holding tank soon despaired for her life.[6] Pauline, as they named her, could not even keep herself upright and had to be supported constantly. On the third day of her captivity, a male dolphin was captured and placed in the same tank. This raised her spirits; the male helped her swim, at times nudging her to the surface. Pauline appeared to make a complete recovery but suddenly died two months later from an abscess caused by the fishhook, whereupon the male refused to eat and died three days later. An autopsy revealed a perforated gastric ulcer, surely aggravated by his mournful fasting.

It would be the end of most species if every bereaved animal died of grief. Such cases must be extreme and unusual. Dying of grief is not the only proof of love and affection in animals, but these incidents do illuminate an emotional range and emotional possibilities. Animals in the wild also grieve for companions other than mates. Lions do not form pairs, yet a lion has been known to remain by the body of another lion that had been shot and killed, licking its fur.[7] As is so often the case, elephants offer examples that are uncannily similar to human feelings. Cynthia Moss, a researcher who has studied wild African elephants for years, describes mother elephants who appear in perfect health but become lethargic for many days after a calf dies and trail behind the rest of the family.

An observer once came across a band of African elephants surrounding a dying matriarch as she swayed and fell. The other elephants clustered around her and tried mightily to get her up. A young male tried to raise her with his tusks, put food into her mouth, and even tried sexually mounting her, all in vain. The other elephants stroked her with their trunks; one calf knelt and tried to suckle. At last the group moved off, but one female and her calf stayed behind. The female stood with her back to the dead matriarch, now and then reaching back to touch her with one foot. The other elephants called to her. Finally, she walked slowly away. [8]

Cynthia Moss describes the behavior of an elephant herd circling a dead companion "disconsolately several times, and if it is still motionless they come to an uncertain halt. They then face outward, their trunks hanging limply down to the ground. After a while they may prod and circle again, and then again stand, facing outward." Finally – perhaps when it is clear the elephant is dead – "they may tear out branches and grass clumps from the surrounding vegetation and drop these on and around the carcass."[9] The standing outward suggests that the elephants may find the sight painful; maybe they want to stay close but find it intrusive to watch such suffering; perhaps it has a ritual meaning we do not yet comprehend.

It was once thought that elephants went to special elephant graveyards to die. While this has been disproved, Moss speculates that elephants do have a concept of death. They are strongly interested in elephant bones, not at all in the bones of other species. Their reaction to elephant bones is so predictable that cinematographers have no difficulty filming elephants examining bones. Smelling them, turning them over, running their trunks over the bones, the elephants pick them up, feel them, and sometimes carry them off for a distance before dropping them. They show the greatest interest in skulls and tusks. Moss speculates that they are trying to recognize the individual.

Once Moss brought the jawbone of a dead elephant – an adult female – into her camp to determine its exact age. A few weeks after this elephant's death, her family happened to pass through the camp area. They made a detour to be with and examine the jaw. Long after the others had moved on, the elephant's seven-year-old calf stayed behind, touching the jaw and turning it over with his feet and trunk. One can only agree with Moss's conclusion that the calf

was somehow reminded of his mother – perhaps remembering the contours of her face. He felt her there. It seems certain that the calf's memory is at work here. Whether he experienced a feeling of melancholic nostalgia, sorrow, perhaps joy in remembering his mother, or was moved by some emotional experience we might not be able to identify, it would be difficult to deny that feelings were involved.

Based on their behavior, the feelings of the Gombe chimpanzees who witnessed one of their number fall to his death seem similarly complex. Three small groups of chimpanzees, mostly males, but including a female in estrus, had come together when Rix, an adult male, somehow fell into a rocky gully and broke his neck. The reaction was immediate pandemonium – apes screaming, charging, displaying, embracing, copulating, throwing stones, barking, and whimpering seemingly at random. Eventually they grew quieter. For several hours the chimps gathered around the corpse. They came close and peered at Rix's body silently, climbed on branches to get a different vantage point. They never touched him. One male adolescent, Godi, seemed particularly intent, whimpering and groaning repeatedly as he gazed at Rix. Godi became highly agitated when several large males drew very close to the body. After several hours the chimpanzees drifted away. Before leaving, Godi leaned over Rix and stared at him intently before hurrying after his companions.[10]

During this episode the chimpanzees repeatedly uttered "wraah" calls, common when chimps are disturbed by strange humans or by Cape buffalo, but also when they sight a dead chimp or baboon. On one occasion chimps *wraahed* for four hours after witnessing the death of a baboon injured in a fight with other baboons.

A chimpanzee at the Arnhem Zoo, rather confusingly named Gorilla, had several babies who died despite her tender care. Each time an infant died she would become visibly depressed. Gorilla would sit huddled in a corner for weeks on end, ignoring the other chimpanzees. At times she would burst out screaming. This story had a happy sequel: Gorilla became a successful mother when she was given the care of Roosje, a ten-week-old baby chimpanzee, whom she was taught to bottle-feed.[11]

LONELINESS

Loneliness appears to affect animals who live in social or family groups. It is probably one factor causing death in many captive animals. For captive beavers, for example, the presence or absence of a companion is an important factor in survival. One wildlife biologist noted that yearling beavers, "if they do not get companionship, may simply sit where they are put down until they die."[12] Loneliness, a frequent result of confinement and domesticity, is often observed in captive animals. A lonely wild beaver could presumably set off in search of other beavers.

Animals seek each other out more than biologists once assumed, perhaps in an effort to avoid feelings of sadness, loneliness, and sorrow. In some species, males who have been "kicked out of the nest" by their mothers form bachelor herds. Male African elephants gather in groups in "bull areas."[13] Many animals are rather sweepingly described as solitary, but careful field studies of animals famous for their solitary natures – tigers, leopards, rhinoceros, and bears – often reveal that they spend more time associating with each other than was previously thought. The European wildcat and the fishing cat are said to be solitary species in which the female and male mate and then separate, and the female raises the kittens alone. In zoos, however, the female and male may be caged in pairs, with interesting results. Usually the male is taken out before kittens are born, in case he should harm them. In the Cracow Zoo this precaution was omitted, and instead of attacking the kittens the male wildcat carried his meat to the entrance of the den and made coaxing sounds. Similarly, in the Magdeburg Zoo the father wildcat guarded the den day and night and, though normally peaceful, attacked the keeper if he came too near. The father brought food to the den, and when the kittens were old enough to come out and play, he hissed and threatened any zoo-goers who startled his kittens. Fishing cats at the Frankfurt Zoo also led a surprisingly warm family life. The male not only brought food, but often curled up in the nest box with the rest of the family. He was such a conscientious parent that if he was out of the nest box and the female also came out, he became anxious and went in the nest box with the kittens.

Possibly these species are less solitary than has been thought, or perhaps this is another demonstration of the flexibility of animal behavior. Paul Leyhausen, who observed these cats, speculates that while males in the wild may have nothing to do with their mates and kittens, in captivity they may be "subjected to stimuli which awaken normally dormant behavior patterns."[14] If so, we are entitled to wonder whether a male fishing cat, wandering by a southeast Asian stream or through a forest, ever gets a twinge from those normally dormant patterns, and feels lonely.

IMPRISONMENT

Even when captive animals are not confined in solitude, their imprisonment may make them sad. It is often said of zoo animals that the way to tell if they are happy is to ask whether the young play and the adults breed. Most zookeepers would not accept this standard of happiness for themselves. As Jane Goodall noted, "Even in concentration camps, babies were born, and there is no good reason to believe that it is different for chimpanzees."[15]

Captivity is undoubtedly more painful to some animals than others. Lions seem to have less difficulty with the notion of lying in the sun all day than do tigers, for example. Yet even lions can be seen in many zoos pacing restlessly back and forth in the stereotyped motions seen in so many captive animals. The concept of *Funktionslust*, the enjoyment of one's abilities, also suggests its opposite, the feeling of frustration and misery that overtakes an animal when its capacities cannot be expressed. If an animal enjoys using its natural abilities, it is also possible that the animal *misses* using them. Although a gradual trend in zoo construction and design is to make the cages better resemble the natural habitat, most zoo animals, particularly the large ones, have little or no opportunity to use their abilities. Eagles have no room to fly, cheetahs have no room to run, goats have but a single boulder to climb.

There is no reason to suppose that zoo life is not a source of sadness to most animals imprisoned there, like displaced persons in wartime. It would be comforting to believe that they are happy there, delighted to receive medical care and grateful to be sure of their next meal. Unfortunately, in the main, there is no evidence to suppose that they are. Most take every possible opportunity to escape. Most will not breed. Probably they want to go home. Some captive animals die of grief when taken from the wild. Sometimes these deaths appear to be from disease, perhaps because an animal under great stress becomes vulnerable to illness. Others are quite obviously deaths from despair-near-suicides. Wild animals may refuse to eat, killing themselves in the only way open to them. We do not know if they are aware that they will die if they do not eat, but it is clear that they are extremely unhappy. In 1913 Jasper Von Oertzen described the death of a young gorilla imported to Europe: "Hum-Hum had lost all joy in living. She succeeded in living to reach Hamburg, and from there, the Animal Park at Stellingen, with all her caretakers, but her energy did not return again. With signs of the greatest sadness of soul Hum-Hum mourned over the happy past. One could find no fatal illness; it was as always with these costly animals: 'She died of a broken heart.'" [16]

Marine mammals have a high death rate in captivity, a fact not always apparent to visitors at marine parks and oceanariums. A pilot whale celebrity at one oceanarium was actually thirteen different pilot whales, each successive one being introduced to visitors by the same name, as if it were the same animal. [17] It takes little reflection to see the great difference in a marine mammal's life when kept in an oceanarium. Orcas grow to twenty-three feet long, weigh up to 9,000 pounds,

and roam a hundred miles a day. No cage, and certainly not the swimming pools where they are confined in all oceanariums, could possibly provide satisfaction, let alone joy. They are believed to have a life expectancy as long as our own. Yet at Sea World, in San Diego, the oceanarium with the best track record for keeping orcas alive, they last an average of eleven years. [18]

If a person's life span were shortened this much, would one still speak of happiness? Asked whether their animals were happy, a number of marine mammal trainers all said yes: they ate, engaged in sexual intercourse (it is extremely rare for an orca to give birth in captivity), and were almost never sick. This could mean that they were not depressed, but does it mean they were happy? The fact that people ask this question again and again indicates a malaise, perhaps profound guilt at subjecting these lively sea travelers to unnatural confinement.

Which animals suffer the most in captivity can be unpredictable. Harbor seals often thrive in oceanariums and zoos. Hawaiian monk seals almost invariably die – sometimes they refuse to eat, sometimes they succumb to illness. One way or another, one observer noted, they have generally "just moped to death." [19]

The issue of the effects of captivity is most painful when one considers animals that can live nowhere but in captivity because their habitat is gone – as is the case for an increasing number of species – or because they are physically incapacitated. When fewer than a dozen California condors were left in the wild, arguments raged about whether to capture the remaining birds for captive breeding or to let the species perish freely, without undergoing the ignominy of captivity. The condor is a soaring bird that can easily fly fifty miles in a day, a life that can hardly be simulated in a cage. In the end the birds were captured, and so for a time there were no California condors in the wild. Since then, captive-bred birds have been released in an attempt to reestablish the species.

The fact that animals can be sad must first be acknowledged before it can be studied and understood. Zookeepers ask whether animals are healthy, and whether they are likely to breed, but rarely ask, "What would make this animal *happy*?" Nor have the studies by animal behaviorists been of much help. The *Oxford Dictionary of Animal Behavior* notes: "It seems reasonable to allow that animals may be distressed by being unable to feed and drink, to move their limbs, to sleep, and to have social interaction with their fellows, but the difficulty of defining distress in an objective and convincing way has been a stumbling-block in the formation of animal welfare legislation even in countries where there is wide-spread public interest in the way that animals are treated."[20]

DEPRESSION AND LEARNED HELPLESSNESS

In humans, extreme sadness is called depression. As used by psychiatrists and psychologists, depression is a catchall diagnosis, referring to melancholy springing from a number of sources. In the quest to validate the medical model of psychiatry, scientists have sought to produce clinically depressed animals in the laboratory – to which end some experimenters have worked to provide animals with spectacularly unhappy childhoods.

Among the most widely reported experiments in the history of animal behavior are those psychologist Harry Harlow performed on rhesus monkeys. The baby monkeys under his aegis who preferred soft, huggable dummy mothers to hard, wire surrogates, even when only the wire ones dispensed milk, are famous and have been used as evidence that psychological studies on animals – really forms of torture – can teach humans about their emotions. While the study suggests that the nurturant feelings in mothering can be even more important than its survival value, surely this gruesome experiment was gratuitously emotionally cruel as well as unnecessary to prove this point.

Other rhesus monkeys, at the age of six weeks, were placed alone in the "depression chamber," or vertical chamber, a stainless-steel trough intended to reproduce a psychological "well of despair."[21] Forty-five days of solitary confinement in the chamber produced permanently impaired monkeys. Even when months had passed since their experience, the once-chambered monkeys were listless, incurious, and almost completely asocial, huddling in one spot and clasping themselves.[22] No knowledge gained, no point proved, can justify such abuse.

Similarly, dogs, cats, and rats in the laboratory have been induced to feel the global pessimism known as "learned helplessness." In the classic experiment, dogs were strapped into a harness and given electric shocks at unpredictable intervals. The shock was inescapable – nothing they could do prevented or lessened it. Afterward they were placed in a divided chamber. When a tone sounded, the dogs needed to jump into the other side of the chamber to avoid being shocked. Most dogs learned this quickly, but two-thirds of the dogs who had been given inescapable shocks just lay still and whined, making no attempt to escape. Their previous experience had apparently taught them despair. This effect wore off in a few days. Yet, if the dogs were subjected to inescapable shocks four times in a week, their "learned helplessness" was lasting. Psychologist Martin Seligman, the principal researcher in the study of learned helplessness (and author of the bestselling book *Learned Optimism*),[23] argues that the shocked animal is frightened at first, but when it comes to believe that it is helpless, sinks into depression. In his explanation of how he came upon the notion of doing experiments on learned helplessness in animals Seligman cites the research of C. P. Richter during the [1950s], "who reasoned that for a wild rat, being held in the hand of a predator like man, having whiskers trimmed, and being put in a vat of hot water from which escape is impossible produces a sense of helplessness in the rat."

Learned helplessness has been experimentally produced in humans, though not by means of shock. People given tasks at which they repeatedly fail quickly come to believe that they will fail at other tasks and do poorly at them, compared to those who have not been put through a sequence of failures. In the real world, battered women may be unable to leave their batterers, although the risks of leaving and the lack of anywhere to go may be as important as their perception that any action on their part to save themselves from continued abuse is pointless. The animal research really shows nothing about humans – the alleged purpose of such research – that one cannot learn by talking to battered women about their lives.[24]

Having produced depressed dogs, Seligman wanted to cure them. He placed "helpless" dogs in the chamber and removed the partition to make it easy for them to cross and avoid shock, but the despondent dogs made no effort to get away and so did not discover escape was possible. Seligman got in the chamber and called them, and offered them food, but the dogs did not move. Eventually he was reduced to dragging the dogs back and forth on leashes. Some dogs were dragged back and forth two hundred times before they discovered that this time they could escape the electric shocks. According to Seligman, their recovery from learned helplessness was lasting and complete. Their experience, however, must have had some lasting effect on them.

Many other experimenters have produced learned helplessness in the laboratory by various means, with sometimes fiendish results. One experimenter raised rhesus monkeys in solitude, in black-walled isolation cages, from infancy until six months, to induce "social helplessness." Then he taped each young monkey to a cruciform restraining device and placed it, for an hour a day, in a cage with other young monkeys. After initial withdrawal, the unrestrained monkeys poked and prodded the restrained monkeys, pulling their hair, gouged their eyes, and pried their mouths open. The restrained monkeys struggled, but could not escape. All they could do was cry out. After two to three months of this abuse, their behavior changed. They stopped struggling, though they still cried out.[25] And as the experimenter noted, "No advantage was taken of numerous opportunities to bite the oppressor which thrust fingers or sex organs against or into its mouth." These monkeys were lastingly traumatized and were terrified of other monkeys even when unrestrained. Like the other experiments, this one is distinguished by its cruelty.

Comparatively few depressed humans became so through being placed in solitary confinement for half their childhoods, or by being raised in solitary confinement and then tortured by peers. Oddly enough, the argument on the part of the scientists conducting these experiments has been that animals are so similar to us in their feelings that we can learn about human depression by studying animal depression. But this raises the important ethical question asked by many animal-rights groups: If animals suffer the way we do, which is the whole justification for the experiments, is it not sadistic to conduct them? Clearly the animals can be made deeply unhappy, but this fact could have been observed under naturally occurring conditions, without subjecting sensitive creatures to pointless cruelty.

Through all these griefs and torments, animals display sorrow through their movements, postures, and actions. Often animal vocalizations provide evidence of sadness. Wolves seem to have a special mourning howl or lonesome howl that differs from their usual convivial howling.[26] Other animals are said to wail, moan, or cry. When Marchessa, an elderly female mountain gorilla, died, the silverback male of her group became subdued and was heard to whimper frequently, the only time such a sound had been heard from a silverback.[27] These two wild gorillas may have spent as much as thirty years of their lives together. One observer wrote of orangutans, "In disappointment the young specimen quite commonly whimpers or weeps, without, however, shedding tears."[28]

No one knows for certain why humans weep. Newborn babies cry, but they do not usually shed tears until they are a few months old. Adults cry less, and some adults never shed tears. Tears have been classified into three kinds: continuous tears, which keep the eye moist; reflex tears, which flush foreign objects or irritating gases out of the eye; and emotional tears, the tears of grief, happiness, or rage. Emotional tears are different in that they contain a higher percentage of protein than other tears.[29] Curiously, since Darwin's survey of the subject in 1872, weeping has been little studied, but it has been speculated that emotional tears may have both physical and social or communicative functions.

Since it is possible for people to feel great unhappiness and not weep, it is also unclear why tears communicate so effectively. It may be that our reaction is instinctive, and perhaps part of the respect accorded to tears comes from the possibility that they are ours alone. It has been suggested that almost every human bodily secretion is considered disgusting (such as feces, urine, and mucus), and its ingestion is taboo with one exception: tears. This is the one body product that may be uniquely human and hence does not remind us of what we have in common with animals.[30]

Perhaps it isn't only humans who are impressed by tears, however. The chimpanzee Nim Chimpsky, who regularly sought to comfort people who looked sad, was particularly tender when he saw tears, which he would wipe away.[31] Since Nim was raised by humans, he may have learned the connection between tears and unhappiness.

It would be interesting to discover whether any animals who have not had the opportunity to learn about tears respond to tears as evidence of sadness in humans or even in other animals. This could be answered experimentally. If a chimpanzee reared with other chimps saw another who appeared to be shedding tears, would it react as Nim did? If a chimpanzee accustomed to humans saw a person cry for the first time, would it behave as though it was a sign of distress?

Tears keep the eyes of animals moist. Their eyes also water when irritated. Tears may spill from the eyes of an animal in pain. Tears have been seen in the eyes of animals as diverse as an injured horse and an eggbound grey parrot.[32] Some animals are more tearful than others. Seals, who have no nasolachrymal ducts into which tears drain, are especially apt to have tears rolling down their faces. This is thought to help them cool down when they are on land.[33]

Charles Darwin, in researching *The Expression of the Emotions in Man and Animals*, looked for evidence that animals did or did not shed emotional tears. He complained, "*The Macacus maurus,*[34] which formerly wept so copiously in the Zoological Gardens, would have been a fine case for observation; but the two monkeys now there, and which are believed to be of the same species, do not weep." He was not able to observe animals shedding emotional tears, and called weeping one of the "special expressions of man."

Darwin noted one exception: the Indian elephant. It was reported to him by Sir E. Tennant that some newly captured elephants in Ceylon (now Sri Lanka), tied up and lying motionless on the ground, showed "no other indication of suffering than the tears which suffused their eyes and flowed incessantly." Another captured elephant, when bound, sank to the ground, "uttering choking cries, with tears trickling down his cheeks." A captured elephant is usually also separated from its family. Other elephant observers in Ceylon assured Darwin that they had not seen elephants weep, and that Ceylonese hunters said they had never seen elephants weep. Darwin put his trust in Tennant's observations, however, because they were confirmed by the elephant keeper at the London Zoo, who said he had several times seen an old female there shedding tears when her young companion was taken out.

In the years since Darwin, the balance of the evidence has been the same: most elephant-watchers have never seen them weep – or have, rarely, seen them weep when injured – yet a few observers have claimed to have seen them weep when not injured. An elephant trainer with a small American circus told researcher William Frey that his elephant, Okha, does cry at times, but that he had no idea why. Okha sometimes shed a tear when being scolded, it is reported, and at least once wept while giving children rides.[35] Iain Douglas-Hamilton, who has spent years working with African elephants, has seen elephants shed tears only when injured. Tears fell from the eyes of Claudia, a captive elephant, during a difficult labor with her first calf.[36]

R. Gordon Cummings,[37] an eighteenth-century hunter in South Africa, described killing the biggest male elephant he had ever seen. He first shot it in the shoulder so that it could not run away. The elephant limped over to a tree and leaned against it. Deciding to contemplate the elephant before killing it, Cummings paused to make coffee and then chose to experimentally determine which were an elephant's vulnerable spots. He walked up to it and fired bullets into various parts of the head. The elephant did not move except to touch the bullet wounds with the tip of his trunk. "Surprised and shocked to find that I was only tormenting and prolonging the sufferings of the noble beast, which bore his trials with such dignified composure," Cummings wrote, he decided to finish him off and shot him nine times behind the shoulder. "Large tears now trickled from his eyes, which he slowly shut and opened; his colossal frame quivered convulsively, and, falling on his side, he expired." This elephant must have been in great pain, however, and that alone would have been cause enough for him to shed tears. Other than humans, no animal runs torture experiments on other animals.

In his book *Elephant Tramp*,[38] George Lewis, an itinerant elephant trainer, reported in 1955 that in the years he had worked with elephants he had seen only one weeping. This was a young, timid female named Sadie, who was being trained along with five others to do an act for the Robbins Brothers Circus. The elephants were being taught their acts quickly, since the show would start in three weeks, but Sadie had trouble learning what was wanted. One day, unable to understand what she was being told to do, she ran out of the ring. "We brought her back and began to punish her for being so stupid." (Based on information Lewis gives elsewhere, they probably punished her by hitting her on the side of the head with a large stick.) To their astonishment, Sadie, who was lying down, began to utter racking sobs, and tears poured from her eyes. The dumbfounded trainers knelt by Sadie, caressing her. Lewis says that he never punished her again, and that she learned the act and became a "good" circus elephant. His fellow elephant trainers, who had never witnessed such a thing, were skeptical. But reports are not confined to animal behaviorists. Victor Hugo wrote in his diary on January 2, 1871: "*On a abbabut l'éléphant du Jardin des Plantes. Il a pleuré. On va le manger.*" ["The elephant in the Jardin des Plantes was slaughtered. He wept. He will be eaten."][39] That elephants weep emotional tears is widely believed in India, where elephants have been kept for many centuries. It is said that when the conqueror Tamerlane captured three thousand elephants in battle, snuff was put in their eyes so they would appear to be weeping at the loss. Douglas Chadwick was told of a young Indian elephant shedding tears when scolded for playing too boisterously and knocking someone down, and also of an elephant that ran away and, when found by its mahout, wept along with him.[40] Observing young orphaned elephants in an Asian stable, Chadwick noticed that one was shedding tears. A mahout told him that the babies often cried when they were hungry and that it was almost feeding time. But after being fed, the baby still wept.[41]

Elephant handlers say that the eyes of elephants water heavily, presumably to keep them moist. Fluid may also stream from their temporal glands, which are between the eye and ear. But no one familiar with elephants would be confused by this. Possibly there is some significance to the fact that many of the elephants shedding tears were lying down, not a usual position for an elephant. Perhaps the position somehow prevents drainage of tears.[42] For all we know elephants often shed tears of grief, but if standing, the tears run through nasolachrymal ducts and down the inside of their trunks.

Emotional tears have been reported in some other species. Biochemist William Frey, who studies human emotional tears, has received reports of dogs – particularly poodles – shedding tears in emotional situations, such as being left behind by their owner, but despite repeated efforts, he has been unable to confirm this in the laboratory. No one but their owners has witnessed these tears, and poodles are a particularly damp-eyed breed even at their most cheerful.

It has been reported that tears rolled from the eyes of adult seals who saw seal pups clubbed by hunters. This is undoubtedly true. But since tears often roll from seals' eyes, there is no proof that these were emotional tears.

Beavers have also been suspected of crying emotional tears. Trappers have said that a beaver in a trap sheds tears, but such beavers may be crying in pain. However, one biologist has reported that beavers also weep copiously when manually restrained.[43] Dian Fossey reported tears shed by Coco, an orphaned mountain gorilla. Coco was three or four years old when her family was killed before her eyes to secure her capture. She had spent a month in a tiny cage before coming into Fossey's possession and was very ill. She was released into an indoor pen with windows. When Coco first looked out the window of her pen at a forested mountainside like the one on which she grew up, she suddenly began "to sob and shed actual tears."[44] Fossey said she never witnessed a gorilla do this before or afterward.

Montaigne, who may be the first Western author to express distaste for the hunt, wrote in his 1580 essay "Of Cruelty":

For myself, I have not even been able without distress to see pursued and killed an innocent animal which is defenseless and which does us no harm. And as it commonly happens that the stag, feeling himself out of breath and strength, having no other remedy left, throws himself back and surrenders to ourselves who are pursuing him, asking for our mercy by his tears ... that has always seemed to me a very unpleasant spectacle.[45]

In the end, it hardly matters whether stags, beavers, seals, or elephants weep. Tears are not grief, but tokens of grief. The evidence of grief from other animal behaviors is strong. It is hard to doubt that Darwin's sobbing elephants were unhappy, even if their tears sprang from mechanical causes. A seal surely feels sad when its pup is killed, whether it is dry-eyed or not. Just as a psychiatrist cannot really know when a person has crossed the border of "normal" grief to "pathological" mourning, so humans cannot know that the world of sorrow is beyond the emotional capacities of any animal. Sadness, nostalgia, disappointment, are feelings we know from direct experience; animals we know intimately hint at their parallel feelings in this dark world. Should science accept their challenge and try to understand animal sorrow, even its accurate description will need to be complex and subtle, well beyond the clumsy categories and reductive causalities that prevail in the psychology of human pain.

NOTES

1. Marcey Cottrell Houle, *Wings for My Flight: The Peregrine Falcons of Chimney Rock* (Reading, MA: Addison-Wesley Publishing Co., 1991), pp. 75–87. The female peregrine had reportedly been shot. The two surviving nestlings fledged successfully.
2. Quoted in H. C. Bernhard Grzimek, ed., *Grzimek's Animal Life Encyclopedia,* Vol. 12 (New York: Van Nostrand Reinhold, 1975).
3. Elizabeth Marshall Thomas, *The Hidden Life of Dogs* (Boston and New York: Houghton Mifflin, 1993).
4. J. Y. Henderson with Richard Taplinger, *Circus Doctor* (Boston: Little, Brown & Co., 1951), p. 78.
5. Karen Pryor, *Lads Before the Wind: Adventures in Porpoise Training* (New York: Harper and Row, 1975), pp. 276–77.
6. Antony Alpers, *Dolphins: The Myth and the Mammal* (Boston: Houghton Mifflin, 1960), pp. 104–5.
7. Elizabeth Marshall Thomas, "Reflections: The Old Way." *New Yorker* (October 15, 1990), p. 91.
8. Cynthia Moss, *Portraits in the Wild: Behavior Studies of East African Mammals* (Boston: Houghton Mifflin, 1975), p. 34.
9. Cynthia Moss, *Elephant Memories: Thirteen Years in the Life of an Elephant Family* (New York: William Morrow, 1988), pp. 272–73.
10. Geza Teleki, "Group Response to the Accidental Death of a Chimpanzee in Gombe National Park, Tanzania," *Folia Primatol* 20 (1973), pp. 81–94.
11. Frans de Waal, *Chimpanzee Politics: Power and Sex Among Apes* (New York: Harper and Row, 1982), pp. 67–70.

12. Lars Wilsson, *My Beaver Colony* , trans. by Joan Bulman (Garden City, NY: Doubleday, 1968), pp. 61–62.

13. Moss, *Elephant Memories,* p. 112.

14. Leyhausen, Paul. *Cat Behavior: The Predatory and Social Behavior of Domestic and Wild Cats*, trans. by Barbara A. Tonkin (New York and London: Garland, 1979), pp. 287–88.

15. Jane Goodall, *Through a Window: My Thirty Years with the Chimpanzees of Gombe* (Boston: Houghton Mifflin, 1990), p. 230.

16. Cited in Robert M. Yerkes and Ada W. Yerkes, *The Great Apes: A Study of Anthropoid Life* (New Haven, CT: Yale University Press, 1929), p. 472.

17. Pryor, *Lads Before the Wind,* pp. 82–83.

18. Robert Reinhold, "At Sea World, Stress Tests Whale and Man," *New York Times,* April 4, 1988, p. A9.

19. Pryor, *Lads Before the Wind,* p. 132.

20. David McFarland, ed., *Oxford Companion to Animal Behavior* (Oxford and New York: Oxford University Press, 1987), p. 599.

21. Harlow said that his "device was designed on an intuitive basis to reproduce such a well [of despair] both physically and psychologically for monkey subjects." See the trenchant criticism by James Rachels in "Do Animals Have a Right to Liberty?" in *Animal Rights and Human Obligations,* Tom Regan and Peter Singer, eds. (Englewood Cliffs, NJ: Prentice-Hall, 1976), p. 211. See also Peter Singer's criticism in Chapter 2 of his *Animal Liberation* (New York Review, 1975).

22. "Do Animals Have a Right to Liberty?" in Regan and Singer, eds., *Animal Rights and Human Obligations*, 1976), p. 211. See also the fine criticism of Harlow's work in Chapter 2 of Peter Singer's influential *Animal Liberation* (New York Review, 1975); the original article by Harlow is written with Stephen J. Suomi: "Depressive Behavior in Young Monkeys Subjected to Vertical Chamber Confinement," *Journal of Comparative and Physiological Psychology* 80 (1972), pp. 11–18. Harlow published his articles in prestigious journals. For example, see his "Love in Infant Monkeys," *Scientific American* 200 (1959), pp. 68–74; and "The Nature of Love," *American Psychologist,* 13 (1958), pp. 673–85. A useful general critique is found in *Psychology Experiments on Animals: A Critique of Animal Models of Human Psychopathology* by Brandon Kuker-Reines for the New England Anti-Vivisection Society, 1982, who remarks in a telling aside that "the apparent quest to reveal the 'true man' through monkey experimentation is symptomatic of an identity crisis rather than scientific progress" (p. 68).

23. Martin E. P. Seligman, *Helplessness: On Depression, Development, and Death* (San Francisco, CA: W. H. Freeman, 1975), pp. 23–25. While restrained, each dog was given sixty-four shocks of 6.0 milliamperes, lasting for five seconds.

24. Lenore Walker has powerfully delineated the role of learned helplessness in the lives of battered women. See her *Terrifying Love: Why Battered Women Kill and How Society Responds* (New York: Harper and Row, 1989).

25. J. B. Sidowski, "Psychopathological Consequences of Induced Social Helplessness During Infancy," in *Experimental Psychopathology: Recent Research and Theory,* H. D. Kimmel, ed. (New York: Academic Press, 1971), pp. 231–48.

26. Russell J. Rutter and Douglas H. Pimlott, *The World of the Wolf* (Philadelphia and New York: J. B. Lippincott, 1968), p. 138; Lois Crisler, *Captive Wild* (New York: Harper and Row, 1968), p. 210.

27. Ian Redmond, "The Death of Digit," *International Primate Protection League Newsletter* 15, No.3, December 1988, p. 7.

28. Yerkes, Robert M. and Yerkes, Ada W. *The Great Apes: A Study of Anthropoid Life* (New Haven, CT: Yale University Press, 1929), p. 161.

29. William Frey, II, *Crying: The Mystery of Tears,* with Muriel Langseth (Minneapolis: Winton Press, 1985). Emotional tears are also called psychogenic tears. It is unclear where tears of pain fit into these categories.

30. S. B. Ortner, "Shera purity," *American Anthropologist* 75 (1973), pp. 49–63. Quoted in Paul Rozin and April Fallon, "A Perspective on Disgust," *Psychological Review* 94 (1987), pp. 23–41.

31. Herbert Terrace, *Nim: A Chimpanzee Who Learned Sign Language* (New York: Washington Square, 1979), p. 56.

32. Wolfgang de Grahl, *The Grey Parrot.* Trans. by William Charlton (Neptune City, NY: T.F.H. Publications, 1987), p. 189.

33. Victor B. Scheffer, *Seals, Sea Lions, and Walruses: A Review of the Pinnipedia* (Stanford, CA: Stanford University Press, 1958), p. 22. Also Frey, *Crying.*

34. *Macacus maurus,* the Celebes macaque, is now denoted *Cynomacaca maurus.* An influential German book in its time, Karl Friedrich Burdach's *Blicke ins Leben* (3 vols, Leipzig: Leopold Woss, 1842), Vol. 2, p. 130, cites examples of female seals who "shed copious tears when they were abused," giraffes who cried when they were removed from their companions, and tears in fur seals when their young were stolen *(geraubt)* and in an elephant seal when it was treated roughly.

35. Frey, *Crying,* p. 141.

36. Volker Ant and Immanuel Birmelin, *Haben Tieren ein Bewusstsein?: Wenn Affen lugen, wenn Katzen denken und Elefanten traurig sind* (Munich: C. Bertelsmann, 1993), p. 154.

37. R. Gordon Cummings, *Five Years of a Hunter's Life in the Far Interior of South Africa* (1850), quoted in Richard Carrington, *Elephants: A Short Account of Their Natural History, Evolution and Influence on Mankind* (London: Chatto & Windus, 1958), pp. 154–55.

38. George Lewis, as told to Byron Fish, *Elephant Tramp* (Boston: Little, Brown, 1955), pp. 52, 188–89.

39. Victor Hugo, *Carnet intime 1870–1871,* publié et présenté par Henri Guillemin (Paris: Gallimard, 7th edn, 1953), p. 88.

40. Chadwick, Douglas H. *The Fate of the Elephant* (San Francisco: Sierra Books, 1992), p. 327.

41. Ibid., p. 384.

42. This suggestion was proposed by Dr. William Frey.

43. L. S. Lavrov, "Evolutionary Development of the Genus *Castor* and Taxonomy of the Contemporary Beavers of Eurasia," *Acta Zool. Fennica* 174 (1983), pp. 87–90.

44. Dian Fossey, *Gorillas in the Mist* (Boston: Houghton Mifflin, 1983), p. 110.

45. D. M. Frame, trans., *The Complete Works of Montaigne,* Vol. 2 (Garden City, NY: Anchor Books, 1960), pp. 105–9.

13

CAREL P. VAN SCHAIK, MARC ANCRENAZ, GWENDOLYN BORGEN, BIRUTE GALDIKAS, CHERYL D. KNOTT, IAN SINGLETON, AKIRA SUZUKI, SRI SUCI UTAMI, MICHELLE MERRILL

Orangutan Cultures and the Evolution of Material Culture*

This article first appeared in the journal *Science* and is the product of the work of a large team of researchers. The members of this team hail from a number of countries, including the US, Canada, Malaysia, Indonesia, Japan, and the Netherlands. Some of the authors are academics working in universities, while others are affiliated with organizations such as the Orang-Utan Conservation Project, Orangutan Foundation International, Sumatran Orangutan Conservation Programme and the Primate Institute. This article provides evidence that great apes possess a material culture. Based on six different sites of wild orangutan populations, the authors document geographic variations in primate behavior that are not the outcome of environmental conditions, but rather the result of social learning or cultural variations. For example, the researchers noted differences between the groups of orangutans in feeding techniques (including tool use) and social signals. The authors argue that while there are differences between human cultures and those of the great apes, orangutans (and chimpanzees) show three of the four elements of culture indicative of social learning – they use labels to mark food preferences and recognize predators, they use socially transmitted signals such as song dialects and they deploy innovative skills such as tool use. The authors conclude that the presence of material culture in orangutans indicates that great ape cultures have existed since the orangutan and African ape branches last shared a common ancestor – 14 million years ago.

Geographic variation in some aspects of chimpanzee behavior has been interpreted as evidence for culture. Here we document similar geographic variation in orangutan behaviors. Moreover, as expected under a cultural interpretation, we find a correlation between geographic distance and cultural difference, a correlation between the abundance of opportunities for social learning and the size of the local cultural repertoire, and no effect of habitat on the content of culture.

---

* Reprinted with permission of the publisher and from Carel P. van Schaik, Marc Ancrenaz, Gwendolyn Borgen, Birute Galdikas, Cheryl D. Knott, Ian Singleton, Akira Suzuki, Sri Suci Utami, and Michelle Merrill (2003) "Orangutan Cultures and the Evolution of Material Culture." *Science* 299, 102–105. Copyright 2005 AAAS.

Hence, great-ape cultures exist, and may have done so for at least 14 million years.

Among the numerous definitions of culture, the idea that it is a system of socially transmitted behavior is particularly useful for comparative purposes.[1] Because the creation of culture under experimental conditions illuminates neither the extent of culture among wild animals nor its content, documenting culture's existence in nature remains essential. Unfortunately, this task is not easy; even if a study lasts long enough to show that a newly observed variant is an innovation, it remains difficult to demonstrate convincingly that the variant's acquisition by others is guided by social transmission. However, recent work on chimpanzees has shown geographic patterns in many behavioral variants that are consistent with the operation of cultural processes. A variant is considered cultural if it is customary (shown by most or all relevant individuals) or habitual (shown by at least several relevant individuals) in at least one site but is absent in at least one other ecologically similar site.[2,3] Intraspecific genetic variation is almost certainly not responsible for these patterns.[4]

Critics have stressed that the geographic approach may generate a type I error, spuriously leading us to conclude that cultures exist, when in fact unrecognized ecological differences between sites have produced within-population convergence and between population divergence through individual learning.[5-7] Hence, further tests are essential to increase our confidence in a cultural interpretation.[8,9]

Orangutans (*Pongo pygmaeus*) showing variation in two forms of tool use consistent with culture[10,11] provide an opportunity for further testing. Here, we systematically apply the geographic approach to six different wild orangutan populations in Borneo and Sumatra[12] and test additional predictions derived from a cultural interpretation.

Table 1 lists three categories of geographic variants[13]: (i) very likely cultural variants, which are behaviors present in at least one site at customary or habitual levels and absent elsewhere without clear ecological differences; (ii) likely cultural variants [as in (i) above] for which ecological explanations for absence, though unlikely, cannot be excluded; and (iii) rare variants that are unlikely to be maintained by social transmission. We shall refer to the first two as "putative cultural variants."

The list of putative cultural variants at the six sites contains 24 elements; an additional 12 local variants did not spread to customary or habitual level at any site. Data from additional sites would expand the list,[14] as it does for chimpanzees.[3] Of the putative cultural variants, 10 involve specialized feeding techniques, including tool use, and 6 are alternative forms of social signals, such as kiss-squeaks. As in chimpanzees,[2,3] some variants may come close to reflecting shared meaning based on arbitrary symbols. In particular, the "raspberry" vocalizations, emitted in the final phase of nest building in Suaq Balimbing[11] and just before its start at Lower Kinabatangan (Table 1), seem to announce that the sender is bedding down for the night. Putatively cultural geographic variation in orangutans, therefore, is very similar to that in chimpanzees.

Human cultures show geographic patterning reflecting innovation and diffusion, and they incorporate more elements if they are open to influences from other societies (successful local innovation being comparatively rare), and within fairly broad limits show only a moderate effect of habitat on their content.[15,16] If these generalizations also apply to orangutans and chimpanzees, it would increase our confidence in the cultural interpretation and the heuristic used here and elsewhere.[2,3,17]

First, the innovation-and-diffusion hypothesis suggests that a behavioral variant often occurs at a site because it was brought there by animals dispersing from the site where it originated. We found the predicted correlation between geographic distance and cultural difference for the putative cultural variants, i.e., those variants that spread well within at least one locality should therefore diffuse between localities as well. This relationship is unlikely to be an artifact because it is not found for the local variants that do not reach customary level at any site and therefore

Table 1. *Geographic variation in orangutan behavior patterns. C, customary; H, habitual; R, rare; P, present with unknown frequency, probably rare; E, absent for ecological reasons; A, absent; ?, unknown.*

	Site and island					
	Gunung Palung (Borneo)	Tanjung Puting (Borneo)	Kutai (Borneo)	Lower Kinaba-tangan (Borneo)	Leuser, Ketambe (Sumatra)	Leuser, Suaq Balimbing (Sumatra)
Observation intensity (increasing ranks):	2	2	1	1	2	1
Very likely cultural variants						
1. Snag riding: Ride on pushed-over snag as it falls, then grab on to vegetation before it crashes on ground	A	C	A	A	A	A
2. Kiss-squeak with leaves: Using leaves on mouth to amplify sound, then drop leaf	C	A	H	A	A	A
3. Kiss-squeak with hands: Using fists (like trumpet) or flat hands on mouth to amplify sound	R	R	H	A	C	H
4. Leaf wipe: Wiping face with fistful of squashed leaves, then drop (in kiss-squeak context)	A	C	A	A	A	A
5. Play nests: Building nest for social play (no resting occurs)	C	C	P	A	C	H
6. Bunk nests: Build a nest a short distance above the nest used for resting (during rain)	A	P	A	H	A	A
7. Sun cover: Building cover on nest during bright sunshine (rather than rain)	A	?	C	C	H	A
8. Hide under nest: Seek shelter under nest for rain	A	R	C	P	R	A
9. Scratch stick: Using detached stick to scratch body parts	A	R	H	A	A	A
10. Autoerotic tool: Using tool for sexual stimulation (female and male)	A	A	P	A	C	A
11. Raspberry: Spluttering sounds associated with nest building	A	A	A	H	A	C
12. Symmetric scratch: Exaggerated, long, slow, symmetric scratching movements with both arms at same time	A	A	A	A	R	C
13. Twig biting: Systematically passing ends of twigs used for lining of nest past the mouth (sometimes including actual bite) during last phase of nest building	A	A	A	A	A	C
14. Leaf napkin: Using handful of leaves to wipe latex off chin	A	A	C	A	A	A
15. Branch as swatter: Using detached leafy branches to ward off bees/wasps attacking subject (who is usually raiding their nest)	R	R	H	H	H	H
16. Leaf gloves: Using leaf gloves to handle spiny fruits or spiny branch, or as seat cushions in trees with spines	A	R	A	A	H	E

	Site and island					
	Gunung Palung (Borneo)	Tanjung Puting (Borneo)	Kutai (Borneo)	Lower Kinabatangan (Borneo)	Leuser, Ketambe (Sumatra)	Leuser, Suaq Balimbing (Sumatra)
17. Tree-hole tool use: Using tool to poke into tree holes to obtain social insects or their products	A	A	A	A	A	C
18. Seed extraction tool use: Using tool to extract seeds from the protected fruits of *Neesia* sp.	A	A	[?]	A	E	C
19. Branch scoop: Drinking water from deep tree hole using leafy branch (water dripping from leaves)	A	A	A	A	A	H
Likely cultural variants (ecological explanation not excluded)						
20. Snag crashing: Aimed pushing of dead standing trees	C	C	C	A	H	C
21. Bouquet feeding: Using lips to pick ants from fistful of dry, fresh, or rotting leaves (nests)	C	C	A	R	C	C
22. Nest destruction: Rummage through old orangutan nests for insects		H	C	P	A	H
23. Dead twig sucking: Breaking hollow (dead) twigs to suck ants from inside	A?	C	A?	A	C	C
24. Slow loris eating: Capture and eat slow loris hiding in dense vegetation	A	A	A	A	H	H
Rare behaviors						
1. Females rubbing their genitals together	R	R	A	A	A	R
2. Use leaf to clean body surface	R	A	A	A	A	A
3. Sneaky nest approach: Building series of nests, while approaching conspecific in fruit tree	R	A	A	A	A	A
4. Leaf bundle while sleeping ("doll")	R	R	A	A	A	A
5. Leaf scoop: Drinking water from the ground, using leaf as vessel (drinking straight from vessel)	R	A	A	A	A	A
6. Bridge nest: Build nest connecting two trees on opposite banks of river	A	R	A	A	A	A
7. Biting through vine to swing Tarzan-like	A	R	A	A	A	R
8. Artistic pillows: Similar twigs lining nest	A	P	?	A	?	?
9. Branch dragging display on ground	A	A	?	R	A	A
10. Stick as chisel: To open termite nest in log on ground	A	A	A	A	R	A
11. Sponging: Drinking water using crumpled leaves	A	A	A	A	R	A
12. Hiding behind detached branch from predators or humans	A	R	P	R	R	A

should diffuse poorly (Mantel tests: chimpanzees, $P = 871/5039 = 0.17$; orangutans, $P = 434/719 = 0.60$).

Second, the size of the local cultural repertoire is the balance between the rates of origination (due to innovation or diffusion from elsewhere) and extinction (due to failed social transmission). Thus, greater size of the local repertoire may reflect (i) higher rates of origination, which in turn reflect greater need for innovation due to marginal ecological conditions (necessity) or more opportunities for playful exploration (free time)[18]; or (ii) higher rates of retention due to better conditions for diffusion between sites and social transmission within sites, caused by frequent tolerant proximity.[19,20] Statistical power is insufficient to establish patterns if both influences are important, but if one predominates it should receive significant support. Across orangutan sites, no support exists for the necessity hypothesis (using percent of feeding time on tree cambium as an index of food scarcity and food-related local variants, cultural or not, as the response variable: $r = -0.812$, $n = 6$, $P < 0.05$, which is opposite to prediction), nor does statistical support exist for the free-time hypothesis (using total minutes in the day spent resting and total number of local variants, respectively: $r = -0.910$, $P < 0.05$, which is opposite to prediction). On the other hand, we did find support for the opportunities for social learning hypothesis as suggested by the pattern in humans: The number of customary and habitual variants in both orangutans (from Table 1) and chimpanzees [from Table 1 in reference 2] is predicted by the percentage of time that nondependent animals spend in association, which is used to index opportunities for learning from individuals other than the mother.[21] Moreover, this relationship is stronger when limited to the customary and habitual variants that are related to feeding, as expected, because acquisition of these variants should, on average, depend more on close-range socially biased learning than does acquisition of other variants. Hence, the size of the cultural repertoire at a given site is best predicted by the opportunities for oblique and horizontal social transmission during development.

Third, habitat may facilitate predictable individual learning and thus may facilitate convergent variant repertoires in separate localities, overriding the effects of the historical process of innovation and diffusion. No habitat effect is found, however, in orangutans, where pairs of sites with similar types of habitats do not have more similar variant repertoires than those with different types of habitats (sea-level floodplains versus mainly dryland forests) (Mantel test: $P = 503/719 = 0.70$; in chimpanzees, habitat effects are difficult to evaluate independently because they coincide with geographic differences).

These additional tests support a cultural interpretation of geographic variation in great-ape behavior and indicate fundamental similarities to human culture. However, because culture, as defined above, may be common among vertebrates,[1,17,22] finer distinctions are needed for meaningful evolutionary reconstruction. Differences in cultures should reflect variation in the complexity of innovation and the mechanisms of socially biased learning. Thus, cultural elements may be (i) labels, where food preferences or predator recognition are socially induced[5,7,23] and which generally involve little innovation; (ii) signals, involving socially transmitted arbitrary innovations as variants on displays, such as kiss-squeaks on leaves or song dialects[17]; (iii) skills, involving rare innovations (including tool use), whose complexity depends on the nature of socially biased learning [which affects the degree of ratcheting, see reference 6]; and (iv) symbols, probably derived from signal variants that became membership badges of the social unit or population.[6,15]

Species are expected to vary in the kinds of cultural elements they display. Only humans have all four kinds of cultural elements, whereas, unique among nonhuman primates, chimpanzees and orangutans show the first three,[2,3,8-11] which are made possible by innovative abilities and sophisticated forms of socially biased learning.[24-26] Human cultures, therefore, differ from those of great apes in having unambiguously symbolic elements,[6,27] far more complex skills, and far greater repertoire sizes, made possible by cognitive differences affecting innovation or observational learning.[1,5,6] The presence in orangutans of humanlike skill (material) culture pushes back its origin in the hominoid lineage to about 14 million years ago, when the orangutan and African ape clades last shared a common ancestor,[28] rather than to the last common ancestor of chimpanzees and humans.

Important tasks for the future include documenting the possible interdependence among these different kinds of cultural elements, identifying the conditions favoring their evolution, and assessing whether they all show the geographic and social correlates known for humans and demonstrated here for great apes.

NOTES

1. R. Boyd, P. J. Richerson, *Proc. Br. Acad.* 88, 77 (1996).
2. A. Whiten *et al., Nature* 399, 682 (1999).
3. A. Whiten *et al., Behaviour* 138, 1481 (2001).
4. F. B. M. de Waal, *Nature* 399, 635 (1999).
5. B. G. Galef Jr., *Hum. Nat.* 3, 157 (1992).
6. M. Tomasello, *The Cultural Origins of Human Cognition* (Harvard Univ. Press, Cambridge, MA, 1999).
7. B. G. Galef Jr., in *The Biology of Animal Traditions*, D. M. Fragaszy, S. Perry, Eds. (Cambridge Univ. Press, Cambridge, in press).
8. C. Boesch, P. Marchesi, N. Marchesi, B. Fruth, F. Joulian, *J. Hum. Evol.* 26, 325 (1994).
9. W. C. McGrew, R. M. Ham, L. J. T. White, C. E. G. Tutin, M. Fernandez, *Intern. J. Primatol.* 18, 353 (1997).
10. C. P. van Schaik, C. D. Knott, *Am. J. Phys. Anthropol.* 114, 331 (2001).
11. C. P. van Schaik, in *The Biology of Animal Traditions*, D. M. Fragaszy, S. Perry, Eds. (Cambridge Univ. Press, Cambridge, in press).
12. After compiling a preliminary list of candidate cultural variants, representatives of all sites with long-term data on wild orangutans convened in San Anselmo, California, from 14 to 17 February 2002 to discuss these variants and to identify new ones through plenary discussion of site descriptions and video footage from multiple sites. We used the same criteria as employed in the chimpanzee comparison, including those for prevalence at a given site (*2, 3*).
13. Included sites had more than 4 years of intensive observations of at least 25 individual orangutans and 10,000 contact hours. Observation intensity is based on numbers of observation hours and total duration of the study as (i) less than 25,000 hours or (ii) more than 25,000 hours. We excluded (i) universals, which are behavior patterns that were found at all sites or were absent for obvious ecological reasons; (ii) variant feeding techniques on the same species of fruit (unless one involved tools), because different morphologies and subtle ecological influences producing independent convergence within sites are difficult to exclude without detailed examination; and (iii) variants with localized distributions that most likely reflect ecological conditions (e.g., lathering of fruit pulp or seeds in the fur of arms, drinking water from natural containers such as pitcher plants, making ground nests, wading through standing water, etc.).
14. E. A. Fox, I. bin'Muhammad, *Am. J. Phys. Anthropol.,* in press.
15. F. M. Keesing, *Cultural Anthropology: The Science of Custom* (Holt, Rinehart, and Winston, New York, 1958).
16. J. C. Hudson, *Geographical Diffusion Theory* (Northwestern University Studies in Geography No. 19, Northwestern Univ., Evanston, IL, 1972).
17. L. Rendell, H. Whitehead, *Behav. Brain Sci.* 24, 309 (2001).
18. H. Kummer, J. Goodall, *Philos. Trans. R. Soc. London Ser. B* 308, 203 (1985).
19. S. Coussi-Korbel, D. M. Fragaszy, *Anim. Behav.* 50, 1441 (1995).
20. C. P. van Schaik, R. O. Deaner, M. Merrill, *J. Hum. Evol.* 36, 719 (1999).
21. In an analysis of covariance (ANCOVA), the effect of association time is significant (ANCOVA: $F[1,7]$ = 9.74, $P < 0.05$), whereas the effects of species and the interaction are not.
22. T. Nishida, in *Primate Societies*, B. B. Smuts *et al.*, Eds. (Chicago Univ. Press, Chicago, 1987), pp. 462–474.
23. E. Curio, in *Social Learning: Psychological and Biological Perspectives*, T. R. Zentall, B. G. Galef

Jr., Eds. (Erlbaum, Hillsdale, NJ, 1988), pp. 75–97.

24. A. Whiten, *Cogn. Sci.* 24, 477 (2000).
25. M. Myowa-Yamakoshi, in *Primate Origins of Human Cognition and Behavior*, T. Matsuzawa, Ed. (Springer, Tokyo, 2001), pp. 349–367.
26. T. Stoinski, A. Whiten, *J. Comp. Psychol.*, in press.
27. R. Tuttle, *Curr. Anthropol.* 42, 407 (2001).
28. M. Goodman *et al.*, *Mol. Phylogenet. Evol.* 9, 58 5 (1998).
29. N. Mantel, *Cancer Res.* 27, 209 (1967).
30. C. Boesch, in *Great Ape Societies*, W. C. McGrew, L. F. Marchant, T. Nishida, Eds. (Cambridge Univ. Press, Cambridge, 1996), pp. 101–113.
31. Y. Sugiyama, *Primates* 9, 225 (1968).
32. Y. Sugiyama, *Primates* 22, 435 (1981).
33. Sponsored by the L.S.B. Leakey Foundation. For contributions to the database, we thank D. Agee, M. Brown, I. Foitova, E. Fox, N. Ghaffar, I. bin'Muhammad, A. Johnson, T. Laman, J. Mitani, T. M. Setia, H. Peters, D. Priatna, and S. Wich. We thank the Indonesian Institute of Sciences (LIPI) and the directorate general of Forest Protection and Nature Conservation Service in the Ministry of Forestry for permission for the various projects. For substantial or long-term support of orangutan field work, we thank the Wildlife Conservation Society; the National Geographic Society; NSF; the Netherlands Organization for Tropical Research; the L.S.B. Leakey Foundation; the Wenner-Gren Foundation for Anthropological Research; the Pittsburgh Zoo; the Conservation, Food, and Health Foundation; the Great Ape Conservation Fund; and the United States Fish and Wildlife Service. We thank C. Boesch, D. Brockman, R. Deaner, J. Galef, M. Huffman, J. Mitani, A. Russon, M. van Noordwijk, and C. Vinyard for help with this paper.

FURTHER READING IN ANIMALS AS REFLEXIVE THINKERS

Allen, Colin and Marc A. Bekoff. 1997. *Species of Mind: The Philosophy and Biology of Cognitive Ethology.* Cambridge, MA: MIT Press.

Bekoff, Marc, Colin Allen, and Gordon M. Burghardt (eds.). 2002. *The Cognitive Animal: Empirical and Theoretical Perspectives on Animal Cognition.* Boston: MIT Press.

Brandt, K. 2004. A Language of Their Own: An Interactionist Approach to Human-Horse Communication. *Society and Animals* 12 (4): 299–316.

Crist, Eileen. 1999. *Images of Animals: Anthropomorphism and Animal Mind.* Philadelphia: Temple University Press.

Darwin, Charles. 1872. *The Expression of the Emotions in Man and Animals.* London: Murray.

Daston, Lorraine and Gregg Mitman. 2005. *Thinking with Animals: New Perspectives on Anthropomorphism.* New York: Columbia University Press.

Dawkins, Marian Stamp. 1998. *Through Our Eyes Only? The Search for Animal Consciousness.* New York: Oxford University Press.

De Luce, J. and H. T. Wilder (eds.). 1983. *Language in Primates: Perspectives and Implications.* New York: Springer-Verlag.

de Waal, Frans. 1997. *Good Natured: The Origins of Right and Wrong in Humans and Other Animals.* Cambridge, MA: Harvard University Press.

Dugatkin L. A. 1997. *Cooperation among Animals: An Evolutionary Perspective.* New York: Oxford University Press.

Dunbar, Robin. 1996. *Grooming, Gossip, and the Evolution of Language.* Cambridge, MA: Harvard University Press.

Gill, Jerry H. 1997. *If a Chimpanzee Could Talk and Other Reflections on Language Acquisition.* Tucson: University of Arizona Press.

Goodall, Jane. 1971/2000. *In the Shadow of Man.* New York: Mariner Books.

Great Ape Project. 2003. *The Great Ape Project Census: Recognition for the Uncounted.* Portland, OR: Great Ape Project Books.

Griffin, Donald R. 2001. *Animal Minds. Beyond Cognition to Consciousness.* Chicago: University of Chicago Press.

Linden, Eugene. 1999. *The Parrot's Lament: And Other True Tales of Animal Intrigue, Intelligence, and Ingenuity.* New York: Dutton.

Lucretius. On the Nature of Things. http://www.gutenberg.org/etext/785, accessed June 14, 2006.

Patterson, Francine and Eugene Linden. 1988. *The Education of Koko.* New York: Henry Holt.

Pepperberg, Irene. 1999. *The Alex Studies: Cognitive and Communicative Abilities of Grey Parrots.* Cambridge, MA: Harvard University Press.

Savage-Rumbaugh, Sue, Stuart G. Shanker, and Talbot J. Taylor. 2001. *Apes, Language, and the Human Mind.* Oxford: Oxford University Press.

Smolker, Rachel. 2002. *To Touch a Wild Dolphin: A Journey of Discovery with the Sea's Most Intelligent Creatures.* New York: Anchor.

Wallman, Joel. 1992. *Aping Language.* Cambridge: Cambridge University Press.

*A*nimals as Domesticates, "Pets" and Food

INTRODUCTION

Animals have such integral roles in human culture that we tend to take their presence for granted. But there was a time when humans encountered animals simply as prey or as predators. With domestication (taming "wild" animals to live with humans by altering their behavior and/or physiology), our relationships with other animals became much more diverse and complex. This section is devoted to the history of animal domestication and two of the primary functions animals have come to serve for humans as a result thereof – as playthings (or "pets") and as food. At first blush it may seem anomalous to include the themes of animals as playthings and food in one section. However, as Yi-Fu Tuan argues, the making of "pets" and the making of "livestock" share utilitarian motivations and both entail the physical and psychological manipulation of animals.

We begin this section with two readings that map the historical landscape of our relationships with animals. The first essay is by archaeologist Steven Mithen and provides an overview of the prehistory of human-animal relationships and a critical appraisal of prior research on early human-animal interactions and the domestication process. Mithen's work is guided by the question, How is it that humans have gone beyond the predator/prey relationship that other animals experience into a new arena of inter-species interactions?

Environmental historian Harriet Ritvo expands upon the discussion of animal domestication, providing insights into the consequences of domestication for the "domesticatees" and the "domesticators," which she describes as the most transformative relationship between humans and other animals. She discusses the link between animal domestication and the spread of some contagious diseases, with particular attention paid to a topic receiving much press of late – the spread of zoonotic diseases (diseases that be transmitted from animals to humans, such as bovine spongiform encephalopathy, or "mad cow disease," and avian influenza, or the "bird flu"). Rigid boundaries between what is animal and what is human are eroding as diseases increasingly traverse the human/animal divide with impunity.

Next, Yi-Fu Tuan examines the connection between aesthetics and exploitation in the "petrification" of animals as playthings. He considers the manipulation of the bodies of domesticated animals nothing more than cruel aesthetic exploitation, questions the loss of "natural vigor" in pet animals and laments that even the highly valued pet is often treated as "a convenience."

The last four readings in this section examine the motivations for, and the consequences of, using animals as food. As Carol Adams reminds us, "meat eating is the most frequent way in which we interact with animals." First we examine a classic reading by Plutarch on "The Eating of Flesh," which is particularly profound given that 2,000 years ago he introduced issues that are widely debated today, such as the maltreatment of "livestock" animals raised for food and the connection between the victimization of animals and the victimization of humans.

Jim Mason and Mary Finelli describe in detail the treatment of food animals in modern factory farms (those that operate on a mass scale, are highly mechanized, and treat the animals as "biomachines"). Not only do they provide insight into the negative effects this system of production has on the animals used as raw material, they also describe the negative consequences this mode of production has on human health and on disappearing farming communities.

The final two readings examine the thought-provoking connection between meat-eating and power. Carol Adams argues that meat-eating is identified with masculinity and male power (usually white males) and that the hierarchy of meat protein (in which "real" men eat meat and everyone else eats plants) reinforces a hierarchy of sex, class and race, particularly when food is scarce. Adams concludes that meat-eating is a symbol of patriarchy that validates masculine privilege. It should be noted that in other work, Adams has demonstrated that the metaphorical intersection of the oppression of certain human groups and of animals has become part of our cultural fabric, particularly in the representation of butchered animals and violence against women.

The culture of capitalism is particularly pernicious in the exploitation of both humans and animals in the search for profit. In the last reading, David Nibert focuses on the relationship between meat consumption and environmental and human-rights crises in the developing world. He writes that the (over)consumption of meat in affluent countries has devastating negative consequences in other parts of the world, consequences that multinational corporations have an interest in perpetuating. Nibert laments that, despite the increased production in modern agribusiness with its huge social and environmental costs, hundreds of millions of humans around the world remain hungry. He concludes with a link between the US food and restaurant industries and their sexist, racist and classist practices that exacerbate the problems of low wages and inadequate health-care coverage for employees. Once again, the animal question hovers at the intersection of the oppression of animals and of marginalized humans.

14

STEVEN MITHEN

The Hunter-Gatherer Prehistory of Human-Animal Interactions*

Steven Mithen is an archaeologist who studies prehistoric hunter-gatherers and early farmers, the evolution of the human mind and computational archaeology. Author of several books, including a study of the origins of music, language, mind and body, Mithen is well known for his ability to make archaeology, human genetics and environmental science accessible to general readers. We reproduce here an article that traces the evolution of the human-animal relationship and the changes in that relationship that came about when animals were no longer viewed merely as sources of meat or predation. He writes that about 100,000 years ago, humans buried their dead with animal body parts and 30,000 years ago humans reproduced animal images in cave paintings and portable art – activities that indicate that animals had become part of human rituals. Further, argues Mithen, there was a "fluidity between the worlds of humans and animals" based on representations from 33,000 years ago that are part-human and part-animal. Mithen chronicles the hunting techniques used by early humans, from the confronted technique used by the Neanderthals to a cooperative ambush and slaughter strategy that by the end of the last Ice Age probably resulted in the extinction of entire species because of overhunting. He concludes with a discussion of the evidence that some animals may have been tamed (domesticated) during the last Ice Age, and that dogs were unambiguously domesticated 12,000 years ago – dog burials with humans indicates "a further collapse" in the boundaries separating the human world from the animal world.

INTRODUCTION

People have a remarkably rich and varied set of relationships with animals: we use them for food and for sport; we use them as companions and loved ones; we use them to entertain and to educate us. Throughout history and throughout the world, animals have played

* "The Hunter-Gatherer Prehistory of Human Animal Interaction" by S. Mithen from *Anthrozoos*, vol. 12, no. 4, pp 195–204. ©1999 Purdue University Press. Reprinted by permission of the publisher. Unauthorized duplication not permitted.

central roles in mythologies and religious beliefs; they have been used as symbols of power
and authority, as beasts of war and as gifts of
friendship. (For a good review see Willis 1990.)
Indeed our day-to-day lives involve such a
variety of interactions with animals that we
hardly spare this remarkable phenomenon a
second thought.

But when we pause to reflect on how one type
of animal – *Homo sapiens* – has come to interact in
such a diversity of ways with so many other types
of animals we realize that we are indeed a rather
peculiar type of animal. We have gone beyond
the predator, competitor and prey relationships
that other animals experience into a whole new
world of inter-species interactions that are unique
to ourselves. How has this come about? How is
it that humans can entertain such a diversity of
relationships with other animal species? These are
important questions, for in other ways humans
are indeed just another animal: we are products
of biological evolution and shared a common
ancestor with the chimpanzee no more than five
to six million years ago.

That common ancestor would most probably
have been quite similar to the chimpanzee today,
and would have had a similar range of interactions with other species: occasionally hunting small monkeys, feeding on insects, being
preyed upon by wild cats and eagles. During the
course of human evolution those interactions
diversified as animals came to play new roles
in society. Indeed, the course of our biological
and cultural evolution is intimately tied up
with the emergence of those new inter-species
relationships.

In this paper I will examine some of the key
moments in the evolution of human relationships
with animals, tracking the emergence of these
new relationships and the impact they have had
on our bodies, our minds and our culture. My
concern is with prehistoric hunter-gatherers. Agriculture, first appearing at *c.*10,000 years ago, is
a very recent development in human society and
comes after humans had already entered into a
diverse range of relationships with animals, including those of domestication.

HUNTER-GATHERERS: PAST AND PRESENT

We all have some familiarity with hunters and
gatherers, although few have first-hand experience. The term conjures up images of the !Kung
of the Kalahari (e.g. Lee 1979), the Inuit of the
Arctic (e.g. Gubser 1965; Saladin D'Anglure
1990) and the aborigines of Australia (e.g. Levitt
1981; Meehan 1982). These societies certainly
have many and varied relationships with animals:
hunting them for meat, using their products for
clothing and tools, depicting them within their
art (e.g. Morphy 1989a). Their mythologies
frequently, perhaps always, involve stories of
animals that could transform themselves into
humans and back again. Many groups have
animals as their totems, species from whom
they claim descent and to whom they attribute
special powers (Willis 1990). In these regards the
human-animal interactions are not significantly
different to ours today – with the exception of
domestication.

These modern hunter-gatherers, however,
may be quite untypical of the hunter-gatherers
who lived during the five million years of humans, *Homo sapiens*, a species that appears in the
fossil record only 100,000 years ago (Stringer
and McKie 1996); also the hunter-gatherers of
the modern world have lived in harsh, marginal
environments, notably dry deserts or tropical
rainforest. The majority of those from prehistory
lived in more temperate settings, not having to
suffer such severe environmental conditions.
In summary, it is most likely that many of our
prehistoric forebears lived very different lives
and had very different types of interaction with
animals than those of hunter-gatherers of the
ethnographic record. The only traces of those
interactions are to be followed in the fossil and
archaeological records.

AUSTRALOPITHECINES AND ANIMALS

We must begin with the earliest direct ancestors
of our species, the australopithecines who lived

in eastern and southern Africa between 4.2 and 1 million years ago. (For a review of australopithecine fossils see Jones et al. 1992; Johanson and Edgar 1996.) The first discovery of these was made in 1929 by the South African anthropologist Raymond Dart and is known as the Taung child. Since that date many specimens have been found showing us that australopithecines came in various shapes and sizes, some rather gracile, perhaps rather like baboons today, others very robust perhaps similar to gorillas. All of the australopithecines had brains about the size of the chimpanzee's (c. 400cc); it is likely that they all used some form of tools, most probably similar to the termite sticks and the hammer stones used by chimpanzees when acquiring food. Whether the australopithecines flaked stone is open to much debate.

What sort of interactions did these earliest hominids have with animals? Forty years ago Raymond Dart thought that they were blood-thirsty hunters, brutally killing antelopes and monkeys (Binford 1983) He had studied the animal bones found associated with the australopithecine fossils in the caves of south Africa and decided that they were hunting weapons, clubs, daggers and missiles. Today we know better, largely thanks to the work of C.K. Brain (1981). During the 1970s he reexcavated the caves and understood how the assemblages of bones were formed: far from the australopithecines having been the hunters, they were the hunted – principally the victims of leopards.

The Taung child itself had been a victim. This was a juvenile australopithecine that had been grabbed by an eagle, perhaps from its mother's side and taken to its aerie – just as eagles do with monkeys today. We know this because of telltale beak and talon marks on the skull and the other animals' bones with which it was found, bones typical of those found within a collapsed aerie (Berger and Clark 1995).

Did the australopithecines hunt at all? Probably not, or at least no more than chimpanzees today. Indeed the robust australopithecines evolved into specialized vegetarians, with massive jaws and chewing muscles fixed onto a crest of bone. So

what role did animals play in the society of our first direct ancestors? It was one of a predator. If you had been an australopithecine, gathering berries, digging for tubers and eating seeds in the woodland savannahs of Plio-Pleistocene Africa, then leopards, eagles and snakes were animals to avoid and to fear.

THE EARLIEST HOMO, BRAIN GROWTH AND THE SIGNIFICANCE OF MEAT

Human-animal interactions began to change after two million years, although the danger from predators continued. At this time, hominid brain size expanded, reaching up to 750cc in some specimens, about 50% of the size of the average human brain today (Jones et al. 1992; Wood 1992). Along with a reduction in the size of dentition and various other anatomical features, this increased brain size is used to denote the first members of our genus, Homo. Specimens are often grouped together as a single species, Homo habilis. But the diversity in size, shape and body form suggests that several different species were present, each with a different type of adaptation to the African environments. They all possessed significantly larger brains than the australopithecines, largely deriving from a significant increase in body size, and it is most probable that they all made stone tools which first appear about 2.5 million years ago.

Such tools are no more than simple flakes of stone and the nodules from which they were struck. Sometimes the artifacts are found surrounding the remains of a single large animal, such as at the HAS site in Koobi Fora where they are associated with a hippopotamus (Isaac 1978). At other sites the artifacts are found amidst dense scatters of bone fragments, representing animals of several species, such as zebras, antelopes and wildebeest. Mary Leakey described these sites as living floors, and believed that they derived from where animals were butchered and consumed. During the 1970s the late Glynn Isaac (1978) thought that these sites reflected substantial sharing of meat at homebases, which laid the basis for a society much like that of hunter-gatherers today.

Just as had happened with the australopith-ecine cave sites in South Africa, the 1980s saw a degree of revisionism about these bone accumulations (Binford 1981; Potts 1989). Microscopic studies on some of the animal bones showed that they had been gnawed by hyenas before they had been cut with stone tools; other studies examined the parts of the carcasses present on these sites finding that there were often bones of marginal utility such as lower legs from which only limited quantities of meat could have been acquired.

So the picture emerged that rather than hunting these animals, early *Homo* had simply been scavenging on the carcasses left behind by carnivores, gaining only tit-bits of meat. The marrow from inside the bones is likely to have been of great value to them and it appears that many of the stone artifacts were used to smash the bones open to access this marrow – a resource not available to the hunting and scavenging carnivores. So while it seems that some hunting and meat sharing did take place, for occasionally sites provide meat-bearing bones with no traces of carnivore damage (Binford 1986; Bunn and Kroll 1986), the earliest members of our genus were not great hunters of wild beasts, but largely sneaky scavengers, creeping in after the lions, hyenas and vultures had had their fill.

This does not suggest that meat and other animal products were not important in the human diet; indeed they seem to have been essential. We know this because of the substantial increase in the size of the brain that occurred after 2.5 million years ago. Brains are metabolically very expensive organs to have: they require 22 times as much energy as an equivalent amount of muscle. So that brain enlargement needed to have been fuelled somehow, and a change of diet appears to be the explanation (Aiello and Wheeler 1995). By eating higher-quality foodstuffs, especially tubers and meat, the overall volume of the gut could have been reduced, freeing metabolic energy to fuel the larger brain.

DISPERSAL FROM AFRICA AND THE EARLY HUMAN MIND

One of these early *Homo* species, most probably *Homo ergaster*, dispersed from Africa and colonized Asia. Quite when this happened remains unclear but it was most probably soon after two million years ago (Gamble 1993). In Asia, *Homo ergaster* evolved into *Homo erectus,* a name also applied to later African Specimens. Europe was most likely colonized around 800,000 years ago, probably by an African descendant of *H. ergaster* referred to as *H. Heidelbergensis* (Parés and Pérez-Gonzalez 1995; Dennell and Roebroeks 1996). As from 1.4 million years ago, a new type of artifact is found in Africa, and then in southern Asia and Europe: the handaxe. This is a bifacially knapped artifact, with an imposed form often appearing in a symmetrical pear shape.

After 1.5 million years ago we enter a period of stasis in human evolution: for the next million years brain size remains static between around 1000 cc (Aiello 1996). There are no significant developments in body size or shape, no new species that we know of, and the archaeological record has a multitude of minor variations on the simple themes of handaxes and Oldowan like tools. At this time there is no evidence for art or ritual behavior, no traces of structures or built hearths. It seems unlikely that these ancestors did not have the use of fire, but there are few traces of this in the archaeological record.

The exploitation of animals is likely to have been important to these human ancestors, particularly those living in northern environments. Direct, unambiguous evidence of hunting was first discovered in 1997 in the form of well-designed, wooden hunting spears found associated with horse bones at Schöningen, Germany, dating to 400,000 years ago (Thieme 1997). There are also unambiguous traces of hunting activity at Boxgrove, England, dating to 500,000 years ago (Roberts 1997). It is clear, therefore, that some big-game hunting was undertaken by these early humans, although this is unlikely to have replaced scavenging in its entirety.

Between 600,000 and 250,000 [years ago] a substantial development occurs in human evolution: a dramatic enlargement of brain size to modern proportions (Ruff et al. 1997). We see this partly within species such as *Homo heidelbergensis*, and then more dramatically with the Neanderthals who lived in Europe between 250,000 and just 29,000 years ago. Quite why brain size increased in this fashion at this particular time is unknown. It is thought to be related principally to the evolution of our language capacities. From specimens such as those from Atapuerca in Spain at 300,000 years ago, and more particularly the Kebara II Neanderthal specimen of 63,000 years ago, we can see evidence for a modern vocal tract (Schepartz 1993). Language is most likely to have evolved hand in hand with other mental capacities, such as that of theory of mind (Mithen 1999).

IN NEANDERTHAL SOCIETY

The Neanderthals are the best known of our prehistoric relatives. They lived in harsh, glaciated conditions of Europe and the Near East, having evolved the form of stout, robust bodies which are most suitable for living in cold climates (Stringer and Gamble 1993; Mellars 1996). We know that the Neanderthals had capacities for spoken language and brains as large as ours today. Indeed specimens such as Amud I had a brain larger than [that of] any known modern humans at 1,750 cc. What is so strange, however, is that their behavior remains quite archaic in nature: we have no unambiguous evidence for art or ritual, for tools made from bone and antler, for a scientific or a religious perspective on the world. Anatomically they look quite modern; behaviorally they appear quite archaic (Mithen 1996a).

With regard to their interactions with other animals we know that the Neanderthals were at times hunters. We have evidence for this in the many assemblages of animal bones that have come from Neanderthal cave sites in Europe and Asia. Detailed meticulous analysis of these by archaeologists, looking at factors such as what parts of the skeletons are present, at cut marks, at gnawing by carnivores and at a host of other factors have shown that some Neanderthals were hunting large game, while others were scavenging on carcasses either killed by other carnivores or which had died of natural causes (e.g. Chase 1986; Stiner and Kuhn 1992). Their main hunting weapons appear to have been short thrusting spears, tipped with stone points. The points themselves required considerable skill to make, but the weapons themselves remained quite simple in design. With such weapons, the Neanderthals appear to have frequently used a confrontational hunting technique. This seems to have been a major cause of the high frequency of bone fractures found on Neanderthal skeletal remains and the high mortality of young adults (Trinkaus 1995).

Why Neanderthals did not invent more effective hunting weapons and methods to avoid such injuries remains unclear. We have no evidence for throwing spears, for bows and arrows, for spear throwers, for pits, traps and snares. Of course such evidence might be forthcoming with new discoveries or interpretations. But at present it appears that for several hundred thousand years Neanderthals relied upon a hunting technology of limited effectiveness. It also appears that Neanderthals did not develop any relationships with animals beyond those of predator/prey as had characterized human ancestors for the previous million years. There are no pictorial depiction of animals, no evidence that animals were used as symbols of power and authority, no trace of totemic thinking.

In summary, it is clear that the role animals played in Neanderthal society was limited. They were hunted, scavenged and used as food; we assume their hides were used for clothing and perhaps for shelters. Their bones are likely to have been used as tools, but in spite of the many thousands of stone artifacts and animal bones from the archaeological record there are no convincing examples of carved bone, antler or ivory which can be attributed to the Neanderthals or any other type of pre-modern human (but see

Marshack 1990, 1997 and Bednarik 1996 for an alternative view).

This is quite astonishing. We are dealing with large-brained humans, some of whom were living no less than 30,000 years ago. But there are hardly any traces of that rich array of relationships that modern humans have with animals today. Why was this? One possibility is that it was due to the type of intelligence that Neanderthals possessed. The technical skill required to make their stone tools, the challenges posed by their ice-age environments, and the likely complexity of their social interactions clearly tell us that Neanderthals were highly intelligent: they had to have been [so, in order] to have survived and made such artifacts. But, as I have argued at length elsewhere (Mithen 1996a), it appears that Neanderthal intelligence was structured in a quite different fashion to that of the modern mind. They appear to have had discrete domains of intelligence, "social," "technical" and "natural history" intelligences, just as Gardner (1983) has argued that modern humans have multiple intelligences. But in contrast to modern humans Neanderthals seem [to have been] unable to integrate knowledge gained in one domain of behavior with that of another. For instance the absence of a sophisticated hunting technology may have been because the detailed and extensive knowledge about animal behavior that they possessed was unable to be integrated with their knowledge about making artifacts so that hunting weapons suitable for killing specific types of animals in specific circumstances could not be designed. Similarly, although it seems most likely that Neanderthals had a well-developed social intelligence, involving a theory of mind, this seems to have been restricted to the dealing with humans alone. Among modern humans, it is quite usual to "apply" our social intelligence to our dealings with animals – we constantly anthropomorphize animals, imposing onto them human-like minds.

THE ORIGIN OF MODERN HUMANS AND NEW ROLES FOR ANIMALS

Anatomically modern humans evolved in Africa, first appearing about 130,000 years ago, and then dispersed throughout the world (Stringer and McKie 1996). They replaced all other human types to leave our species as the only living member of our genus. How was this replacement achieved? The Neanderthals had lived in Europe for thousands of years with bodies physiologically adapted to those cold environments. Yet modern humans with a gracile stature best suited to hot equatorial regions not only colonized Europe but pushed this cold adapted species into extinction, as they did with other archaic populations throughout the world. Many archaeologists now believe that lying at the root of the success of modern humans was a profound cognitive difference between our species and all of our ancestors and relatives. Part of the evidence for this contrast derives from the new types of interaction with other animals to which we can now turn.

Some of the earliest evidence for this is the use of animal body parts in ritual behavior. Although Neanderthals had buried some of their dead (e.g. at Kebara, Bar-Yosef et al. 1992) there are no unambiguous traces of ritual, such as grave goods placed with the bodies. (See Gargett 1989 for a critical discussion of the evidence.) The earliest known burials of modern humans, however, dating to at c. 100,000 years ago in the caves of Skhul and Qafzeh (Israel), involved the placement of animal parts with the dead. At Skhul the head and antlers of a deer were placed on top of a child (McCown 1937), while in Qafzeh cave the jaw of a wild boar was laid in the hands of a deceased male (Vandermeersch 1970). Were these animals the totemic species for the dead? Were these animal parts offering to the afterworld? We do not know, but we have the first evidence that animals were no longer viewed just as sources of meat or predation.

ANIMALS IN THE ART OF THE ICE AGE

The most dramatic evidence for this change comes with the very first representational art, that made between 30,000 and 10,000 years ago by the first modern humans who colonized Europe. Within their caves, on pieces of bone and stone and on open rock faces they painted, engraved and carved animals. (For a review see Bahn 1996.) Bison, horse and deer dominate this art, often painted in magnificent panoramas such as those on Altamira ceiling or in the caves of Lascaux or Chauvet. Dangerous animals were also depicted such as lions and hyenas, as were fish, birds and even on one occasion an insect.

The quality of these paintings is astounding. They often demonstrate substantial technical skill and have considerable emotive power. The latter is especially the case when the paintings are seen by the light of a flickering candle within the otherwise dark and cold cave.

What motivated these people to make such art? Ever since it was discovered theories have been proposed as to why during the harshest periods of the last ice age people went into caves to paint and draw animals, sometimes going deep underground, or constructing scaffold to reach high vaults. Did they do it as hunting magic, to ensure success in the hunt? Was it fertility magic to ensure constant supplies of game? Was it as a means of recording their mythologies and as a means to pass on these to the next generation? Was it to educate children about the natural world, about the habits of game and how to hunt? Or was it simply to celebrate the beauty of their ice age world? All of these theories have been put forward and argued at length during the last century (as critically reviewed in Bahn 1996).

It seems unlikely that any one explanation will suffice for this art that stretches from southern Spain to Siberia, and lasted for over 20,000 years. We know from the art of recent hunter-gatherers, such as Aborigines, that paintings often had multiple meanings: fish painted beside a lake, for instance, might mean on the one hand that the lake is a good place to go fishing; on the other hand the fish will act as a symbol of life by having the quality of rainbowness. As individuals grow and mature in Australian aborigine societies they gradually learn additional meanings of images, moving from the most literal interpretations to those which rely on a profound knowledge of mythology (Morphy 1989b; Taylor 1989). So too may it have been with the paintings from the last ice age: on one level I suspect that these paintings do relate to hunting practices, providing information about what and how to hunt (Mithen 1988); but on another level these images must surely relate to the mythological world of the ice-age people about which we can know very little.

The specific meaning of these paintings may be beyond our powers of deduction, but we can be sure that they reflect new types of relationships between humans and animals. One of these is aesthetic appreciation. Would it have been possible to have painted such animals without appreciating their beauty and grace? Another is that the sharp boundaries between humans and animals that had existed throughout human evolution had now collapsed.

We know that this had happened, for within the art are images of beings that are part animal and part human. We have, for instance, the 33,000-year-old lion man from Hohlenstein Stadel in Germany, a carving from mammoth ivory with the head of a lion and the torso and legs of a man. There is also the 30,000 year old painting from Chauvet cave with the head and shoulders of a bison and the legs of a man (Chauvet et al. 1996). And there is the famous sorcerer from Trois Frères, an entity constituted by bits of a human, of deer, of feline, of horse and perhaps seal (Bahn 1996). What are these images? Are they of hunters in disguise? Of shamans in costume who could communicate with the spirit world? Or of supernatural beings? We don't know. But whatever they are they testify to a fluidity between the worlds of humans and animals.

NEW TOOLS, HUNTING METHODS AND LATE PLEISTOCENE EXTINCTIONS

Human-animal interactions were changing in other ways. Unlike their predecessors, modern humans appear to have made far greater use of animal products. Their bones and ivory were carved not just into objects of art, but also into new types of hunting weapon. Some of the smallest tools were the most important: consider the impact [of bone needles, first made 18,000 years ago, on making adequate clothing and shelter]. With their new tools modern humans hunted more intensively and effectively. Whereas the Neanderthals had confronted and killed individual animals, the modern humans now ambushed and slaughtered whole herds at river crossings or in narrow gullies. To do so they must have predicted the animals' movements with great care, geared up their tools, cooperated in the hunt and then processed and stored the meat from their slaughter (Mithen 1990). More generally, as from 30,000 years ago a wide range of sophisticated hunting methods and complex technology can be identified in the archaeological record showing how modern communities rapidly adapted to new environments in a quite different fashion to [that of] all previous human types. (Peterkin et al. 1993 contains a very useful collection of papers describing the hunting and animal exploitation in the Upper Palaeolithic and Mesolithic periods.)

Such hunting technology, cooperation and planning created a new type of human-animal interaction: enforced extinction due to over-hunting. We normally think of this as a phenomenon of the modern day, a consequence of our pollution and greed for the earth's resources. But toward the end of the last ice age a vast array of animals in Europe, Asia, Australia and North America became extinct (Martin and Klein 1984). These were all mega-fauna such as giant wombats and kangaroos, enormous ground sloths and most famously the mammoth – although a small population of these survived in the Siberian Arctic for a few thousand years. For many years a debate has raged as to whether it was humans or the environmental changes at the end of the ice age that pushed these animals into extinction. The answer is that it was probably the combined effects of these two forces. Certainly if we look at either the Americas or Australasia the coincidence between the timing of human colonization and mega-faunal extinction appears too great for there to be no relationship. The extinction of the mammoth in North America has been most intensively studied and argued about. Scenarios of extinction have varied from a "blitzkreig extermination" by Clovis hunters as the first colonists of North America (e.g. Mosimann and Martin 1975) to starvation due to changing vegetation patterns associated with Pleistocene/Holocene transition (e.g. Guthrie 1984). The most convincing scenario is that by Haynes who argues that many mammoths were in an emaciated state at the end of the Pleistocene due to drought and the Clovis hunters principally made "Coup de Grace" killings of animals that were already close to death (Haynes 1991). Even a small amount of additional hunting may have been sufficient to push the mammoth into extinction, as has been demonstrated by computer simulation (Mithen 1996[b]).

THE FIRST DOMESTICATED ANIMALS

While some species may have been hunted to extinction by Late Pleistocene humans, others appear to have been undergoing the first stages of domestication. There is an intriguing drawing of a horse's head from St Michael d'Arudy made during the last ice age, that has lines which appear to depict the wearing of a harness – this is many thousands of years before the first domesticated horses. Whether or not it is a harness has been debated for more than 100 years with no resolution (White 1989); it may simply be the depiction of bone structure or coloration. But it is tantalizing evidence that during the last ice age animals were tamed for the very first time, perhaps domesticated. A reindeer bone from the archaeological site of Isturitz in the French

Pyrenees provides further evidence. This is from an injured reindeer, whose injuries appear to have been too severe for it to have survived by itself in the wild. Yet we can see from the bone that the deer did survive and some of its injuries healed. So was this deer cared for by humans?

The most convincing archaeological evidence for the first domesticated animals comes after the end of the last ice age from the hunter-gatherers who lived in the thick forests that covered Europe and the open oak woodland of the Near East. Perhaps not surprisingly those animals were dogs. As such, this contrasts substantially with the claimed date of 100,000–130,000 years for the separation of the dog and wolf lineages based on MtDNA evidence (Vila et al. 1997). There are claims of domesticated dogs from the Magdalenian period of Europe (c. 17,000–10,000 B.P.), from the sites of Oberkassel and Teufelsbrucke in Germany (Benecke 1987, Musil 1984), but the status of the canid bones at these sites remain unclear. The earliest unambiguous examples of domesticated dogs come from the Natufian culture of the Near East at c. 12,000 B.P., notably from the sites of Ein Mahalia (Davis and Valla 1978) and Hayonim Terrace (Tchernov and Valla 1997), where dogs are found buried with humans. Further examples come from the Mesolithic of Southern Scandinavia, at c. 6,500 B.P., notably in the cemetery of Skateholm (Larsson 1984 1990). This cemetery includes a variety of dog burials, some with humans and some alone, some seemingly to have been casually dumped into a grave, and others very carefully positioned. Some of the dogs were buried with grave goods similar to those placed elsewhere with humans. Quite why dogs became domesticated long before other animals remains unclear. Various hypotheses have been put forward: as scavengers, hunting aides, companions, or guard dogs (see e.g. Clutton-Brock 1995; Coppinger and Schneider 1995). The archaeological evidence suggests that dog domestication was associated with the first sedentary communities, and it seems most likely that dogs fulfilled a variety of roles within those prehistoric societies.

These dog burials testify to a further collapse of the boundaries between the human and animal world. This was, of course, extended by the domestication of sheep and goats at about 8,000 years ago that provided the basis for the first agricultural societies which followed the Natufian in the Near East.

CONCLUSION

In this paper I have described some of the main turning points in the role that animals played within prehistoric hunter-gatherer [societies] during the last 5 million years of human evolution. Three million years ago animals were just predators of our australopithecine ancestors. By two million years ago, the first members of our genus were scavenging on animal tissues; by 500,000 years ago the large-brained early humans were hunting animals. But it was only in the last 100,000 years, and possibly just the last 30,000, that animals came to occupy that immensely diverse set of roles in our society that they have today: animals as sources of food, animals as companions; animals as the subject of stories, myths and paintings; animals as metaphors; animals as objects to abuse.

When we take such a broad sweep through human prehistory what appears surprising is that animals remained simply as either prey or as predators for such a long period of time. Even the Neanderthals who possessed brains as large as ours and had some form of language, do not appear to have entered into any more complex or varied relationships with animals. The most likely explanation for this relates to the nature of the Neanderthal mind and intelligence, as I discussed above. Along with all other premodern humans, Neanderthals seem to have lacked a capacity for symbolic thought. This was a serious constraint on the type and range of relationships that could be formed with animals. The first modern humans, and especially those after 50,000 years ago, seem quite different and not only hunted animals on a more effective basis, but developed that diverse range of relationships with animals that we see in the modern world today. One of the key mental developments lying behind these new relationships seems to be that of anthropomorphizing animals. As long ago as 500,000 years ago, our human ancestors are likely to have evolved a theory of mind: interpreting the behavior of other human individuals by attributing to them beliefs and desires different to one's own (Mithen 1999; for definitions and discussion of theory of mind see Carruthers and Smith 1996). This ability would have been essential for the development of more complex human societies, as originally argued by Humphrey (1976). After 50,000 years ago, it seems that this way of thinking was also applied to animal minds, one manifestation of what I [have] termed the emergence of "cognitive fluidity" (Mithen 1996a). In this regard, attributing to animals human-like minds brought those animals into the world of human culture and society.

ACKNOWLEDGEMENTS

I am most grateful to Dennis Turner and an anonymous referee for comments on an earlier version of this manuscript and to Anna Dahlstrom for help with its production. I would also like to thank the organizers of the 8th International Conference on Human-Animal Interactions, Prague 10–12 September 1998 for inviting me to the meeting at which a Version of this paper was delivered.

REFERENCES

Aiello, L. 1996. Hominine preadaptations for language and cognition. In *Modelling the Early Human Mind*, 89–102, ed. P Mellars and K Gibson. Cambridge: McDonald Institute Monograph Series.

Aiello, L. and Wheeler, P. 1995. The expensive tissue hypothesis. *Current Anthropology* 36: 199–221.

Bahn, P. 1996. *Journey through the Ice Age*. London: Weidenfeld & Nicolson.

Bar-Yosef, O, Vandermeersch, B, Arensburg, B, Belfercohen, A, Goldberg, P, Laville, H, Meignen, L, Rak, Y, Speth, J D, Tchernov, E, Tillier, A M and Weiner, S, 1992. The excavations in Kebara Cave, Mt Carmel. *Current Anthropology* 33: 497–551.

Bednarik, R 1995. Concept mediated marking in the Lower Palaeolithic. *Current Anthropology* 36: 605–634.

Benecke, N 1987. Studies of early dog remains from Northern Europe. *Science* 14: 31–49.

Berger, L R and Clark, R J 1995. Eagle involvement in accumulation of the Taung child fauna. *Journal of Human Evolution* 29: 275–299.

Binford, L 1981. Bones: *Ancient Men and Modern Myths*. New York: Academic Press.

Binford, L 1983. *In Pursuit of the Past*. London: Thames & Hudson.

Binford. L 1986. Comment on "Bunn, H and Kroll, E M, 1986. Systematic butchery by plio-pleistocene hominids at Olduvai Gorge, Tanzania." *Current Anthropology* 27: 247–266.

Brain, C K 1981. *The Hunters or the Hunted?* Chicago: Chicago University Press.

Bunn, H and Kroll, E M 1986. Systematic butchery by plio-pleistocene hominids at Olduvai Gorge, Tanzania. *Current Anthropology* 27: 247–266.

Carruthers, P and Smith, P K 1996. *Theories of Theories of Mind*. Cambridge: Cambridge University Press.

Chase, P 1986. *The Hunters of Combe Grenal: Approaches to Middle Palaeolithic Subsistence in Europe*. Oxford: British Archaeological Reports International Series S286.

Chauvet, J-M, Deschamps, E B and Hillaire, C 1996. *Chauvet Cave: the World's Oldest Paintings*. London: Thames & Hudson.

Clutton-Brock, J 1995. Origins of the dog: domestication and early history. In *The Domestic Dog: Its Evolution, Behaviour and Interactions with People*, 8–20, ed J Serpell. Cambridge: Cambridge University Press.

Coppinger, R and Schneider, R 1995. Evolution of working dogs. In *The Domestic Dog: Its Evolution, Behaviour and Interactions with People*, 24–47, ed. J Serpell. Cambridge: Cambridge University Press.

Davis, S and Valla, F R 1978. Evidence for the domestication of the dog 12,000 years ago in the Natufian of Israel. *Nature 276*: 608–610.

Dennell, R and Roebroeks, W 1996. The earliest occupation of Europe: a short chronology revisited. *Antiquity* 68: 489–503.

Gamble, C 1993. *Timewalkers: the Prehistory of Global Colonisation*. Stround: Alan Sutton.

Gardner, H 1983. *Frames of Mind: The Theory of Multiple Intelligences*. New York: Basic Books.

Gargett, R 1989. Grave shortcomings: the evidence for Neanderthal burial. *Current Anthropology* 30: 157–190.

Gubser, N J 1965. *The Nunamiut Eskimos: Hunters of Caribou*. New Haven: Yale University Press.

Guthrie, D 1984. Mosaics, allelochemics and nutrients; An ecological theory of late Pleistocene magafaunal extinctions. In *Quaternary Extinctions*, 259–298, ed. P S Martin and R G Klein. Tuscon: University of Arizona Press.

Haynes, G 1991. *Mammoths, Mastodonts and Elephants: Biology, Behavior and the Fossil Record*. Cambridge: Cambridge University Press.

Humphrey, N 1976. The social function of intellect. In *Growing Points* in *Ethology*, 303–317, ed. P P G Bateson and R A Hinde. Cambridge: Cambridge University Press.

Isaac, G 1978. The food-sharing behaviour of proto-human hominids. *Scientific American* 238 (April): 90–108.

Johanson, D and Edgar, B 1996. From *Lucy to Language*. London: Weidenfeld & Nicolson.

Jones, J S, Martin, R and Pilbeam, D eds 1992. *The Cambridge Encyclopedia of Human Evolution*. Cambridge: Cambridge University Press.

Larsson, L 1983. The Skate holm Project – A Late Mesolithic settlement and cemetery complex at a southern Swedish bay. *Meddelanden fran* Lunds *Universitets Historiska* Museum 1983–84: 4–38.

Larsson, L 1990. Dogs in fraction – symbols in action. In *Contributions to the Mesolithic* in *Europe*, 153–160, ed P M Vermeersch and P van Peer. Leuven: Leuven University Press.

Lee, R B 1979. *The Kung San: Men, Women and Work in a Foraging Society*. Cambridge: Cambridge University Press.

Levitt, D 1981. *Plants and People: Aboriginal Uses of Plants* on *Groote Eylandt*. Canberra: Australian Institute of Aboriginal Studies.

Marshack, A 1990. Early hominid symbolism and the evolution of human capacity. In *The Emergence of Modern Humans*, 457–498, ed P Mellars. Edinburgh: Edinburgh University Press.

Marshack, A 1997. The Berekhat Ram figurine: A late Acheulian carving from the Middle East. *Antiquity* 71: 327–337.

Martin, P S and Klein, R C eds 1984. *Quaternary Extinctions: A Prehistoric Revolution*. Tuscon: University of Arizona Press.

McCown, T 1937. Mugharet-es Skhul: description and excavation. In *The Stone Age of Mount Carmel*, 91–107, ed D Garrod and D Bate. Oxford: Clarendon.

Meehan, B 1982. From *Shell Bed to Shell Midden*. Canberra: Australian Institute of Aboriginal Studies.

Mellars, P 1996. *The Neanderthal Legacy*. Princeton: Princeton University Press.

Mithen, S J 1988. Looking and Learning: Upper Palaeolithic Art and Information Gathering. *World Archaeology* 19: 297–327.

Mithen, S J 1990. *Thoughtful Foragers: A Study of Prehistoric Decision Making*. Cambridge: Cambridge University Press.

Mithen, S J 1996a. *The Prehistory of the Mind*. London: Thames & Hudson.

Mithen, S J 1996b. Simulation mammoth hunting and extinction: implications for North America. In *Time, Process and Structured Transformation* in *Archaeology*, 176–215, ed S van de Leeuw and J McGlade. London: Routledge.

Mithen, S J 1999. Palaeoanthropological perspectives on the theory of mind. In *Understanding Other Minds: Perspectives from Autism* and *Cognitive Neuroscience*, 494–508, ed S Baron-Cohen, H T Ausberg and O Cohen. Oxford: Oxford University Press.

Morphy, H 1989a. *Animals into Art*. London: Unwin Hyman.

Morphy, H 1989b. On representing Ancestral beings. In *Animals into Art*, 144–160, ed H Morphy. London: Unwin Hyman.

Mosimann, J E and Martin, P. 1975. Simulating overkill by palaeoindians. *American Scientist* 63: 305–313.

Musil, R 1984. The first known domestication of wolves in Central Europe. In *Animals and Archaeology: 4. Husbandry* in *Europe*, 23–26, ed C Grigson and J Clutton-Brock. Oxford: BAR International.

Pares, J M and Pérez-Gonzalez, A 1995. Palaeo-magnetic age for hominid fossils of Atapuerca archaeological site, Spain. *Science* 269: 830–832.

Peterkin, G L, Bricker, H and Mellars, P eds 1993. *Hunting and Animal Exploitation* in *the Later Palaeolithic and Mesolithic of Eurasia*. Archaeological Papers of the American Anthropological Association No 4.

Potts, R 1989 *Early Hominids Activities* at *Olduvai Gorge*. New York: Aldine de Gruyter.

Roberts, M 1997. Boxgrove. *Current Archaeology* 153: 324–333.

Ruff, C B, Trinkaus, E and Holliday, T W 1997. Body mass and encephalisation in Pleistocene Homo. *Nature* 387: 173–177.

Saladin D'Angulare, B. 1990. Nanook, super 1 male: the polar bear in the imaginary space and social time of the Inuit of the Canadian Arctic. In *Signifying Animals: Human Meaning in the Natural World*, 173–195, ed R G Wills. London: Unwin Hyman.

Schepartz, L A 1993. Language and modern/human origins. *Yearbook of Physical Anthropology* 36: 91–126.

Stiner, M and Kuhn, S 1992. Subsistence, technology and adaptive variation in Middle Palaeolithic Italy. *American Anthropologist* 94: 12–46.

Stringer, C and Gamble, C 1993. *In Search of the Neanderthals*. London: Thames & Hudson.

Stringer, C and McKie, R 1996. *African Exodus*. London: Jonathon Cape.

Taylor, L 1989. Seeing the 'inside': Kunwinjku paintings and the symbol of the divided body. In *Animals into Art*, 371–389, ed H Morphy. London: Unwin Hyman.

Tchernov, E and Valla, F 1997. Two new dogs and other Natufian dogs from the southern Levant. *Science* 14: 65–95.

Thieme, H 1997. Lower Palaeolithic hunting spears from Germany. *Nature* 385: 807–810.

Trinkaus, E 1995. Neanderthal mortality patterns. *Journal of Archaeological Science* 22: 121–142.

Vandermeersch, B. 1970. Une sépulture moustérienne avec offrandes découverte dans la grotte de Qafzeh. *Comptes rendus Hebdomadaires des seances de l'Académie des Sciences* 270: 298–301.

Vila, C, Savolainen, P, Maldonado, J, Amorim, I, Rice, J, Honeycutt, L, Crandall, K, Lundeberg, J and Wayne, R 1997. Multiple and ancient origins of the domestic dog. *Science* 276: 1687–1689.

White, R 1989. Husbandry and herd control in the Upper Palaeolithic. *Current Anthropology* 23: 169–192.

Willis, R G ed. 1990. *Signifying Animals: Human Meaning in the Natural World*, 173–195. London: Unwin Hyman.

Wood, B. 1992. Origin and evolution of the genus Homo. *Nature* 355: 783–790.

15

HARRIET RITVO

Animal Planet*

Harriet Ritvo is an environmental historian and studies British cultural history, the history of natural history and the history of human-animal relations. She is the author of the influential book, *The Animal Estate: The English and Other Creatures in the Victorian Age* and *The Platypus and the Mermaid* which deals with the paradoxes of Victorian attempts to classify the natural world. She is editor of the book series "Animals, History, Culture," and is currently working on a study of the Victorian environment. In the article reproduced here, Ritvo provides an overview of the myriad ways that animals figure in the narratives of environmental history. She discusses hunting and the exploitation of animals as a commercial resource as major issues in the extinction of animal species, the spread of contagious diseases as one of the "downsides" of animal domestication, episodes of zoonotic diseases (such as mad cow disease which appears to have been the result of feeding cattle food made from the carcasses of diseased animals), and the practices of animal breeding and pet-keeping [examined further in the following reading by Yi-Fu Tuan]. Ritvo writes that "(w)ith animals the question of us and them is always close to the surface" and that the boundaries between what is wild and what is domesticated, what is animal and what is human are becoming increasingly blurred – animals are not only representative of the natural world, they are also cast as representative of human groups, a topic that is taken up again in Section 5.

It is hard to count the ways in which other animals figure in the stories that environmental historians tell.[1] They are part of our epic tales – those with the longest chronological reach – about the movements of early hunters and gatherers. They are part of the grand narrative of domestication and the transformation of human existence through agriculture. They often have represented nature (however nature has been understood) in religious and scientific thought. Animals also play a large role in our novellas – that is, accounts of distinctively modern concerns (or distinctively modern variations on these age-old themes), such as species loss through habitat destruction, the simplification of ecosystems through monoculture and invasion, and the modification of organisms by means of biotechnology. Their ubiquitous presence has helped establish the city

* This chapter was adapted from an article entitled "Animal Planet" Vol. 9(2), 204–220, originally published in the journal *Environmental History* (www.foresthistory.org/ehmain) published by the American Society of Environmental History and the Forest History Society, Durham, NC. Reproduced with permission of the publisher.

and the suburb as appropriate settings for environmental history. None of these stories – long or short – has yet come to a definitive conclusion: certainly, at least from the perspective of the animals themselves, no happy endings are in sight. That may be one reason that animals have been appearing with increasing frequency in the work of environmental historians and of scholars in related disciplines. Another may be that many of the difficult issues at the intersection of academic studies of the environment (historical or otherwise) and environmental politics have an animal dimension, or even an animal-triggered flash point: preservation of threatened ecosystems, overexploitation of resources such as fisheries, emergent diseases, and cloning, to name a few.

Environmental historians are not alone in their heightened interest in animals, nor is scholarly attention to animals completely new. Livestock traditionally has attracted the attention of economic historians who focus on agriculture. Important animal-related institutions, from humane societies to zoos, have had their chroniclers. The history of zoology is a well-established branch of the history of science, most conspicuously in relation to the development of evolutionary ideas. People distinguished in their association with animals, whether as breeders or hunters or scientists, have had their biographers, as, indeed, have some animals distinguished in their own right – from Jumbo to Seabiscuit. Historians have investigated the moral and legal rights and responsibilities of animals, as well as animal-related practices, such as vivisection.[2]

Nevertheless during the last several decades, the attitude of historians in general toward the study of animals has shifted significantly: To put it briefly, animals have been edging toward the mainstream. No longer is the mention of an animal-related research topic likely to provoke surprise and amusement, as was the case twenty years ago. There is now enough new work and enough interest in reading it to support a book series on the theme of "Animals, History, Culture," published by the Johns Hopkins University Press, and a series of annual edited volumes, the

Colloques d'histoire des connaissances zoologiques, published at the University of Liège in Belgium. There are several ways to understand this shift. Animals can be seen as the latest beneficiaries of a democratizing tendency within historical studies. As the labor movement, the civil rights movement, and the women's movement inspired sympathetic scholars, so have, in their turn, the advocates of hunted whales, poached tigers, abandoned dogs, and overcrowded pigs. Even in fields like agricultural history, where animal topics have been routine, farmyard creatures have become less likely to be abstracted through quantification, and more likely to appear as individuals, or at least groups of individuals. Straws in this wind include Susan D. Jones's recent study of veterinary treatment of livestock and horses, and the conference on "The Chicken: Its Biological, Social, Cultural, and Industrial History, from the Neolithic Middens to McNuggets," sponsored in 2002 by the Yale Program in Agrarian Studies.[3] In addition, of course, the vigorous growth of environmental history has helped direct the attention of other kinds of historians toward animals.

At least in the United States, environmental history originally developed from the history of the frontier. The field has moved away from these pioneer beginnings, both geographically and theoretically, as is perhaps most clearly indicated by the gradual problematization of the concept of wilderness. But concern with the relation between the sphere of human domination and what lies (or seems to lie) outside remains strong. This concern often has been mediated through the study of the relationship between people and wild animals, a focus that links modern ways of living with those of our earliest ancestors. The longest story ever told – at least the longest one with people as characters – chronicles the development of human cultures and societies. It exists in numerous variants, depending, among other things, on whether the story is limited to *Homo sapiens,* or whether it includes extinct congeners like *H. neanderthalensis* and *H. habilis.* or stretches still further back to the australopithecines, or moves laterally to embrace our living pongid cousins. All versions agree, however, on the importance of predation. Even if, as with the chimpanzees studied by Jane Goodall, hunting was a relatively infrequent activity, and meat an occasional dietary supplement rather than a dependable source of calories, the skill and cooperation required to kill small and medium-sized game provided significant social and intellectual stimulation.[4] In most pre-agricultural human groups, hunting was more routine and more important. The archaeological record suggests that small nomadic groups also had to worry about becoming the objects of other creatures' hunts, which doubtless served in a complementary way to sharpen wits and enhance cooperation.[5]

In addition, hunting provides the earliest example of the disproportionate human power to affect the rest of the environment. Even though prehistoric human populations were relatively small, they may have had a significant impact on the large herbivores who provided the most rewarding and challenging objectives and, secondarily, on the large carnivores who also ate them. It frequently has been argued, most conspicuously by the biologist Edward O. Wilson, that the spread of modern humans outside their African homeland caused the rapid decline and, in many cases, the extinction of large animal species (and even genera) along their paths of migration.[6] Certainly the coincidence between the arrival of *H. sapiens* in Australia, North America, and South America and the subsequent impoverishment of their indigenous megafauna is very suggestive, especially as these continents, in contrast to Eurasia – where the impact of modern humans appears to have been less dramatic – had not been inhabited by earlier hominid species. This account has always been controversial, however, for several reasons. Inevitably, evidence is sparse and the argument relies heavily on inference. To acknowledge that small pre-agricultural human groups could have such an overwhelming impact on large animal species is to acknowledge that there was never any period or state of human society that existed in a completely harmonious or static relation to the rest of the environment – literally or metaphorically, no garden of Eden.

Reluctance to relinquish this notion accounts for some of the emotion provoked by Shepard Krech's suggestion that PaleoIndians bore some responsibility for the Pleistocene extinctions in North America.[7] There are possible alternative explanations, of which the most prominent is that the same climatic changes that encouraged human migration, especially into the Americas, also altered the habitats to which the enormous Pleistocene animals had adapted. From this perspective, the cold-adapted fauna ultimately was displaced by competitors better suited to a more temperate climate.[8] It is probably an indication of the enduring fascination of these animals, even to people with no opportunity or desire to hunt them, that the cause of their extinction has inspired learned and popular debate since their rediscovery in the nineteenth century.[9]

In many respects, the activities of modern hunters resemble those of their earliest forebears. In an overview of hunting from the Pleistocene to the present, Matt Cartmill has shown how, nevertheless, those activities have altered or been contested, along with shifting understandings of nature. The hunter has figured variously as heroic provider, as protector of threatened outposts, as sensitive intermediary between the human and the divine prey, as gallant sportsman, as brutal butcher, and as agent of extinction.[10] The last two epithets are the most recent, and they have become increasingly prominent in the course of the last century or so. This is not to suggest that no animal species had been eliminated between the Pleistocene and the late nineteenth century, at least on a local basis. In Britain, for example, the wolf, the bear, the wild boar, and the beaver disappeared as a result of the activities of medieval hunters, and, with the possible exception of the beaver, they were not regretted. On the contrary, their absence was greatly appreciated. The last aurochs, the wild bovines from which domesticated cattle are descended, died in Poland in the seventeenth century, not long before the last dodos were killed on Mauritius. Their passing engaged the interest of naturalists and antiquaries, but it was not until the great imperial expansion of the eighteenth and nineteenth centuries that the diminution and disappearance of animal populations began to arouse concern.

Commercial interests raised the first real alarm. Overexploitation radically reduced the productivity of the North American fur trade from the middle of the eighteenth century, when the annual harvest of Canadian beaver skins was over 150,000, to the early nineteenth century, when a territory four times as large provided one-third the yield.[11] Naturalists and hunters (often the same people wearing different hats) corroborated this worrisome sense that even substantial animal populations might not be indefinitely resilient. Visitors to the Cape Colony at the southern tip of Africa observed that neither naturalists nor hunters could find much to amuse them, and that one species of antelope, the blaubok, had been killed off completely; similar complaints were made with regard to the parts of India most accessible to colonial sportsmen. Extinction even of more numerous species was ultimately recognized as a real possibility (a recognition that was inconsistent with some versions of creationist theology, although not so troublesomely inconsistent as evolution proved to be). As formerly blank spaces on the map were filled in, the sparseness or complete absence of wild animals from areas where they had formerly been abundant no longer could be explained as their retreat to the unknown interior. Response to these dawning perceptions was mixed. Like Theodore Roosevelt several generations later, many enthusiastic sportsmen accepted the diminution of game as part of the march of progress. Throughout the nineteenth century, authorities in many parts of the world subsidized the extermination of wild animals perceived as threats to or economic competitors with farmers and their livestock.[12]

The near disappearance of the vast North American bison herds in the middle of the nineteenth century, followed by the actual disappearance of the quagga, a close relative of the zebra, from southern and eastern Africa, began to convert perception into action. Still symbolic of uncivilized nature, wild game was transformed from an obstacle into a valuable resource in need of protection. Yellowstone National Park was founded in 1872 to protect the remaining animals; for several decades the success of this endeavor remained in doubt.[13] Yellowstone and the many reserves and national parks that followed it represented a novel twist on an old idea. Restricted game parks had a long history in Europe and in parts of Asia where their purpose had been at least as much to defend the exclusiveness of hunting as to preserve the animal targets. This spirit permeated the preservation laws that were enacted by many British colonies in Africa and Asia in the late nineteenth and early twentieth centuries. They often specified differential access, quotas, and licensing fees, clearly privileging colonial officials and visiting dignitaries over both indigenous inhabitants and humble European settlers. They also discriminated among animal species, so that large carnivores were excluded from the protective umbrella; indeed their slaughter was often encouraged with bounties. This complex of motives and goals was embodied in the "Conventions for the Preservation of Wild Animals, Birds, and Fish in Africa," which was signed in London in 1900 by representatives of various European governments with colonial holdings, although most of them subsequently failed to ratify it or to honor its provisions. The Society for the Preservation of the Wild Fauna of the Empire, founded in 1903 by a distinguished group of sportsmen and colonial administrators, proved more durable, although (or perhaps because) its membership encompassed strongly conflicting viewpoints. By the time of the society's diamond anniversary, the authors of its official history characterized these early members as "penitent butchers."[14]

Efforts to protect wild animal populations have continued to provoke conflict, both internal and external. Some early campaigners for wild-bird preservation wore elaborate feather hats, and so opened themselves to criticism as hypocrites (by the unconvinced) or as dilettantes (by their more rigorously logical coadjutors).[15] Poaching was an issue when game was protected only for the entertainment of elite hunters, and it continued to be an issue after the animals also became intended beneficiaries.[16] Nor was the need for wild-animal protection universally acknowledged. In many places, competing human interests, alternative sources of information, and inconsistent official motivations meant that protections were not enforced or even enacted until targeted populations were severely reduced or entirely gone. Thus the last thylacine (also known as the Tasmanian tiger and the marsupial wolf) died in a zoo in 1936. Legal protection for its species in Tasmania was enacted just fifty-nine days before it expired. (Thylacines had been hunted to extinction on the Australian mainland long before any Europeans set foot there.) Subsequently the thylacine has been the object of a great deal of apparently heartfelt but inevitably impotent regret.[17] The fate of the tiger in Indonesia and Malaysia depended on the opinions of a variety of colonized and colonizing groups, possibly in addition, Peter Boomgaard gently suggests, to those of the tigers themselves.[18] And individuals always could change their minds – or be of several minds. In *Man-Eaters of Kumaon*, Jim Corbett chronicled his triumphs over numerous lethal tigers, mostly in the classic colonialist mode: That is, claiming to protect Indian villagers who could not defend themselves. By the time of its original publication during [the Second] World War, he had become an ardent conservationist. (A national park in the Himalayan foothills was named in his honor after he died [and] in 1973, Project Tiger, which aims to save the tiger from extinction, was founded there.) Yet he wrote for a public that thrilled to the chase and the kill.[19] Very recent history offers many more examples of competing human claims to the resources represented by wild animals. *Eating Apes* by Dale Peterson explores one of the most extreme and problematic cases.[20]

If hunting represents the primeval relationship between humans and the rest of the animal kingdom, then domestication represents the most transformative one, from the perspectives of both the domesticators and the domesticatees. With the possible single exception of the dog, which may have been part of human social groups long before people began to settle down,

animals were domesticated in conjunction with the development of agriculture. The period when domesticated dogs first appeared and the means by which wolves became dogs are highly controversial. Raymond Coppinger and Lorna Coppinger argue strongly that dog domestication was an indirect product of early agriculture – that is, that dogs who were inclined to scavenge in village waste sites domesticated themselves, much as cats inclined to hunt in rodent-infested grain stores did several thousand years later. Other zoologists prefer explanations that emphasize the human penchant for adopting wild pets and the similar hunting practices of humans and canids.[21] But cattle, sheep, goats, pigs, horses, donkeys, camels, and llamas all were domesticated by agriculturalists or proto-agriculturalists. It is a commonplace of the most sweeping environmental histories that, although domesticated animals were not essential to the development of agriculture, they made a tremendous difference. They supplemented human labor, enhanced transportation, and provided skins and fiber, as well as meat and milk (and selective pressure in favor of the evolution of adult lactose tolerance in some human groups).[22] They have often been identified by contemporary historians as the reason for the competitive success of societies ultimately derived from ancient southwest Asia, especially in comparison with the indigenous societies of the Americas and Oceania. In the nineteenth century, racialist thinkers sometimes read this comparison in reverse, and used the absence of domesticated animals or even the failure to domesticate a particular kind of animal, as a way of denigrating human groups. Africans, for example, were criticized for not taming the elephant, which had proved so valuable in Asia.

Like most aspects of what is normally celebrated as progress, the domestication of animals had a downside, although the connection was not recognized until much later. Archaeological evidence suggests that small nomadic groups were relatively untroubled by the contagious diseases that repeatedly have decimated most settled communities. The size and the mobility of these groups had contributed to this happy situation, and both these attributes altered as people settled down to farm. Increased population meant larger reservoirs for disease and fixed residences meant permanent proximity to waste, whether disposed of in middens or in nearby watercourses. If people had domesticated only plants, these changes would only have exposed them more intensively to disease organisms that they already harbored. But the domestication of wild ungulates – animals which, though mobile, lived in groups large enough to incubate contagions – brought people into contact with a new set of diseases. Such human diseases as smallpox and measles – and diseases of other domestic animals, such as cat and dog distemper – resulted from contact with viruses that originally caused livestock diseases.[23] Over the millennia, it has been theorized by environmental historians, all but the most isolated old-world populations became accustomed to these diseases. Their social impact was minimized through childhood exposure and their individual impact was possibly reduced through maternally transmitted or inherited resistance.[24] But the human inhabitants of the Americas, who had left northeast Asia before the domestication of herds or flocks, had not enjoyed this protracted opportunity to adapt to the microbial cocktail to which European adventurers began to expose them in the late fifteenth century.[25] Most environmental historians of the contact have concluded that this exposure caused the dramatic drop in indigenous populations throughout the Americas in the ensuing centuries, although David Jones has recently suggested that social factors should be weighted more heavily.[26]

Of course epidemic disease was not the only effect that old-world animals had on new-world people. More direct, or at least more obvious, was the impact of the animals themselves, many of which escaped and multiplied vigorously in favorable habitats throughout the Americas. Elinor Melville characterizes such enthusiastic adaptations as ungulate irruptions. Unlike that of contagions, their impact was mixed. As they had done in Europe, Asia and North Africa, these animals provided food, power, and

transportation to indigenous people as well as to colonists, while also subjecting some fragile environments to unsustainable strains.[27]

Although vaccines against most of these ancient scourges had been developed by the late twentieth century, and it had even become possible to contemplate the absolute extinction of a few of them, human epidemiological vulnerability to our vast dense populations of meat animals is not a thing of the past. Influenza returns each year, slightly reengineered in southeast Asia – probably a product of the mode of farming practiced there, in which people, chickens, pigs, and wild fowl live in sufficient proximity for their flu viruses to trade genetic material. Epidemiologists watched the avian flu that decimated flocks of chickens last winter with apprehension based only partly on fear of its economic impact on the poultry industry and on the few cases in which it spread (lethally) to people. They realized that the virus that caused the influenza pandemic of 1918 was derived from a different bird virus that developed the ability to infect mammals; possibly its avian origins made it more difficult for people to resist. Nor do animals need to be domesticated to transmit zoonotic disease, although when wild animals play this role, they usually have been incorporated into human economy if not human society. Thus SARS (severe acute respiratory syndrome), which shut down travel to east Asia and to Toronto in 2003, apparently has been traced to civets, as AIDS has been traced to nonhuman African primates (both chimpanzees and monkeys). In each case, the attribution of responsibility has a blame-the-victim aspect.

The most compelling recent episode of zoonotic transmission is mad cow disease or BSE (bovine spongiform encephalopathy), an affliction that clearly was produced by human practices and human politics. The disease, which spread widely among British cattle in the 1980s – and in a limited number of cases to members of other species, including humans and cats – seems to have originated in cattle feed enriched with material from sheep carrying scrapie, a similar disease.[28] Although feeding cattle with material derived from fellow ungulates – a practice de-nounced by some excitable critics as enforced cannibalism – is not traditional, in a sense it represents an extension of a well-established technique. Since the eighteenth century, livestock farmers have attempted to streamline the inherently inefficient diets of their animals. Cattle fed on food like oilcake – a much richer source of calories than the grass they evolved to metabolize – matured earlier and gained weight faster, and thus became marketable more rapidly and more profitably. But if physical factors produced BSE, it was the Conservative British government of the 1980s that turned the disease into an epizootic. A philosophy that defined government as the protector of commercial enterprise rather than of its citizens meant that official concern with beef-industry profits consistently overshadowed official concern with public health. Further, the British response to BSE (shared by some members of the public as well as government officials) was shaped by such elusive factors as national pride and national passion. Of course, any significant commodity can serve as a metonym for the nation that produces or consumes it, but animals have been particularly likely to fill such roles, and beef and beef cattle had occupied a particularly powerful emblematic position in Britain for several hundred years.[29] Not only were citizens urged to show their patriotism by continuing to eat British burgers, but non-British responses often suggested reciprocal national feeling. Thus the stalwart commitment proclaimed by other European governments to defend the health of their citizens against the British bovine menace could seem less absolute when BSE was rumored in their own herds. Although American politicians recently have taken alarm at a single detected case, rather than waiting, as was the case in Britain, for animals to succumb in their tens of thousands, they seem similarly inclined to view protection of the beef industry as their first priority, and to use the national border to distinguish among cattle suffering from the same affliction.

The vulnerability of livestock to diseases also has affected the human environment in various non-epidemic ways. That is, epizootics, such as outbreaks of cattle plague or foot and mouth disease, repeatedly have wreaked economic havoc without making people sick. Since both cattle and horses are susceptible to sleeping sickness, the prevalence of the tsetse fly made it difficult for the European biological assemblage, which had proved so effective in expediting the colonization of the temperate Americas and Australia, to move into large tracts of Africa. The waste produced by industrial concentrations of animals in stockyards and factory farms continues to strain sewage facilities. Nevertheless, as greatly as domesticated animals have influenced human existence, our impact on them has been greater still. Simply in terms of numbers, these few favored species now account for a much larger proportion of the world's biomass than did their pre-agricultural ancestors. In several cases – the camel and the cow – the wild progenitors of domesticates have disappeared. In others, such as the wolf, their populations are dwarfed by those of their domesticated relatives. If *Canis familiaris* were to be reclassified as *C. lupus* on the basis of willingness to interbreed and ability to produce fertile hybrid offspring, it would be difficult to argue for the protection of the wolf as an endangered species. So domestication has given target species an enormous evolutionary advantage, if evolutionary success is measured simply in terms of quantity.

In addition to exponentially increasing certain animal populations, the process of domestication has changed the very nature of its subjects. Archaeological evidence suggests that the early stages of domestication produced similar changes in a variety of species: reduced body size in general and brain size in particular, increased diversity in superficial characteristics like ear shape and coat color, and shortening of the face (part of a set of skeletal and behavioral changes that can be explained as the retention of juvenile characteristics into adulthood).[30] It is likely that people originally selected animals for tractability and for distinctiveness – characteristics that would make it easier to manage the creatures and to tell them apart. Once domesticated populations were firmly distinguished from their wild relatives, however, people probably began to breed for more specialized qualities. Modern breeders often claim that their favorite variety of dog or horse or cow has ancient roots, but although it is clear that distinct strains existed in earlier times, it is difficult to make direct connections from them to particular modern types. (Of course every living animal has ancient forebears, just as every living human does; in both cases the problem is to figure out who they might be.) Over the past three centuries animal breeding has become a highly technical, self-conscious, and institutionalized process – a form of bioengineering before the fact. By the middle of the nineteenth century, breeding (or artificial selection) had become so widely understood, that Charles Darwin used it to introduce his audience to the less familiar process of natural selection in the opening pages of *On the Origin of Species*.[31]

When modern breeding practices were taking form in the eighteenth century or a little before, the aim of breeders was to enhance quality in ways that could be assessed quantitatively. The first kinds of animals for which elaborate public breeding records were kept – the kind that could sustain pedigrees – were the thoroughbred horse and the greyhound, both bred for speed, which could be easily measured. The first livestock breed to receive this kind of formal attention was the shorthorn cow, the subject of a herd book published in 1822. But careful breeding had been going on long before, validated by market prices if not by paper trails. On the contrary, the best-known stock breeder of the eighteenth century, Robert Bakewell, made a point of obscuring the descent of his prized bulls, rams, boars, and stallions. The quality of his animals was a matter of judgment, guaranteed by his name rather than those of his animals. His own success was calibrated by the size of the stud fees. Although Bakewell often has been credited with developing the breeding techniques that he applied and marketed so brilliantly, it is likely that his fame obscured the earlier labors of modest breeders,

whose unsung achievements served as the basis for his celebrated ones.[32]

By the nineteenth century, as pet keeping became a popular pastime among members of the middling and less-than-middling orders of Western societies, the infrastructure of breeding was applied to dogs, cats, rabbits, rodents, and various kinds of birds. It often had been difficult to decide what made a cow or pig excellent – there were heated controversies over, for example, whether morbid obesity was a prime desideratum or the reverse. With animals whose major function was to provide companionship and amusement, however, such decisions could approach the impossible. Or at least, they were likely to be very arbitrary, often reflecting an appreciation simply of the human power to manipulate. Sometimes this power was exercised to the obvious disadvantage of established useful traits, and sometimes it was exercised capriciously enough to produce creatures that were perceived as monstrosities. For example, when collies became popular pets in the Victorian period, they lost many of the characteristics that made them effective herd dogs. Particularly lamented was their intelligence, which was sacrificed when their skulls were reshaped to feature a long elegant nose. As information about genetics filtered into the pet-fancying world during the twentieth century, breeders' techniques became more focused and powerful. They even were able to achieve some goals that had long eluded them, such as a canary colored red rather than yellow.[33]

The shift from breeding livestock to breeding pets was also ordinarily, although not inevitably, a shift from the country to the city. Animals are most frequently associated with rural settings, but cities always have been full of them. Before the development of modern technologies of refrigeration and transportation, towns needed to accommodate both dairies and abattoirs.[34] Dairy animals mostly stayed out of sight, while livestock bound for slaughter often marched through the streets, but both groups added significantly to the urban waste stream. Many people, including those living in tenements, kept their own chickens and even pigs. Before the twentieth century, all urban thoroughfares were choked with horses, which disappeared only gradually with the advent of the internal-combustion engine. To some extent, at least in the affluent cities of the industrial world, these utilitarian animals have been replaced by burgeoning pet populations. Several zoonotic diseases typically have occurred in urban settings. Rabies is most frequently transmitted to people by dogs, and so is most feared where dog populations are densest, although rural dogs and various wild animals are also carriers. The black death of the Middle Ages and the early modern period, whether or not it was the same as the modern contagion called bubonic plague, was focused on cities, although its traditional association with rats and fleas has recently been questioned.[35] But whether or not they spread the great fourteenth-century plague, rats of several species would figure prominently in an animal census of most urban environments, along with other creatures similarly adapted to scavenging or parasitism (which is to say, semi-tame, if not semi-domesticated), including mice, pigeons, and stray dogs and cats. Also making their homes in cities are many animals ordinarily categorized as wild –monkeys in Calcutta, foxes in London, raccoons and coyotes in Boston.

Of course, it is as difficult to decide what makes animal wild as to define wildness or wilderness in any other context. The Royal Ontario Museum in Toronto once introduced its display of stuffed specimens with a diorama featuring a pair of large raccoons vigorously toppling a garbage can. The diorama (now gone, unfortunately) evoked a set of incongruities or paradoxes – not only which animals are wild and which are not, but which are suitable subjects for scrutiny in cultural and educational settings. Thus most past and present zoos have preferred to collect exotic wild animals, segregating any resident domesticates into petting zoos for children; one of the things that distinguishes the Walter Rothschild Zoological Museum at Tring (now a branch of the Natural History Museum in London) is its large collection of stuffed dogs. And animals, especially domesticated ones, breach other boundaries as well. Or, to put it another way, they help expose some of the assumptions that underlie the stories that we tell, in particular stories about the extent to which we are part of or separate from our environmental subject. With animals the question of us and them is always close to the surface. Not only have they often functioned – even the most ingratiating of them – as representatives of the natural world, but they often have been selected as obvious representatives of human groups, whether as totems or national emblems or team mascots.[36]

This liminality is most obvious – and most problematic – with regard to the animals who resemble us most closely. From its Enlightenment beginnings, formal taxonomy has recognized not only the general correspondence between people and what were then known as quadrupeds (that is, mammals), but also the particular similarities that human beings shared with apes and monkeys. It was the nonfunctional details that proved most compelling: the shape of the external ear, for example, or the flatness of fingernails and toenails. On this basis, the celebrated eighteenth-century systematizer Carolus Linnaeus located people firmly within the animal kingdom: He constructed the primate order to accommodate humans, apes, monkeys, prosimians, and bats.[37] Humans also were claimed to demonstrate their animal affinities in ways that were less abstract and more sensational. In an age fascinated by hybrids, humans were sometimes alleged to be the objects or the originators of potentially fruitful relationships with orangutans and chimpanzees, although scientific accounts of such episodes tended to be carefully distanced by skepticism or censure.[38] Outside the community of experts, claims could be less restrained; in the nineteenth century, non-Europeans who were unusually hairy or adept with their toes were ballyhooed as products of an ape-human cross. Physical and mental similarities between people and other primates often were foregrounded in zoo displays that featured chimpanzees who not only wore clothes, but ate with silverware, drank from cups, and turned the pages of books.

Such displays were not universally appealing, however, and as evolutionary theory suggested a more concrete and ineluctable connection, it provoked increasingly articulate resistance. As Darwin sadly noted at the end of *The Descent of Man,* written a decade after the appearance of the *Origin* in 1859, "The main conclusion arrived at in this work, namely that man is descended from some lowly organized form, will, I regret to think, be highly distasteful to many persons."[39] In the century and more since Darwin wrote, his evolutionary theory has been enshrined as biological orthodoxy. But some of the questions that troubled his Victorian critics continue to complicate modern narratives, whether told for a scientific or scholarly audience or for a less specialized one. Remote from the reflections of historians, animals clog the airwaves. A majority of the extravagantly produced commercials for Superbowl XXXVIII featured animal actors, although this was not their most frequently remarked attribute. An entire cable channel is devoted to animals, and zoological documentaries appear frequently on other networks. Many of these programs present an environmental context and an elegiac environmentalist message, at the same time as they celebrate the physical triumph of fit, canny trappers or photographers (hunters transformed to suit modern sensibilities) over dangerous beasts. It is often hard to know who is the hero of the story, let alone what the moral is meant to be.

NOTES

1. I will continue to assume that we are animals too, but for the sake of euphony, I will refer to nonhuman animals just as "animals" for the rest of this essay.
2. The literature on animal rights and responsibilities is relatively sparse and eccentric: See for example E. P. Evans, *The Criminal Prosecution and Capital Punishment of Animals: The Lost History of Europe's Animal Trials* (1906; reprint, London: Faber 1987); and Vicki Hearne, *Bandit: Dossier of a Dangerous Dog* (New York: HarperCollins 1991). The literature on vivisection is denser and more conventional: See for example Nicolaas A. Rupke, ed., *Vivisection in Historical Perspective* (London: Routledge 1987); and Richard D. French, *Antivivisection and Medical Science in Victorian Society* (Princeton: Princeton University Press 1975).
3. Susan D. Jones, *Valuing Animals: Veterinarians and Their Patients in Modern America* (Baltimore: Johns Hopkins University Press, 2003). For further reflections on this topic see Harriet Ritvo, "History and Animal Studies," *Society and Animals* 10 (2002): 403–6. This issue of *Society and Animals* also includes essays on the relation of animal studies to other disciplines in the humanities and social sciences.
4. Jane Goodall, *The Chimpanzees of Gombe: Patterns of Behavior* (Cambridge: Harvard University Press 1986), chapter 11.
5. See for example C. K. Brain, *The Hunters or the Hunted? An Introduction to African Cave Taphonomy* (Chicago: University of Chicago Press 1981).
6. Edward O. Wilson, *The Diversity of Life* (Cambridge: Harvard University Press 1992), ch.12.
7. Shepard Krech III, *The Ecological Indian: Myth and History* (New York: W.W. Norton, 1999), chapter 1.
8. Discussions of the evidence for alternative points of view can be found in E. C. Pielou, *After the Ice Age: The Return of Life to Glaciated North America* (Chicago: University of Chicago Press 1991), chapter 12; and Tim Flannery, *The Eternal Frontier: An Ecological History of North America and Its Peoples* (New York: Grove Press, 2001), chs. 14–17.
9. Claudine Cohen, *The Fate of the Mammoth: Fossils, Myth, and History,* trans. William Rodarmor (1994: Chicago: University of Chicago Press, 2002), especially chapter 12. See also A. Bowdoin Van Riper, *Men among the Mammoths: Victorian Science and the Discovery of Human Prehistory* (Chicago: University of Chicago Press 1993).
10. Matt Cartmill, *A View to a Death in the Morning: Hunting and Nature through History* (Cambridge MA: Harvard University Press 1993).
11. For statistical analysis of the consequences of the fur trade, see Arthur Radclyffe Dugmore, *The Romance of the Beaver; being the History of the Beaver in the Western Hemisphere* (London: William Heinemann 1914), chapter 4; and

Briton Cooper Busch, *The War against the Seals: A History of the North American Seal Fishery* (Kingston and Montreal: McGill-Queen's University Press 1985).

12. Harriet Ritvo. *The Animal Estate: The English and Other Creatures in the Victorian Age* (Cambridge MA: Harvard University Press 1987), chs. 5–6.

13. For an elaborate account of the decimation and partial recovery of the North American bison herd, see Andrew C. Isenberg, *The Destruction of the Bison* (Cambridge: Cambridge University Press, 2000).

14. John M. MacKenzie, *The Empire of Nature: Hunting, Conservation and British Imperialism* (Manchester: Manchester University Press 1988); and Richard Fitter and Peter Scott, *The Penitent Butchers: 75 Years of Wildlife Conservation: The Fauna Preservation Society 1903–1978* (London: Fauna Preservation Society 1978).

15. For an extensive discussion of this campaign in the United States and Britain, see Robin W. Doughty, *Feather Fashions and Bird Preservation: A Study in Nature Protection* (Berkeley: University of California Press 1975).

16. Karl Jacoby, *Crimes against Nature: Squatters, Poachers, Thieves, and the Hidden History of American Conservation* (Berkeley: University of California Press, 2001); and Louis S. Warren, *The Hunter's Game: Poachers and Conservationists in Twentieth Century America* (New Haven: Yale University Press 1997).

17. Robert Paddle, *The History and Extinction of the Thylacine* (Cambridge: Cambridge University Press, 2000).

18. Peter Boomgaard broaches the possibility of writing history, environmental or otherwise, that incorporates the perspective of animals, but regretfully decides to keep to the conventional path. Both his decision and his regret are understandable. Peter Boomgaard, *Frontiers of Fear: Tigers and People in the Malay World, 1600–1950* (New Haven: Yale University Press. 2001).

19. Jim Corbett. *Man-Eaters of Kumaon* (1944; reprinted Oxford: Oxford University Press 1993).

20. Dale Peterson, *Eating Apes* (Berkeley: University of California Press, 2003).

21. Raymond Coppinger and Lorna Coppinger. *Dogs: A New Understanding of Canine Origin, Behavior, and Evolution* (Chicago: University of Chicago Press, 2001). For an alternative view, see Juliet Clutton-Brock, A *Natural History of Domesticated Mammals* (Cambridge: Cambridge University Press 1987), chapter 3.

22. For example William McNeill and John R. McNeill, *The Human Web: A Bird's-Eye View of World History* (New York: W.W. Norton, 2003); Alfred W. Crosby, *Ecological Imperialism: The Biological Expansion of Europe, 900–1900* (Cambridge: Cambridge University Press. 1986); and Jared Diamond, *Guns, Germs, and Steel: The Fates of Human Societies* (New York: W.W. Norton 1997).

23. For overviews of the relation between humans and other animals as mediated by disease, see Lise Wilkinson, *Animals and Disease: An Introduction to the History of Comparative Medicine* (Cambridge: Cambridge University Press 1992); and Joanna Swabe, *Animals, Disease and Human Society: Human-Animal Relations and the Rise of Veterinary Medicine* (London: Routledge 1999).

24. Classically, in William McNeill, *Plagues and Peoples* (New York: Anchor 1976).

25. The process that began in 1492 or thereabouts arguably continued until the flu pandemic of 1918. For a description of that event, see Alfred W. Crosby, *America's Forgotten Pandemic: The Influenza of 1918* (Cambridge: Cambridge University Press 1990); and Gina Kolata, *Flu: The Story of the Great Influenza Pandemic of 1918 and the Search for the Virus that Caused It* (New York: Farrar, Straus & Giroux. 1999).

26. David S. Jones. *Nationalizing Epidemics: Meanings and Uses of American Indian Mortality since 1600* (Cambridge MA: Harvard University Press, 2004), chs. 1–2. For the standard explanation, see Alfred W. Crosby, *The Columbian Exchange: Biological and Cultural Consequences of 1492* (1973; reprinted Westport, CT: Praeger, 2003). While the fact of population decline is uncontested, the extent of the demographic disaster is highly controversial, on historical, scientific, and political grounds, as Krech explains in *Ecological Indian*, chapter 3.

27. Elinor G. K. Melville, A *Plague of Sheep: Environmental Consequences of the Conquest of Mexico* (Cambridge: Cambridge University Press 1994).

28. For a scientific discussion of BSE, see Pierre-Marie Lledo, *Histoire de la vache folle* (Paris: Presses Universitaires de France, 2001).

29. For an account of BSE in Britain, see Harriet Ritvo, "Mad Cow Mysteries," *American Scholar* (Spring 1998): 113–22.

30. Clutton-Brock, *Natural History* of *Domesticated Mammals,* chapter 1.

31. Charles Darwin, *On the Origin of Species* (1859; reprinted Cambridge MA: Harvard University Press 1964), chapter 1. Darwin later wrote a very long book dealing exclusively with this subject: *The Variation* of *Animals and Plants under Domestication,* 2 vols. (1868; reprinted Baltimore: Johns Hopkins University Press, 1998).

32. For accounts of early breeding, see Nicholas Russell, *Like Engend'ring Like: Heredity and Animal Breeding in Early Modem England* (Cambridge: Cambridge University Press 1986); Harriet Ritvo, "Possessing Mother Nature: Genetic Capital in 18th. Century Britain," in *Early Modern Conceptions of Property,* ed. Susan Staves and John Brewer (London: Routledge 1994), 413–26; and Ritvo, *Animal Estate,* chapter 2.

33. Modern breeding efforts are discussed in Margaret E. Derry, *Bred for Perfection: Shorthorn Cattle, Collies, and Arabian Horses since 1800* (Baltimore: Johns Hopkins University Press, 2003); and Tim Birkhead, *A Brand New Bird: How Two Amateur Scientists Created the First Genetically Engineered Animal* (New York: Basic Books, 2003).

34. On the development of modern abattoirs, see Nöelie Vialles, *Animal to Edible,* trans. J. A. Underwood (Cambridge: Cambridge University Press 1994).

35. See David Herlihy, *The Black Death and the Transformation of the West* (Cambridge: Harvard University Press 1997), introduction and chapter 1.

36. Keith Thomas has discussed the development of the association between animals and nature in *Man and the Natural World: A History of the Modem Sensibility* (New York: Pantheon 1983), especially in chapters 3, 4, and 6.

37. Carolus Linnaeus, *Systema Naturae: Regnum Animale* (1758; reprinted London: British Museum [Natural History] 1956).

38. For an extended discussion of eighteenth- and nineteenth-century hybrids and crossbreeds, see Harriet Ritvo, *The Platypus and the Mermaid, and Other Figments of the Classifying Imagination* (Cambridge MA: Harvard University Press 1997), chapter 3.

39. Charles Darwin, *The Descent of Man* (1871; reprinted New York: Modern Library 1950), 919.

16

YI-FU TUAN

Animal Pets: Cruelty and Affection*

Yi-Fu Tuan is considered the father of humanistic geography. One of the most influential scholars of our time, Tuan has reshaped how we think about culture and nature. While he spent his early childhood in China surrounded by war and poverty, Tuan emerged from the experience with intellectual ambition, compassion, and a "yearning for the great triad" – the True, the Beautiful, and the Good. Over his 30-year career as an academic (and a self-described maverick), he has written 10 books and numerous essays on "systematic human geography," a way of thinking about how politics, culture and the economy shape human interaction with the environment. Influenced by phenomenology (thus opposed to naturalism or objectivism), Tuan made the concept of "place" (locality, landscape, territory) central to the study of human geography. We reproduce a chapter from Tuan's influential book, *Dominance and Affection: The Making of Pets*, in which he argues that domestication means domination. He is concerned with how aesthetic exploitation, or the mistreatment of nature, is particularly cruel when it is considered "playful." Tuan labels a variety of things as "playthings" or "pets," such as water displayed in showy fountains and the diminutive "penjing" and "bonsai" gardens (domesticated by the "exquisite means of torture"). In this extract, Tuan examines the "petrification" of animals, with a focus on goldfish and dogs, and describes their domestication, manipulation and domination by humans as acts that combine cruelty and affection.

[...] consider two well-documented animals, the goldfish and the dog, the one bred purely as an animal pet and the other for a variety of reasons. Since the nineteenth century, the goldfish has become one of the most popular pets in the world, and nowhere more so than in its earliest homes – China and Japan. No Chinese home is complete without a *chin-yü*, which might be housed in a muddy pond or, at the other extreme, in a carved ivory and gilded aquarium. Every large marketplace in Japan has a *kingyo* stall at which connoisseurs of all ages discourse expertly on the relative merits of each specimen. In the Western world, almost every pet shop sells goldfish. Goldfish in small, glass bowls were at one time popular prizes at funfairs.

* Reproduced with permission of the publisher and from Yi-Fu Tuan (1984) *Dominance and Affection: The Making of Pets*. New Haven; London: Yale University Press. Copyright © 1984 by Yale University.

Now, at American county and agricultural fairs they may be given away in plastic bags. London backdoor hawkers used to exchange goldfish for old clothes. Although these practices have been on the wane since the 1930s, the use of the goldfish for interior decorations remains in favor. For a room furnished in the Oriental style, an aquarium stocked with black-colored Moors is considered an elegant touch. For a modem room, the aquarium may be chromium plated and stocked with an American breed known as the Comet, developed in the 1880s. In the 1930s, society hostesses fashionably substituted a bowl of goldfish for a bowl of flowers on their dining room table.[1]

The wild goldfish (*Carassius auratus*, or *chi yü*) is native to Chinese fresh waters. It is a greenish or grayish fish, not much esteemed as ornament but sold in markets as food. Red scales appear as a variant, and this striking color has been noted by the Chinese perhaps as early as the fourth century AD. Even in its natural state the goldfish displays a broad range of variations, a fact that the Chinese took advantage of when they decided to interbreed the abnormal specimens to produce varieties that appealed to their aesthetic sense and even to their appetite for the monstrous. Domestication is known to have begun early in the Sung dynasty (960–1279). By the year 1200, we have firm evidence of the existence of a fancy breed, described as having a snow-white body with black spots, beautiful markings, and a varnish-like luster. By the seventeenth century, the Chinese were breeding goldfish of many different colors in large quantities. In a work written in 1635, the two authors noted in detail the following colors and color combinations: deep red, lustrous white, white with ink spots, red with yellow spots, white with vermilion on the brow, vermilion with white on the spine, vermilion on the spine with seven white spots, white spine with eight red lines, and other banded varieties.

The shape of the body and of the fins and such anatomical details as the shape, size, and position of the eyes have undergone major changes during the sixteenth century and later. In the sixteenth century, goldfish with three, five, and even seven tails began to appear. Fish with compact and stunted bodies, known as the Egg Fish, emerged in the same period, as did the Telescope Fish, a variety with large, protuberant eyes. Ideally, the eyes of the Telescope Fish should be well-rounded, of equal size, and equally protuberant. However, it sometimes happens that only one eye bulges out in the desired manner, or that both bulge out but not equally. The Telescope Fish appears unable to adapt itself to the enlarged eyeballs. As an adult it is likely to injure them by swimming against hard objects and thus become blind.[2] Moreover, in a pond the protuberant balls may be sucked out by another fish. Minnows are notorious offenders in this regard. Among the more monstrous of the goldfish breeds is a latecomer, developed in Japan in the nineteenth century, widely known as the Lion-head, but also called the Hooded Goldfish, or the Buffalo-head in the United States and the Tomato-head in Germany. This breed is distinguished by wartlike excrescences that first emerge on the top of the head and then gradually spread downward over the cheeks and gill-covers, leaving only a small area under the mouth comparatively free. The excrescences are soft to the touch, and usually red, pink, or white in color. In the best specimens every excrescence is about the same size, and the fish has been aptly described as having an unripe raspberry for a head.

The goldfish is a pet. It has to be fed and cared for. As early as the tenth century, the monk Kao Tsan-ning wrote: "If goldfish eat the refuse of olives or soapy water then they die; if they have poplar bark they do not breed lice."[3] These lines provide evidence of the most careful observation and experimentation. It may be that monks who lived in large Buddhist estates with fine gardens have played an important role in breeding fancy goldfish. Emperors, we know, have enjoyed them as pets. Billardon de Sauvigny, in a tract on the goldfish first published in 1780, observes that the emperors make much of the fish and consider feeding them with their own hands among their daily amusements, but that nonetheless "it is the apartments of the women, where they are so much feted and lauded, petted and loved, that have made their fortune and spread them throughout the empire."[4]

For many centuries the Chinese people, high and low in society, have been able to enjoy the goldfish as pet. To the leisured class, however, it can also be treated as an art object. The fish in its aquarium, set upon a stool, is in its own world – one that does not impinge on ordinary human living space. In this respect, the goldfish differs from hard-to-confine pets, such as the dog, and is more like a potted plant or an inanimate work of art. The goldfish is also like an art object because new varieties can be produced so quickly through skilful human intervention. It occasionally happens that a fish fancier is so impatient that he bypasses the process of selective breeding altogether and seeks to impose change directly by dubious devices such as etching Chinese characters on the fish's body with acid or painting flower and other patterns on it.[5] Of course, it is fakery to offer such decorated pieces as the products of nature. Note, however, that this criticism cannot be directed at artifice itself, for the process of mating to produce the right breeds is at least as manipulative. Here, for example, is a semitechnical account of how to hand-spawn goldfish.

A mature male and female goldfish are placed for from twelve to twenty-four hours in a medium-sized aquarium, with some aquatic plants. As soon as the female has shed a few eggs, the male is removed and the female taken in hand and allowed to wriggle. Squeezing her is not necessary. The wriggling results in the ejection of a large number of eggs, fully as many as are ejected in the normal way. As soon as all the eggs are shed, the female fish is placed aside, the water given a gentle stir, to distribute the eggs over the plants, and the male taken in the hand. By gently squeezing him in the anal region the sperms are ejected and carried by the same wave to fertilize the eggs. This method almost guarantees all the eggs being fertilized.[6]

Remember that the procedure, described above in such a dry manner, has no other aim than to produce something appealing and decorative.

It is an exercise in fantasy, another attempt to bend nature not so much to human needs as [to their] moods. Certainly the names given to the different breeds of goldfish are fanciful. Among those used by Chinese fanciers toward the end of the seventeenth century were: Seven Stars (a reference to the constellation *Ursa Major*), Eight Diagrams (a reference to divination), Lotus Terrace, Embroidered Coverlet, Eight Melon Seeds, Crane Pearl, Silver Saddle, and Red Dust.[7]

Goldfish is a special case of domestication, one that enjoys the advantage of being exceptionally well documented in literature and art for a period of one thousand years. The story of the goldfish is, of course, a mere detail in the broad sweep of the history of animal domestication, to which we will now turn. Domestication means domination: the two words have the same root sense of mastery over another being – of bringing it into one's house or domain. With a small animal like the goldfish, domination is not a problem. People can always control and play with it. Training is not in question. Although there are stories of how fish have been trained to respond to the call of a single master or mistress, the ability to perform on cue is not essential to its standing as a pet. Because fishes are confined to ponds and aquariums they cannot be a nuisance. The one real challenge, then, lies in altering their shape rather than their behavior. With large land animals, domination must be established if they are to be used or enjoyed. Certain large mammals can be tamed without domestication (where *domestication* means altering the genetic constitution of a species through selective breeding). Elephants, the largest land mammal, are an example. Although not domesticated, they are easily tameable. They have been trained to do everything from hauling timber to standing on their hind legs, wearing a petticoat, for the amusement of circus spectators.[8] Apart from the inherent difficulties of breeding elephants, which have a long gestation period followed by a long period of immaturity, there was no compelling need for humans to alter and control them by such means. With most other large animals, there was such need. Humans have found it necessary to tinker with their biological makeup because, unless this was done, such animals could not be tamed easily and, moreover, remain tame through their adult lives.

What were the directions of change? How have humans established their dominance over beasts that in a wild state were too large and fierce to be manageable? One direction of change was toward diminished size. A large animal was reduced to a smaller one – to a pet, the literal meaning of which is "small." Animal domestication began in prehistoric times, more than 10,000 years ago. One criterion by which archaeologists are able to tell whether the skeletons found at a prehistoric settlement belong to a domesticated species is size. How was the reduction effected? Could it have been deliberate? Even when attempts at control and taming were deliberate, the reduced size might have come about by more or less accidental means. At least this is the view of F. E. Zeuner, who thinks that farmers in early Neolithic times lacked the knowledge to bring about a diminishment in the size of large bovines in a calculated manner. Rather, he believes that something like the following sequence of events happened. Contact with humans first occurred when wild bovines, as was their wont, began to rob the fields. The farmers, already experienced with such domesticated species as the dog, the sheep, and the goat, took tentative steps to induct the bovines into the human fold. One step in that direction was to capture the young individuals and keep them as pets around camp. Some of these appealing captives were surely treated with kindness, but they could not as a whole have received consistent attention and care. Neolithic farmers, who made only modest demands on themselves for housing and food, were unlikely to provide the best possible living conditions for their captives. Animals thus kept deteriorated in health. Compared with their wild ancestors, their progenies became smaller and weaker and hence also more docile. Throughout the Neolithic period, the size of cattle decreased until, during the Iron Age, specimens were bred that would be considered dwarfs by modern standards. The height of their withers was little more than a meter.[9]

Manageability or control was the real aim. The smaller size helped. Another device, more direct and perhaps practiced as early as Neolithic times, was castration, which made the male animals more docile. Cutting off the testes of some specimens and not others meant that humans could and did interfere directly with the breeding process. In time, they gained mastery over even the large bovine. Once an animal became fully domesticated and docile, humans could deliberately seek ways to alter it so that it was even more useful and pleasing to them. They might try to make their cattle larger so as to yield more meat or be better draft animals without, however, making them at the same time more fierce; and they might try to lengthen and alter the shape of the horns for religious reasons. With the horse, in a later stage of domestication history, humans have tried to make the animal both larger and smaller. Thus we have now at one extreme Shire horses and at the other extreme Shetland ponies. Certain aesthetic criteria probably also applied. In wild horses as well as in asses and zebras the mane is short and stands erect rather than falling gracefully to one side as in all breeds of the domestic horse. Moreover, the domestic horse boasts a longer and more elegant tail.

All young animals are docile toward the adults of the species. It suits human purpose, therefore, to breed animals such that they retain juvenile anatomical and behavioral traits through their entire life span. Other than size, the retention of foetal and juvenile traits is used by archaeologists as a criterion for evaluating whether a particular skeleton belongs to a wild or a domesticated animal. Among juvenile traits are a shortening of the jaw and of the facial region. Dogs commonly display these characteristics, but so do other animals – sometimes to an exaggerated degree – as in certain breeds of pig (Middle White, for example) and in cattle such as the South American variety known as Niatu.[10] With the dog, reduction in the size of the muzzle results in smaller teeth. Not even the Great Dane and the Saint Bernard have teeth as large as those of their wild progenitor, the wolf, even though their body may be larger. Other juvenile traits in the domesticated dog are the short hair, curly tail, skin folds like the dewlap, and the hanging ears of many breeds. Hanging ears give the dog a conspicuously submissive look: think of the spaniel. Police dogs should have erect and pointed ears to avoid even the appearance of submission. Although docility is a desirable feature in a pet, it can become excessive. Fawning can be cloying and friendliness toward humans indiscriminate. Such behavioral traits, Konrad Lorenz believes, is a result of exaggerated infantilism. Dogs of this kind "are always over-playful, and long after their first year of life, when normal dogs have sobered down, they persist in chewing their master's shoes or shaking the curtains to death; above all, they retain a slave-like submission which in other dogs is supplanted after a few months by a healthy self-confidence."[11]

The impact of domestication on the dog merits a closer look for several reasons. One is that the dog is almost certainly the first animal to have been domesticated. In its long association with humans the dog has become diversified to an extraordinary degree, perhaps more so than any other animal species. Moreover, in the Western world at least, the dog is the pet par excellence. It exhibits uniquely a set of relationships we wish to explore: dominance and affection, love and abuse, cruelty and kindness. The dog calls forth, on the one hand, the best that a human person is capable of – self-sacrificing devotion to a weaker and dependent being, and, on the other hand, the temptation to exercise power in a wilful and arbitrary, even perverse, manner. Both traits can exist in the same person.

An outstanding fact about the dog, to the naked eye, is its variability. The range in size is so large that it is hard to believe that its members all belong to the same species; and indeed the largest dog cannot breed with the smallest one for obvious physical reasons. A Chihuahua may weigh 4 pounds and a full-grown Saint Bernard 160 pounds, or forty times as much.

Legs vary from the squat extremities of dachshunds to the long, graceful limbs of greyhounds and salukis. At opposite extremes we see the undershot jaws and foreshortened heads of bulldogs and pugs, and the long, narrow heads of the borzois. Tails vary from a tight curl to a sickle shape. Manifold variations in the color, length, and texture of hair exist and there is even a permanently bald breed, the Mexican hairless, contrasting with the poodle with its continuously growing hair.[12]

The wild relatives of the dog – the wolf, the coyote, and the jackal – also show wide ranges in size, but their ranges do not match that of the dog. Moreover, none of them exhibits the anatomical contrasts and differences in hair color and length that appear in the domesticated canines. There is not, for example, the equivalent of the dachshund and the borzois among wolves. Skeletons of dogs from Neolithic settlements reveal as yet little differentiation: they all resemble those of the modern Eskimo dog. By 3000 BC, however, distinct breeds were known in Mesopotamia: one was the heavy mastiff (a guard dog) and the other was the much more slender greyhound or saluki. From the art of ancient Egypt, we gather that several distinct varieties existed; and from the length of time covered by the representations and the consistency of type, we surmise that their distinctiveness was maintained with care.[13]

In Near Eastern antiquity, already, the dog was treated as an animal whose breeding line could be controlled and modified for human purposes. What were these purposes? What motivated humans to make changes in the breeding line? Foremost among the motivations, from antiquity to the modern period, was use – the use of the dog in hunting and as a guardian of the home. Dogs that helped the hunter were an instrument of survival. On the other hand, in agricultural civilizations hunting was relegated more and more to a subsidiary role in survival while taking on, increasingly, the status and function of a sport, not only among the elite but even – in time – among peasants. Thus, as early as the fourteenth century, farm laborers and servants in England might keep greyhounds and use them in hunting for sport, although no doubt they welcomed the game captured and killed as additions to their pantry.[14]

Once hunting became a specialized sport, the dog served as an instrument for attaining specific ends, defined by the nature of the sport but serving the larger general purpose of pleasure. Dogs that were at first only instruments of pleasure could later be the direct source of satisfaction whether as a status symbol or as a toy, or both. Nearly all the smaller dogs, which we now think of primarily as pets – playthings for the lap and boudoir – were once bred for hunting. Terriers, for example, derive their name from the French *terre* and were bred to creep into the ground and drive out small animals like foxes and badgers. They were known to English hunters at least as early as the sixteenth century. Spaniels originated in Spain and were used both for hawking and for hunting birds with nets. Richard Blome, writing in 1686, noted how the spaniel could be trained to "couch and lie close to the ground," then trained to lie still while a bird net was dragged across him, and then taught to associate lying down with the scent of a partridge. Toy breeds existed in the sixteenth century, and these later came to be known as King Charles spaniels. It is hard to see what purpose they served other than as pets. Loyalty was early recognized as one of their most distinctive traits. Thus Blome, in a book devoted to the recreational employment of dogs, nonetheless took space to write: "Spaniels by Nature are very loving, surpassing all other Creatures, for in Heat and Cold, Wet and Dry, Day and Night, they will not forsake their Master. There are many Prodigious Relations, made in several Grave and Credible Authors, of the strange Affections which Dogs have had, as well to their Dead and living Masters; but it is not my business to take notice of them here."[15]

The poodle is another example. It seems a frivolous and pampered creature that has no conceivable use other than as a plaything and a social symbol. Yet it was bred originally as a hunter. The word *poodle* comes from the German *pudeln* (to splash in water). It was and is used extensively by the French as a gun dog, and especially for duck hunts. A clipped poodle looks ridiculous.

What is called the lion clip (hair shorn from the back and hind parts so that the dog looks like a heavy-maned miniature lion) is more than three hundred years old; and far from being a mere playful fantasy the clipping was done to make it easier for the dog to progress through water. As for the ribbon tied to the hair on the head and on the tail, this too was done originally for a practical end, namely, so that the animal could be seen easily as it moved among the reeds. However, by the reign of Louis XVI (1774–92) the poodle had already become a fashionable pet in France. Poodle barbers practiced a lucrative trade along the banks of the Seine. They ingeniously shaved various patterns on these long-suffering animals, including true lovers' knots and monograms. Thus a topiary art was applied to the hair of an animal.[16]

One breed of dog that seems to have lost all connection to practical use, if it ever had any, is the Pekinese. It is hard to imagine how this hairy and cuddly dog, which could be as small as 4½ pounds, might have the wolf as a distant ancestor. Yet in anatomy and physiology, in internal and external parasites, the wolf and the Pekinese are remarkably alike. Unique in the Pekinese is its exceptional retention of such babyish traits as a very short facial region of the skull, large brain case, big eyes, short legs, curly tail, and soft fur. Juvenility makes it easy to train the Pekinese into a pet and performer. On the other hand, the animal is reputed to be highly intelligent and independent. This combination of virtues, together with the appeal of its babyish features, accounts for the popularity of the Pekinese among European toy dog fanciers ever since it was introduced from China in the nineteenth century.

The story of the Pekinese in China is unclear. Writers on the subject differ widely as to when the breed appeared.[17] Miniature dogs were known in China by the first century AD. They could be fitted under the table, which during the Han dynasty had very short legs. Small dogs were in vogue at court during the T'ang dynasty (618–907). Some of these were probably the Maltese type brought into China from Fu Lin or Byzantium. The prestige of these small hairy dogs, whether they were Maltese or proto-Pekinese, received a boost when they came to be associated with the legend of Buddha's lion. Lamaist Buddhism focused on the lion as a symbol of passion which Buddha was able to subdue; the subdued passion, in the shape of a diminutive lion, trotted by Buddha's heels like a pet. Kublai Khan (1215–94), as emperor of China, favored Lamaist Buddhism. Lions were a part of his menagerie, and a tame lion or two even roamed his court. About this time the expression "lion dog" came into use. Dog of a certain type served as an emblem of the lion, acquiring its prestige as a mighty beast but also the prestige of that beast's association with Buddha. Were the Pekinese, then, a popular pet during the Yuan dynasty? We do not know. We do know that they flourished during the Manchu (Ch'ing) dynasty (1644–1911). Art works dating from the early K'ang-hsi (1662–1722) to the late Tao Kuang period (1821–50) clearly depict the Pekinese as well as other breeds of dogs. All Manchu rulers appear to have been partial to the Pekinese. They also favored the idea of the Pekinese as lion dog because of the implied comparison between themselves and Buddha.

To Chinese fanciers, the ideal Pekinese should have round cheeks "like dumplings." Their eyes should be large and somewhat protuberant, like those of a goldfish. The front legs were to be short, not straight and sticklike; they were to be shorter than the hind legs, with the intention of producing a rolling gait, the movement of a "plentifully finned goldfish."[18] Thus the Pekinese was compared not only with the lion but also with the goldfish, that other favored pet among the Chinese. The comparison with goldfish implies the desirability of traits opposite to those of a lion: the Pekinese should be diminutive in size – an animal that one could handle as one would a small toy. Manchu breeders sought to produce specimens of tiny size such that they could be tucked into the sleeves of women's coats. During Tao Kuang emperor's reign, unscrupulous men tried to stunt the growth of the Pekinese through the use of drugs and various manipulative devices. Dowager Empress Tsu-hsi (1834–1908), who took her sobriquet of "Old Buddha" seriously, discouraged these practices while promoting the achievement of the same end through inbreeding. She was not very successful. Knavish fanciers continued to alter the size and shape of the Pekinese by devious means. One method lay in curtailing the exercise a dog should have over the period from the third month to maturity, with the aim of reducing its appetite and food consumption and hence rate of growth. A pup might be put in a close-fitting wire cage and kept there until it had reached maturity. Another method lay in holding a pup in the hand for days at a time, inducing by gentle pressure of the fingers a slight exaggeration of width between the shoulders. To achieve the desired result of a small snub nose, some owners broke the cartilage of the nose with their thumbnail or with a chopstick when the pup was from three to seven days old. Others massaged the nose daily in the hope of restraining its growth.[19]

Imperial patrons and respectable society frowned on all these practices for their cruelty but also because they were illegitimate shortcuts. The approved method was the slow one of selective breeding. In the case of the Pekinese, this procedure had been applied under the patronage of Manchu emperors and the supervision of chief eunuchs over a period of several hundred years. The result was an appealing, healthy, and intelligent animal that was capable of performing all sorts of tricks and of living to the ripe old age of 25 years.

Dogs, then, can be bred to some arbitrarily constructed standard without doing damage to their health and liveliness. On the other hand, examples can readily be cited of purebred dogs that do suffer from genetic and physiologic deterioration. The basic problem can be stated simply. It is rarely possible to breed a dog to arbitrary criteria of beauty and appeal and still have it retain functional vigor and intelligence. As Konrad Lorenz has pointed out, "Circus dogs which can perform complicated tricks demanding great intelligence are very rarely equipped with a pedigree; this is not because the 'poor' artists are unable to pay the price of a well bred dog – for fabulous fees are paid for talented circus dogs – but because it is mental rather than physical qualities that make good performing animals." As one example of rapid degeneration, among many that can be cited, Lorenz mentions the Chow. In the early 1920s, Chows were still natural dogs whose pointed muzzles, obliquely set Mongolian eyes, and pointed, erect ears called to mind their wolf-blooded ancestors. Modern breeding of the Chow, however, has "led to an exaggeration of those points which gives him the appearance of a plump bear: the muzzle is wide and short ... the eyes have lost their slant in the compression of the whole face, and the ears have almost disappeared in the overgrown thickness of the coat. Mentally too, these temperamental creatures, which still bore a trace of the wild beast of prey, have become stodgy teddy bears."[20]

An animal may lose much of its natural vigor and still be serviceable as a pet. It is even desirable that a pet not be endowed with too much vigor and initiative. The pet, if it is to find acceptance in a well-run household, must learn to be immobile – to be as unobtrusive as a piece of furniture. The single most important trick taught a dog is instant obedience to the order "sit" or "lie down." A well-trained dog will lie down for hours at a stretch, upon command, even in a strange place, while its master goes off on business. The ability to stay put is a necessity in a hunting dog and it is clearly a great convenience to humans in a busy, modern household, where time is tightly organized. However, to some people, a dog's submission to command is desirable in itself. Power over another being is demonstrably firm and perversely delicious when it is exercised for no particular purpose and when submission to it goes against the victim's own strong desires and nature. Dog shows cater to the usual human vanity and competitiveness, but they also provide the occasion and the excuse to demonstrate openly and to public applause the power to dominate and humble another being. Here is an account of a dog obedience show which the author offers

in all innocence but which may well serve as a prime example of refined cruelty.

Perhaps the hardest test required that the dog should be brought into the ring hungry and, when given a plate of his favourite food, sit by it until he was told to eat; the time was four minutes and the owner had to go out of sight, leaving the dog alone with his tempting plate. Hundreds of people were watching when, on one occasion, Beeswing [a tiny Pekinese] came into the ring. He was ravenous and the four minutes must have seemed interminable; he endured for two and then, without moving from his post, slowly got up and, in Miss Cynthia's words, "sat on his bottom and begged." The crowd roared but he did not move a muscle. He had not broken the rules but instead of sitting on four legs sat on two; after another two minutes the judge called her; Beeswing saw his mistress come into the ring but knew he still must not move as she walked up and stood beside him. She had to wait for the word from the judge. It came, she released Beeswing who literally jumped on the food and gobbled it.[21]

In modern society, the owner of a dog may have someone else do the disciplining and training. He enjoys the product – a docile and friendly pet. The harsh story behind the making of a pet is forgotten. And the story must be harsh because the basis of all successful training is the display of an unchallengeable power. The dog must not be in doubt as to who is the master and as to the consequences of disobedience. Another repressed side of the story, so far as a genteel buyer-owner is concerned, are the processes of mating and breeding. These processes are either subsumed under "pedigree," when the past is in question, or steps to be taken under the supervision of specialists, when the progeny or future is in question. Breeding animals to achieve and maintain certain traits calls for an indifference to individual lives that is suggestive of nature's own vast wastefulness. "As soon as the bitch hath littered," explains a seventeenth-century English handbook, "it is requisite to choose them you intend to preserve, and throwaway the rest;" and the kennel book of a Yorkshire dog-breeder

(1691–1720) contains such laconic entries as, "three of this litter given to Br. Thornhill, the rest hanged, because not liked."[22] A modern breeder is well aware of the perils of inbreeding, which must nonetheless be carried through to fix a pattern. "Nature uses it extremely," one twentieth-century specialist on the subject says, "but nature is harsh and, if it leads to deterioration, nature has no mercy." The breeder must also show no mercy. He must be scientific and cruel in his play. He "must watch the effect of inbreeding as if through a microscope, and at the very first sign of deleterious effects, not only down must come the guillotine, but the litter that showed them must be destroyed: a step too far has been taken, a step back is necessary."[23]

Mating with the aim to produce progeny of a certain kind is, of course, a highly calculative and manipulative process. We have seen how the goldfish might be handled to produce the desired effect. A much larger literature, which reads at times like a laboratory manual and at times like pornography, exists for canines. That compelling desire to intervene decisively in the life of another finds a certain satisfaction in dog breeding. Life's urges and processes are, however, often imprecise; the breeder encounters difficulties that must be overcome. One is the time to mate, which varies with different breeds, within the same breed, and "even between individual bitches bred from the same parents. Dogs, also, vary in their attitude toward in-season bitches. Many will not touch a bitch until the red discharge has ceased. Some will mate a bitch at any time, if the bitch herself will permit it." Often she will not permit it. She has someone else in mind other than the well-groomed mate chosen by the breeder. Waiting for her to relent is useless. Force has to be applied. An expert advises: "Get a good firm grip on her ears. Someone else should then put a hand underneath her to steady her for the dog. With the other hand, a little helpful push at the right moment behind the dog might make all the difference. Steady him whilst he is tying the bitch; then when you are quite sure that the tying has taken place, gently turn him round, back to back with the bitch."[24] To ease

the process of mating, it may even be necessary to put vaseline on the vagina and take the dog's member "into the palm of one's hand and exert a slight warming pressure." At unscrupulous kennels, where breeding is a profitable business, bitches that do not show willingness are helped, and if they resist the help, they are forced, that is, muzzled and put into a sling to prevent them from resisting.[25]

The procedures just sketched are the impolite backstage activities. In front, for all to see, are the owners and their pets. How do people relate to the animals they keep in their house? How have attitudes changed in the course of time? Was affection – that personal involvement with the welfare of an individual animal – a common element of the bond? To these large questions I can provide here only suggestive answers. The key question for us, namely, the importance of affection in the bond, is also the most elusive for historical periods. That dogs have been highly valued pets since ancient times is beyond dispute. For example, remains of small dogs have been discovered in the tombs of Egyptian pharaohs, dating back to 2000 BC. One specimen had ivory bracelets on its legs, and others had collars of twisted leather. The teeth of many of these dogs were in bad condition, which indicates that they suffered from pyorrhoea – a consequence of being fed soft food.[26] In China, dogs were treasured and pampered by many emperors, notably by Ling Ti (168–90), whose favorites were given official titles; they ate the choicest rice and meat and slept on costly carpets.

On both sides of the Eurasian continent, historical records abundantly attest to the importance of the dog in high society. Difficult to ascertain now is the precise character of the relationship between master or mistress and pet. Without doubt, fine breeds served as a symbol of social worth. They were protected and treated with as much care as other precious possessions. However, unlike other possessions, the animal offered entertainment; it could be picked up and played with or used in some way (as a rug or hand warmer, for instance); and it could be put aside anytime, even kicked aside, when one's mood changed. Hints have come down to us that in the past, as in the present, pets served a wide variety of purposes, that they could be a source of pride and yet treated with cruel arbitrariness, that even when human affection toward them was genuine and strong it was more likely to be directed to a type or breed than to particular individuals. Roman ladies were fond of little dogs. Pliny the Elder observed, however, that they also served a practical purpose. "As touching the pretty little dogs that our dainty dames make so much of, called Meltaei in Latin, if they be ever and anon kept close unto the stomach, they ease the pain thereof."[27] Alcibiades possessed a large and beautiful dog, noted in particular for its long, feathered tail. It was an animal he could be proud of and which he surely valued, and yet, according to Plutarch, he caused the tail to be cut off so that the Athenians might focus on this eccentricity of behavior rather than on something worse.[28] The behavior *was* eccentric and intended to shock. Still, we may wonder whether an attitude of indifference, interspersed with bursts of effusive attention, was not rather common for his time – and, indeed, of what historical period would this attitude toward animals be untrue?

From the Renaissance period onward, portraits of notables often show a dog or two, sometimes prominently placed in the center foreground, along with other precious possessions – rich fabrics, furnishings, and glimpses of landscape and landed property – all drawn with attention to detail so as to suggest their material substance and tangibility. The dogs in such a world were certainly valued, but did they, individually, capture the affection of their master or mistress? Were they, for example, given personal names? In general, probably not. Thus G. S. Thomson, who studied the household of the fifth earl of Bedford at Woburn Abbey as it existed in the second half of the seventeenth century, has this to say:

Many a dog appeared with his master or mistress in the portraits on the walls of the gallery at Woburn. Chiefly, these were spaniels, but one painting at least of the Earl himself, not at Woburn but at Chatsworth, shows a beautiful coursing greyhound standing by his master's side. But to be put into a picture was the only tribute paid to the dogs. No dog in the accounts, whether a spaniel or a coursing hound, is ever mentioned by name, or assumes the individuality of Tomson, the hawk. The entries are always on purely general lines–so many dogs to be fed and looked after.[29]

Fox hunting became a popular sport among aristocrats and the squirearchy in seventeenth-century England and continued to be so for the next two hundred years. The social flavor of the sport had not a little to do with the hunters' sartorial discrimination and with the presence of fine horses and dogs, which in the eighteenth century might well live in quarters more substantial than those of common laborers or of the servants who took care of them. And yet horses and hounds could also be treated harshly – whipped or kicked – when their masters and mistresses saw fit to do so, in a foul mood or in the heat of a chase. After a day in the field, wrote a riding-master in 1655, it "would pity the heart of him who loveth a horse to see them so bemired, blooded, spurred, lamentably spent, tired out." When worn out they were quickly discarded.[30]

Wherever animals were kept and brought up around the home compound, genuine affection toward them would develop, if only temporarily and sporadically, if only by the women who nurtured them and by young children who hugged and played with them. In Europe, society as a whole seemed to show a warmer feeling toward domestic animals from the seventeenth century onward. Dutch genre paintings of the period support this view. Whether the paintings are of landscapes or of house interiors, the dog is a common and conspicuous figure. Furthermore, just as the people and the interiors shown lack pretension – they are of the bourgeoisie and of low life – so the dogs depicted are not the prized possessions, the emblems of rank and wealth, but well-fed household animals and the mangier specimens of the countryside and the streets. Dogs in a bourgeois household were members of the family, participants in its daily round of activities as well as in its more festive occasions, and valued as such rather than for their pedigree.[31] There was sentiment, but of an unselfconscious and practical kind. More effusive sentiment – the hothouse product of a softer city life – emerged later, in the early decades of the nineteenth century. It was then that maudlin dog books began to reach many readers. Joseph Taylor's *The General Character of the Dog*, first published in 1804, enjoyed enough success to warrant two sequels, *Canine Gratitude* in 1806 and *Four-Footed Friends* in 1828. Schoolchildren were besieged by storybooks preaching kindness to animals.[32] In the same period appeared the immensely popular animal pictures of Edwin Landseer. Unlike the dogs drawn by such past masters as Paolo Veronese, Titian, and Velasquez, which showed the animals as they were engaged in their own thoughts and business, Landseer's dogs were drenched in human feelings and morality.

This highly sentimentalized view of animals was uniquely developed in western Europe and, later, in North America. What were the contributory causes? One general cause was simply the growing distance between people and nature. Wild animals and even farm animals were becoming less and less the common experience of men and women in an increasingly urbanized and industrialized society. It was easy to entertain warm feelings toward animals that seemed to have no other function than as playthings. Moreover, humans needed an outlet for their gestures of affection and this was becoming more difficult to find in modern society as it began to segment and isolate people into their private spheres, to discourage casual physical contact, and to frown upon the enormously satisfying stances of patronage, such as laying one's hand on another's shoulder.

To appreciate the *depth* of the bond between individual humans and their animals, we do well to read the numerous personal stories that have been recorded at different times and places. From antiquity, for example, are the well-known accounts of the devotion of Alexander the Great to his horse Bucephalus. He once risked war with an aggressive mountain tribe, the Mardians, when they abducted his horse. Alexander hand-reared his favorite dog, Peritas. At least one town in central Asia was named after the dog; in addition, a monument was built to its honor. With the world at their feet, potentates still seemed to need the blind devotion of animals, and to the animals they in turn might show the utmost concern and affection. Thus Louis XIV, to whom men and women constantly deferred, yet required the company of his setter bitches and always had seven or eight in his rooms. He fed them with his own hands so that they could learn to know him. Thomas Carlyle in his biography of Frederick the Great tells several stories of the king's tender feelings for his dogs. He is reported to have been found "sitting on the ground with a big platter of fried meat, from which he was feeding his dogs. He had a little rod, with which he kept order among them, and shoved the best bits to his favourites." In 1774, "wrapped in solitude, the King shut himself up in Sans Souci with his dogs, and afterwards he asked to be buried under the terrace of this little summer palace at Potsdam among his dogs." As he lay on his deathbed in 1786, he noticed that his greyhound bitch, which lay on a stool by his bed, was shivering. "Throw a quilt over it," he said, and they were probably his last words on earth.[33]

A tender romance of our time is that between the lonely writer T. H. White and his dog, a red setter named Brownie. The romance started coolly on White's part. He recalled how at first he thought of his pet as simply "the dog," rather as one thinks of "the chair" or "the umbrella." "Setters," he said, "are beautiful to look at. I had a beautiful motor car and sometimes I wore a beautiful top hat. I felt that 'the dog' would suit me nearly as nicely as the hat did." This casual appreciation deepened later into love. Brownie's near fatal sickness and White's nursing the setter back to health triggered the change. When, after eleven years of companionship, the dog did die, White wrote to David Garnett: "I stayed with the grave for a week, so that I could go out twice a day and say, 'Good girl: sleepy girl: go to sleep, Brownie.' It was a saying she understood ... Then I went to Dublin, against my will, and kept myself as drunk as possible for nine days, and came back feeling more alive than dead." More alive than dead. White, obviously, had to keep on living. Even before burial, when Brownie's body was still by his side, he wondered whether he should buy another dog or not. He pondered in a practical manner: "I *might* live another 30 years, which would be two dogs' lifetimes ... and of course they hamper one very much when one loves them so desperately."[34]

Konrad Lorenz, in his book *Man Meets Dog*, makes two points that may serve as defining the limits of human affection. One is the lingering tendency to treat even a valued pet as a convenience. Lorenz puts it thus: "If I ask a man who has just been boasting of the prowess and other wonderful properties of one of his dogs, I always ask him whether he has still got the animal. The answer is all too often ... 'No, I had to get rid of him – I moved to another town – or into a smaller house.'" In this regard, it is significant that the mean age of household pets in California is only 4.4 years, with more than half being under 3 years. Household dogs are well looked after and yet they rarely grow old in the human family: they are disposed of long before they reach a ripe old age. The second point that Lorenz raises touches on the individuality of an animal. The death of a faithful dog may cause as much grief as the death of a beloved person. But Lorenz says, there is one essential detail that makes the former event easier to bear:

The place which the human friend filled in your life remains for ever empty; that of your dog can be filled with a substitute. Dogs are indeed individuals, personalities in the truest sense of the word and I should be the last to deny this fact, but they are much more like each other than are human beings ... In those deep instinctive feelings which are responsible for their special relationship with man, dogs resemble each other closely, and if on the death of one's dog one immediately adopts a puppy of the same breed, one will generally find

that he refills those spaces in one's heart and one's life which the departure of an old friend has left desolate.[35]

NOTES

1. George F. Hervey and Jack Hems, *The Goldfish* (London: Faber and Faber, 1968), 248–49. I have depended on this work for the section on goldfish.
2. *Japanese Goldfish: Their Varieties and Cultivation* (Washington, D.C.: W. F. Roberts, 1909), 37.
3. Quoted by Hervey and Hems, *Goldfish,* 77.
4. George Hervey, *The Goldfish of China in the Eighteenth Century* (London: The China Society, 1950), 33.
5. Ibid., 26.
6. Hervey and Hems, *Goldfish*, 228.
7. Ibid., 240.
8. H. H. Scullard, *The Elephant in the Greek and Roman World* (Ithaca: Cornell University Press, 1974), 250–59.
9. Frederick E. Zeuner, *A History of Domesticated Animals* (New York: Harper and Row, 1963), 36–43, 46–49, 51–63.
10. Juliet Clutton-Brock, *Domesticated Animals from Early Times* (Austin: University of Texas Press, 1981), 22–24.
11. Konrad Lorenz, *Man Meets Dog* (Harmondsworth: Penguin, 1964), 24.
12. John Paul Scott and John L. Fuller, *Genetics and the Social Behavior of the Dog* (Chicago: University of Chicago Press, 1965), 29.
13. M. Hilzheimer, *Animal Remains from Tell Asmar,* Studies in Ancient Oriental Civilization, no. 20 (Chicago: University of Chicago Press, 1941); P. E. Newberry, Beni Hasan, part I, in F. L. Griffeth, ed., *Archaeological Survey of Egypt,* Egypt Exploration Fund (London: Kegan Paul, Trubner Co., 1893).
14. G. M. Trevelyan, *English Social History* (London: Longman, Green, 1942), 22–23.
15. Richard Blome, *The Gentlemans Recreation* (London: S. Roycroft, 1686), quoted in Scott and Fuller, *Social Behavior of the Dog,* 46–47.
16. Grace E. L. Boyd, "Poodle," in *The Book of the Dog,* ed. Brian Vesey-Fitzgerald (London: Nicholson and Watson, 1948), 598–99.
17. V. W. F. Collier, *Dogs of China and Japan in Nature and Art* (New York: Fredrick A. Stokes,

1921); Annie Coath Dixey, *The Lion Dog of Peking* (London: Peter Davies, 1931); Clifford L. B. Hubbard, "Pekinese," in Vesey-Fitzgerald, *Book of the Dog*, 583–86.

18. Rumer Godden, *The Butterfly Lions: The Pekinese in History, Legend and Art* (New York: Viking, 1978), 137.

19. Collier, *Dogs of China and Japan*, 53–54.

20. Lorenz, *Man Meets Dog*, 88–90.

21. Godden, *Butterfly Lions*, 159.

22. Nicholas Cox, *The Gentleman's Recreation* (1677; reprint, East Ardsley, 1973); quoted in Keith Thomas, *Man and the Natural World: A History of Modern Sensibility* (New York: Pantheon, 1983), 60.

23. W. L. McCandlish, "Breeding for Show," in Vesey-Fitzgerald, *Book of the Dog*, 84.

24. Winnie Barber, "The Canine Cult," in ibid., 105.

25. J. R. Ackerley, *My Dog Tulip* (New York: Fleet, 1965), 68, 77, 84.

26. A. Croxton-Smith, "The Dog in History," in Vesey-Fitzgerald, *Book of the Dog*, 24.

27. *Pliny's Natural History* in *Philemon Holland's Translation*, P. Turner, ed. (London: Centaur, 1962), 316.

28. "Alcibiades," in *Plutarch's Lives* (New York: Modern Library, n.d.), 238.

29. Gladys Scott Thomson, *Life in a Noble Household 1641–1700* (London: Jonathan Cape, 1937), 234.

30. Thomas de Grey, *The Compleat Horse-Man*, 3d edn, 1656; quoted in K. Thomas, *Man and the Natural World*, 100; see Trevelyan, *English Social History*, 280–81, 406–07.

31. Brian Vesey-Fitzgerald, *The Domestic Dog: An Introduction to Its History* (London: Routledge & Kegan Paul, 1957), 67.

32. Turner, *Reckoning with the Beast*, 19.

33. Mary Renault, *The Nature of Alexander* (Harmondsworth: Penguin, 1983), 158, 168; Lucy Norton, *Saint-Simon at Versailles* (London: Hamish Hamilton, 1958), 260; Thomas Carlyle, *History of Friedrich II of Prussia called Frederick the Great*, ed. John Clive (Chicago: University of Chicago Press, 1969), 469.

34. Sylvia Townsend Warner, *T. H. White* (London: Jonathan Cape, 1967), 72, 211–13.

35. Lorenz, *Man Meets Dog*, 138–39, 194–95.

17

PLUTARCH

The Eating of Flesh*

Plutarch (Mestrius Plutarchus) was born in a small town in Greece in the first century CE. Over his approximately 80-year lifetime, he was a historian, a philosopher, a biographer and a priest at the Oracle of Delphi. He also studied mathematics and rhetoric, and left a large collection of writings that have been very influential on later scholars, including Montaigne who drew inspiration from Plutarch's Moralia (Moral Essays). We reproduce one of Plutarch from his Moralia, "The Eating of Flesh," in which he discusses the ethical and social issues related to eating animals. The essay begins with reference to the Greek scholar Pythagoras' abstention from eating meat. Pythagoras is reported to have objected to meat-eating because he believed humans had a kinship with other animals, and he had a large following who abstained from eating meat. [Before the term "vegetarian" was coined, those who did not consume animals were called Pythagoreans.] Instead of explaining and justifying why Pythagoras did not eat meat, Plutarch questions how the practice of consuming animals began in the first place. He points to human physiology (such as how slowly the human stomach digests food) as evidence that the consumption of animals by humans is unnatural. He further argues that the consequences of consuming animals extend beyond the biological into the social realm, proposing that the slaughter of animals inclines humans toward the destruction of each other. Plutarch was one of the first to articulate the connection between humanity's victimization of animals and human social problems.

TRACT I

You ask of me then for what reason it was that Pythagoras abstained from eating of flesh. I for my part do much wonder in what humor, with what soul or reason, the first man with his mouth touched slaughter, and reached to his lips the flesh of a dead animal, and having set before people courses of ghastly corpses and ghosts, could give those parts the names of meat and victuals, that but a little before lowed, cried, moved, and saw; how his sight could endure the blood of slaughtered, flayed, and mangled bodies; how his smell could bear their scent; and how the very nastiness happened not to offend the taste, while it chewed the sores of others,

* These extracts are in the public domain and are reprinted from Plutarch's *The Complete Works Volume 3, Essays and Miscellanies*, obtained from eBooks@Adelaide, The University of Adelaide Library, at the following website: http://etext. library.adelaide.edu.au/p/plutarch/essays/complete.html.

and participated of the saps and juices of deadly wounds.

Crept the raw hides, and with a bellowing sound
Roared the dead limbs; the burning entrails groaned.

("Odyssey," xii. 395)

This indeed is but a fiction and fancy; but the fare itself is truly monstrous and prodigious, – that a man should have a stomach to creatures while they yet bellow, and that he should be giving directions which of things yet alive and speaking is fittest to make food of, and ordering the several kinds of the seasoning and dressing them and serving them up to tables. You ought rather, in my opinion, to have inquired who first began this practice, than who of late times left it off.

And truly, as for those people who first ventured upon eating of flesh, it is very probable that the whole reason of their so doing was scarcity and want of other food; for it is not likely that their living together in lawless and extravagant lusts, or their growing wanton and capricious through the excessive variety of provisions then among them, brought them to such unsociable pleasures as these, against Nature. Yea, had they at this instant but their sense and voice restored to them, I am persuaded they would express themselves to this purpose:

Oh! happy you, and highly favored of the gods, who now live! Into what an age of the world are you fallen, who share and enjoy among you a plentiful portion of good things! What abundance of things spring up for your use! What fruitful vineyards you enjoy! What wealth you gather from the fields! What delicacies from trees and plants, which you may gather! You may glut and fill yourselves without being polluted. As for us, we fell upon the most dismal and affrighting part of time, in which we were exposed by our production to manifold and inextricable wants and necessities. As yet the thickened air concealed the heaven from our view, and the stars were as yet confused with a disorderly huddle of fire and moisture and violent fluxions of winds. As yet the

sun was not fixed to a regular and certain course, so as to separate morning and evening, nor did the seasons return in order crowned with wreaths from the fruitful harvest. The land was also spoiled by the inundations of disorderly rivers; and a great part of it was deformed with marshes, and utterly wild by reason of deep quagmires, unfertile forests, and woods. There was then no production of tame fruits, nor any instruments of art or invention of wit. And hunger gave no time, nor did seed-time then stay for the yearly season. What wonder is it if we made use of the flesh of beasts contrary to Nature, when mud was eaten and the bark of wood, and when it was thought a happy thing to find either a sprouting grass or a root of any plant! But when they had by chance tasted of or eaten an acorn, they danced for very joy about some oak or esculus, calling it by the names of life giver, mother, and nourisher. And this was the only festival that those times were acquainted with; upon all other occasions, all things were full of anguish and dismal sadness. But whence is it that a certain ravenousness and frenzy drives you in these happy days to pollute yourselves with blood, since you have such an abundance of things necessary for your subsistence? Why do you belie the earth as unable to maintain you? Why do you profane the lawgiver Ceres, and shame the mild and gentle Bacchus, as not furnishing you with sufficiency? Are you not ashamed to mix tame fruits with blood and slaughter? You are indeed wont to call serpents, leopards, and lions savage creatures; but yet yourselves are defiled with blood, and come nothing behind them in cruelty. What they kill is their ordinary nourishment, but what you kill is your better fare.

For we eat not lions and wolves by way of revenge; but we let those go, and catch the harmless and tame sort, and such as have neither stings nor teeth to bite with, and slay them; which, so may Jove help us, Nature seems to us to have produced for their beauty and comeliness only. [Just as if one seeing the river Nilus overflowing its banks, and thereby filling the whole country with genial and fertile moisture, should not at all admire that secret power in it that produces plants and plenteousness of most sweet and useful fruits, but beholding somewhere a crocodile swimming in it, or an asp crawling along, or mice (savage and filthy creatures), should presently affirm these to be the occasion of all that is amiss, or of any want or defect that may happen. Or as if indeed one contemplating this land or ground, how full it is of tame fruits, and how heavy with ears of corn, should afterward espy somewhere in these same cornfields an ear of darnel or a wild vetch, and thereupon neglect to reap and gather in the corn, and fall a complaining of these. Such another thing it would be, if one – listening to the harangue of some advocate at some bar or pleading, swelling and enlarging and hastening toward the relief of some impending danger, or else, by Jupiter, in the impeaching and charging of certain audacious villanies or indictments, flowing and rolling along, and that not in a simple and poor strain, but with many sorts of passions all at once, or rather indeed with all sorts, in one and the same manner, into the many and various and differing minds of either hearers or judges that he is either to turn and change, or else, by Jupiter, to soften, appease, and quiet – should overlook all this business, and never consider or reckon upon the labor or struggle he had undergone, but pick up certain loose expressions, which the rapid motion of the discourse had carried along with it, as by the current of its course, and so had slipped and escaped the rest of the oration, and, hereupon undervalue the orator.]

But we are nothing put out of countenance, either by the beauteous gayety of the colors, or by the charmingness of the musical voices, or by the rare sagacity of the intellects, or by the cleanliness and neatness of diet, or by the rare discretion and prudence of these poor unfortunate animals; but for the sake of some little mouthful of flesh, we deprive a soul of the sun and light, and of that proportion of life and time it had been born into the world to enjoy. And then we fancy that the voices it utters and screams forth to us are nothing else but certain inarticulate sounds and noises, and not the several deprecations, entreaties, and pleadings of each of them, as it were saying thus to us: "I deprecate not thy necessity (if such there be), but thy wantonness. Kill me for thy feeding, but do not take me off

for thy better feeding." O horrible cruelty! It is truly an affecting sight to see the very table of rich people laid before them, who keep them cooks and caterers to furnish them with dead corpses for their daily fare; but it is yet more affecting to see it taken away, for the mammocks remaining are more than that which was eaten. These therefore were slain to no purpose. Others there are, who are so offended by what is set before them that they will not suffer it to be cut or sliced; thus abstaining from them when dead, while they would not spare them when alive.

Well, then, we understand that that sort of men are used to say, that in eating of flesh they follow the conduct and direction of Nature. But that it is not natural to mankind to feed on flesh, we first of all demonstrate from the very shape and figure of the body. For a human body no ways resembles those that were born for ravenousness; it hath no hawk's bill, no sharp talon, no roughness of teeth, no such strength of stomach or heat of digestion, as can be sufficient to convert or alter such heavy and fleshy fare. But even from hence, that is, from the smoothness of the tongue, and the slowness of the stomach to digest, Nature seems to disclaim all pretence to fleshy victuals. But if you will contend that yourself was born to an inclination to such food as you have now a mind to eat, do you then yourself kill what you would eat. But do it yourself, without the help of a chopping-knife, mallet, or axe, – as wolves, bears, and lions do, who kill and eat at once. Rend an ox with thy teeth, worry a hog with thy mouth, tear a lamb or a hare in pieces, and fall on and eat it alive as they do. But if thou hadst rather stay until what thou greatest is become dead, and if thou art loath to force a soul out of its body, why then dost thou against Nature eat an animate thing? Nay, there is nobody that is willing to eat even a lifeless and a dead thing as it is; but they boil it, and roast it, and alter it by fire and medicines, as it were, changing and quenching the slaughtered gore with thousands of sweet sauces, that the palate being thereby deceived may admit of such uncouth fare. It was indeed a witty expression of a Lacedaemonian, who, having purchased a small fish in a certain inn, delivered it to his landlord to be dressed; and as he demanded cheese, and vinegar, and oil to make sauce, he replied, if I had had those, I would not have bought the fish. But we are grown so wanton in our bloody luxury, that we have bestowed upon flesh the name of meat [Greek omitted in the original translation], and then require another seasoning [Greek omitted in the original translation], to this same flesh, mixing oil, wine, honey, pickle, and vinegar, with Syrian and Arabian spices, as though we really meant to embalm it after its disease. Indeed when things are dissolved and made thus tender and soft, and are as it were turned into a sort of a carrionly corruption, it must needs be a great difficulty for concoction to master them, and when it hath mastered them, they must needs cause grievous oppressions and qualmy indigestions.

[...]

TRACT II

[...]

Who, then, were the first authors of this opinion, that we owe no justice to dumb animals?

> Who first beat out accursed steel,
> And made the lab'ring ox a knife to feel.

In the very same manner oppressors and tyrants begin first to shed blood. For example, the first man that the Athenians ever put to death was one of the basest of all knaves, who had the reputation of deserving it; after him they put to death a second and a third. After this, being now accustomed to blood, they patiently saw Niceratus the son of Nicias, and their own general Theramenes, and Polemarchus the philosopher suffer death. Even so, in the beginning, some wild and mischievous beast was killed and eaten, and then some little bird or fish was entrapped. And the desire of slaughter, being first experimented and exercised in these, at last passed even to the laboring ox, and the sheep that clothes us, and to the poor cock that keeps the house; until by little and little, unsatiableness, being strengthened by use, men came to the slaughter of men, to bloodshed and wars. Now even if one cannot demonstrate and make out, that souls in their regenerations make a promiscuous use of all bodies, and that that which is now rational will at another time be irrational, and that again tame which is now wild, – for that Nature changes and transmutes everything,

> With different fleshy coats new clothing all, –

this thing should be sufficient to change and show men, that it is a savage and intemperate habit, that it brings sickness and heaviness upon the body, and that it inclines the mind the more brutishly to bloodshed and destruction, when we have once accustomed ourselves neither to entertain a guest nor keep a wedding nor to treat our friends without blood and slaughter.

[...]

18

JIM MASON and MARY FINELLI

Brave New Farm?*

Jim Mason is an internationally known scholar who has used his diverse background as a journalist, lecturer, environmentalist, and attorney to advocate for animals, nature, and the environment. Mason is author of *An Unnatural Order: Why We Are Destroying the Planet and Each Other*, which chronicles the historical and cultural roots of the Western belief in dominionism and how it has compromised our relations with nature and especially animals. [He coined the word "misothery" to refer to a widespread hatred and contempt for animals.] Mason has co-authored numerous books with Peter Singer on the ethics of food choice and factory farming, has written award-winning magazine essays, has appeared on radio and television speaking on a variety of animal issues, and was the founding editor of *The Animal's Agenda*, a news magazine of the animal-rights movement. Mary Finelli is an animal activist for farm animals, the first editor of *Farmed Animal Watch*, an online news digest reporting on farmed animal issues, and a representative of United Poultry Concerns at workshops and conventions. We reproduce their chapter from Peter Singer's recent edited volume, *In Defense of Animals*, where they trace the development of factory farms, describe the current processes of raising/producing chicken, pigs, cows, and aquatic animals, and outline the consequences of factory farming on animals, humans, and rural communities.

In our mind's eye the farm is a peaceful place where calves nuzzle their mothers in a shady meadow, pigs loaf in the mudhole, and chickens scratch about the barnyard. These comforting images are implanted in us by calendars, coloring books, theme parks, petting zoos, and the countrified labeling and advertising of animal products.

The reality of modern farmed animal production, however, is starkly different from these scenes. Now, virtually all poultry products and most milk and meat in the US come from animals mass-produced in huge factory-like systems. In some of the more intensive confinement operations, animals are crowded in pens and in cages stacked up like so many shipping crates.

* Reproduced with permission of the publisher and from Jim Mason and Mary Finelli (2006) "Brave New Farm?" in Peter Singer (ed.), *In Defense of Animals: The Second Wave*. Malden; Oxford: Carlton Blackwell, pp. 104–122.

In these animal factories there are no pastures, no streams, no seasons, not even day and night. Growth and productivity come not from frolics in sunny meadows but from test-tube genetics and drug-laced feed.

Animal factories allow producers to maintain a larger number of animals in a given space, but they have created serious problems for consumers, farmers, and the environment, and they raise disturbing questions about the degree of animal exploitation that our society permits.

The animal factory is a classic case of technology run horribly amok: it requires high inputs of capital and energy to carry out a simple, natural process; it creates a costly chain of problems and risks; and it does not, in fact, produce the results claimed by its proponents. Moreover, the animal factory pulls our society one long, dark step backward from the desirable goal of a sane, ethical relationship with the natural world and our fellow inhabitants.

FACTORIES COME … FARMS GO

Right under our noses agribusiness has wrought a sweeping revolution in the ways in which animals are kept to produce meat, milk, and eggs. It began in the years before World War II, when farmers near large cities began to specialize in the production of chickens to meet the constant demand for eggs and meat. By supplementing the birds' diet with vitamin D, they made it possible for them to be raised indoors without sunlight. The first mass-producers were able to turn out large flocks all the year round. Large-scale indoor production caught on fast around the urban market centers, but the new methods created a host of problems. Nightmarish scenes began to occur in the crowded, poorly ventilated sheds. Birds pecked others to death and ate their remains. Contagious diseases were rampant, and losses multiplied throughout the budding industry.

The boom in the chicken business attracted the attention of the largest feed and pharmaceutical companies, which put their scientists to work on the problems of mass-production. Someone found that losses from pecking and cannibalism could be reduced by burning off the tips of chickens' beaks with a blowtorch. Soon an automatic "debeaking" machine was patented, and its use became routine. Richer feeds made for faster-gaining birds and a greater number of "crops" of chickens each year. Foremost of the developments, however, was the discovery that sulfa drugs and antibiotics could be added to feed to help hold down diseases in the dirty, crowded sheds.

Chickens themselves were not entirely ready for mass-production, and the poultry industry set about looking for a better commercial bird. In 1946, the Great Atlantic and Pacific Tea Company (now A&P) launched the "Chicken of Tomorrow" contest to find a strain of chicken that could produce a broad-breasted body at low feed cost. Within a few years poultry breeders had developed the prototype for today's "broiler" – a chicken raised for meat who grows to a market weight of about five pounds in seven weeks or less. The pre-war ancestor of this bird took twice as long to grow to a market weight of about three pounds.

The egg industry went to work on engineering their own specialized chicken – the "layer" hen, who would turn out eggs and more eggs. Today's model lays twice as many eggs per year as did the "all-purpose" backyard chickens of the 1940s. Egg producers also tried to follow the "broiler" industry's factory ways, but they were faced with a major problem: confined hens produce loads of manure each week. "Broiler" producers had the manure problem with their large flocks too, but the birds were in and out within twelve weeks, and accumulations could be cleaned out after every few flocks. (Today, it can be years between complete litter changes.) Egg producers, however, kept their birds indoors for a year or more, so they needed a means of manure removal that would not disturb the hens or interfere with egg production. Unfortunately for the hens, they found it: producers discovered they could confine their chickens in wire-mesh cages suspended over a trench to collect droppings. At first they placed hens one to each cage, but when they found that birds were cheaper than wire and buildings, crowded cages became the rule. Although crowding caused the deaths of more hens, this cost was considered "acceptable" given the increased total egg output.

Having reduced chickens to the equivalent of living machinery, entrepreneurs and government scientists began looking about for ways to extend factory technology to other farmed animal species. In the 1960s they began developing systems for pigs, cattle, and sheep that incorporated the principles of confinement, mass-production, and automated feeding, watering, ventilation, and waste removal. The wire cage, which made everything possible for the egg industry, would not work for these heavier, hoofed animals. But slatted floors – rails of metal or concrete spaced slightly apart and built over gutters or holding pits – did much the same job. Now large numbers of animals could be confined indoors and held to rigid production schedules, for the laborious tasks of providing bedding and mucking out manure had been eliminated.

The basics of factory husbandry had been established. Now the job of refining mass-production systems and methods fell to husbandry experts, opening up a great new field for them. It opened up, as well, great new markets for the agribusiness companies that could profit from the expanded sales of feed, equipment, drugs, and the other products required by the new capital-intensive technology. Humanity and concern retreated further as animal scientists – funded by these companies and by government – worked out the "bugs" in the new systems.

THE FACTORY FORMULA

Factory methods and equipment vary from species to species, but the principles are the same: keep costs down and manipulate animals' productivity upward. These principles ensure that animals are crowded in barren environments, restricted, stressed, and maintained on drug-laced, unnatural diets.

The modern chicken comes from the sterile laboratories of a handful of "primary breeders" worldwide. In the US, these companies sell animals for breeding to some 300 "multipliers" or hatcheries (down from 11,405 in 1934), which in turn produce the chicks who are used for egg and meat production. At the multipliers, birds have the run of the floor in the breeding houses, for freedom and exercise promote health and a higher percentage of fertile eggs.

If the hatchery is turning out birds for egg factories, the first order of business is to destroy half the "crop" of chicks. Males don't lay eggs, and the flesh of these specialized layer breeds is of poor quality – "not fit to feed," as one hatchery worker put it. These chicks, by the millions annually, have for decades been thrown into plastic bags to be crushed or suffocated. Large-scale hatcheries have moved toward the use of gas asphyxiation or "macerators," which grind up the live chicks at high speeds. About three-fourths of the female chicks ("pullets") are reared in cages, the other fourth raised loose in floor facilities. Shortly before they begin to lay eggs, at between eighteen and twenty weeks of age, they are moved to the egg factory.

Today, 98 percent of commercial layer hens in the US are caged. At an industry average of eight birds per cage, each hen gets about 50 square inches of floor space. In 2002, under pressure from public opinion, the industry trade group United Egg Producers announced "Animal Care Certified" guidelines that will, over a six-year period, gradually increase the space allowance to a minimum of 67 inches per hen, or seven birds per cage. Studies have shown, however, that hens require 71–5 square inches of space just to stand and lie down, and about twice that much space to stretch their wings. In major egg-producing states, operations with flocks of 100,000 hens are common, some housing as many as 200,000 hens in a single building. The owner of a planned 2.4 million-hen facility explained: "We used to have one person for 10,000 chickens. Now we have one for every 150,000."

After a year in the cages, hens' egg productivity wanes and it becomes unprofitable to feed and house them. The manager may decide to use "force molting," a procedure which causes the birds to grow new feathers and accelerates and synchronizes another cycle of egg production. This is usually accomplished by reducing light and depriving the hens of food for ten to fourteen days. In a large study, mortality doubled during the first week of the molt and then doubled again during the second week. Aggression also increases among the starving birds. After a forced molt or two the hens are deemed "spent" and are removed from the cages to make room for the next flock. There is a poor market for the birds in these days of mass-produced "broiler chickens," so they, too, are thrown into macerators, buried alive, or killed by having their neck broken. Now that these gruesome methods have created controversy, a few firms are beginning to experiment with other ways of killing hens, such as electrocution and gassing. Whatever the method of killing, millions go to renderers to be turned into companion-animal food and feed supplements, to incinerators, or to landfills.

With "broiler chickens," both sexes are kept and raised for meat. The chicks are dumped into a huge "shed" with some type of litter covering the floor. Not that these birds have it all that much better than their cousins in the layer cages: generations of inbreeding for rapid growth have produced crippled birds prone to heart attacks and a slew of other health problems. They spend their short lives packed together by tens of thousands on manure-soaked floors, breathing dust and ammonia. The situation is similar for turkeys, and the numbers are huge: roughly nine billion birds go through factory systems to slaughter each year in the USA alone (up from about 1.6 billion in 1960).

Specialized buildings similar to those used in the poultry industries are used to breed, wean, and fatten ("finish") pigs. About 83 percent of female pigs used for breeding ("sows") give birth in total confinement facilities, and some 82 percent of piglets are put in total confinement nurseries. While some operations keep male and female pigs to produce litters of piglets, most pigs marketed today are probably produced by artificial

insemination. Roughly 70 percent of sows are artificially inseminated for at least their first two matings, according to United States Department of Agriculture (USDA) figures.

The factory sow's misery deepens in the "gestation crate," a stall so narrow that she cannot turn around or groom herself. It is the most common type of housing for female pigs used for breeding. She remains in it for her entire four-month gestation period. Her normal urges to forage, socialize, and build a nest are completely frustrated. As with cows, and birds used to breed fast-growing offspring, to prevent the sow from gaining weight and becoming unable to reproduce, her feed will be severely restricted, resulting in extreme hunger and distress. She may be fed only once every two days or so.

About a week before her piglets are due, she is moved to a narrow "farrowing crate." This device permits her to lie and stand, but she cannot walk or turn around; its purpose is to keep her in position only to eat, drink, and keep her teats exposed to the baby pigs. Soon after birth, the piglets' teeth are clipped; their tails are cut off, their ears are notched for identification, and males are castrated – all without any anasthetic. In a few weeks, the sow goes back to the breeding area, and the piglets are moved to pens in the "finishing" buildings, where they spend about sixteen weeks until they reach a slaughter weight of about 250 pounds.

Most of the milk produced in the US comes from cows in intensive confinement, most commonly kept tethered to a stall. Increasingly popular in the West and Southwest are drylots: dirt or concrete lots devoid of vegetation and often without shade. They are only thoroughly cleaned once or twice a year, allowing manure to build up from the thousands of cows they hold. Partial tail amputation ("docking"), purportedly for cleanliness but actually for worker convenience, has become a popular practice.

From 1950 to 2000, owing to genetics and other factors, the number of cows used for milk production in the US decreased by 67 percent while the amount of milk produced tripled. By 2002, over 20 percent of the 9 million cows were being injected with synthetic bovine growth hormone to increase milk production. (The drug is banned in other countries due to animal health concerns.) The dramatic increase in milk production has been accompanied by deterioration in most measures of cow health. High-producing cows are particularly prone to metabolic disorders, lameness, mastitis (inflammation of the udder, a disease that costs the dairy industry $1.7 billion annually), and infertility. Crowding also leads to a higher incidence of "production diseases." Although cows do not reach full maturity until four years of age, they are typically sent to slaughter by about five years. Even at that early age many are already debilitated, the problem of non-ambulatory ("downer") animals being most common with the dairy industry.

Veal production has been considered by many to be the cruelest of all the confinement systems. In the US, every year about 750,000 calves – mostly males, who are of little use to the dairy industry – are taken from their mothers within a day of birth and turned into sickly, neurotic animals to provide the luxury-grade "milk-fed" veal preferred by gourmet cooks and fancy restaurants. The young calves, stressed by separation from their mothers, are placed in narrow wooden stalls, lined up row on row in the confinement building. For between eighteen and twenty weeks, each calf is confined to a space scarcely larger than his own body, and is tied at the neck to restrict movement further. He is fed only "milk replacer," a liquid mixture of dried milk products, starch, fats, sugar, antibiotics, and other additives. The milk replacer is deficient in iron to induce subclinical anemia – a necessary condition if the producer's calves are to have flesh white enough to fetch the market price for "prime" veal. No hay or other roughage is permitted, for that too might darken the flesh. Even the wooden stalls and neck chains are part of the plan, as these restrictions keep the calf from licking his own urine and feces to satisfy his craving for iron.

In "beef cattle" feedlots, stress from crowding, exposure, and an unnatural diet adversely affect the animals' health. Liver abscesses are common in these animals because their digestive tracts are geared more to roughage than to the steady diet of high-energy grain and growth promotants that they receive. Cattle may be dehorned and branded, and males are castrated, all without anesthesia.

Ducks are raised both for meat and to produce foie gras ("fatty liver"), which involves a most brutal practice. Total-confinement housing is the most common method of raising ducks, with thousands of birds kept in a single, dark building. Being aquatic animals, they need to submerse their head in water in order to keep their eyes healthy. But the only water they are provided with is for drinking, from nipple-like devices. The tip of their sensitive bill is burned off with a hot knife, often resulting in chronic pain and debilitation. At about four months of age, ducks used for foie gras are put in small pens or are kept virtually immobilized in individual cages. For two to three weeks, up to two pounds of a corn/fat mixture are forced down their throat through a 12- to 16-inch pipe attached to a motorized pump. The massive quantities of food cause the bird's liver to swell to up to ten times its normal size, a clinical disease state called "hepatic steatosis." Many of the birds also suffer blindness, lameness, throat injuries, and ruptured livers.

Aquatic animals account for 16 percent of the animal protein consumed worldwide. Official figures on the number of aquatic animals killed for food in the US are not kept but estimates exceed 15 billion annually. This is far more than all the other farmed animal species combined. Aquaculture, the factory farming of aquatic species, supplies 30 percent of all seafood consumed globally, up from 10 percent two decades ago. It's a $56 billion global enterprise that is rapidly being consolidated by a few big companies. About a third of the seafood consumed in the US, including nearly all of the catfish and trout and about two-thirds of the salmon and shrimp, is from captive-raised animals. With wild fish populations having been drastically reduced, in order to just maintain world fish consumption levels it is predicted that aquaculture will have to grow seven-fold in the next twenty-five years.

Aquaculture is being promoted as the "Blue Revolution," an aquatic version of the Green Revolution which vastly multiplied agricultural output in non-industrialized countries. Critics warn of environmental havoc, as was seen with the Green Revolution. Algicides, pesticides, antibiotics, and other drugs are heavily used in aquaculture, and federal inspection of fish farms is lacking. Coastal waters are degraded by the discharge of aqua-farm chemicals and wastes, with shrimp farming said to be particularly destructive. Environmentally superior techniques are expensive and difficult to employ on a large-scale basis. Feed conversion is also inefficient. For example, between two and five pounds of other fish are needed as feed to produce one pound of farmed salmon.

Increasingly, fish are being raised in cages floating in the ocean. Sea lice proliferate in these crowded confines, boring holes in the skin of fish and feasting on their flesh. Schools of fish inevitably escape through torn nets, flooding, or accidental release during transport. Once free, they spread disease and compete with wild native fish. Genetically engineered fish, made to grow at much faster rates, pose an even greater potential threat.

Many farmed fish species spend most of their lives in steel buildings, crowded into shallow cement troughs. According to the 2002 Compassion in World Farming report "In Too Deep," twenty-seven one-foot-long trout share the equivalent of a bathtub of water. At high densities, fish exhibit abnormal behaviors, such as increased aggression; suffer widespread injuries, deformities, and disease; and have high parasitic infestations. Scientific research has shown that fish are capable of experiencing pain and distress. Veterinary medicine for fish is very limited, and pre-slaughter mortality rates are high.

Fish are commonly starved for seven days or more prior to slaughter. To increase shelf life, many are left to suffocate on bins of ice. Others are rendered immobile rather than insensible at slaughter, resulting in their being processed while still alive and fully capable of immense suffering. Stunning methods include clubbing and gassing. Slaughter methods include bleeding and electrocution. Less inhumane methods are being researched.

FACTORY PROBLEMS, FACTORY SOLUTIONS

The industrialization of animal production has provided farmers with tighter controls over their herds and flocks and it has eliminated much of the labor of feeding, waste removal, and other chores, but it has also created a whole new set of problems for producers. These problems have in turn created whole new industries of research and experts who churn out increasingly elaborate management schemes and expensive inputs needed to keep the factory system producing. Continual manipulations of animals' heredity, anatomy, physiology, and environment are required to hold down health problems and maintain mass commodity production at a profitable level. Chief among these factory-caused health problems is stress.

In confinement, animals are subjected to a variety of stressors. In addition to acute stresses such as early weaning, debeaking, dehorning, tail docking, and castration, other causes of stress in the factory farm are constant. The animals have no relief from crowding and monotony. In a less restrictive environment they would relieve boredom by moving; confined animals cannot. Nor have they relief from social disturbances caused by factory conditions. When animals are crowded and agitated, they are more likely to fight. In the restricted space of confinement pens, less aggressive animals cannot get away to make the instinctive show of submission. With caged birds, for example, each cage contains a small "flock," with one member at the bottom of the social ladder. This unfortunate bird cannot escape her tormentors. When growing pigs are moved to larger pens and mixed with unfamiliar pigs, fighting can occur, leaving pigs injured or dead.

In pigs, stress-induced aggression or "cannibalism" takes the form of tail biting, best described by a swine expert for Hog Farm Management back in 1976, when such practices had not yet raised controversy and farming publications were more plainspoken than they are today: "Acute tail biting is often called cannibalism and frequently results in crippling, mutilation and death ... Many times the tail is bitten first and then the attacking pig or pigs continue to eat further into the back. If the situation is not attended to, the pig will die and be eaten."

In dealing with these stress-related problems, animal-factory managers manipulate both animal and environment rather than eliminating the primary underlying cause – crowded, inappropriate conditions. Prevented from forming stable social structures, birds may engage in abnormal and potentially injurious pecking behavior. (Genetics and other faulty management factors can also precipitate this.) To control it, birds are debeaked, an operation that removes the front third to one-half of the bird's beak. Chickens used by the egg industry and those used for breeding purposes are debeaked anywhere from one day to eighteen weeks of age. The procedure is sometimes later repeated. Turkeys and ducks are also debeaked, but today's "broilers" are not, because they are too young and listless to become aggressive. According to United Egg Producers, welfare impairments "may include the bird's ability to feed itself following beak trimming, short-term pain, perhaps chronic pain, and acute stress." Poultry ethologist Dr. Ian Duncan explains that the tip of the beak is richly innervated and contains pain receptors. Therefore, cutting and heating the beak will lead to acute pain. Additionally, the behavior of debeaked birds is radically altered for many weeks, which, along with neurophysiological evidence, indicates the birds experience chronic pain. Dr. Duncan states: "Chopping off parts of young animals in order to prevent future welfare problems is a very crude solution." (Incidentally, the poultry industry coined the term "debeaking" and used it for generations until the controversies over factory methods surfaced; since then it has preferred the term "beak trimming.")

At the same time they are debeaked, turkeys and some chickens have part of their toes amputated, often by the same hot-knife machine. This is done to prevent them from using their claws to cause injuries. The combs and wattles of males used for breeding are also cut off to prevent them from being injured, since injuries reduce production. All of these procedures are performed without anesthesia.

Problematic genetics and production demands take their toll on stressed animals in other ways. Pigs bred for leanness and rapid growth are prone to a condition that we would probably call "shock" if it occurred in humans; the pig industry calls it "porcine stress syndrome," or simply "PSS." Pigs may literally drop dead from stress when they are weaned, moved to a new pen, mixed with strange pigs, or shipped to market. Cattle bred similarly for meat production are also highly excitable, making them hard to manage and prone to injury. A condition affecting about a third of flocks in the US egg industry is termed "caged layer fatigue." The exhausted birds have brittle or broken bones and a pale, washed-out appearance in their eyes, combs, beaks, and feet. The relentless calcium demand for eggshell production causes the mineral to be withdrawn from hens' bones and muscles. Afflicted birds are left unable to stand and may die if unable to reach food or water. It occurs only in caged birds, due to their lack of exercise, and is exacerbated by crowding. In "broiler" operations, "Acute Death Syndrome," also known as "Flip-Over Syndrome," occurs in fast-growing birds. They have been observed suddenly jumping into the air, giving a loud squawk, and falling over dead. Metabolic diseases associated with fast growth have become more of a problem than infectious diseases for the poultry meat industry. One chicken farmer wrote, "Aside from the stupendous rate of growth ... the sign of a good meat flock is the number of birds dying from heart attacks."

To speed up reproductive cycles, babies are prematurely separated from their mothers. In nature, a calf might nurse and run with his or her mother for about a year; on a dairy farm they're lucky to spend more than a day together. Sows and their piglets are left together an average of about nineteen days (down from fifty-six days). In addition to the manipulation of sex and reproduction, managers control lighting to increase production. Egg producers try to create the illusion of perpetual spring by keeping the lights on a little longer each day.

BIOTECH BARNYARD

Not satisfied with the innovations described above, some scientists are now looking at the prospect of cloning and genetic engineering to further optimize production. These reproduction technologies raise grave concerns.

Cloning can be carried out with embryo cells or with somatic (i.e. body) cells. In the technically simplest form, egg and sperm from prized animals are "harvested" and combined in a laboratory to form an embryo. Once the cell has multiplied to a certain stage it is divided and each section is implanted as a separate embryo into a lesser-valued surrogate mother for gestation. This enables more highly valued animals to be produced than could be through normal reproduction. This type of cloning, called "embryo splitting" or "embryo twinning," has been commercially employed for a decade or two but on an extremely limited basis due to its expense and the unpredictability of results. In the more highly publicized form of cloning, somatic cell nuclear transfer (SCNT), a nearly exact genetic copy of a parent animal is produced by putting the nucleus of a differentiated cell from the parent into a denucleated egg cell from a surrogate mother, who then gestates the embryo. In theory, farmed animals with particularly desirable characteristics can be mass-produced this way. In practice, however, hundreds of attempts are needed to produce a single healthy animal. In the US, the Food and Drug Administration has asked that animals produced this way, and products from them, not

be allowed in the human or animal food supply on account of food safety and animal welfare concerns.

Genetic engineering has been used to insert genes from another life form – usually another species and not necessarily an animal – into animals in order to produce specific benefits for humans. It is hoped that these "transgenic" animals will have an increased quantity and quality of food and fiber production, or will produce pharmaceutical proteins in their milk, eggs, or urine: animal "pharming." Additional research is underway to produce transgenic pigs with organs that will be able to be transplanted into humans without being rejected.

Repeatedly subjecting individual animals to invasive procedures in order to obtain eggs for cloning is likely to cause them pain and distress. "Large Offspring Syndrome" occurs with cloned cattle and sheep, putting the animals used as surrogate mothers at increased risk for difficult pregnancies and caesarean sections. Attempts to clone animals through SCNT often produce deformed animals who suffer and die at an early age. Genetically engineered animals may also suffer from bizarre maladies. Additionally, opponents argue that these technologies will only benefit large corporations while further exacerbating the loss of small farms, and that poor countries won't be able to afford them.

HUMAN HEALTH CONCERNS

"In current agricultural practice, raising animals for food depends heavily on the use of pharmacologically active compounds: drugs," states a 1999 National Academy of Science report. ("Broiler chicken" feed, for example, almost always contains an antibiotic, a coccidiostat for internal parasites and improved feed efficiency, and arsenic to color the birds' skin yellow and increase growth.) This is no wonder because factory animals are genetically more susceptible to infectious diseases, and the stresses of factory life further debilitate their immune defenses. Animal factories breed germs – leaner, meaner germs and more kinds of them – that easily spread throughout the crowded, dirty buildings. Stressed from discomfort and frustration, and breathing dusty, noxious air, factory animals are highly vulnerable to infection. If not suppressed with drugs and chemistry, flocks and herds would be even more disposed to disease epidemics.

Antibiotics have been the main tool for growth promotion and disease control since the 1950s. Nearly all US factory animals – poultry, pigs, cattle in feedlots, and calves raised for veal – routinely get antibiotic-laced feed. In 2001, the Union of Concerned Scientists (UCS) "conservatively" estimated that 24.6 million pounds of antibiotics was administered to US cattle, pigs, and poultry for nontherapeutic purposes. According to UCS, this was equivalent to 70 percent of the country's total anti-microbial use, and eight times the amount used in human medicine.

Individual bacteria that are able to withstand the effects of antibiotics can multiply, creating resistant bacteria. As bacteria evolve very rapidly, many species have developed resistance to our "wonder drugs." For example, the types of bacteria that cause diarrhea, septicemia, salmonella, gonorrhea, pneumonia, tuberculosis, typhoid, and childhood meningitis have long developed drug-resistant strains. Harmless bacteria that develop resistance can transfer resistant genes to infectious bacteria. So, if you are infected by one of these strains, a course of antibiotics will not help as it might have a decade or so ago. Because of this, the World Health Organization (WHO) and the American Medical Association recommend that antibiotics not be used to promote animal growth. The European Union is set to ban the practice in 2006. It has already been banned in Denmark and Sweden.

The factory system has also created an alarming new kind of pollution. Reportedly, up to 75 percent of an antibiotic may pass undigested through an animal's body. The trillions of pounds of manure produced in the US every year (1.4 billion tons in 1997) contain antibiotics and astronomical amounts of bacteria, including antibiotic-resistant bacteria. Much of the manure is used as fertilizer, from which resistant bacteria can leach into the soil and groundwater, altering microbial ecosystems in the environment.

Top "broiler" companies recently announced that they are phasing out the use of certain antibiotics that are similar to ones used in human medicine, and leading fast-food chains say they are no longer purchasing chickens treated with certain antibiotics. The National Chicken Council claims overall antibiotic usage in animals of all kinds has been in decline since 1999. However, industry data don't provide specifics about antibiotic use and the government doesn't collect such data. If there has in fact been a decline, at least part of the reason for the industry change may be because antibiotics have lost much of their growth-promoting effectiveness.

Over the past three decades, many studies have pointed to the dangers posed by rampant chemical and pharmaceutical use and abuse in animal factories. There are many instances of widespread sales and abuse of illegal drugs, and there are many instances of abuses of legal drugs. For example, in late March 2004, US federal regulators discovered that growth hormones were being used in up to 90 percent of calves raised for veal production, an illegal practice the industry admitted to having engaged in for decades. USDA testing for drugs in animal tissues has been much criticized. A string of reports, including ones by the Government Accountability Office, have concluded that the government's inspection and testing programs are inadequate to protect the public from either drug residues or bacterial contamination.

Aside from drug-resistant diseases, people (and other animals) can come down with "ordinary" food poisoning caused by the animal factory's prolific production of germs. Some of these cases are not so ordinary, with factory farms and the debilitated animals in them providing the ideal environment in which pathogenic bacteria and viruses can become more virulent. The Center for Disease Control and Prevention (CDC) estimates that food-borne diseases cause approximately 76 million illnesses, 325,000 hospitalizations, and 5,000 deaths in the US each year. Other public health authorities put the food-poisoning estimates at 250 million illnesses and 9,000 deaths each year. In an analysis of food-borne illnesses occurring between 1990 and 2003, the Center for Science in the Public Interest found seafood, poultry, beef, and eggs to be among the top five vehicles for which a single food was identified as responsible. Collectively, they were responsible for 88 percent of the outbreaks and 79 percent of the cases. Two of the most common pathogens, salmonella and *E. coli,* are most frequently linked to animal waste that can contaminate produce via the billions of pounds of manure spread on cropland as fertilizer. In addition to acute illness, animal products pose long-term risks to human health due to their cholesterol and fat content, and their lack of fiber and complex carbohydrates. This combination is implicated in heart disease, cancers, obesity, kidney disease, diabetes, hypertension, and other chronic illnesses.

The recklessness of the factory system manifested for industry, governments, and consumers when "mad cow disease" (bovine spongiform encephalopathy [BSE]) was identified in 1986. The disease, caused by feeding cattle the rendered remains of sheep, also infected human beef consumers. Since then, there have been some 190,000 reported cases of BSE in twenty-five countries, with several million cattle killed in an attempt to eradicate the disease. There have been 153 cases of the human form of the disease, new variant Creutzfeldt-Jakob Disease, which is always fatal. It has now been found that the disease can spread through the blood supply. Some scientists warn that the human cases may just be the beginning of a "timebomb."

Avian influenza (AI) is another disease that has crossed the species barrier. Wild aquatic birds are the natural hosts of AI. The viruses ordinarily do not cause disease in them, but in a new host, such as chickens, they dangerously mutate. According to Dr. Robert Webster, director of the World Health Organization Collaborating Center for Studies on the Ecology of Influenza in Animals and Birds, humans have created optimal conditions to generate flu epidemics. A single factory farm provides hundreds of billions of replication cycles with an exponentially greater risk of a pathogenic strain arising. In early 2004, virulent AI raced through Asia, infecting thirty-four people, twenty-three of them fatally. An estimated 200,000,000 birds were killed in an attempt to control the disease. If avian virus merges with a human virus, it could more easily transmit between people and rapidly spread. Some scientists fear avian influenza may become the human plague of the twenty-first century.

FARMERS (AND THE REST OF US) ARE VICTIMS TOO

Ironically, the trend toward complex, expensive husbandry systems hurts farmers and rural communities. Those huge buildings full of specialized floors and feeding equipment don't come cheap. Financial burdens are so great that factory farmers must continuously keep their buildings at capacity, working longer and harder than ever just to meet their loan payments. The tendency to operate at capacity in order to cover capital costs creates chronic overproduction in the poultry, pork, and dairy industries and drives down market prices. In this situation, many smaller and non-factory farmers cannot make a living so they quit raising animals altogether. Moreover, the high capital investment required tends to attract agribusiness companies, urban investors, and other non-farm interests with deep pockets. Thus, more and more production has fallen into the hands of the largest, most intensive operations. Government subsidies have also helped accelerate this trend.

The poultry industry, the originator of factory systems, offers a clear example of how the trend toward capital intensification affects farmers. Chickens and eggs, along with pigs, used to be the mainstay of the small, independent family farm before the poultry scientists and agribusiness companies got involved. In 1950, independent operators raised 95 percent of the chickens produced for meat. Today, nearly all chickens raised for meat are produced and processed under contracts between "growers" and processors. Prior to 1950, nearly all egg production was conducted by independent operators. Today, nearly 40 percent of eggs are produced under contract, with the remainder produced through vertical integration (whereby various stages of production and processing are controlled by a single company). The farm family has been reduced to the status of "poultry peons" who turn out company birds on company feed according to company schedules and specifications. Similarly, in 1970 nearly all pigs were sold on the open market. By 2001, only about 25 percent were, the rest having been produced under contract.

There are many, many costs in the new factory methods and systems for raising animals, although agribusiness experts would have us hear only their talk of benefits. They are fond of using cost/benefit analyses to justify crowding animals, the use of antibiotics in feed, and converting farming communities to factory towns. They assert that the benefits to consumers from these practices outweigh the risks involved. But if this sort of test is to have any validity in agricultural affairs it must take into account all the costs of factory methods, which harm:

• farmed animals, who are restricted, mutilated, manipulated, and ultimately killed;
• the health of consumers, who are put at much greater risk for both acute and chronic disease;
• the land, much of which is used to grow animal feed or is degraded by overgrazing;
• wildlife, whose habitat is destroyed and who are killed by agricultural predator control programs;
• the environment, polluted by pesticides and toxic animal wastes;
• our limited supply of fossil fuels, their procurement causing environmental destruction and escalating international strife;
• the atmosphere, polluted by fossil fuel use and methane gas, generated by the immense numbers of ruminant farmed animals, adding to global warming;

• prospects for alleviating world hunger, by the depletion of fresh water and other natural resources;
• farm families and rural communities, whose livelihood is stolen by high-tech factory systems;
• citizens, who pay for subsidies that prop up costly systems, and farmers – and ultimately all residents – in other countries who are unable to compete with the "cheap" imports;
• human dignity and self-respect, as a result of carrying on all of the above and on such a massive scale.

Quite possibly the greatest threat factory farming poses now is its expansion in "developing" countries. Worldwatch Institute's *State of the World 2004* explains:

> Global meat production has increased more than fivefold since 1950, and factory farming is the fastest growing method of animal production worldwide. Industrial systems are responsible for 74 percent of the world's total poultry [meat], 50 percent of pork production, 43 percent of the beef, and 68 percent of the eggs. Industrial countries dominate production, but developing nations are rapidly expanding and intensifying their production systems. According to the U.N. Food and Agriculture Organization (FAO), Asia has the fastest-developing livestock sector, followed by Latin America and the Caribbean.

LAWS AND STANDARDS

Farmed animals in the US have little to no legal protection. Hundreds of millions of them die every year prior to the time they would be slaughtered, yet there is no federal law that regulates the treatment of farmed animals on farms. (Farmed animals are essentially exempted from the protections of the Animal Welfare Act.) The Twenty-Eight Hour Law prohibits the transport of animals across state lines for more than twenty-eight hours without being unloaded for at least five hours of rest with access to food and water. However, the law does not apply to trucks, by far the most common means of transporting farmed animals. Furthermore, the law is rarely enforced and the maximum penalty is only $500. The Humane Methods of Slaughter Act requires that slaughter "be carried out only by humane methods" to prevent "needless suffering." Yet birds and fish, who constitute about 98 percent of slaughtered animals, are not covered by the Act. In a 1996 slaughter plant audit commissioned by the USDA, 64 percent of the cattle plants and 36 percent of the pig and sheep plants were rated "not acceptable" or a "serious problem" in regard to stunning procedures. Enforcement of the law was found to be so lacking that, in 2002, Congress passed a resolution entitled Enforcement of the Humane Slaughter Act of 1958. In February 2004, the government's General Accounting Office reported that the Act was still not being adequately enforced.

In the absence of federal law, state law does little better. The majority of US states exempt customary farming practices from their anti-cruelty statutes, and it is industry that determines what is customary. In other words, industry determines what is an acceptable way to treat farmed animals. Convictions are extremely difficult and infrequent, and fines are relatively minimal. Forty-one states currently have animal anti-cruelty statutes with felony penalties, but only in seven states do they effectively apply to farmed animals. In Florida in 2002, a law banning gestation crates for pregnant pigs was passed by a 55 percent majority vote. It is said to be the first US measure banning a particular farming practice on the grounds of cruelty. However, ballot initiatives are difficult and expensive, and twenty-six states do not allow them.

Industry – including farmed-animal trade groups, supermarkets, and fast-food restaurant chains – has recently responded to public pressure by formulating minimal, voluntary standards, some with third-party inspections. But there are grounds for skepticism about the efficacy of industry codes and standards. In the US, the United Egg Producers authorized the use of an "Animal Care Certified" logo to mark cartons of eggs from operations enrolled in their welfare standards program. In 2004, the Better Business Bureau deemed this logo misleading because the program did not ensure that animals were cared for. In the same year, an undercover investigation by People for the Ethical Treatment of Animals (PETA) at a slaughter plant operated by Pilgrim's Pride, the second-largest chicken company in the US, revealed sadistic abuse of birds, involving laborers, supervisors, foremen, and managers. In responding, the President and CEO assured the public that "Pilgrim's Pride strictly adheres to the animal welfare program recommended by the National Chicken Council (NCC)."

The national organic standards, implemented by the USDA in 2001 after a decade of formulation, require outdoor access for farmed animals, with notable exceptions. However, the standards are vague about the type of space, and do not specify the amount of space or the length of time animals must have access to it.

Animal advocacy organizations have also formulated farmed-animal welfare standards. They include the Animal Welfare Institute, American Humane ("Free Farmed"), and Humane Farm Animal Care ("Certified Humane"), the latter two of which are predicated on the Freedom Food program of the UK's Royal Society for the Protection of Animals (RSPCA). Additionally, Whole Foods Market, the world's largest retailer of natural and organic foods, is in the process of devising standards. (See Karen Dawn's interview with John Mackey and Lauren Ornelas in *In Defense of Animals: The Second Wave*.) Promoted as "humane," such standards lead to conditions that are at best less inhumane than conventional production practices. For example, Certified Humane – which is endorsed by the American Society for the Protection of Animals (ASPCA), Animal People, the Humane Society of the US, and ten other humane societies and SPCAs – does not require outdoor access for animals. It also, among other objectionable points, permits castration, tail docking, dehorning, and debeaking, all without anesthesia, albeit with limitations.

Farmed-animal abuse didn't begin with factory farming nor is it unique to it. Welfare standards for alternative production are usually vague if not altogether lacking, and auditing programs are being questioned. While alternative, "humane" animal agriculture is growing in popularity and may be preferable to factory farming, virtually all animal agriculture involves a substantial degree of animal suffering and death. As long as eating meat is considered acceptable, farmed animals will not rise above the status of consumables. Eating eggs and dairy products may actually be worse than eating meat, since the hens and cows used to produce them are among the animals who suffer the longest and the worst, after which they, too, are killed. We need to question the very concept of marketing sentient beings. Welfare reforms can lessen their suffering but will not make it right.

19

CAROL J. ADAMS

The Sexual Politics of Meat*

Carol Adams, a graduate of Yale Divinity School, is a feminist author and an antiviolence activist. In the 1970s, she co-founded a hotline for battered women and directed a rural ministry program that worked to combat issues of poverty, racism and sexism in rural New York. Adams is internationally known for studies of the links between forms of violence against humans and those against other animals. She has written several influential essays on feminism, animal rights, and the relationship between animal abuse and domestic violence, as well as books on vegetarianism and the connection between sexual violence and meat-eating. The extract reproduced below is from Adams's ground-breaking book *The Sexual Politics of Meat: A Feminist-Vegetarian Critical Theory*, in which she describes how sexism, racism, and classism are implicated in patterns of meat consumption. In this extract Adams explains that many societies reserve meat for the powerful (privileged men) and soldiers in times of war, while less powerful groups have had to be content with consuming fruits, vegetables, and grains. On the other hand, during times when meat is plentiful it is expected that all will consume it. Thus, she argues that meat has been equated with male dominance and privileged masculinity and has become ascendant in our culture over types of food not derived from the flesh of animals, and "[t]he foods associated with second-class citizens are considered to be second-class protein." In this extract and in her larger body of work Adams demonstrates how the marginalization of oppressed groups of humans and other animals are mutually reinforced conceptually. The next reading by David Nibert examines a substantive case of the linking of these forms of oppression.

MYTH FROM THE BUSHMAN:

In the early times men and women lived apart, the former hunting animals exclusively, the latter pursuing a gathering existence. Five of the men, who were out hunting, being careless creatures, let their fire go out. The women, who were careful and orderly, always kept their fire going. The men, having killed a springbok, became desperate for means to cook it, so one of their number set out to get fire, crossed the river and met one of the women gathering seeds. When he asked her for some fire, she invited him to the feminine camp. While he was there she said, "You are very hungry.

Just wait until I pound up these seeds and I will boil them and give you some." She made him some porridge. After he had eaten it, he said, "Well, it's nice food so I shall just stay with you." The men who were left waited and wondered. They still had the springbok and they still had no fire. The second man set out, only to be tempted by female cooking, and to take up residence in the camp of the women. The same thing happened to the third man. The two men left were very frightened. They suspected something terrible had happened to their comrades. They cast the divining bones but the omens were favorable. The fourth man set out timidly, only to end by joining his comrades. The last man became very frightened indeed and besides by now the springbok had rotted. He took his bow and arrows and ran away.[†]

I left the British Library and my research on some women of the 1890s whose feminist, working-class newspaper advocated meatless diets, and went through the cafeteria line in a restaurant nearby. Vegetarian food in hand, I descended to the basement. A painting of Henry VIII eating a steak and kidney pie greeted my gaze. On either side of the consuming Henry were portraits of his six wives and other women. However, they were not eating steak and kidney pie, nor anything else made of meat. Catherine of Aragon held an apple in her hands. The Countess of Mar had a turnip, Anne Boleyn – red grapes, Anne of Cleaves – a pear, Jane Seymour – blue grapes, Catherine Howard – a carrot, Catherine Parr – a cabbage.

People with power have always eaten meat. The aristocracy of Europe consumed large courses filled with every kind of meat while the laborer consumed the complex carbohydrates. Dietary habits proclaim class distinctions, but they proclaim patriarchal distinctions as well. Women, second-class citizens, are more likely to eat what are considered to be second-class foods in a patriarchal culture: vegetables, fruits, and grains rather than meat. The sexism in meat eating recapitulates the class distinctions with an added twist: a mythology permeates all classes that meat is a masculine food and meat eating a male activity.

MALE IDENTIFICATION AND MEAT EATING

Meat-eating societies gain male identification by their choice of food, and meat textbooks heartily endorse this association. *The Meat We Eat* proclaims meat to be "A Virile and Protective Food," thus "a liberal meat supply has always been associated with a happy and virile people."[1] *Meat Technology* informs us that "the virile Australian race is a typical example of heavy meat-eaters."[2] Leading gourmands refer "to the virile ordeal of spooning the brains directly out of a barbecued calf's head."[3] *Virile: of or having the characteristics of an adult male,* from *vir* meaning *man.* Meat eating measures individual and societal virility.

Meat is a constant for men, intermittent for women, a pattern painfully observed in famine situations today. Women are starving at a rate disproportionate to [that of] men. Lisa Leghorn and Mary Roodkowsky surveyed this phenomenon in their book *Who Really Starves? Women and World Hunger.* Women, they conclude, engage in deliberate self-deprivation, offering men the "best" foods at the expense of their own nutritional needs. For instance, they tell us that "Ethiopian women and girls of all classes are obliged to prepare two meals, one for the males and a second, often containing no meat or other substantial protein, for the females."[4]

In fact, men's protein needs are less than those of pregnant and nursing women and the disproportionate distribution of the main protein source occurs when women's need for protein is the greatest. Curiously, we are now being told that one should eat meat (or fish, vegetables, chocolate, and salt) at least six weeks before becoming pregnant if one wants a boy. But if a girl is desired, no meat please, rather milk, cheese, nuts, beans, and cereals.[5]

Fairy tales initiate us at an early age into the dynamics of eating and sex roles. The king in his countinghouse ate four-and-twenty blackbirds in a pie (originally four-and-twenty naughty boys) while the Queen ate bread and honey. Cannibalism in fairy tales is generally a male activity, as Jack, after climbing his beanstalk, quickly learned. Folktales of all nations depict giants as male and "fond of eating human flesh."[6] Witches – warped or monstrous women in the eyes of a patriarchal world – become the token female cannibals.

A Biblical example of the male prerogative for meat rankled Elizabeth Cady Stanton, a leading nineteenth-century feminist, as can be seen by her terse comment on Leviticus 6 in *The Woman's Bible:* "The meat so delicately cooked by the priests, with wood and coals in the altar, in clean linen, no woman was permitted to taste, only the males among the children of Aaron."[7]

Most food taboos address meat consumption and they place more restrictions on women than on men. The common foods forbidden to women are chicken, duck, and pork. Forbidding meat to women in nontechnological cultures increases its prestige. Even if the women raise the pigs, as they do in the Solomon Islands, they are rarely allowed to eat the pork. When they do receive some, it is at the dispensation of their husbands. In Indonesia "flesh food is viewed as the property of the men. At feasts, the principal times when meat is available, it is distributed to households according to the men in them … The system of distribution thus reinforces the prestige of the men in society."[8]

Worldwide this patriarchal custom is found. In Asia, some cultures forbid women from consuming fish, seafood, chicken, duck, and eggs. In equatorial Africa, the prohibition of chicken to women is common. For example, the Mbum Kpau women do not eat chicken, goat, partridge, or other game birds. The Kufa of Ethiopia punished women who ate chicken by making them slaves, while the Walamo "put to death anyone who violated the restriction of eating fowl."

Correspondingly, vegetables and other non-meat foods are viewed as women's food. This makes them undesirable to men. The Nuer men think that eating eggs is effeminate. In other groups men require sauces to disguise the fact that they are eating women's foods. "Men expect to have meat sauces to go with their porridge and will sometimes refuse to eat sauces made of greens or other vegetables, which are said to be women's food."[9]

MEAT: FOR THE MAN ONLY

> There is no department in the store where good selling can do so much good or where poor selling can do so much harm as in the meat department. This is because most women do not consider themselves competent judges of meat quality and often buy where they have confidence in the meat salesman. (Hinman and Harris, *The Story of Meat*)[10]

In technological societies, cookbooks reflect the presumption that men eat meat. A random survey of cookbooks reveals that the barbecue sections of most cookbooks are addressed to men and feature meat. The foods recommended for a "Mother's Day Tea" do not include meat, but readers are advised that on Father's Day, dinner should include London Broil because "a steak dinner has unfailing popularity with fathers."[11] In a chapter on "Feminine Hospitality" we are directed to serve vegetables, salads and soups. The New *McCall's* Cookbook suggests that a man's favorite dinner is London Broil. A "Ladies' Luncheon" would consist of cheese dishes and vegetables, but no meat. A section of one cookbook entitled "For Men Only" reinforces the omnipresence of meat in men's lives. What is for men only? London Broil, cubed steak and beef dinner.[12]

Twentieth-century cookbooks only serve to confirm the historical pattern found in the nineteenth century, when British working-class families could not afford sufficient meat to feed the entire family. "For the man only" appears continually in many of the menus of these families when referring to meat. In adhering to the mythologies of a culture (men need meat; meat gives bull-like strength) the male "breadwinner" actually received the meat. Social historians report that the "lion's share" of meat went to the husband.

What then was for women during the nine-teenth century? On Sundays they might have a modest but good dinner. On the other days their food was bread with butter or drippings, weak tea, pudding, and vegetables. "The wife, in very poor families, is probably the worst-fed of the household," observed Dr. Edward Smith in the first national food survey of British dietary habits in 1863, which revealed that the major difference in the diet of men and women in the same family was the amount of meat consumed.[13] Later investigators were told that the women and children in one rural county of England, "eat the potatoes and look at the meat."[14]

Where poverty forced a conscious distribution of meat, men received it. Many women emphasized that they had saved the meat for their husbands. They were articulating the prevailing connections between meat eating and the male role: "I keep it for him; he *has* to have it." Sample menus for South London laborers "showed extra meat, extra fish, extra cakes, or a different quality of meat for the man." Women ate meat once a week with their children, while the husband consumed meat and bacon, "almost daily."

Early in the present century, the Fabian Women's group in London launched a four-year study in which they recorded the daily budget of thirty families in a working-class community. These budgets were collected and explained in a compassionate book, *Round About a Pound a Week*. Here is perceived clearly the sexual politics of meat: "In the household which spends 10s or even less on food, only one kind of diet is possible, and that is the man's diet. The children have what is left over. There must be a Sunday joint, or, if that be not possible, at least a Sunday dish of meat, in order to satisfy the father's desire for the kind of food he relishes, and most naturally therefore intends to have." More succinctly, we are told: "Meat is bought for the men" and the leftover meat from the Sunday dinner, "is eaten cold by him the next day."[15] Poverty also determines who carves the meat. As Cicely Hamilton discovered during this same period, women carve when they know there is not enough meat to go around.[16]

In situations of abundance, sex role assumptions about meat are not so blatantly expressed.

For this reason, the diets of English upper-class women and men are much more similar than the diets of upper-class women and working-class women. Moreover, with the abundance of meat available in the United States as opposed to the restricted amount available in England, there has been enough for all, except when meat supplies were controlled. For instance, while enslaved black men received half a pound of meat per day, enslaved black women often found that they received little more than a quarter pound a day at times.[17] Additionally, during the wars of the twentieth century, the pattern of meat consumption recalled that of English nineteenth-century working-class families with one variation: the "worker" of the country's household, the soldier, got the meat; civilians were urged to learn how to cook without meat.

THE RACIAL POLITICS OF MEAT

The hearty meat eating that characterizes the diet of Americans and of the Western world is not only a symbol of male power, it is an index of racism. I do not mean racism in the sense that we are treating one class of animals, those that are not human beings, differently than we treat another, those that are, as Isaac Bashevis Singer uses the term in *Enemies: A Love Story:* "As often as Herman had witnessed the slaughter of animals and fish, he always had the same thought: in their behavior toward creatures, all men were Nazis. The smugness with which man could do with other species as he pleased exemplified the most extreme racist theories, the principle that might is right."[18] I mean racism as the requirement that power arrangements and customs that favor white people prevail, and that the acculturation of people of color to this standard includes the imposition of white habits of meat eating.

Two parallel beliefs can be traced in the white Western world's enactment of racism when the issue is meat eating. The first is that if the meat supply is limited, white people should get it; but if meat is plentiful all should eat it. This is a variation on the standard theme of the sexual politics of meat. The hierarchy of meat protein reinforces a hierarchy of race, class, and sex.

Nineteenth-century advocates of white superiority endorsed meat as superior food. "Brainworkers" required lean meat as their main meal, but the "savage" and "lower" classes of society could live exclusively on coarser foods, according to George Beard, a nineteenth-century medical doctor who specialized in the diseases of middle-class people. He recommended that when white, civilized, middle-class men became susceptible to nervous exhaustion, they should eat more meat. To him, and for many others, cereals and fruits were lower than meat on the scale of evolution, and thus appropriate foods for the other races and white women, who appeared to be lower on the scale of evolution as well. Racism and sexism together upheld meat as white man's food.

Influenced by Darwin's theory of evolution, Beard proposed a corollary for foods; animal protein did to vegetable food what our evolution from the lower animals did for humans. Consequently:

> In proportion as man grows sensitive through civilization or through disease, he should diminish the quantity of cereals and fruits, which are far below him on the scale of evolution, and increase the quantity of animal food, which is nearly related to him in the scale of evolution, and therefore more easily assimilated.[19]

In his racist analysis, Beard reconciled the apparent contradiction of this tenet: "Why is it that savages and semi-savages are able to live on forms of food which, according to the theory of evolution, must be far below them in the scale of development?" In other words, how is it that people can survive very well without a great deal of animal protein? Because "savages" are

> little removed from the common animal stock from which they are derived. They are much nearer to the forms of life from which they feed than are the highly civilized brain-workers, and can therefore subsist on forms of life which would be most poisonous to us. Secondly, savages who feed

on poor food are poor savages, and intellectually far inferior to the beef-eaters of any race.

This explanation – which divided the world into intellectually superior meat eaters and inferior plant eaters – accounted for the conquering of other cultures by the English:

> The rice-eating Hindoo and Chinese and the potato-eating Irish peasant are kept in subjection by the well-fed English. Of the various causes that contributed to the defeat of Napoleon at Waterloo, one of the chief was that for the first time he was brought face to face with the nation of beef-eaters, who stood still until they were killed.

Into the twentieth century the notion was that meat eating contributed to the Western world's preeminence. Publicists for a meat company in the 1940s wrote: "We know meat-eating races have been and are leaders in the progress made by mankind in its upward struggle through the ages."[20] They are referring to the "upward struggle" of the white race. One revealing aspect of this "upward struggle" is the charge of cannibalism that appeared during the years of colonization.

The word "cannibalism" entered our vocabulary after the "discovery" of the "New World." Derived from the Spaniards' mispronunciation of the name of the people of the Caribbean, it linked these people of color with the act. As Europeans explored the continents of North and South America and Africa, the indigenous peoples of those lands became accused of cannibalism – the ultimate savage act. Once labeled as cannibals, their defeat and enslavement at the hands of civilized, Christian whites became justifiable. W. Arens argues that the charge of cannibalism was part and parcel of the European expansion into other continents.[21]

Of the charges of cannibalism against the indigenous peoples, Arens found little independent verification. One well-known source of dubious testimony on cannibalism was then plagiarized by others claiming to be eyewitnesses. The eyewitnesses fail to describe just how they were able to escape the fate of consumption they report witnessing. Nor do they explain how the language barrier was overcome enabling them to report verbatim conversations with "savages." In addition, their reports fail to maintain internal consistency.

One cause of cannibalism was thought to be lack of animal protein. Yet most Europeans themselves during the centuries of European expansion were not subsisting on animal protein every day. The majority of cultures in the world satisfied their protein needs through vegetables and grains. By charging indigenous peoples with cannibalism (and thus demonstrating their utterly savage ways, for they supposedly did to humans what Europeans only did to animals) one justification for colonization was provided.

Racism is perpetuated each time meat is thought to be the best protein source. The emphasis on the nutritional strengths of animal protein distorts the dietary history of most cultures in which complete protein dishes were made of vegetables and grains. Information about these dishes is overwhelmed by an ongoing cultural and political commitment to meat eating.

MEAT IS KING

During wartime, government rationing policies reserve the right to meat for the epitome of the masculine man: the soldier. With meat rationing in effect for civilians during World War II, the per capita consumption of meat in the army and navy was about two-and-a-half times that of the average civilian. Russell Baker observed that World War II began a "beef madness ... when richly fatted beef was force-fed into every putative American warrior."[22] In contrast to the recipe books for civilians that praised complex carbohydrates, cookbooks for soldiers contained variation upon variation of meat dishes. One survey conducted of four military training camps reported that the soldier consumed daily 131 grams of protein, 201 grams of fat, and 484 grams of carbohydrates.[23] Hidden costs of warring masculinity are to be found in the provision of male-defined foods to the warriors.

Women are the food preparers; meat has to be cooked to be palatable for people. Thus, in a patriarchal culture, just as our culture accedes to the "needs" of its soldiers, women accede to the dietary demands of their husbands, especially when it comes to meat. The feminist surveyors of women's budgets in the early twentieth century observed:

It is quite likely that someone who had strength, wisdom, and vitality, who did not live that life in those tiny, crowded rooms, in that lack of light and air, who was not bowed down with worry, but was herself economically independent of the man who earned the money, could lay out his few shillings with a better eye to a scientific food value. It is quite as likely, however, that the man who earned the money would entirely refuse the scientific food, and demand his old tasty kippers and meat.[24]

A discussion of nutrition during wartime contained this aside: it was one thing, they acknowledged, to demonstrate that there were many viable alternatives to meat, "but it is another to convince a man who enjoys his beefsteak."[25] The male prerogative to eat meat is an external, observable activity implicitly reflecting a recurring fact: meat is a symbol of male dominance.

It has traditionally been felt that the working man needs meat for strength. A superstition analogous to homeopathic principles operates in this belief: in eating the muscle of strong animals, we will become strong. According to the mythology of patriarchal culture, meat promotes strength; the attributes of masculinity are achieved through eating these masculine foods. Visions of meat-eating football players, wrestlers, and boxers lumber in our brains in this equation. Though vegetarian weight lifters and athletes in other fields have demonstrated the equation to be fallacious, the myth remains: men are strong, men need to be strong, thus men need meat. The literal evocation of male power is found in the concept of meat.

Irving Fisher took the notion of "strength" from the definition of meat eating as long ago as 1906. Fisher suggested that strength be measured by its lasting power rather than by its association with quick results, and compared meat-eating athletes with vegetarian athletes and sedentary vegetarians. Endurance was measured by having the participants perform in three areas: holding their arms horizontally for as long as possible, doing deep knee bends, and performing leg raises while lying down. He concluded that the vegetarians, whether athletes or not, had greater endurance than meat eaters. "Even the *maximum* record of the flesh-eaters was barely more than half the *average* for the flesh-abstainers."[26]

Meat is king: this noun describing meat is a noun denoting male power. Vegetables, a generic term meat eaters use for all foods that are not meat, have become as associated with women as meat is with men, recalling on a subconscious level the days of Woman the Gatherer. Since women have been made subsidiary in a male-dominated, meat-eating world, so has our food. The foods associated with second-class citizens are considered to be second-class protein. Just as it is thought a woman cannot make it on her own, so we think that vegetables cannot make a meal on their own, despite the fact that meat is only secondhand vegetables and vegetables provide, on the average, more than twice the vitamins and minerals of meat. Meat is upheld as a powerful, irreplaceable item of food. The message is clear: the vassal vegetable should content itself with its assigned place and not attempt to dethrone king meat. After all, how can one enthrone women's foods when women cannot be kings?

THE MALE LANGUAGE OF MEAT EATING

Men who decide to eschew meat eating are deemed effeminate; failure of men to eat meat announces that they are not masculine. Nutritionist Jean Mayer suggested that "the more men sit at their desks all day, the more they want to be reassured about their maleness in eating those large slabs of bleeding meat which are the last symbol of machismo."[27] The late Marty Feldman observed, "It has to do with the function of the male within our society. Football players drink beer because it's a man's drink, and eat steak because it's a man's meal. The emphasis is on 'man-sized portions,' 'hero' sandwiches; the whole terminology of meat-eating reflects this masculine bias."[28] Meat-and-potatoes men are our stereotypical strong and hearty, rough and ready, able males. Hearty beef stews are named "Man-handlers." Chicago Bears' head football coach, Mike Ditka, operates a restaurant that features "he-man food" such as steaks and chops.

One's maleness is reassured by the food one eats. During the 1973 meat boycott, men were reported to observe the boycott when dining out with their wives or eating at home, but when they dined without their wives, they ate London Broil and other meats.[29] When in 1955 Carolyn Steedman's mother "made a salad of grated vegetables for Christmas dinner," her husband walked out.[30]

GENDER INEQUALITY/SPECIES INEQUALITY

The men ... were better hunters than the women, but only because the women had found they could live quite well on foods other than meat.

Alice Walker, *The Temple of My Familiar*[31]

What is it about meat that makes it a symbol and celebration of male dominance? In many ways, gender inequality is built into the species inequality that meat eating proclaims, because for most cultures obtaining meat was performed by men. Meat was a valuable economic commodity; those who controlled this commodity achieved power. If men were the hunters, then the control of this economic resource was in their hands.

Women's status is inversely related to the importance of meat in nontechnological societies:

The equation is simple: the more important meat is in their life, the greater relative dominance will the men command ... When meat becomes an important element within a more closely organized economic system so that there exist rules for its distribution, then men already begin to swing the levers of power ... Women's social standing is roughly equal to men's only when society itself is not formalized around roles for distributing meat.[32]

Peggy Sanday surveyed information on over a hundred nontechnological cultures and found a correlation between plant-based economies and women's power and animal-based economies and male power. "In societies dependent on animals, women are rarely depicted as the ultimate source of creative power." In addition, "When large animals are hunted, fathers are more distant, that is, they are not in frequent or regular proximity to infants."[33]

Characteristics of economies dependent mainly on the processing of animals for food include:

- sexual segregation in work activities, with women doing more work than men, but work that is less valued
- women responsible for child care
- the worship of male gods
- patrilineality

On the other hand, plant-based economies are more likely to be egalitarian. This is because women are and have been the gatherers of vegetable foods, and these are invaluable resources for a culture that is plant-based. In these cultures, men as well as women were dependent on women's activities. From this, women achieved autonomy and a degree of self-sufficiency. Yet, where women gather vegetable food and the diet is vegetarian, women do not discriminate as a consequence of distributing the staple. By providing a large proportion of the protein food of a society, women gain an essential economic and social role without abusing it.

Sanday summarizes one myth that links male power to control of meat:

The Mundurucu believe that there was a time when women ruled and the sex roles were reversed, with the exception that women could not hunt. During that time women were the sexual aggressors and men were sexually submissive and did women's work. Women controlled the "sacred trumpets" (the symbols of power) and the men's houses. The trumpets contained the spirits of the ancestors who demanded ritual offerings of meat. Since women did not hunt and could not make these offerings, men were able to take the trumpets from them, thereby establishing male dominance.[34]

We might observe that the male role of hunter and distributer of meat has been transposed to the male role of eater of meat and conclude that this accounts for meat's role as symbol of male dominance. But there is much more to meat's role as symbol than this.

"VEGETABLE": SYMBOL OF FEMININE PASSIVITY?

Both the words "men" and "meat" have undergone lexicographical narrowing. Originally generic terms, they are now closely associated with their specific referents. Meat no longer means all foods; the word *man,* we realize, no longer includes *women.* Meat represents *the essence or principal part of something,* according to the *American Heritage Dictionary.* Thus we have the "meat of the matter," "a meaty question." To "beef up" something is to improve it. Vegetable, on the other hand, represents the least desirable characteristics: *suggesting or like a vegetable, as in passivity or dullness of existence, monotonous, inactive.* Meat is *something one enjoys or excels in,* vegetable becomes representative of someone who does not enjoy anything: a *person who leads a monotonous, passive, or merely physical existence.*

A complete reversal has occurred in the definition of the word vegetable. Whereas its original sense was to *be lively, active,* it is now viewed as dull, monotonous, passive. To vegetate is to lead a passive existence; just as to be feminine is to lead a passive existence. Once vegetables are viewed as women's food, then by association they become viewed as "feminine," passive.

Men's need to disassociate themselves from women's food (as in the myth in which the last Bushman flees in the direction opposite from women and their vegetable food) has been institutionalized in sexist attitudes toward vegetables and the use of the word *vegetable* to express criticism or disdain. Colloquially it is a synonym for a person severely brain-damaged or in a coma. In addition, vegetables are thought to have a tranquilizing, dulling, numbing effect on people who consume them, and so we can not possibly get strength from them. According to this perverse incarnation of Brillat-Savarin's theory that you are what you eat, to eat a vegetable is to become a vegetable, and by extension, to become woman-like.

Examples from the 1988 Presidential Campaign in which each candidate was belittled through equation with being a vegetable illustrates this patriarchal disdain for vegetables. Michael Dukakis was called "the Vegetable Plate Candidate."[35] Northern Sun Merchandising offered T-shirts that asked: "George Bush: Vegetable or Noxious Weed?" One could opt for a shirt that featured a bottle of ketchup and a picture of Ronald Reagan with this slogan: *"Nutrition Quiz:* Which one is the vegetable?"[36] [...]

The word vegetable acts as a synonym for women's passivity because women are supposedly like plants. Hegel makes this clear: "The difference between men and women is like that between animals and plants. Men correspond to animals, while women correspond to plants because their development is more placid."[37] From this viewpoint, both women and plants are seen as less developed and less evolved than men and animals. Consequently, women may eat plants, since each is placid; but active men need animal meat.

MEAT IS A SYMBOL OF PATRIARCHY

In her essay, "Deciphering a Meal," the noted anthropologist Mary Douglas suggests that the order in which we serve foods, and the foods we insist on being present at a meal, reflect a taxonomy of classification that mirrors and reinforces our larger culture. A meal is an amalgam of food dishes, each a constituent part of the whole, each with an assigned value. In addition, each dish is introduced in precise order. A meal does not begin with a dessert, nor end with soup. All is seen as leading up to and then coming down from the entree that is meat. The pattern is evidence of stability. As Douglas explains, "The ordered system which is a meal represents all the ordered systems associated with it. Hence the strong arousal power of a threat to weaken or confuse that category."[38] To remove meat is to threaten the structure of the larger patriarchal culture.

Marabel Morgan, one expert on how women should accede to every male desire, reported in her *Total Woman Cookbook* that one must be careful about introducing foods that are seen as a threat: "I discovered that Charlie seemed threatened by certain foods. He was suspicious of my casseroles, thinking I had sneaked in some wheat germ or 'good-for-you' vegetables that he wouldn't like."[39]

Mary McCarthy's *Birds of America* provides a fictional illustration of the intimidating aspect to a man of a woman's refusal of meat. Miss Scott, a vegetarian, is invited to a NATO general's house for Thanksgiving. Her refusal of turkey angers the general. Not able to take this rejection seriously, as male dominance requires a continual recollection of itself on everyone's plate, the general loads her plate up with turkey and then ladles gravy over the potatoes as well as the meat, "thus contaminating her vegetable foods." McCarthy's description of his actions with the food mirrors the warlike customs associated with military battles. "He had seized the gravy boat like a weapon in hand-to-hand combat. No wonder they had made him a brigadier general – at least that mystery was solved." The general continues to behave in a bellicose fashion and after dinner proposes a toast in honor of an eighteen-year-old who has enlisted to fight in Vietnam. During the ensuing argument about war the general defends the bombing of Vietnam with the rhetorical question: "What's so sacred about a civilian?" This upsets the hero, necessitating that the general's wife apologize for her husband's behavior: "Between you and me," she confides to him, "it kind of got under his skin to see that girl refusing to touch her food. I saw that right away."[40]

Male belligerence in this area is not limited to fictional military men. Men who batter women have often used the absence of meat as a pretext for violence against women. Women's failure to serve meat is not the cause of the violence against them. Yet, as a pretext for this violence, meat is hardly a trivial item. "Real" men eat meat. Failing to honor the importance of this symbol catalyzes male rage. As one woman battered by her husband reported, "It would start off with him being angry over trivial little things, a trivial little thing like cheese instead of meat on a sandwich."[41] Another woman stated, "A month ago he threw scalding water over me, leaving a scar on my right arm, all because I gave him a pie with potatoes and vegetables for his dinner, instead of fresh meat."[42]

Men who become vegetarians challenge an essential part of the masculine role. They are opting for women's food. How dare they? Refusing meat means a man is effeminate, a "sissy," a "fruit." Indeed, in 1836, the response to the vegetarian regimen of that day, known as Grahamism, charged that "Emasculation is the first fruit of Grahamism."[43]

Men who choose not to eat meat repudiate one of their masculine privileges. The *New York Times* explored this idea in an editorial on the masculine nature of meat eating. Instead of "the John Wayne type," epitome of the masculine meat eater, the new male hero is "Vulnerable" like Alan Alda, Mikhail Baryshnikov, and Phil Donahue. They might eat fish and chicken, but not red meat. Alda and Donahue, among other men, have repudiated not only the macho role, but also macho food. According to the *Times,* "Believe me. The end of macho marks the end of the meat-and-potatoes man."[44] We won't miss either.

NOTES

† H. R. Hays, *The Dangerous Sex: The Myth of Feminine Evil* (New York: Pocket Books, 1964), p. 37.

1. P. Thomas Ziegler, *The Meat We Eat* (Danville, IL: The Interstate Printers and Publishers, 1966), pp. 5, 1.
2. Frank Gerrard, *Meat Technology: A Practical Textbook for Student and Butcher* (London: Northwood, 1945, 1977), p. 348.
3. Waverley Root and Richard de Rochemont, *Eating in America: A History* (New York: William Morrow, 1976), p. 279.
4. Lisa Leghorn and Mary Roodkowsky, *Who Really Starves? Women and World Hunger* (New York: Friendship Press, 1977), p. 21.
5. Lloyd Shearer, "Intelligence Report: Does Diet Determine Sex?", summarizing the conclusions of Dr. Joseph Stolkowski, *Parade* 27 June 1982, p. 7.
6. William S. Baring-Gould and Ceil Baring-Gould, *The Annotated Mother Goose* (New York: Bramhall House, 1962), p. 103.
7. Elizabeth Cady Stanton, *The Woman's Bible: Part I* (New York: European Publishing Co., 1898; Seattle: Coalition Task Force on Women and Religion, 1974), p. 91.
8. Frederick J. Simoons, *Eat Not This Flesh: Food Avoidances in the Old World* (Madison: University of Wisconsin Press, 1961, 1967), p. 12. The quotation in the following paragraph is found in Simoons, p. 73.
9. Bridget O'Laughlin, "Mediation of Contradiction: Why Mbum Women do not eat Chicken," *Woman, Culture, and Society,* ed. Michelle Zimbalist Rosaldo and Louise Lamphere (Stanford: Stanford University Press, 1974), p. 303.
10. Robert B. Hinman and Robert B. Harris, *The Story of Meat* (Chicago: Swift & Co., 1939, 1942), p. 191.
11. Sunset Books and Sunset Magazines, *Sunset Menu Cook Book* (Menlo Park, CA: Lane Magazine and Book Co., 1969), pp. 139, 140.
12. *Oriental Cookery* from ChunKing and Mazola Corn Oil.
13. Edward Smith, M.D., *Practical Dietary for Families, Schools and the Labouring Classes* (London: Walton and Maberly, 1864), p. 199.

14. Laura Oren, "The Welfare of Women in Laboring Families: England, 1860–1950," *Feminist Studies* 1, no. 3–4 (Winter/Spring 1973), p. 110, quoting B. S. Rowntree and May Kendall, *How the Labourer Lives: A Study of the Rural Labour Problem* (London: Thomas Nelson and Sons, 1913). The quotations in the following paragraph are from Oren, p. 110, quoting Rowntree and Maud Pember Reeves, *Round About a Pound a Week.*

15. Maud Pember Reeves, *Round About a Pound a Week* (G. Bell and Sons 1913, London: Virago Press, 1979), pp. 144 and 97.

16. Cicely Hamilton, *Marriage as a Trade* (1909, London: The Women's Press, 1981), p. 75.

17. Todd L. Savitt, *Medicine and Slavery: The Diseases and Health Care of Blacks in Antebellum Virginia* (Urbana and Chicago: University of Illinois Press, 1978), p. 91.

18. Isaac Bashevis Singer, *Enemies: A Love Story* (New York: Farrar, Straus and Giroux, 1972), p. 257.

19. George M. Beard, M. D., *Sexual Neurasthenia (Nervous Exhaustion) Its Hygiene, Causes, Symptoms and Treatment with a Chapter on Diet for the Nervous* (New York: E. B. Treat & Co., 1898, New York: Arno Press, 1972). This and succeeding quotations are found on pp. 272–78.

20. Hinman and Harris, *The Story of Meat,* p. 1.

21. W. Arens, *The Man-Eating Myth: Anthropology and Anthropophagy* (New York: Oxford University Press, 1979).

22. Russell Baker, "Red Meat Decadence," *New York Times* 3 April 1973, p. 43.

23. Aaron M. Altschul, *Proteins: Their Chemistry and Politics* (New York: Basic Books, 1965), p. 101.

24. Reeves, p. 131.

25. Helen Hunscher and Marqueta Huyck, "Nutrition," in *Consumer Problems in Wartime,* ed. Kenneth Dameron (New York and London: McGraw-Hill, 1944), p. 414.

26. Irving Fisher, "The Influence of Flesh Eating on Endurance," *Yale Medical Journal* 13, no. 5 (March 1907), p. 207.

27. Quoted in "Red Meat: American Man's Last Symbol of Machismo," *National Observer* 10 July 1976, p. 13.

28. Marty Feldman, quoted in Rynn Berry Jr., *The Vegetarians* (Brookline, MA: Autumn Press, 1979), p. 32.

29. *New York Times* 15 April 1973, p. 38.

30. She concludes, "and I wish he'd taken us with him." Carolyn Steedman, "Landscape for a Good Woman," in *Truth, Dare or Promise: Girls Growing Up in the Fifties,* ed. Liz Heron (London: Virago Press, 1985), p. 114.

31. Alice Walker, *The Temple of My Familiar* (San Diego, New York: Harcourt Brace Jovanovich, 1989), p. 50.

32. Richard E. Leakey and Roger Lewin, *People of the Lake: Mankind and Its Beginnings* (New York: Doubleday & Co., 1978, New York: Avon Books, 1979), pp.210–11.

33. Peggy Sanday, *Female Power and Male Dominance: On the Origins of Sexual Inequality* (Cambridge and New York: Cambridge University Press, 1981), pp. 65, 66.

34. Sanday 1981, p. 39.

35. Sandy Grady, "The Duke as Boring as Spinach," *Buffalo News* 26 March 1988.

36. From a catalog from Northern Sun Merchandising, 2916 E. Lake Street, Minneapolis, MN, 55406.

37. From Hegel's *Philosophy of Right,* para. 166, p. 263, quoted in Nancy Tuana, "The Misbegotten Man: Scientific, Religious, and Philosophical Images of Women," unpublished manuscript.

38. Mary Douglas, "Deciphering a Meal," in *Implicit Meanings: Essays in Anthropology* (London: Routledge & Kegan Paul, 1975), p. 273.

39. Marabel Morgan, *Marabel Morgan's Handbook for Kitchen Survival: The Total Woman Cookbook* (New Jersey: Fleming H. Revell Co., 1980), p. 13.

40. Mary McCarthy, *Birds of America* (New York: Harcourt Brace Jovanovich, 1965, New York: New American Library, 1972), pp. 167, 180, 183.

41. R. Emerson Dobash and Russell Dobash, *Violence Against Wives: A Case Against the Patriarchy* (New York: The Free Press, 1979), p. 100.

42. Erin Pizzey, *Scream Quietly or the Neighbours will Hear* (Harmondsworth: Penguin, 1974), p. 35.

43. James C. Whorton, "'Tempest in a Flesh-Pot': The Formulation of a Physiological Rationale for Vegetarianism," *Journal of the History of Medicine and Allied Sciences* 32, no. 2 (April 1977), p. 122.

44. Editorial, *New York Times,* 17 August 1981.

20

DAVID NIBERT

The Promotion of "Meat" and its Consequences*

David Nibert, a sociologist who has worked as a tenant organizer and community activist, studies the historical and contemporary entanglement of the oppression of humans and other animals. With a focus on the prevention of mistreatment and violence against devalued groups, he has published in journals devoted to child welfare, interpersonal violence, victimization of women and children, and critical sociology. The extract reproduced below is from his book, *Animal Rights /Human Rights: Entanglements of Oppression and Liberation*, which describes the myriad ways capitalist culture and the profit motive cause the oppression of humans and other animals. Nibert extends Carol Adams's analysis of the patriarchal text of meat by drawing attention to the larger ways in which the capitalist system similarly exploits less powerful groups of people and animals, arguing that the chief reason for the oppression of human groups and animals is monetary gain. Additionally, he describes his own analysis as supplementing Adams's work by "suggesting that the hunting of other animals not only produced 'food' primarily consumed by the ruling class and patriarchy but that it also was entangled with the origins of the systematic subordination and oppression of women – and eventually became entangled with countless systems of oppression, past and present." In his chapter on Agribusiness and Global Oppression, Nibert explores the connection between current agribusiness practices, meat consumption, global environmental problems and starvation in less developed countries. He uses examples from Central America to describe how US corporate interests have propped up dictators who have violently taken land from citizens so that it could be used for "beef" production. [You will note that Nibert uses quotation marks around words such as "beef" to problematize the language we use that serves to obscure and justify the oppression of animals.] In the extract we reproduce below from that chapter Nibert argues that the connection between the oppression of humans and animals is rooted in the capitalist political economic system, with consequences that play out across the boundaries of nation-states.

* Reprinted with permission of the publisher and from David Nibert (2002) *Animal Rights and Human Rights: Entanglements of Oppression and Liberation*. Lanham, Boulder, New York, and Oxford: Rowman & Littlefield Publishers, Inc.

The focus of agribusiness giants on highly profitable sales of "meat," milk, and egg "products" is based on a long-standing manipulation of cultural practices and consumer preferences.

Earlier in US history, "meat" consumption was much lower than it is today,[1] and pigs were the most widely consumed "meat." However, in the late nineteenth century, large "meat" producers like Armour and Swift greatly increased their production of more profitable "beef". Fat from pigs' bodies, once used as lubricants and illuminants, was being replaced by petroleum, and by-products derived from the skin and other body parts of cows – such as "cowhide" – could fetch far more revenues than pig corpses. Much US "beef," however, was exported for consumption by the privileged in Europe.

In the post-World War II period, when the United States enjoyed economic domination of the Western world, the increased incomes of many in the United States facilitated increased domestic consumption of "beef." New businesses were created, such as White Castle and McDonald's. The industry boosted market demand – through relentless advertising – and capitalized on the increasing consumption of "steers" and "unproductive" cows, particularly in the form of "hamburgers." By 1977, nearly 40 percent of all "beef" consumed in the United States was in the form of "ground beef." Unlike "steaks" and other "choice cuts" of flesh, hamburgers are largely derived from the bodies of grass-fed "steers," as opposed to grain-fed "steers" who produce more desirable "cuts." Much of the grass-fed "cattle" raised in Central America is exported to North America.[2]

Consumption of other animals as food in the United States grew, especially in the latter half of the twentieth century, as agribusiness aggressively marketed the growing supply of "goods." Between 1950 and 1976, the US per capita consumption of "beef" alone more than doubled, from 63.4 to 129.4 pounds annually.[3] Profitable fast-food chains flourished as they promoted the growth and expansion of the "hamburger culture." With greater production and consumption of "farm" animals facilitated by the Green Revolution – other animals increasingly being fed grain to facilitate rapid weight gain and reduce "production" time – the use of agricultural land shifted, until about 80 percent of the grain crops were raised to be used as feed for the hundreds of millions of other animals who were exploited for their milk or eggs or slaughtered for their flesh. Today an enormous amount of land in the United States alone, more than 302 million hectares, is used to produce food for the billions of other animals relegated to the social position of "livestock"; of this land, about 272 million hectares are pasture and 30 million are used for cultivation of various "feed" grains.[4]

Increased exploitation of billions of other animals as food is deplorable not only because of the misery of the other animals and the exploitation of agricultural workers but also because agribusiness's self-interested pursuit of short-term profits prevents the development of a rational, sustainable, and ethical form of food production. Jacques Leslie is among those who see the link between escalating "meat" consumption and the destruction of land and depletion of water. He writes:

> Livestock have already grown so numerous that 20 percent of the earth's rangeland has lost productivity because of overgrazing … A ton of potatoes … needs 500 to 1,500 tons of water, while a ton of chicken needs 3,500 to 5,700 tons of water, and a ton of beef needs 15,000 to 70,000 tons of water.[5]

A report by a panel of scientists whose work appeared in a 2001 article in the journal *Science* projects an increase in the human population from six billion in 2000 to nine billion by 2050. This increase will "double the world's food demands by mid-century, partly because people in wealthy countries will want diets rich in meat, which takes more resources to produce."[6] The report states that "the projected 50 percent increase in global population and demand for diets richer in meat" by the wealthier world "are projected to double global food demand by 2050." They suggest that, if contemporary forms of agriculture persist, by 2050 the global agricultural land base will have to increase by at least 109 hectares of land, resulting in the worldwide loss of forests and "natural ecosystems" in a total area larger than the United States. The displacement, destruction, and death brought on by appropriation of so much of the remaining homeland of devalued humans and other animals would be cataclysmic. The panel writes, "Because of regional availabilities of suitable land, this expansion of agricultural land is expected to occur predominantly in Latin America and sub-Saharan Africa. This could lead to the loss of about a third of remaining tropical and temperate forests, savannas, and grasslands and of the services, including carbon storage, provided by these ecosystems."[7]

Feeding a vastly increasing human population, especially under contemporary agribusiness with its emphasis on "meat" production, would require even greater levels of deforestation, increase desertification (the destruction of soil, rendering it infertile and desert-like), add to air pollution (caused in no small part by the vast amounts of methane gas generated by huge populations of other animals, particularly hundreds of millions of cows), exhaust freshwater supplies, and compound already-critical levels of water pollution. Such wide-scale environmental havoc in the name of food production is likely to leave a large segment of the increased global population undernourished (and leave few life-sustaining resources for future generations of humans and other animals) as long as the agricultural production under capitalism exists to make profits rather than to feed the world.[8] Recall E. P. Thompson's observation on the spirit that sparked agricultural improvements in the eighteenth century under conditions of early capitalism: "[T]he spirit of agricultural improvement in the 18th century was impelled less by altruistic desires to banish ugly wastes or – as the tedious phrase goes – to 'feed a growing population' than by the desire for fatter rent-rolls and larger profits."[9]

Precisely the same observation can be made of agriculture after two centuries of capitalist-based

social development. It is as sad as it is ironic that, despite the suffering and social and environmental costs of modern agribusiness methods, there has been little compensating lessening of hunger for hundreds of millions of humans around the world. Indeed, the Green Revolution and capitalist-controlled food production have exacerbated hunger. Modern agribusinesses produce food for everyone who can afford it, not for everyone who needs it.

For example, seeking increasing supplies of low-cost "beef" and "feed," giant US agribusinesses turned increasingly to Central American countries where many "cattle" are now raised and from which "feed" grains are imported at low cost – that is, at low cost to the corporations. Jeremy Rifkin writes:

> The increasing demand for beef in post-World War II Europe and the United States spurred renewed interest in the land of Latin America. In the 1960s, with the help of loans from the World Bank and the Inter-American Development Bank, governments throughout Central and South America began to convert millions of acres of tropical rain forests and cropland to pastureland to raise cattle for the international beef market ... Much of Central America was turned into a giant pasture to provide cheap beef for North America. In South America the Amazon rain forests were cleared and burned to make room for cattle grazing, largely to supply the beef needs of England and Europe ...
>
> At the same time, countries like Brazil are using more and more land to produce feed for livestock. When the land is seeded with soy, far less corn is available for human consumption, resulting in higher grain prices ...
>
> Mexico is devoting an increasing amount of its agricultural production to sorghum to feed cattle and other livestock ... This in a country where millions of people are chronically malnourished.[10]

Millions of humans in those nations have been forced from their homes and off small, subsistence farms by the economic elite in their countries, who appropriated huge areas of land and supplies of freshwater for cultivating feed crops and the flesh of other animals for export to wealthier nations rather than producing food for their own populations. Frances Moore Lappe and Joseph Collins note:

> [M]any of the countries in which hunger is rampant export much more in agricultural goods than they import. It is the industrial countries, not third world countries, that import more than two-thirds of all food and farm commodities in world trade. Imports by the 30 lowest-income countries, on the other hand, account for only 6 percent of all international commerce in food and farm commodities.[11]

Increasingly, then, Third World masses are no longer able to produce food for themselves, and they find it extremely difficult to afford food from countries like the United States. Modern agribusinesses produce food for those who can afford their products, not for those who need them. *Estimates of world hunger range "from 550 million to 1.3 billion,"[12] and those affected are disproportionately women and children.*

Interestingly, advocates for both humans and other animals frequently urge that, if privileged humans would only eat "meat" less often, enough food would be available to feed all the hungry humans in the world.[13] Such pleas are laudable; however, they are symptomatic of justice movements that downplay, or are not aware of, the structural forces underlying varying forms of oppression and its effects, including world hunger. Food is produced in capitalist society to generate profit. Unless the millions of hungry and malnourished have the resources to "demand" (i.e., to afford) the surplus food, it would likely be considered a "glut," and production simply would be scaled back accordingly in order to keep prices at profit-producing levels.

The "solution" to global hunger that agribusiness promotes is biotechnology. Biotech-produced crops are genetically altered to do such things as resist weed-killing chemicals and even to release their own insecticides, measures designed to increase yield per acre. Consumer groups and health organizations are deeply concerned about the "long-term health consequences of eating foods that are armed with insecticides and foreign genes."[14] Critics of genetically modified organisms, or GMOs, suspect that agribusiness has deliberately inundated the world market with genetically altered seeds to "pre-emptively settle the question of whether or not to accept biotechnology."[15] (Few, however, are complaining loudly about feeding other animals GMO grain; "the bulk of US grain sold for domestic and international use goes into animal feed.")[16] The plethora of critical problems thrust upon the world by agribusiness practices are thus to be "solved" by further expansion of chemical-based agriculture and genetically modified food (with little known about their long-term effects). Humans and other animals are increasingly left with little choice but to ingest biotech food. Still unanswered, however, is how the hundreds of millions around the world with few resources will be able to "demand" their share of the "brave new" food.

Many humans in the Third World, displaced from land now used to raise other animals or feed crops, have migrated to urban areas to look for jobs – a common historical pattern. There, those lucky enough to find employment are exploited by businesses, including many US-based multinational corporations seeking low-cost laborers, often to work in sweatshops. Ironically, apologists for the exploitation of these workers speak of the much-needed assistance multinational corporations are contributing to the "underdeveloped" economies of the Third World.

Poverty and "underdevelopment" in Third World countries, scholar and activist Michael Parenti observes, is not "an original historic condition" but, rather, the result "of the pillage they have endured."[17] Many in the United States are not aware that the "Communist threats" to the United States from Central and South American "guerrilla movements" they have occasionally heard about were, and continue to be, largely efforts by masses of dispossessed humans to regain land that had been expropriated by elites in their countries. The elites used much of the land to raise "cattle," "livestock" feed, and other "cash crops" that are sold to multinational corporations. Such US corporations as Borden, United Brands, International Foods, Cargill, Ralston Purina, and Weyerhaeuser have invested heavily in Latin American "beef" production.

While US corporations had expropriated resources and raw materials, such as cotton, coffee, and bananas, from Central America for decades, the increase in "cattle" raising in the latter half of the twentieth century required much more land and motivated the expropriation of marginal agricultural areas in which countless humans had maintained subsistence plots and tiny farms. Robert G. Williams observes:

> Beef's contribution to instability in Central America was less subtle than cotton's. The beef boom placed greater stress on the rural population than cotton or any other export boom. Coffee, sugar, bananas, cotton, and other export crops had very definite geographical limits outside of which production on a commercial basis was unprofitable. In contrast, cattle could be raised practically anywhere.
>
> With very little starting capital and relatively little effort, ranchers could claim large expanses of land. Physical barriers to cattle ranching were temporary: forests were felled and roads were built. Cotton placed stress on peasants by claiming high-yielding lands from corn production, but cattle competed for the marginal lands as well. Moreover, cattle ranching differed from other export activities in that it offered very little employment for the evicted ...
>
> The removal of peasants from lands they had cleared was not always easy ... The peasantry did not accept slow death through starvation as inevitable but struggled against the ranchers at every step of the way.[18]

Seeking to protect the United States' "national interest" (read "corporate interest"), the US military and the Central Intelligence Agency (CIA) helped, indeed encouraged, corporate-anointed Central American dictators to ruthlessly smash efforts by tens of thousands of the displaced for political democracy and social and economic justice. Take, for instance, Guatemala, where

"less than 3 percent of the population owns 70 percent of the agricultural land, much of it used for cattle ranching."[19] Sociologist Daniel Faber describes the "brutal oppression" that occurred there:

> Between 1950 and 1964 ... Zacapa, Izabal and Chiquimula experienced heavy deforestation and peasant displacement by large cattle ranchers. During this period, pasture acreage tripled in Izabal and nearly doubled in Zacapa. Deforestation was particularly severe along a road running eastward from Guatemala City through the richly forested Motagua River Valley to Puerto Barrios and Matias de Galvez, major beef ports on the Caribbean.
>
> Discontent quickly ripened into rebellion at the edge of the rainforests. By the mid-1960s, as in Matagalpa, Nicaragua, a guerrilla organization emerged. Rebel Armed Forces (FAR) formed widespread alliances with desperately poor peasant villages in Zacapa and Izabal to resist the appropriation of their land ...
>
> In 1966, at the urging of the U.S. State Department, the Guatemalan government declared these eastern districts a counterinsurgency zone, launching a series of merciless attacks on peasant communities to break the resistance. U.S. supplied-and-piloted helicopter gunships, T-3 fighter jets, and B-26 "invader" bombers armed with napalm and heavy bombs assisted the Guatemalan army in the carnage, killing some 6,000 to 10,000 people between 1966 and 1968.[20]

By 1972, the number of Guatemalans resisting the appropriation of their land and the exploitation of their labor who were killed was estimated to be over thirteen thousand, and by 1976 (the year of the highly celebrated marking of the United States bicentennial of liberation from British tyranny – millions in the United States observed the occasion by barbecuing "steaks" and "hamburgers") the count in Guatemala exceeded "20,000, murdered or disappeared without a trace."[21] Daniel Faber writes:

> The "success" of these military campaigns quickly opened up the farms and rainforests found on the "agricultural frontier" to huge cattle ranches owned by landed oligarchs, local and national government officials, and paramilitary personnel. The U.S.-

trained commander of the counterinsurgency, Colonel Carlos Arana, known as "The Butcher of Zacapa," became one of the largest ranchers in northeast Guatemala and later president of the military government.[22]

Former State Department official (turned journalist) William Blum expands on the nature and extent of US involvement in the extermination of those who were "impediments" to capitalist expansion and profitable "beef" production.

> The U.S. Agency for International Development (AID), its Office of Public Safety (OPS), and the Alliance for Progress were all there to lend a helping hand. These organizations with their reassuring names all contributed to a program to greatly expand the size of Guatemala's national police force … Senior police officers and technicians were sent for training at the Inter-American Police Academy in Panama, replaced in 1964 by the International Police Academy in Washington, at a Federal School in Los Fresnos, Texas … and other educational establishments, their instructors being CIA officers operating under OPS cover …
>
> The glue which held this package together was the standard OPS classroom tutelage, similar to that given to the military, which imparted the insight that "communists", primarily the Cuban variety, were behind all the unrest in Guatemala; the students were further advised to "stay out of politics", that is, support whatever pro-U.S. regime happens to be in power."[23]

Continued expropriation of land by ranchers and would-be ranchers in the late 1970s formed the context of the ruthless massacre in Panzos, Guatemala […] As Robert G. Williams observed, countless families were forced into marginal agricultural areas after being displaced by the military to make way for "cattle" ranchers. As "cattle" depleted the ill-acquired rangelands, ranchers expropriated the newly settled lands, and thousands of again-dispossessed subsistence farm families – including the Quiche – were subjected to violent and murderous displacement.

The Quiche villagers sent to Panzos by Guatemalan soldiers were confronted by the area's largest ranchers, who joined the military in trapping and slaughtering them at the town plaza. Like the other animals in Hinckley, the inhabitants of the area were obstacles to profitable use of the land under capitalist arrangements. (In much the same way, the quest for cheap "wool" resulted in the murder and displacement of the Native American inhabitants of the Ohio territory in the eighteenth and nineteenth centuries and the subsequent massacre of the other animals at Hinckley; similar incidents have been repeated again and again.) The massacre at Panzos permitted greedy ranchers and military leaders to accumulate more wealth by acquiring or expanding grazing lands to raise "cattle" for export to North America, where McDonald's and Burger King could sell affordable "quarter pounders."

After the massacre at Panzos, many indigenous Guatemalans joined resistance movements, but their overt and ruthless repression continued well into the 1980s, exemplified in the following horrific statement given to Amnesty International in 1982 by a seventeen-year-old Quiche woman:

> The soldiers came; we went to the mountains; there we found tree trunks and stones where we hid. A group of soldiers came from behind us. They seized three of us; they took them to the mountains; they tied them up in the mountains and killed them with machetes and knives. There they died. Then they asked me which ones were the guerrillas, and I didn't tell them, so they slashed me with the machete; they raped me; they threw me on the ground and slashed my head; my breasts, my entire hand. When dawn came, I tried to get home. By then I could hardly walk. I came across a girl from our village and she was carrying some water. She gave me some and took me to her house.
>
> The army also seized my 13-year-old brother Ramos and dragged him away and shot him in the foot and left him thrown on the ground. My brother and my parents and my other brothers and sisters had been in the house. The soldiers said "They are guerrillas, and must be killed." My brother saw how they killed my parents, my mother, my brothers and sisters and my little

one-year-old brother; the soldiers machine-gunned them to death when they arrived in the village. Only my brother Ramos and I are alive. Our friends are giving us injections and medicines. We can't go to the hospital in Caban. I think they would kill us there.[24]

The calamity visited upon just *one* Third World country, during a single period, represents only a bare glimpse at the international machinations of the US government in the service of corporate interests, in this case in the practices used to acquire cheap "beef."

Much of the horrific violence perpetrated in Guatemala and throughout Central and South America is unquestionably entangled with the oppression of other animals; the more cows raised to be slaughtered for food, the more humans were forced from the land. Ironically, and tragically, some of the tens of thousands driven off their lands in Central America, and their descendants, are recruited for and exploited in slaughterhouses and other "food-processing" operations in the United States. Once here, they are frequently snubbed and harassed by resentful locals, threatened by white supremacists, and sexually exploited by supervisors and managers.

For example, in 2000 W. R. Grace and Company agreed to pay twenty-two women workers from Central America $850,000 to settle a lawsuit alleging egregious sexual harassment at Grace Culinary Systems (a restaurant food-processing plant specializing in soup and "poultry dishes") in Laurel, Maryland. Plant managers and supervisors "engaged in systemic harassment that included exposing themselves, demanding oral sex and touching workers' breasts, buttocks and genital areas."[25] Women who rejected the advances were fired. An Equal Employment Opportunity Commission (EEOC) attorney stated that the harassment had lasted four years and "was one of the worst sexual harassment cases we've seen."[26] In 1999, a major California agribusiness, Tanimura & Antle, agreed to pay $1.85 million to a group of Latino women who complained they were pressured to submit to sexual acts.[27] In 2001, the EEOC filed a lawsuit

against DeCoster Farms in Iowa, alleging that Latino women egg packers were raped by supervisors "who threatened to have them fired or killed if they didn't submit."[28] Meanwhile, the EEOC was investigating allegations of egregious sexual harassment of African American women line workers at a Birmingham, Alabama, chicken "processing" plant.[29]

It is important to note that the US food and restaurant industries are deeply grounded in, and profit from, racist, sexist, and classist traditions and practices.[30] The restaurant industry continually uses its considerable political clout to resist any initiatives that would decrease access to "affordable" immigrant labor, to forestall increases in the minimum wage and to fight efforts to expand health care coverage for their employees.[31] Not surprisingly, the industry has been a big advocate of "welfare reform." For example, between 1997 and 2000 Burger King alone has hired more than ten thousand humans subjected to "welfare-to-work" initiatives.[32]

NOTES

1. Benjamin F. Miller, Lawrence Galton, and Daniel Brunner, *Freedom from Heart Attacks* (New York: Simon & Schuster, 1972).

2. The majority of grass-fed cows imported to the United States today come from Australia and New Zealand. However, Mark Edelman observes that "what may seem of minor significance in the United States looks different when seen from Central America, where pasture is often the major land use and beef a key source of foreign exchange." See Mark Edelman, "From Costa Rican Pasture to North American Hamburger," in *Food and Evolution: Toward a Theory of Food Habits,* ed. Marvin Harris and Eric B. Ross (Philadelphia: Temple University Press, 1987), 545.

3. Eric Ross, "Patterns of Diet and Forces of Production: An Economic and Ecological History of the Ascendancy of Beef in the United States Diet," in *Food and Evolution,* 190.

4. Roger Segelken, *U.S. Could Feed 800 Million People with Grain That Livestock Eat* (Ithaca, N.Y.: Cornell University Science News, 1997);

www/news/cornell.edu/science/Aug97livestock.hrs.html.

5. Jacques Leslie, "Running Dry: What Happens When the World No Longer Has Enough Freshwater," *Harper's Magazine* 301, no. 1802 (July 2001): 50.

6. Jill Mahoney, "Environmental Havoc Forecast," *Dayton Daily News,* 16 April 2001, 9A.

7. Tilman et al., "Forecasting Agriculturally Driven Global Environmental Change," 283.

8. Jeremy Rifkin, *Beyond Beef: The Rise and Fall of the Cattle Culture* (New York: Plume, 1992), 127.

9. Edward Palmer Thompson, *The Making of the English Working Class* (New York: Pantheon/Random House, 1964), 217.

10. Rifkin, *Beyond Beef,* 147, 148, 149.

11. Frances Moore Lappe and Joseph Collins, *Food First: Beyond the Myth of Scarcity* (New York: Ballantine, 1979), 11.

12. Robert K. Schaeffer, *Understanding Globalization: The Social Consequences of Political, Economic and Environmental Change* (New York: Rowman & Littlefield, 1997), 165.

13. See for example Norine Dworkin, "22 Reasons to Go Vegetarian Right Now," *Vegetarian Times* 260 (April 1999): 90–93.

14. David Barboza, "As Biotech Crops Multiply, Consumers Get Little Choice," *New York Times,* 10 June 2001, A28.

15. Barboza, "As Biotech Crops Multiply, Consumers Get Little Choice," A28.

16. Barboza, "A1; Biotech Crops Multiply, Consumers Get Little Choice," Al8.

17. Michael Parenti, *Against Empire* (San Francisco: City Lights, 1995), 7.

18. Robert G. Williams, *Export Agriculture and the Crisis in Central America* (Chapel Hill: University of North Carolina Press, 1986), 158–59, 151.

19. Rifkin, *Beyond Beef,* 193.

20. Daniel Faber, *Environment under Fire: Imperialism and the Ecological Crisis in Central America* (New York: Monthly Review Press, 1993), 127–28.

21. William Blum, *Killing Hope: U.S. Military and CM Interventions since World War II* (Monroe, Maine: Common Courage, 1995), 232.

22. Faber, *Environment under Fire,* 128.

23. Blum, *Killing Hope,* 234.

24. Amnesty International, *Political Killings by Governments* (London: Author, 1983), 27.

25. Steven Greenhouse, "Companies Pay $1 Million in Harassment Suit," *New York Times,* 2 June 2000, A12.

26. Greenhouse, "Companies Pay $1 Million in Harassment Suit," A12.

27. Cathleen Ferraro and Eric Young, "Huge Ag Sex-Harass Suit Ends: Lettuce Grower to Pay Victims $1.85 Million," *The Sacramento Bee,* 24 February 1999; http://cgi.sacbee.com/news/beetoday/newsroom/biz/O22499/biz02.html.

28. Emily Gersema, "Female Workers Raped at Iowa Plants, Suit Alleges," *Seattle Post-Intelligencer,* 23 August 2001; http://seattlepi.nwsource.com/business/36156_assault23.shtml.

29. http://www.eeoc.gov/press/4-10-01.html.

30. See for example Glenn Collins and Monte Williams, "In Restaurants with the High Tips, Black Waiters Are Few," *New York Times,* 30 May 2000, A13; Robert Klara, "Don't Ask, Don't Tell," *Restaurant Business* (15 January 2000): 30–36.

31. Victor Wishna, "You've Got Issues: From Capitol Hill to the Town Hall, This Year's Legislative Battles Are Already Brewing," *Restaurant Business* (15 January 2000): 21–27.

32. Wishna, "You've Got Issues," 22.

FURTHER READING IN ANIMALS AS DOMESTICATES, "PETS" AND FOOD

Alger, Janet and Steven Alger. 2003. *Cat Culture: The Social World of a Cat Shelter*. Philadelphia: Temple University Press.

Anderson, Virginia DeJohn. 2004. *Creatures of Empire: How Domestic Animals Transformed Early America*. Oxford and New York: Oxford University Press.

Arluke, Arnold. 2006. *Just a Dog: Animal Cruelty, Self, and Society*. Philadelphia: Temple University Press.

Beirne, Piers. 1999. For a Nonspeciesist Criminology: Animal Abuse as an Object of Study. *Criminology*, 37, 117–147.

Clutton-Brock, Juliet. 1999. *A Natural History of Domesticated Mammals*. Cambridge and New York: Cambridge University Press.

Coren, Stanley. 2003. *The Pawprints of History: Dogs and Course of Human Events*. New York: Free Press.

Eisnitz, Gail. 1997. *Slaughterhouse: The Shocking Story of Greed, Neglect, and Inhumane Treatment Inside the U.S. Meat Industry*. Amherst, NY: Prometheus Books.

Emberly, Julia V. 1998. *The Cultural Politics of Fur*. Ithaca, NY: Cornell University Press.

Fitzgerald, Amy J. 2005. *Animal Abuse and Family Violence: Researching the Interrelationships of Abusive Power*. Lewiston, NY: Edwin Mellen Press.

Garber, Marjorie. 1996. *Dog Love*. New York: Simon & Schuster.

Goldberg, David and Michiel Korthals. 2004. *Before Dinner: Philosophy and Ethics of Food*. Norwell MA: Springer.

Harris, Marvin. 1987. *The Sacred Cow and the Abominable Pig: Riddles of Food and Culture*. New York: Touchstone Books.

Hribal, Jason. 2003. "Animals Are Part of the Working Class": A Challenge to Labor History, *Labor History* 44, 435–453.

Kete, Kathleen. 1994. *The Beast in the Boudoir: Petkeeping in Nineteenth-Century Paris*. Berkeley: University of California Press.

Irvine, Leslie. 2004. *If You Tame Me: Understanding our Connection with Animals*. Philadelphia: Temple University Press.

Manning, Aubrey and James Serpell (eds.). 1994. *Animals and Human Society: Changing Perspectives*. London and New York: Routledge.

Peterson, Dale. 2004. *Eating Apes*. Berkeley: University of California Press.

Rifkin, Jeremy. 1992. *Beyond Beef: The Rise and Fall of the Cattle Culture*. New York: Dutton.

Ritvo, Harriet. 1987. *The Animal Estate: The English and Other Creatures in the Victorian Age*. Cambridge, MA: Harvard University Press.

Robbins, Louise E. 2002. *Elephant Slaves and Pampered Parrots: Exotic Animals in Eighteenth-Century Paris*. Baltimore: Johns Hopkins University Press.

Serpell, James. 1986/1996. *In the Company of Animals: A Study of Human-Animal Relationships*. Cambridge and New York: Cambridge University Press.

Tester, Keith. 1991. *Animals and Society*. London and New York: Routledge.

Thomas, Keith. 1983/1996. *Man and the Natural World*. New York: Oxford University Press.

*A*nimals as Spectacle and Sport

Introduction

We humans have always been fascinated by the spectacles of nature, particularly animals in combat, having long embraced the notion that animals are, by their very nature, violent and aggressive. Rarely do we emphasize animals' playful and frolicsome side, as in the two polar bears playing underwater in the image opening this section. Thus, confrontation between animals (and between animals and men) was common in Mesopotamian art, much of which reflected ongoing struggles between the uncivilized and civilized. Indeed, the first epic poem ever written was a story of the battle between "nature" (Enkidu) and "culture" (Gilgamesh). The notion of an ongoing confrontation between the wild and the tame is a theme that runs throughout this section on animals as spectacle and sport.

The ancients depicted hunting as a royal battle of valor between kings and wild beasts. "Paradise parks" enclosed exotic animals close to landowners' estates so that owners could hunt at will and visitors could easily observe the action. The countryside parks and the infamous Roman arena hunts both provided the opportunity to see wild animals destroyed, thus affirming the superiority of culture over nature.

We begin with an ancient writer on animal spectacles, Pliny the Elder. It is important to note that even the ancients occasionally questioned the rigid hierarchical distinction between humans and animals. Pliny the Elder often wrote about animals in anthropomorphic ways, as in the essay on elephant combats reproduced in this section. He recounts how the audience protested the shabby treatment of elephants at one of Pompey's games lamenting that the animals were human-like in their struggle against getting slaughtered, also noting that elephants are caring of others and even altruistic at times.

Staged games and athletic contests were common in antiquity, and there is much visual evidence that animals have long been pitted against humans and other animals in entertainment and other sport spectacles. Bullfights were a popular funerary motif in Egyptian tomb decorations as long ago as 2600 BC, leaping over bulls was a sport of agility in 1450 BC in Minoan society, and baiting humans with dogs was practiced in Etruscan society in 510 BC.

The next two articles discuss the meaning of pitting animals against humans or against other animals in the context of providing humans with something they need. In Garry Marvin's essay, bullfighting is a spectator sport that represents the opposition between nature and culture, with the wild bull eventually tamed (killed) by the civilized, cultured *matador*. The process of "taming" (or domesticating) animals in public spectacles is an excellent example of Yi-Fu Tuan's dictum in the last section, "domestication means domination." In the article by Evans, Kalich (Gauthier) and Forsyth, dogfighting in the southern US is revealed as an activity that reflects and validates the masculinity and honor of the white males who participate in the sport.

Seeing, observing, and looking at the spectacles of nature, whether in events of the slaughter of wild animals or just gazing at exotic animals in confined places, is a central theme in this section. Randy Malamud writes that all institutions that bring together captive animals as spectacles for humans to gaze at (zoos, circuses, carnivals, sea worlds, wildlife centers) help shape the cultural representation of animals. This last point is driven home by Malamud when he links Michel Foucault's ideas about power and surveillance with the famous menagerie at Versailles and Jeremy Bentham's panopticon, a useful design for any institution that required the continual watching of the activities of others. Many of the themes that make an appearance in this section on spectacle and sport are discussed throughout the volume, particularly on how issues of power and control figure in the human-animal relationship.

We end this section with an essay by Matt Cartmill that focuses on the meaning of the human-animal and culture-nature boundaries in the history of hunting in Western culture. In antiquity, hunting was armed confrontation between humans and the untamed wilderness, or wild, hostile animals. (Cartmill's logic is clear when he writes, "You can kill cows in the dairy barn, but you cannot hunt them.") Anti-hunting sentiments gained popularity with the rise of the notion in the 1500s that the human-animal boundary was arbitrary and that humans were not superior to other animals. The symbolic nature of the distinction between animals and humans (and the lack thereof) has been expressed by many writers, and we turn to that topic in Section 5.

21

PLINY THE ELDER

Combats of Elephants*

Pliny the Elder (Gaius Plinius Secundus) was born in northern Italy in AD 23. He began his career in the army in Germany and held several imperial official positions in Gaul, Africa, and Spain. Pliny the Elder is best known for writing seven encyclopedic works in the four years before his death, of which only one has survived, the *Natural History*. Pliny worked continuously and was carried about Rome in a sedan chair to save walking time; he slept very little, insisting that "To live is to be awake." While part of the *Natural History* is devoted to recording the state of Roman scientific knowledge, it is best known as a comprehensive (if sometimes inaccurate) account of what was known about animal behavior and physiology in the first century AD. Pliny was particularly fond of writing about the details of the spectacles of nature, such as fierce battles between different animal species, baiting elephants with dogs, cooperative fishing between dolphins and humans, spearing trapped killer whales, and combats between elephants [the latter is detailed in the extracts below]. Much of his writings were based on first-hand accounts. [Indeed, he died from sulphurous fumes while watching the eruption of Vesuvius in AD 79.] "The Combats of Elephants," is a retrospective account of numerous staged arena (or Circus) events that included elephant combat and (usually) slaughter. One of the events described by Pliny in this passage is the slaughter of elephants in Pompey's arena games in 55 BC, an event that has been retold innumerable times as the only known example of popular protest against the centuries-long tradition of animal slaughter in the Roman amphitheaters.

There is a famous combat mentioned of a Roman with an elephant, when Hannibal compelled our prisoners to fight against each other. The one who had survived all the others he placed before an elephant, and promised him his life if he should slay it; upon which the man advanced alone into the arena, and, to the great regret of the Carthaginians, succeeded in doing so. Hannibal, however, thinking that the news of this victory might cause a feeling of contempt for these animals, sent some horsemen to kill the man on his way home. In our battles with

---

* The extract reprinted here is from Pliny the Elder's *The Natural History*, which is in the public domain and was obtained from The Perseus Digital Library at the following website link: http://www.perseus.tufts.edu/cgi-bin/ptext?lookup=Plin .+Nat.+8.7. The text is based on the following book: *The Natural History*. Pliny the Elder. John Bostock, M.D., F.R.S., H.T. Riley, Esq., B.A. London. Taylor and Francis, Red Lion Court, Fleet Street. 1855.

Pyrrhus it was found, on making trial, that it was extremely easy to cut off the trunks of these animals. Fenestella informs us, that they fought at Rome in the Circus for the first time during the curule ædileship of Claudius Pulcher, in the consulship of M. Antonius and A. Postumius, in the year of the City 655; and that twenty years afterwards, during the curule ædileship of the Luculli, they were set to fight against bulls.

In the second consulship of Pompeius, at the dedication of the temple of Venus Victrix, twenty elephants, or, as some say, seventeen, fought in the Circus against a number of Gætulians, who attacked them with javelins. One of these animals fought in a most astonishing manner; being pierced through the feet, it dragged itself on its knees towards the troop, and seizing their bucklers, tossed them aloft into the air: and as they came to the ground they greatly amused the spectators, for they whirled round and round in the air, just as if they had been thrown up with a certain degree of skill, and not by the frantic fury of a wild beast. Another very wonderful circumstance happened; an elephant was killed by a single blow. The weapon pierced the animal below the eye, and entered the vital part of the head. The elephants attempted, too, by their united efforts, to break down the enclosure, not without great confusion among the people who surrounded the iron gratings. It was in consequence of this circumstance, that Cæsar, the Dictator, when he was afterwards about to exhibit a similar spectacle, had the arena surrounded with trenches of water, which were lately filled up by the Emperor Nero, when he added the seats for the equestrian order. When, however, the elephants in the exhibition given by Pompeius had lost all hopes of escaping, they implored the compassion of the multitude by attitudes which surpass all description, and with a kind of lamentation bewailed their unhappy fate. So greatly were the people affected by the scene, that, forgetting the general altogether, and the munificence which had been at such pains to do them honour, the whole assembly rose up in tears, and showered curses on Pompeius, of which he soon afterwards became the victim. They fought also in the third consulship of the Dictator Cæsar, twenty of them against five hundred foot soldiers. On another occasion twenty elephants, carrying towers, and each defended by sixty men, were opposed to the same number of foot soldiers as before, and an equal number of horsemen. Afterwards, under the Emperors Claudius and Nero, the last exploit that the gladiators performed was fighting singlehanded with elephants.

The elephant is said to display such a merciful disposition towards animals that are weaker than itself, that, when it finds itself in a flock of sheep, it will remove with its trunk those that are in the way, lest it should unintentionally trample upon them. They will never do any mischief except when provoked, and they are of a disposition so sociable, that they always move about in herds, no animal being less fond of a solitary life. When surrounded by a troop of horsemen, they place in the centre of the herd those that are weak, weary, or wounded, and then take the front rank each in its turn, just as though they acted under command and in accordance with discipline. When taken captive, they are very speedily tamed, by being fed on the juices of barley.

22

GARRY MARVIN

On Being Human in the Bullfight*

Garry Marvin is an anthropologist who specializes in the sociology and anthropology of travel and tourism, visual anthropology and human-animal relations. Marvin has published widely on cockfighting, bullfighting and zoos, and his book *Bullfight*, from which we have extracted a portion to include here, was the subject of his doctoral dissertation. Marvin decided to write about bullfighting while attending a Spanish *corrida*. Hoping to provide a balanced and sensitive ethnography of the event, he writes about the cultural context of bullfighting and makes an attempt to avoid both negative and positive judgments of the sport. Marvin argues that the *corrida* is symbolic of the opposition between nature and culture. In a culture that is centered by the notion of human control and that to be civilized is to be removed from nature and its unpredictability, bullfighting is a confrontation between untamed nature (the wild bull) and culture (the human bullfighter), a confrontation of force (the bull's natural instincts) and intelligence (the human's ability to exert self-control, make logical moves and plan ahead). The bull's strength is gradually diminished by the skills of the *matador* (Spanish for "the killer"), the animal's body is denatured when decorated with the colorful *banderillas* (harpoon sticks wrapped in bright paper which are thrown so that they pierce the animal's shoulders). When the bull is finally killed he is no longer a wild animal – he has been tamed, and that process of "taming" is a public spectacle with great cultural significance.

Corbin and Corbin in their aptly entitled *Urbane Thought* (1987),[1] a study of systems of Andalusian cultural meanings based on research in the city of Ronda, have suggested that Andalusian culture can be interpreted as a statement of what it means to be civilized and that the people who live within the terms of this culture are fundamentally concerned with the expression of this quality. The central argument in this chapter is that the cultural significance of the *corrida* can be best understood if it is interpreted as an event which both encapsulates and succinctly and dramatically summarizes the important structural oppositions of nature and culture which underlie the idea of what it means to be civilized or truly human as expressed in terms of Andalusian thought. It is essential to discuss the meaning of the terms of this distinction, and how the *corrida* involves a dramatic representation of them, in order to show that the *corrida* is an event which

---

makes a statement not only about what it means to be human, but more specifically about what it means to be a human male in this culture.

To understand the *corrida* in these terms it is first necessary to appreciate that Andalusians make a fundamental distinction between "urban" and "rural." "Urban" can refer to both a *ciudad* (city) and a *pueblo* (a small town or village) for, as the Corbins write, urbanity "is a matter of density of dwellings, not the size of settlement" (1987, 22). The notion of "density" is most important here because the density of buildings, particularly human dwellings, gives rise to the intense social activity and close human contact so highly valued by Andalusians as constituents of proper human life. Those who live in the country, away from human settlements, are felt to be isolated and therefore unable to partake of a full social life.

The central focus of this clustering is the main *plaza* or *plazas* (town squares). These key points of social gathering are described by Lopez Casero as "the centre for relaxation, the centre of criticism and the centre of information" (1972, 123). The *plaza* is where men gather in the morning if they are not working, where people meet friends, where people stroll in the evening – it is the location for a concentration of social activity. In smaller towns and villages, where there is only one important *plaza,* the church, the town hall and other important buildings will be found around it. Not only is the *plaza* a place to meet, it is also prestigious to live in a house on it, or at least close to it, and the desirability of residence decreases the further one moves from the centre. As Gilmore points out, the wealthy live around the important *plazas,* for: "To live on them implies not only wealth and social position but also a close connection to the community's cosmopolitan institutions and nearness to the pulse of life" (1977, 442). It is felt that as one moves further from the centre, so the quality of life gradually diminishes, because at the far limits of the town there are few bars, shops and *plazas* where people gather, all of which are, as Gilmore comments "highly valued for lending *ambiente* (spirit or atmosphere) and *vida* to a

residential district" (p. 441). It is the mingling of many people which gives a place *ambiente,* which in turn is the social basis for the claim of urbanity.[2]

The importance of being close to the centres of social activity and the importance of the urban ethos in this culture is succinctly illustrated in a recent study by Henk Driessen of a small town near Cordoba. A new quarter was built on the edge of town; one of the streets was said to have more *ambiente* than the others, and consequently most of the houses there were occupied whereas in other streets houses were vacant. The street with *ambiente* was one of the inner streets, with houses on both sides, where most of the social traffic between neighbours took place. Two of the outer streets faced the Cordoba plains, and in order to get people to live in those houses members of the cooperative had to draw lots. As Driessen comments, one might have thought that people would have wanted these houses because of the view they commanded, but that was exactly what the people did *not* want; they wanted the close presence of neighbours and the feeling of sociability they offered. As one of them said to him, "We see enough of the country. When at home, we want to see neighbours" (1981, 27). Driessen draws an important observation from this example:

> In general, proximity to the social centre determines the desirability of houses and the *ambiente* of streets. This kind of distance is obviously cultural and has little to do with geography. The people who are living in the new *barrio* complain of 'the great distance to the *pueblo*' although it is only five to ten minutes' walk. (p. 27)

In Andalusian terms, urban space is human space; it is created by humans and is an environment of order, controlled and sustained by human will. In contrast the *campo* (the countryside) is perceived as subhuman space, the realm of plants and animals and subject to the control of the forces of nature.[3] The life of those who earn their living in the country is felt to be a continual struggle against nature, something which is felt to be more powerful than people.

Here humans attempt to control, to impose order, to impose their will, but they are not always successful. A farmer might plough, weed, plant and fertilize his land and do all in his power to ensure a good crop, but the rain might not come at the right time; he might have built up a good stock of animals, but some might not breed, or they might be struck by a disease. In terms of the perception of those living in the urban centres, country dwellers cannot be fully civilized because their lives are too bound up with the processes of the natural world and with elements which they cannot easily control.[4]

This notion of human control and where, how and when it is exercised is a fundamental concern in this culture. To be fully civilized is to be in control of one's self, in control of one's life and in control of one's environment. This control is a function of will which people put into operation to overcome, on the personal level, their own human animal nature and, more generally, the world around them. Control is thus the domain of culture; lack of it signals the domain of nature. To be fully civilized is to be fully removed from nature, especially to be removed from the effects of its unpredictable elements. To be civilized is demonstrated by living in the urban realm with fellow human beings, by emphasizing that which is distinctively human (as opposed to animal) in terms of behaviour – for, as the Corbins note, "animality is particularly the quality humanity seeks to transcend" (1987, 18) – and by the successful demonstration of human will and control.[5] The general point which Sherry Ortner makes about culture, that it "at some level of awareness asserts itself to be not only distinct from, but superior to nature, and that some sense of distinctiveness and superiority rests precisely on the ability to transform – to 'socialise' and 'culturalise' nature" (1974, 73), is certainly true for the Andalusian context.

Nowhere is this subordination and "culturizing" of nature, in Andalusian terms, more dramatically demonstrated than in the *corrida.* It is an urban event intimately linked with the country, which brings together, in the centre of human habitation, an uncontrolled wild bull, an item from the realm of nature, and a man who represents the epitome of culture in that, more than any ordinary man, he is able to exercise control over his "natural" fear (the fear felt by the human animal), an essential prerequisite if he is to control the wild animal. In terms of this culture there is a strong demarcation between humans and animals, and the entirely appropriate relationship of the subordination of animal will to human will is indicated by the fact that people are able to control and make use of animals for their own ends. Normally this relationship is completely unproblematic, but in the *corrida* it is explored and expressed in a dramatic context. The event is constructed in such a way that the imposition of human will is extremely uncertain because of the difficult circumstances; a situation which in turn generates tension, emotion and dramatic interest.

It is significant that the *corrida* takes place in urban space, where it is expected that people should exercise control, and it is interesting to contrast it for a moment with aspects of the hunt, another event in which people also attempt to kill wild animals in difficult circumstances, but in which they do so in rural space. An essential contrast in terms of processes is that of the passage between these two spaces. In the *corrida* the animal is brought out of its natural habitat to be acted on by a man in *his* natural habitat, whereas in the hunt it is the human who moves, attempting to locate, pursue and kill a wild animal in the country. The human being enters the realm of nature and attempts to impose human will there, but this is an attempt fraught with difficulties because the animal is in control of its own will and can escape. The hunter must pit human skill against it in order to defeat it.[6] At one level both the *torero* and the hunter are attempting something similar; to resolve a challenge presented by a wild animal, to impose their will successfully, to dominate their opponent and thus demonstrate their superiority.

The relationship between the *torero* and the bull is actually much closer than that between the hunter and the animal hunted, in that, in being brought from the country and released into an enclosed space in the city, the bull is unable to exercise a fundamental aspect of its will. It is physically contained, it is unable to escape – something it might well want to do – and it is therefore forced to defend itself – something it does by attacking those who attempt to engage it. Apart from the fact that this confrontation in the form of an attack rarely happens in most hunting in Spain, because, except in the case of wild boar, the animals are not the sort which could effectively attack a human being, the event is structured so that the animals can avoid any engagement. The creature which is pursued avoids engagement either by effectively concealing itself or by fleeing from any approach, and at the last moment, if the hunter is a poor shot and is unable to kill the animal, it will still be able to escape. The hunt is a balance between the animal having the ability to use its instinct and physical ability to escape and the human being attempting, by skill and intelligence, to prevent this happening. It is this balance which is the essence of the hunt, for if there were no escape for the animal there would be no sport for the human.

Hunters must also voluntarily reduce or set limits to their ability to kill the animal. The efficiency of modern weapons has improved the odds so much in favour of the hunters that, were they not to operate within these limiting conditions, the balance between the human skill and the animal's ability to escape would be destroyed, and the hunt would be no longer a matter of chance and skill but a simple matter of mechanical slaughter and destruction. Like the hunter, the *matador* must have limits set to his ability to kill the bull. It is easy to kill a bull with a gun from the safety of the barrier; it would also be easy to kill the bull if those in the arena were allowed to carry a variety of weapons with which they could attack it; but if this were done it would not be a *corrida* but simply a piece of unpleasant butchery. In both cases it is not simply the fact that the man triumphs over the animal by killing it; the real triumph comes from the way in which it is killed.

Viewed from the perspective of patterns of the Andalusian cultural model, the domestication of animals involves the subjection of their will to that of human will. People decide how the animals live, what food they may eat, when they may breed and when they must die. In dealing with female animals, domestication usually involves no special process except that of physical control, although sows are sometimes castrated if they are only going to be used for food. It might be argued that females do go through a special process, artificial insemination, but this is unlike castration in that it does not involve a permanent alteration of the nature of the animal. In the case of male animals (except for those used for breeding), their domestication involves castration. Maleness in this culture is equated with wilfulness (which in turn is associated with sexuality), a condition which is undesirable in domestic animals. Castration is the removal of sexual potency and potential, and results in an animal which is *manso* (meek, tame). Such an animal is passive; it has lost its will and is easily controlled. It is interesting to note, as has already been mentioned, that the word *manso* is also used of a man who is unassertive and retiring and therefore by analogy somewhat like a castrated male animal; he is not acting like a true man. [...] The ideas of masculinity, sexual potency, willfulness, assertiveness and independence are all closely associated in this culture, as are those of femininity, passivity (in the sense of lack of sexual assertiveness), lack of competitive assertiveness and controllability, which are their opposites. It is argued below that human males must not only be assertive and control others, but must also exercise *self-control,* something which male animals and to some extent human females are not thought to be able to do.

Most domesticated animals are controlled in this culture simply by enclosing them, or (in the case of sheep, goats and cattle) by herding them in pastures, but apart from that people have little contact with them and they are certainly not usually responded to as individuals. Animals are not anthropomorphized, and pet keeping is not popular. There is, however, one animal which is most important in this culture, and with which humans have a more complex relationship, and that is the horse. Horses are not herded (except maybe when they are very young) but used individually, and thus the exercise of control by the rider over the mount is elaborate and ongoing. It is important to consider the process and the vocabulary of the breaking and taming of horses because the bull in the *plaza* passes through a similar process, although, because of the concentrated nature of that process, it is less immediately obvious.

Unbroken horses are not referred to as *bravo* and are not thought of as wild animals in the sense that bulls are. The only equivalent word I ever heard used with regard to horses was *cerrero* or *cerril* (a *cerro* is a hill and *cerril* refers to rough or mountainous terrain; both, therefore, are images of the countryside), which means "unbroken" or "untamed" when referring to an animal, and "uncouth, ill-behaved and rough" when referring to a person. Even so this word, like *bravo*, points toward the realm out of human control, the realm of nature. In the case of the horse it refers to that aspect of it which humans have yet to control, and in the case of a person it points to someone who is closer to the natural rather than the cultural realm, in that the baser animal nature is allowed to dominate over the truly human which should be dominant.

The actual breaking of a horse is called *desbravando* (literally, "dewilding") [...] the translation of the word *bravo* [is] "wild." *Desbravando* involves bringing the animal under control, making it manageable and subjecting its will to that of humanity. Once that stage has been reached it still has to be taken through a further process, for it must be trained to accept a saddle and to respond to the will of the rider, a process called *domar* ("to train" or, figuratively, "to control, master or repress"). Most male horses are castrated as part of the initial process of bringing them under control, but some are left sexually intact, and stallions are used for both breeding and riding. The stallion is regarded as an extremely wilful animal, a condition which is thought to be associated with its sexual potency. In fact, there is some ambiguity about the breaking of the stallion because it is not castrated, and thus its behaviour is liable to move back toward that of its unbroken state and make it a difficult animal to manage. It seemed, in my conversations with those closely associated with horses, that by association this wilfulness confers increased masculinity (for it was usually only men who rode stallions) on the man who is masterful enough to subject this animal to his will, for an aspect of masculinity is the proven ability to dominate and control others. The more difficult and dangerous these "others" are to control, the greater the reputation and prestige which is gained. As will be shown later, the prestige a *torero* gains and the esteem in which he is held arise precisely because of his willingness to challenge an extremely difficult and dangerous "other."

In terms of the conceptual scheme under discussion, the bull is the quintessential wild animal and the quintessential male animal, its aggressive male qualities once again being associated with great sexual potency. But none of these qualities are significant when it is living in the country; they are not qualities with which man has to deal. The challenge which the bull offers to man only comes about because it is transposed from one environment to another. The *corrida* is, as it were, a problem which man sets for himself. The bull is forced into the position of being "out of place"; the situation is a contrived anomaly, which man then attempts to resolve in order to emphasize dramatically the correct relationship between man and animal, between civilization and the natural world. When the bull is in the country it is in its proper domain, *bravo* and *campo* being associated concepts. In the *plaza*, however, the bull is out of its proper domain. It is deliberately put there to inject an inappropriate element, wild untamed nature, into the city, the site *par excellence* of culture. The city is not the proper place for animals and if they do pass through it, they should be controlled. In fact, horses are often ridden through the city, and even in a city as large as Seville, one sometimes finds animals being herded through the outskirts.[7] Wild animals (except for vermin and some birds, most of which people attempt to remove) are certainly not found in cities, except perhaps in the exceptional case of zoos, where the animals are strictly separated and controlled, in the crude sense that they are physically restrained by being caged and are dependent on humans for food.

In the *corrida* the contrived meeting between the bull and the man is a confrontation between nature and culture, which is worked out in a controlled environment in a stylized and regulated way. That this is a cultural event is emphasized by the fact that it *is* a contrived meeting – contrived by man – and subject to regulations and controls invented by man; by its urban setting (significantly, *corridas* never take place in the country); and by its being held on a holiday or a special day. It usually takes place, moreover, in a building constructed especially for this purpose, a location which closely parallels the main town square in the sense that it is a public place (one must pay to enter the *plaza de toros* but there is no restricted access; anyone who cares to buy a ticket may enter), a place to meet with friends, to enjoy oneself, and to criticize and comment about what is going on. López Casero's comment about the town *plaza* as a place where "one goes to meet all the village" (1972, 125) is particularly appropriate for the way the *plaza de toros* is used in Andalusian villages during the *corrida* or *novillada* held as part of the *feria*. Other factors which emphasize the cultural nature of the event are the music, the pageantry and the costumes of the *toreros*. The suit of lights, with its bright colours and floral and geometric designs picked out in elaborate gold and silver embroidery, emphasizes, by exaggeration, the cultural status of the *torero*. The significance of the suit of lights is actually more complex than this. [...]

As was suggested earlier in this section, the city in Andalusian culture is perceived as a place of order and control, a place from which nature has been expelled: and yet the *corrida*, which involves the injection of chaos and disorder in the form of wild uncontrolled nature, takes place in a public arena in the city which is consciously made dangerous and unfit for ordinary humans.

This aspect is even more dramatically demonstrated when the *corrida* takes place in a sealed-off public square in a town which does not have a proper *plaza de toros*. The *plaza* is then closed off by sealing the streets leading into it with barriers made from wooden poles, farm carts and trailers, and generally with whatever is available. For example, in Algaba, a village near Seville, this tradition of using old wooden farm wagons is still preserved. They are drawn into a three-quarter circle, the other quarter being formed by a set of specially constructed banked seats. Those who do not have a seat sit in the wagons and between the wheels to watch the event.

The key to understanding the cultural significance of the *corrida* is in recognizing that, in terms of the Andalusian conceptual scheme, it can be interpreted as a resolution of the culturally created anomalous situation of a wild animal in the centre of a city threatening humans and attempting to dominate an urban space. The starting point of the event is chaos and danger, and it is for the man to impose order progressively. By organizing the activity in the arena, by establishing regularity and patterns where there had been chaos, and by controlling the bull, the man publicly demonstrates his separation from and his domination of nature, and thus asserts his humanness. This is not to claim that this is the only way that man demonstrates his humanness in this culture, but it is certainly the most dramatic.

When the bull first comes into the arena it usually charges powerfully and erratically, and is extremely difficult to control. Slowly the *matador* forces it to charge the way he wants it to charge and where he wants it to charge; he bends its will to his will. The great critic Antonio Díaz Cañabate said that the basis of the performance should be that the man is able "to make the bull go where it doesn't want to go" (1980, 40). If the *matador* is unable to control the animal he will have failed in his task, for the minimum expected of him is that he control the bull. The creation of an artistic performance is secondary to this and dependent on this basic level of control. [...] If the man is unable to control the bull, the meaning of the event collapses, for then it is the bull which is imposing its will on the man. As Gregorio Corrochano comments, "To *torear* is to command the bull, to do what one wants with the bull, to have *toreo* in the palm of one's hand; if one does not command the bull, if the bull does not go where the *torero* wants it to go, the *torero* is not *toreando,* it is the bull who is *toreando*" (1966, 219).

Toreros, aficionados and commentators alike emphasize the fundamental importance of human intelligence in *toreo;* however brave the *torero,* he must have intelligence and understanding to direct that bravery if he is to survive. He must also have intelligence to be able to work through the problems created by the bull if he is to dominate and control the animal. The great *matador* Paco Camino was called "El Niño Sabio" ("The Wise Child") when he was younger because of his extraordinary ability to make the bull do exactly what he wanted it to do, and his first precept for *toreros* was "*Que tenga mucha cabeza en la plaza*" (literally, "That one has 'much head' in the plaza") (McCormick and Mascareñas, 1967, 244), meaning that in order to *torear* it is essential to be able to use one's head, to be intelligent. The highly successful present-day *matador* Niño de la Capea (Pedro Gutiérrez Moya) also emphasized the importance or intelligence as a necessary quality for a *torero,* a quality without which he is unable to survive the confrontation with the greater physical power of the bull:

> The exact nature of the superiority of the man, of the *torero,* consists in putting his intelligence to the test with that of the bull and thus arriving at the point that the animal, being less intelligent, does what the man wants. The superior intelligence in this case is always that of the man. There can be no doubt that the animal has a lot more power but when it becomes aware that its intelligence has been overcome by the *torero* it gives up. (*El Mundo de los Toros* 22 August 1978, No. 664, 6)

This is not a confrontation of force by force. As mentioned in the quotation above, the bull is obviously more powerful than the man. It is a confrontation of force by intelligence. The man uses his intelligence and his ability to control himself, to plan ahead, to react with logic rather than instinct, or more precisely with a logic which has become instinct, to deceive the bull and by the successful use of deceit to survive. (This is in contrast to the bull which is not expected to exert control but to obey its natural instincts.) The bull charges at that which moves and the *torero* must learn to direct that charge. His deception is basic and consists of keeping his body still and moving the cape or *muleta* in order to persuade the bull to follow that rather than attack his body. This is why it is of such importance to have a bull which has never had the experience of a man and a cape before it comes into the ring: a bull which has had that experience will ignore the cape and will attack the man's body. Deceit is fundamental to *toreo;* indeed, the *muleta* is often called an *engaño,* literally, a "deceit" (from the verb "*engañar,*" "to deceive"). Yet although deceit is an essential and acknowledged part of *toreo,* there are some forms which are unacceptable and forbidden, and this can be seen as constituting a limitation on the means available to the *torero.* For example, assistants sometimes stand close to the *burladero* (the wooden protection barrier) and incite the bull to charge, so that when the cape is moved the animal crashes into the barrier, thus dazing and damaging itself. A *matador* may also *dobla* (double) the bull by cutting a pass short, an action which forces the bull to turn sharply on itself, a movement which severely weakens and thus tires it. These sorts of action are likely to bring censure from the public.

To return for a moment to the points made about breaking horses, an important aspect of *desbravando* is that of tiring it so much that its will is weakened and thus it is made easier for people to impose their will on it. This is usually carried out by putting a bridle attached to a long rope on the horse; a man then holds the rope and runs the horse around him in a circle. Once the horse is tired he is able to start to put the saddle and other parts of the harness on it. This tiring of an animal to bring it under control is an important aspect of the *corrida*, but it must be managed extremely carefully (indeed, it is part of the skill of the *torero* to know how to pace the process), because if the bull is tired too quickly it will not charge and the *torero* will not be able to perform well – that is, artistically – with it.

The strength of the bull is slowly reduced by the skilled capework of the *matador* and his assistants and by the pike work of the *picador*. The placing of *banderillas* is also important for achieving a balance between reducing the strength of the bull and yet at the same time keeping it lively. It is usually argued that the amount of running which the bull has to do in this act helps to liven it up a little after the sluggishness which comes as a result of the act with the *picadores*. Although some people argue that the *banderillas* themselves have some physical effect in terms of further weakening the bull, in fact the harpoon points do very little damage. What is most obvious about the sticks is the bright coloured paper in which they are wrapped, a marked contrast to the naked wooden pole of the *picador*. The significant aspect of this act is that the bull is decorated or adorned, a sign of the imposition of culture on nature and a further sign of the gradual denaturing of the bull. The reducing of the bull's strength and the process of bringing it under control constitute, in conceptual terms, its domestication; but this use of "domestication" needs some qualification.

It is not a domestication in the morphological sense. The exhausted bull which is killed by the *matador* has not gone through a domestication process in the sense that agriculturalists or zoologists would use the term (see Marvin, 1988/1994, chapter 6 and Ingold, 1980, 82), but in terms of the perception of members of the audience, based on the interpretation of the behaviour of the bull, it is brought closer to those animals normally classed as domestic. The removal of the will of the animal or the domination of the will of the animal by that of the man is indicated by the behaviour of the latter – by its behaviour being controlled by man. A similar process occurs in the breaking of a horse; once it responds to the human will it passes into the

realm of domestic animals. The important thing is that behaviourally and conceptually the bull is no longer a wild animal when it is killed; it has been tamed. This taming of a wild animal, though, is not as simple as, for example, in the context of wild animals in a circus. In a circus lions are "tamed," but conceptually they are still regarded as wild animals, whereas in terms of the perception of members of the audience at the *corrida*, there is a change in the nature of the bull as it passes through the various acts of the event. To quote from Gines Serran Pagan ... "without wildness," the quality removed by the various impositions of man, "the bull was no longer a true bull" (1979, 127).

The nature of the relation between the man and the bull presents some problems for definition, especially so because it occupies such a short time. It is certainly a taming (although not in the sense of making docile prior to developing a performance) in that the man brings a wild animal under control. What is peculiar is that he does this in public as a performance. The only other event in this culture in which a man confronts a wild animal has already been mentioned, and that is in certain acts in the circus, but here the relationship between man and animal has an essential difference.

The animals in the circus are certainly controlled by man, but they are also trained to perform certain actions which are then repeated on different occasions over a considerable time span. What the audience sees at the circus is a finished performance. The animals go through their actions supervised by the trainer, and although they are in fact severely controlled, the trainer may make this control appear threatened and thus add to the drama of the event.[8] The man is called a "lion tamer," but this "taming" is not part of the public performance, although the man might make both taming and training *appear* to be part of the act. In the *corrida*, the *matador* does not perform as a trainer; the event is about the taming of a wild animal in the sense of bringing it under control. Once this state has been achieved the animal is killed; there is no second level of training and the animal certainly does not perform tricks. The audience at a *corrida* sees what the audience at a circus does not see; they see the *process* of taming. In terms of this culture, the transformation of the bull occurs as its *bravura* (wildness), which is closely linked to its will, is removed.

Desbravando and *domando* are clearly seen as two processes in the context of breaking horses, but in the *corrida* it is not really possible to isolate them as separate in time. The two occur concurrently, and the *torero* may be more or less successful in imposing his will on the animals. Members of the audience are certainly aware of the process and will talk at length about how it ought to be developed with regard to each individual bull. They talk of *rompiendo* (breaking) the bull, a term associated with *desbravando* (although *desbravando* as a term is not actually used), and *mandando* (ordering), *templando* (moderating), *enseñando* and *educando* (teaching and educating) which are associated with *domando*, a term which is used to refer to the effect of the man on the bull. Hemingway, describing a performance of the great Ronda *matador* Antonio Ordóñez, captures exactly this sense of the man imposing his will on the bull and modifying its character and behaviour:

> His first bull was worthless. He was hesitant with the horses and did not want to charge frankly but Antonio picked him up with the cape delicately and suavely, fixed him, taught him, encouraged him by letting him pass closer and closer. He fabricated him into a fighting bull before your eyes. Antonio in his own enjoyment and knowledge of the bull seemed to be working the bull's head until the bull understood what was wanted of him. If the bull had a worthless idea Antonio would change it for him subtly and firmly. (1985, 26)

The *matador* kills the bull once it has been dominated, but this killing is not a simple process, and it is worth comparing it for a moment with the killing of other animals in this culture. The slaughter of animals for domestic consumption is largely unproblematic and, apart from the domestic slaughter of the pigs or poultry which some families raise, it is nowadays an industrial process carried out by specialists working in factory-like buildings, out of public view. Death here is certain, regulated, unelaborated culturally and involves no challenge or risk to human beings. The killing of animals in the hunt has already been mentioned. Here an essential feature is that the death is uncertain because of the possibility that the animal might escape. Although there is a challenge there is usually no risk to the hunter, either because the animals which are hunted are wild but not dangerous, or because there is a considerable distance between the hunter and the hunted. The killing of the animal is also non-public in that, although there may be several people in a hunting party, it takes place outside human habitation. The death of the fighting bull is rather special because it is a public spectacle, and it is the subject of great cultural elaboration. Although it is known that the bull will die, that death is made uncertain in the sense that it is not known how the *matador* will bring it about, or, indeed, whether the bull will be able to reverse the proper relationship and kill or injure the man. The uncertainty comes from the difficulty and danger of the challenge to kill correctly and from the risk to his own life which the *matador* must accept.

There are special rules which stipulate how the killing must be performed and the types of implement to be used (Marvin, 1988, see chapter 1 and Gilpérez García and Fraile Sanz, 1972, article 131). The *matador* must approach the bull from the front and the sword must pass through the lower part of the neck of the bull. This means that at the moment the sword goes in, the body of the *matador* ought to pass over the bull's horns (or to be more precise, over the right horn), a movement which involves great risk because if the bull lifts its head at this moment the man is almost certain to be gored. The potential for failure, in the sense of killing properly, if the man is unable to control or dominate his fear is therefore built into the event until the last moment. If the *matador* gives in to his fear and approaches the bull in a less dangerous manner, if he is incompetent in producing a kill because of this unwillingness to risk himself, the audience is likely to shout *"¡asesino!"* ("murderer!"), a term which suggests an unacceptable killer, someone who, because he kills another is, in one sense, dehumanized. It is not that the audience is attributing humanity to the bull and suggesting that the man is immoral, but rather that they are denying the proper humanity of the man – denying the very quality which he is attempting to emphasize. If the *matador* kills successfully he shows that he has not succumbed to the threat posed by the animal; he has dominated it and, through his mastery of it, triumphantly asserted his humanity.

A *matador* can fail in several ways. If he is unable to bring the bull under control because he has not mastered his own fear, then his failure is total. If, on the other hand, he has demonstrated his courage and been willing to commit himself, but has been unable to perform well either because the bull was simply impossible to work with or because he did not have sufficient knowledge or technical resources with which to resolve the problems, then he will probably be criticized but forgiven. Similarly, for the man to be caught and injured by the bull is not necessarily a sign of total failure. Although in one sense it does indicate that the bull has imposed itself on the man, this can also be accepted as the result of an error of judgement on the part of the man, or the result of a completely unpredictable piece of behaviour on the part of the bull. In other words, it is regarded as bad luck and evokes a sympathetic response. In the world of *los toros* there is no great emphasis on the idea of being wounded and having scars as an indication of masculinity. Press and television reports dealing with a particular *torero* might mention the bad scars he has, but the emphasis is that these are the price one has to pay to be a *torero* rather than indicative of his great courage. Scars are not borne proudly in the way that they were by duelists of the [nineteenth] century.

The *corrida* is a cultural event which puts the definition of humanity, especially male humanity, [...] in jeopardy precisely so that it may be dramatically reaffirmed in the most difficult of circumstances. To be an adult human male in this culture is to be an active agent, to be capable of control, and yet the *matador* risks his ability to control when he enters the arena. It is an audacious act, a supreme folly, for a man voluntarily to put himself in this precarious position, where the public can observe him attempting to prove himself and where he risks not being able to master the situation. In this culture, neither men nor women are normally willing to present themselves in uncertain circumstances and in such a way as to allow fellow humans to publicly comment on and critically evaluate their character and behaviour. In the *corrida,* however, the *torero* does just that; he offers himself to the public for them to judge whether or not he justifies his claim that he is this very special person, a *matador.* Anyone in the *plaza* is free to comment loudly about his behaviour and character and to abuse him publicly, and yet the *matador* may not respond to such attacks (except by improving his performance so that they may cease), and indeed can be fined if he argues with the public. This is a very odd position for a man in this culture to be in, for such an attack and such abuse would provoke an immediate response in any other public place (Brandes 1980 and Driessen 1983).

At the beginning of the afternoon, by his presence in the arena, the man asserts his claim to be a man worthy of the title *matador.* The event then progresses, through a period of doubt and the necessary demonstrations of his character and skill to support the claim, to a final acceptance of the claim by the audience. The *corrida,* however, also allows for the possibility of failure, a possibility which gives the event an element of uncertainty and dramatic tension. The arena contains sets of relationships which are loaded with peril for the human performers as they attempt to establish a proper order. Members of the audience are aware of the difficulties of the situation and they are there to watch the performers overcome these, for that is what the *matador's* artistry consists of – the elegant and stylish resolution of both the difficulty of mastering himself and his fear and the dangerous process of bringing the bull under his control. In a sense the *matador*, although performing as and judged as an individual, is a representative of humanity; he is a figure in whom key human qualities valued by this culture are epitomized, and it is those qualities the audience comes to see asserted.

Although these are human qualities and the fundamental distinction in the arena is between human and animal, one cannot fully understand the *corrida* without understanding that it is a totally male-orientated event, and that the values which underlie it and give cultural sense to it are essentially masculine values – that is, they are values which are held by men concerning proper and expected behaviour of both themselves and other men. It is therefore necessary to focus on that particular aspect of humanity, and on how the *corrida* may be interpreted as a statement in a dramatic form of what it means to be a human male in this culture.

NOTES

1. Much of the interpretation in this chapter [...] constitutes a development of ideas developed in Corbin and Corbin 1987, an anthropological work which attempts to construct and interpret an Andalusian cosmology.

2. Writing specifically about Seville, Murphy emphasizes the importance of the concept of *ambience* in the assessment of the quality of a place or a situation:[...]"Sevillanos spontaneously make judgements about whether or not a social place or situation has *ambiente*. *Ambiente* is at once a feeling in the air and a quality of human interaction. A lack of *ambience* means that a place or a situation is colourless and unstimulating and not conducive to interesting or pleasant social interactions. Furthermore, a place or a type of situation may have *ambiente* or character which distinguishes it from other places or situations [...]" (1978, 23).

3. For an elaboration of these arguments, see Corbin and Corbin 1987; chapter 2.

4. Driessen gives several examples of the view that those who live in the town have of the life and character of those who live in the country: [..."] For Santaellanos their *pueblo* is endowed with positive qualities *ambiente, cultura,* comfort and cleanliness, and all these 'civilised' qualities are lacking in the rural settlements. Life in the country is said to be slow, primitive, uncomfortable and filthy. They consider their counterparts as people of a different *raza* (race). They do not belong to the same community ... 'Vivir en el campo', to live in the country, and 'gente del campo' are pejorative expressions [...] (1981, 53) [...] It should be pointed out that this is a view from the village or the town toward the country. There is also another perspective to this, in that villagers who consider themselves to be urban are considered by those in the city to be rural. Although the urban ethos is important, there is also an ambivalent view of the big city (in this case Cordoba) by villagers or by those in small towns and villages (see Driessen, 65ff; Caro Baroja, 1963).

5. People should avoid behaviour which indicates the animalistic side of humanity, so, for example, drunkenness, explicit sexuality or violence is inappropriate behaviour in public. They should also dress correctly for being in public; men should wear shoes, trousers and shirts, and women should wear shoes, a dress, or skirt and blouse (nowadays it is also acceptable for them to wear trousers) – in other words they should be decently covered. As Corbin and Corbin write: "'Nakedness'is appropriate to wild beasts, to human beings cavorting in the countryside, to infants, to domesticated animality in the house. Civilized people, when not 'enclosed'within the house, should not allow their bodies to be *abierto al aire* (open to the air) in the street" (1987, 28). Their argument is developed further in the chapter from which the quotation is taken.

6. Howe, in a recent study of the ritual of fox hunting, comments generally that rituals which feature animals have been created by human beings in order to "make statements about themselves through the medium of those beings" (1981, 282). In the hunt, because of the skills necessary to locate and finally kill a wild animal in its own habitat, people make a statement about the human condition (see also Ortega y Gasset, 1968).

7. Driessen points to the gradual removal of rural elements, including animals, from the urban realm, as constituting an aspect of the growth of the urban ethos in Santaella: "In 1923 municipal decrees tried to ban dunghills from the built-up area, prohibited the slaughtering of pigs in private houses and the passage of flocks of sheep and goats through the town ... Rural elements like animals, dung and mud are increasingly considered unclean and removed to rural space" (1981, 198, 191).

8. For a detailed discussion of the construction of big cat acts in circuses see Bouissac 1971 and 1976.

REFERENCES

Bouissac, P. 1971. "Poetics in the lion's den: the circus act." *Modern Language Notes*, 86, 845–857.

Bouissac, P. 1976. *Circus and Culture: A Semiotic Approach*. Bloomington: Indiana University Press.

Brandes, S. 1980, *Metaphors of Masculinity: Sex and Status in Andalusian Folklore*. Philadelphia: University of Pennsylvania Press.

Caro Baroja, Julio. 1963, "The city and the country: reflections on some ancient commonplaces." In J. Pitt-Rivers (ed.), *Mediterranean Countrymen*, Paris: Mouton and Co.

Corbin, J. R. and Corbin, M. D. 1987, *Urbane Thought: Culture and Class in an Andalusian City*. Aldershot: Gower Publishing Company Ltd.

Corrochano, G. 1966, *¿Que es Torear? Introducción a las Tauromaquias de Joselito y de Domingo Ortega*. Madrid: Revista de Occidente.

Días Cañabate, A. 1980, *Los Toros*. Vol. 5. Madrid: Espasa Calpe.

Driessen, H. 1981, *Agro Town and Urban Ethos in Andalusia*. Nijemen: Katholieke Universiteit.

Driessen, H. 1983, "Male sociability and rituals of masculinity in rural Andalusia." *Anthropological Quarterly*, 56, 3, 125–33.

Gilmore, D. 1977, "The social organization of space: class, cognition and residence in a Spanish Town." *American Ethnologist*, 4, 3, 437–51.

Gilpérez García, L. and Fraile Sanz, M. 1972, *Reglamentación Taurina Vigente: Diccionario Comentada*. Seville: Gráficas del Sur. 2nd edn.

Hemingway, E. 1985, *The Dangerous Summer*. London: Hamish Hamilton.

Howe, J. 1981, "Foxhunting as ritual." *American Ethnologist*, 8, 2, 278–300.

Ingold, T. 1980, *Hunters, Pastoralists and Ranchers: Reindeer Economics and their Transformations*. Cambridge: Cambridge University Press.

López Casero, L. 1972, "La plaza, estructura y procesos en un pueblo de la Mancha." *Ethnica*, 4, 89–133.

Marvin, G. 1988/1994, *Bullfight*. New York: Basil Blackwell.

McCormick, J. and Mascarenas, M. S. 1967, *The Complete Aficionado*. London: Weidenfeld and Nicolson.

Murphy, M. 1978, "Between the Virgin and the whore: local community and the nuclear family in Seville, Spain." Unpublished Ph.D. thesis, University of California, San Diego.

Ortega y Gasset, J. 1968, *La Caza y los Toros*. Madrid: Revista de Occidente.

Ortner, S. 1974, "Is female to male as nature is to culture?" In M. Z. Rosaldo and L. Lamphere (eds), *Women, Culture and Society*, Stanford, California: Stanford University Press, 67–87.

Serran Pagan, G. 1979, "El toro de la Virgen y la industria textil de Grazalema." *Revista Española de Investigaciones Sociológicas*, 5, 119–35.

23

RHONDA EVANS, DEANN KALICH (GAUTHIER) and
CRAIG J. FORSYTH

Dogfighting: Symbolic Expression and Validation of Masculinity*

Rhonda D. Evans, DeAnn Kalich (Gauthier), and **Craig J. Forsyth** are on the faculty at the University of Louisiana at Lafayette. Their areas of research intersect in the sociology of deviance, criminology, and gender issues. Evans (Criminal Justice), Kalich (Anthropology) and Forsyth (Sociology) have collaborated on numerous studies of gender and deviance investigating a wide range of activities, such as prison relationships, crack cultures, and underage drinking. Their interest in subcultural normative systems has produced insightful analyses of unusual lifestyles such as rodeo groupies and the study of dogfighting reprinted here. The authors examine dogfighting as a symbolic expression of the subculture of white masculinity in the southern United States, particularly for the working class. The fighting dogs, mostly Pit Bull Terriers, are reflections of their owners and thus the instruments of the owners' prowess. Dogs are expected to fight bravely (like a man), penalties are levied on dogs who behave cowardly (like a "cur"), and dogs who refuse to fight are quickly killed, allowing the owner to regain some of the status lost because of the dog's poor performance. Thus, the sport of dogfighting provides validation of masculinity for some Southern working-class men. The confirmation of what it means to be a man and the expectations for appropriate masculine behavior are themes that run throughout many observations of the human deployment of animals in blood sport.

This study examines the issue of masculinity in dogfighting. Dogfighting is an illegal gaming sport centered in the Southern United States. The data for this study were obtained via ethnographic fieldwork over a period of two years. Interviews were conducted with 31 dogmen, approximately 90% of whom were white males. In addition the authors attended 14 dogfights and numerous pre-fight meetings. We argue that specific elements of this sport represent symbolic attempts at attaining and maintaining honor and status, which, in the (predominantly white,

* Reproduced from Rhonda Evans, DeAnn K. Gauthier, and Craig J. Forsyth (1998) "Dogfighting: Symbolic Expression and Validation of Masculinity." Sex Roles 39(11–12): 825–832, © 1998 Plenum Publishing Corporation/Springer, with permission from Springer Science and Business Media.

male, working-class) dogfighting subculture, are equated with masculine identity. We further argue that pursuit of symbolic masculinity through dogfighting is more important to working-class men, who possess fewer alternative avenues for achieving status than do middle-class or professional men. The implications of this research for the larger culture of masculinity in the United States are also explored.

In all societies, manhood means more than simply being born male. Manhood is a status that must be achieved through socially constructed means. Gilmore (1990, 17) states that

> true manhood is a precious and elusive status beyond mere maleness, a hortatory image that men and boys aspire to and that their culture demands of them as a measure of belonging.

If manhood is seen as precious in all cultures one would expect this status to be even more precious in patriarchal systems where the concept of manhood embodies privilege and power. The United States is a prime example of such a culture. In particular, the Southern region of the U.S., where recent empirical research suggests gender roles have a more marked tendency toward traditionalism and patriarchy (Hurlbert and Bankston, 1998), offers the ideal context in which to study aspirations toward, and expressions of, masculinity.

Traditional qualities of masculinity in the United States include a focus on action: assertiveness, aggressiveness, strength, and competitiveness (O'Neill, 1982; Hantover, 1978). Many of these traits which are considered characteristic of the ideal man are also characteristics of the ideal American who is expected to strive for success. These traits are associated with the traditional roles of men as breadwinner and provider (Craib, 1987), though when these traits were first being defined as "manly" in the latter part of the nineteenth century, they often were perceived as virtuous regardless of their relationship to such utilitarian gender role behaviors. Action, especially in the form of dangerous or daring competitions, was viewed as an end in itself,

synonymous with manhood. Previous ideals of manliness had emphasized reserve over passion, and inaction over action. But as Rotundo (1993, 239) argues, the new masculine values came to be integrated with the old through the venue of competitive athletics:

> The significance of sport went beyond its growing popularity as a pastime; it was also important as a cultural phenomenon. This dimension was what gave athletics its special significance for the redefinition of manhood at the turn of the century.

Among other claims, sports came to be seen as a source of manhood; in particular, they were viewed as providing training in the fighting virtues, and as a means for building manly character. Indeed, competition itself became a masculine obsession, extending from contests directly between men (as in opposing football or baseball teams) to contests in which animals represented men (as in horseracing and cockfighting). Of course, neither category of contests was new to nineteenth-century men (Fischer, 1989; Enquist and Leimar, 1990); rather, it was the meaning and importance of these contests which changed.

Likewise, Gibson (1994) argues convincingly that the recent surge of interest in paramilitary culture is, in part, the result of males continuing to create social arenas in which they can express and validate masculine identity. They accomplish this through imaginary battles (such as The National Survival Game, or paintball, as it has come to be known) that obscure the boundary between counterfeit and genuine violence by allowing men to physically "attack" other men without risking real injury to themselves or their opponent. These special contexts allow men, in the safety of the game environment, to validate their masculine identities while remaining only on the periphery of actual violence. Such arenas are important in building solidarity between men, united against a common "enemy." We argue here that the modern-day dogfight provides a symbolic battlefield for accomplishing the same.

REVIEW OF THE LITERATURE: SPORT AND MASCULINITY

Most research on masculinity and sport has studied mainstream activities, while other sports, which lie outside of the dominant culture, have been ignored. The sport of dogfighting, which is illegal in all 50 states, continues to be the sport of choice for thousands of American men (predominately Southerners) most of whom are otherwise law-abiding citizens, yet researchers who study masculinity and sport have neglected to investigate this potentially rich data source. The current study seeks to explore the sport of dogfighting as a symbolic arena for developing, expressing, and validating masculinity.

Dogfighting can be defined as the act of baiting two dogs against one another for entertainment or gain. It involves placing two dogs into a pit to fight until one either quits or dies. In addition to the dogs, there are two handlers and a referee in the pit, watched by numerous spectators, who begin betting on the outcome once the fight begins. This phenomenon originated in the seventeenth century to test dogs who would perform as protectors of human life and property (Jones, 1988). Although dogfighting originally arose to serve a vital function, it quickly progressed from utility to entertainment. In its early years, dogfighting served as entertainment for all sectors of society and could not yet be defined as a sport by which men gained status (Matz, 1984).

The transformation of dogfighting from entertainment to sport coincided with industrialization. In the nineteenth and twentieth centuries dogfighting came to be defined as an exclusive male sport in which individual men can earn status within the dogfighting subculture, through the accomplishments of their dogs. Today, a subculture exists (predominantly among the Southern, white, working class) which is dedicated to the continued survival of the sport of dogfighting. The sport is now highly organized, and elaborate rules have been constructed which reflect and reinforce the traditional masculine characteristics of competitiveness, aggression, strength, toughness, and courage.

Because the defining characteristics of and opportunities for expressing masculinity in the U.S. vary between subcultures (Hantover, 1978), one important context for understanding masculine ideals in this study is the subculture of honor which exists among Southern (and predominantly white) males. As Cohen et al. (1996, 946) argue, the Southern propensity for violence is tied directly to a culture of honor, "... in which affronts are met with violent retribution." Males in the South are expected to act in this manner in order to maintain their status as men (McWhiney, 1988; Wyatt-Brown, 1982). Fischer (1989, 690) elaborates: "Honor in this society [means] pride of manhood in masculine courage, physical strength, and warrior virtue." Dogmen are enmeshed in this subculture, and therefore their own attitudes and actions should be shaped and fashioned along similar lines. Placing the sport of dogfighting in its proper Southern manhood context, then, will be necessary before an understanding of dogmen's motivations and perceived rewards may be developed.

A second important context for understanding masculine ideals in this study concerns the socioeconomic status of dogmen and the perpetuation of dogfighting in an era which no longer accords the sport the same reputability it once held. The baiting sports were first introduced to society by royalty and aristocrats (Atyeo, 1979), and during the nineteenth century, attending a dogfight came to be considered a right of passage into manhood for wealthy young men (Matz, 1984). It was a reputable activity of the time. Such a fact is important, when considered in light of Veblen's theory of the leisure class, where the standards of worth and manner of life considered reputable for "the leisure class ... become incumbent upon all classes lower in the scale" (1994, 84). Veblen maintained that this is true of sports as well. Thus, sports favored by the upper classes become those which are held in high repute among all classes. For example, Veblen (1994, 143) attributed the popularity of horse racing among the leisure class to this notion of emulation when he asserted:

> The utility of the fast horse lies largely in his efficiency as a means of emulation; it gratifies the owner's sense of aggression and dominance to have his own horse outstrip his neighbor's. This use being not lucrative, but on the whole pretty consistently wasteful, and quite conspicuously so, it is honorific, and therefore gives the fast horse a strong presumptive position of reputability.

Though Veblen mentions other sports, such as cockfighting, which served the same purposes, he does not write directly of dogfighting as a means of emulation. Still, we argue that it is within this same context that dogfighting originally emerged as a means of adherence to the standards of the leisure class, and as an attempt at emulation, in which the traits of honor and reputability (as proscribed by the leisure class of the time) could be aspired to by the lower classes of society.

Furthermore, Veblen argues that throughout history, once the upper classes of society have dictated which institutions of society are to be considered reputable, these institutions become accepted into habits of thought and are resistant to change. Veblen's contention that forms of honorific expenditure, once accepted and habitual, are resistant to change is central to the understanding of the persistence of dogfighting in modern society. Though dogfighting no longer conveys the reputability it once did (particularly among the middle and upper classes of modern society, from which animal-rights activists draw most of their support), and is illegal in all 50 states, it has continued to thrive as a sport. This is especially true in the South, a region Veblen (1994, 326) characterized as predatory (or violent) in temperament, and possessing a "livelier sense of honour." Recent research agrees that the Southern heritage of violence remains present to this day (Nisbett, 1993; Nisbett and Cohen, 1996), perhaps "... because [it has] become embedded in social roles, expectations, and shared definitions of manhood" (Cohen et al., 1996, 958). Thus, although the sport of

dogfighting may have its origins in the upper classes of pre-modern times, its continued persistence in the modern era may be explained as one manifestation of the Southern subcultural expectation of violence.

Furthermore, within the larger context of Southern violence and culture of honor norms may lie important socioeconomic bases for differences among dogmen in levels of commitment to the sport. Though today dogmen are drawn overwhelmingly from the working-class, some participants come from the middle and upper classes as well. Just as the defining characteristics of and opportunities for expressing masculinity in the U.S. vary between subcultures, so too do they vary between social classes. Thus, while strength and aggression are the preferred masculine qualities in working-class subcultures, rationality is the valued characteristic in middle-class subcultures (Craib, 1987). Differential constructs, by social class, of masculinity, may be related to opportunities for obtaining masculinity. Research suggests that men from lower-class backgrounds, who lack opportunities for expression of masculinity through occupational success, tend to rely on more accessible routes of expression which emphasize aggression, violence, and strength (Toby, 1975). This is evident in the arena of sport where participants in boxing, football, and wrestling are disproportionately drawn from the working-class sectors of society (Loy, 1969; Weinberg and Arond, 1952). Thus, with the sport of dogfighting, it may be true that there are differences in meanings derived from participation by men of different socioeconomic statuses.

METHODOLOGY

The primary data for this study are interviews with an availability sample of men who fight dogs for sport (N = 31). The interviews range from 2 to 4 hours each, and were held at dog fights, the homes of dogmen, or at pre-fight meetings. In addition, primary data include ethnographic observations of all activities and participants at

14 dog fights and numerous pre-fight meetings. The research locations include several parishes in Louisiana and counties in Mississippi. The racial/ethnic composition of our sample is approximately 90% white. Secondary data are taken from historical accounts of dogfighting.

FINDINGS

Symbolic Meaning and the Southern Culture of Honor

Public sporting events provide opportunities for generation and illustration of character, if the contestants are able to demonstrate valued qualities such as courage, gameness, integrity, and composure (Birrell, 1981). We argue that in the sport of dogfighting, the actual combatants serve as symbols of their respective owners, and therefore any character attributed to the dogs is also attributed to the men they represent. Dogfighting is centered in the South, a region whose inhabitants are well-known for their love of sports and "… any event that [promises] the excitement of deciding the inequalities of prowess among men, or among men and beasts" (Wyatt-Brown, 1982, 339). As such, gaming of all sorts (including cards, dice, horse racing, cockfighting, and dogfighting) qualifies. But as Wyatt-Brown (1982) notes, these activities mean much more than a chance to turn a profit; they provide for the distribution of honor and status to participants, while nonparticipation signifies cowardice. For our purposes, an even more meaningful observation is the one that among Southerners "… the union of the individual with the instrument of his prowess – the horse, cocker, cards, marksman's gun, or dice – [has] a sacred character" (Wyatt-Brown, 1982, 344). This, we argue, is the case between dogmen and their dogs. If the dogs behave as heroes, then the men must be heroes also. As Porpora (1996, 211) notes:

> heroes are better conceptualized not as idols of worship, but as an idealized reference group: one

seeks to stand with one's heroes rather than to be one's heroes in actuality, and heroes thus are one mechanism we use to tell ourselves what it is we stand for. For those who have them, then, heroes are an important inner marker of identity. They are part of the landscape of the soul.

The hero in this case is the American Pit Bull Terrier, the exclusive breed employed in dogfighting today. The dog is expected to fight under stringent rules and "take it like a man." The rules of the sport are primarily concerned with penalizing any dog (and the owner of the dog) who behaves cowardly (or as the members of the fraternity would say, shows signs of being a "cur"). The rules are further concerned with rewarding dogs (and their owners) who display masculine characteristics with status and prestige.

The term "cur" is considered by dogmen to be extremely derogatory. Their ultimate goal is to prove that their dog possesses the most admirable quality within the sport of dogfighting: gameness. Gameness is defined as "an awesome persistence that flows out of an invincible will" (Jones, 1988, 249). The dog who displays gameness and is persistent in this display will win and the dog that shows weakness or any signs of being a cur will lose. Jones (1988, 293) notes that gameness is an essential quality of heroism and that

> the dogfighters, more than anything else, [are] hero worshippers. They [seek], through the test of the pit, to find the unstoppable dog … the dog, within which [dwells] a mighty force, a will which [enables] him to push forward, unbroken and unbreakable, in spite of pain or injury, to victory or to death. The dogfighters [are] in the business of creating heroes. They [are] artists who [sculpt] in flesh, men who [aim], by the application of scientific breeding principles, to produce Sir Lancelot for real. Characters in a book [are] fine for timid souls, but not for them. They [want] heroes that [live] and [breathe] and [walk] on Earth.

Our research confirms that the dogs employed in the sport of dogfighting do serve as symbols for the traditional masculine ideal of heroism that exists within the subculture of dogfighters and they are the symbols through which their owners gain status as men. As one dogfighter puts it, "… these dogs are a reflection on the man. Mean and tough guys have the kind of dogs that [demonstrate] they are men." Our informants repeatedly confirmed to us that the sport serves an important purpose by validating their masculinity. For example, one participant notes the significance of dogfighting as an arena for gaining status as men, by stating: "There's an old saying about this game, that the truth of it is you're an honest and tough guy. If you're faking, the truth comes out in the pit." Another owner states outright: "I only expect a dog to be as good as the man behind him, not any more, not any less. If a man brings a no good dog to the pit, he's usually not 100 percent either." Still another fighter concurs: "I expect the same thing out of my dog as I expect out of myself. A dog is only as good as his master."

In fact, because fighting dogs are seen by dogmen as reflections of their owners, they are expected to aspire to mythical ideals of masculinity within the context of the Southern culture of honor. The following meaningful statement by a dogman vividly expresses these expectations:

> To us a game dog is one that will try aggressively to beat you and not stop until he is physically or mentally unable. He tries to fight the other dog by putting out a frontal assault, not backing up, running, like you sometimes see in boxing. Whenever I was raised up, Saturday night fights with my grandfather … you never saw them old fighters back up and dodge their opponent. That's the kind of dogs we want. Like Mike Tyson, that's the kind of bulldog I want. No Sugar Ray Leonards in our breed.

This comparison between the fighting styles of Tyson and Leonard is indicative of the importance of the symbolic expression of a macho identity in these dogmen. Mike Tyson is widely perceived as tough, aggressive, and fearless. He is a fighter who is not afraid of punishment. Leonard, on the other hand, is known for strategically trying to avoid punishment. Significantly, Southern dogmen indicated to us that they feel validated as men when their dogs behave as Tyson would, yet they fear the scorn associated with dogs that fall short of this heroic mark. Other dogmen echo this sentiment in the following statements:

> The dog that stays there and keeps it going regardless of if he's getting whipped, is what I'm talking about.

> If the dog is capable of standing on his feet, he should keep fighting and never quit. I would condemn any dog that chooses to quit.

All respondents note that they expect their dogs to display this quality of gameness in extreme proportions. Dogs that prove to be curs are considered poor reflections on the sport, and as such, disposable. The fate of participants who fail to display the masculine qualities which have come to define gameness is severe:

> If one of my dogs proves to be a cur, I put him to sleep. I don't give curs away or sell them for any amount of money. We don't want curs being bred; it looks bad on the sport.

Not only are curs considered to reflect poorly on the sport, but inappropriate resolution of the problem they present can damage the man's reputation as well.

> A true dogman will put a dog that quits (a cur) to sleep, instead of letting someone else have him [even as a pet]. A person who would take a dog that quit, is not a true dogman.

Thus, dogs who prove to be curs are killed, not only because of their perceived negative impact on the sport but also because they are perceived to reflect badly on the men who own them. Status is gained by bringing game dogs to the pit; status is questioned or lessened for any man who brings a cur. As one respondent notes:

> No man should come to the pit with a cur dog. He should know what he has before he enters the pit.

Bringing a dog to the pit who proves to be a cur, leads to the humiliation of the owner. In a sport where the dog symbolizes the man, there is no place for cowards. All respondents told us that if they ever have a dog that quits in the pit, it faces certain death. What is striking about this declaration is that in every fight, the structured nature of the sport is such that one contestant must be declared the loser. Unless that dog has proven itself in previous fights, it will not be given even one more chance to do so. Losing dogs with proven histories of gameness may gain one, perhaps two, additional chances to redeem themselves in the pit, but no more. Yet, the crucial sociological question is: what is so important to these dogmen that their cur dogs must be killed?

The official reason given by the dogfighters for killing cur dogs (to prevent the transmission of bad character through procreation) seems incomplete, as neutering the dog would accomplish the same goal. Symbolically, however, it may be important to execute the curs because this provides an aggressive and violent end to a nonaggressive, nonviolent (or at least not sufficiently aggressive or violent) life. It is a symbolic reinstatement of the (by virtue of his losing dog) fallen man to the masculine ideal. In this way, status lost via a cur dog is regained via quick and aggressive action to extinguish the problem. In fact, as we note above, failure to dispense with the dog quickly is judged harshly by onlookers as evidence of weakness of character. This is an additional confirmation that the man is "no better than his dog." The threat to the losing dogman, then, is much more than a simple loss in the pit; the threat is a loss of masculinity and status in the eyes of his dogfighting peers.

Furthermore, since the overwhelming majority of dogfighters are drawn from the working class, we argue that alternative opportunities (such as occupational success) for validating masculinity may be perceived by these working-class men to be less accessible, thus making a loss in the pit much more threatening in terms of their masculine identities. These males may already feel they are "losers" in the game of life,

and they may therefore be more inclined to rely on validating rituals such as the execution of cur dogs to keep from being stigmatized as "losers" in this situation as well. The ritual of violence becomes intelligible when considered in context: in the Southern culture of honor, humiliations are met with violent rejoinders. As one respondent states:

> I don't care how long my dog fights, if he is still able to keep going and chooses to quit, he's not coming home with me. He's a dead dog.

SYMBOLIC MEANING AND SOCIOECONOMIC STATUS

Our sample of dogfighters is drawn primarily from the working class, a fact which lends some support to the findings of other researchers (Loy, 1969; Weinberg and Arond, 1952) that participants in aggressive, violent sports are disproportionately drawn from the working class.

However, a small portion of our sample includes middle-class business owners. These two groups provide the opportunity to explore a second important context for understanding masculine ideals: the socioeconomic status of dogmen and the perpetuation of the sport into the modern era. Our sample allows us to explore possible differences in the symbolic meaning of this sport to men of different socioeconomic status.

All of our respondents, regardless of class, view the sport of dogfighting as an arena in which they can compete with other men for status. However, there are notable differences between participants from the working and middle classes. The most significant difference lies in the degree of importance ascribed to the sport by each class of men. While working-class men tend to express extreme commitment to the sport and describe it as having a primary role within their lives, the responses of middle-class participants indicate that they are not nearly as committed to the sport and view it merely as a hobby. To demonstrate the strength of this difference, note the following remark by one married, working-class dogman (a construction worker) who describes the significance of the sport to him as follows:

> I eat, sleep, and drink bulldogs. That's the only thing that I live for. This is my life. My goal is to one day be an old man and have people say this was a gentleman who had some of the best dogs.

This individual, like many of the other dogmen with whom we spoke, hopes that the actions of his dogs may come to have enduring symbolic value; his dogs may be his only means to display attributes of his own character unseen in other arenas of life. Another working-class dogman expresses his commitment to the sport by saying:

> I told my girlfriend that if she ever thinks there will be a day that I won't fool with these dogs, then we could just end our relationship now. That ain't happening. I won't give it up. I gave it up once and those were the worst two years of my life.

These responses, and others like them, suggest that this sport occupies a primary position in the lives of participants. Though winning is always important, it is not the solitary goal of these participants: the camaraderie among the dogmen is just as important. Being a member of this subculture allows participants to maintain a sense of belonging and solidarity with other men. They share similar risks, ranging from potential betting losses to legal detection (and the ensuing consequences) of their involvement in illegal activities. It is this shared association and sense of group identity that holds the subculture of dogfighters together. It is this same togetherness that causes dogmen to return when they have left the group, for they report feeling lost without it. This idea is common among sports competitors in general: that belonging is just as, perhaps even more important, than winning.

Additionally, working-class dogmen seem to view their sport as an avenue by which the playing field has been leveled between men. Here, too, is an idea that is common among sports competitors in general: wealth has less to do with winning than brute strength and determination. Sports have long been heralded as a place where rich and poor, black and white, can meet and play with some consciousness of a level playing field. On the contrary, in other areas of social life, working-class dogmen correctly perceive the fields to be tilted in favor of those with more social weight. One respondent put it this way:

> In this sport I can compete with someone who is really wealthy and whose ancestors have been in the sport for 60 or 70 years. I can beat them. If I bring a good dog to the pit, I stand just as good a chance of winning as they do. It doesn't matter if they are richer than I am.

Winning, in terms of the masculine ideal, is paramount to maintaining masculine status for working-class males in particular. Though middle-class participants "enjoy" winning, they do not focus as strongly on that goal. While working-class participants repeatedly assert their dedication to the sport as a part of their everyday lives, middle-class participants indicate that the sport is not central to their lives at all, but more an amusing distraction from the serious business of their lives. The following response of a middle-class business owner is representative of the responses of the other middle-class participants with whom we spoke:

> I enjoy competing in the sport; but, it's just a hobby to me. I try not to let it interfere with my business.

The literature on sports documents a connection between socioeconomic status and the meaning participants attribute to sport (Messner, 1990). Though baiting sports were once viewed as reputable standards by the upper classes, meanings attributed to the sport have changed in modern times. Yet, as Veblen (1994) noted, once standards become established, they are highly resistant to change. This may be even more the case when the lower classes, still in pursuit of status, find new standards of repute blocked from access. Thus, the differential meaning attributed to the sport of dogfighting by men from different socioeconomic ranks suggests that, for working-class men, restricted means of asserting masculinity and gaining status through other routes (such as workplace/economic success) may motivate them to rely more heavily on an older standard (such as the sport of dogfighting) as an alternate path toward masculine status.

CONCLUSIONS

The symbolic battlefield on which the dogfight is waged may be the primary route for some men, entrenched in a Southern culture of honor, to validate their masculinity without risking physical injuries to themselves or their human adversaries. Gaming, in this context, functions to distribute honor and status among males who have little access to alternate routes for legitimate successes which might allow them to "measure up" as "real" men. Instead, these men hope to breed unbreakable heroes of their dogs, who will then be considered mere shadows of them as men. Should they fail in this regard, the dogmen seek to insure future success by killing all curs, while simultaneously defending their threatened honor as men.

The men who participate in this sport face the possibility of legal prosecution and yet they continue to participate in ever increasing numbers (Semencic, 1984). We maintain their reasons for participation include the symbolic status they gain from the sport. The sport offers an arena in which they can aspire to the masculine ideal through their dogs. The findings of this study also indicate that there are differences in the meaning attributed to sport by participants from different socioeconomic status. We suspect these differences stem from differential legitimate opportunities to achieving masculine status. Working class men face limited opportunities for masculine expression and validation within or through their jobs, and may be more likely to see sport as a primary means for validating their masculinity.

Though not a focus of the present research, one avenue for future study might be to explore the activities of participants who play the role of spectator to these events. Most individuals present at the dogfights are not fighting dogs in the current match, but have in the past, or will be in the future. In other words, individuals rotate between the roles of spectator and handler. As spectators, the primary behavior is one of betting on the outcome of the fight. Research on horseracing and poker suggests that only bettors that take chances are considered capable of displaying character (Scott, 1968; Birrell, 1981). Geertz (1972) argues the same is true of Balinesian cockfights, where "deep play" refers to the custom of betting more than one can afford to lose. This practice is not considered foolish among the Balinese, but honorable. Future analyses of dogfight bettors should examine what role, if any, masculine honor plays in guiding betting practices.

In this paper, we have argued that the sport of dogfighting provides masculine validation for the men who participate in it. The study of this sport as an arena for expressing masculinity offers insight into the lengths men will go to in order to prove they are "real men." Furthermore, the implications of our findings are not restricted to the Southern, working-class subculture but extend to the larger culture of masculinity in the United States. Though violence may receive heightened emphasis among Southerners, the emphasis on violence is found to exist in definitions of masculinity across the nation as a whole. We see this emphasis in the violent rites of passage demanded of male gang members. We see it in the continued persistence of rape myths which suggest that rape is an act of passion on the part of "real" men driven by masculine impulses. We see it in the military hazing of young (particularly male) recruits as a prerequisite to combat training. Certainly, we also see it in sports such as hockey (where violence is central to the game itself). Even the "non-contact" sports such as basketball and baseball assure elevated status among their peers to men who "foul" their opponents with violence, or who "bean" the batters with the ball. Thus, the code of honor to which dogmen aspire is but a reflection of a more universal code which exists among men in most walks of life. Violence is viewed as culturally legitimate, and masculine, and as such it aids in shaping men's ideas about who they are as men. Violence as a legitimate element of masculinity has succeeded in assuring men as a group of their relationship to each other, to women, and to society.

As long as the status of manhood continues to be "precious" (Gilmore, 1990) and defined as something that must be earned, males will continue to seek avenues by which to validate their status as men. Males who face limited opportunities for masculine expression within the boundaries proscribed by the dominant culture may seek avenues outside of these boundaries, even if they are illegal. In U.S. society, failure to achieve (or even failure to aspire to) the culturally constructed and defined goal of masculinity is often considered, by many males, far worse than any legal penalties they might incur in the process.

REFERENCES

Atyeo, D. (1979). Blood and buts, violence in sports. New York: Paddington Press.

Birrell, S. (1981). Sport as ritual. Social Forces, 60, 354–376.

Cohen, D., Bowdle, B. F., Nisbett, R. E., & Schwarz, N. (1996). Insult, aggression, and the southern culture of honor. Journal of Personality and Social Psychology, 70, 945–960.

Craib, I. (1987). Masculinity and male dominance. Sociological Review, 38, 721–743.

Enquist, M. & Leimar, O. (1990). The evolution of fatal fighting. Animal Behavior, 39, 1–9.

Fischer, D. H. (1989). Albion's seed: Four British folkways in America. New York: Oxford University Press.

Geertz, C. (1972). Deep play: Notes on the Balinese cockfight. Daledalus, 101, 1–27.

Gibson, J. W. (1994). Warrior Dreams: Violence and manhood in post-Vietnam America. In E. Disch (Ed.), Reconstructing gender, Mountain View, CA: Mayfield Publishing.

Gilmore, D. D. (1990). Manhood in the making: Cultural concepts of masculinity. New Haven, CT: Yale University Press.

Hantover, J. P. (1978). The Boy Scouts and the validation of masculinity. Sociological Issues, 34, 184–195.

Hurlbert, J. S. & Bankston, W. B. (1998). Cultural distinctiveness in the face of structural transformation: The "New" Old South. In D. R. Hurt (Ed.), Social change in the rural South, 1945–1995. Baton Rouge: Louisiana State University Press.

Jones, M. (1988). The dogs of capitalism Book 1: Origins. Cedar Park, TX: 21st Century Logic.

Loy, John W., Jr. (1969). The study of sport and social mobility. In G. S. Kenyon (Ed.), Aspects of Contemporary Sport Sociology. Chicago: The Athletic Institute.

Matz, K. S. (1984). The pit bull: fact and fable. Sacramento, CA: De Mortmain Publishing.

McWhiney, G. (1988). Cracker culture: Celtic ways in the Old South. Tuscaloosa: University of Alabama Press.

Messner, M. A. (1990). Boyhood, organized sports, and the construction of masculinities. Contemporary Ethnography, 18, 416–444.

Nisbett, R. E. (1993). Violence and U.S. regional culture. American Psychologist, 48, 441–449.

Nisbett, R. E. & Cohen, D. (1996). Culture of honor: The psychology of violence in the South. Boulder, CO: Westview Press.

O'Neill, J. M. (1982). Gender role conflict and strain in men's lives. In K. Soloman & N. B. Levy (Eds.), Men in transition: Theory and therapy. New York: Plenum Press.

Porpora, D. V. (1996). Personal heroes, religion, and transcendental metanarratives. Sociological Forum, 11, 209–229.

Rotundo, E. A. (1993). American manhood. New York: Basic Books.

Scott, M. (1968). The racing game. Chicago: Aldine.

Semencic, C. (1984). The world of fighting dogs. Neptune City, New Jersey: T. F. H. Publications.

Toby, J. (1975). Violence and the masculine ideal: Some qualitative data. In S. K. Steinmetz & M. A. Straus (Eds.), Violence in the Family. New York: Dodd Mead.

Veblen, T. (1994). The theory of the leisure class. New York: Penguin Books.

Weinberg, S. K. & Arond, H. (1952). The occupational culture of the boxer. American Journal of Sociology, 57, 460–469.

Wyatt-Brown, B. (1982). Southern honor: Ethics and behavior in the Old South. New York: Oxford University Press.

24

RANDY MALAMUD

Zoo Spectatorship*

Randy Malamud is a Professor of English who studies modern literature, ecocriticism, postcolonial studies and cultural studies. These specializations provide the conceptual framework for his highly regarded book *Reading Zoos: Representations of Animals and Captivity*, an analysis of "zoo stories" from literary sources that shows how zoos are problematized in cultural representations, such as fiction, songs, cartoons, and advertising. Malamud is unapologetic in his disdain for zoos. He writes that the preservation of animals in zoos is a "token" project that permits humans to "repress the reality of the danger people pose to the natural world." Zoos are "high-profile cultural attractions" that put animals on display for amusement and spectacle. This chapter from *Reading Zoos* addresses the issue of spectatorship and how humans watch animals in the zoo from a position of power and control over the watched "specimens." Malamud finds zoo spectatorship passive, vicarious behavior that does not lend itself to an appreciation of nature, but rather to an objectification of animals and a privileging of the human by spectators who, in their unimpeded view of other animals, consider themselves "masters of all they survey." Finally, animal-watching is not confined to zoos. Television documentaries and the internet are increasingly popular ways for humans to gaze upon animals. Malamud argues that while nature shows have some potential for a better understanding of animals with their offer of a view of animals in their natural habitats, internet sites, digital media and virtual zoos are particularly compelling devices that distance humans from other animals.

Few if any wild animals ... would choose to live in full view of human beings, yet in a zoo they must.

A. H. N. Green-Armytage, *Bristol Zoo* 1865–1965

There is no higher use to which a wild bird or mammal can be devoted than to place it in perfectly comfortable captivity to be seen by millions of persons who desire to make its acquaintance.

William Hornaday, Founding Director, Bronx Zoo

The animal scrutinises [man] across a narrow abyss of non-comprehension ... The man too is looking across a similar, but not identical, abyss of non-

* Reproduced with permission of the publisher and from Randy Malamud (1998) *Reading Zoos: Representations of Animals and Captivity*. New York: New York University Press.

comprehension. And this is so wherever he looks. He is always looking across ignorance and fear.

John Berger, "Why Look at Animals?"

I live only to be stared at.
The throng they call people comes here.
They like to tease me.
They enjoy it when my rage rattles the bars.

José Emilio Pacheco, "Baboon Babble"

This chapter will examine how spectators watch animals at zoos. What, exactly, do they see? How does the seemingly oxymoronic *activity of spectatorship* affect their consciousness – morally, imaginatively, socially? What does zoo spectatorship fundamentally involve, and how do the characteristics of watching reflect on the enterprise of zoos? What can we see when we watch people watching, and watch *how* people watch? I hypothesize that zoo spectatorship is passive, minimally imaginative, cheaply vicarious, at least slightly distasteful, conducive to a range of socially inappropriate or undesirable behavior, and inhibitive, rather than generative, of the creative experience and appreciation of nature. Both zoo stories and zoo culture suggest that spectators tend to display few of the nobler instincts of inquiry or epistemological and experiential appetite as they pass from cage to cage. S. A. Omrod reflects a sense of the tawdry when he writes, "Most [zoos] are simply peep-shows, the animals merely goods displayed to the public in return for hard cash" ("Wild Animals in Captivity," in Magel, 121).

At the extreme, the most audacious spectators may pose tangible harm to animals and to other zoogoers, manifesting aggression and social dysfunctionality. Bob Mullan and Garry Marvin describe accounts of vandalism motivated by, in addition to sadism,

probably simply the end of being intrusive, or demanding attention or interaction. In Bombay Zoo crocodiles have been stoned to death in futile attempts to stir them ... Peter Batten ... observes that it is "doubtful whether any American zoo has escaped vandalism in some form by sadistic,

ignorant, or dimwitted humans ... zoo animals are maimed, mutilated and killed quite frequently." (135)

Bernard Livingston expands upon the potential menaces of spectatorship, recounting keepers' accounts of public nuisances who haunt zoos: among the most common

are the "dirty old men" of the zoo ... These voyeurs hang around the zoo for hours on end hoping to see animals copulate. Every zoo has them and mostly they are harmless except for an occasional exhibitionist ... Another type of sexual pervert who occasionally plagues zoos is the sodomist. The wild ass, the deer, the aoudad, young llamas and other more or less docile hoofed beasts are usually the choice for this night-visiting predator, chiefly because these animals are similar to the kind of animal he victimized on the farm where the habit often started. [Zoo director Heini] Hediger adds to the sexual perverts mentioned above "the type who concentrates not on the animals but on women, young people and children, eying them in dark and secluded corners of the zoo. There are also people who apparently are sexually stimulated by the sight of some particular animal or other, e.g., a long-necked terrapin, and consequently visit it with inordinate frequency." (48–50)

Marie Nimier's *The Giraffe* (1993) illustrates similar instances of unbalanced behavior: her zoo visitor reflects upon

a Sunday I'll remember all my life. I was standing at my favorite vantage point ... Directly across from me, I saw a man begin to masturbate. It was a fine day and crowds streamed boisterously through the park, but the man seemed completely oblivious. His leather-gloved hand moved back and forth like a forlorn bird, steadily, coldly. His glazed eyes followed the crimson rump of an old female baboon climbing on the boulders (29).

The deviant activity is contagious:

I think he noticed me, for his hand stopped moving when mine reached inside my fly. I ducked behind the wooden shutters. The man removed his jacket and used it to cover himself. I found him attractive ... I was impressed with the controlled, workmanlike nature of his stroking. Almost involuntarily, I began to copy him, following his rhythm, breathing along with him. (30–1)

This behavior manifests a kind of spectatorial exuberance gone wild, and probably, too, a warped exertion of power (shocking and offending "normal" zoogoers, transgressing mores of social propriety). The masturbation betokens exhibitionism (the possibility of being seen by other spectators titillates) as well as voyeurism (part of the men's thrill deriving from masturbating while watching animals and other people), representing a zoo-based variant on the psychiatric characterization of voyeurism:

> The essential feature of this disorder is recurrent, intense, sexual urges and sexually arousing fantasies ... involving the act of observing unsuspecting people, usually strangers ... The act of looking ("peeping") is for the purpose of achieving sexual excitement ... Orgasm, usually produced by masturbation, may occur during the voyeuristic activity, or later in response to the memory of what the person has witnessed ... the person with Voyeurism is aroused by the secretive, illegal nature of his peeping.[1]

In *The Giraffe*, the autoerotic spectators' transgressions result from what Nimier portrays as the objectification of zoo animals: the situation of animals at a great remove from people, and the refusal to dignify their stature in what we regard as our world; the construction of a zoo as a place where normal behavioral guidelines – toward fellow human as well as nonhuman creatures – do not apply. For example, the narrator muses about a giraffe (the zoo animal that most obsesses him, yet which he still fails to appreciate or respect except as a fetish for his own sensibilities): "She seemed so different from me, at the time, so distant. I preferred to ignore her, she was only an object, the object of my attentions, nothing more." (25–6) Here and in other zoo stories, spectators' perceptions that the zoo does

not nurture or require considerate standards of deportment facilitates misbehavior. It is as if offending spectators perceive the zoo's abrogations of social/natural beneficence (its sadistic strain, hegemonic chauvinism, constraint) that make transgressive behavior seem less proscribed than in ordinary society. The zoo, in such cases, fosters sociopathy – or, at least, provides people with sociopathic tendencies an amenable environment for their expressions.

Another zoo voyeur appears in Brigid Brophy's *Hackenfeller's Ape* (1953), where the interests of science provide a cover for Professor Darrelhyde's study of the apes' sexuality. "There was no record that any white man had witnessed the mating of Hackenfeller's Ape." (19) The professor becomes as obsessed with these animals as Nimier's spectator is with the giraffe, sublimating his emotions to the advancement of biological knowledge. "When he observed the mating fervour seize the apes, he came as near as his temperament allowed to ambition," imagining that he would be cited in "a footnote in every future monograph on the species. What he hoped was to replace the confused, anonymous, undated tradition, which had been preserved among untrained minds, by a couple of sentences, packed and precisely descriptive" (19), describing the animals' copulation. Brophy depicts voyeurism masquerading as a quest for scientific insight, order, truth.

Certainly most zoo spectators are not latent perverts; but many do behave badly, inappropriately, in less extreme ways than the overt degenerates. Spectators' opportunity to watch everything animals do resembles on some level the power and pleasure that characterizes the disorder of voyeurism. Peeping – watching everpresent and compliant subjects, *carte blanche* – encompasses zoo visitors' role, their *raison d'être*. "Staring," writes Stephen St C. Bostock, "is in a way the essence of a zoo" (100).

Yet if zoo spectatorship taps into subconscious cravings for voyeuristic arousal by tantalizing patrons with exotic and forbidden stimuli, it can also frustrate visitors' fantasies and cravings. John Berger writes:

The zoo cannot but disappoint. The public purpose of zoos is to offer visitors the opportunity of looking at animals. Yet nowhere in a zoo can a stranger encounter the look of an animal. At the most, the animal's gaze flickers and passes on. They look sideways. They look blindly on. They scan mechanically. They have been immunised to encounter, because nothing can any more occupy a *central* place in their attention. Therein lies the ultimate consequence of their marginalisation. That look between animal and man, which may have played a crucial role in the development of human society, and with which, in any case, all men had always lived until less than a century ago, has been extinguished. Looking at each animal, the unaccompanied zoo visitor is alone. As for the crowds, they belong to a species which has at last been isolated (28).

The spectators' position is circumscribed by paradox: the zoo promises it will allow them to see everything, but they may really see nothing. The spectatorial role, people presume, privileges us magisterially. But according to Berger, animals deflate the human gaze we conceive as so puissant, by cutting us in return – refusing to dignify or acknowledge our self-important ritual of looking. A king may look at a cat, but perhaps a cat disdains to look back at a king. The zoo situates spectators in a position suggesting that they will regard unimpeded, imperiously, omnivorously, masters of all they survey. But the actual visual pickings may prove less grand: eager for quick and lurid thrills, spectators may instead discover isolation and frustration.

Michel Foucault's ideological insights further despoil spectators' purportedly innocent pleasures. The logical extrapolation of the zoo, Foucault writes in *Discipline and Punish*, is the prison; in both, authority figures exercise power via surveillance. He discusses Jeremy Bentham's model for the panopticon prison, an architectural enterprise famously devoted to regulation, discipline, separation between a figure of power and a subjugated other, and the enforced imposition of order upon unwilling subjects. "Bentham does not say whether he was inspired, in his project,

by La Vaux's menagerie at Versailles: the first menagerie in which the different elements are not, as they traditionally were, in a park" (203); but Foucault infers that La Vaux exerted an institutional influence upon Bentham.

In the Versailles menagerie, "At the centre was an octagonal pavilion which, on the first floor, consisted of only a single room, the king's *salon*; on every side large windows looked out onto seven cages ... containing different species of animals" (203). Both zoo and panopticon show "a similar concern with individualizing observation, with characterization and classification, with the analytical arrangement of space" (203). For the prisoners always potentially under scrutiny – who know always that the guardian *could be* watching, although not that he necessarily is – "Visibility is a trap" (200). The major effect of this "trap" is "to induce in the inmate a state of consciousness and permanent visibility that assures the automatic functioning of power ... Surveillance is permanent in its effects, even if it is discontinuous in its action" (201). Whether or not someone happens to be watching, the caged creature is there to be exhibited, and thus endures the constant servility of the subject under surveillance. Via surveillance, the institution ensures "that the perfection of power should tend to render its actual exercise unnecessary" (201). In the prison, the ramifications of such surveillance obviously assist the processes of keeping prisoners captive. In the zoo, Foucault's analysis implies, people watch animals as a means of symbolically celebrating (or supplanting, or satisfying vicariously) a desire to exert power over them more explicitly.

The institutional dynamics of spectatorship as a power stance inhere in the zoo whether or not its patrons consciously opt to exercise them. Foucault suggests how zoo spectatorship reiterates the prison warden's position with its power of unbounded, one-way surveillance. Other appraisals of zoo culture, too, confirm the praxis he describes as operant in zoos. "The problem with staring," writes Bostock, is "that staring with many species, including ourselves, is a threat"

(100). "The traditional menagerie," as Mullan and Marvin describe, "allow[ed] the humans the closest visual experience of the animals. The notion that an animal was entitled to some sort of privacy, that it could absent itself from the human gaze, was totally alien to this sort of exhibition. It was on display, the public had paid to see it and therefore it should be visible" (70). As unfortunate as this scenario is for animals, I am more interested in what this incessant sense of entitlement to absolute spectatorial control says about the people who relish the power that accompanies total visual access. If, as Foucault suggests, zoos resemble prisons semiotically and institutionally, it is unsurprising that the relationship between the watcher and the watched should embody antagonism.

One of the most popular spectatorial activities is feeding time at the zoo – both keepers' scheduled feedings and visitors' *ad hoc* offerings. A 1930 *Cook's Handbook to London* notes, under its entry for the London Zoo: "The feeding time of the lions and tigers is 4 p.m., except from November to February, when it is one hour earlier; the sea lions and seals are fed at 4.30 (November to February 3.30); pelicans 2.30" (238).[2] And still, in 1996, the zoo distributes a brochure, "London Zoo: Your Day in Our Life," listing special events including "1.30: Pig out! You are welcome to come and watch our rare breeds make pigs of themselves at lunch. Better than that, you can even help feed them!"; "2.30: Fast food. It's down in one when the penguins p-p-p-pick up a fish and generally make a meal of feeding time. See for yourself why it's one of the Zoo's top attractions"; "2.30: Fishy goings-on. Piranha pounce, sharks attack, archer fish aim and angel fish angle for a bite in the aquarium." (An advertisement in that brochure, headlined "Feeding Time at the Zoo," promotes several restaurants and kiosks where *people* can eat; outside the cages as well as inside, ingestion features as a prominent zoo activity.) "Eating, especially for animals, is still an act overlaid with magical associations," argues Boria Sax, explaining the appeal of watching animals feed.

"In a very visceral way, people have always been inclined to judge types of animals by the things and manner in which they eat."

Louis MacNeice's *Zoo* (1938) depicts what a spectator at the Regent's Park lion house sees at feeding time:

> the heavy rumbling of the meat-trolley, an outburst of growls, general galvanization … The keeper began with the jaguar in the cage at the west end, undoing the slat at the bottom of the bars and thrusting in a joint of horse. The animals struck at him with left hooks through the bars, growling breathily. Some went on growling even when the meat was in their mouths. Most of the leopards took their pieces up to their high shelves, like a cat jumping on to a table, but most of the lions subsided plumb in the front of their cages facing the crowds behind the barrier and, bending their heads to one side, lazily ground up the bones (100–1).

MacNeice may or may not intend the unsavory and unsettling tinge I perceive in his account. While the activity of eating is literally natural and common, it appears colored here with a subliminal guilty embarrassment, even repulsion. The antagonistic oppression Foucault identifies, and the disappointing emptiness Berger posits, indeed seem present – in terms of a pervasive and otherwise inexplicable sense of anger, and an almost grotesque viciousness – as MacNeice describes spectators watching animals eat.

E. F. Benson's essay "The Zoo" (1893) provides a more explicitly critical and disturbed reaction to Regent's Park feeding displays:

> I once saw the snakes fed; the public are now no longer allowed to see it, and quite rightly. There were about a dozen people in the snake-house, at the time, and I think we were all silent as we went out, when the feeding was over. The snake I watched was a live python from South America … and he was given a live rat, for they will not eat the dead food. The rat was let in through a small wire grating, and seemed quite at his ease at first, for the snake was asleep. He ran about the cage for a little while, and eventually walked

across two of the reptile's coils. At that moment the other opened his eyes and saw the rat. He was in no hurry, and stretched himself slowly ...

The rat was still unconcerned, he was sitting in a corner, performing his last toilet, which was not worth while, and it was very pitiful. Presently he looked up, and saw that which made him drop down on all-fours, and tremble. The snake had fully awoke, he was hungry, and it was dinner time; two small eyes were looking towards the living meal ... it was horrible.

It is many years since I saw that sight. It was, I think, the most terrifying thing I ever beheld. In sleep, the horror of it sometimes still reaches me. I am in a dim unfamiliar room, alone at first, but as I sit there, something wakes into existence which is horrible, evil, not understood, and I cannot get away (158–60).

My point – and I believe Benson's as well – is not that animals eating is disgusting; obviously it is a fundamental facet of natural behavior. But something seems askew, inappropriate, about feeding rituals as they occur at the zoo, and about spectators' presence. Both MacNeice's and Benson's accounts (but more explicitly the latter) project a sense that it is wrong for people to be watching – yet spectators queue up nevertheless, as directed by timetables, to see. Benson's final passage extends beyond describing the feeding, focusing ultimately on himself: his own troubled memory of the event. He indicates, as I argue, that what happens in zoos is essentially not about animals but about people, and that it is about us in disturbing ways. Despite the copious anthropomorphism, I do not think Benson means to address the situations of the rat or the snake: they are on their own as predator and prey, just as they would be in nature. Rather, he expresses the troubling qualities of *human* behavior, the spectator's traumatic anagnorisis. What is significant (and most disturbing) about the feeding scene as he describes it is, specifically, the human presence.

Penelope Lively's *Moon Tiger* (1987) offers a tawdry depiction of how feeding the animals generates revenue and spectatorial attraction at the Cairo Zoo: "The hippos share a small lake with flamingos and assorted duck; a keeper stands alongside with a bucket of potatoes – five piastres buys a couple of potatoes which you then throw into the pink maw of the hippo. The adult hippos wallow with their mouths permanently agape while two young ones, who have not yet got the idea, cruise fretfully up and down, occasionally struck by inaccurate potatoes"; a spectator remarks that the display resembles "an exotic form of hoop-la" (106).

In Edward Kamau Brathwaite's "The Zoo" (1989), feeding animals explicitly represents one element in the repertoire of degradation that spectators exert: the poem catalogues dozens of animals, who

are merely gathered here so we can gape &
celebrate their public idiosyncrasies –
so we can pause, point, peel oranges,
buy buns to throw (48).

Another account of public feeding appears in John Irving's *Setting Free the Bears*:

I watched them feed the Big Cats. Everyone in the zoo seemed to have been waiting all day for that ... First, this keeper came and flipped a horse steak through the bars to the lioness; the keeper flipped it right in a puddle of her pee. Everyone snickered ... the keeper was more professional with the cheetah; he slid the meat in on a little tray, shook it off, and the cheetah pounced on it, snapping it around in his mouth. Just the way a house cat breaks a mouse's neck. But the cheetah shook his meat too hard; a big hunk flew off and plopped on the ledge outside the bars. Everyone was hysterical. You see, the cheetah couldn't quite reach it, and being afraid someone would steal it, the poor animal set up this roar ... Someone pranced in front of the cheetah, pretending to make a grab for the meat on the ledge. The cheetah, must have lost his mind, trying to jam his head between the bars (107–8).

When the animal finally grabs the food, "he ate up that meat in two terrible bites and swallows – not one bit of chewing – and sure enough, he gagged, finally spewing it all back up. And when I left the Cat House, the cheetah was bolting down his vomit" (108). Irving infuses the scene with the spectators' tawdry, sadistic glee: the people act entertained by the animals' difficulty in eating, titillated by the visceral incontinence of their gross appetites. What the spectators watch, of course, hardly resembles animals' natural feeding behavior – Irving's emphasis on the cage, the bars, the animals' difficulty reaching the food, the food's proximity to urine and vomit all specifically connote how animals eat in zoos; *wild* animals eat without these obstacles. Irving implies that people come to zoos precisely to see the antics of a public feeding spectacle. Mullan and Marvin describe the sensational appeal of watching animals feed: "members of the public . . . seem to be fascinated by the spectacle of [a lion] eating portions of [a cow]. Many zoo directors have stopped such public feeding of the big cats as they feel that the snarling, growling and generally agitated behaviour which is displayed by the animals at this time is a poor ethological representation of their true behaviour and merely panders to popular misconceptions" (6).

Many zoos today attempt to ban spectators' attempts to feed animals themselves, "because of what we know of the harm done to animals' health by uncontrolled public feeding" (Bostock, 183). In Chile's Santiago Zoo, for example, "An African elephant died after undergoing numerous operations to remove plastic bags, nails, and other items from its stomach. Zoo workers said visitors, who until recently were allowed to feed the animals, often gave the elephant lighted cigarettes" (Sims). Even if prohibitions exist, throwing popcorn through bars remains a highlight of a zoo visit for many spectators, as irrepressible as tossing pennies in a fountain. Despite the nutritional dangers, write Mullan and Marvin, understimulated animals will often beg for food simply to alleviate boredom, which "the public often responds to positively because it allows them to interact with the animals" (134). While no zoos that they studied encouraged public feeding, "so concerned are most zoo visitors to influence what goes on in an enclosure and to cause activity among the animals, that in all but a few zoos, we found a variety of animals are fed" (134).

They conclude, "rather than the animals needing to be fed, it is humans wanting to feed them. Zoos are ostensibly about going to view animals, an activity in which the people are not important except as passive viewers. But this is not how it works in practice. In the zoo the humans *demand* to be noticed by the animals" (134).

A. A. Milne illustrates Mullan and Marvin's observation in *When We Were Very Young* (1965), showing how feeding represents spectators' attempt to bridge an otherwise absolute division between people and animals:

> If you try to talk to the bison he never quite understands;
> You can't shake hands with a mingo – he doesn't like shaking hands,
> And lions and roaring tigers hate saying, "How do you do?" –
> But I give buns to the elephant when I go down to the Zoo (46–7).

And Yi-Fu Tuan describes zoo visitors' spontaneous feeding in a vein that recalls the Foucauldian model of the spectator as authority: "One of the pleasures of visiting a zoo is feeding the animals. The act is generous and the pleasure is innocent, although both derive from a base of superiority and power. Making another being eat out of our hand – *that* yields a special thrill all the greater if the animal is first made to beg and if it is large enough to crush us in another setting less structured in our favor" (80).

[. . .]

[M]any zoo stories seem predicated on a cultural sense that zoos are somehow inherently "manly": more attractive to men and more repellent to women. The zoo's semiotic resonances of aggressive adventure, patriarchal control/exploitation, and imperial bravado probably appeal more to men than women; perhaps women are more sensitive than men to the suffering of animals, and to the inauthenticity of a construct shaped by the stereotypically male sociocultural provenances of capture, imperial bravado, and elaborate testimony to physical mastery. Significantly gendered attitudes are discernible in numerous zoo stories. For instance, consider Jerry's unsociable, anti-domestic hostility from Albee's *The Zoo Story*, a play tinged with homosocial misogyny. In Stafford's "At the Zoo," constraining, autocratic zoo imagery metaphorically threatens the sisters' integrity and autonomy; the resonance of a zoo seems especially constrictive to young girls. The futile, driven machismo of the hunger artist's ego in Kafka's story seems specifically masculine, like Yank's blundering self-destructiveness in O'Neill's *The Hairy Ape*; zoos pointedly affect both characters' outlooks. Drabble's Jane Grey, in *The Waterfall*, manifests maternal instincts that resist zoos. Doyle's Paddy Clarke and Edgar from Doctorow's *World's Fair* express uneasily ambiguous feelings about zoos shaped by their awkward adolescent sense of "proper" gender behavior: the socially prescribed masculinity script, dissuading acknowledgment of sensitivity, conflicts with more sympathetic boyish strains, resulting in their inability to situate themselves comfortably, definitively, with respect to the zoo. Zoos offer men sanctuary from women they perceive as threats, as in Garnett's *A Man in the Zoo* and *The Hairy Ape*. The personae in Hughes's "The Jaguar" and Dickey's "Encounter in the Cage Country" exhibit particularly masculine spectatorial stances of entitlement and heedlessness of the disempowered.

Zoo 78, Victor Burgin's photographic exhibition depicting Berlin, presents more variations on the theme of spectatorship, evoking blatantly exploitative and tawdry sexual zoo associations colored by voyeurism, oppression, and constraint. Like Leonard Woolf, Viktor Schklovsky, and Nicolás Guillén, Burgin represents zoos' politically allegorical resonances: for example, juxtaposing zoo cages with the Berlin Wall. *Zoo 78* features eight diptychs about "the idea of enclosure," comprising photographs of zoo animals in a prison-like compound, dwarfed and barely visible amid several sets of cages, obscured by signage; voyeuristic shots of a bored-looking nude woman posed degradingly in a commercial sex show; a scene of impassive patrons at a cafe counter, who look as displaced and decontextualized as if they were zoo animals; and forbidding images of a tattered, claustrophobic, industrially foreboding Cold War Berlin (which, like the zoo photograph, feature excessive and ominous signage). The photographs include an overlaid text with phrases describing various processes of surveillance, but the texts conspicuously mismatch the photographs on which they are printed. The photograph of the peep-show, for example, includes a caption describing a panopticon:

> The plan is circular: at the periphery, an annular building; at the centre, a tower pierced with many windows. The building consists of cells; each has two windows: one in the outer wall of the cell allows daylight to pass into it; another in the inner wall looks onto the tower, or rather is looked upon by the tower, for the windows of the tower are dark, and the occupants of the cells cannot know who watches, or if anyone watches (72).

And on the zoo photograph:

> A circular revolving stage, within four walls of booths, the size of telephone boxes. A window in each booth looks onto the stage, but only when a coin is put in a slot, causing a blind to be withdrawn: 1 Minute – 1 Mark. The stage is lit, exposed; the cells are in darkness, their occupants concealed (70).

Describing the thematic connections between all these images, Burgin explains:

> the centre, where the main railway-station is, is called "Zoo" – Zoologischer Garten – the actual zoo is right alongside the station – and all around the same area are sex shows called "peep-shows," where a naked girl dances on a small revolving stage with booths all around it which you can enter and, by putting a coin in a slot, get a peep at the girl. Of course, not so far away there's the Wall with men peeping through slits in concrete boxes. I was interested in the possible links between these different forms of surveillance (78).

Burgin's aesthetic fuses several themes associated with zoo spectatorship: the Foucauldian power dynamics, the voyeuristic perspective, the zoo as a venue for symbolically playing out issues of human sexuality – straightforwardly or ironically. The disparate scope of images in *Zoo 78* suggests that the sensibility the zoo represents (or exudes) transcends zoos, manifesting a milieu, an ethos, detectable in numerous diversely oppressive situations. If Burgin's 1978 exhibit is identified as *"Zoo 78,"* then presumably there exists also a *Zoo 77*, a *Zoo 79*, and so forth. The misplaced textual descriptions of surveillance make the point that they are all interchangeable – variations on a theme. Burgin's exhibition argues for the importance of appreciating spectatorship's manifold range of apparitions. Most important, his photographs explicitly identify the central perspective of this zoo sensibility as being associated with his camera, with the viewer's stance, with the relationship of the seer to the seen. The activity of watching may seem innocent and harmless, but Burgin's vision situates it as archly powerful, ominous, deadening – an element of totalitarianism. Burgin does not elucidate or prove the zoo's specific implication in these dark forces; he simply observes, suggestively but vaguely, "possible links between these different forms of surveillance" that his photographs depict. His work points toward a network of relations growing out of the spectatorial paradigm, wherein his titular zoo represents the overarching exemplar of a nefarious milieu.

Julio Cortázar's "Axolotl" (1967) demonstrates metaphorically the dangers of watching – of getting too close and falling through the looking glass (or in this case, the aquarium tank glass): spectators who see too much get caught. At the end of Kafka's "A Hunger Artist," the audience hovers enthralled outside the cage: on the verge of becoming implicated in, or infected by, ignominies comparable to what the creature on display experiences. "Axolotl" picks up from that point, and also recalls the sensibility from Jacques Tourneur's film *Cat People*, where a person obsessed with a zoo animal becomes somehow fused with that animal – interconnected, even interchangeable.

"There was a time when I thought a great deal about the axolotls," begins the narrator of Cortázar's surrealist story. "I went to see them in the aquarium at the Jardin des Plantes and stayed for hours watching them, observing their immobility, their faint movements. Now I am an axolotl" (3). Almost immediately, "I knew that we were linked, that something infinitely lost and distant kept pulling us together" (4). As he watches, the narrator perceives the misery of the animals' constraint, seeing the "axolotls huddled on the wretched narrow (only I can know how narrow and wretched) floor of moss and stone in the tank" (4).

His empathy only makes him feel guiltier about watching them. "Disconcerted, almost ashamed, I felt it a lewdness to be peering at these silent and immobile figures heaped at the bottom of the tank" (4). While he perceives that his spectatorship, in some way, involves the pain of those animals he finds so compelling, he is nevertheless powerless to stop watching: trapped, as if obsessed or addicted. (He might have profited from the insight Russell Hoban's character Neaera, in *Turtle Diary*, reaches at the aquarium: "The fish all look bored to death but of course fish aren't meant to be looked at closely, will not bear close examination" (30).)

The narrator finds the axolotls beautiful – "I saw a rosy little body, translucent (I thought of those Chinese figurines of milky glass) ... what obsessed me was the feet, of the slenderest nicety" (5) – illustrating how zoo spectators may *intend* the most eloquent enterprise of aesthetic appreciation: savoring beautifully sublime facets of nature. But his train of thought undercuts a stance of respectful, imaginative homage to natural beauty: "And then I discovered its eyes, its face. Inexpressive features, with no other trait save the eyes, two orifices, like brooches, wholly of transparent gold, lacking any life but looking, letting themselves be penetrated by my look" (5). The spectator's experience deteriorates from his contemplation of the pure, delicate splendor of biological existence. His description of the fish as inert and insensate (inexpressive ... transparent ... lacking any life) belies his initial sensitivity to their attractiveness. The simile comparing the animals' eyes to gold brooches invokes a reference to a mineral that has become appropriated as the consummate currency of human cultural power: something that represents not nature but human exploitation and usurpation of natural beauty. (Imaginative cultural imagery rarely extols gold in its natural condition: it acquires its allure only after it has been mined, smelted, artificed – only after humankind has transformed it almost unrecognizably.) The spectator perceives (or fantasizes about) the lizard acquiescing passively to his appropriation, his control. A golden lifeless mass is "penetrated *by my look*" – indicating its submissive vulnerability. Power permeates Cortázar's praxis of spectatorship: to see is to penetrate, to violate, to determine the subject's condition.

The narrator watches, with the most extreme intensity of attention possible. He reaps the rewards of spectatorship, and eventually, more than he bargained for – he begins to get sucked in: "Once in a while a foot would barely move, I saw the diminutive toes poise mildly on the moss. It's that *we* don't enjoy moving a lot, and the tank is so cramped" (5, emphasis added). He slips, accidentally using the wrong pronoun: first-person plural instead of third-person (-animal?). The more he stares, the more he realizes how much he resembles them: "Above all else, their eyes obsessed me … their handsome eyes so similar to our own" (6); and "They were not human beings, but I had found in no animal such a profound relation to myself" (7). As Cortázar narrows in on the essence of spectatorship – intensively scrutinizing the spare, elemental tableau that his story situates, of a man outside a tank staring at a reptile within – a reversal becomes gradually apparent: "The golden eyes continued burning with their soft, terrible light; *they continued looking at me* from an unfathomable depth which made me dizzy" (6, emphasis added). And the act of looking, the narrator intimately realizes – all the more keenly as he begins to become the spectatorial subject – is keenly loaded, dangerous. "'You eat them alive with your eyes, hey,' the guard said, laughing … What he didn't notice was that it was they devouring me slowly with their eyes, in a cannibalism of gold" (7).

The story's power, and danger, derive from its eventual uncertainty about exactly who watches whom. Cortázar challenges the zoo spectator's traditional position of absolute privileged supremacy. Turnabout is fair play: the watchers in Cortázar's fantastic story become the watched, in a Möbius-strip version of spectatorship. His point is that spectatorship, which he depicts as evil in its exploitative consumption of an objectified animal, debases the watcher as well as the watched. The culmination of spectatorship, as Cortázar sees it – the most acute condition of watching something, visually devouring the subject, obsessively craving to see the animal in captivity – is to become what one is looking at. The narrator exerts spectatorship so fiercely that he becomes the subject of his own visual subjection. This narcissistic strain implies that zoos are more about people than animals: it is in some way as if this spectator is finally looking at himself – seeking the spectacular beauty of life, he ultimately discovers an incarnation of his own reflection to be the most stunning image of all.

Cortázar's zoo story suggests a disturbing allegory: temporarily, zoos celebrate people's power over animals – our *penetrating* ability to keep them and watch them. Human control over zoo animals celebrates an imperial relation toward the realm of nature, and its subordination to our whims. But in the long term, a human society that expresses its relationship to the natural world via the institution of zoos risks foundering amid our imperious ecological ethos. At the apex of modern Western culture, we act as if we control everything in the world; but the tables will turn. As the bumper sticker puts it, Nature bats last. Eventually, people risk finding ourselves victims of the lifestyles and habits we have enjoyed (of which zoo spectatorship is one isolated symbol, or symptom). Indeed, by many accounts, we are already beginning to suffer the toll of a reckless exploitation of nature; we may become as disempowered, in a biotic meltdown, as the creatures we now revel over in the zoo.

In the narrator's waning final moments of privilege as a spectator, he imagines the axolotls' cry: "Save us, save us." (7) The irony is thick: it is still not too late for him. If only the spectator (and by implication, I posit, all zoo spectators) could appreciate the moral import of what he is seeing in the zoo; if only he (*we*) could *truly* empathize with the animals; if only he could perceive the dangers of zoos. But he cannot, so he is sentenced, in the mode of Dantean *contrapasso*, to suffer what he has consigned others to. (I suggest that *contrapasso* is not just a literary motif, but a law of nature.)

Finally, Cortázar depicts the narrator's metamorphosis from man to amphibian, from spectator to specimen in the tank, as inevitable – the necessary culmination of the aquarium construct, of spectatorship, "that had to occur":

> there was nothing strange in what happened. My eyes were attempting once more to penetrate the mystery of those eyes of gold without iris, without pupil. I saw from very close up the face of an axolotl immobile next to the glass. No transition and no surprise, I saw my face against the glass, I saw it on the outside of the tank, I saw it on the other side of the glass. Then my face drew back and I understood (7–8).[3]

The narrator's transformation into a zoo exhibit resembles the denouement of *The Hairy Ape*, when Yank becomes like the escaped zoo animal to whose place he was relegated. However, in Cortázar's zoo story, the human-animal exchange occurs not just spatially but physically as well: "He was outside the aquarium ... I was an axolotl," or, more specifically, "prisoner in the body of an axolotl, metamorphosed into him with my human mind intact, buried alive in an axolotl" (8). The story ends with the narratorial consciousness, now stuck in the aquarium tank, watching a man outside the tank who watches the axolotls. "He returned many times, but he comes less often now" (9). Who is "he" – a shade of the former human self now trapped in the reptile's body? A replacement spectator, the next generation of exploitative watcher-cum-victim? The last words of "Axolotl" identify "him" with the story's author: "in this final solitude to which he no longer comes, I console myself by thinking

that perhaps he is going to write a story about us, that, believing he's making up a story, he's going to write all this about axolotls" (9).

"Axolotl" illuminates a tension between zoo and zoo story – one that, I find, infuses most zoo stories. Cortázar's final frame pronouncedly privileges the zoo story over the zoo. This zoo devours the integrity of all – whether caged animal or human spectator – inside its inviolable clutches. It might (to invoke Dante again) fittingly bear on its gates the legend from the gates of hell: Abandon all hope, you who enter here. The only antidote to the existentially vacant despair festering at the end of this parable lies in the writer's presence: "he's going to write all this about axolotls" (as, obviously, he just has). Like a missive smuggled out of prison, this story embodies the only possible transcendence of the subjugation suffered by those stuck inside. It is the zoo story alone that can attempt to make sense of, or order, or mediate, or expose, the miasma Cortázar describes. What happens in the zoo here is nightmarish, deadening; but what happens in the zoo story is at least decipherable, comprehensible – even clever, neat, symmetric, vital in its artifice – within, and by recourse to, certain conventions of avant-garde narratology. However much the *fabula* (i.e., what happens in Cortázar's zoo *per se)* is unsettling, horrible, deadening, ineffable, the *sjuzet* – the narrative working of the *fabula* – flourishes within a rich tradition of imaginative expression. The zoo story often posits a kind of contest between itself and the zoo, and – unsurprisingly – here, as often, the zoo story wins.

The rampant dysfunctionality surrounding Cortázar's spectator invites further attention to the psychiatric condition of voyeurism, which resonantly underlies the trope of spectatorship. Mass zoo spectatorship relates to the clinical occurrence of voyeurism in a way that cannot quite be literally categorized as such, according to the technical psychiatric definition; but the spectator is a voyeur in much more than simply a metaphorical sense. In "Representation, Voyeurism, and the Vacant Point of View," Joel

Rudinow establishes a model that elucidates a potent strain of voyeurism inherent in spectatorship. He delineates a network of symptoms and sensibilities common to voyeurism and spectatorship, arguing "that the consumption of representations generally is voyeuristic" (179), and advancing a paradigm I find neatly applicable to the "consumption of representations" (i.e., spectatorship) at zoos.

Rudinow's definition of what he terms a "voyeuristic project" resembles my characterization of zoo spectatorship. "The voyeur seeks a spectacle, the revelation of the object of his interest, that something or someone should be open to his inspection and contemplation; *but no reciprocal revelation or openness is conceded*" (176, author's emphasis). This criterion applies to zoos: animals are there for people to look at, but, as Berger writes, the look is not returned. Zoo stories rarely describe a reciprocity of watching: instead, they depict caged animals ignoring the public scornfully (Smith's "The Zoo"); or offending spectators, as if to discourage further watching (cummings's Poem XVIII, Vonnegut's "Welcome to the Monkey House," Edgar's "The Lion and Albert"); or serving as impassively victimized subjects incapable of exchanging glances (Johnson's *Cries from the Mammal House,* Babel's "The Beast Grows Silent," the beginning of Cortázar's "Axolotl," and Rilke's "The Panther" – where the animal becomes literally blind). Berger asserts that spectators want their looks returned, while Rudinow suggests they do not; but both cases finally demonstrate a lack of reciprocity in the viewing arrangement. I regard the zoo's fundamental, imperial inequity to be its absolute establishment of a *one-way* power-based relationship between viewer and subject, which is undesirable in and of itself, and, more dangerously, sets the tone for manifold other human practices that exploit animals and nature based upon principles of non-reciprocity.

"The voyeur understands his act of viewing as an act of aggression, specifically invasion," Rudinow continues, "and accordingly as something ideally to avoid suffering himself" (176). The invasiveness of bona fide voyeurs is apparent – they look at things (people's personal and private behavior) that the victims would not wish to be seen. The parallel invasiveness of zoo spectators features in copious zoo stories: in Neaera's admission of guilt about watching zoo animals in Hoban's *Turtle Diary*, and in the extensive meditation on his invasiveness Cortázar's spectator conducts in "Axolotl." Voyeuristic invasiveness is a kind of aggression, Rudinow asserts, and – from Albee's Jerry to O'Neill's Yank – manifestly aggressive zoogoers are legion. I believe at least some zoo spectators, like participants in Rudinow's more generic voyeuristic projects, *do* indeed understand the aggressive, invasive elements of their behavior. Indeed, this consciousness may even increase the experience's flattering appeal. Many activities in a society predicated upon the ethos of capitalist/imperialist exploitation accrue cachet in proportion to the ensuing toll borne by others. The consciousness of aggression in spectatorship/voyeurism leads Rudinow to argue:

viewing is understood by the voyeur to be destructive, to spoil the view. I believe this understanding to be based on the voyeur's profoundly accurate perception that to treat something as a voyeuristic spectacle is to ruin it for other more fundamental human purposes: it cannot be touched, one cannot be touched by it, one cannot reveal oneself to it. In general, one cannot enter into any relationship with it which is mutual, reciprocal, or symmetrical, insofar and so long as one treats it voyeuristically (176).

If we find this assessment an apt approximation of zoo spectatorship, we must recognize how impossible it is for zoos to fulfill their nominal goals of facilitating natural appreciation and ecological ethics. Some zoo stories explicitly delineate the destructiveness in which spectators are implicated, as in Murakami's "The Zoo Attack," where the soldiers' sole function as zoo visitors is to kill every animal, or Lispector's "The Buffalo," featuring a woman thinking "of the carnage she had come in search of in the zoological gardens … she would have destroyed these monkeys leaping around inside the cages," she fantasizes, "with fifteen sharp bullets" (147–8). But even in the absence of such extreme spectatorial destruction, many zoo stories suggest that people who look at animals in zoos do not leave the visual subject unaffected, uninjured: viewers somehow corrupt what they view. Spectators regarding a herd of Asian animals in their local zoo see, in addition to the animals present, immediate physical/visual confirmation that they have spoiled a comparable view in Asia. Cutting-edge zoos pride themselves on offering *recreations* of natural biotas; semantically, recreating implies having destroyed.

Rudinow asserts that the voyeur manifests a "paradoxical care for the spectacle which he would destroy" (177), which explains why the zoos I characterize as such retrograde institutions are nevertheless enveloped with a thick discourse of solicitous concern on the parts of patrons and keepers. The workings of voyeurism, Rudinow explains, involve voyeurs' "attempts not only to consume and destroy the spectacle, but also, and in the same gaze, to preserve it as a continuing object of view" (176–7). His theory illuminates the apparent paradox of strong public support for zoos that coexists with our destruction of the natural world – whether willfully and sadistically, or through benign neglect, laziness and selfishness – at an unprecedented pace. Zoos capitalize on spectators' commitment to lovingly preserving what they simultaneously destroy. Indeed, as I have suggested earlier, token support for preservation may be a way of repressing awareness of, or alleviating guilt about, large-scale ecological desecration.

Voyeurs, finally, have "not a chance of gaining satisfaction" (178), Rudinow writes, however determinedly they embrace their voyeuristic project. This seems instinctively true of psychiatrically certified deviant voyeurs: at least we (the nondeviant) would like to believe that such invasive, withdrawn, antisocial, non-reciprocal relationships as voyeurs crave cannot prove gratifying. Cortázar's spectator offers one example of the zoo voyeur's absolute frustration; and I believe he stands metaphorically for many more spectators in zoo stories and zoos alike.

Spectators may look as intently as possible, in zoos that are as good as they can be, and still the experience may well prove unfulfilling. This strain infuses zoo stories consistently, explaining the sordid, unpleasant proclivities that repeatedly tend to indict zoos. As evidence of the voyeur's constant frustration, Rudinow cites "the multitude of genuine innovations and finicky adjustments which continue to be made in the devices and settings for voyeuristic observation and in the descriptions and formulations of what constitutes the voyeur's satisfaction" (178). The voyeurs' view, their experience, is never quite good enough: they can never see as much as they want for as long as they want, or derive from the sight as much pleasure as they want, so they fidget to grasp more of what continues to elude satisfaction. And keepers tinker with innovations and adjustments, trying to make zoos better places to see more authentic, appealing, stimulating, "natural" vistas of animals. The view in the zoo is not good enough, and never can be; but keepers and patrons obsessively continue striving simply (and impossibly) to establish a more satisfying spectatorial experience.

There are other ways of watching animals besides in zoos or in their native habitats: two popular modes are television programs and Internet sites. The genre of nature shows dates back even before the advent of television – in the 1930s Marlin Perkins hosted a live radio nature show ("until the day he brought on an electric eel that got a little overexcited and sent a charge through him, his assistant, and the microphone, blowing out the entire network" (Siebert, "Artifice", 47–8). In the early days of television, Charles Siebert writes, "most people's idea of a nature show was still *The American Sportsman*: Curt Gowdy and Mickey Mantle duck hunting on Saturday afternoons (46); such shows, and even Perkins's later *Mutual of Omaha's Wild Kingdom* series, featured what Siebert calls "television's cowboy naturalists" (47). Hosts chased, trapped, and often physically grappled with the animals they filmed, sometimes shooting them with tranquilizers; the television personalities who mediated the viewer's relationship to the animals were very interactive with them, in a way I consider inappropriately intrusive: hindering an understanding of how animals live when people are not around them; conveying an undesirable sense of how people should behave toward animals; reinforcing the habits of what Jim Mason calls a dominionist sensibility toward nature.

A rich tradition of nature programming has grown out of these early ventures (comprising a significant portion of American Public Broadcasting, and a cable network, the Discovery Channel, that devotes a considerable amount of its schedule to productions about animals and nature). Perkins's successors include Jacques Cousteau in the 1970s – "our first existentialist naturalist," as Siebert terms him, featuring "the hushed, somber, guilt-tinged tone that has become the hallmark of nature-show narration" (45) – and "today's definitive nature-show host" Sir David Attenborough, escorting us like a knowledgeable and omnipresent museum guide, his voice respectfully trailing off into gaspy whispers whenever he gets very close to the proceedings" (49). Another mainstay of the genre comes from National Geographic productions, which embody the vintage Smithsonian naturalistic discourse of precise, encyclopedic coverage.

I find documentaries about wild animals potentially appealing – many are of high quality, educationally profuse, sensitive to a range of issues about animals' lives and interrelated ecological concerns regarding the shared world of people and other species. They can help offer viewers exposure to animals' worlds in ways that I believe zoos cannot. At the same time, nature shows remain vulnerable to many of the criticisms (or close variants thereof) that I launch against zoos.

Cliff Tarpy, who advocates new and improved zoos (as he regards them), credits television with uplifting spectators' standards. He quotes a zoo director who says: "In the '70s you could see a shift in the public's attitude toward zoos. Wildlife shows on television were a big influence. They showed you animals running free in the wild, their behavior, the importance of ecosystems"

(11). This zoo director is probably correct that nature shows have made spectators more intolerant of the most egregious zoo conditions; and I regard this as a point in their favor, illustrating how they enlighten viewers about desirable and undesirable ways of representing and experiencing nature. But on the other hand, I worry that Tarpy's scenario coopts the ideal consequences of ecological education: that is, I would hope such awareness would lead viewers to oppose not just "bad" zoos but all zoos. Indeed, I think some people do respond to nature shows with a wholehearted dismissal of the approach to nature embodied in zoo culture. Personally, as I began to find zoos increasingly unpalatable, I turned to nature shows; finding it possible to satisfy my interest in wild animals through this outlet (among others) coincided with my conviction that zoos were not necessary or even adequate providers of natural education. Zookeepers, like the proprietors of any mass-oriented industry with a long-term record of success, cannily note changes in the winds among target audiences, and reposition/repackage themselves to maintain their market share. The phenomenon Tarpy describes – zoos making themselves look a bit more like animals' natural worlds as nature programming makes people increasingly familiar with natural biotas, and aware of how vastly they differ from zoo cages – represents an example of such consumeristic adaptation geared toward the industry's survival. Nevertheless, I think that continued exposure to effective nature shows can lead audiences beyond tolerating old zoos with a new facade. Television alone cannot be a universal panacea for artificial, convenient misrepresentations of nature – the education must occur along several fronts; but nature documentaries can offer one effective effort in this regard.

Two compelling critiques come from Siebert and Steve Baker. Baker's *Picturing the Beast* examines numerous incidences of what he calls the manipulative and inauthentic appropriations of animals' integrity that inhere in the semiotics of cultural representation. One false type of animal representation, he argues, is the nature show, in which the desired truth or reality of the animal seems to elude the viewer, forever slipping out from the edge of the image. A television reviewer writes wistfully: "Wildlife programmes have grown to become such a televisual industry that ... you can watch more than a dozen over any seven days. All beautiful, all leaving you frustrated at the brief and distant glimpses you get, at best, of the real thing." Umberto Eco says much the same thing about the role of the realistic fake wild animal in Disneyland. The crucial thing is its "obedience to the program": it is there when viewers want to see it, and it stays there (194).

Although television representations of wild animals offer viewers close, insightful approximations of animals' lives, Baker argues, their problem

> is that we can hardly know in any very meaningful way what it is that we are seeing (or rather, merely glimpsing). Tim Ingold puts it plainly: "for the Western television viewer, observing the antics of a strange and exotic animal on his screen, he might as well be watching a work of science fiction as a nature documentary" (194).

Siebert, making arguments resembling mine against zoos, rejects television nature shows because he believes they domesticate and distort the real world. Indeed, he notes at least one example of an explicit connection between nature shows and zoos, recounting an episode of *Wild Kingdom* from the early 1960s in which Perkins "is thrashing about in a South American river with an anaconda round his neck, his face going red as he tries to get the snake into a burlap bag for some zoo in Europe" (46–7).) Siebert objects to an unnatural convenience: "to sit here in front of a nature show is to have one's ego fed shamelessly," he writes, "via the distilled essence of that original place whose indifference and gradualness we can no longer abide" (48). That is, nature is too slow and undramatic for the modern temperament; the television-age sensibility demands that nature conform to the narratives, the pace, the style, that audiences expect of any stimuli emanating from television sets. The discourse of

nature shows, Siebert writes, is "above all else, extravagant animal opera, dramatizing, scoring, voicing in human terms the vast backdrop of inhuman action" (43). Actual and televised nature "have little to do with each other. The woods are so wide, old, and slow as to be dismissive of me ... and what I might wish and wait to see. The show, by contrast, is rapid, focused, and framed, a potent distillation of someone else's waiting designed precisely for me" (44). The profusion of shows has made us "a race of armchair naturalists," and even when we do venture into the wilds to visit "the places and creatures whose stories we've watched," what we have seen on television conditions our expectations: "We go as nature tourists ... expectant of seeing those characters, as though visiting the various sets of a Universal Studios theme park" (50). Just as I consider zoos, with their artifice and contrivance, inauthentic because they are a subset of human culture, Siebert accuses television nature shows of lacking their own integrity and being a subset of television culture.

A modern nature show offers "a clean and well-lighted simultaneity of the unseen; of things you'd never see in a thousand walks in the wild," while nature's wonders themselves are remarkable "for precisely the reasons a nature show cannot convey. It is the mostly hidden and non-reflective enormity of their life forces, behemoth and belittling, that has most to show and tell us" (48). Siebert parallels my main objection to zoos when he argues that television transforms real nature into *our* nature, distanced and distinct from the original: "The more facts we compile about the animals' days, the more human the tales we tell of them. We've come so far from actual nature" (45).

But finally, while I cannot wholly dismiss Siebert's provocative and well-reasoned objections, I consider nature shows much the lesser of two evils. It is crucial for people to learn about animals and their natural settings, their native worlds, and it is both unreasonable and undesirable to expect that this understanding could be achieved at first-hand on a mass scale. Some sort of sociocultural mediation, therefore, is necessary, and such mediation should be as un-obtrusive as possible; if representations are destined to distort reality in some way, they should strive to do so as little as possible. If the process of interacting with animals must occur within a system of commercial capitalism, it should strive to be as little as possible tainted by this. (In America, nearly all nature shows appear on public broadcasting stations or low-key cable outlets, rather than the big business networks; those who create and produce nature shows are at the low-status end of the television and film industry; financial support for such documentaries comes from government grants, public-interest foundations, and ecologically attuned educational and advocacy organizations, rather than mainstream commercial interests.)

Zoos are one response to people's need and desire to know animals, and nature shows are another; I side with nature shows. Both are artificial constructs, profoundly ensconced in human discourse: but I believe the documentaries offer a greater potential for people to understand how animals really exist (while doing less damage than zoos to animals and their habitats). Animals shown on nature shows almost always appear *in situ*, behaving naturally, and – in today's shows, which have evolved beyond Perkins's wrestling matches – depicted in a condition unmediated by human contact (or, if human proximity *is* involved, the implications of such proximity are explored, instead of ignored and repressed as in zoos). If an element of dominionist bravado remains ("Look at the amazing places a few people can visit and document with cameras") it is much less dangerous than what zoos celebrate ("Look how many millions of 'us' can enjoy easy access to something we have spirited away from 'there'"). Granting Siebert the shortcomings and distortions inherent in the neat editing, the musical background, the contextualizing "nature voice" with its cultural biases, and the artificial concentration of action, I still finally believe that benefits outweigh drawbacks. Television shows about animals explicitly acknowledge the distance between us and them, unlike zoos,

which pretend that animals are very close to us. Certainly it could be argued that television sucks its viewers into a vicarious fantasy world where armchair spectators are induced to pretend they can transport themselves magically to all the places the documentaries show, and are, even more than zoo visitors, in a position of ultimate (and delusory) mastery. But I think that for most viewers, the literal inaccessibility of what documentaries show is clearly presented and understood, in a way that the zoo fudges, finesses.

Television depicts the difference between the animals' world and ours. Nature shows teach people about animals, usually in great detail, with careful scientific and ecological information of weighty content, which dwarfs the zoo's main educational medium, signs. One of the chief functions zoos invoke to justify their existence is arousing audiences' sympathies for the plight of endangered species and habitats, and spurring financial/socio-political motivation to support conservationism. I believe television shows can accomplish ecological advocacy as effectively as zoos – probably even more so, since the medium of television is so conducive to promotion.

But if television seems to offer a palatable techno-cultural medium for watching animals, the heir apparent to its media prominence – the computer – offers less sanguine prospects. Internet sites and CD-ROMs offer a new postmodern twist to reading zoos: watching, via the isolated distance of the computer terminal, something that isn't there. Computers promise ultimate control over the subject; compared with zoos, they distance viewers even further from animals, but compensate with more (and instant) data and knowledge. Animals are trapped not in a cage, but in the net, which represents the logical consequence, and at the same time the *reductio ad absurdum*, of zoo spectatorship. Wild animals are infinitely decontextualized, to the point where spectators enjoy complete access to what is physically absent. Viewers retain cultural/cognitive mastery over animals, without the smell of shit.

NOTES

1. *Diagnostic and Statistical Manual of Disorders,* 3rd edn. Washington: American Psychiatric Association, 1987, pp. 289–90.
2. *Cook's Handbook to London.* London: Simpkin, Marshall, 1930.
3. Cortázar's focus on eyes throughout the story draws attention to the instruments, the organs, of spectatorship. The device is metonymic: the part – the eye – represents the whole – the spectator.

REFERENCES

Babel, Isaac. "The Beast Grows Silent." In *Isaac Babel: The Forgotten Prose.* Trans. Nicholas Stroud. Ann Arbor, MI: Ardis, 1978.

Baker, Steve. *Picturing the Beast: Animals, Identity and Representation.* Manchester: Manchester University Press, 1993.

Benson, E. F. "The Zoo." 1893. In *Six Common Things.* London: Osgood.

Berger, John. "Why Look at Animals?" In *About Looking.* New York: Vintage Books, 1980.

Bostock, Stephen St C. *Zoos and Animal Rights: The Ethics of Keeping Animals.* London: Routledge, 1993.

Brathwaite, Edward Kamau. "The Zoo." In *Sappho Sakyi's Meditations.* Mona, Jamaica: *Savacou* 16, 1989. 45–50.

Brophy, Brigid. *Hackenfeller's Ape.* London: Allison & Busby, 1953.

Burgin, Victor. *Zoo* 78. In *Between.* Oxford: Blackwell, 1986. 61–87.

Cortázar, Julio. "Axolotl." In *End of the Game and Other Stories.* Trans. Paul Blackburn. New York: Pantheon, 1967. 3–9.

cummings, e. e. "The Secret of the Zoo Exposed." In *E. E. Cummings: A Miscellany.* Ed. George J. Firmage. New York: Argophile, 1958.

cummings, e. e. "[Poem] XVIII." From *ViVa.* 1931. Poem 30. From 50 *Poems.* 1940. In *Complete Poems: 1904–1962.* Ed. George J. Firmage. New York: Liveright, 1991. 328, 516.

Edgar, Marriott. "The Lion and Albert." 1933. In *The World of Stanley Holloway.* London: Francis, Day & Hunter. 1972. 2–5.

Foucault, Michel. *Discipline and Punish: The Birth of the Prison.* Trans. Alan Sheridan. New York: Pantheon, 1977.

Guillén, Nicolás. *¡Patria O Muerte! The Great Zoo and Other Poems.* Trans. Robert Marquez. New York: Monthly Review, 1972.

Hoban, Russell. *Turtle Diary.* New York: Random House, 1975.

Irving, John. *Setting Free the Bears.* 1968. New York: Pocket, 1979.

Johnson, Terry. *Cries from the Mammal House.* 1984. In *Plays: One.* London: Methuen, 1993. 137–209.

Lispector, Clarice. "The Buffalo." 1960. In *Family Ties.* Trans. Giovanni Pontiero. Austin: U of Texas Press, 1972.

Lively, Penelope. *Moon Tiger.* New York: Grove, 1987.

Livingston, Bernard. *Zoo Animals, People, Places.* New York: Arbor House, 1974.

MacNeice, Louis. *Zoo.* Illus. Nancy Sharp. London: Michael Joseph, 1938.

Magel, Charles R. *Keyguide to Information Sources in Animal Rights.* London: Mansell, 1989.

Milne, A. A. *When We Were Very Young.* London: Methuen, 1965.

Mullan, Bob, and Garry Marvin. *Zoo Culture.* London: Weidenfeld & Nicolson, 1987.

Murakami, Haruki. "The Zoo Attack." Trans. Jay Rubin. *The New Yorker* 71.22 (31 July 1995): 68–74.

Nimier, Marie. *The Giraffe.* 1993. Trans. Mary Feeney. New York: Four Walls Eight Windows, 1995.

Rilke, Rainer Maria. "The Panther," "The Gazelle," and "The Flamingos." In *The Selected Poetry of Rainer Maria Rilke.* Trans. Stephen Mitchell. New York: Viking, 1989.

Rudinow, Joel. "Representation, Voyeurism, and the Vacant Point of View." *Philosophy and Literature* 3.2 (Fall 1979): 173–86.

Schklovsky, Viktor. *Zoo, or Letters Not About Love.* Trans. Richard Sheldon. Ithaca, NY: Cornell University Press, 1971.

Siebert, Charles. "The Artifice of the Natural: How TV's Nature Shows Make All the Earth a Stage." *Harper's* February 1993: 43–51.

Sims, Calvin. "Chile Zoo Called Hostile Setting for Man and Beast." *New York Times* 23 June 1996: A4.

Smith, Stevie. "The Zoo." In *The Collected Poems of Stevie Smith.* New York: Oxford, 1976.

Tarpy, Cliff. "New Zoos: Taking Down the Bars." *National Geographic* 184.1 (July 1993): 2–37.

Tourneur, Jacques (dir.). *Cat People.* Writer, DeWitt Bodeen. RKO, 1942.

Tuan, Yi-Fu. *Dominance and Affection: The Making of Pets*. New Haven. CT: Yale UP, 1984.

Vonnegut, Kurt, Jr. *Slaughterhouse-Five*. 1969. New York: Dell, 1971.

Vonnegut, Kurt, Jr. "Welcome to the Monkey House." In *Welcome to the Monkey House*. New York: Delacourte, 1968. 27–45.

Woolf, Leonard. "Fear and Politics: A Debate at the Zoo." In *In Savage Times: Leonard Woolf on Peace and War*. New York: Garland, 1973. 5–24.

25

MATT CARTMILL

Hunting and Humanity in Western Thought*

Matt Cartmill is a biological anthropologist who studies the history of ideas and the history and philosophy of science in addition to human origins, animal consciousness and the functional anatomy of people and other primates. Cartmill is widely known for his work in humanistic science, including the ape-language controversy and, the topic of the article reproduced here, the intellectual history of hunting. In this article, Cartmill traces the transformation of attitudes toward hunting from a noble aristocratic sport to widespread anti-hunting sentiment in Western art and literature, a process that has resulted in a growth of contradictory and conflicted positions on hunting. Cartmill argues that conflicted attitudes about hunting begin with the very concept of what constitutes an appropriate hunt, specifically the pursuit of an animal that is free to flee or attack the hunter, without traps, cages or baiting [a concept that is seriously compromised by the penchant for "canned hunting," an activity that was common even in antiquity when exotic animals were enclosed in parks for the exclusive hunting pleasure of Assyrian kings]. Cartmill writes that medieval hunting rights were ever more the purview of the aristocracy, giving rise to popular ballads about Robin Hood and other forest fugitives that symbolized the meaning of the hunt for peasants (freedom, feasting, and rebellion). It wasn't until the Renaissance that anti-hunting sentiment gained any real purchase, particularly with writers such as Michel de Montaigne who challenged the rigid boundary between humans and other animals [see Section 2]. Cartmill argues that since the human-animal boundary is only an arbitrary construct [a theme which runs throughout this volume], hunting other animals is nothing more than a form of butchery.

Five hundred years ago, when Henry VIII occupied the throne of England, a Portuguese mariner named Raphael Hythloday left the company of Amerigo Vespucci's third expedition and travelled south from India into the imaginary countries of Terra Australis Incognita, one of which (so Thomas More assures us) is an island called Utopia. Here Hythloday found a land full of paradoxical excellences. The Utopians worked very little; and yet they were all rich. They abhorred the death penalty; and yet they had little crime. Most of the few criminals they did have were sentenced to terms of temporary slavery, in which they were made to do the

* Reprinted with permission of the publisher and from Matt Cartmill (1995) "Hunting and Humanity in Western Thought." *Social Research* 62(3): 773–786.

menial jobs nobody else wanted to do. And here was another paradox: one of those menial jobs was *hunting*.

Hunting was an activity that More's fellow Englishmen held to be so delicious – and so expressive of power – that it was reserved for the aristocracy, who spent thousands of man-hours every year riding through the countryside on horseback in search of game. But More wrote,

> The Utopians think that this whole business of hunting is beneath the dignity of free men, and so they have made it a part of the butcher's trade – which, as I said before, they foist off on their slaves. They regard hunting as the lowest and vilest part of butchery, and the other parts of it as more useful and honorable, since they kill animals only to meet human needs, whereas the hunter seeks nothing but pleasure from murdering a poor innocent beast (Thomas More, *Utopia*, np).

Medieval moralists (Rogers, 1881, 224; Pike, 1938, 23; Hobusch, 1978, 74) had protested against the hunt as oppressive to the peasants, who had to open their lands and furnish their labor to the hunting aristocrats; but nobody in the Middle Ages had ever complained that hunting was oppressive to the *animals*. Erasmus (*Praise of Folly*, 1.18) and others had denounced hunters as idle fools and wastrels; but nobody before More had ever branded them as murderers and perverts.

Yet More did both, and we encounter similar attitudes in the works of later sixteenth-century writers. Since then, anti-hunting sentiment has become ever more common in Western art and literature. It has grown to be more or less the norm in modern America. In recent opinion polls, most Americans express agreement with the proposition that hunting for sport or for trophies, or for any purpose other than putting meat on the table, should be forbidden by law. In what follows, I want to sketch some of the history of this transformation, and to examine some factors that have gone into the growth of our own contradictory and conflicted attitudes toward hunting.

Those contradictions and conflicts grow out of the very concept of the hunt, as we define it. Hunting, for us, is not simply a matter of killing animals. A successful hunt ends in an animal's death, but it has to be a special animal, killed in a special way. It must be free, able to flee or attack the hunter. It must be killed on purpose, and by violence, and in person: no traps, no cages, no poisoned baits, no road kills. Above all, it must be a *wild* animal; and what that means for the hunter is that it must be *hostile*, not friendly to human beings or submissive to their authority. You can kill cows in the dairy barn, but you cannot hunt them. Hunting is thus by definition an armed confrontation between the human world and the untamed wilderness, between culture and nature; and it has been defined and praised and attacked in those terms throughout Western history, from antiquity onward.

Hunting had great mythical and symbolic significance for the Greeks. Three of their major deities – Apollo, Artemis, and Dionysus – were closely associated with the hunt in myth and ritual. Dionysus and Artemis (or Diana, as the Romans called her) are paired with each other in a symbolic opposition that shows up in various forms again and again in Western thought about hunting. Artemis is a perpetual virgin; Dionysus is the dissolute god of wine. She is a masculinized female (real Greek women did not hunt); he is an effeminate male. Artemis leads a troop of maiden archers in an orderly program of wildlife management; but Dionysus dances at the head of a band of drunken crazies who tear their quarry apart with their bare hands and eat the bloody flesh, like predatory beasts. The followers of Artemis discipline the wilderness, but the followers of Dionysus *participate* in it. The maenad's costume of fawnskins, lynx pelts, and live serpents symbolizes a union with nature just as surely as do the buckskins and the raccoon cap on the mythic American frontiersman.

This tension between the images of the hunter as a park ranger and the hunter as a beast of prey is a corollary of the way we define hunting, as something that occurs on the boundary between the human domain and the wild. Throughout

Western history, from the myths of Artemis and Dionysus down to our own stories of mythic hunters like Daniel Boone and Davy Crockett, the hunter has been seen as a liminal and ambiguous figure, now a fighter against wilderness and now a half-animal participant in it, who stands with one foot on either side of the boundary and swears no perpetual allegiance to either side. Perhaps the reason that hunting plays such a large part in Greek myth – and in our own stories about human origins – is that it takes place on that boundary, and thus marks the edge of the human world.

The Greek fascination with hunting was mirrored in the recurrence of mythic hunts and divine huntresses throughout the mythologies of the ancient Middle East, from Egypt all the way over to India. But it had no equivalent in the rest of Europe. Like More's Utopians, the early Romans saw hunting as a farm chore, with no more symbolic or mythical importance than catching rats. Some Roman authors denounced sportive hunting on the Greek model as a silly or vicious affectation, and the first anti hunting sentiments in Europe appear in Roman history and literature. In 55 BC, the crowd in the Roman arena rose up to protest the butchering of a score of elephants in a staged hunt. Cicero wrote to a friend about it: "What pleasure can a cultured man get in seeing ... a noble beast run through with a hunting spear?" (*Ad Familiares*, 7.1.3). This difference between Greek and Roman attitudes, which is partly a rural versus urban difference (provincial Romans sound more like Greeks [Martial, *Epigrams*, 1.49, 12.14; Nemesianus, *Cynegetica*]), recurs in their respective national epics. When the mighty Odysseus kills a stag in Homer's *Odyssey*, the event is described in cheerfully bloodthirsty terms, all full of hock joints and vertebrae (10.161–84). But when one of Aeneas's companions shoots a stag in Virgil's *Aeneid*, it turns out to be somebody's pet, and it runs home to *complain*: "And the animal, I wounded, fled back to his familiar roof; / moaning, he reached his stall, and suppliant / and bleeding, filled the house with his lament" (7.500–502, Mandelbaum, 1961, 179).

Literary Roman expressions of distaste for the hunt and pity for the hunter's quarry represent one historical source of modern anti-hunting sentiments, from Thomas More onward. Another ancient line of thought that is woven into those sentiments is the traditional Christian view of human beings as inherently wicked, and of nature as degraded by human sin, which introduced death and predation into the peaceable kingdom of Eden:

> The World did in her Cradle take a fall,
> And turn'd her brains, and took a general maim
> Wronging each joint of th' universal frame.
> The noblest part, man, felt it first; and than
> Both beasts and plants, curs'd in the curse of man
> (Donne, "The First Anniversarie," lines 196–200).

A third ingredient was the hallowing of the forest in medieval thought. For the Greeks and Romans, forests were generally threatening and scary places. The Greek and Latin words that mean "woodsy" (*hylaios, sylvaticus*) have the secondary meaning of "savage." In early Christian thought, the wilderness is a sort of natural symbol of hell, and the wild animals that live there in a state of perpetual rebellion against the sons of Adam typify demons and sinners in rebellion against God. But this image was undermined from the very beginning of the Christian era by the counterimage of John the Baptist and other hermit saints in the wilderness, attended by friendly wild animals that the saint's holiness has restored to the docility of Eden. And since the wild animals treated the saints better than most people did, the odor of sanctity soon began to rub off on the forest creatures themselves. In an apocryphal gospel of the eighth century, Jesus, being adored by wild animals, turns to his friends and declares; "How much better than you are the beasts which know me and are tame, while men know me not" (James, 1924).

Other changes in the significance of wild places and creatures during the latter part of the Middle Ages reflect changes in the social significance of hunting. Before the tenth century, small farmers throughout northern Europe had been allowed to hunt more or less freely on their own land. But as new techniques of agriculture produced a surge in medieval crop yields and population, and Europe's forests retreated before the ax and the plow, hunting rights were increasingly taken over by the aristocracy, who put the remaining patches of woods off limits as royal hunting preserves and ruthlessly punished any peasants suspected of taking game (White, 1962, 39ff; Dalby, 1965, v; Eckardt, 1976, 27–31; Hobusch, 1978, 117–19).

Hunting thus took on opposite connotations for the peasants and the aristocracy. For the elite, the hunt became an elaborate ritual encrusted with jargon and courtly ceremony, which served to validate the aristocratic credentials of the hunters. The peasantry, on the other hand, associated hunting with freedom, feasting, and rebellion against the authorities in the songs and stories they soon began to tell about Robin Hood and other deer-poaching forest fugitives, from the eleventh century onward (Keen, 1961).

But in both the high and low traditions, there were important late medieval changes in the symbolic meaning of the wilderness. As the forests contracted into exclusive aristocratic playgrounds, they became transformed in the European imagination from the gloomy wasteland of earlier tradition into the gay and magical greenwood of late medieval literature. The deer, who are the symbolic inhabitants of the wilderness and give it its English name – etymologically a *wild-deer-ness* – also took on a new symbolic importance. From the eleventh to the fourteenth century, words that had meant "animal" or "wild beast" in several European languages narrowed semantically to mean "deer" or "doe" in particular – English *deer*, French *biche*, German *Wild*, and so on – and words for "deer" and "hunting" became conflated, so that deer became both ideal animals and the ideal objects of the hunt.

In late medieval and Renaissance art and literature, down through the sixteenth century, the deer hunt becomes a recurrent metaphor for erotic love (Thiébaux, 1974); and deer, which had been symbols of cowardice for the Greeks and Romans the way rabbits and chickens are for us, take on symbolic nobility in both folk ballads and high culture. The stag hunt becomes a metaphor for the tragic fall of a noble victim, as in the speech that Shakespeare's Mark Antony makes over the corpse of Caesar:

> Here wast thou bay'd, brave hart;
> Here didst thou fall; and here thy hunters stand,
> Sign'd in thy spoil, and crimson'd in thy lethe.
> O world, thou wast the forest to this hart;
> And this indeed, O world, the heart of thee.
> How like a deer, strucken by many princes,
> Dost thou here lie! (*Julius Caesar*, 3.1.204–210)

In the extreme form of this metaphor, the hunted deer becomes the crucified Christ, whom one medieval poem describes as the stag "whose hoof is stained/with blood, for he ransomed us at so great a price," and who appears as a hunted deer (commonly with a cross between his horns) again and again in medieval art and literature (Thiébaux, 1974, 185–228).

Yet in spite of all this symbolic equation of hunting with tragedy and crucifixion, there are no significant medieval sources of anti-hunting sentiment. The hunt did not start to become a symbol of injustice and bloody tyranny until the beginning of the northern Renaissance, when Erasmus condemned the hunt as a "bestial amusement" in 1511 and More denounced it five years later in *Utopia*. A similar revulsion toward hunting is evident in the essays of Montaigne and the plays of Shakespeare, who employs the hunt almost always as a symbol of murder, usurpation, and rape (Shakespeare, *Macbeth*, 4.3; *As You Like It*, 2.1; *Love's Labour's Lost*, 4.1; *Titus Andronicus*, 2.1, 2.2, 3.1). We see it also in some of the artwork of the period – for example, in Albrecht Dürer's disturbing 1504 drawing of the severed head of a stag with a crossbow bolt in its skull and its eye turned backward to look at the viewer.

Perhaps the most surprising place where anti-hunting sentiment crops up in the sixteenth century is in hunting manuals, which from 1561 on contain rhymed complaints by the game animals denouncing the senseless cruelty of Man the Hunter. The standard English hunting manual of the period, the 1576 *Book of Venerie* by the poet George Turberville, puts these words into the mouth of the hunted hare:

> Are minds of men become so void of sense,
> That they can joy to hurt a harmless thing?
> A silly beast, which cannot make defense?
> A wretch? a worm that cannot bite, nor sting?
> If that be so, I thank my Maker than,
> For making me a Beast and not a Man.
>
> ...So that thou show'st thy vaunts to be but vain,
> That brag'st of wit, above all other beasts,
> And yet by me, thou neither gettest gain
> Nor findest food to serve thy glutton's feasts:
> Some sport perhaps: yet *Grievous is the glee*
> *Which ends in blood*, that lesson learn of me.
> (Turberville, [1576] 1908, 176–78)

This is strange stuff to find in a handbook for hunters. One might as well expect to see *Field and Stream* putting out a monthly column on animal rights signed by Bambi and Thumper.

Why, after sportive hunting had been admired and respected all through the Middle Ages, did it start to get attacked in the 1500s? Some of these attacks reflected middle-class antagonism toward the hunting gentry; but that explanation does not hold for Montaigne or Shakespeare or Turberville. Some of these new negative attitudes toward the hunt were associated with rising doubts about the meaning and reality of other established hierarchies, including the boundary between people and animals (Cartmill, 1993, 87–91). In 1580, Montaigne denied the existence of that boundary, and concluded that "it is [only] by foolish pride and stubbornness that we set ourselves before the other animals and sequester ourselves from their condition and society" (*Essays*, 2.12, "Apology for Raimond Sebond").

The scientific revolution of the 1600s, and the exponential growth of science that has taken place in the succeeding three centuries, have further eroded the animal-human boundary to the vanishing point. This erosion of human distinctiveness is inherent in the nature of science. Because science tries to find universally applicable explanations for the causes of all things, and justifies its search in practical terms as a means to securing power over nature, it inevitably tends toward a vision of the universe as a collection of lumps of uniform, neutral matter, all obeying the same universal laws and all valuable only as means to human ends. The bargain that science offers us is a Faustian one: in exchange for getting control over these lumps, we must ourselves consent to become lumps of the same uniform stuff.

From the late 1600s on, successive schools of Western thought about the natural order have been looking for loopholes in the contract we have made with science. Descartes and his followers tried to draw an absolute distinction between the world of matter and the world of the spirit, depicting animals as insensate machines made of meat. But almost everybody else has attacked the problem by trying to extend some limited form of citizenship to the animals and drawing them into the moral order – with predictable effects on the symbolic meanings attached to hunting.

The animal condition first began to take on serious moral dimensions in the eighteenth century, when a surprising range of thinkers, from the atheist Julien de la Mettrie at one extreme to John Wesley at the other, agreed in seeing the human mind as only a souped-up version of facilities shared by many other animals (Cartmill, 1993, 98–100). Animal suffering now came to be seen for the first time as a serious natural and moral evil, and the intelligentsia began to try to do something about it by preaching kindness to animals through the mass media of the time: sermons, cheap prints, and the first children's books. In this climate of opinion, hunting came increasingly to be seen as just another cruel entertainment, like bull baiting.

It was a commonplace of eighteenth-century thought that the natives of North America represented the natural state of man, and that they lived chiefly by hunting. If hunting is both morally wrong and the primordial human enterprise, then the hunt naturally begins to be seen as a sign of man's innate depravity. These considerations combined with the early Romantic vision of Nature as a kind of virgin territory, exempt from man's polluting presence, to yield the first foreshadowings of our own familiar image of *Homo sapiens* as a crazed killer ape cutting a bloody swath across the face of sweet green Nature. Alexander Pope, in his *Essay on Man*, identified the advent of human predation with the Fall of Adam (3.147–168); and in 1774, 84 years before the *Origin of Species*, Lord Monboddo came out with the whole killer-ape theory in a pre-Darwinian package. Human beings in a state of nature Monboddo argued, are not American Indians, but chimpanzees and orangutans. Thousands of years ago, these apes had multiplied to the point where the fruits of the earth could no longer sustain them; and some of them were forced to take up killing and eating other animals, and to invent language and weapons to help them in the chase. "This change of man from a frugivorous to a carnivorous animal must have produced a great change in character," wrote Monboddo. "He grew fierce and bold, delighting in blood and slaughter. War soon succeeded to hunting; and the necessary consequence of war was, the victors eating the vanquished, when they could kill or catch them; for, among such men, war is a kind of hunting" (Burnett, 1774, 270–313, 367, 392–97, 416–20).

Monboddo's misanthropic vision of Man the Hunter was to recur two centuries later in the literature of my own professional discipline, physical anthropology. The anatomist Raymond Dart, who discovered and named our Pliocene ancestor, the so-called man-ape *Australopithecus*, was largely responsible for launching the killer-ape theory of human origins that dominated the anthropological textbooks of the 1960s and 1970s. This theory portrayed hunting as a sort of original sin, which had not only started the human lineage off on a different historical course from the apes but had alienated us from nature and turned us into innately vicious and violent creatures. Dart described the fossil man-apes as "confirmed killers: carnivorous creatures, that seized living quarries by violence, battered

them to death, tore apart their broken bodies, dismembered them limb from limb, slaking their ravenous thirst with the hot blood of victims and greedily devouring livid writhing flesh." Poring over the cracked and battered man-ape fossils from the South African caves, Dart began to find – or imagine – evidence that *Australopithecus* was not only a killer, but a murderer and cannibal, who "ruthlessly killed fellow australopithecines and fed upon them as he would upon any other beast" (Dart, 1953; Dart and Craig, 1959, 201). All the worst traits of human beings were there to be read in – or into – the bones from the South African caves, and they all represented a murderous legacy from our killer-ape ancestry.

The killer-ape image of human beings as sick animals, alienated from the harmony of nature by their destructive technology, has been shared by many influential modern scientists, writers, and artists (Cartmill, 1993, 11–14, 20–24, 211ff). It is a central part of anti-hunting sentiment in the twentieth century. It seems significant in this regard that some people, who will wax indignant about Southern white males driving their Broncos into the forest and blasting away at the wildlife, are not at all perturbed when Southern Cherokees or Seminoles do the same thing. The reason, I think, is that what disturbs us about the hunt is not the killing of animals as such. If that were what bothered us, we would see more picket lines around slaughterhouses. What we are really disturbed by is the armed confrontation between technology and the wilderness, between sinful human history and the timeless harmonies of nature. And in that confrontation, we continue to see the American natives, as we have always seen them, as being outside of human history: part of the natural landscape of America, along with the buffalo and the prairie grasses and the passenger pigeon. They cannot offend against the natural order, because in our imagination they are part of it.

Oddly enough, this same opposition that we like to pose between the pollution of civilization and the purity of nature provides an important motive for sport hunting as practiced in modern America. It should be stressed here that people hunt for different and sometimes conflicting reasons. Some hunters' rationales contradict those of others, and some hunters' rationales are self-contradictory. For instance, many hunters like to describe their sport as a foraging activity, a thrifty harvest of Nature's gratuitous bounty. The trouble with that description is that (according to the figures I have seen) each pound of venison brought home by the average American deer hunter costs about 20 dollars in cash and five hours of labor. On the whole, the average hunter would be better off harvesting some prime rib in a good restaurant. Another delusory rationale for hunting is the notion that we have a moral responsibility to keep game animals from overpopulating their ranges and starving to death in the snows of winter. The difficulty here is that hunters are among the first to protest when coyotes or feral dogs or wild cats move in and threaten to take over the job of population control. Significantly, this argument is always focussed on those eternal martyrs of the wildwood, the deer. Not even the most conscientious of hunters trudges off into the winter woods to find starving ravens and weasels and put them out of their misery (Cartmill, 1993, 28, 231–32).

But the most literate hunters, the ones who are apt to write books and columns about the joys of hunting, generally agree that the chiefest of these joys is the pleasure of a temporary union with the natural order. "I must know," writes one sporting columnist, "that I am part of, and have common bond with, the wilderness" (Simpson, 1984). Another calls the hunt "a promise with the land" that keeps the huntsman from being "isolated from the natural world" (Holt, 1990). Valerius Geist describes hunting as an "intercourse with nature" (Geist, 1975, 153). "The human being," wrote the hunting philosopher Ortega y Gasset, "tries to rest from the enormous discomfort and all-embracing disquiet of history by 'returning' transitorily, artificially to nature in the sport of hunting." Hunting, said Ortega, "permits us the greatest luxury of all, the ability to enjoy a vacation from the human condition" (Ortega y Gasset, 1972, 139).

This rationale is a product of the way we define hunting, in terms of a symbolic opposition between the wild kingdom of nature and the polluted domain of human culture and history. That symbolic opposition is what precludes our hunting in the dairy barn. But at bottom that opposition, and the hunter's motives that are grounded in it, are no less delusory than the notion of the hunt as harvest or the hunt as birth control for Bambi. Our scientific knowledge of the nature of life and the history of this planet impel us to the certain conviction – whether we like it or not – that people are animals and the descendants and cousins of animals, and that the human condition is simply one aspect of the animal condition. We cannot participate in one condition, or enjoy a vacation from the other, by the act of seeking out and killing unfriendly animals of other species.

The facts of evolutionary biology have far-reaching implications, some of which have been traced by other participants in this symposium. They have an obvious bearing on the moral status of recreational hunting. If the human-animal boundary, and the parallel boundary that we like to draw between culture and nature, are as arbitrary a pair of constructs as evolutionary biology leads us to think, then the distinction between wild and domestic animals, between *Wildtiere* and *Haustiere*, is equally arbitrary. If so, it makes eminently good sense to see hunting as More's Utopians did, as just another species of butchery. And if we accept all this, then it seems hard to avoid coming to the same conclusion that Thomas More came to four hundred and eighty years ago: that butchery is not, in the final analysis, an appropriate recreation for a free people.

REFERENCES

Burnett, J., *Of the Origin and Progress of Language*, 2/e (Edinburgh: J. Balfour, 1774).

Cartmill, M., *A View to a Death in the Morning: Hunting and Nature through History* (Cambridge, MA: Harvard University Press, 1993).

Dalby, D., *Lexicon of the Medieval German Hunt* (Berlin: Walter de Gruyter, 1965).

Dart, R.A., "The Predatory Transition from Ape to Man," *International Anthropological and Linguistic Review* 1 (1953): 201–217.

Dart, R.A. and Craig, D., *Adventures with the Missing Link* (New York: Harper, 1959).

Eckardt, H.W., *Herrschaftliche jagd, bäuerliche Not und bürgerliche Kritik: Zur Geschichte der fürstlichen und adligen Jagdsprivilegien vornehmlich im südwestdeutschen Raum* (Göttingen: Vandenhoeck und Ruprecht, 1976).

Geist, V., *Mountain Sheep and Man in the Northern Wilds* (Ithaca: Cornell University Press, 1975).

Hobusch, E., *Von den edlen Kunst des Jägens: Eine Kulturgeschichte der Jagd und der Hege der Tierwelt* (Innsbruck: Pinguin, 1978).

Holt, C., *Durham (N.C.) Morning Herald*, 11 November 1990, p. B-I0.

James, M.R., *The Apocryphal New Testament* (Oxford: Oxford University Press, 1924).

Keen, M., *The Outlaws of Medieval Legend* (London: Routledge and Kegan Paul, 1961).

Mandelbaum, A., trans, *The Aeneid of Virgil* (New York: Bantam, 1961).

More, Thomas, *Utopia* (for the 1901 transcription by Cassell & Company Edition by David Price, see the Project Gutenberg eBook version edited by Henry Morley at http://www.gutenberg.org/etext/2130).

Ortega y Gasset, J., *Meditations on Hunting* (New York: Scribner's, 1972).

Pike, J.B., *Frivolities of Courtiers and Footprints of Philosophers* (Minneapolis: University of Minnesota Press, 1938).

Rogers, J.E.T., ed., *Loci e Libro Veritatum* (Oxford: Oxford University Press, 1881).

Simpson, B., *Raleigh (NC) News and Observer*, 28 October 1984, p. B–14.

Thiébaux, M., *The Stag of Love: The Chase in Medieval Literature* (Ithaca: Cornell University Press, 1974).

Turberville, G., *The Book of Venerie* (Oxford: Oxford University Press, [1576] 1908).

White, Jr., L., *Medieval Technology and Social Change* (Oxford: Oxford University Press, 1962).

FURTHER READING IN ANIMALS AS
SPECTACLE AND SPORT

Acquaroni, José Luis. 1966. *Bulls and Bullfighting*, trans. Charles David Ley. Barcelona: Editorial Noguer.

Anderson, J. K. 1985. *Hunting in the Ancient World*. Berkeley: University of California Press.

Baratay, Eric and Elisabeth Hardouin-Fugier. 2002. *Zoo: A History of Zoological Gardens in the West*. London: Reaktion.

Bentham, Jeremy. 1787/1995. Panopticon, in *The Panopticon Writings*, ed. Miran Bozovic, 29–95. London: Verso (http://cartome.org/panopticon2.htm, accessed July 26, 2005).

Bergman Charles. 1996. *Orion's Legacy: A Cultural History of Man as Hunter*. New York: Plume/Penguin.

Darnton, Robert. 1984/2001. *The Great Cat Massacre and Other Episodes in French Cultural History*. New York/London: Basic/Penguin.

Desmond, Jane C. 1999. *Staging Tourism: Bodies on Display from Waikiki to Sea World*. Chicago, IL: University of Chicago Press.

Davis, Susan G. 1997. *Spectacular Nature: Corporate Culture and the Sea World Experience*. Berkeley: University of California Press.

Dizard, Jan E. 2003. *Mortal Stakes: Hunters and Hunting in Contemporary America*. Amherst: University of Massachusetts Press.

Foucault, Michael. 1977/1995. *Discipline & Punish: The Birth of the Prison*, trans. Alan Sheridan. New York: Vintage.

Geertz, Clifford. 1973. Deep Play: Notes on the Balinese Cockfight. In Clifford Geertz, *The Interpretation of Cultures*, 412–453. New York: Basic Books.

Kalof, Linda and Amy Fitzgerald. 2003. Reading the Trophy: Exploring the Display of Dead Animals in Hunting Magazines. *Visual Studies* 18(2), 112–122.

Kyle, Donald G. 1998. *Spectacles of Death in Ancient Rome*. New York: Routledge.

Luke, Brian. 1998. Violent Love: Hunting, Heterosexuality, and the Erotics of Men's Predation *Feminist Studies* 24, 627-655.

Mullan, Bob and Garry Marvin. 1987. *Zoo Culture*. London: Weidenfeld & Nicolson.

Nájera-Ramírez, Olga. 1996. The Racialization of a Debate: The Charreada as Tradition or Torture. *American Anthropologist* 98(3): 505–511.

Ortega y Gasset, José. 1972. *Meditations on Hunting*. New York: Charles Scribner's Sons.

Pink, Sarah. 1997. *Women and Bullfighting: Gender, Sex and the Consumption of Tradition*. Oxford: Berg.

Pitt-Rivers, Julian. 1993. The Spanish Bull-Fight and Kindred Activities. *Anthropology Today* 9, 11–15.

Rothfels, Nigel. 2002. *Savages and Beasts: The Birth of the Modern Zoo*. Baltimore: Johns Hopkins University Press.

Thiébaux, Marcelle. 1974. *The Stag of Love: The Chase in Medieval Literature*. Ithaca: Cornell University Press.

SECTION 5

*A*nimals as Symbols

INTRODUCTION

Charting our experience of the world using animal signs has occupied and sustained humans from the earliest times. While we don't know the range of significance of animals for our Paleolithic ancestors, it is clear from their art that animals were greatly admired, and perhaps much like zoomorphic cultures, their worlds were experienced in animal forms and attributes. This veneration of animals continued for as long as humans kept to an agrarian way of life, but disappeared with the rise of cities and increasing urbanization. We begin this section with John Berger's classic essay, "Why Look at Animals?" While animals were our first symbols, Berger argues, the human veneration of animals has disappeared with urbanization and, further, animals themselves (*real* animals – not Donald Duck, pets, stuffed animals, or zoo animals) have disappeared from our lives.

The second extract is from Claude Lévi-Strauss's "Totemism," and includes one of the most widely cited phrases in animal studies – animals are "good to think." While Berger mourns the loss of animal explanations, names, and characters for human experiences, Lévi Strauss argues from his analysis of food taboos in certain societies that our relations with animals are in fact real, not symbolic, and that totemic animals have a "perceptible reality" that enhances the "embodiment of ideas." Animals are not conceived as direct ancestors or relatives or emblems of human clans, but rather incarnates of a clan's god(s) and the respect accorded them is gained indirectly, through a unique relationship that the clan has with the animal in its specific natural environment. Thus, humans have a special way of thinking about animals.

In the third essay, Boria Sax applies Lévi-Strauss's ideas to the notion of "animals as tradition." Sax argues that a respectful relationship with animals and the natural world comes with understanding the stories told about animals throughout human history. Stories and myth figure importantly in Sax's work on animal symbolism, with frog kings and animal brides indicative of a human merger with animals through magic, metaphor, and fantasy. As does Berger, Sax considers animals integral to "our heritage as human beings."

Human-animal mergers are also central to the work of postmodern animal studies, particularly in motifs that reconfigure the animal form representing multiple meanings and blurred boundaries. These are characteristics that define postmodern art and engage with Deleuze and Guattari's notion of *becoming-animal* discussed in Section 1. Steve Baker's work is exemplary in this regard – his project is to "read" art and philosophy in relation to each other. In the essay reproduced here from *The Postmodern Animal*, Baker examines what he calls *animal-sceptical* art which critiques the notion that the value of animals lies in what they mean for humans. Postmodern animal art is body-focused, such as "botched" taxidermy and animal biotechnology that render the corporeal unrecognizable, awkward, fragmented and disrupted.

The last essay in this section, Jonathan's Burt's "Illumination of the Animal Kingdom," elaborates on the concepts central to Baker's work – visual imagery, bodies and technology. Burt draws on late nineteenth-century British history to analyze the link between the visual and the moral [Here we suggest readers reflect on William Hogarth's *Three Stages of Cruelty* as a superb example of the power of this connection.] Burt examines two kinds of technology in relation to the visibility of animals that construct their representation [symbolization]: technology that enhances their visibility such as film and zoo display, and technology that conceals their visibility such as the use of electrical stunning in slaughterhouses. He concludes that seeing animals as metaphors for human attributes is "too limiting" and that animal representation is related to ethical practices and social control.

26

JOHN BERGER

Why Look at Animals?*

John Berger is one of the world's most influential writers of the last half century. An art historian, novelist, screenwriter, and critic, Berger lives and works in a small village in the French Alps and is internationally known as a "maverick Englishman." Berger's huge body of work [often collaborative projects built on the notion of democracy and open exchange of ideas] is centered by concern for the "lived experience of the oppressed," and upon earning a Booker Prize for one of his novels in the early 1970s he donated half of the award money to the Black Panthers and the other half to fund research into contemporary migration. Berger's *Ways of Seeing*, a BBC documentary that was published as a small book in 1972, is widely known for having uncovered the power and politics embedded in fine art. For example, he argued that post-Renaissance European art depicted men acting and women appearing – men (as spectator-owners) looked at women (as objects) and women watched themselves being looked at. This notion of spectatorship-ownership and the oppressive observation of women was linked to the observation of animals in the article reproduced here, entitled "Why Look at Animals?" With his enduring focus on the meaning of visual representations in which subjects become observed objects, moving from women to animals as "objects of sight" was not a large leap for him to make, and the juxtaposition of women's bodies with animal bodies was a theoretical breakthrough that will be taken up again in Section 6 on science. In this essay, Berger mourns the loss of real animals who in the nineteenth century began to gradually disappear from human lives because of commercial exploitation and mechanization, and today are "co-opted" into the family (as pets) and into spectacles (as in zoo animals). Particularly problematic are the conditions of the zoo animal, who, like the objectified female in fine art, is always the observed and never the observer. While the zoo provides humans with the opportunity to look at other animals, it is a one-way gaze, as is the male gaze upon the female. Berger draws on the concept of totemism [discussed in the next reading, by Lévi-Strauss] in a lament of the loss of "the universal use of animal-signs for charting the experience of the world" and argues [in assertions similar to those in Section 2] that the much-maligned process of anthropomorphism is actually beneficial because it expresses the proximity between human and animal.

For Gilles Aillaud

The nineteenth century, in Western Europe and North America, saw the beginning of a process, today being completed by twentieth-century corporate capitalism, by which every tradition which has previously mediated between man and nature was broken. Before this rupture, animals constituted the first circle of what surrounded man. Perhaps that already suggests too great a distance. They were with man at the centre of his world. Such centrality was of course economic and productive. Whatever the changes in productive means and social organization, men depended upon animals for food, work, transport, clothing.

Yet to suppose that animals first entered the human imagination as meat or leather or horn is to project a nineteenth-century attitude backwards across the millennia. Animals first entered the imagination as messengers and promises. For example, the domestication of cattle did not begin as a simple prospect of milk and meat. Cattle had magical functions, sometimes oracular, sometimes sacrificial. And the choice of a given species as magical, tameable, *and* alimentary was originally determined by the habits, proximity, and "invitation" of the animal in question.

> White ox good is my mother
> And we the people of my sister,
> The people of Nyariau Bul…
> Friend, great ox of the spreading horns,
> which ever bellows amid the herd,
> Ox of the son of Bul Maloa
> (*The Nuer: a description of the modes of livelihood and political institutions of a Nilotic people*, by Evans-Pritchard)

Animals are born, are sentient, and are mortal. In these things they resemble man. In their superficial anatomy – less in their deep anatomy – in their habits, in their time, in their physical capacities, they differ from man. They are both like and unlike.

We know what animals do and what beaver and bears and salmon and other creatures need, because once our men were married to them and they acquired this knowledge from their animal wives. (Hawaiian Indians quoted by Lévi-Strauss in *The Savage Mind*)

The eyes of an animal when they consider a man are attentive and wary. The same animal may well look at other species in the same way. He does not reserve a special look for man. But by no other species except man will the animal's look be recognized as familiar. Other animals are held by the look. Man becomes aware of himself returning the look.

The animal scrutinizes him across a narrow abyss of noncomprehension. This is why the man can surprise the animal. Yet the animal – even if domesticated – can also surprise the man. The man too is looking across a similar, but not identical, abyss of noncomprehension. And this is so wherever he looks. He is always looking across ignorance and fear. And so, when he is *being seen* by the animal, he is being seen as his surroundings are seen by him. His recognition of this is what makes the look of the animal familiar. And yet the animal is distinct, and can never be confused with man. Thus, a power is ascribed to the animal, comparable with human power but never coinciding with it. The animal has secrets which, unlike the secrets of caves, mountains, seas, are specifically addressed to man.

The relation may become clearer by comparing the look of an animal with the look of another man. Between two men the two abysses are, in principle, bridged by language. Even if the encounter is hostile and no words are used (even if the two speak different languages), the *existence* of language allows that at least one of them, if not both mutually, is confirmed by the other. Language allows men to reckon with each other as with themselves. (In the confirmation made possible by language, human ignorance and fear may also be confirmed. Whereas in animals fear is a response to signal, in men it is endemic.)

No animal confirms man, either positively or negatively. The animal can be killed and eaten so that its energy is added to that which the hunter already possesses. The animal can be tamed so that it supplies and works for the peasant. But always its lack of common language, its silence, guarantees its distance, its distinctness, its exclusion, from and of man.

Just because of this distinctness, however, an animal's life, never to be confused with a man's, can be seen to run parallel to his. Only in death do the two parallel lines converge and after death perhaps, cross over to become parallel again: hence the widespread belief in the transmigration of souls.

With their parallel lives, animals offer man a companionship which is different from any offered by human exchange. Different because it is a companionship offered to the loneliness of man as a species.

Such an unspeaking companionship was felt to be so equal that often one finds the conviction that it was man who lacked the capacity to speak with animals – hence the stories and legends of exceptional beings, like Orpheus, who could talk with animals in their own language.

What were the secrets of the animal's likeness with, and unlikeness from man? The secrets whose existence man recognized as soon as he intercepted an animal's look.

In one sense the whole of anthropology, concerned with the passage from nature to culture, is an answer to that question. But there is also a general answer. All the secrets were about animals as an *intercession* between man and his origin. Darwin's evolutionary theory, indelibly stamped as it is with the marks of the European nineteenth century, nevertheless belongs to a tradition almost as old as man himself. Animals interceded between man and their origin because they were both like and unlike man.

Animals came from over the horizon. They belonged *there* and *here*. Likewise they were mortal and immortal. An animal's blood flowed like human blood, but its species was undying and each lion was Lion, each ox was Ox. This – maybe the first existential dualism – was reflected in the treatment of animals. They were subjected *and* worshipped, bred *and* sacrificed.

Today the vestiges of this dualism remain among those who live intimately with, and depend upon, animals. A peasant becomes fond of his pig and is glad to salt away its pork. What is significant, and is so difficult for the urban stranger to understand, is that the two statements in that sentence are connected by an *and* and not by a *but*.

The parallelism of their similar/dissimilar lives allowed animals to provoke some of the first questions and offer answers. The first subject matter for painting was animal. Probably the first paint was animal blood. Prior to that, it is not unreasonable to suppose that the first metaphor was animal. Rousseau, in his *Essay on the Origins of Languages,* maintained that language itself began with metaphor: "As emotions were the first motives which induced man to speak, his first utterances were tropes (metaphors). Figurative language was the first to be born, proper meanings were the last to be found."

If the first metaphor was animal, it was because the essential relation between man and animal was metaphoric. Within that relation what the two terms – man and animal – shared in common revealed what differentiated them. And vice versa.

In his book on totemism, Lévi-Strauss comments on Rousseau's reasoning: "It is because man originally felt himself identical to all those like him (among which, as Rousseau explicitly says, we must include animals) that he came to acquire the capacity to distinguish *himself* as he distinguishes *them* – i.e., to use the diversity of species for conceptual support for social differentiation."

To accept Rousseau's explanation of the origins of language is, of course, to beg certain questions. (What was the minimal social organization necessary for the break-through of language?). Yet no search for origin can ever be fully satisfied. The intercession of animals in that search was so common precisely because animals remain ambiguous.

All theories of ultimate origin are only ways of better defining what followed. Those who disagree with Rousseau are contesting a view of man, not a historical fact. What we are trying to define, because the experience is almost lost, is the universal use of animal-signs for charting the experience of the world.

Animals were seen in eight out of twelve signs of the zodiac. Among the Greeks, the sign of each of the twelve hours of the day was an animal. (The first a cat, the last a crocodile.) The Hindus envisaged the earth being carried on the back of an elephant and the elephant on a tortoise. For the Nuer of the southern Sudan (see Roy Willis's *Man and Beast),*

> all creatures, including man, originally lived together in fellowship in one camp. Dissension began after Fox persuaded Mongoose to throw a club into Elephant's face. A quarrel ensued and the animals separated; each went its own way and began to live as they now are, and to kill each other. Stomach, which at first lived a life of its own in the bush, entered into man so that now he is always hungry. The sexual organs, which had also been separate, attached themselves to men and women, causing them to desire one another constantly. Elephant taught man how to pound millet so that now he satisfies his hunger only by ceaseless labour. Mouse taught man to beget and women to bear. And Dog brought fire to man.

The examples are endless. Everywhere animals offered explanations, or more precisely, lent their name or character to a quality, which like all qualities, was, in its essence, mysterious.

What distinguished man from animals was the human capacity for symbolic thought, the capacity which was inseparable from the development of language in which words were not mere signals, but signifiers of something other than themselves. Yet the first symbols were animals. What distinguished men from animals was born of their relationship with them.

The *Iliad* is one of the earliest texts available to us, and in it the use of metaphor still reveals the proximity of man and animal, the proximity from which metaphor itself arose. Homer describes the death of a soldier on the battlefield and then the death of a horse. Both deaths are equally transparent to Homer's eyes, there is no more refraction in one case than in the other.

"Meanwhile, Idomeneus struck Erymas on the mouth with his relentless bronze. The metal point of the spear passed right through the lower part of his skull, under the brain and smashed the white bones. His teeth were shattered; both his eyes were filled with blood; and he spurted blood through his nostrils and his gaping mouth. Then the black cloud of Death descended on him." That was a man.

Three pages further on, it is a horse who falls: "Sarpedon, casting second with his shining spear, missed Patroclus but struck his horse Pedasus on the right shoulder. The horse whinnied in the throes of Death, then fell down in the dust and with a great sigh gave up his life." That was animal.

Book 17 of the *Iliad* opens with Menelaus standing over the corpse of Patroclus to prevent the Trojans stripping it. Here Homer uses animals as metaphoric references, to convey, with irony or admiration, the excessive or superlative qualities of different moments. *Without the example of animals,* such moments would have remained indescribable. "Menelaus bestrode his body like a fretful mother cow standing over the first calf she has brought into the world."

A Trojan threatens him, and ironically Menelaus shouts out to Zeus: "Have you ever seen such arrogance? We know the courage of the panther and the lion and the fierce wild-boar, the most high-spirited and self-reliant beast of all, but that, it seems, is nothing to the prowess of these sons of Panthous ...!"

Menelaus then kills the Trojan who threatened him, and nobody dares approach him. "He was like a mountain lion who believes in his own strength and pounces on the finest heifer in a grazing herd. He breaks her neck with his powerful jaws, and then he tears her to pieces and devours her blood and entrails, while all around him the herdsmen and their dogs create a din but keep their distance – they are heartily scared of him and nothing would induce them to close in."

Centuries after Homer, Aristotle, in his *History of Animals,* the first major scientific work on the subject, systematizes the comparative relation of man and animal.

> In the great majority of animals there are traces of physical qualities and attitudes, which qualities are more markedly differentiated in the case of human beings. For just as we pointed out resemblances in the physical organs, so in a number of animals we observe gentleness and fierceness, mildness or cross-temper, courage or timidity, fear or confidence, high spirits or low cunning, and, with regard to intelligence, something akin to sagacity. Some of these qualities in man, as compared with the corresponding qualities in animals, differ only quantitatively: that is to say, man has more or less of this quality, and an animal has more or less of some other; other qualities in man are represented by analogous and not identical qualities; for example, just as in man we find knowledge, wisdom, and sagacity, so in certain animals there exists some other natural potentiality akin to these. The truth of this statement will be the more clearly apprehended if we have regard to the phenomena of childhood: for in children we observe the traces and seeds of what will one day be settled psychological habits, though psychologically a child hardly differs for the time being from an animal …

To most modern "educated" readers, this passage, I think, will seem noble but too anthropomorphic. Gentleness, cross-temper, sagacity, they would argue, are not moral qualities which can be ascribed to animals. And the behaviourists would support this objection.

Until the nineteenth century, however, anthropomorphism was integral to the relation between man and animal and was an expression of their proximity. Anthropomorphism was the residue of the continuous use of animal metaphor. In the last two centuries, animals have gradually disappeared. Today we live without them. And in this new solitude, anthropomorphism makes us doubly uneasy.

The decisive theoretical break came with Descartes. Descartes internalized, *within man,* the dualism implicit in the human relation to animals. In dividing absolutely body from soul, he bequeathed the body to the laws of physics and mechanics, and, since animals were soulless, the animal was reduced to the model of a machine.

The consequences of Descartes' break followed only slowly. A century later, the great zoologist Buffon, although accepting and using the model of the machine in order to classify animals and their capacities, nevertheless displays a tenderness toward animals which temporarily reinstates them as companions. This tenderness is half envious.

What man has to do in order to transcend the animal, to transcend the mechanical within himself, and what his unique spirituality leads to, is often anguish. And so, by comparison and despite the model of the machine, the animal seems to him to enjoy a kind of innocence. The animal has been emptied of experience and secrets, and this new invented "innocence" begins to provoke in man a kind of nostalgia. For the first time, animals are placed in a *receding* past. Buffon, writing on the beaver, says this:

> To the same degree as man has raised himself above the state of nature, animals have fallen below it: conquered and turned into slaves, or treated as rebels and scattered by force, their societies have faded away, their industry has become unproductive, their tentative arts have disappeared; each species has lost its general qualities, all of them retaining only their distinct capacities, developed in some by example, imitation, education, and in others, by fear and necessity during the constant watch for survival. What visions and plans can these soulless slaves have, these relics of the past without power?
>
> Only vestiges of their once marvelous industry remain in far deserted places, unknown to man for centuries, where each species freely used its natural capacities and perfected them in peace within a lasting community. The beavers are perhaps the only remaining example, the last monument to that animal intelligence …

Although such nostalgia toward animals was an eighteenth-century invention, countless *productive* inventions were still necessary – the railway, electricity, the conveyor belt, the canning industry, the motor car, chemical fertilizers – before animals could be marginalized.

During the twentieth century, the internal-combustion engine displaced draught animals in streets and factories. Cities, growing at an ever increasing rate, transformed the surrounding countryside into suburbs where field animals, wild or domesticated, became rare. The commercial exploitation of certain species (bison, tigers, reindeer) has rendered them almost extinct. Such wildlife as remains is increasingly confined to national parks and game reserves.

Eventually, Descartes's model was surpassed. In the first stages of the industrial revolution, animals were used as machines. As also were children. Later, in the so-called post-industrial societies, they are treated as raw material. Animals required for food are processed like manufactured commodities.

> Another giant [plant], now under development in North Carolina, will cover a total of 150,000 hectares but will employ only 1,000 people, one for every 15 hectares. Grains will be sown, nurtured and harvested by machines, including airplanes. They will be fed to the 50,000 cattle and hogs ... those animals will never touch the ground. They will be bred, suckled and fed to maturity in specially designed pens. (Susan George's *How the Other Half Dies*)

This reduction of the animal, which has a theoretical as well as economic history, is part of the same process as that by which men have been reduced to isolated productive and consuming units. Indeed, during this period an approach to animals often prefigured an approach to man. The mechanical view of the animal's work capacity was later applied to that of workers. F.W. Taylor, who developed the "Taylorism" of time-motion studies and "scientific" management of industry, proposed that work must be "so stupid" and so phlegmatic that he (the worker) "more nearly resembles in his mental make-up the ox than any other type." Nearly all modern techniques of social conditioning were first established with animal experiments. As were also the methods of so-called intelligence testing. Today behaviourists like Skinner imprison the very concept of man within the limits of what they conclude from their artificial tests with animals.

Is there not one way in which animals, instead of disappearing, continue to multiply? Never have there been so many household pets as are to be found today in the cities of the richest countries. In the United States, it is estimated that there are at least forty million dogs, forty million cats, fifteen million cage birds and ten million other pets.

In the past, families of all classes kept domestic animals because they served a useful purpose – guard dogs, hunting dogs, mice-killing cats, and so on. The practice of keeping animals regardless of their usefulness, the keeping, exactly, of *pets* (in the sixteenth century the word usually referred to a lamb raised by hand) is a modern innovation, and, on the social scale on which it exists today, is unique. It is part of that universal but personal withdrawal into the private small family unit, decorated or furnished with mementoes from the outside world, which is such a distinguishing feature of consumer societies.

The small family living unit lacks space, earth, other animals, seasons, natural temperatures, and so on. The pet is either sterilized or sexually isolated, extremely limited in its exercise, deprived of almost all other animal contact, and fed with artificial foods. This is the material process which lies behind the truism that pets come to resemble their masters or mistresses. They are creatures of their owner's way of life.

Equally important is the way the average owner regards his pet. (Children are, briefly, somewhat different.) The pet *completes* him, offering responses to aspects of his character which would otherwise remain unconfirmed. He can be to his pet what he is not to anybody or anything else. Furthermore, the pet can be conditioned to react as though it, too, recognizes this. The pet offers its owner a mirror to a part that is otherwise never reflected. But, since in this relationship the autonomy of both parties has been lost (the owner has become the-special-man-he-is-only-to-his-pet, and the animal has become dependent on its owner for every physical need), the parallelism of their separate lives has been destroyed.

The cultural marginalization of animals is, of course, a more complex process than their physical marginalization. The animals of the mind cannot be so easily dispersed. Sayings, dreams, games, stories, superstitions, the language itself, recall them. The animals of the mind, instead of being dispersed, have been co-opted into other categories so that the category *animal* has lost its central importance. Mostly they have been co-opted into the *family* and into the *spectacle*.

Those co-opted into the family somewhat resemble pets. But having no physical needs or limitations as pets do, they can be totally transformed into human puppets. The books and drawings of Beatrix Potter are an early example; all the animal productions of the Disney industry are a more recent and extreme one. In such works the pettiness of current social practices is *universalized* by being projected on to the animal kingdom. The following dialogue between Donald Duck and his nephews is eloquent enough.

DONALD: Man, what a day! What a perfect day for fishing, boating, dating or picnicking – only I can't do *any* of these things!

NEPHEW: Why not, Unca Donald? What's holding you back?

DONALD: The Bread of Life boys! As usual, I'm broke and it's eons till payday.

NEPHEW: You could take a walk Unca Donald – go birdwatching.

DONALD: (groan!) I may *have to!* But first, I'll wait for the mailman. He may bring something good newswise!

NEPHEW: Like a cheque from an unknown relative in Moneyville?

Their physical features apart, these animals have been absorbed into the so-called silent majority.

The animals transformed into spectacle have disappeared in another way. In the windows of bookshops at Christmas, a third of the volumes on display are animal picture books. Baby owls or giraffes, the camera fixes them in a domain which, although entirely visible to the camera, will never be entered by the spectator. All animals appear like fish seen through the plate glass of an aquarium. The reasons for this are both technical and ideological: technically the devices used to obtain ever more arresting images – hidden cameras, telescopic lenses, flashlights, remote controls and so on – combine to produce pictures which carry with them numerous indications of their normal *invisibility*. The images exist thanks only to the existence of a technical clairvoyance.

A recent, very well-produced book of animal photographs (*La Fête Sauvage* by Frederic Rossif) announces in its preface: "Each of these pictures lasted in real time less than three-hundredths of a second, they are far beyond the capacity of the human eye. What we see here is something never before seen, because it is totally invisible."

In the accompanying ideology, animals are always the observed. The fact that they can observe us has lost all significance. They are the objects of our ever-extending knowledge. What we know about them is an index of our power, and thus an index of what separates us from them. The more we know, the further away they are.

Yet in the same ideology, as Lukacs points out in *History and Class Consciousness,* nature is also a value concept. A value opposed to the social institutions which strip man of his natural essence and imprison him. "Nature thereby acquires the meaning of what has grown organically, what was not created by man, in contrast to the artificial structures of human civilisation. At the same time, it can be understood as that aspect of human inwardness which has remained natural, or at least tends or longs to become natural once more." According to this view of nature, the life of a wild animal becomes an ideal, an ideal internalised as a feeling surrounding a repressed desire. The image of a wild animal becomes the starting-point of a daydream: a point from which the day-dreamer departs with his back turned.

The degree of confusion involved is illustrated by the following news story: "London housewife Barbara Carter won a 'grant a wish' charity contest, and said she wanted to kiss and cuddle a lion. Wednesday night she was in a hospital in shock and with throat wounds. Mrs. Carter, 46, was taken to the lions' compound of the safari park at Bewdley, Wednesday. As she bent forward to stroke the lioness, Suki, it pounced and dragged her to the ground. Wardens later said. 'We seem to have made a bad error of judgment. We have always regarded the lioness as perfectly safe.'"

The treatment of animals in nineteenth-century romantic painting was already an acknowledgement of their impending disappearance. The images are of animals *receding* into a wildness that existed only in the imagination. There was, however, one nineteenth-century artist who was obsessed by the transformation about to take place, and whose work was an uncanny illustration of it. Grandville published his *Public and Private Life of Animals* in instalments between 1840 and 1842.

At first sight, Grandville's animals, dressed up and performing as men and women, appear to belong to the old tradition whereby a person is portrayed as an animal so as to reveal more clearly an aspect of his or her character. The device was like putting on a mask, but its function was to unmask. The animal represents the apogee of the character trait in question: the lion, absolute courage; the hare, lechery. The animal once lived near the origin of the quality. It was through the animal that the quality first became recognizable. And so the animal lends it his name.

But as one goes on looking at Grandville's engravings, one becomes aware that the shock which they convey derives, in fact, from the opposite movement to that which one first assumed. These animals are not being "borrowed" to explain people, nothing is being unmasked; on the contrary. These animals have become prisoners of a human/social situation into which they have been press-ganged. The vulture as landlord is more dreadfully rapacious than he is as a bird. The crocodiles at dinner are greedier at the table than they are in the river.

Here animals are not being used as reminders of origin, or as moral metaphors, they are being used *en masse* to "people" situations. The movement that ends with the banality of Disney began as a disturbing, prophetic dream in the work of Grandville.

The dogs in Grandville's engraving of the dog-pound are in no way canine; they have dogs' faces, but what they are suffering is imprisonment *like men.*

The bear is a good father shows a bear dejectedly pulling a pram like any other human bread-winner. Grandville's first volume ends with the words "Goodnight then, dear reader. Go home, lock your cage well, sleep tight and have pleasant dreams. Until tomorrow." Animals and populace are becoming synonymous, which is to say the animals are fading away.

A later Grandville drawing, entitled *The animals entering the steam ark,* is explicit. In the Judaeo-Christian tradition, Noah's Ark was the first ordered assembly of animals and man. The assembly is now over. Grandville shows us the great departure. On a quayside a long queue of different species is filing slowly away, their backs toward us. Their postures suggest all the last-minute doubts of emigrants. In the distance is a ramp by which the first have already entered the nineteenth-century ark, which is like an American steamboat. The bear. The lion. The donkey. The camel. The cock. The fox. Exeunt.

"About 1867," according to the *London Zoo Guide,* "a music hall artist called the Great Vance sang a song called *Walking in the zoo is the OK thing to do,* and the word 'zoo' came into everyday use. London Zoo also brought the word 'Jumbo' into the English language. Jumbo was an African elephant of mammoth size, who lived at the zoo between 1865 and 1882. Queen Victoria took an interest in him and eventually he ended his days as the star of the famous Barnum circus which travelled through America – his name living on to describe things of giant proportions."

Public zoos came into existence at the beginning of the period which was to see the disappearance of animals from daily life. The zoo to which people go to meet animals, to observe them, to see them, is, in fact, a monument to the impossibility of such encounters. Modern zoos are an epitaph to a relationship which was as old as man. They are not seen as such because the wrong questions have been addressed to zoos.

When they were founded – the London Zoo in 1828, the Jardin des Plantes in 1793, the Berlin Zoo in 1844, they brought considerable prestige to the national capitals. The prestige was not so different from that which had accrued to the private royal menageries. These menageries, along with gold plate, architecture, orchestras, players, furnishings, dwarfs, acrobats, uniforms, horses, art and food, had been demonstrations of an emperor's or king's power and wealth. Likewise in the nineteenth century, public zoos were an endorsement of modern colonial power. The capturing of the animals was a symbolic representation of the conquest of all distant and exotic lands. "Explorers" proved their patriotism by sending home a tiger or an elephant. The gift of an exotic animal to the metropolitan zoo became a token in subservient diplomatic relations.

Yet, like every other nineteenth-century public institution, the zoo, however supportive of the ideology of imperialism, had to claim an independent and civic function. The claim was that it was another kind of museum, whose purpose was to further knowledge and public enlightenment. And so the first questions asked of zoos belonged to natural history; it was then thought possible to study the natural life of animals even in such unnatural conditions. A century later, more sophisticated zoologists such as Konrad Lorenz asked behaviouristic and ethological questions, the claimed purpose of which was to discover more about the springs of human action through the study of animals under experimental conditions.

Meanwhile, millions visited the zoos each year out of a curiosity which was both so large, so vague, and so personal that it is hard to express in a single question. Today in France 22 million people visit the 200 zoos each year. A high proportion of the visitors were and are children.

Children in the industrialized world are surrounded by animal imagery: toys, cartoons, pictures, decorations of every sort. No other source of imagery can begin to compete with that of animals. The apparently spontaneous interest that children have in animals might lead one to suppose that this has always been the case. Certainly some of the earliest toys (when toys were unknown to the vast majority of the population) were animal. Equally, children's games, all over the world, include real or pretended animals. Yet it was not until the nineteenth century that reproductions of animals became a regular part of the decor of middle-class childhoods – and then, in this century, with the advent of vast display and selling systems like Disney's – of all childhoods.

In the preceding centuries, the proportion of toys which were animal was small. And these did not pretend to realism, but were symbolic. The difference was that between a traditional hobby horse and a rocking horse: the first was merely a stick with a rudimentary head which children rode like a broom handle: the second was an elaborate "reproduction" of a horse, painted realistically, with real reins of leather, a real mane of hair, and designed movement to resemble that of a horse galloping. The rocking horse was a nineteenth-century invention.

This new demand for verisimilitude in animal toys led to different methods of manufacture. The first stuffed animals were produced, and the most expensive were covered with real animal skin – usually the skin of still-born calves. The same period saw the appearance of soft animals – bears, tigers, rabbits – such as children take to bed with them. Thus the manufacture of realistic animal toys coincides, more or less, with the establishment of public zoos.

The family visit to the zoo is often a more sentimental occasion than a visit to a fair or a football match. Adults take children to the zoo to show them the originals of their "reproductions" and also perhaps in the hope of re-finding some of the innocence of that reproduced animal world which they remember from their own childhood.

The animals seldom live up to the adults' memories, while to the children they appear, for the most part, unexpectedly lethargic and dull.

(As frequent as the calls of animals in a zoo, are the cries of children demanding: Where is he? Why doesn't he move? Is he dead?) And so one might summarize the felt, but not necessarily expressed question of most visitors as: Why are these animals less than I believed?

And this unprofessional, unexpressed question is the one worth answering.

A zoo is a place where as many species and varieties of animal as possible are collected in order that they can be seen, observed, studied. In principle, each cage is a frame around the animal inside it. Visitors visit the zoo to look at animals. They proceed from cage to cage, not unlike visitors in an art gallery who stop in front of one painting, and then move on to the next or the one after next. Yet in the zoo the view is always wrong. Like an image out of focus. One is so accustomed to this that one scarcely notices it any more; or, rather, the apology habitually anticipates the disappointment, so that the latter is not felt. And the apology runs like this: What do you expect? It's not a dead object you have come to look at, it's alive. It's leading its own life. Why should this coincide with its being properly visible? Yet the reasoning of this apology is inadequate. The truth is more startling.

However you look at these animals, even if the animal is up against the bars, less than a foot from you, looking outward in the public direction, *you are looking at something that has been rendered absolutely marginal;* and all the concentration you can muster will never be enough to centralize it. Why is this?

Within limits, the animals are free, but both they themselves, and their spectators, presume on their close confinement. The visibility through the glass, the spaces between the bars, or the empty air above the moat, are not what they seem – if they were, then everything would be changed. Thus visibility, space, air, have been reduced to tokens.

The decor, accepting these elements as tokens, sometimes reproduces them to create pure illusion – as in the case of painted prairies or painted rock pools at the back of the boxes for small animals. Sometimes it merely adds further tokens to suggest something of the animal's original landscape – the dead branches of a tree for monkeys, artificial rocks for bears, pebbles and shallow water for crocodiles. These added tokens serve two distinct purposes: for the spectator they are like theatre props: for the animal they constitute the bare minimum of an environment in which they can physically exist.

The animals, isolated from each other and without interaction between species, have become utterly dependent upon their keepers. Consequently most of their responses have been changed. What was central to their interest has been replaced by a passive waiting for a series of arbitrary outside interventions. The events they perceive occurring around them have become as illusory in terms of their natural responses as the painted prairies. At the same time this very isolation (usually) guarantees their longevity as specimens and facilitates their taxonomic arrangement.

All this is what makes them marginal. The space which they inhabit is artificial. Hence their tendency to bundle toward the edge of it. (Beyond its edges there may be real space.) In some cages the light is equally artificial. In all cases the environment is illusory. Nothing surrounds them except their own lethargy or hyperactivity. They have nothing to act upon – except, briefly, supplied food and – very occasionally – a supplied mate. (Hence their perennial actions become marginal actions without an object.) Lastly, their dependence and isolation have so conditioned their responses that they treat any event which takes place around them – usually it is in front of them, where the public is – as marginal. (Hence their assumption of an otherwise exclusively human attitude – indifference.)

Zoos, realistic animal toys, and the widespread commercial diffusion of animal imagery all began as animals started to be withdrawn from daily life. One could suppose that such innovations were compensatory. Yet in reality the innovations themselves belonged to the same remorseless movement as was dispersing the animals. The zoos, with their theatrical decor for display, were in fact demonstrations of how animals had been rendered absolutely marginal. The realistic toys increased the demand for the new animal puppet: the urban pet. The reproduction of animals in images – as their biological reproduction in birth becomes a rarer and rarer sight – was competitively forced to make animals ever more exotic and remote.

Everywhere animals disappear. In zoos they constitute the living monument to their own disappearance. And in doing so, they provoked their last metaphor. *The Naked Ape, The Human Zoo,* are titles of world bestsellers. In these books the zoologist Desmond Morris proposes that the unnatural behaviour of animals in captivity can help us to understand, accept, and overcome the stresses involved in living in consumer societies.

All sites of enforced marginalization – ghettos, shanty towns, prisons, madhouses, concentration camps – have something in common with zoos. But it is both too easy and too evasive to use the zoo as a symbol. The zoo is a demonstration of the relations between man and animals; nothing else. The marginalization of animals is today being followed by the marginalization and disposal of the only class who, throughout history, has remained familiar with animals and maintained the wisdom which accompanies that familiarity: the middle and small peasant. The basis of this wisdom is an acceptance of the dualism at the very origin of the relation between man and animal. The rejection of this dualism is probably an important factor in opening the way to modern totalitarianism. But I do not wish to go beyond the limits of that unprofessional, unexpressed but fundamental question asked of the zoo.

The zoo cannot but disappoint. The public purpose of zoos is to offer visitors the opportunity of looking at animals. Yet nowhere in a zoo can a stranger encounter the look of an animal. At the most, the animal's gaze flickers and passes on. They look sideways. They look blindly beyond. They scan mechanically. They have been immunized to encounter, because nothing can any more occupy a *central* place in their attention.

Therein lies the ultimate consequence of their marginalization. That look between animal and man, which may have played a crucial role in the development of human society, and with which, in any case, all men had always lived until less than a century ago, has been extinguished. Looking at each animal, the unaccompanied zoo visitor is alone. As for the crowds, they belong to a species which has at last been isolated.

This historic loss, to which zoos are a monument, is now irredeemable for the culture of capitalism.

27

CLAUDE LÉVI-STRAUSS

The Totemic Illusion*

Claude Lévi-Strauss pioneered the structural study of anthropology, in which cultural activities such as rituals, food preparation, and entertainment are examined to discover the deep structures that produce meaning in a culture. Lévi-Strauss argues that all cultures have a system of symbolic communication that produce ways of thinking which are similar for all humans and which organize and categorize their worlds. Lévi-Strauss rejects the notion that modern or "civilized" societies are more advanced than "primitive" societies, thus also rejecting one of the most widely known classification systems known to anthropologists – totemism, the tradition of associating, through metaphor, a human group or clan with an animal (and less frequently with a plant, an object, or a natural phenomenon). In this extract from his classic essay, Lévi-Strauss discusses the origin of the word "totem" (which means "a relative of mine") and argues that totemism represents a unique relationship between a human clan and its specific natural environment and is expressed as a metaphor that groups use to classify themselves from other groups. He famously observes that animal-eating prohibitions are not totemic, and that beliefs and prohibitions about animal or plant species exist independently of the species' relationship to the human clan. Humans have opposite attitudes toward plants and animals; relations with plant species are symbolic, and relations with animals are real. Thus, food taboos apply to animals not plants, with "marked" plants always edible but "marked" animals never edible. Lévi-Strauss advances his well-known criticism of the traditional anthropologists' view that an animal only becomes totemic if it is first good to eat, with the argument that species are chosen as totems "not because they are 'good to eat' but because they are 'good to think'."

It is well known that the word totem is taken from the Ojibwa, an Algonquin language of the region to the north of the Great Lakes of North America. The expression *ototeman*, which means roughly, "he is a relative of mine," is composed of: initial *o-*, third-person prefix; *-t-*, epenthesis serving to prevent the coalescence of vowels; *-m-*, possessive; *-an*, third-person suffix; and, lastly, *-ote*, which expresses the relationship between Ego and a male or female relative, thus defining the exogamous group at the level of the generation of the subject. It was in this way that clan membership was expressed: *makwa nindotem*, "my clan is the bear"; *pindiken nindotem*, "come in, clan-brother," etc. The Ojibwa clans mostly have animal names, a fact which Thavenet – a French missionary who lived in Canada at the end of the eighteenth century and the beginning of the nineteenth – explained by the memory preserved by each clan of an animal in its country of origin, as the most handsome, most friendly, most fearsome, or most common, or else the animal usually hunted.[1]

This collective naming system is not to be confused with the belief, held by the same Ojibwa, that an individual may enter into a relationship with an animal which will be his guardian spirit. The only known term designating this individual guardian spirit was transcribed by a traveler in the middle of the nineteenth century as *nigouimes*, and thus has nothing to do with the word "totem" or any other term of the same type. Researches on the Ojibwa show that the first description of the supposed institution of "totemism" – due to the English trader and interpreter Long, at the end of the eighteenth century – resulted from a confusion between clan-names (in which the names of animals correspond to collective appellations) and beliefs concerning guardian spirits (which are individual protectors).[2] This is more clearly seen from an analysis of Ojibwa society.

These Indians were, it seems, organized into some dozens of patrilineal and patrilocal clans, of which five may have been older than the others, or, at any rate, enjoyed a particular prestige.

A myth explains that these five "original" clans are descended from six anthropomorphic supernatural beings who emerged from the ocean to mingle with human beings. One of them had his eyes covered and dared not look at the Indians, though he showed the greatest anxiety to do so. At last he could no longer restrain his curiosity, and on one occasion he partially lifted his veil, and his eye fell on the form of a human being, who instantly fell dead "as if struck by one of the thunderers." Though the intentions of this dread being were friendly to men, yet the glance of his eye was too strong, and it inflicted certain death. His fellows therefore caused him to return to the bosom of the great water. The five others remained among the Indians, and "became a blessing to them." From them originate the five great clans or totems: catfish, crane, loon, bear, and marten.[3]

In spite of the mutilated form in which it has been handed down to us, this myth is of considerable interest. It affirms, to begin with, that there can be no direct relationship, based on contiguity, between man and totem. The only possible relationship must be "masked," and thus metaphorical, as is confirmed by the fact, reported from Australia and America, that the totemic animal is sometimes designated by another name than that applied to the real animal, to the extent that the clan name does not immediately and normally arouse a zoological or botanical association in the native mind.

In the second place, the myth establishes another opposition, between personal relation and collective relation. The Indian does not die just because he is looked at, but also because of the singular behavior of one of the supernatural beings, whereas the others act with more discretion, and as a group.

In this double sense the totemic relationship is implicitly distinguished from that with the guardian spirit, which involves a direct contact crowning an individual and solitary quest. It is thus native theory itself, as it is expressed in the myth, which invites us to separate collective totems from individual guardian spirits, and to stress the mediating and metaphorical character of the relationship between man and the eponym of his clan. Lastly, it puts us on our guard against the temptation to construct a totemic system by accumulating relationships taken one by one, and uniting in each case *one* group of men to *one* animal species, whereas the primitive relation is between two systems: one based on distinction between groups, the other on distinction between species, in such a fashion that a plurality of groups on the one hand, and a plurality of species on the other, are placed directly in correlation and in opposition.

According to the reports by Warren, who was himself an Ojibwa, the principal clans gave birth to others:

Catfish: merman, sturgeon, pike, whitefish, sucker
Crane: eagle
Loon: cormorant, goose
Bear: ——
Marten: moose, reindeer

In 1925 Michelson recorded the following clans: marten, loon, eagle, bull-head salmon, bear, sturgeon, great lynx, lynx, crane, chicken. Some years later, and in another region (Old Desert Lake), Kinietz found six clans: water-spirit, bear, cat-fish, eagle, marten, chicken. He added to this list two more clans which had recently disappeared: crane, and an undetermined bird.

Among the eastern Ojibwa of Parry Island (in Georgian Bay, part of Lake Huron), Jenness compiled in 1929 a series of "bird" clans: crane, loon, eagle, gull, sparrowhawk, crow; a series of "animal" clans: bear, caribou, moose, wolf, beaver, otter, raccoon, skunk; a series of "fish" clans: sturgeon, pike, cat-fish. There was also another clan, waxing moon, and a whole list of names of clans which were hypothetical or which had disappeared from the region: squirrel, tortoise, marten, fisher, mink, birch-bark. The still existing clans were reduced to six: reindeer, beaver, otter, loon, falcon, and sparrowhawk.

It is also possible that the division was into five groups, by sub-division of the birds into "celestial" (eagle, sparrowhawk) and "aquatic" (all the others), and the mammals into "terrestrial" and "aquatic" (those inhabiting swampy zones, such as the cervidae of Canada, or which live on fish, such as the fisher, mink, etc.)

However this may be, it has never been reported of the Ojibwa that they believe members of a clan to be descended from the totemic animal; and, the latter was not the object of a cult. Thus Landes remarks that although the caribou has completely disappeared from southern Canada, this fact did not at all worry the members of the clan named after it: "It's only a name," they said

to the investigator. The totem was freely killed and eaten, with certain ritual precautions, viz., that permission had first to be asked of the animal, and apologies be made to it afterward. The Ojibwa even said that the animal offered itself more willingly to the arrows of hunters of its own clan, and that it paid therefore to call out the name of the "totem" before shooting at it.

The chicken and the pig – creatures of European importation – were used in order to attribute a conventional clan to the half-caste offspring of Indian women and white men (because the rule of patrilineal descent would otherwise have deprived them of a clan). Sometimes such persons were also assigned to the eagle clan, because this bird figures on the arms of the United States, well known from its currency. The clans were themselves divided into bands designated by the parts of the clan animal, e.g., head, hindquarters, subcutaneous fat, etc.

In thus assembling and comparing the evidence from several regions (each of which furnishes only a partial list, since the clans are not equally represented everywhere), we may discern a tripartite division: *water* (water spirit, cat-fish, pike, sucker, sturgeon, salmonidae, and so on, i.e., all the "fish" clans); *air* (eagle, sparrowhawk, then crane, loon, gull, cormorant, goose, etc.); *earth* (first the group consisting of caribou, moose, reindeer, marten, beaver, raccoon, then that of fisher, mink, skunk, squirrel, and lastly bear, wolf, and lynx). The place of the snake and of the tortoise is uncertain.

Entirely distinct from the system of totemic names, which is governed by a principle of equivalence, there is that of the "spirits" or *manido*, which are ordered in a hierarchized pantheon. There was certainly a hierarchy of clans among the Algonquin, but this did not rest on a superiority or inferiority attributed to the eponymous animals other than in jokes such as, "My totem is the wolf, yours is the pig ... Take care! Wolves eat pigs!"[4] At most there were reported hints of physical and moral distinctions, conceived of as specific properties. The system of "spirits," to the contrary, was plainly ordered along two axes: that of greater and lesser spirits, and that of beneficent and maleficent spirits. At the summit, the great spirit; then his servants; then, in descending order – both morally and physically – the sun and moon, forty-eight thunderers opposed to mythical snakes, "little invisible Indians," male and female water spirits, the four cardinal points, and finally hordes of *manido*, named and unnamed, which haunt the sky, the earth, the waters, and the chthonian world. In a sense, therefore, the two systems – "totems" and *manido* – are at right angles to each other, one being approximately horizontal, the other vertical, and they coincide at only one point, since the water spirits alone are unambiguously present in both the one and the other. This may perhaps explain why the supernatural spirits in the myth related above, who are responsible for the totemic names and for the division into clans, are described as emerging from the ocean.

All the food tabus reported from the Ojibwa derive from the *manido* system, and they are all explained in the same way, viz., as prohibitions communicated to the individual in dreams, on the part of particular spirits, against eating a certain meat or a certain part of the body of an animal, e.g., the flesh of the porcupine, the tongue of the moose, etc. The animal concerned does not necessarily figure in the list of clan names.

	MANIDO	SYSTEM
	great	spirit
	sun	moon
	thun-	derers
	cardinal	points
"TOTEMIC"	eagle, goose, water	spirits, pike, sturgeon, etc.
SYSTEM		
	chtonian	snakes
	et	c.

Similarly, the acquisition of a guardian spirit came as the consummation of a strictly individual enterprise which girls and boys were encouraged to undertake when they approached puberty. If they succeeded they gained a supernatural protector whose characteristics and circumstances of appearance were signs informing the candidates of their aptitudes and their vocations. These favors were only granted, however, on condition of behaving with obedience and considerateness

toward the protector. In spite of all these differences, the confusion between totem and guardian spirit into which Long fell may be explained in part by the fact that the latter was never "a particular mammal or bird, such as one might see by day around the wigwam, but a supernatural being which represented the entire species."[5]

Let us now look at another part of the world, described by Raymond Firth in accounts which have contributed greatly to the exposure of the extreme complexity and heterogeneous character of beliefs and customs too hastily lumped together under the label of totemism. These analyses are all the more illuminating in that they concern a region – Tikopia – which Rivers thought to furnish the best proof of the existence of totemism in Polynesia.

But, says Firth, before advancing such a view:

> ... it is essential to know whether on the human side the relation [with the species or natural object] is one in which people are involved as a group or only as individuals, and, as regards the animal or plant, whether each species is concerned as a whole or single members of it alone are considered; whether the natural object is regarded as a representative or emblem of the human group; whether there is any idea of identity between a person and the creature or object and of descent of one from the other; and whether the interest of the people is focused on the animal or plant *per se*, or it is of importance primarily through a belief in its association with ancestral spirits or other deities. And in the latter event it is very necessary to understand something of the native concept of the relation between the species and the supernatural being.[6]

This suggests that to the two axes which we have distinguished, viz., *group-individual* and *nature-culture*, a third should be added on which should be arranged the different conceivable types of relation between the extreme terms of the first two axes: emblematic, relations of identity, descent, or interest, direct, indirect, etc.

Tikopia society is composed of four patrilineal but not necessarily exogamous groups called *kainanga*, each headed by a chief (*ariki*) who stands in a special relationship to the *atua*. This latter term designates gods properly speaking, as well as ancestral spirits, the souls of former chiefs, etc. As for the native conception of nature, this is dominated by a fundamental distinction between "edible things" (*e kai*) and "inedible things" (*sise e kai*).

The "edible things" consist mainly of vegetables and fish. Among the vegetables, four species are of first importance in that each has a particular affinity with one of the four clans: the yam "listens to" or "obeys" *sa Kafika*; and the same relation obtains between the coconut and the clan *sa Tafua*, the taro and the clan *sa Taumako*, the breadfruit and the clan *sa Fangarere*. In fact, the vegetable is thought to belong directly, as in the Marquesas, to the clan god (incarnated in one of the numerous varieties of freshwater eels or those of the coastal reefs), and the agricultural rite primarily takes the form of a solicitation of the god. The role of a clan chief is thus above all to "control" a vegetable species. A further distinction between species is necessary: the planting and harvesting of the yam or taro, and the harvest of the breadfruit tree, are of a seasonal nature. This is not the case with coconut palms, which reproduce spontaneously, and the nuts of which ripen all year round. This difference may perhaps correspond to that between the respective forms of control: everybody possesses, cultivates, and harvests the first three species, and prepares and consumes their products, while only the clan in charge of them performs the ritual. But there is no special ritual for coconut palms, and the clan which controls them, Tafua, is subject to only a few tabus; in order to drink the milk, its members have to pierce the shell instead of breaking it; and in order to open the nuts and extract the flesh they may use only a stone, and no other tool.

These differential modes of conduct are not interesting solely because of the correlation they suggest between rites and beliefs on the one hand and certain objective conditions on the other. They also support the criticism advanced above against the rule of homology formulated by Boas, since three clans express their relationship to the natural species through ritual, and the fourth through prohibitions and prescriptions. The homology, therefore, if it has, has to be sought at a deeper level.

However this may be, it is clear that the relationship of men to certain vegetable species is expressed under two aspects, sociological and religious. As among the Ojibwa, a myth is resorted to in order to unify them:

A long time ago the gods were no different from mortals, and the gods were the direct representatives of the clans in the land. It came about that a god from foreign parts, Tikarau, paid a visit to Tikopia, and the gods of the land prepared a splendid feast for him, but first they organized trials of strength or speed, to see whether their guest or they would win. During a race, the stranger slipped and declared that he was injured. Suddenly, however, while he was pretending to limp, he made a dash for the provisions for the least, grabbed up the heap, and fled for the hills. The family of gods set off in pursuit; Tikarau slipped and fell again, so that the clan gods were able to retrieve some of the provisions, one a coconut, another a taro, another a breadfruit, and others a yam. Tikarau succeeded in reaching the sky with most of the foodstuffs for the feast, but these four vegetable foods had been saved for men.[7]

Different though it is from that of the Ojibwa, this myth has several points in common with it which need to be emphasized. First, the same opposition will be noted between individual and collective conduct, the former being negatively regarded and the latter positively in relation to totemism. In the myths, the individual and maleficent conduct is that of a greedy and inconsiderate god (a point on which there are resemblances with Loki of Scandinavia, of whom a masterly study has been made by Georges Dumézil). In both cases, totemism as a system is introduced as *what remains* of a diminished totality, a fact which may be a way of expressing that the terms of the system are significant only if they are *separated* from each other, since they alone remain to equip a semantic field which was previously better supplied and into which a discontinuity has been introduced. Finally, the two myths suggest that direct contact (between totemic gods and men in one case; gods in the form of men and totems in the other), i.e., a relation of contiguity, is contrary to the spirit of the institution: the totem becomes such only on condition that it first be set apart.

On Tikopia, the category of "edible things" also includes fish. However, there is no direct association at all between the clans and edible fish. The question is complicated when the gods are brought into the picture. On the one hand, the four vegetable foods are held to be sacred because they "represent" the gods – the yam is the "body" of the deity Kafika, the taro is that of Taumako; the breadfruit and coconut are respectively the "head" of Fangarere and of Tafua – but, on the other hand, the gods "are" fish, particularly eels. We thus rediscover, in a transposed form, the distinction between totemism and religion which has already been discerned in the opposition between resemblance and contiguity. As among the Ojibwa, Tikopian totemism is expressed by means of metaphorical relations.

On the religious plane, however, the relation between god and animal is of a metonymic order, first because the *atua* is believed to *enter* the animal, but does not change into it; secondly because it is never the *totality* of the species that is in question but only a single animal (therefore a *part* of the species) which is recognized, by its unusual behavior, as being the vehicle of a god; lastly because this kind of occurrence takes place only intermittently and even exceptionally, while the more distant relation between vegetable species and god is of a more permanent nature. From this last point of view, one might almost say that metonymy corresponds to the order of events, metaphor to the order of structure.[8]**

That the plants and edible animals are not themselves gods is confirmed by another fundamental opposition, that between *atua* and food. It is in fact inedible fish, insects, and reptiles that are called *atua*, probably, as Firth suggests, because "creatures which are unfit for human consumption are not of the normal order of nature … [In the case of animals] it is not the edible, but the inedible elements which are associated with supernatural beings." If, then, Firth continues, "we are to speak … of these phenomena as constituting totemism it must be acknowledged that there are in Tikopia two distinct types of the institution – the positive, relating to plant food-stuffs, with emphasis on fertility; the negative, relating to animals, with emphasis on unsuitability for food."[9]

The ambivalence attributed to animals appears even greater in that the gods assume many forms of animal incarnation. For the *sa Tafua*, the clan god is an eel which causes the coconuts of its adherents to ripen; but he can also change into a bat, and as such destroy the palm plantations of other clans. Hence the prohibition on eating bats, as well as water hens and other birds, and also fish, which stand in a particularly close relationship to certain deities. These prohibitions, which may be either general or limited to a clan or lineage, are not, however, of a totemic character: the pigeon, which is closely connected with Taumako clan, is not eaten, but there are no scruples against killing it, because it plunders the gardens. Moreover, the prohibition is restricted to the first-born.

Behind the particular beliefs and prohibitions there is a fundamental scheme, the formal properties of which exist independently of the relations between a certain animal or vegetable species and a certain clan, sub-clan or lineage, through which it may be discerned.

Thus the dolphin has a special affinity for the Korokoro lineage of Tafua clan. When it is stranded on the beach, members of this kin group make it an offering of fresh vegetable foodstuffs called *putu*, "offering on the grave of a person

---

** Seen in this perspective, the two myths of the origin of totemism which we have summarized and compared may also be considered, as myths concerning the origin of metaphor. And as a metaphorical structure is, in general, characteristic of myths, they therefore constitute in themselves metaphors of the second degree.

recently deceased." The meat is then cooked and shared between the clans, with the exception of the kin group in question, for which it is *tapu* because the dolphin is the preferred form of incarnation of their *atua*.

The rules of distribution assign the head to the Fangarere, the tail to the Tafua, the forepart of the body to the Taumako, and the hindpart to the Kafika. The two clans whose vegetable species (yam and taro) is a god's "body" are thus entitled to "body" parts, and the two whose species (coconut, breadfruit) is a god's "head" receive the extremities (head and tail). The form of a system of relations is thus extended, in a coherent fashion, to a situation which at first sight might appear quite foreign to it. And, as among the Ojibwa, a second system of relations with the supernatural world, entailing food prohibitions, is combined with a formal structure while at the same time remaining clearly distinct from it, though the totemic hypothesis would incline one to confuse them. The divinized species which are the objects of the prohibitions constitute a separate system from that of clan functions which are themselves related to plant foodstuffs: e.g., the octopus, which is assimilated to a mountain, the streams of which are like its tentacles, and, for the same reason, to the sun and its rays; and eels, both fresh-water and marine, which are objects of a food tabu so strong that even to see them may cause vomiting.

We may thus conclude, with Firth, that in Tikopia the animal is conceived neither as an emblem, nor as an ancestor, nor as a relative. The respect and the prohibitions connected with certain animals are explained, in a complex fashion, by the triad of ideas that the group is descended from an ancestor, that the god is incarnated in an animal, and that in mythical times there existed a relation of alliance between ancestor and god. The respect observed toward the animal is thus accorded to it indirectly.

On the other hand, attitudes toward plants and toward animals are opposed to each other. There are agricultural rites, but none for fishing or hunting. The *atua* appear to men in the form of animals, never of plants. Food tabus, when they exist apply to animals, not plants. The relation of the gods to vegetable species is symbolic, that to animal species is real; in the case of plants it is established at the level of the species, whereas an animal species is never in itself *atua*, but only a particular animal in certain circumstances. Finally, the plants which are "marked" by differential behavior are always edible; in the case of animals the reverse obtains. Firth, in a brief comparison of Tikopian facts with the generality of Polynesian reports, expresses almost word for word the formula of Boas, drawing the lesson that totemism does not constitute a phenomenon *sui generis* but a specific instance in the general field of relations between man and the objects of his natural environment.[10]

[...]

Radcliffe-Brown's demonstration ends decisively the dilemma in which the adversaries as well as the proponents of totemism have been trapped because they could assign only two roles to living species, viz., that of a natural stimulus, or that of an arbitrary pretext. The animals in totemism cease to be solely or principally creatures which are feared, admired, or envied: their perceptible reality permits the embodiment of ideas and relations conceived by speculative thought on the basis of empirical observations. We can understand, too, that natural species are chosen not because they are "good to eat" but because they are "good to think."

NOTES

1. See Cuoq, J. A. *Lexique de la langue algonquine.* Montreal, 1886, pp. 312–313.
2. *Handbook of North American Indians North of Mexico.* Bureau of American Ethnology, Smithsonian Institution, *Bulletin* 30, 2 vols. Washington, 1907–1910. "Totemism."
3. Warren, W., "History of Ojibways," *Collections of the Minnesota Historical Society,* Vol. V. Saint Paul, Minn., 1885, pp. 43–44.
4. Hilger, M. I., "Some Early Customs of the Menomini Indians," *Journal de la Société des Américanistes,* Vol. XLIX (n.s.), 1960, p. 60.

5. Jenness, D., "The Ojibwa Indians of Parry Island: Their Social and Religious Life," *Bulletin of the Canadian Department of Mines,* No. 78. Ottawa, 1935, p. 54.

6. Firth, R., "Totemism in Polynesia," *Oceania,* Vol. I, No. 3, 1930–31, p. 292.

7. Firth, R., "Totemism in Polynesia," *Oceania,* Vol. I, No. 3, 1930–31, p. 296. This book was already in proof when there came into our hands a very recent work by Firth (1961) in which other versions of the same myth are to be found.

8. Jakobson, R. and Halle, M., *Fundamentals of Language.* s-Gravenhage, 1956, Chap. V.

9. Firth, R., "Totemism in Polynesia," *Oceania,* Vol. I, No. 3, 1930–31, pp. 300, 301.

10. Firth, R., "Totemism in Polynesia," *Oceania,* Vol. I, No. 4, 1930–31, p. 398.

28

BORIA SAX

Animals as Tradition*

Boria Sax studies global environmental history, rural and agricultural history, and communication and rhetoric and is the founder of Nature in Legend and Story, a non-profit organization dedicated to the promotion of an understanding of the bonds between humans and the natural world. Sax is an accomplished lecturer on nature/culture topics, with televised appearances, such as on the History Channel's "Rats, Bats, and Bugs." Much of his writing focuses on the symbolic meaning of the depiction of animals in human narratives, such as stories, pictures, and scientific accounts. We reproduce an extract from his recent book, *The Mythical Zoo*, that takes up the notion of "animal as tradition" that could provide new, more respectful, and cautious ways for humans to relate to animals and the natural world. You will see that Boria Sax's work highlights the importance of Claude Lévi-Strauss's phrase discussed in the previous excerpt, "animals are good to think." Sax suggests that we think of every animal as a tradition, arguing that to know, respect, and preserve animals, we must understand them through the stories that have surrounded them throughout human history. He describes animals as tradition in five categories of "lore," or traditional knowledge: "metamorphosed animals" (such as shape changers, including Frog Princes and totemic animals), "divine animals" (such as gods incarnated as cats), "demonic animals" (such as devils incarnated as spiders), "satiric animals" (animals such as Renard the Fox who teach lessons about human frailties), and "political animals" (the deployment of animals to degrade and mock others). Because of genetic engineering and modern domestication [see Sections 3 and 6], we can no longer define animals in terms of biology, but defining animals as tradition draws on the history of the human-animal relationship, links animals to human culture, and encourages respect.

There are more things in heaven and earth, Horatio,
Than are dreamt of in your philosophy.

William Shakespeare, *Hamlet*, act 1, scene 5

You are sitting in the park and your eyes meet those of a squirrel. What do you see? The Vikings saw a messenger that moved back and forth between the underworld and the abodes

* Reproduced with permission of the publisher and from Boria Sax (2001) *The Mythical Zoo: An Encyclopedia of Animals in World Myth, Legend, and Literature.* Santa Barbara; Denver; Oxford: ABC-CLIO, Inc.

of humans and gods. The Ainu saw the worn, discarded sandals of the god Aioina. For late medieval people, the squirrel was sometimes a form taken by a witch. Simply by saying the name "squirrel," however, we dissipate part of the mystery.

In the second biblical tale of creation, Adam gains dominance over the animals by naming them (Gen. 2:20). Did he give them names as species such as "Elephant"? Did he give them individual names such as "Babar"? In the language of God, words fit reality so perfectly that there was no need for such distinctions. Since human beings were scattered after Babel, we have lost that perfect language. A single creature is "Rover," "dog," "pet," "canid," "mammal," and many other things besides.

> Without the primal language of Adam, the act of naming the animals is a continuous process. Aristotle first systematized the classification of animals. In the modern era, the Aristotelian system of classification was greatly refined by Carolus Linnaeus. Before the eighteenth century, bats were usually considered winged mice. After looking carefully at their anatomy, Linnaeus decided that bats were really primates. Reconsidering, he finally placed them in a separate family, and that is where they have stayed ever since. The classifications we use in everyday life are usually rough, informal versions of those that have been worked out by scientists over the centuries.

Scientists generally regard animals as belonging to different species when they do not habitually mate together. Although dogs, wolves, jackals, and coyotes are capable of mating together, they generally do not do so in the wild, so each of these is considered a distinct species. In contexts of domestication, however, such a definition becomes problematic. A horse and an ass not only can mate but also are often induced to do so to produce a mule, which retains useful qualities of both species. Today, with food animals the genetic manipulation is so intense that sometimes one can no longer speak of species at all. The turkeys that are sold for Thanksgiving have such large breasts that they cannot reach one another to mate but must be reproduced through artificial insemination.

With gene splicing, it is now possible to cross divisions not only of species and genus but even between plants and animals. Scientists have produced a cross between a sheep and a goat, known as a "geep." They have inserted genes from flounder into the genetic code of tomatoes to increase resistance to frost, and they have inserted genes from chickens into tomatoes to make the plants more resistant to disease. They have placed human genetic material in pigs to produce organs that will not be rejected when transplanted into human beings. These creatures are like the monsters of folklore, and it may well be that in the future we will see crosses between human beings and chimpanzees or gorillas. Contemporary genetic theory views animals, including human beings, less as individuals or representatives of species than as repositories of hereditary information. As we examine new ways of thinking about animals, it is best not to forget the older ones. These traditional perspectives are intimately linked to cultural values and practices that we have developed over millennia.

When it comes to establishing the identity of an animal, biology is not nearly enough. Often we are so impressed with the success of science that we forget it is merely one aspect of a larger tradition. Every name places an animal in a tradition that is constantly developing. It surrounds the animal with ideas and associations. My dictionary defines *tradition* as "an inherited pattern of thought and action." It comes from *trade,* which originally meant "track." To study a tradition is to track a creature, as though one were a hunter, back through time. The names we give animals carry intricate expectations and assumptions. As we learn of the traditions that have grown up around animals, they regain something of the numinous quality that they had in cave paintings of prehistoric times.

Tradition does not mean uncritically following precedents but simply retaining continuity with the values of the past. Some people are suspicious of tradition because they associate it with cruelty and injustice – as in the Inquisition, for example.

Yet it is the values embedded in tradition that enable us to protest such abuses. The Christian value of love, for example, proved more basic than injunctions against heresy, and so the Inquisition was ended. Traditions develop in an organic way, which is a bit like the evolution of living organisms. Like many species of animals and plants, traditions are vanishing.

To define a kind of animal strictly in terms of biology is too narrow, too technical, and too restrictive. It is not even very meaningful under conditions of domestication, whether on a farm or in a zoo, where animals do not necessarily choose the partners with which they breed. It becomes almost meaningless with genetic engineering, where breeders exchange genes across lines of species. Suppose we work to preserve either a species in the wild or a breed in domesticity. What exactly are we preserving? A collection of physical characteristics? A piece of genetic code? A part of a habitat?

If we define each sort of animal as a tradition, our definition includes all of these and more. It also includes stories from myth, legend, and literature. All of these, with the love and fear they may engender, are part of an intimate relationship with human beings that has been built up over millennia. To regard each sort of animal as a tradition also encourages respect. Why should we care about species extinction? Why should we care about the welfare of strays? Appeals to transcendent reasons do not satisfy people in our secular society. Appeals to pragmatic reasons, such as preserving the ecosystem, are easily subject to challenge. Tradition links animals to the ideas, practices, and events that make up human culture.

Perhaps the greatest of the many ethical problems faced by human beings at the beginning of a new millennium is deciding the extent to which we are entitled to alter the natural world for our convenience. Unprecedented capabilities such as genetic engineering and the harnessing of atomic energy give us far more power than wisdom. The idea of every animal as a tradition will not give us a simple answer to our dilemmas, but it will at least provide a way in which to think of them.

Traditions tend to degenerate when they are not adjusted to changing conditions, but alterations are generally made in a cautious and respectful manner. To preserve an animal as a tradition, we must know it intimately, we must be familiar with the lore that has grown up around the creature since time immemorial.

METAMORPHOSED ANIMALS

Remember the Frog Prince from a famous fairy tale by the Grimm brothers, the very first in their collection? Well, he had a long and distinguished history, though it is not mentioned in books for children. Long ago in the days of the mammoths, he was a powerful totem, sacred to human beings. During the Middle Ages, he joined forces with the Devil to become the animal companion, or "familiar," of a witch. Then, probably in the eighteenth or nineteenth century, he reformed. A young woman transformed him into a human prince by – depending on which version of the story you prefer – giving him a kiss, throwing him against a wall, or chopping off his head.

In tribal societies, human form is not always important. All beings are forever changing their shapes, like waves breaking on the shore. Human beings may become ravens, while hares may turn into human beings. You become what you eat; you become what you are eaten by. Death is simply a transition, a bit like the passage from girl to woman or boy to man.

Totems are animals from which a tribe traces its ancestry. Beyond that, they are guardians of the tribe, at times revisiting the members in trances or in dreams. Among the Indo-Europeans, the tribal totem was perhaps most frequently the wolf. Going into battle, warriors would be possessed by the spirit of the wolf, and our legends of werewolves are a legacy of that archaic time. A mother wolf suckled Romulus and Remus, the legendary founders of Rome; a woodpecker fed them. Among people of the Far North, totems were most often birds. For the Native Americans of the Northwest coast, the favorite totem was frequently the raven, sometimes the bear; for tribes farther south, it might have been the coyote, beaver, or jaguar.

Legends of totemistic societies commemorate learning the arts of civilization from observation of animals. The Navaho Indians, for example, tell how women learned to weave from Spider Woman. Other stories may tell of learning to build from beavers or to hunt from wolves. Traditional dances often imitate the motions of animals, while music sometimes mimics their sounds. Observing what bears or snakes would eat has revealed many herbal medicines. Many totems from archaic societies lived on as the helpful animals in fairy tales – the cat in Charles Perrault's "Puss in Boots," for example. Today the legacy of totemism is everywhere, from the mascots of sports teams to heraldic animals on coins.

Marriages of people with animals often led to the founding of a tribe. As they hunted or went off to war, men told tales of animal brides. As they sat together and spun, women told of animal grooms. For both men and women, the animal was that mystery in a partner that no intimacy could fully overcome. In each other's eyes, lovers still are "squirrel" and "dove."

Among many tribal peoples, the ability to take the form of an animal had been the sign of a great shaman, but this changed in urban societies. In the *Metamorphoses* of the Roman poet Ovid, taking the form of an animal was generally a punishment. The maiden Arachne was changed into a spider for being arrogant. Zeus changed King Lycaon into a wolf for serving his guests human flesh. The goddess Diana changed the hunter Actaeon into a stag for intruding upon her bath. Buddhists and Hindus believed that animals needed many reincarnations spread across millennia to become human beings.

DIVINE ANIMALS

The prehistoric cave paintings of France and Spain are among the most ancient works of art that we have. The human beings in these paintings are usually crude stick figures that the artists must not have considered very important. The animals are painted with far more care and passion. The first clearly identifiable religious shrines in history are at Çatal Hüyük in Anatolia and date from around the middle of the seventh millennium BC. They were dedicated to animals, especially bulls, but also vultures, foxes, and others. The ancient Egyptians believed their creator god Ptah was incarnated in a bull named Apis that could be recognized by specific markings. Apis was kept in a temple and honored in sacred rites. The Egyptians also worshipped their gods as incarnated in cats, ibises, and many other creatures.

Over millennia, anthropomorphic goddesses and gods slowly replaced the animal deities. The archaic divinities accompanied their more human successors, often as mascots or alternate forms. Athena, for example, was pictured with an owl, Zeus with an eagle; Odin was accompanied by ravens and by wolves; Mary, mother of Christ, was often shown with a dove. The monkey-god Hanuman, who fought alongside the hero Rama in the epic *Ramayana,* is now perhaps the most popular figure in the Hindu pantheon. There is a bit of an archaic mother-goddess in the "wicked witch" of Halloween, pictured with a faithful spider at her side.

As tribes were absorbed into kingdoms and empires, their religions were fused and local deities were combined. Archaic practices sometimes continued as local cults or customs. In Rome, people would sometimes keep a snake in their home, believing it the spirit of an ancestor. This practice survived into modern times in parts of Italy. A few holy men and women retained the shaman's gift of speaking with creatures of the woods and fields. Saint Francis preached to the birds, while Saint Anthony evangelized the fish.

Figures that blend human and animal features became common with the transition from hunting and gathering to agriculture. The gods and goddesses of ancient Egypt often had a human torso and the head of an animal – crocodile, baboon, jackal, cat, falcon, or ibis. The Greeks had their centaurs and satyrs, while the Hebrews had cherubim and seraphim. Garuda, the carrier of the Hindu god Vishnu, had the torso and face of a man but the wings and beak of an eagle. Yet another fantastic animal was al-Borak, the steed on which Mohammed made his flight to Heaven; she had the body of a horse and the face of a woman, and she could see the dead.

The unicorn, usually shown as a horse with the horn of a narwhal, became the most popular fantastic animal in the Middle Ages. Edward Topsell, a zoologist of Renaissance England, rebuked those who doubted the existence of the unicorn, saying that that was to doubt the power of God. In the early modern period, many sailors told of encountering mermaids, creatures that embodied the wonder and terror of the sea.

DEMONIC ANIMALS

The Hebrews constantly struggled against the old animal cults. Moses killed thousands of people for introducing the Hebrews to worship of the golden calf. The old totems would not simply disappear; they often became devils. A devil will often have the horns of a bull, the teeth of a wolf, the legs of a goat, the tail of a monkey, and the tusks of a boar. One poor weaver who was convicted of sorcery in early modern Scotland described demons as being "like flies dancing around a candle" (Scott 1832, 249).

In witch trials of the Renaissance, especially in Britain, people claimed that demons would visit a sorcerer as an animal companion. The demon was frequently a cat, and felines might be burned along with a convicted witch. Often, it was a snake, toad, lizard, spider, cat, or dog. A suspect was sometimes forced to sit in the middle of a room where she would be deprived of sleep and watched for 24 hours. Inquisitors made a hole in her door, and any creature that approached her, whether spider or cat, was considered her familiar. For the poor and vulnerable, keeping pets or even feeding animals could arouse suspicion of witchcraft.

Furthermore, witches themselves were often shape shifters. In sixteenth-century Scotland,

Isobel Gowdie confessed without compulsion to being a witch. She said that witches commonly took the form of animals such as crows or cats. Once she took on the form of a hare to deliver a message for the Devil. A neighbor's hounds began to chase her; she jumped into her home and took refuge behind a chest. Finally, Isobel managed to elude the dogs long enough to say a charm that returned her to human form. A mark where a dog had nipped at her remained on her back.

SATIRIC ANIMALS

In *The Epic of Gilgamesh,* from Mesopotamia around 2000 BC, the hero undertook a journey to the world below and found the plant of immortality. A snake stole the plant, shed its skin, and lived eternally. Ever since human beings have striven to be heroes, animals have deflated human pretensions. Along with the story of Gilgamesh, archeologists digging up the library of Assyrian king Ashurnasirpal found the first animal epic, known as *The Fable of the Fox,* where lion, dog, and wolf all boast and plead, acting as pretentious and vulnerable as human beings.

After Homer wrote of the heroes of the Trojan War, an unknown Greek wrote *Batrachyomachy,* the epic battle between frogs and mice. These mighty warriors clashed around a pond, as Zeus and all the gods looked on. The invincible mouse-hero Meridarpax seemed about to lead his men – or, rather, mice – to victory, when Zeus sent armored crabs to drive the invaders away.

According to Judeo-Christian tradition, animals spoke to Adam and Eve in the Garden of Eden. Countless tales all over the world begin with a formula like "In the days when animals talked like people ..." The fables of Aesop, who lived on the Greek island of Sámos in the sixth century before Christ, are set in a world where all beings, from gnat to lion, can speak to one another like human beings. In epic stories of animals, such as the Hindu *Panchatantra* or the Arab *Kalila wa Dimna,* animals have a society unto themselves. They bargain, quarrel, and make friends with little regard for species.

In the folklore of the Merovingians, who ruled Germany and much of France at the beginning of the Middle Ages, the creatures of the forest have a court. The lion is king, while the bear and stag are nobles. Every year at the summer solstice they meet to hear lawsuits and dispense justice. As human rulers in Europe appeared less glamorous and more corrupt, people also took a more jaundiced view of the animal kingdom. In stories of Renard the Fox, told throughout Europe toward the end of the Middle Ages, the king of beasts was just a fool for all his pomp. The wolf and fox quarreled over chicken stolen from the coop, in the language of piety and romance.

Brer Rabbit outwitted the fox and wolf in tales told among people of African descent in the Caribbean and the South of the United States. Satirists such as J. J. Grandville drew goats and roaches parading about in formal clothes. On the editorial pages of newspapers, politicians today become newts and dogs.

POLITICAL ANIMALS

Animals became degraded as giant industries took agriculture over from smaller farms and private homes. Once feared and killed with ceremony, animals are now raised in cramped cells and according to rigid regimens, and then they are slaughtered on assembly lines. And yet this degradation and helplessness makes human beings identify with animals. The experimental lab where several million rats and rabbits are killed every year has often been used as a metaphor for Bolshevik Russia; the industrial abattoir has become a common metaphor for the concentration camps in Nazi Germany.

Animal Farm by George Orwell, first published in 1946, begins with the animals revolting and driving the farmers away. Gradually, however, the pigs become more and more like human beings, as they learn to sell, slaughter, imprison, and exploit the other creatures. The novella ends, "The creatures outside looked from man to pig, and from pig to man again; but already it was impossible to say which was which" (128).

Animals are constantly used in propaganda. Portrayed as apes, people might be mocked. Or people might be called "pigs" or "sheep," so they could be slaughtered. They might be called "wolves" or "bears" so they could be hunted down, or "viruses" so they could be exterminated. In *Maus* (1991), a comic book telling of his father's life in Auschwitz, cartoonist Art Spiegelman made inmates into mice, the Nazis into pigs or cats. In 1988 the prime minister of Israel said he would crush the Palestinians "like grasshoppers." A sales pitch for mouthwash shows little creatures cowering in terror and tells us, "They're germs; they deserve to die." One advertisement for Orkin pest control shows the barrel of a large high-tech gun pointed by an exterminator with the caption "The last thing a bug sees." Still another, this one for Combat Roach Bait, shows a bunch of dead cockroaches lying on their backs with the caption "Tired of living with thousands of strangers" – a clear appeal to resentment against recent immigrants (Boxer 1995, section 4, 2).

THE MODERN PERIOD AND AFTER

People usually think that there is a big difference between animals and ourselves, but just what it is, is very hard to say. Is it our intellect? Emotion? Stupidity? Technology? Tragic destiny? Religion? Language? Success? Morality? Wickedness? Power? War? Our use of fire? Our upright stance?

Modern scientific culture began in the seventeenth century with René Descartes. He described animals as intricate machines, yet few people could believe that of a beloved dog. As pets proliferated, so did their stories: a cat had learned to open all the locks in her home; a pig could do arithmetic and spell; a nightingale gave singing lessons to other birds from inside its cage; dogs beat all comers in card games. Toward the end of the sixteenth century, Michel de Montaigne in France collected anecdotes in "Apology for Raymond Sebond" to show that human intelligence was not so special. He explained that tuna must know mathematics since they move in regular patterns; they must also know astrology, since they guide themselves by stars.

In the Romantic Movement of the late eighteenth and early nineteenth centuries, a revolt against the constraints of civilization led to the celebration of wild animals. Georges-Louis Leclerc de Buffon, the most popular naturalist of the time, believed that all animals once had a civil society with laws, before they were murdered and enslaved by human beings. The last remnants could be found in the New World, where beavers still built villages, created constitutions, and held courts of law.

In the eighteenth century, Linnaeus classed human beings as primates, placing them in the same genus as apes, monkeys, and lemurs. Then in 1859 Charles Darwin proclaimed his theory of evolution in *The Origin of Species,* suggesting (at first, he did not dare say it outright) that humanity evolved from something like an ape. There were passionate debates and embarrassed snickers; people joked about having gorillas for grandfathers. Racists depicted those from other cultures – Africans, Irish, Jews, and Japanese – as being like apes. The targeted people were drawn as slouched over with dangling arms and receding foreheads.

But modern people have feared above all the "animal" in themselves. The metaphor of "the beast within" was used in the Victorian era to explain all sorts of vices, from lechery to gluttony. Physiognomists looked for animal features in the faces of human beings. Sigmund Freud and his disciples divided human character into the "id," which represented the beast (or instinct) in human beings, and the "ego," or self – the two of which were in constant conflict.

Today anthropomorphic animals are everywhere we look: tigers sell cornflakes and gasoline; talking cows sell milk; bulls and ducks represent sports teams. Centerfolds of undressed women in *Playboy* are called "bunnies," while in *Penthouse,* a rival magazine, they are called "pets." The cartoon character Joe Camel was so effective in selling cigarettes to teenagers that massive protests forced the tobacco company to discontinue ads with him in 1997.

Hatred as well as love can still "humanize" other creatures. Demonic animals fill our horror stories, such as *Cujo* by Stephen King (1981), named after a beloved pet who goes on a rampage of lurid murders. Perhaps Cujo was infected with rabies by a bat? Perhaps Cujo is a reincarnation of a policeman who killed many women? The author leaves the reader to decide. Diabolic animals also fill the silver screen, from the shark in *Jaws* to the tyrannosaurus in *Jurassic Park* and the snake in *Anaconda.*

Over the millennia, the greatest trend in our understanding of animals has been an increasing secularization. In early human settlements, animal gods replaced the totems of tribal societies. These deities, in turn, were generally subordinated to anthropomorphic gods and goddesses. By the Middle Ages, the predominant view of animals was symbolic and allegorical, and it became increasingly naturalistic in the modern period. Today, countless species are driven to extinction, and people, who are becoming increasingly urban, have ever less contact with animals on a daily basis. This has resulted in two seemingly contradictory trends.

On the one hand, there is ruthless exploitation of animals in factory farms and in industry. In 1989, an animal was patented for the first time: a mouse genetically engineered to develop cancer. The cloning of a sheep named Dolly in 1997 has largely broken down the boundary between living organisms and manufactured objects. There are now entire varieties called "pharm animals," developed solely to produce certain chemicals.

At the same time, our current estrangement from animals seems to have revived some of the numinous qualities they had in the archaic past. They connect us with a history in which people often seemed to live on a grander and more heroic scale than they do today. Now the discipline of ecology makes animals guardians of the ecosystem, and their fate is linked with that of human beings. Ecologists count frogs and butterflies to learn about a possible apocalypse; these researchers are a bit like the ancient priests of Greece or Babylon who would foretell the future from the flight of birds. Scientists have tried to decipher the languages of animals, from bees to monkeys.

Every animal is a tradition, and together animals are a vast part of our heritage as human beings. No animal completely lacks humanity, yet no person is ever completely human. By ourselves, we people are simply balls of protoplasm. We merge with animals through magic, metaphor, or fantasy, growing their fangs and putting on their feathers. Then we become funny or tragic; we can be loved, hated, pitied, and admired. For us, animals are all the strange, beautiful, pitiable, and frightening things that they have ever been: gods, slaves, totems, sages, tricksters, devils, clowns, companions, lovers, and far more. When we contemplate the inner life of animals, myth is finally our only truth.

REFERENCES

Boxer, Sarah. 1995. Look Into Those Big Bug Eyes and Shoot. *New York Times* 4 (August 27), 2.

Cooper, J. C. 1992. *Symbolic and Mythological Animals.* London: Aquarian/Thorson's.

Griffin, Donald R. 1976. *The Question of Animal Awareness: Evolutionary Continuity of Mental Experience.* New York: Rockefeller University Press.

King, Stephen. 1981. *Cujo.* New York: New American Library.

Le Guin, Ursula. 1987. *Buffalo Gals and Other Animal Presences.* New York: New American Library.

Montaigne, Michel de. "Apology for Raymond Sebond." In *The Complete Essays of Montaigne*, 2 vols. Trans. Donald M. Frame. Stanford: Stanford University Press, 1959, vol. 1, 428–561.

Orwell, George. 1946. *Animal Farm.* New York: Harcourt, Brace, Jovanovich/Signet Classics.

Rifkin, Jeremy. 1998. *The Biotech Century: Harnessing the Gene and Remaking the World.* New York: Jeremy P. Tarcher/Putnam.

Sax, Boria. 1990. *The Frog King: On Legends, Fables, Fairy Tales, and Anecdotes of Animals.* New York: Pace University Press.

———. 1990. *The Parliament of Animals: Legends and Anecdotes, 1775–1900.* New York: Pace University Press.

———. 2000. The Mermaid and Her Sisters: From Archaic Goddess to Consumer Society. *ISLE* 72 (summer), 43–54.

Scott, Sir Walter. 1832. *Letters on Demonology and Witchcraft.* J. and J. Harper.

Spiegelman, Art. 1991. *Maus: A Survivor's Tale.* 2 vols. New York: Pantheon.

29

STEVE BAKER

What is the Postmodern Animal?*

Steve Baker is an art historian who studies the history and theory of modern and contemporary art, with a focus on attitudes toward animals in art, philosophy, and popular culture. He is a founding member of the Animal Studies Group, a collection of UK scholars who work toward the promotion of the study of human-animal relationships in the humanities. Baker's research is centered by contemporary ethical issues and the ways that artists engage with animal biotechnology and "botched" (or subverted) taxidermy, an art motif that reconfigures the animal form. His first book, *Picturing the Beast*, examined the humorous and anthropocentric ways that animals are depicted in contemporary visual popular culture, and his recent *The Postmodern Animal* [from which we have extracted a portion for you to read here] assesses large ethical questions about animals, such as whether living animals can be justifiably used in works of art and whether art can be used to advocate for animals. While Lévi-Strauss's structuralism focused on the elements of culture that are organized around binary oppositions, poststructuralists such as Baker analyze elements that are not accounted for in a structuralist view, such as the multiple meaning of art forms. This multiplicity of meanings resonates with the central characteristic of the work of Deleuze and Guattari, which we discussed in Section 1 on animals as philosophical and ethical subjects. Baker argues that postmodern art is about creating distance from animals, producing an unsettled view of them that is fractured and awkward (such as skinned dogs, cats with modeled heads and dirty white toy seals). In this extract, Baker makes a distinction between animal-endorsing art (which would align itself with animal advocacy) and animal-skeptical art (which would question the cultural construction and classification of animals to make them meaningful to humans). He also argues that the future of the human is intimately linked to that of the animal, thus compromising the classic human-animal dualistic thinking endorsed by Descartes and other Enlightenment philosophers. Finally, Baker emphasizes that the focus of postmodern art is on the look of the animal body, a notion that will become increasingly important in our discussion of animals as scientific objects in Section 6.

* Extracted from *The Postmodern Animal* by Steve Baker, Reaktion Books, pp. 7–25 (London, 2000), with permission of the publisher.

De l'animal peut-on parler?

Jacques Derrida, 'L'Animal que donc je suis'[1]

At one end of the deep gallery space, the viewer is allocated a narrow corridor of clear floor across which to move. Beyond this, starting at knee height and rising unevenly like a choppy sea to the other distant end of the gallery, are piled large and impossibly bright white rectangles of polystyrene, in a surprisingly convincing approximation to the look of a cracked Arctic ice floe. There, up at the far end, beached on one of the higher ridges, and visible from either side of a Géricault-like raft of "ice" in the viewer's foreground, are what appear to be three grubby white stuffed toy seals.

Their appearance is slightly disconcerting, without it being easy to fix on a reason for this. They certainly call to mind the American artist Mike Kelley's views on the uncanny manner in which dirty homemade stuffed toys offend against art's demand for perfect form. At the same time, basking there in the inaccessible distance, they both interrupt and offer a point of focus for any viewing of the piece. It is perhaps no accident that the polystyrene ice floe, each fragile sheet of which could serve in another context as a fair-sized minimalist painting, is somehow sullied by the presence and centrality of these tatty creatures.

Spoiling the view, they are read as out of place. As anthropomorphic and romanticized images of the alienated human (the artist is invariably one such human), the seals invite viewers to stage their own mental confrontation between sentimental compassion and aesthetic satisfaction. Nietzsche, it seems certain, would have relished the sight of this futile battle between polystyrene sheets and stuffed toys, staged in the mock-serious imagery of Caspar David Friedrich and Géricault. This is the strange accomplishment of the piece; viewers *are* moved, even as they see that they are being manipulated. It is as though the artists are offering, ingenuously, the raw materials from which their viewers might care to spin out a meaning.

The effect of the installation, General Idea's *Fin de Siècle*, is easier to convey in words than in reproduction. This fact in itself reveals something of the awkwardness of thinking about the postmodern animal. This thing, this chosen creature, which is often the image of the artist or viewer at one remove (in this postmodern context the roles of artist and viewer are largely interchangeable), is difficult to reduce to what it looks like. As one commentator has written of *Fin de Siècle*, it threatens "the disappearance of visibility, the dissolution of bodies." [2]

There is a widespread perception that life is led differently now, faster and more precariously, for both humans and animals. If in part postmodernism embraces this, in the spirit of Nietzsche's injunction to "live dangerously!", it also sees the necessity of charting those new dangers, with a view to contesting them. In 1990 the philosopher Gilles Deleuze expressed the view that "we are at the beginning of something," and that to deal with the new circumstances there was "no need to fear or hope, but only to look for new weapons."[3] In art and in philosophy, postmodernism is both a theoretical and a practical enterprise, and its resistance to the dissolution of human and animal bodies often therefore takes the form of what has been called "an argument for *pleasure* in the confusion of boundaries and for *responsibility* in their construction."[4]

ENDORSEMENT AND SCEPTICISM

In *What is Nature?*, Kate Soper addresses a distinction in contemporary thinking about "nature" between the apparently practical concerns of ecology on the one hand, and the more theoretical emphases of postmodernism on the other. The former is concerned primarily with "the 'nature' that we are destroying, wasting and polluting;" the latter with "the ways in which relations to the nonhuman world are always historically mediated." Since in her view both perspectives may have necessary and complementary roles "in shaping a particular political outlook" on nature, she proposes "to speak of a contrast between what might be termed 'nature-endorsing' and 'nature-sceptical' arguments with no presumption being made that these reflect some simple antithesis between a 'green' and a 'postmodernist' politics."[5]

This promises to be a fruitful basis from which to begin to think more specifically about the diverse ways in which postmodern art has dealt with the animal, across a spectrum ranging from the *animal-endorsing* to the *animal-sceptical*. These terms, clumsier than Soper's, nevertheless point to the complexity of what it is that is called "animal" here. Animal-endorsing art will tend to endorse animal life itself (and may therefore align itself with the work of conservationists, or perhaps of animal advocacy), rather than endorsing cultural constructions of the animal. Animal-sceptical art, on the contrary, is likely to be sceptical not of animals themselves (as if the very existence of nonhuman life was in question), but rather of culture's means of constructing and classifying the animal in order to make it meaningful to the human.

A comparison of the use of animal imagery in the work of the American artist Mark Dion, and in that of the British artists Olly and Suzi, will help to clarify matters. All three artists admittedly share certain ecological and environmental concerns, but aside from this, their approaches appear to have little in common. Their differing perspectives are evident even in their exhibition titles: Dion's first major British exhibition, in 1997, was called *Natural History and Other Fictions*; Olly and Suzi's, in 1998, was called *Raw*.[6]

Dion is in many respects a typical postmodern artist – the epitome of what the philosopher Richard Rorty has called the postmodern "ironist theorist," whose responsibility is to call received wisdom into question.[7] Dion engages directly with theoretical perspectives. His interest in nature as "a constantly reinvented rhetorical construction," and in how such constructions have "articulated cultural anxieties about difference that separated *Homo sapiens* from other living creatures," is shaped in part by commentators on science such as Stephen Jay Gould and Donna Haraway.[8] He

has also expressed particular interest in the social anthropologist Tim Ingold's important book, *What is an Animal?*[9]

The subject common to many of his installations is not so much the animal itself, but rather the attempts of science and philosophy to devise secure hierarchies and taxonomies in which to place it. A typically complex (if visually concise) example of his work, from 1990, is *Taxonomy of Non-Endangered Species*. It places Georges Cuvier, the founder of comparative anatomy, halfway up a ladder in the guise of Mickey Mouse. The subject of his monologue – the animated speaking body is activated by a floor button – is to be the two orderly shelves of preserving jars, labelled in Latin, into which have been stuffed the whole and perfect bodies of Pluto, the Pink Panther, Babar the elephant, and others.

Conceived in response to the development of the EuroDisney complex, and exhibited in Paris to coincide with its opening, the piece has been described as "appropriating Cuvier's theories to expose the authoritarian world of Disney," whose theme parks include their own tableaux in which "animal characters proselytize about 'truths'" concerning the natural world.[10] For Dion the role of the artist as environmental activist is to employ "the rich set of tools, like irony, allegory and humour," which are less readily or imaginatively employed by the institutions which seek to promote particular "truths," such as science or the entertainment industry.[11]

Olly and Suzi's work, which principally takes the form of paintings and drawings of wild animals in their natural habitat, could hardly be more different. They intend their paintings of endangered predators to convey a simple and direct message which is entirely free of postmodern irony: "the animals are here now, they just might not be for much longer."[12] Their images attempt to express directly their sense of the beauty and perfection of these animals. This approach, which is perhaps unusually straightforward in the context of contemporary art, undoubtedly prompts the question of whether the naturalistic representation of animals can really be called postmodern. There are compelling reasons for saying that it can.

Since 1993 the artists have sought to make pieces which reflect their immediate encounters and interactions with animals in the wild. The *Raw* exhibition, of work made since 1995, included paintings of lions, zebra, wild dogs, and rhinoceros in the African bush, polar bears in the Arctic tundra, tigers and elephants in Nepal, leopards and tigers in India, white sharks in the ocean off South Africa, and ravens, wolves, and deer in Minnesota. Often operating in difficult or dangerous circumstances, as close as they can get to these animals, and "reacting to everything that's around us," they typically work on white or cream paper with materials such as natural pigments, soil, plant colourings, blood, inks, and dyes. The two of them work simultaneously on each image, "hand over hand."

Aside from an absence of sentimentality or "prettifying" in their work, two further features distinguish them from more traditional "wildlife" artists. One is that the making of the pieces is extensively documented, "as a performance," by the photographer Greg Williams, who travels with them. The other is that whenever possible the depicted animals are encouraged, without manipulation or coercion, to "interact" with the work and mark it further themselves. This may take the form of bears or elephants leaving prints or urine stains on the image, or of chunks being bitten off a piece by a wolf or a shark. Exceptional cases, where the "artistic interaction" did not go entirely to plan, include a leopard dragging a painting away and destroying it, and a rhinoceros eating a whole piece.

COMMON GROUND: TRUTH AND AUTHORSHIP

The comparison of Dion with Olly and Suzi indicates something of the range of serious contemporary art employing animal imagery. Beyond some level of ecological engagement and an interest in animals themselves, there are, however, surprising areas and issues of common concern in their attitudes to art and to the responsibilities of the artist.

The question of truth is one such issue. Postmodern scepticism about the operation of truth and knowledge has undoubtedly complicated any thinking about animals: about what counts as "authentic" experience, about the experience of wonder or fear as antidotes to anthropocentrism, and about the extent to which it is possible to shed what Olly and Suzi call the "baggage" of their Western thought. Dion has explained his interest "in pre-Enlightenment collections like curiosity cabinets and *wunderkammers*" in terms of the way they "tested reason" and attested to the marvellous. Questioned as to how he might provoke a contemporary sense of the marvellous, he replied: "One thing is to tell the truth, which is by far more astounding than any fiction. (I cringe as the word 'truth' passes my lips, but I always mean it with a lower case 't'.)"[13] Olly and Suzi, when specifically asked whether their work sought to communicate a "truth" about animals, have been similarly cautious about the word: "Our way of working aims to express our view of the world, which is our 'truth' ... We can't really say that there is one truth and we're aiming to get at that."

In the incorporation of marks made by animals in some of their finished pieces, however, there is a very specific attempt to overcome viewers' postmodern sense of not knowing or believing what they are seeing. A work such as *Shark Bite*, exhibited along with the ragged corner ripped off by the shark, spat out and subsequently recovered, attests to the presence or existence of the living animal. The photographic documentation of the event, also exhibited in *Raw*, offers an important but somehow *lesser* – or at least more conventional, familiar, and thus more easily ignored – record of its existence. It is only the painting as object, as thing, marked by the animal itself, which can indelibly record the immediacy and "truth" of the encounter.

In this respect, as far as the artists' environmental message (as opposed to their aesthetic sensibility) is concerned, it could be said that it hardly matters what the painting looks like. The key thing is its status as the mark of the real, the wound, the touch: "by the end of the trip this paper's been transformed from its clinical state into a document, it's like a piece of parchment, a genuine artifact of the event." While an artist like Dion might question the feasibility of any such unmediated communication with the viewer, hedged around as it is by the institutional trappings of its display, he would at least be sympathetic to the attempt to overcome the typically deadening effect of galleries and museums, in which "the viewer is always passive."[14]

In addition to the question of truth, there is significant common ground between Dion and Olly and Suzi in terms of how they position themselves as artists. They share an interest not only in Joseph Beuys's use of animals in his art, but in how he drew together the roles of artist, environmental activist, and educator. The title of one of Olly and Suzi's paintings, *Deer for Beuys*, is a direct tribute to the artist they see as "the foremost environmentalist in the art world." In the educational dimension of their work, and in their field trips, both they and Dion necessarily work closely and cooperatively with individuals who do not see themselves as artists. Dion has said that "making art is no longer confined to the institutional spaces that we've created for such activity. It's more in the 'field' now. The focus is on relations and processes – an ecology of art if you will."[15] Much the same could be said of Olly and Suzi's approach: they abandoned studio work in 1993.

Such working procedures are by no means wholly new, of course. In addition to Beuys, Dion is conscious of other influences on his own disruption of "the notion of an originating author." They include the activist aesthetics of his former teacher, Hans Haacke, and the example of Marcel Broodthaers's subversion of the authority of both artist and museum in his *Musée d'Art Moderne, Département des Aigles* in the early 1970s.[16] Broodthaers's provocative project included labelling each eagle exhibit with the caption "This is not a work of art."

New or not, the kind of unassuming "complex authorship" responsible for the production of these contemporary artists' work – most strikingly evident not only in Olly and Suzi's collaborative "hand over hand" technique, but in the occasional participation of animals themselves in the mark-making – has recently been characterized specifically as "a strategy for the times."[17]

THE LIVING ANIMAL AS POSTMODERN ANIMAL

A further word must be said about the significance of the living animal for these artists, and the "use" they make of it. In 1993 Dion made a complex installation entitled *Library for the Birds of Antwerp*, which incorporated eighteen living African finches. The installation was sited in the city's Museum of Contemporary Art, and during the exhibition the finches flew freely around the gallery space, perching on the tree-like structure at its centre. Like much of Dion's work, the piece was both a site-specific response to local history and a commentary on broader ecological issues such as the extinction of bird species.

As Norman Bryson explains in a thoughtful essay on this piece, the birds were purchased in Antwerp's Vogelmarkt, which continues a trade in exotic birds that began in the sixteenth century. The installation included signs of this trade, such as wooden cages, metal traps and cartridges of birdshot, as part of a wider set of references to extinction (the image of a dodo, books on extinct bird species from the Americas), all wedged into or hung from the branches of the apparently diseased tree. Bryson reads the tree as a "by now ironic image of man's place at the pinnacle of the evolutionary hierarchy."

It is the living birds, however, which do the real work of the piece. "Through the conceit that birds are readers," Bryson writes, the book-laden tree stages an encounter between "man-made systems of knowledge on one side, and on the other side a realm beyond those systems, a Nature whose properties remain radically unknown and unknowable." This seems a fair assessment of Dion's approach, which seeks to demystify human blinkeredness rather than human fascination with the nonhuman world. As Bryson puts it, the birds in the piece mark a reality which exists "as an excess lying beyond the scope of representation, as a reserve which the production of truth draws upon, but cannot exhaust or contain."[18]

For Olly and Suzi too, the animal is a reminder of the limits of human understanding and influence, but also of the value of working *at those limits*. The very existence of dangerous wild animals "keeps us in check," they state, and serves to warn that humans (including artists) are "not the boss of everything." The reality of the animals' existence, and the artists' physical proximity to those animals, is central to their work. Whatever else happens, "we have to have an experience in the bush," and the work emerges directly from that experience. They recognize that the benefits of their experiences and interactions with animals "are, in the short term at least, in our favour, despite our long-term objectives of helping the animals' predicament,"[19] but their work, like Dion's, stands as a marker – a concise encapsulation – of what they perceive as the interdependence of humans and animals in the contemporary world.

The comparison of these artists' work was introduced with Soper's modification of the distinction between "green" and postmodern priorities. Rather like Soper, though across a wider range of cultural, scientific, and political issues, Wendy Wheeler has also recently stressed the common ground here. She describes the postmodern not only in terms of a calling into question of earlier certainties about "the value of science, rationality and progress" (a familiar enough description), but also as a new sensibility: "the Cartesian dualism which has so fundamentally structured the modern world is in the process of being replaced by what is, in the broadest possible sense, an ecological sensibility." In this "more holistic" new perspective, notions of order, reason and the body are, she contends, being expanded "through a growing understanding of the creative complexity of the world, and of the creatures amongst whom we move and in whom we have our being – as do they in us."[20]

Although the implications of this last phrase are not drawn out in detail by Wheeler, it is striking to find an account of the postmodern which alludes so directly to animals, and which proposes that the future of the human in the postmodern world is so intimately and creatively bound up with that of the animal. From this perspective, the classic dualism of human and animal is not so much erased as *rendered uninteresting* as a way of thinking about being in the world.

ART AND PHILOSOPHY

A postmodern artist or writer is in the position of a philosopher...

Jean-François Lyotard[21]

Some of the most adventurous and influential developments in recent Western art and philosophy have taken a deeply sceptical view of what has come to be seen as the divisive and defensive "common-sense" account of identity. Whether described in terms of the heritage of Enlightenment rationalism or liberal humanism, this account of the privileged and empowered individual, often epitomized by the figure of the creative artist or author, has for several decades been the object of a destabilizing rhetoric. In 1966 Foucault had envisaged the possibility of circumstances arising in which "man's mode of being as constituted in modern thought" might "crumble." By the 1990s the rhetoric (not always backed by sound historical argument) proposed that the postmodern should also be considered a *posthuman* condition.[22]

It is in the culture's art forms that the evidence of this changed condition has often been sought. It has been plausibly suggested, for example, that Ted Hughes's poem "Wodwo" – in which a creature, strange to itself, searches for clues to its possible identity – "inhabits a world beyond humanism, in which the human can no longer be taken for granted, but must be rediscovered anew in each encounter with a ceaselessly changing reality."[23] Such views are current in the various manifestations of poststructuralist theory, and in postmodern art's intense and critical focus on the body. The encounters they address will often be difficult or uncomfortable. Donna Haraway gives clear expression to this view. Acknowledging that there seems to be an inescapable need for "something called humanity," she writes: "We also know now, from our perspectives in the ripped-open belly of the monster called history, that we cannot name and possess this thing which we cannot not desire."[24]

Many postmodern or poststructuralist artists and writers seem, at one level or another, to adopt or to identify with the animal as a metaphor for, or as an image of, their own creativity. Whether it connotes a sense of alienation from the human or a sense of bodily freedom and unboundedness, this willing taking-on of animal form casts the fixity of identity as an inhibition of creativity. Is this part of a genuinely open-minded process of thinking anew, or just another badge with which to secure an intelligible identity? Questions of identity on the one hand, and of creativity on the other, represent two major and interlocking strands of *The Postmodern Animal's* investigation.

In that investigation, art and philosophy offer complementary perspectives; as Mary Midgley neatly expresses it, "our imagination needs both art and philosophy." Among some of the more poetic philosophers, at least, there is agreement that art (in the widest sense) offers access to a kind of truth to which a more narrowly defined philosophy is blind. Heidegger writes of there being "fundamentally different *kinds of truth*," of which art is one, and Adorno specifically suggests that art and philosophy each address gaps in the other's view of the world: "Only in combination," as Albrecht Wellmer summarizes it, "are they capable of circumscribing a truth which neither alone is able to articulate."[25]

Much of *The Postmodern Animal* therefore tries to read examples of the art and the philosophy in relation to each other, looking not only for correspondences but for ways in which each might test the other. The notion of the postmodern adopted here is broadly that envisaged by Lyotard in *The Postmodern Condition*. The postmodern stands for the forms in which imaginative thought necessarily challenges the complacency of the age, an unthinking "consensus" of politics and of taste which would prefer "to put an end to experimentation," "to liquidate the heritage of the avant-gardes," and instead "to offer the reader or viewer matter for solace and pleasure."[26] These remarks have lost none of their relevance in the years since Lyotard made them, and they have a particular pertinence in relation to questions of the animal. No rethinking of human or animal identity is likely to emerge, it is clear, if art and philosophy choose to present the animal primarily as matter for human "solace and pleasure."

[…]

WHAT WAS THE MODERN ANIMAL?

Mark Dion and Olly and Suzi share a common perception that their concerns, as artists, have only recently come to be recognized as serious and valid. Dion notes of his own development that in "the slick world of Conceptual and media-based art" in the early 1980s, "no one seemed interested in problems of nature"; Olly and Suzi recognize a continuing widespread reservation over the idea of the animal "as a serious subject in contemporary art."[27] If the postmodern animal appears awkwardly to lurch or stumble into being in recent art, this is perhaps because it does not follow in the steps of a modern animal.

The very idea of a "postmodern" animal, however loosely the term is employed, inevitably provokes the question "what was the *modern* animal?" *The Postmodern Animal's* hypothesis is that there was no modern animal, no "modernist" animal. Between nineteenth-century animal symbolism, with its reasonably secure hold on meaning, and the postmodern animal images whose ambiguity or irony or sheer brute presence serves to resist or to displace fixed meanings, lies modernism at its most arid. This hypothesis, it must be said, is essentially art-historical in its emphases: it is specifically to do with *the look of the animal body*, and with what that look was understood to say about the artist responsible for the representation.

For modern art, the imperatives of formalism and abstraction rendered the image of the human difficult enough. The image of the animal was further hampered by memories of the unashamedly anthropomorphic sentiment of an earlier age, which could hardly have been more at odds with the values of the self-consciously serious modernist avant-gardes. The animal is the very first thing to be ruled out of modernism's bounds. From then onwards it was what a picture must be understood to be "before being a battle horse" which would count, according to the classic modernist dictum.[28]

There are therefore no animals in major cubist works ... So might begin a rather tedious listing of the animal's absence from much of the twentieth century's most adventurous and imaginative visual art. Such a list would need to explain that even when the animal was visually present, it could be explained away, and that one function of modernist art criticism was to do so. So the animals in *Guernica* or in Heartfield's photomontages were a necessary part of the political symbolism of those works; those in the paintings of Marc, or of Pollock, were a mere step on the ladder toward a more mature abstraction; those in Brancusi's sculptures should not be taken too seriously because he was better understood as one of those key modernists who "derive their chief inspiration from the medium they work in;"[29] and so on.

No matter that Brancusi regarded as "imbeciles" those who called his work abstract; in his own view his realism stemmed from the fact that "what is real is not the exterior form but the idea, the essence of things."[30] Modernist criticism had little apparent interest in doing so, but it is certainly possible to read Brancusi's animal motifs (the fish, the turtle, the birds) as examples of the human imagining-itself-other. They represent the dream of unimpeded movement through air or water: a nonhuman, *non-pedestrian* movement in the strange imaginative spaces of the animal.

Perhaps the most striking example in the art of the early twentieth century of an attempt to think outside the secure perspectives of the human, however, is Franz Marc's 1911 essay "How does a horse see the world?" Arguing that it was "typical of our best painters that they avoid living subject matter," Marc outlined his alternative:

> How does a horse see the world, how does an eagle, a doe, or a dog? It is a poverty-stricken convention to place animals into landscapes as seen by men ... It's the doe that feels, therefore the landscape must be 'doe-like.' That is its predicate. The artistic logic of Picasso, Kandinsky, Delaunay, Burljick, etc., is perfect. They don't 'see' the doe and they don't care. They project *their* inner world ... I could paint a picture called *The Doe*. Pisanello has painted them. I may also want to paint a picture, *The Doe Feels*. How infinitely more subtle must the painter's sensitivity be in order to paint that![31]

In a matter of a few years, however, Marc had moved away from such exercises in proprioception, and had begun more closely to embrace abstraction as the style appropriate to a heroic conception of modern art. He justified his new priorities as "nothing other than the highly conscious, action-hungry determination to overcome sentimentality."[32]

As the example of modernist art history as a whole suggests, the animal comes to be least visible in the discourses which regard themselves as the most serious. The modern animal is thus the nineteenth-century animal (symbolic, sentimental), which has been *made to disappear*. On the rare occasions it is anything other than the absented image of this earlier creature, it is the proto-postmodern animal of surrealism, for example, and perhaps of some very early Disney animations: that which disturbs.

It is therefore perhaps unsurprising that it is in its less disturbing and more abstracted form that the modernist animal meets with critical success, as in Henry Moore's monumental bronze *Sheep Piece*, from the early 1970s. This piece has been described as "a landmark in the evolution of

Moore's sculpture," and is said to be regarded by Anthony Caro as one of Moore's finest works.[33] When set alongside a very different rendering of the same animal, Edwina Ashton's 1997 video performance *Sheep*, it offers an opportunity to see what is at stake in the shift from a modernist to a postmodern disposition or sensibility with regard to animals.

Although close in time to Moore's *Sheep Sketchbook*, drawn from nature in 1972, whose animals Peter Fuller has remarked "could not be more sharply observed," *Sheep Piece* in fact derives from a maquette made in 1969. Like many of his "animal" sculptures, it owes "more to the imagination than to observation." According to one account, at least, the finished bronze acquired its title not from its subject matter but from the fact that it became "a rubbing and sheltering post for sheep" in the field in which it was first placed.[34] Moore himself admitted "I can see animals in anything, really." Commentators have followed him in this, seeing the piece as "a summing up of his feeling about sheep form," or variously finding in it "suggestions of a ram mounting a ewe or of a lamb nuzzling its mother."[35]

The animals in Ashton's *Sheep* are envisaged quite differently. The piece runs for four minutes, and is seen on two adjacent video screens. On the right, a figure dressed as a sheep looks across, as it were, to the other screen, on which an apparently identically dressed figure, in much the same setting, sits at a desk with its script. In a faltering voice, and endlessly, agitatedly wringing its "hands," this second sheep recites a series of truly dreadful sheep jokes. "Why do sheep hate pens? Because they can't write." "Can you stop making that noise with the paper. Why? Because I hate sheep rustlers." Most of the jokes are told hesitantly or badly. "My dad, my dad's car got nicked. Oh no – who by? A ram raider." "What do you call a lady with a dog on her head? Mutton Mutton."

There is a peculiar play of engagement and disengagement in the piece. Both performers are Ashton herself, but with her voice disguised: "I don't want to be in them," she has said of all her video performances. The animal was chosen not for its appeal but because, in her view, "sheep are hideously ugly." A long time was spent "trying to get the faces right" on the hand-made costumes, to achieve "a sufficient degree of blankness" while nevertheless keeping a kind of "haphazard" look. The speaking sheep's voice, in contrast, is intended to be entirely human (but not recognizably Ashton's) rather than attempting to imitate the animal.[36]

What can be learned from Moore's and Ashton's contrasting takes on sheep form, if read as rather arbitrarily chosen representatives of modern and postmodern perspectives? Neither perspective, significantly, need involve a *sympathy* for the animal: it would be quite wrong automatically to associate animal imagery in postmodern art with any overtly pro-animal stance.

Nevertheless, there is a proximity to and engagement with the animal in Ashton's video which is absent from Moore's sculpture. For Moore the sheep is always outside, a thing quite separate from himself. It is a thing to be addressed and presented (whether through observation *or* imagination) by means of the authority and expertise of the artist, who surrenders nothing to it. Ashton is literally stuck inside her sheep, uncomfortably so, wringing her hands and disguising her voice, telling bad jokes at the expense of the animal identity she has taken on, which itself is only stated in "haphazard" fashion. *Sheep Piece* is not about animal identity: the artist secures his own identity by keeping his distance from the animal. *Sheep*, on the other hand, is wholly about problematized identity, about awkward conjunctions of human and animal which seem typical of much postmodern art but which have few parallels in modernism.

There is of course a severe risk of caricaturing the distinction in any such comparison, and of overstating both modernism's concern with purity and wholeness and postmodernism's preparedness to cast aside the secure trappings of human identity. It may also be that such distinctions, to the extent that they are justified at all, can be traced just as readily within differing manifestations of the postmodern itself.

Among the proliferating theories of the post-modern in recent times, there are several instances of the idea of there being two distinct postmodern "moments." In the field of art, for example, Hal Foster distinguishes the work of "early postmodernists" who appeared to "delight in the sheer image," from that of "later postmodernists" who sought instead to "possess the real thing." This is not presented as an unproblematically good thing – it marks a shift in artists' preoccupations from "the highs of the simulacral image" to "the lows of the depressive object" – but Foster's language certainly implies a shift from superficiality to seriousness.[37]

Wendy Wheeler has similarly proposed two distinct stages of the postmodern. The first stage often involved (at a safe theoretical distance from its effect on real lives) an indulgent and rather inhuman celebration of "the fragmenting of texts and bodies," in forms that were typically "ironic or parodic." The second, more constructive contemporary stage she characterizes as "a 'postmodern' rebuilding," oriented toward ways of "rethinking human beings" and readdressing the world; it is a wholly serious and creative attempt "to imagine differently reconstituted communities and selves" and to heal the destructively fragmented experience of the contemporary world.[38]

Foster and Wheeler seem primarily concerned to describe successive stages in the historical development of the postmodern condition: an early superficial postmodernism of the 1970s and 1980s; and a later and more mature postmodernism, the effects of which are still operative at the start of the new millennium. [...] It is important to understand, however, that these two postmodernisms are at the very least *open to being read* as something other than stages in a history which moves from a blinkered "then" to an enlightened "now." They represent alternative dispositions, perspectives or emphases, which coexist and often compete.

If the book [*The Postmodern Animal*]'s emphasis ... is almost exclusively on the "second" of these dispositions, this is not because it seems more optimistic, or appears to hold out the prospect of a "better" future for animals, but because it is more genuinely curious and engaged. It is closer, in other words, to Lyotard's understanding of the work of the postmodern artist or philosopher. Regardless of whether its priorities are judged to be more humane or less humane, it is undoubtedly more serious about the animal, and is just possibly less fearful of it.

NOTES

1. Jacques Derrida, "L'Animal que done je suis (à suivre)", in *L'Animal autobiographique: Autour de Jacques Derrida*, ed. M.-L. Mallet (Paris, 1999), p. 271.
2. Joshua Decter, "General Idea: The Sensuous Whiteness of Life's Interruptions", in *General Idea*, exh. cat.: Camden Arts Centre, London (London, 1998), unpaginated.
3. Gilles Deleuze, "Postscript on the Societies of Control", *October*, LIX (1992), pp. 7, 4.
4. Donna J. Haraway, *Simians, Cyborgs, and Women: The Reinvention of Nature* (New York, 1991), p. 150.
5. Kate Soper, *What is Nature?: Culture, Politics and the non-Human* (Oxford and Cambridge, MA, 1995), pp. 3–4.
6. See *Natural History and Other Fictions: An Exhibition by Mark Dion*, exh. cat. by J. Leslie: Ikon Gallery, Birmingham; Kunstverein, Hamburg; De Appel Foundation, Amsterdam (Birmingham, Hamburg and Amsterdam, 1997); and *Raw: Olly and Suzi*, exh. cat. by K. Pierrepont: Blains Fine Art, London (London, 1998).
7. Richard Rorty, *Contingency, Irony, and Solidarity* (Cambridge and New York, 1989), p. 96.
8. Lisa Graziose Corrin, "Mark Dion's Project: A Natural History of Wonder and a Wonderful History of Nature", in Lisa Graziose Corrin, Miwon Kwon, and Norman Bryson, *Mark Dion* (London, 1997), pp. 39, 47.
9. Mark Dion, conversation with the author, May 1998. See *What is an Animal?*, ed. T. Ingold (London, 1988).
10. Corrin, "Mark Dion's Project", pp. 55–7.
11. Mark Dion, "Interview", in Corrin, Kwon, and Bryson, *Mark Dion*, p. 33.

12. Olly and Suzi, unpublished interview with the author, London, August 1998. All further quotations from the artists are from this interview.

13. Dion, "Interview", pp. 17–18.

14. Ibid., p. 17.

15. Ibid., p. 22.

16. See Corrin, "Mark Dion's Project", pp. 49, 46, 50.

17. Richard Johnson, "Complex Authorships: Intellectual Coproduction as a Strategy for the Times", *Angelaki*, III/3 (1998).

18. Norman Bryson, "Mark Dion and the Birds of Antwerp", in Corrin, Kwon, and Bryson, *Mark Dion*, pp. 92, 96–7.

19. Olly and Suzi, interview with the author, August 1998, and correspondence with the author, September 1998.

20. Wendy Wheeler, *A New Modernity?: Change in Science, Literature and Politics* (London, 1999), pp. 7, 5.

21. Jean-François Lyotard, *The Postmodern Condition: A Report on Knowledge*, trans. G. Bennington and B. Massumi (Manchester, 1984), p. 81.

22. Michel Foucault, *The Order of Things: An Archaeology of the Human Sciences* (London, 1970), p. 344; Robert Pepperell, *The Post-Human Condition* (Oxford, 1995), passim.

23. Tony Davies, *Humanism* (London and New York, 1997), p. 135.

24. Donna Haraway, "Ecce Homo, Ain't (Ar'n't) I a Woman, and Inappropriate/d Others: The Human in a Post-humanist Landscape", in *Feminists Theorize the Political*, eds J. Butler and J. W. Scott (New York and London, 1992), p. 88.

25. Mary Midgley, *Utopias, Dolphins and Computers: Problems of Philosophical Plumbing* (London and New York, 1996), p. 25; Martin Heidegger, quoted in Will McNeill, *Heidegger: Visions: Of Animals, Others and the Divine* (Warwick, 1993), p. 40; Albrecht Wellmer, *The Persistence of Modernity: Essays on Aesthetics, Ethics, and Postmodernism*, trans. D. Midgley (Cambridge, MA, 1991), p. 7.

26. Jean-François Lyotard, *The Postmodern Condition*, pp. 71, 73, 81.

27. Dion, "Interview," p. 8; Olly and Suzi, artists' statement, 1998.

28. Maurice Denis, "Definition of Neotraditionism" (1890), in *Theories of Modern Art: A Source Book by Artists and Critics*, ed. H. B. Chipp (Berkeley, Los Angeles, and London, 1968), p. 94: "It is well to remember that a picture before being a battle horse, a nude woman, or some anecdote – is essentially a plane surface covered with colours assembled in a certain order."

29. Clement Greenberg, "Avant-Garde and Kitsch" (1939), in *Art in Theory 1900–1990: An Anthology of Changing Ideas*, eds C. Harrison and P. Wood (Oxford, 1992), p. 532.

30. Constantin Brancusi, "Aphorisms (ca. 1957)", in *Theories of Modern Art*, ed. H. B. Chipp, p. 365.

31. Franz Marc, "How Does a Horse See the World?", in *Theories of Modern Art*, pp. 178–9.

32. Franz Marc, "Aphorisms, 1914–1915", in *Theories of Modern Art*, p. 181.

33. W. J. Strachan, *Henry Moore: Animals* (London, 1983), p. 75; Roger Berthoud, *The Life of Henry Moore* (London and Boston, 1987), p. 344.

34. Peter Fuller, *Henry Moore: An Interpretation* (London, 1993), p. 54; Strachan, *Henry Moore: Animals,* p. 10; Berthoud, *The Life of Henry Moore*, p. 344.

35. Strachan, *Henry Moore: Animals,* pp. 9 (quoting Moore), 75; Berthoud, *The Life of Henry Moore*, p. 344.

36. Edwina Ashton, unpublished interview with the author, London, April 1999.

37. Hal Foster, *The Return of the Real: The Avant-Garde at the End of the Century* (Cambridge, MA and London, 1996), p. 165.

38. Wheeler, *A New Modernity?*, pp. 90, 8, 74.

30

JONATHAN BURT[1]

The Illumination of the Animal Kingdom: The Role of Light and Electricity in Animal Representation*

Jonathan Burt is an animal historian with a diverse set of interests including art, music, geography, world history, film history and environmental and agricultural history. He edits *Animal*, a book series devoted to the cultural history of individual animals, and is a founding member of the Animals Studies Group [as is Steve Baker]. Burt is the author of *Animals in Film*, an examination of the relationship between animals, cinema, and photography and how the animal as a visual object structures human responses toward animals. This thesis is also reflected in the article reproduced here, an essay that focuses on animal imagery and technology in three important arenas of human-animal relationships: films, zoos, and slaughterhouses. Burt argues that changes in animal representations in the public domain set the boundaries for the acceptable treatment of animals. Emphasizing the historical link between visual images of cruelty to animals and moral concern, he examines film (particularly those that show the killing of animals) and zoo display (obstruction-free enclosures intended to display the animal in a "natural" environment) as technologies that enhance animal visibility and thus change human emotions and reactions to animals. Burt concludes with a history of the use of electrical stunning in slaughterhouses. Electrocution was considered morally acceptable because of the perception that it was a clean form of killing, more civilized and technologically advanced than the "barbarous" act of hanging to death, and because decent meat depended on decent treatment of the meat animal, electrical stunning reduced stress and anxiety at slaughter. In all three examples, the issue of what is considered humane is tied to technological development, and animal representations are subjects framed by technology.

This essay addresses the subject of animal representation via a historical account of the place of the animal in visual culture. It emphasizes the relationship between the animal as a visual image and the technology that produces this image. It explores three examples in a period covering *c.*1895 to the 1930s, in Britain, that analyze the relations between animal representation,

* Reprinted from Jonathan Burt (2001) "The Illumination of the Animal Kingdom: The Role of Light and Electricity in Animal Representation," *Society and Animals* 9(3): 203–228, with permission from Brill Academic Publishers.

technology, and the public domain. These are film, zoo display, and slaughterhouse practice. The overall goal of the essay is to move away from emphasis on the textual, metaphorical animal, which reduces the animal to a mere icon, to achieve a more integrated view of the effects of the presence of the animals and the power of its imagery in human history.

> "[s]i l'animal a le temps, s'il est «constitué» par un «temps»" ["[w]hether the animal has time, whether the animal is 'constituted' by a 'time'"]. (Derrida 1999, 273)

The history of animals is, among other things, the history of the disappearance of the animal, and there are two slightly different senses in which we might understand the idea of this "history of disappearance." The first relates to a process that has been going on for a long time but in recent decades has accelerated alarmingly, namely the gradual disappearance of species of all forms of wildlife and the reduction in global biodiversity.

The second sense, which might be expressed more accurately by the term "effacement" rather than "disappearance," concerns the ways in which the representation of the animal – indeed the history of animal representation – is limited to a human framework or where the animals are depicted as if they were quasi-human (anthropomorphism). In such instances, the animal is overlaid with metaphors of human characteristics or becomes the bearer of purely human concerns.

Clearly, the second sense of disappearance is not as absolute and certainly is more partial than the first. However, modes of representation have a widespread impact on the way animals are culturally conceived, and structure our attitudes to the real disappearances of animals. Furthermore, and this is the main concern of this essay, the way in which we portray animal representation has a crucial bearing on how we portray the place of animals in history and the trajectory such a history is conceived to take.

One of the ironies of animals' not speaking is that so much should be written about the animal as a symbol conveying human meaning. Most of the relations humans have with animals and their reactions to animals are founded in the realms of emotion, instinct, and, in problematic ways, desire. There are exceptions: communication is significant in companion-animal caretaking and, more directly, in the ape-language projects. Furthermore, many aspects of animal-human relations are bizarre.

One of the most commonly noted examples of this is the inconsistency between the celebration of animals in, say, nature films or pet-keeping and the simultaneous sanctioning of, or presiding over, the destruction of animal life on an enormous scale. It is, perhaps, to avoid the full implications of this strangeness that we choose to find a place for them in a well-organized cultural logic that divides the animal world into categories like pet, vermin, threatened species, and expendable species. Certainly, a logic of sorts can be identified at the practical interface between animals and humans, but, in truth, it is multi-faceted, and the representations that arise there [are] usually over-determined and contradictory.

Generally, problems that arise in relation to the representation of animals are exacerbated by the conceptual dyad of human-animal and, by extension, culture-nature. These oppositions concentrate on, in the sense of bringing into focus, issues of symbolic difference and human identity, but there is a temptation to make this the template, or dominant terminology, by which we write about animals. This also leads to a tendency to make animals fit in with the dominant concerns and anxieties of a particular period, playing down the ways that they may be read against the grain of an epoch or culture. A good instance of this can be found in a study of the London Zoo in the nineteenth century: "[A]nimals were to be viewed as metonyms of imperial triumph, civic pride, and the beneficence of God or scientific discovery" (Jones 1997, 5). Such a remark ignores other more ambivalent and contradictory discourses that surrounded the Zoo at the time, such as those that saw the Zoo as a site of animal indecency or cruelty.[2] In addition, the metaphorical or metonymic status of the animal leads to the animal being treated as a type of *tabula rasa* that can signify anything we wish. A contemporary example of this can be found in Lippit (2000): Animals "simply transmit ... [they are] unable to withhold the outflow of the flow of signals and significations with which they are endowed" (21).

It is ironic that within the strictures of the human-animal divide the animal should have such an arbitrary and shifting representational status. It is a measure of how difficult it is to escape from this pattern of thinking that even when the terms "human" and "animal" are explored in ways that radically contest their familiar meanings, as in Derrida (1999), the conclusion, of this text at least, is a series of questions. They start with, "What is an animal?" and end with a question about self-identity, "Who am I?" (301). Ironically, given the conceptual radicalism of much post-modernist writing, Derrida here follows a predictable path: the passage from the animal that always leads back to the human.

The problem that arises for the study of animals in history is that treating the animal as an icon, paradoxically, places the animal outside history. The role is purely symbolic; it reflects historical processes without truly being part of them. Being detached from what might be called the historical dynamics of a culture makes it difficult to assess the manner in which animals influence these dynamics. This is one of the reasons why the animal often is associated with the archaic and nostalgic rather than change, "progress," or even modernity. Historians who have tended to focus on the human meanings conveyed or embodied in animals have reinforced this sense of the ahistorical. Kete (1994) describes the bourgeois pet in 1860s and 1870s Paris as the "counter-icon of the scientific, and dehumanised, age" (7). French (1975) considers the anti-vivisectionists of the late nineteenth century in England to be protesting at the "shape of the century to come" (212). Ritvo (1987) describes the early nineteenth-century attitude to nature as one of sentiment and nostalgia because nature has "ceased to be a constant antagonist" (3).

To associate the animal with types of conservatism emphasizes that many histories of animal representation also are subject to the same structural principles as the ones they are describing. In addition, the choices of themes such as pedigree and breeding, civic values, and empire give animals a formidable cultural weight while reducing their role to one that is merely totemic. (I hasten to add that these studies are invaluable, and it is more a question of supplementing than rejecting them.)

To supplement such studies with an account of representation that is driven more by the idea of animals as figures in their own right does not mean writing a more optimistic or sunnier history of human-animal relations. In this particular study, which involves looking at the impact of electricity and illumination on various aspects of animal representation, the animal has a prototypical status derived from being an experimental object. Although this status evolves from its role in science, the technological aspects of animal representation that derive from this science are very much part of the popular domain. Thus, animals have complicated roles to play. Animals become central figures in the presentation of new and "progressive" technology. They are represented as acting beings in their own right. They are locked into discourses of health, moral improvement, conservation, and vitality.

These discourses, to a large extent, are future-oriented and concern the improving paths society needs to take. In this instance, animals do not lead back to the human in quite the way they do in anthropomorphic discourse. Instead, the animal has a more ambivalent role because these technologies entail other ramifications such as social control and efficiency. It also is important to note that the media of animal representation are crucial to its analysis; in such a context, whether we are dealing with the twentieth century or earlier, the relations of animal to technology are just as important as relations to the human.

CHANGING CONFIGURATIONS OF ANIMAL VISIBILITY AND INVISIBILITY

The disappearance of species and the effacement of the animal in anthropomorphism have no intrinsic relation to each other as such. However, there is an important argument famously proposed by Berger (1980) to suggest a causal relation between the disappearance and extinction of animals and an increasing diffusion of animal imagery, particularly given that they coincide historically during the nineteenth century (24). In other words, animal representation comes to compensate for the growing absence of the animal in daily life.

At one level, Berger (1980) is incorrect, given the widespread variety of animal representation. Furthermore, the growth of animal representation in film, photography, and print, which is particularly noticeable toward the end of the nineteenth century, coincides with the expansion of the animal-welfare movement and nature conservation (Kean 1998; Grove 1995). Berger, however, does point us in an important direction, because the ways in which the animal is seen and not seen – the connection between presence and absence – do change in the nineteenth century and, thus, have a direct bearing on animal representation. Changes in configurations of animal visibility and invisibility not only determine the style of presentation of animals in the public domain but also demarcate the boundaries of how animals should be treated in a civilized society. Unfortunately, as I shall now show, the interaction of animals with the technologies of visual culture, which in many ways determine their representation, cause these boundaries to be highly porous.

The link between vision and cruelty already was an important component in the history of animal welfare from the early years of the nineteenth century on, and has considerable impact in making the animal, in certain moral and political contexts, a powerful visual image. A great part of animal-welfare history in the nineteenth century, both at the level of state legislation and in the activities of societies such as the Royal Society for the Prevention of Cruelty to Animals (RSPCA), dealt with the question of how animals were seen to be treated and implicitly linked the issue of cruelty to the visual order. This was manifested in a succession of bills beginning with the 1809 *Act to prevent malicious and wanton cruelty to animals*.

One of the inspirations behind the formation of the RSPCA in 1824 was the sight of animals being driven to Smithfield Market in London. The issue of visual order was an important factor in increasing control exercised over all sorts of different domains of animal-related practice – including bear baiting, vivisection, slaughter, or the clearing of the city streets of strays. An interesting feature of a Bill in 1857 was that children under 14 should not be permitted in slaughterhouses to witness killing.[3] In the 1876 Act laying down the rules for vivisection, public lectures involving vivisection were banned and restrictions placed on its use in illustrating lectures in medical schools. If cruelty was to take place, it was to be behind closed doors and under license.[4] Vialles (1994) describes parallel events in France. Napoleon's reforms of the meat trade in 1806 slowly led to slaughterhouses being moved from the centers of towns and made increasingly anonymous architecturally. This transformation was paralleled textually in the twentieth century in successive editions of the Larousse encyclopedia in which pictures of activities within the abattoir were replaced in the 1982 edition by a diagram of its functions (24–27).

In all these instances, the emphasis is not just on visibility but also on what might be called the appropriate seeing of the animal. In the context of some remarks on the early nineteenth century, Kean (1998) writes,

> [C]hanges that would take place in the treatment of animals relied not merely on philosophical, religious or political stances but the way in which animals were literally and metaphorically seen. The very act of seeing became crucial in the formation of the modern person (26–27).

I would like to extend this remark by adding the phrase, "and the modern animal." What this also means is that the seeing of the animal becomes, in certain circumstances, a complex act that combines a preoccupation with the humane alongside codes that sanction animal killing or experimentation in areas outside the field of public vision. Where animals are seen, they become in some respects – to adapt a book title (Rose 1986) – bearers of morality in the field of vision.

The contemporary counterpart of this can be found in the centrality of visual imagery to animal politics. Jasper and Paulsen (1995) emphasize this in a comparative study of anti-nuclear and animal-rights protesters whereby the image of the animal is understood as a powerful condensing symbol for a range of human emotions and reactions: "[T]he visual images used in animal rights recruitment have a simple but effective structure based on good versus evil" (505).[5]

The historical background that links the visual to the moral is important in explaining the power of animal imagery, but it also needs to be considered in conjunction with the technology of the media that articulates these images. Not only are animals linked in to a progressive, or improving, framework of civilized behavior, they also are, in a parallel manner, integrally related to the development of a technology that will enhance their visibility. I am now going to take two examples of this: moving film and changing contexts of animal display at the London Zoo in the early twentieth century.[6]

FILM

In the early decades of moving film, from 1895 on, animals appeared in an extraordinary diverse and flourishing medium. Striking examples include (a) Edison's "Electrocuting an Elephant" (1903), (b) the microscopic insect films and stop motion studies of Percy Smith, (c) Cherry Kearton's hunting film from Africa, and (d) the racy entertainments of Colonel Selig.

In these instances, the novelty of film was reinforced by the novelty value of animals as well as birds and insects. However, the significance of the animal was due not only to imagery as such but also to the integral links between the powerful potential of representing animals and the technological challenges such a complex object for depiction presented. Animals were an important motive force in driving the new technology of moving film as well as being, in some senses, its inspiration.[7] Historically, the sequential photographic work of Eadweard Muybridge, Jules-Etienne Marey and Ottomar Anschütz in the 1870s and 1880s depicted all manner of living creatures and explored techniques important to the development of moving film; namely, increasingly refined timing mechanisms, fast film, and precision in camera design to capture the rapid movement of animal and human bodies.[8]

It could be said that, until recently, the tremendous significance of the representation of animals in moving film and still photography was in inverse proportion to scholarly interest in the topic.[9] To some extent, this has been due to an emphasis on the textual animal at the expense of the visual animal and explains the predominant focus on animals as metaphors or signs.

This does not mean that these symbolic elements are absent from animal representation on film. The power of the film image, however, and its relationship to the visual status of the animal in public contexts means that this type of animal representation relates much more to collective aspects of the field of human-animal relations than to particular instances within it. In fact, film straddles a number of cultural fault-lines –most notably those that relate to entertainment and education – as well as crossing back and forth over the dividing line between the humane and the cruel.

In line with the idea that the good treatment of animals in public connotes a decent standard of civilization, early animal films also were seen as improving. A National Council of Public Morals (1917) report was primarily concerned with the need to raise the tone of cinema programs.

Educational films, such as nature studies, were considered an important tool in this process. But the report also recognized that these would not be able to compete with, say, Charlie Chaplin films or the exploits of Elaine, unless they, themselves, were in some ways entertaining (National Council of Public Morals, lix).[10]

In theory, however, humane concerns were to balance the needs of entertainment. From the inception of the British Board of Film Classification in 1913, animal cruelty was one of the grounds listed for cutting or banning a film. This category became more detailed in subsequent years specifying activities like cock-fighting, branding, and – more bizarrely – animals gnawing men and children (Robertson 1985, 20–21; Low 1997, 91). However, the inevitable tension between the need for entertainment and the humanitarian and educational potential of nature films was never resolved, and this was reflected most profoundly in the occasional examples of animal death on film. Nor did this rule out instances in which the making of film entailed fatal consequences for animals. When death did occur, however, it usually was treated as the consequence of a natural process, not something unnecessarily contrived for the camera.

The killing of animals on film has a long precedent. One of the first films made was of a Seville Bullfight in 1896. The limitation of short lengths of film in the early motion pic-ture cameras meant that only snatches of the bullfight were captured – but enough to see a horse being gored and, at the end of the film, the dead carcass being dragged from the arena. Other early examples include Cherry Kear-ton's *Lion Hunting in Africa* (1910), in which the Masai kill a lion. Some scenes of animal death were more contrived, such as the setting up of artificial animal combat, a photographic tradition that goes back to Muybridge, or the provoking of wild animals to charge onto the camera and then shooting them. This marked a number of safari films in the 1920s and 1930s (Bousé 2000, 42–43; Imperato and Imperato 1992, 112).[11]

The comparison with pornography that Bousé (2000) makes when discussing the issue of animal death on film highlights the particularly charged nature of animal imagery. Taking the parallel further, it also draws attention to the combination of repulsion and fascination that marks a response to certain kinds of animal representation and relates, in turn, to the problematic negotiation between coexisting humane and cruel impulses. Even with the most worthy of intentions, such as in the cause of animal welfare, the photographic exploration of cruelty has a strong voyeuristic streak. In 1914, the *Times* (Anonymous 1914) reported a film made by the RSPCA to protest at decrepit horse traffic. Toward the end of the film,

> [B]y way of an argument in favour of a humane killer, the film shows a primitive method of slaughtering the unfortunate beasts by driving a knife into the chest. As the blood surges out the animal's death struggles are seen with repulsive realism. The Society itself admits that these pictures cannot be shown in public, however vividly they prove the need for some improvement of existing conditions (6).

As the above example shows, the issue of voyeurism is determined also by the rules of what should be seen publicly, creating taboo imagery and associating the idea of animal cruelty with concealment and invisibility. Hence, as an ironic repetition of the secret filming of wildlife … present-day secret filming in laboratories and other institutions by animal-rights activists is a further consequence of a long process that has, in so many contexts, saturated the visual animal image with moral connotations.

ZOO DISPLAY

These considerations are not confined to film. Another example, which again relates animal representation to technology as part of a vision of historical progress, concerns changes in zoo display at the London Zoo during the 1903 to

1935 secretaryship of Peter Chalmers Mitchell. In a similar situation to that of film – and it was a parallel of which the Zoo was well aware – the Zoo needed to achieve a balancing act between entertainment and its interest in animal welfare. Under Mitchell, programs were instituted to improve the health and longevity of animals in captivity, which Mitchell saw as the main purpose of the Zoo (Mitchell 1911, 545). An important example of this was the creation of displays exploiting fresh air and light, particularly for primates.[12]

Because the health anxieties of the Zoo were comparable to those of the population at large – especially with regard to rickets and tuberculosis – the solutions explored, such as improved ventilation and exposure to sunshine, also were similar. Exposing animals to increased doses of ultra-violet light using either quartz bulbs or a special window glass – labeled appropriately as "Vitaglass" – that did not filter out ultra-violet rays from the sun, was another feature of this process.

As discussed above, there are a number of respects in which this policy had a direct bearing on the issues of visual representation. As with film, the significance and attractiveness of the animal in the zoo was that the animal was not simply an object but also an event. From an entertainment point of view, the more dynamic the event the greater the interest, and the need for dynamism was directly related to the issue of animal health. Mitchell (1929) claimed that some of his ideas concerning fresh air had derived from the work of Hill, a one-time colleague of his at the London Hospital Medical School (189). Hill had published a number of studies that promoted the idea that bodily vigor and good health were derived from exposure to sunlight and fresh, preferably cold, air. Confinement in "still, warm atmospheres and lack of open-air exercise dull the fire of life and, together with lack of sunlight, produce the deleterious effects of city life on the physical development" (Hill 1925, 107).

The show-piece manifestations of this thinking at the Zoo were bare environments that, in the interests of cleanliness, avoided clutter and gave clear passage to the elements deemed important for health. They also served to make the animal even more starkly visible. In the Experimental Monkey House, a temporary building erected in 1925 and designed to exploit the advantages of fresh air and ultraviolet light, all the surfaces were made of some form of impermeable material – whether glazed bricks, concrete, or asphalt. The Monkey Hill, a display of a community of Hamadryas baboons on an artificial rockscape separated from the public by a ditch, was another example of this. Inside the Hill were heated quarters containing quartz bulbs for ultra-violet lighting. Opened in 1925, this exhibit placed no obstruction such as bars or mesh between the viewer and the animals and intended to highlight the animal as living in a near-natural state.

Many aspects of the Monkey Hill lent the display to anthropomorphic readings – particularly in the treatment given to it by the popular press – but it is worth highlighting the way the display was peculiarly like film. Given that there was no need to forage for food, which takes up a vast amount of time in the wild, the baboons became hyperactive socially, spending disproportionate amounts of time in sexual behavior and fighting. Rather in the way that film cuts down on the mundane to focus on the exciting, so a significant part of baboon behavior had been effectively edited out.

There also was a stage-like quality to the rockscape with its small semi-concealed entrances leading back into the rock, and it is no coincidence that another theatrical display, the chimpanzee's tea party, was introduced a short time afterwards in 1927. It also exploited its prototypical quality as an expression, or representation, of the healthy community in an urban environment. Some newspapers picked up on the implications of the display for human health, asking why monkeys at the Zoo should be given a treatment that was not made widely available to children and slum-dwellers. "Should baboons have the sun and air that babies are denied?" (Saleeby 1926). It was suggested that the design principles at the Zoo should be extended to the dwellings of human beings. However, Monkey Hill also combined these utopian intentions, as far as issues of collective health were concerned, with tragedy. The fighting due to pressure of space and sexual-dominance conflicts led to numerous fatalities, mainly among the female baboons (Zuckerman 1981, 219–223). As with film, the baboons represented the idea of social improvement while suffering from the framing structures that illuminate such representation.

INVISIBILITY AND HUMANE KILLING

My final example, which concerns the history of electrical stunning in slaughterhouses, relates to concealment and invisibility. Although this subject has a different relationship to representation in the public domain from film and zoo display, in many respects the practices in all these examples are structured in similar ways. Historically, animals were crucial to both the exploration of the properties of electricity and its conceptualization. Apart from rudimentary experiments exploring the effects of the electrocution on animals and birds, the first significant experiment that incorporated part of the animal body into an electric current was performed in 1753 by Giambatista Becaria. He demonstrated the stimulation of muscular contractions by passing an electric spark through the exposed thigh muscles of a live cock (Rowbottom and Susskind 1984, 34). Toward the end of the eighteenth century, Galvani and Volta made significant contributions to the development of electrical theory, particularly through their debates on the nature of what was termed "animal electricity," basing much of their work on the electrical stimulation of parts of animal (and human) bodies (Pera 1991; Galvani 1953). Through its use in medicine in the later eighteenth and nineteenth centuries, electricity came to be seen as both cathartic and rejuvenating. Paralyzed limbs could be revitalized, and, later, as electro-convulsive therapy (ECT) appeared to demonstrate from the late 1930s on, obstacles to sound mental functioning could

be cleared. In fact, the experimental groundwork for working out the dosages for ECT was conducted by Ugo Cerletti on hogs in a Rome slaughterhouse. From a cultural point of view, the cleansing aspect of electricity incorporated both moral and physical connotations. However, the most significant historical episode in the development of the electrical stunning of animals was the development of execution by electrocution, and two elements of this particular story concern us here.

First, electrocution was seen as a "cleaner," and hence morally more acceptable form of killing. Second, it reflected a shift from what was seen by some as the barbarism of public hangings to something more private and efficient. In other words, it was a process in keeping with a more civilized and technological modernity. Again, animals were crucial to its development.

Alfred Southwick, a dentist from Buffalo and an important promoter of this mode of execution in the 1880s, excited the interest of the head of the Buffalo Society for the Prevention of Cruelty to Animals, who had been looking for an alternative to drowning unwanted pets and strays (Brandon 1999, 20ff).[13] Furthermore, during this period, animals, particularly strays, were used in large numbers in experiments to establish what constituted a lethal dose (Brandon 1999, 59). Sometimes, this even was done in a public demonstration, including Harold Brown's notorious "canine execution show" (not the actual title of his lecture series!) that traveled round New York State electrocuting up to a dozen dogs in an evening (Brandon 1999, 78). In 1887 and 1888, Edison also presided over similar experiments at his West Orange laboratory in New Jersey. Some were attended by members of the public and journalists in an atmosphere, summarized by one recent commentator, as "a cross between a circus side show and an abattoir" (Metzger 1996, 99). These experimental displays eventually included the killing of larger animals in response to the criticism that dogs were too small and not comparable to the human body. When the electric chair was installed at Auburn prison in 1889, it was tested with a horse and a four week old calf (Metzger 1996, 112–114).

Considerations that brought together the issue of civilized, or humane, behavior and technology also were important to the meat industry.[14] Despite the increasing importance of technology in the processing of meat from the early nineteenth century on, it had long been recognized that, to produce decent meat, animals had to be treated decently. They could not be subjected to stress or anxiety. As Wynter (1854) put it, somewhat dramatically, " ... for anything like fright or passion is known to affect the blood, and consequently the flesh. Beasts subjected to such disturbances will often turn green within twenty-four hours after death" (284). In what essentially was the first scientific text book for the meat industry, Leighton and Douglas (1910) described the goal of the industry as the ability to produce the optimum amount of meat of the best quality in the shortest time (87ff).

Later, from about 1927, experiments in electrical stunning before slaughter offered new possibilities for attaining such a goal. As with execution by electrocution, electrical stunning offered options of efficiency, low cost, and hygiene as well as meeting humane considerations. In addition, it was a technology that could be operated with relatively little skill compared to, say, wielding a poleaxe. In the words of Müller (1932), one of its pioneers, it indicated, "the higher standard of modern civilisation" (487).[15] As Müller (1929) wrote elsewhere,

> [T]he setting up of electrical stunning devices for the slaughtering of animals will further the cause of humanity. The question of the stunning of animals for slaughter, to the humane slaughterman, is a matter which is not a party, political, or religious one, but one that must be answered from the point of view of humanity and justice to animals (166).

In the production of meat, the need to bleed the animal thoroughly is essential as residual blood causes damage to the carcass and can lead to the spoiling of the meat. This problem was called "splashing ... the term commonly applied to a more or less disfigurement of dressed carcasses, which takes the form of haemorrhagic areas" (Parker 1929, 197). Splashing was recognized as particularly apparent in carcasses of animals who had had long journeys before slaughter or who had shown fear or been difficult to handle. This was one of the main reasons why the inhumane treatment of animals needed to be avoided. Stunning seemed a partial solution to this by offering an efficient method of pacifying the animal and calming the atmosphere of the slaughterhouse. A number of scientists such as Hill (1935) noted how unusually quiet the slaughterhouse was when electrical stunning was being used (53). Thus, slaughter was to be not only unseen but also unheard.

Early efforts at electrical stunning had not been entirely satisfactory, mainly because of the difficulty of establishing correct voltage levels (Ducksbury and Anthony 1929). Too heavy a voltage could lead to a convulsion in the animal severe enough to cause skeletal damage. Too low a voltage, and it could not be guaranteed that the animal would be unconscious when it actually was killed. This debate, incidentally, has continued to be an issue to this day (Hickman 1954, 501; Roberts 1954, 565; Eisnitz 1977, 64–66).

In late 1931, a new model improving on the Müller-Weinberger machine, known as the S. R. V. Electrolethaler 2, was demonstrated in Britain with favorable results (Anthony 1932, 380–381). However, Dryerre and Mitchell pointed out in a 1933 report on stunning to the RSPCA that the requirements for electrical work were not likely to be promoted when slaughterhouse workers were operating under the pressure of time. All that the worker really required was for the animal to be pacified before hoisting, which could mean that correct voltages were not necessarily applied. Whether an animal was truly unconscious would not necessarily be a primary consideration (Longley 1950, 264). This argument over unconsciousness versus bodily paralysis really could not be decided. However, its ramifications extended beyond a simple matter of the humane precisely in those areas that Müller (1929;

1932b) saw as irrelevant to modern slaughter: religion and politics.

When Müller (1929; 1932b) wrote that stunning should not be a religious matter, he had in mind primarily the Jewish method of slaughter, which he considered barbaric. This practice, known as *shechita*, involves the cutting of the throat of the animal in one swift action with an extremely sharp knife. The animal is not permitted to suffer any kind of bleeding, external or internal, before this act. This form of killing had been the focus of much debate throughout Europe and was banned in a number of northern European countries, beginning with Switzerland in 1893 (Sax 2000). Müller believed that electrical stunning would be acceptable in *shechita* because no blood would be spilt before slaughter.[16] However, the debate raised an issue that went to the heart of whether stunning was a humane practice – the possibility that animals actually may not lose consciousness when stunned. With *shechita*, it was claimed that loss of consciousness was virtually instant. In the debate, as conducted in the pages of British veterinary journals, two Dutch scientists pointed out that Leduc's electrocution experiments on himself in 1903 led to the loss of motor functions and speech but not consciousness (Roos and Koopmans 1934). One response to the Dutch was to suggest that their arguments were flawed because they were Jewish: "[B]y his explanations, Professor Roos perhaps intends to assist his co-religionists in the question of killing according to the Jewish rite" (Müller 1934, 413). Roos was compelled to respond, "in Holland a Jewish professor is as credible as any other" (Roos 1935, 64).

CONCLUSION

This debate over stunning crystallized many themes concerning the relation of the animal to technology and culture. In all three examples, the issue of the humane is bound up with technological development at some level. The animal is not outside the changing dynamics of this technology but integrally related to both its development and its articulation in the public domain. The changing configurations of visibility and invisibility – indeed, one cannot consider one without the other – are what determine both the nature and power of animal representation. To see animals as straightforward metaphors for human attributes, whether individual or social, is too limiting. Animal representation is related to a much broader and ambivalent structure of ethical practices and social control. This seems to me to be central to the way we might express the animal's relation to modernity. To refer to Derrida's (1999, 273) question that I quoted at the very beginning of this essay, animals inevitably are constituted by the time in which they live. They also have time, but it is edited – by film – manipulated, and reorganized – by zoo display – and accelerated – by the mechanization of slaughter. This is the temporality of modernity for all creatures, human and animal. Thus, in many ways, animals are representations of themselves as subjects to the technology that frames them.

NOTES

1. Correspondence should be sent to Jonathan Burt, Ferry House, Bottisham Lock, Waterbeach, Cambridge, CB4 9LN, United Kingdom. This paper has been inspired and influenced by two very important articles. The first is by Erica Fudge (1999) [Editors' note: Full citation missing in original] and examines the particular problems presented by animals to historiography; and the second by Diana Donald (1999) dealing with the animal in the visual culture of nineteenth-century London. My thanks also to Steve Baker, Bob Mckay, Roger Yates, and Nicolette Zeeman.

2. For a reading of the contradictory problems the zoo presents for animal representation see my article, Violent health and the moving image: The London Zoo and Monkey Hill, In M. Henninger-Voss, Mary (ed.), *Animals in Human History: The Mirror of Nature and Culture* (University of Rochester Press, 2002). Material in the discussion of the London Zoo is drawn from part of this study.

3. This concern continues for a long time. [...]

4. *Parliamentary Papers* (1857). A Bill to amend the act for the more effectual prevention of cruelty to animals. 1, 4. *Parliamentary Papers* (1876). A Bill entitled an Act to amend the law relating to the cruelty to animals. 1, 3.

5. See also Munro's study of the relationship between the Australian Coalition against Duck Shooting and the media.

6. With the exception the work of Gregg Mitman and Derek Bousé, the lack of detailed analyses of animals and film has been surprising. Furthermore, even less attention has been given to the already existing visual contexts of animals, as outlined above, that moving film relates to as it develops at the *fin-de-siècle*. However, it is perhaps no coincidence that the focus on animal metaphor in historical writing has avoided the subject of film, as well as still photography, given that animal representation in film bears a more abstract, ambivalent relationship to the idea of the human. On the relation of film to other art forms in the nineteenth century see my *Animals in Film*, London: Reaktion Books, 2002.

7. Bousé writes, "It is tempting to propose a variation on the … statement that 'the history of animal art must begin at the beginning of all art,' and to say that *the history of wildlife film must begin at the beginning of all film*" (41).

8. Anschütz began making pictures in 1882 and his experiments on equine and aerial locomotion was undertaken for the Prussian military from 1885. See Braun, Haas.

9. There has also been a spate of anthologies of still photography recently. Interesting examples include Hall, Merrit and Barth.

10. See also Mitman for parallel concerns in the United States (8–9).

11. For a colourful, contemporary, account of the more chaotic side of using animals in early films see Delmont.

12. For Mitchell's account of this see the chapter entitled Air, Heat, Light and Monkeys in Mitchell (1929, 187–208). On the relationship between zoo architecture and health one might also note the design of Lubetkin's 1932 Gorilla House at the London Zoo in relation to his plans for London clinics: see Allan (114–117, 202), Coe and Reading (140–144).

13. On electrocution as means of killing strays in London by the RSPCA and the Battersea Dogs' Home, see Cottesloe (68ff).

14. On histories of the meat industry contemporary with the period under discussion see Critchell and Raymond, Cronshaw and Anthony.

15. Gregory mentions that the very first account of electrical stunning was in 1775 involving the stunning and resuscitation of two chickens using a Leyden Jar (82).

16. A number of people raised the possibility that electrical stunning might involve some tissue damage, for example Hill (1935, 53). See also Hyamson, Sassoon. It is worth bearing in mind that protests against kosher slaughter came from many different sides of the political spectrum. See for instance Bell (13).

REFERENCES

Allan, J. (1992). *Berthold Lubetkin: Architecture and the tradition of progress*. London: RIBA Publications.

Anonymous. (1914, February 27). A film of decrepit horse traffic. *The Times*, 6.

Anthony, D. J. (1932). Electricity for the slaughter of animals. *Veterinary Record*, 12, 380–386.

Bell, E. (1904). *The humane slaughtering of animals*. London: Humanitarian League.

Berger, J. (1980). Why look at animals? In J. Berger (Ed.), *About Looking* (pp. 1-26). London: Writers and Readers.

Bousé, D. (2000). *Wildlife films*. Philadelphia: University of Pennsylvania Press.

Brandon, C. (1999). *The electric chair: An unnatural American history*. Jefferson, NC: Macfarland.

Braun, M. (1992). *Picturing time: The work of Etienne-Jules Marey 1830–1904*. Chicago: University of Chicago Press.

Coe, P. and Reading, M. (1981) *Lubetkin and Tecton – architecture and commitment: A critical study*. London: Arts Council of Great Britain and University of Bristol.

Cottesloe, G. (1979). *The story of the Battersea Dogs' Home*. Newton Abbot, UK: David and Charles.

Critchell, J. T. and Raymond, J. (1912). *A history of the frozen meat trade*. London: Constable

Cronshaw, H. B. and Anthony, D. J. (1927). *The meat industry: A text book for meat traders and others engaged in various branches of the meat industry*. London: Baillière, Tindall and Cox.

Delmont, J. (1925). *Wild animals on the films*. London: Methuen.

Derrida, J. (1999). L'animal que donc je suis (à suivre) The animal that I am (to follow). In M.-L. Mallet (Ed.), *L'animal autobiographique: Autour de Jacques Derrida* (pp. 251–301). Paris: Éditions Galilée.

Donald, D. (1999). "Beastly sights": The treatment of animals as a moral theme in representations of London, *c.*1820–1850. *Art History*, 22, 514–44.

Ducksbury, C. H. and Anthony, D. J. (1929). Stunning of the pig by electricity before slaughter. *Veterinary Record*, 9, 433–4.

Eisnitz, G. A. (1977). *Slaughterhouse: The shocking tale of greed, neglect, and inhumane treatment inside the American meat industry*. New York: Prometheus Books.

French, R. D. (1975). *Antivivisection and medical science in Victorian society*. Princeton: Princeton University Press.

Fudge, E. (2002). A left-handed blow: Writing the history of animals. In N. Rothfels (Ed.). *Representing animals*. Bloomington: Indiana University Press, 3–18.

Galvani, L. (1953). *A translation of Luigi Galvani's "De viribus electricitatis in motu musculari commentarius"* (R. M. Green, Trans.). Baltimore: Waverly Press.

Gregory, N. G. (1998). *Animal welfare and meat science*. Wallingford, UK: CABI.

Grove, R. (1995). *Green imperialism: Colonial expansion, tropical island Edens and the origins of environmentalism 1600–1860*. Cambridge: Cambridge University Press.

Haas, R. B. (1976). *Muybridge: Man and motion*. Berkeley: University of California Press.

Hall, L. (2000). *Prince and others 1850–1940*. London: Bloomsbury.

Hickman, J. (1954). The electrical stunning of animals prior to slaughter. *Veterinary Record*, 66, 498–501.

Hill, L. (1925) *Sunshine and the open air, their influence on health with special reference to the Alpine climate* (2nd ed.). London: E. Arnold and Co.

Hill, L. (1935). Electrical methods of producing humane slaughter. *Veterinary Journal*, 91, 51–57.

Hyamson, M. (1923). *The Jewish method of slaughtering animals from the point of view of humanity.* London: Williams, Lea, and Co.

Imperato, P. J. and Imperato, E. M. (1992). *They married adventure: The wandering lives of Martin and Osa Johnson*. New Brunswick, NJ: Rutgers University Press.

Jasper, J. M. and Paulsen, J. D. (1995). Recruiting strangers and friends: Moral shocks and social networks in animal rights and anti-nuclear protests. *Social Problems*, 42, 493–512.

Jones, R. W. (1997). "The sight of creatures strange to our clime": London Zoo and the consumption of the exotic. *Journal of Victorian Culture*, 2, 275–294.

Kean, H. (1998). *Animal rights: Political and social change in Britain since 1800*. London: Reaktion.

Kete, K. (1994). *The beast in the boudoir: Petkeeping in nineteenth century Paris*. Berkeley: University of California Press.

Leighton, G. R. and Douglas, L. M. (1910). *The meat industry and meat inspection*. 5 vols. London: Educational Book Co.

Lippit, A. M. (2000). *Electric animal: Toward a rhetoric of wildlife*. Minneapolis: University of Minnesota Press.

Longley, E. O. (1950). Electroplectic anaesthesia in animals and man. *British Veterinary Journal*, 106, 283–291.

Low, R. (1997). *A history of British film 1906–1914*. London: Routledge.

Merritt, R. and Barth, M. (2000). *A thousand hounds*. Cologne: Taschen.

Metzger, T. (1996). *Blood and volts: Edison, Tesla, and the electric chair*. New York: Author.

Mitchell, P. C. (1911). On the longevity and relative viability in mammals and birds; with a note on the theory of longevity. *Proceedings of the Zoological Society of London*, 425–548.

Mitchell, P. C. (1929). *A centenary history of the Zoological Society of London*. London: Zoological Society.

Mitman, G. (1999). *Reel nature: America's romance with wildlife on film*. Cambridge, MA: Harvard University Press.

Müller, M. (1929). The electric stunning of animals for slaughter from the humane standpoint. *Veterinary Journal*, 85, 164–166.

Müller, M. (1932a). The electric stunning of pigs from the standpoint of the meat industry and animal protection. *Veterinary Journal*, 88, 452–454.

Müller, M. (1932b). Slaughtering by Jewish and non-Jewish methods. *Veterinary Journal*, 88, 483–489.

Müller, M. (1934). The spasms of animals stunned electrically as a sign of unconsciousness. *Veterinary Journal*, 90, 412–416.

Munro, L. (1997). Narratives of protest: Television's representation of an animal liberation campaign. *Media International Australia*, 83, 103–112.

National Council of Public Morals (1917). *The cinema: Its present position and future possibilities*. London: Williams and Norgate.

Parker, T. (1929). Humane slaughtering and some experiments by various methods of stunning with special reference to the condition known as splashing. *Veterinary Journal*, 85, 187–206.

Pera, M. (1991). *The ambiguous frog: The Galvani-Volta controversy on animal electricity*. Princeton: Princeton University Press.

Ritvo, H. (1987). *The animal estate: The English and other creatures in the Victorian age*. Cambridge, MA: Harvard University Press.

Roberts, T. D. M. (1954). Cortical activity in electrocuted dogs. *Veterinary Record*, 66, 561–566.

Robertson, J. C. (1985). *The British Board of Film Censors: Film Censorship in Britain 1896–1950*. London: Croom Helm.

Roos, J. (1935). The so-called stunning of animals. *Veterinary Journal*, 91, 61–5.

Roos, J. and Koopmans, S. (1934). Studies on the so-called electrical studies of animals. *Veterinary Journal*, 90, 232–245.

Rose, J. (1986). *Sexuality in the field of vision*. London: Verso.

Rowbottom, M. and Susskind, C. (1984). *Electricity and medicine: History of their interaction*. San Francisco: San Francisco Press, Inc.

Saleeby, W. (1926, September 26). Feed the baboons, forget the babies. *Sunday Chronicle*.

Sassoon, S. D. (1955). *A critical study of electrical stunning and the Jewish method of slaughter (Shechita)*. Letchworth, UK: Letchworth.

Sax, B. (2000). *Animals in the Third Reich: Pets, scapegoats, and the Holocaust*. New York: Continuum International.

Vialles, N. (1994). *Animal to edible*. Cambridge: Cambridge University Press.

Wynter, A. (1854). The London Commissariat. *Quarterly Review*, 95, 271–308.

Zuckerman, S. (1981). The social life of monkeys and apes. London: Routledge & Kegan Paul.

FURTHER READING IN ANIMALS AS SYMBOLS

Baker, Steve. 1993/2001. *Picturing the Beast: Animals, Identity, and Representation*. Urbana: University of Illinois Press.

Benton, Janetta Rebold. 1992. *The Medieval Menagerie: Animals in the Art of the Middle Ages*. New York: Abbeville Press.

Boehrer, Bruce. 2002. *Shakespeare among the Animals: Nature and Society in the Drama of Early Modern England*. New York: Palgrave.

Bousé, Derek. 2000. *Wildlife Films*. Philadelphia: University of Pennsylvania Press.

Burt, Jonathan. 2005. John Berger's "Why Look at Animals?": A Close Reading. *Worldviews* 9(2), 203–218.

Clark, Kenneth. 1977. *Animals and Men: Their Relationship as Reflected in Western Art from Prehistory to the Present Day*. New York: William Morrow.

Donald, Diana. 1999. "Beastly Sights": The Treatment of Animals as a Moral Theme in Representations of London, 1820–1850. *Art History* 22(4), 514–544.

Franklin, Adrian. 1999. *Animals and Modern Cultures: A Sociology of Human-Animal Relations in Modernity*. London: Sage.

Fudge, Erica. 2002. *Perceiving Animals: Humans and Beasts in Early Modern English Culture*. Urbana: University of Illinois Press.

Ham, Jennifer and Matthew Senior (eds.). 1997. *Animal Acts: Configuring the Human in Western History*. New York: Routledge.

Hogarth, William and 18th Century Print Culture. McCormick Library of Special Collections. http://www.library.northwestern.edu/spec/hogarth/main.html.

Kalof, Linda. 2007. *Looking at Animals in Human History*. London: Reaktion.

Klingender, Francis, *Animals in Art and Thought to the End of the Middle Ages*, eds. Evelyn Antal and John Harthan (Cambridge, MA: MIT Press, 1971).

Lippit, Akira Mizuta. 2000. *Electric Animal: Toward a Rhetoric of Wildlife*. Minneapolis: University of Minnesota Press.

Mitman, Gregg. 1999. *Reel Nature: America's Romance with Wildlife on Film*. Cambridge, MA: Harvard University Press.

Rothfels, Nigel (ed.). 2002. *Representing Animals*. Bloomington: Indiana University Press.

Rowlands, Mark. 2002. *Animals Like Us*. London: Verso.

Shepard, Paul. 1996. *The Others: How Animals Made Us Human*. Washington, DC: Island Press.

Simons, John. 2002. *Animal Rights and the Politics of Literary Representation*. New York: Palgrave.

Tambiah, S.J. 1969. Animals Are Good to Think, and Good to Prohibit. *Ethnology* 8(4), 423–459.

Toynbee, J.M.C. 1973. *Animals in Roman Life and Art*. London: Thames & Hudson.

Willis, R.G. (ed.). 1990. *Signifying Animals: Human Meaning in the Natural World*. London: Unwin Hyman.

*A*nimals as Scientific Objects

INTRODUCTION

The readings in this section echo the concerns expressed by those writing on animals as symbols – the representation of animals transcends seeing them as metaphors for human attributes or experiences and is related to broader social issues such as ethics and power. The use of animals in science is an objectifying process that has deep ethical implications. Using animals as objects of scientific speculation, classification, and experimentation has a long tradition in human history. Animals have been dissected by Aristotle, Leonardo da Vinci, and George Stubbs; vivisected by Galen, Vesalius, and Descartes; and used by very many to test scientific hypotheses, such as Frederick II who took some vultures, sewed their eyelids shut, kept their noses free, and observed whether or not they located meat by smell or by sight [the vultures went hungry].

These essays address some of the most hotly debated animal issues in contemporary society – vivisection, cloning, and the "obligatory, constitutive, protean" relationship between dogs and humans in technoscience. We begin with a chapter from Coral Lansbury's classic book, *The Old Brown Dog*, which recounts the social context surrounding the anti-vivisection movement of the early 1900s in the UK. The movement was popular among women and the working class (both groups identified with exploited and trapped animals) and was eventually defeated by the scientific community, with particularly effective protests by the local medical students. Lansbury argues that the cause for animals is not well served when animals stand in as surrogates for others, such as woman or workers.

In Lynda Birke's essay we are drawn into the laboratory itself with her analysis of the lab's gendered and hierarchical social relationships (between scientists, technicians, and animals). She argues that this network of relationships has much to tell us about systems of domination and control in the pursuit of scientific objectivity, and that caring and compassion are labeled feminine and largely devalued.

Networked relationships also figure importantly in the next essay in this section, Sarah Whatmore's "Hybrid Geographies." From the lens of geography, Whatmore argues that the spaces that constitute nature and society are too "purified," or categorized according to binary oppositions such as real/ ideal, natural/social, objective/subjective. These places need to be reconfigured as fluid networks composed of actants-in-relation, including humans, nonhumans, technologies, the organic and the mechanic. Whatmore's work draws very heavily on Deleuze and Guattari's conceptualizations of multiplicity, fluidity, and affinity relations discussed in Section 1.

Sarah Franklin's article on the making of Dolly, the first cloned sheep, also addresses the thorny question of the meaning of nature. With the emergence of new reproductive and genetic technologies in science, animal reproduction is separated from their genealogy, producing a commodification of animal bodies that transcends maternity, paternity, gender, and sex.

We end with another piece on the construction of animals in technoscience – Donna Haraway's "Cyborgs to Companion Species." This essay is well-suited to end the volume; it makes important links with our discussion of philosophical foundations (Section 1), reflexive thinkers (Section 2), domestication and "pets" (Section 3), and symbols (Section 5). Haraway outlines the distinction between "cyborgs" and "companion species," noting that while cyborgs are multiple, subjective, and transformative, companion species are made of two things in interaction (and those "things" can be a multiplicity that consists of humans, animals, technologies, or artifacts). In her discussion, Haraway focuses on the long history of our relationship with dogs, and considers it useful to think of them in non-anthropomorphic ways – while dogs have much agency, they are not projections "nor the telos of anything," they are just dogs. She concludes that the "materially semiotically engaged" and "fleshly significant" companion species figure enhances understanding of eugenics, technology, embodiment, and the histories of class, race, gender, and nation.

31

CORAL LANSBURY

The Brown Dog Riots of 1907*

Coral Lansbury was a distinguished scholar of nineteenth-century English literature, a Guggenheim Fellow, and an accomplished writer of contemporary women's fiction. With a feminist center, Lansbury's work has remarkable relevance to contemporary women's issues, whether she is writing fiction or history. Her major scholarly work, *The Old Brown Dog: Women, Workers, and Vivisection in Edwardian England*, examined the growth of the anti-vivisection movement among women and the working class, groups that identified with exploited animals. Nineteenth-century women empathized with trapped and tortured animals, linking the gynecological examinations (particularly of poor women) to the experiments conducted on animals, both of whom were strapped to a table with their bodies exposed and inspected by medical students. The working class was similarly suspicious that surgeons experimented on animals because they had no easy access to human bodies, and they lived in constant fear that their bodies would end up on the dissector's table. We reproduce Chapter 1 from Lansbury's *The Old Brown Dog*, in which she describes the events leading up to the Brown Dog Riots of 1907, emphasizing the symbolic meaning of the practice of vivisection for both sympathizers and opponents. Lansbury concludes that the antivivisection movement was unsuccessful because the concern for animals was blurred with women's rights and worker's rights, with antivivisection coded as working-class socialism and/or feminism. She argues that a pro-animal cause must be based on the animals' own existence, rather than as surrogates for women or workers. We will see from the other readings in this section that the question of animals in scientific practice is often coded with messages of sacrifice and sexual victimization.

In 1980 there was only one old resident of Battersea who could recall the Brown Dog Riots of 1907, when police, feminists, medical students, and trades unionists fought over the statue of a brown dog in the Latchmere Recreation Ground.[1] It was a time when the most unlikely allies found common cause, and for a few turbulent weeks some of the most passionate issues of the day were debated violently in the streets. Cecil Hart, ninety years old, a retired solicitor and vestryman of St Luke's Church remembered the riots vividly but thought they were concerned with the antivivisection hospital in Battersea Road. The dog was – and clearly he was

* Lansbury, Coral. *The Old Brown Dog*. © 1985. Reprinted by permission of the University of Wisconsin Press.

at a loss to account for the dog's role at the time – the dog was just an "advertizing story."

For Cecil Hart, memory had established its own logic and hierarchy of events, and what had been for many the very heart and cause of the riots had dwindled into a commercial fiction. We will have reason to discuss memory and the tricks it plays in the course of our investigation: the ways in which memory edits and interprets the past, and the tendency of fictions to live longer than the experiences which inspired them. The brown dog of Battersea had once been a living creature; later it came to be a symbol of feminist outrage and working-class resentment. Those in authority in society sought to destroy it, denouncing it as the embodiment of traditions and attitudes that had been shaped by a past beyond conscious recall. For these people it stood as a denial of progress, relic of a time when sorcery and sentimentality dragged at the skirts of science. Again and again the opponents of the brown dog declared that they were rational and reflective men of science, whereas the women and workers defending the dog were emotional and irresponsible acolytes of a brutal and unsanitary past. On both sides statements were made that were not the logical consequence of circumstance but the result of accumulated experiences going back to forgotten social rites and customs. What people said and did at that time was shaped as much by literature as by history, and the fears and phantoms invoked by the brown dog were often more real than the actual events. William Hogarth was present at the riots; so too were Black Beauty and the body snatchers, Burke and Hare. Fiction collided continually with facts, and in a sense Cecil Hart was wiser than he knew when he described the brown dog as a "story." What we will try to do now is to explore the subterranean motives and ideas that erupted in Battersea and spread across the river to Trafalgar Square, where two cavalry charges of police were required to disperse the "brown-doggers" and their opponents.

Let us begin then with appearances, the superficial structure of the story, remembering that the most discreet and uniform streets may well conceal the landscape of another world,

another time. Gillian Tindall has described how Kentish Town erected bricks and cement across sleeping fields and walled over the streams that once carried a freight of ships down to the Thames.[2] Stroll along St Pancras Way and you are passing over the buried Fleet; in Battersea it is the Falcon Brook which runs under the corner of Battersea Rise and St John's Road, only making its presence felt in the occasional flooded basement along Falcon Road. It is an image that speaks to the heart of this study, for what happened in 1907 was, like most riots, a congeries of apparently inexplicable actions performed by an eccentric and disparate cast of players having nothing in common except a brown dog. And yet for each of those people the dog was a potent symbol capable of determining action and belief.

First, we can walk around Battersea and see for ourselves where the riots began, then set up a narrative, remembering always that dates and even events are no more than signposts which may often point to a lost age as well as to a present place. The Lavender Hill of 1900, with its respectable small shops and ranked cottages, was once a garden where lavender was grown and its fragrance then dried or preserved in oil for medicines and perfumes. Battersea lavender was as well known in the eighteenth century as Battersea enamel with its primly pastel arcadian patterns. John Burns, president of the Local Government Board and member of the House of Commons, had moved up to Lavender Hill, to "Athelstane," a square, shuttered house, in 1906. We will meet him soon as one of the main opponents of the brown dog.

Nine Elms, colored black and blue as a place of "most degraded poverty" in Charles Booth's maps, was where in the 1800s the Battersea artichoke was cultivated and asparagus blanched for West End dinner tables.[3] That was the time when there were farms and market gardens from the river's edge to Clapham Common, and a century before that, sheep grazed on Battersea Rise. A report issued in 1813 mentions that "the garden-grounds at Battersea occupying a dry and kindly soil, are much famed for the seeds of vegetables grown on them, and the gardeners at Clapham and some other places in the neighbourhood procure their seed from the former parish. In consequence of this demand for seed, much of the garden ground in the Parish of Battersea is employed in raising vegetables for seed."[4]

It was not always easy to find that agricultural past under the streets of Battersea in 1907; nonetheless, the countryside was not so remote from the factories and tenements as it is today. Sally Plornish of Bleeding Heart Yard in *Little Dorrit* had a rustic cottage painted on her living room wall to remind her father of his childhood home, but the people of Battersea did not need pictures to recall the country. Most of them had heads well furnished with rural memories, and those who may have forgotten the open fields and farm animals had only to walk down Latchmere Road, "Pig Hill," when the cattle and pigs were being driven to Chesney Street and Semple's slaughterhouse. Indeed, one small farm could still be seen on the corner of Battersea Rise and Limburg Road until the First World War.[5] Rabbits and chickens were kept behind the cottages along Battersea Road and children sent there for fresh eggs. But all this was changing at the turn of the century: tenants were not permitted to keep livestock in council houses, and blocks of flats had begun to displace cottages.

Gypsies used to camp in the fields by Usk Road; by the turn of the century the fields were gone, but the gypsies still returned in winter to put up their caravans in stable yards and bring the sounds and smells of the country with them. Horses were flogged up the Battersea Rise in icy weather, and many people would stop to pity the straining animals and remember the sufferings of Black Beauty on Ludgate Hill. Anna Sewell's book was not only a perennial favorite in the Battersea Municipal library; it was also prescribed as a school text and a regular Sunday school prize. Down by the river, the two hundred acres of Battersea Park were set out with lawns and trees and flowering shrubs, and here family groups from Battersea came to picnic in the summer, and children could feel grass

under their feet and look up through leaves to the sky. A number of artists and writers lived by the park, among them, G. K. Chesterton, John Burns's friend and ally in his campaign against the brown dog.

From Battersea Rise to Clapham Common the houses were larger, and professional people and tradesfolk made their homes there. This was South Battersea, which worked in the West End like Cecil Hart and insisted that its address was Wandsworth. Rents, land, and servants were cheaper here than across the river; Cecil Hart had a live-in maid and "morning's only" cleaner for seven and sixpence a week. It was a part of Battersea that tried to hold itself aloof, politically and socially, from the factories and slums by the river.

Battersea in 1907, belching smoke across the river, was the creation of the nineteenth century and the railroads."[6] The population had grown from 6,617 in 1841 to 168,907 in 1901, and a good proportion of the men had come to find work in the railway yards and shunting stations. It was the railway which dominated Battersea: the large flat lands where artichokes and asparagus once flourished were now found to be ideal for depots and sidings. Battersea was on the approach to two major terminals, Waterloo and Victoria, and here in Nine Elms the air was always heavy with coal dust and greasy with oil fumes. Today it is the site of Covent Garden Markets, and boxes and barrows of fruit and flowers recall its buried agricultural past: underneath the cement floors of the produce sheds is still that "dry and kindly soil" where vegetables were once grown for seed.

In 1907 Nine Elms was "an area shaped like a narrow triangle lying on its side, bounded on the north by the Thames and on the other two sides by railway lines … In the centre of the triangle, dominating Nine Elms, were the gasometers, retorts, and purifiers of the London Gas Light Company. Nearby there were limeworks, flour mills, breweries, and an iron foundry."[7] With only two exits from the area, both to the south, Nine Elms was, to use Booth's phrase, "a poverty trap," but it was here in the most squalid part of a degraded neighbourhood that one of the main supporters of the brown dog chose to make her home. We will meet Charlotte Despard – feminist, novelist, and social reformer – when she leaves Currie Street to defend the statue of the brown dog against her arch-enemy, John Burns.

Across the river, people said you could smell Battersea long before you saw it. Ernest Morris, who worked at Morgan's Crucibles for over forty years, remembered Battersea as a place of dirt and foul odors where the stench from paint manufacturers contended with the sulphur fumes of the gasworks: "But the Daddy of them all was the Morgan Crucible Co. then known as the plum which blackened the borough with its lamp black, carbon, and plumbago and the dust carried over the Thames into Chelsea."[8] But it's an ill wind, and Battersea women took in washing by the basket and the cart load. As Booth observed, "Central London washes its dirty linen at home. Battersea undertakes this duty for a large part of the West End."[9]

Over in the city, Battersea was famous for more than its reeking smokestacks; it was notorious as a hotbed of radical politics and militant trades unionism. People had not forgotten August 19, 1889, when John Burns marched with the striking dockworkers around the City of London, the same year that the Battersea gas workers went on strike and secured an eight-hour working day. In 1902 the Battersea Borough Council, controlled by the local Trades and Labour Council, belligerently refused to sign the loyal address to the King, and in December would not even consider a donation from Andrew Carnegie for the municipal library because Carnegie's cash was "tainted with the blood of the Pittsburg strikers."[10]

It was also true that if Battersea was mentioned in a music hall, there would be an immediate chorus of barks and howls because of the Battersea Dogs' Home, the largest of its kind in England. Despite the jokes from neighboring boroughs, Battersea residents regarded the Home with a good deal of affection. Part of the folklore of Battersea which found its way into the South-Western Star and the Battersea Mercury turned upon tales of distraught owners reunited with lost dogs at the kennels. When it was suggested in 1907 that Battersea Dogs' Home should supply animals for vivisection, the chairman of the board, the Duke of Portland, rejected the suggestion as "not only horrible, but absurd … and entirely unacceptable to the Home."[11] The Battersea Dogs' Home, the Battersea Polytechnic, and the Antivivisection Hospital were landmarks like Arding and Hobbs' store at Battersea Rise. In the Town Hall with its sweeping staircase and fluted columns, the Borough Council had gained the reputation of being "the most democratic council in the metropolis ever since the London Government Act was passed."[12] Certainly the Council could point with considerable pride to its housing estates: the Town Hall and Shaftesbury Estates set a standard for the many private and cooperative building societies in the area.

The Latchmere Housing Estate was formally opened in 1902, and John Burns stood with Mayor Howarth in the centre of the Recreation Ground, where four years later the statue of the brown dog was to be erected. Burns was at his magniloquent best, and after lauding the virtues of hearth and home, he pronounced a general blessing on all those who were going to rent the small detached houses at seven and sixpence a week: "May this little colony never know the curse of drink or the blight of betting; may it be free from the minor nuisances of life; may its children be bright and cheerful, and may all its members be as mindful of their proper neighbours as the Borough Council has been public-spirited in looking after them."[13] It was a fair sample of Burns's bombast and the patronage that was beginning to make him sound more like Mr. Honeythunder than a radical labor leader. The South-Western Star observed that a number of unionists present had jeered at his rhetoric, and noted with approval that the three thousand inhabitants of the Latchmere Estate had failed to go cap in hand to Burns to thank him for his generosity. Battersea workers were never known for their deference.

These were the workers who became the champions and defenders of the brown dog when it was placed in the very centre of the Recreation Ground: a bronze statue of a terrier dog, muzzle lifted, staring pensively toward the houses, the fountain at its base inviting people and animals to drink. Now, drinking fountains had always been a touchy subject among the working class, for they were frequently erected by temperance societies as well as by those who sincerely wanted to slake the thirst of horses and dogs. A workingman resented being told to forgo his pint of bitter and drink alongside his horse, so these monuments to middle-class concern for working-class sobriety were regarded as being particularly offensive. In 1903, when the Battersea Council was run by Progressives, it flatly turned down an offer from the Metropolitan Drinking Fountain and Cattle Trough Association to donate a drinking fountain and dog trough with the terse response that "the Council regret that they have no available site."[14] As many people suspected, when the brown dog and its fountain were placed in Latchmere with the authority of the Council, it was there for other reasons than those of alleviating thirst.

Here then in Battersea we have the scene for our story, and now we must cross the river and meet some of the men and women who made the brown dog the expression of their most fervent beliefs. The immediate cause of the riot was in the physiology laboratory of University College, where Louise Lind-af-Hageby and her friend Liese Schartau witnessed the vivisection of a brown dog and noticed that the dog had an unhealed wound in its side which indicated that it had recently been used for another experiment. They both made a record of the incident in their diaries.

Louise Lind-af-Hageby was twenty-four when she enrolled with her friend at the London School of Medicine for Women, with the deliberate intention of becoming medical students in order to master the science of physiology and then use that knowledge to expose the practice of vivisection. Both of them were scornful of those sentimental women who drowned themselves and their listeners in floods of tears when they spoke about the suffering of animals under the vivisector's knife: they were determined to arm themselves with the language and arguments of the enemy and speak as doctors. The resolution to dedicate their lives to the antivivisection movement had been born during a visit to the Pasteur Institute in Paris, when they had seen hundreds of animals dying in agony. Fortunately, Louise Lind-af-Hageby came from a wealthy Swedish family and possessed a woman's passport to independence in those days, "private means." She knew that in England the antivivisection movement was strong and well organized if divided in the means required to protect animals from experimental use.

English antivivisectionists were grouped in two main societies, with a number of smaller associations that often seemed more at odds with each other than opposed to vivisection. Despite its fragmentation, however, the movement had won a number of victories with the 1876 Act to Amend the Law Relating to Cruelty to Animals standing as the only legal restriction in the world against the experimental use of animals.[15] But vivisection was still being practiced, and it was known that men who held licenses to vivisect were on the council of the Royal Society for the Prevention of Cruelty to Animals, and were even appointing the inspectors whose charge it was to regulate the Act.[16]

The British Union for the Abolition of Vivisection, under Dr. Robert Walter Hadwen, had been founded in 1898 when Frances Cobbe demanded that the National Antivivisection Society seek the total abolition of vivisection through a single legislative act. The Hon. Stephen Coleridge, a barrister and son of Sir John Coleridge, lord chief justice of England, argued that abolition could be accomplished only by means of successive legislative amendments. It was on this issue of gradualism versus instant and revolutionary change that the movement had split into two distinct societies, with Coleridge assuming the presidency of the National Antivivisection Society, and Frances Cobbe founding the British Union. Far from being unique to the antivivisection movement, these two attitudes reflected theories of change that were being propounded daily by feminists and leaders of the working class. Millicent Fawcett was calling for women's suffrage to be accomplished by successive electoral reforms; the Pankhursts of Manchester were demanding votes for women by means of one legislative act. H. M. Hyndman predicted violent social revolution, whereas John Burns had pledged himself to a piecemeal progress so slow that his critics claimed he was walking backward into the arms of the Liberals.

Louise Lind-af-Hageby and Liese Schartau, like most educated young women, had been taught to keep diaries, and in vivid and dramatic prose they recorded what they had seen at University College in the Department of Physiology. Later we will spend some time with the language and metaphors that these young women chose to use in their diary; unconsciously they were evoking images that went beyond, and often contradicted, the immediate meaning. Over a period of months they compiled a series of vignettes which they felt could become a book. They took what they had written to Stephen Coleridge at the Antivivisection Society offices in Victoria Street, and he immediately saw that if what they had recorded was correct, then there had been a serious infringement of the 1876 Act. Under the Act a vivisected animal could not be revived after one experiment and used for another: it had to be destroyed. But the young women, in a section called "Fun," had described a brown terrier dog with a recent abdominal wound which had been carried into the laboratory strapped to a board. The dog was then subjected to an operation in the throat by Professor William Bayliss. The dog had struggled throughout the course of the demonstration and was still alive when it was taken from the lecture room.

Coleridge questioned the two women and, when convinced of the accuracy of their observations, helped them find a publisher for the diary.[17] As soon as *The Shambles of Science* was in print, Coleridge publicly charged the physiologist,

Bayliss, with having broken the law. Bayliss in turn had no recourse but to sue Coleridge for libel in order to protect his reputation, and the case was heard in November 1903. Coleridge did not expect to win the case: what he wanted was publicity and an opportunity to ventilate the deficiencies and anomalies of the 1876 Act.

The case was widely reported, but already, clear social divisions could be seen in the press. The *Times* referred to the diary as a mischievous work, and Coleridge's actions were impugned in the *Telegraph*; but the Liberal and working-class press – the *Star*, the *Daily News*, the *Sun*, the *Standard*, and the *Tribune* – came out strongly in support of Coleridge. The *Daily News* published the court proceedings in full and concluded:

> Let us grant for the moment that man has the right to make use of animals for experimentation in the means of alleviating human suffering and saving life. But surely there must be some limit to this right. Has it not been reached in such a case as this? Here is an animal which worships and trusts mankind with an unreasoning fidelity. The dog may almost be said to have surrendered himself into our safe keeping. Does not this overwhelming trust – this absolute confidence that glistens in the dog's eye – lay upon us some obligation?
>
> Is it not worth considering whether the human race may not pay too heavy a penalty, for knowledge acquired in this manner? Are we to leave out of count altogether the hardening of heart and searing of sensitive feeling that must be produced by the constant spectacle of such unmerited suffering? Let us suppose that the Swedish ladies were wrong, and that this dog was anaesthetized. But a correspondent points out that the certificate possessed by Dr Bayliss is not the only certificate allowed by law. There are other physiologists who are permitted to perform such operations as these on conscious animals and no one who alleged that the animals were conscious would be saying anything libellous.[18]

Implicit in this statement is not merely a concern for animals, but a challenge to a form of social authority sanctioned by law. For reasons that we will examine in some detail the antivivisectionist movement had become associated with radical politics and the interests of the working class and women. Coleridge had anticipated the outcome of the trial. The chief justice ordered that the section "Fun" be removed from *The Shambles of Science*, and Louise Lind-af-Hageby and Liese Schartau complied in all subsequent editions, replacing the offending vignette with a lengthy account of the trial. Since the burden of proof lay on the defendant, the jury found for Bayliss: Coleridge was fined two thousand pounds to the delighted cheers of the medical students who packed the court throughout the trial – their behavior had been described by the *Times* as "medical hooliganism." The *Daily News* immediately opened a subscription fund to pay Coleridge's damages, and the money was oversubscribed within the month.[19] If Coleridge and Lind-af-Hageby had lost in court, they were not vanquished in public opinion. The case had brought them the publicity they desired, and the sales of *The Shambles of Science* increased. Yet the verdict rankled, for William Bayliss had been found innocent of any charge of cruelty or failure to abide by the provisions of the 1876 Act. Moreover, the medical students were jubilant, and at every antivivisection meeting they added three cheers for Professor Bayliss to their usual catcalls and groans. If there is a mob in this story, it is not the Battersea workers, but these medical students who now had a long tradition of noisy opposition to antivivisectionists.

As early as 1830 medical students in London had rioted and forced the professor of anatomy, G. S. Pattison, from his chair because of his "*total ignorance of* and *disgusting indifference* to new anatomical views and researches."[20] All Pattison's attempts to lecture were shouted down by the students, and eventually the college council was forced to compromise between the students' protests and Pattison's obdurate refusal to learn new methods by appointing him to the chair of surgery. There was always considerable tolerance of medical students' boisterous behavior because it was felt that the nature of their work made such outbursts necessary. What would never have been countenanced in a law student was accepted in a medical student because he had

frequently to do the work of a butcher on living flesh. For this reason many early physiologists like Koch believed that the cries of vivisected animals helped to habituate the student to the pain of a human patient – an argument which continued after the introduction of anaesthesia.

For William H. Lister, a medical student at University College, the Bayliss case was less an instance of "old women of both sexes" holding back the cause of science than an opportunity to set gown against town and in the process make London University students behave and feel like Oxford and Cambridge undergraduates. Lister's ambition was to create a political estate from the students of London University and, if possible, to represent those students himself.[21] He was to seize that opportunity three years later at the Latchmere Recreation Ground.

Antivivisection vied for public attention with a great many other issues, foremost among them unemployment and women's suffrage. The old spontaneous market and election riots bore little relation to the planned and occasionally rehearsed demonstrations of public anger in Trafalgar Square and through the streets of the City of London. The liveliest cause of the day was women's suffrage, and Charlotte Despard, as secretary of the Women's Social and Political Union, was one of the leaders of the radical wing, always ready to march and harangue politicians. For her, as for many feminists, one of the greatest obstacles was John Burns, member of Parliament for Battersea.

In 1906 Burns was prepared to renounce his radical past and run for election as a Liberal with the cabinet post of President of the Local Government Board as his reward. Over the years Charlotte Despard had grown to dislike and despise John Burns. She had led deputations of the unemployed to his door, she had begged him to give his support to women's suffrage like her friend George Lansbury in Poplar, and Burns had always dismissed her with a mouthful of platitudes. A shrewd politician, Burns knew that workingmen had never shown the slightest interest in giving women the vote. For Charlotte Despard, Burns was the great apostate, Mr. Bumble incarnate, and she was not alone in this opinion. The Socialists and many of the Progressives in Battersea abhorred the man. Unfortunately for the radicals of the electorate, Burns proved he had a political base that did not require the support of the Trades and Labour Council or even his own union, the Amalgamated Society of Engineers. In 1906 the TLC presented its own slate of candidates for the borough elections and was successful in capturing forty of the fifty-four Council seats, but they could not break Burns's majority in the parliamentary election. Battersea laughed at Burns's bombast, but it continued to vote for him.

Burns was at his ebullient best in January of 1906. His friend and admirer G. K. Chesterton had spoken on his behalf at the Battersea Town Hall, and Chesterton's dazzling paradoxes met with enthusiastic applause. George Bernard Shaw had just attacked Burns's policies, or the lack of them, in a speech at the Latchmere Baths, and Charlotte Despard followed Shaw with a bitter denunciation of Burns's failure to help women and the unemployed. However, with a majority of over two thousand votes in the election, Burns could afford to disregard his enemies. What the socialists and the suffragettes feared was that as President of the Local Government Board Burns would now be controlling one of the greatest sources of patronage in London.

At this point we can see a number of angry and frustrated individuals: Louise Lind-af-Hageby was still outraged by the Bayliss verdict; Stephen Coleridge was appalled when a commission was appointed to review the working of the 1876 Act and it was proposed to include known vivisectors among the commissioners, closing all its inquiries to the press and the public; Charlotte Despard together with a great many disappointed electors in Battersea deplored the election of John Burns. Into this group now came Miss Louisa Woodward, secretary of the Church Antivivisection League, a wealthy woman from an old Wiltshire family and a close friend of the vicar of St Luke's Church, where Cecil Hart worshipped. The vicar, Erskine Clarke, was not only an antivivisectionist, but was also a supporter of Charlotte Despard and her work among the poor of Nine Elms. Louisa Woodward met Louise Lind-af-Hageby, and the two decided to present the Battersea Council with a most unusual drinking fountain. Stephen Coleridge discussed the plan with the mayor and council, which approved the design and the inscription on the base of the statue. It was agreed that it should be placed in the Latchmere Recreation Ground.[22]

The fountain was designed to be provocative. The inscription rang out like a challenge: "In Memory of the Brown Terrier Dog Done to Death in the Laboratories of University College in February, 1903, after having endured Vivisection extending over more than Two Months and having been handed over from one Vivisector to Another Till Death came to his Release. Also in Memory of the 232 dogs Vivisected at the same place during the year 1902. Men and women of England, how long shall these Things be?" That there was strong antivivisection sentiment in the Council is obvious. Only the conservatives and a few of the radicals were opposed to accepting the fountain, warning that there might be legal action from London University. Indeed, when University College did threaten to take proceedings against the Battersea Borough Council unless the memorial was removed from the statue, the Council bluntly told the university to mind its own business.[23]

There was a large crowd on September 15, 1906, when the fountain was unveiled, and for once, John Burns was not invited. However, Charlotte Despard was there with Louisa Woodward, George Bernard Shaw, and the Reverend Charles Noel, who spoke on behalf of the Anti-Vivisection Council. It was a public snub for Burns, who had always looked on the Latchmere Estate as a testimony to his beneficent care of the borough. The Mayor of Battersea, J. H. Brown, welcomed the statue and all that it stood for. Brown was a thirty-eight-year-old trades unionist, honorary secretary of the General Labourers' Union and secretary of the Battersea Trades and Labour Council.[24] As well as being a vocal critic of Burns for having taken office under a Liberal government, Brown was an antivivisectionist and remained one of the strongest supporters of the brown dog. When the ex-mayor of Chelsea praised Battersea for its bravery in accepting such a gift, Brown said that Battersea would always lead the way in improving conditions for the working class. Clearly, for Brown vivisection was a means used to oppress the working class, and his words were met with cheers. Sufficient to record now that it was a stirring occasion brought to a conclusion by the Reverend Noel, who led the crowd in singing "Ring the Bells of Mercy," the antivivisectionist hymn.[25]

The fountain was in place, the brown dog stared across to the neat ranks of council houses, and if ever a riot had been deliberately instigated, this was it. The wonder is that it took so long for the medical students to respond to the challenge. The *South-Western Star* wrote enticingly: "It is rumoured that the students of the hospital intend to pull it down and that electric bells have been placed on the statue to give notice of any such attempt."[26] However, it was just over a year before the students crossed the river into Battersea. Of course, those who have had some experience of student demonstrations will appreciate that they occur most frequently on campus; there is a marked disinclination to walk any distance for the purpose of rioting. In this case, it is doubtful if the London University students would have done more than complain had they not been organized and led by that politically astute young medical student William Lister.

In Battersea the Socialists were still complaining about John Burns and threatening to run their own candidate against him in the next elections. They were joined by the antivaccinationists, who were outraged when Burns voted in favor of the Vaccination Act, which made inoculation a condition of employment in government service.[27] Half a century later Cecil Hart may have forgotten the brown dog, but he did not forget the Battersea General Hospital and what it stood for in the borough. "The Old Anti" had

always served the working folk of Battersea, but now abruptly it was refused funds from the Metropolitan Hospital Sunday Fund.[28] The Battersea Council saw John Burns's influence at work here and organized carnivals to raise money for the hospital and what it stood for – an institution where every doctor was pledged not to engage in any form of vivisection.

It was a time of furious activity for Charlotte Despard; she led deputations of Battersea's unemployed to the Town Hall, and smaller groups of women to see John Burns, who was no longer able to conceal his contempt for this angry old woman. The Pankhursts, however, were delighted to have Charlotte Despard as secretary of the Women's Social and Political Union, and they made it known that the reason she had not been arrested was that the government feared a riot in Battersea and that there was alarm that her brother might resign from the army – Sir John French being regarded as the most promising general and Haldane's choice for Inspector-General of the Forces.[29] Neither statement was true, but the violence and incoherence of the threats was typical of many of Emmeline Pankhurst's utterances.

In November William Lister decided the time had come to attack the brown dog in Battersea. He had campaigned vigorously throughout the university and felt he had sufficient support to conduct something more elaborate than the customary heckling at antivivisection rallies. On November 20, 1907, an exceptionally foggy day, Lister summoned a group of thirty students from University College and Middlesex Hospital. They purchased a massive hammer and crowbar and set out a little after three to their meeting place at the top of the Tottenham Court Road, where other medical students had assembled. They all caught a Royal Blue Omnibus to Battersea and then quietly, concealed by the fog, made their way along Battersea Park Road to the Latchmere Recreation Ground. But the police had been warned, and when the students rushed to the fountain and one man "took a mighty blow at the creature with the sledge hammer," he was seized by two plain-clothes policemen.[30] Battersea men rushed out of the council houses and helped the police arrest ten of the students, who were formally charged and fined five pounds each the following day at the South-West London Police Court. The magistrate, Paul Taylor, not only rebuked the students: he sent them off with a warning of two months' prison with hard labor and no option of a fine if they created any further disturbances.[31]

Lister now had a cause which would rouse his fellow students to action, and they responded with bonfires in front of University College and demonstrations against Paul Taylor. What infuriated these young men was that they had been treated in the same manner as the suffragettes, who were now being routinely arrested after their disturbances and given prison sentences. Charlotte Despard, for example, had served twenty-one days in Holloway after her part in the February 12 riot in front of the Commons. Despite the fact that some suffragettes were known to approve of vivisection, the students began to attack every women's suffrage meeting with howls, barks, and cries of "Down with the Brown Dog!" Millicent Fawcett, a close friend of several noted vivisectionists and the sister of the medical pioneer Elizabeth Garrett Anderson, had her suffrage meeting at the Paddington Baths broken up in disorder on December 5.[32] Even Edward K. Ford, who wrote a contemporary account of the riots, was puzzled at this association of antivivisection with the women's cause when men like Coleridge and Hadwen had not shown any particular sympathy for women's suffrage.[33] Yet, for the students and increasingly for the public, antivivisection and women's rights were now part of the same movement. Inevitably, as we shall see, each was to lose by this association.

The medical students were now an organized body, and Lister drew up a campaign to destroy the statue. On November 25 students made another attempt to enter the Latchmere Recreation Ground and were driven back in considerable disarray, so Lister planned a demonstration in Trafalgar Square. He knew that on December 10 the Oxford and Cambridge undergraduates would be in town for the Varsity Rugby football

match: if only he could enlist their support, then London men would be seen standing shoulder to shoulder with their Oxbridge companions. The demonstration was advertised, and the police made ready.

Lister was chagrined when the Oxford and Cambridge men down for the match refused to join his cause, but decided to sally forth without them. Shouting and singing, the medical students marched in procession down Kensington High Street, holding aloft effigies of the brown dog and the magistrate Paul Taylor. In Trafalgar Square fights broke out between students and groups of workingmen. Immediately the mounted police moved in, scattering the crowd and arresting several students. Lister led the main band across the river to Battersea, where there were more police and a hostile crowd.

Driven out of the Latchmere Ground the students fought their way down Battersea Park Road, where they tried to attack the Antivivisection Hospital. Again the crowd forced the students back, and when one fell from the top of a tram and was slightly injured, the *Daily Chronicle* reported that the crowd had shouted jubilantly, "That's the brown dog's revenge!"[34] His friends tried to carry him across to the Antivivisection Hospital, but a group of workers barred the door and refused to let him enter.

Battersea's new mayor at this time was Fred Worthey, a master printer, Congregational temperance worker, and fervent antivivisectionist. When the Police Commissioner asked the Battersea Council to pay for the cost of the two policemen who were now required to guard the brown dog twenty-four hours a day, Worthey told the Commissioner to stop badgering the Council and start doing the job for which he was paid.[35] It was a chance for the borough to assert itself against the city and, indirectly, show the London County Council that it could not bully Battersea. A Conservative member of the Battersea Council, A. E. Runeckles, then suggested that the inscription be removed, but the Council had the following statement recorded in the minutes: "That the inscription on the memorial being founded on ascertained facts, the Council declines to sanction the proposal to remove it, and that the Chief Commissioner of Police be informed in reply to his letter that the care and protection of public monuments is a matter for the police and any expense occasioned thereby should be defrayed out of the public rate to which this Borough contributes so largely; also that the Council considers more strenuous efforts should be made to suppress any renewal of the organised ruffianism which has recently taken place in the Metropolis in connection with the Memorial."[36] Letters supporting the Council's stand were received from rate-payers and from an incongruous group of supporters: The Battersea Labour League wanted to see the students removed from Battersea before anyone thought of moving the brown dog, the National Canine Defence League formally applauded the Council for its actions, and the Battersea branch of the Operative Bricklayers' Society pledged its members to defend the statue. Working-class support for antivivisection was now a matter of public record. If medical students had identified the movement with women, people were now beginning to see it as a working-class issue.

When Louise Lind-af-Hageby held a ticketed antivivisection meeting at the Acton Central Hall on December 16, 1907, she had a guard of Battersea workers, yet over a hundred students managed to smuggle their way in, and soon the meeting was pandemonium, with broken chairs, fistfights, and smoke bombs. Again, police were required to restore order and arrest the rioters.[37] The students appealed to Sir Philip Magnus, M.P. for London University, to have the inscription removed from the fountain, and he in turn asked the Home Secretary at question time in the Commons what it was costing the government to protect the Brown Dog Memorial, assuring the House that "a large body of students in the London University were quite prepared to remove this offensive monument free of charge."[38] A petition signed by over a thousand London University students was presented to the Battersea Council demanding that the libellous inscription be erased.[39]

At a public meeting in the Battersea Town Hall on January 15, 1908, Stephen Paget speaking as president of the newly formed Research Defence Society, moved that another inscription be placed on the statue. Stephen Paget was the son of Sir James Paget, who had once remonstrated with Queen Victoria over her opposition to vivisection. The younger Paget was by no means as eminent a doctor as his father, but for several years he had been secretary of the Association for the Advancement of Medicine by Research. On this occasion the students rioted in their customary fashion, and more than three hundred stewards were required to drag the demonstrators from the hall.[40]

The following month in London the Municipal Reformers defeated the Progressives for control of the London County Council. Sir Herbert Jessel had waged a brilliant campaign for the Municipal Reformers, appropriating Socialist slogans and images and using them against the Progressives. Campaign songs were promoted, and one poster showed a Progressive with "a bloated ugly face, chewing a cigar and wearing a top hat, hand outstretched, with the caption *It's Your money we want!*"[41] Battersea was caught up in the same struggle, but here the issues were increasingly debated in terms of the brown dog and the Antivivisection Hospital.

The Battersea General Hospital had always been controlled by a board of local residents: three of the four vice-presidents were women, and these women were antivivisectionists.[42] With its painted sign announcing its principles and practice to passersby the hospital was felt to be an insult to a modern medical profession dedicated to research by means of animal experimentation, Sir William Church of the Metropolitan Hospital Fund declared that "no self-respecting medical man would for one moment consent to the governing body of a hospital which consisted mainly of laymen." Thomas Bryant stated in the same report that the "Antivivisection Hospital casts a great slur upon the profession generally, and that they ought not to support a hospital which was ratified upon such principles."[43]

Cutting off funds to the hospital was one means of closing it, but here the Hospital Fund had not reckoned with the loyalties of men like Cecil Hart and the local trades unions, which helped run carnivals and collect money for the "Old Anti."[44] Finding it impossible to close the hospital by starving it financially, the Hospital Fund charged it with neglecting its patients. This charge was upheld in the Battersea Coroner's Court in December 1909, when the coroner, John Troutbeck, investigated the depths of two patients who had initially received treatment at the hospital. He observed that there had been "great neglect at the Anti-Vivisection Hospital."[45] In consequence the hospital was closed and patients transferred to the Wandsworth Infirmary, where doctors sat on the governing board and there were no restrictions against vivisectors being allowed to practice.

Throughout 1908 the Moderates campaigned to take control of the Battersea Council, and when an additional threepence on the pound was imposed on ratepayers to assist the unemployed, the Moderates knew they could count on an increased vote. After all, not every man could vote under the restricted franchise of this period. In 1907 only 22,914 in a population of more than 180,000 could go to the polls, and these were ratepayers and heads of household most affected by the increase in rates. There were complaints of a Socialist Council pouring money into the pockets of "the wastrels and loafers of that Borough."[46] And the symbol of Socialist authority in Battersea was now the brown dog.

Meetings were held, each more riotous than the last, but it was clear now that so long as the Socialists and Progressives held a majority in the Council the brown dog would remain in Battersea. Nevertheless, at the 1908 elections the Moderates were able to gain control and among the first acts of the new Council was an order to remove the statue. The mayor, Peter Haythornthwaite, a Moderate, tried at first to persuade the Council to alter the inscription to one suggested by Stephen Paget:

> The dog was submitted under profound anaesthesia to a very slight operation in the interests of science. In two or three days it was healed, and remained perfectly well and free of all pain. Two months later it was again placed under profound anaesthesia for further experiment, and was killed under the anaesthetic. It knew nothing of what was being done to it on either occasion. None of us can count on so easy death. We doubtless shall suffer pain or distress, both mental and physical. This dog was free alike from fear and suffering. It died neither of starvation nor of overfeeding, nor of burdens from old age. It just died in its sleep.[47]

The fatuous stupidity of Paget's declaration did not go unremarked, and even the *Daily Mail* wondered if the dog had felt in the best of health between the two operations.[48] Louise Lind-af-Hageby was outraged that known facts should be falsified by a new inscription from an acknowledged vivisector. This was not what she had seen in the laboratory of University College, and she demanded the right to speak again at the Battersea Town Hall. Even though she was met with wild applause, the same fights and brawls broke out between medical students and the stewards.

William Lister was now convinced that in the brown dog he had at last found a cause to unify the London University students, and he led them from one antivivisection and women's suffrage meeting to another. The Police Commissioner was still insisting that the Battersea Council pay for the protection of the statue, and on February 10, 1910, the Council moved that the fountain should be returned to its donor, Louisa Woodward of the Church Antivivisection Society. She promptly sought a restraining injunction from Chancery, and Charlotte Despard and Louise Lind-af-Hageby addressed a mass meeting at the Latchmere Recreation Ground. The ex-mayor Fred Worthey said the Council was making "a concession to organised violence," and handed out pamphlets which he had composed and printed at his own cost.[49]

Before Miss Woodward could secure the restraining injunction, the Council had acted, and about two o'clock on the morning of March 10, four Council workmen guarded by 120 police carried the statue away and hid it in a bicycle shed.[50] Battersea exploded in rage, but now there were mounted police ringing the Recreation Ground. Speakers who tried to place a box there and address the crowd were led away, and the demonstration was effectively quashed.

Ten days later over three thousand people assembled in Trafalgar Square to hear the leaders of the antivivisection movement demand the return of the brown dog. Scuffles broke out between medical students and police, but this time the speakers – Sir George Kekewich, Louise Lind-af-Hageby, and Stephen Coleridge – made themselves heard.[51] Despite their fiery pronouncements and the enthusiasm of the crowd it was clear that the brown dog had gone from Battersea and would never return. Indeed, three weeks later it was broken up in the Council yard.

Most of the participants declared themselves well satisfied with the results of the riots. Stephen Paget regarded it as a victory for progress and science; William Lister felt that a corporate spirit had been created in the "*disjecta membra* of the University"; G. K. Chesterton playfully suggested that the Battersea banner should have a brown dog rampant although he would have preferred a chrysanthemum himself, and Stephen Coleridge stated that the brown dog had been "a splendid advertisement for our cause."[52] Louisa Woodward continued trying to secure legal redress against the Council, but even when she failed, she declared that the cause had become better known, Louise Lind-af-Hageby maintained the struggle by means of her own society and rented shops where antivivisection literature was displayed and sold, George Bernard Shaw continued to write and lecture against vivisection, but there was a *fin de siècle* feeling about the movement by this time, and for many the issues had become so influenced by other social movements that it was difficult to distinguish antivivisection from feminism or working-class socialism.

A chronological narrative like this is always as enigmatic and intrinsically superficial as the passing traveller's perception of a crowded street. You may be able to see London from the top of a bus, but you cannot hope to know and understand it. Just as the slums and suburbs of Battersea defined an obscure geography wherein architecture concealed the life and purpose of the inhabitants, the ranked tenements and paved streets concealed fields and streams which made their presence felt by covert means and unsuspected signs, like those half-forgotten memories which yet have the power to determine present action. Why people behaved and thought as they did at this particular time cannot be explained by reference to changes in local government or the rivalry between town and gown; there are too many incongruities and contradictions in this particular riot.

An immediate problem in such a brief narrative is the conjunction of workers and suffragettes, for if there was one issue which had no support among the trades unions and with working-class men generally, it was the demand that women be given the vote. Labour men routinely pledged their support for the cause, but when it was put to the test in a mass union vote it failed. Working-class men who were threatened with unemployment had no desire to enfranchise the cheap labor of women, and every strong union sought to exclude women, not give them added authority at the polling booth. George Lansbury discovered this in 1912 when he ran for his old seat in Poplar as a suffrage candidate: a majority of 863 became a minority of 731, and his biographer, Raymond Postgate, saw it as the most serious blunder of his career.[53] Yet in Battersea the suffragettes and trades unionists had worked for a common cause – a brown dog.

This straightway gives rise to another difficulty: R. D. French assures us that antivivisection was a dead letter for the working class. Indeed, all efforts to organize the workers ended in failure, and "the ultimate stumbling block emerged in the profound indifference of laborers towards the issue."[54] Who then were those cloth-capped stewards at Louise Lind-af-Hageby's lectures, and what were the local iron-workers doing when they voted to defend a memorial to a vivisected dog? In Battersea we find unionists protecting that dog, and men and women prepared to use their fists and meagre funds to support an antivivisection hospital. The RSPCA always maintained that the working class was callous in its treatment of animals, but perhaps this particular society was less concerned with protecting animals than with policing the workers. Statements of this order cannot be explicated in terms of events but only by exploring those attitudes which translate emotion into action, and we may well find that the workers of Battersea are typical of their class and that their concern with antivivisection is more deeply felt than that of any other social group.

French also notes the involvement of women with antivivisection, "among the very highest for movements without overtly feminist objectives."[55] Women like Frances Cobbe, Anna Kingsford, and Louise Lind-af-Hageby were willing to give their lives to this cause. Anna Kingsford even volunteered to give her own body for vivisection in order to save an animal.[56] Is this passionate involvement really the "displacement of guilt" that the prosperous middle class transferred from their employees to animals, as James Turner argues?[57] Surely the emotions are too extreme to make such an ingenious thesis possible, even if the middle class carried such a burden of guilt over the suffering of the working class. Certainly, many of the middle-class women did not show the same concern for children or the poor, and it is doubtful whether guilt was as pervasive in Victorian society as it is with us today. It may well be that here we shall find a very dark river running beneath the architecture of social forms, a river bounded on one side by pornography and on the other by conventional medical practice.

The doctors of the future, the medical students of our narrative, behaved like a hooligan mob, but not only E. K. Ford was perplexed by their belligerent insistence that women's suffrage and antivivisection were parts of the same objectionable cause. A number of prominent antivivisectionists like Anna Kingsford, the novelist "Ouida," and Robert Hadwen were opposed to any extension of the suffrage, while among the suffragists there were many like Millicent Fawcett who saw antivivisection as an obstruction to scientific progress. It also may be that the young men denouncing the brown dog and its supporters were unconsciously responding to the same force that had drawn women into this cause, although there were few who recognized the nature of that force and fewer still who would have been prepared to acknowledge it if they had.

Eventually the whole incident became a question of opposed symbols in shop windows, and Cecil Hart's recollection of an "advertizing story" now has considerable point. The Anti-Vivisection Council set out a display in a shop front in Oxford Street.[58] Behind the glass were displayed saws, scalpels, and straps; boards designed to hold animals for vivisection; and a centrepiece which Patrick White describes in his novel *The Vivisector*:

> It was one of the greyest days, pierced by black monuments. Hurtle lost the others for a moment: they had all floated apart in the drizzle, the sound of wheels revolving in wet, the tramping of galoshes; when he found himself staring into a display window of horrible purpose. There was a little, brown, stuffed dog clamped to a kind of operating table. The dog's exposed teeth were gnashing in a permanent and most realistic, agony. Its guts, exposed too, and varnished pink to grey-green, were more realistic still.[59]

Next to this shop was one managed by the Research Defence Society with photographs of Pasteur and the picture of a smiling young woman with a baby on her knee, and underneath it the inscription: "Which will you save – your child or a guinea pig?"[60] The images were contradictory, but the conclusion was plain in terms of symbol if not of fact. It was a case where fiction had supplanted reality; the icon of mother and child and the sacrifice of a dog concealed another grotesque image of a woman strapped to a surgical bed struggling to escape. Women's suffrage had very little in common with antivivisection, but the two had become confusedly entwined through the accident of circumstance: the image of the vivisected dog blurred and became one with the militant suffragette being force-fed in Brixton Prison.

There are many reasons why the antivivisection movement dwindled and almost disappeared between these years and the present surge of interest and concern, but one predominating cause is that people no longer saw it in actual terms but through coded messages of scientific progress, sacrificial redemption, and sexual victimization. It was at the time of the Brown Dog Riots that these messages first came to signify reality, but the origin of the messages goes back to the early years of the nineteenth century.

NOTES

1. *Reflections on Battersea,* collected by the Vocational Committee of the Rotary Club Battersea (Battersea: Rotary Club of Battersea, 1980), 9.

2. Gillian Tindall, *The Fields Beneath* (London: Granada, 1977), 22–28.

3. Charles Booth, *Life and Labour of the People in London,* 3d ser., 5 (London: Macmillan, 1902), 150.

4. Sherwood Ramsbury, *Historic Battersea* (pamphlet, Battersea, n.d.), 2.

5. Mrs. W. Chapman, in *Reflections on Battersea,* 19.

6. Janet Roebuck, *Urban Development in Nineteenth-Century London: Lambeth, Battersea, and Wandsworth,* 1838–1888 (London: Phillimore, 1979), 121–22.

7. Andro Linklater, *An Unhusbanded Life: Charlotte Despard* (London: Hutchinson, 1980), 68.

8. *Reflections on Battersea,* 33.

9. Booth, *Life* and *Labour of the People in London,* 9 (1903), 312.

10. *Daily Mail,* 23 May 1902 and 9 December 1902.

11. *Second Royal Commission on Vivisection,* Parl. Papers 1907, Cd. Q. 11624.

12. *Tribune,* 3 October 1906. The Progressive campaign for the 1906 election was managed by the Trades and Labour Council, which represented nearly forty political and labor organizations in the borough. Forty Progressive candidates were nominated, comprising eight laborers, three compositors, two bricklayers, three carpenters, two plasterers, three painters, two general foremen, one electrician, one school attendance officer, one insurance agent, three schoolmasters, an organizer of Polytechnic lectures, one barrister, and three "independent gentlemen."

13. *South-Western Star,* 23 September 1902.

14. Battersea *Council Records,* Minutes of Proceedings, 13 May 1903, 2, 60.

15. *Law Reports, Public General Statutes,* 39 & 40 Vict. c. 77. The provisions and limitations of the act are outlined in Richard D. French's study, *Antivivisection* and *Medical Science in Victorian Society* (Princeton: Princeton University Press, 1975).

16. Stephen Coleridge succeeded in forcing Lord Cromer, president of the Research Defence Society, to resign from the Council of the RSPCA in 1911. Cromer argued that his membership in a society dedicated to animal research did not affect his work for the RSPCA, but after Coleridge had addressed the members, he was forced out of office by a vote of 55 to 48. Coleridge then demanded the resignation of Stewart Stockman, who actually held a number of licences for animal experimentation. *Lancet,* 27 May 1911.

17. Lizzy Lind Af Hageby and Leisa K. Schartau [*sic*], *The Shambles of Science: Extracts from the Diary of Two Students of Physiology* (London: Ernest Bell, 1903).

18. *Daily News,* 19 November 1903.

19. Ibid., 20 December 1903.

20. *Lancet,* 1830, 751.

21. W. H. Lister, then a medical student, was one of two representatives examined by the Commission on University Education in London in 1909. When questioned about the value of representation on the senate, Lister replied: "'What was at the back of our minds was not so much the fact that representation would be of value, but that the actual election would be the great point if you granted us this. That the election taking place once in two years or something of that sort would be a most tremendous help in bringing to the students of London the realisation that they are units of one whole University, especially if carried out on party grounds …' 'Political party grounds?' asked one of the commissioners. 'Yes,' was the reply." Quoted in Eric Ashby and Mary Anderson, *The Rise of the Student Estate in Britain* (Cambridge, MA: Harvard University Press, 1970), 54.

22. Battersea *Council Records,* 11 July 1906, 7, 109.

23. Ibid. At Coleridge's advice the Church Anti-vivisection Society remained the nominal owner of the statue and indemnified the council to the extent of £300 in any possible action for libel. *Lloyd's,* 16 September 1906. A description of the fountain and the popular songs which it inspired are found in a pamphlet by Edward K. Ford, *The Brown Dog and His Memorial* (London: Miss Lind-Af-Hageby's Anti-Vivisection Council, 1908).
24. *South London Mail,* 16 November 1906.
25. *Lloyd's,* 16 September 1906.
26. *South-Western* Star, 17 September 1906.
27. Ibid., 22 August 1907.
28. *Tribune,* 4 May 1907.
29. Linklater, *An Unhusbanded Life,* 112.
30. Walter Seton, *William Howard Lister* (London: Medici Society, 1919), 20.
31. The fine was noted with considerable approval by the Battersea Council, 17 November 1907.
32. *Daily Express,* 6 December 1907.
33. Ford, *The Brown Dog and His Memorial,* 9.
34. *Daily Chronicle,* 15 November 1907.
35. *Battersea Council Records,* 22 January 1908.
36. Ibid.
37. *Tribune,* 17 December 1907.
38. *Daily Chronicle,* 7 February 1908.
39. *Daily Graphic,* 15 Januaary 1908.
40. Stephen Paget became the first secretary of the AAMR in 1882. In 1908 he became secretary of the Research Defence Society. At the annual general meeting of the British Union for Abolition of Vivisection, Robert Hadwen described the RDS as "a nine days' wonder [which] will shortly fizzle out like predecessors of a similar type." *Abolitionist,* 20 May 1908.
41. Ken Young, *Local Politics and the Rise of Party* (Leicester: Leicester University Press,1975), 93.
42. Flyer, 1908, Battersea Municipal Library. Anti-vivisection hospitals were without exception controlled by boards of lay people. The Battersea General was the last of its kind in England; two years before, St. Francis Hospital in New Kent Road had been an antivivisection institution, but a group of local doctors campaigned against the board and gained a majority.
43. *Hospital,* 31 July 1909.
44. E. G. Morris remembered the street carnivals for the "Old Anti" with floats, horses, and decorated carts, walkers, and bands. *Reflections* on *Battersea,*19–20.
45. *Daily Telegraph,* 29 December 1909.
46. *Tribune,* 29 January 1907. It was noted that Battersea was more affected than any other division by the "latch-key" decision and that the Moderates were organizing most effectively.
47. *Municipal* Gazette *and London Argus,* 13 December 1907.
48. *Daily Mail,* 7 December 1909.
49. *Morning Leader,* 22 February 1910.
50. Letter from Marjorie F. M. Martin, daughter of borough surveyor, Battersea, in *British Medical Journal,* 15 September 1956.
51. *Daily Graphic,* 21 March 1910.
52. *Daily Express,* 8 January 1908.
53. Raymond Postgate, *The Life of George Lansbury* (London: Longman Green, 1951), p. 128.
54. French, *Antivivisection and Medical Science,* 239.
55. Ibid., 240.
56. Edward Maitland, *Life of Anna Kingsford* (London: Macmillan, 1913), 1, 309.
57. James Turner, *Reckoning with the Beast* (Baltimore: Johns Hopkins University Press, 1980). Turner argues that the self-interest of the middle class required them to divest the guilt they felt about the working poor upon animals. Brian Harrison challenges this view in his review of Turner's work in the *Times Literary Supplement,* 29 January 1982.
58. *Abolitionist,* 1 August 1912.
59. Patrick White, *The Vivisector* (London: Allen Lane, 1973), 135.
60. *Abolitionist,* 1 August 1912.

32

LYNDA BIRKE

Into the Laboratory*

Lynda Birke is a biologist who studies how feminism links with animal issues in science. Most of her scientific research has focused on animal behavior, but from a feminist standpoint, such as her critique of the taken-for-granted notion that animal behavior is determined by hormones. Birke has also produced a substantial body of work on feminist science studies, including a wide range of topics from arguments against biological determinism to the ethics of animal experimentation. Birke's work is centered by a set of key questions that frame much feminist theory: how science uses bodies (both human and other animal) and the links between objectivity, masculinity, and scientific knowledge. Birke emphasizes animal consciousness and subjectivity (animal agency), and much of her work makes important connections to the readings in Section 2 on Animals as Reflexive Thinkers. One of Birke's best contributions to feminist science studies of animals is her 1994 book, *Feminism, Animals and Science: The Naming of the Shrew*. Birke's use of the word "shrew" in the title provides an interesting link between feminism and animals – a shrew is a small mouse-like animal, an abusive term for women, and the title of a Bristol-based feminist newsletter of the late 1960s and early 1970s. In the chapter reproduced here, Birke continues the discussion of vivisection begun with Lansbury, but in the context of what happens in the laboratory, rather than in the outside community. Birke analyzes human-animal social relationships as expressed in the laboratory setting, noting that since the use of animals in the laboratory is rooted in systems of domination and control, the practice of vivisection is deeply gendered. For example, the typical laboratory's "social pecking order," with scientists and inspectors (usually male) at the top, technicians (usually female) in the middle, and animals of course at the bottom, constitutes a network of gendered and power-driven relationships. While she does not suggest that only women can empathize with lab animals, caring and connectedness are stereotypically associated with femininity, and thus typically devalued in the pursuit of scientific objectivity and detachment.

* Reprinted with permission from Lynda Birke (1994) *Feminism, Animals and Science: The Naming of the Shrew.* Buckingham; Philadelphia: Open University Press.

In her short story, "Mazes," Ursula LeGuin describes how an alien torments an intelligent creature, putting it into mazes, expecting it to learn how to press buttons for food rewards or to avoid punishment. The creature ponders on what motivates the alien; it

> has never once attempted to talk with me. It has been with me, watched me, touched, handled me, for days: but all its motions have been purposeful, not communicative. It is evidently a solitary creature, totally self-absorbed. This would go far to explain its cruelty. (LeGuin 1987b, 64)

The story, she points out, is not about rats. Nor is it about how humans might be treated by aliens from another world. The alien in the story is human, the trapped creature clearly a highly intelligent one from another world. LeGuin's tale powerfully reminds us of the assumptions we make in keeping other animals in laboratories.

Animals are clearly part of what science studies, both in and out of the laboratory. Scientists interested in the behaviour or ecology of a particular species usually study those animals in the field; others, interested in physiology, say, study how animal bodies work in the laboratory. Still others may use animals as part of a series of tests to ensure the safety of particular products – drugs or cosmetics, for example. These developments have meant that animals are usually purpose-bred for research, and kept in locations specifically designed for the purpose. But their use is increasingly questioned by people outside science, many of whom feel that at least some uses of animals in research are of dubious benefit. In that context (and the context of personal threats to researchers from animal rights protesters), it is hardly surprising that those involved in doing biological research are often ambivalent about it.

Science itself is, in its practice, ambivalent about the use of animals. Their use in experiments is sometimes justified on the grounds that animals can provide "models" of human physiology; rats and mice, for instance, are thought to be sufficiently similar to us that they are used to test products such as potential drugs. Yet their difference from us is also clear in the way that scientists must justify their use of animals to a wider public; experiments cannot ethically be justified on people, the reasoning goes, but animals can be used because of their different (lesser) ethical value.

In this part of the book, I focus upon how scientists deal with the ethical dilemmas of using animals. My primary concerns here are twofold; first, I will explore some themes about the place of animals and people in scientific research. The meanings of the animal in the laboratory are located in a web of social relationships; what the animal means to the technician is different from what it means to the scientist. What it means to the anti-vivisectionists is clearly very different again. These meanings depend not only on social relationships, but also on beliefs about animals/nature, and about the ethics of using animals for human gain. [...]

The controversy over "vivisection" is an old one, as we have seen. Although feminist involvement in the anti-vivisection campaigns is perhaps not as strong as it was in the late nineteenth century, there is undoubtedly concern among some feminists today for animal rights. A US group calls itself Feminists for Animal Rights, for example, and many feminists have become involved in anti-vivisection work. If feminism is concerned with issues of oppression and exploitation, the argument goes, then we should care about the exploitation of animals.

In addressing the question of how animals are treated in science, I am assuming that there can be something to say about it from a feminist perspective. I believe that there is; as I will argue, my stance is that feminist standpoints can yield particular insights. Whatever one's personal feelings about animal rights in general or anti-vivisection in particular, the use of animals in the laboratory is problematic. In the first place, the ethical debates are grounded in assumptions about domination and superiority that feminism, and any other social movement seeking an end to oppression, should challenge. The testing of innumerable products on animals, for example, is demanded within a capitalist society; both consumer demand and the profit margins of industry maintain that practice. It is deeply rooted in systems of domination.

Second, the place of animals in science is particularly important for feminists because it is within the ideology of science that naturalizing definitions either arise or are justified. The pursuit of the "homosexual rat" in scientific research is a short hop away from seeking biological bases for homosexuality in people – a search that, as I write, is rapidly gaining momentum with claims for evidence of homosexual brains, or homosexuality-inducing genes on the X-chromosome. *How* animals are used in the creation of such ideology and how that practice is written about raise important questions for feminist critiques of science.

Standing in stark contrast to the unemotional and detached language of the scientific reports (to which I return in more detail later), are the emotive images and language of anti-vivisectionist writing. A report from the British Union for the Abolition of Vivisection, for example, invites you to imagine driving down a quiet English lane and coming across a building that is obviously high security:

> behind those brick walls and blanked out windows are thousand upon thousands of animals being forced to take part in toxicological research. Something you could not possibly have known from simply driving past. But then you weren't supposed to. It was here … that I was soon to become an employee in an attempt to uncover the secrets so carefully stowed away from public scrutiny. (Kite 1990)

The writer is present, clearly inviting the reader to ponder the atrocities within; the photographs of pathetic beagles reinforce the emotional impact. Scientists in anti-vivisectionist literature often seem to be seen as ogres, intent on causing animals to suffer. At the very least, they seem to be divorced from any finer feelings about the possible suffering of the animals they use in their experiments. Such images occur in feminist writing too, where the emphasis is largely on the fact that scientists are more often men; Andree Collard, for example, counterposes masculine science to what she sees as women's values, asking "Women especially must do some serious thinking and reconnect, if not to our gynocentric roots, at the very least to the history of man's violence to animals. For what has been done to animals has always preceded what has been done to us" (1988, 98). To her, scientists must be "emotionally dead" if they can torture animals in the way that she describes (67).

BECOMING A SCIENTIST

Emotionality and empathy are qualities that, by contrast, a trainee dentist must learn to suppress; they get in the way of the quintessential "objective pursuit of truth." Somehow I knew, as a 17-year-old, that I had to swallow my disgust when confronted with a white rabbit with pink ears for dissection; after all, I wanted to be a dentist, didn't I? Learning to be objective means learning to distance yourself from those feelings. To become a scientist I had to leave emotion behind and learn to construct a façade of scientific authority. That is not to say that I no longer felt those emotions (though some dentists, perhaps, would deny that they felt them at all), but I had learned not to admit to them. I had also learned that, despite those emotional reactions, I did enjoy learning science. For all my disgust at seeing the rabbit, there was undoubtedly a fascination about observing first-hand what the organs and tissues actually looked like, and how they fitted together.

For "new recruits" to the biology laboratory, one important task is killing animals. In her analysis of animals as "other" in feminist writing about science, Zuleyma Tang Halpin has suggested, for example, that an important rite of passage for trainee biologists is the "pithing of the frog." This task separates those "who have what it takes from those who do not … The message … is clear: if you want to be a dentist you cannot let your emotions get in the way" (Halpin 1989, 286).

Objective detachment is, as feminist writers have pointed out, stereotypically masculine in our culture (Bleier 1984; Keller 1985), while "not letting your emotions get in the way" is reminiscent of suppressing something feminine. Women in science have to take on board that fundamental contradiction; going through processes of desensitization toward animals is an essential part of attaining the required level of detachment. To identify with your animals (a more "feminine" position) is to cease to be objective.

In making this point, I should emphasize that I am *not* saying that only women can identify with their subjects of study. What I am suggesting, rather, is that this feeling of empathy, of connectedness is gendered; it is stereotypically associated with femininity in our culture (and has been explored in explicitly feminist contexts). To become a scientist means acquiring some desensitization; it also means learning to speak and write in ways that gloss over some of the deep ambivalence that many scientists – male and female – often experience. This is how we learn in science to speak of "sacrifices," or learn to make (unnecessarily) complex sentences in written papers that omit any reference to agency. Part of that learning process is to acquire the social skills of appearing not to be affected by emotions.

I can remember, for example, aged about 20, being in an undergraduate laboratory. We were asked to do experiments with frog skin, to find out about how different chemicals passed through the cells. The frogs (laboratory-bred animals) had been pithed before pieces of skin were removed from their back; even though I knew intellectually that the animals were brain-dead, I felt sick at the sight of the pile of newly-pithed frogs. But I nonetheless swallowed my feelings of disgust, and I still conducted the experiment on my bit of skin. Meanwhile, I hid the emotions (or tried to; hiding feelings is not something I can claim to be good at). Social pressure to conform, to be a "real scientist" is strong, perhaps especially so at that age.

EMPATHY VERSUS EXPERIMENT

Beliefs that empathizing with experimental animals is totally at odds with good experimental practice were evident very early in the Scientific Revolution. Some scientists worried that torturing animals might distort results; the microscopist Robert Hooke expressed doubt in 1665, for example, asking whether by "dissecting and mangling creatures whils't there is life yet within them, we find her [nature] indeed at work, but put into such disorder by the violence offer'd" (Guerrini 1989, 401). Hooke may also have been more sensitive to the gendered basis of science than many of his contemporaries, including his mentor Robert Boyle. Boyle was both avowedly anti-feminist (Potter 1988) and quite prepared to justify animal suffering for the benefit of science (Guerrini 1989).

Scientific method was, moreover, itself portrayed at that time in terms of active male sexuality, "thrusting" into her (nature's) secrets (Keller 1985). Most experimenters of the seventeenth century knew that the animals felt pain (despite Descartes' advocacy of animals as machines), but they believed that this was "legitimately inflicted for the benefit of man and ... for the glorification of God through natural philosophy" (Guerrini 1989, 407) – nature yielding her painful secrets to the determinedly masculine methods of science.

Concern for experimental animals, on the other hand, connotes "feminine" pity – an association that may well be one good reason for the repeated failures of anti-vivisectionist feeling. Women's involvement in the nineteenth-century campaigns led, perhaps predictably, to accusations of hysteria, or of being "old maids" (Ryder 1989). More recently, "the British entomologist Miriam Rothschild has described the process of desensitization that she went through in becoming a scientist, noting that other zoologists of her acquaintance feared being dubbed "unmanly" if they showed compassion towards their animals (Rothschild 1986, 50).

This apparent gender contradiction did not, it seems, deter Rothschild, not least because students of biology were, she felt, brain-washed and "disinclined to think." It was another 30 years of research before she

> began to take the matter seriously … This fortunate, but traumatic experience I owe to my eldest daughter who, as a schoolgirl resolutely marched out of her zoology classroom never to return. She refused to kill and then dissect an earthworm. The penny dropped. (Rothschild 1986, 50–51)

Being (or trying to be) detached from the world that the scientist is observing is central to scientific objectivity; it is also stereotypically masculine. Gender connects to the issue of animal use by science in two ways; it is suspiciously unmanly to object to invasive procedures on animals, and ideas of masculinity are culturally associated with the objectivity demanded of scientists (Keller 1985). Women entering the life sciences have to overcome these associations. The problem besetting potential recruits to biological sciences is clear; it is you who has to change. If you object, or are too squeamish, then your only choice is to get out of doing biology altogether. At the moment at least, the practice of science is unlikely to change.

Empathy, a more "feminine" characteristic, may not be explicitly acknowledged in scientific discourse; yet it is well known within the scientific community that some people are simply better than others at understanding or handling animals. These may not necessarily be women (although women working as animal technicians were felt by some scientists to be "better" with animals in laboratory manuals earlier this century); an article published in 1947 suggested for example that "the right technical assistant (preferably female)" was "by far the most important feature in the management of any rat colony" (McGaughey et al. 1947, 111).

Similarly, Arnold Arluke (1992a) has described what he calls the "ethical culture" of two very different primate labs in the US. In one, the attitudes are cavalier toward the animals; the lab workers are "cowboys." In the other, the attitudes are more companionate and caring; these are "animal people." The gender connotations in his descriptions of caring animal people versus macho cowboys are clear. In her "undercover story" for the British Union for the Abolition of Vivisection, Sarah Kite describes how laboratory workers forced tubes down beagles' throats for oral dosing of drugs, how terrified the animals looked, and how they were subsequently thrown back into their cages. The uncaring, "macho" behaviour she describes seems to accord with Arluke's account, and contrasts with her use of the language of emotions – how "terrified" the animals looked, for instance.

The image of the macho scientist is of someone who does not express feelings, may even seem cavalier in his (or her) attitudes toward the animals used. Researchers, of course, may sometimes seem cavalier out of ignorance; the philosopher and scientist Bernard Rollin suggests that they are often "ignorant regarding many features of the animals they use, and receive little or no training in dealing with animals"; anecdotally, he cites a researcher who asked when mice grew up to be rats, and another who sent a batch of beagles back because they were feverish (dogs normally have a higher body temperature than we do) (Rollin 1989, 125–6). Such anecdotes abound, at least among those willing to acknowledge them.

I have no doubt that such scenes as the anti-vivisectionists describe can sometimes be observed: similar behaviour toward animals (and worse) can be witnessed in slaughterhouses, in intensive agriculture, in people's homes. Every day, the animal welfare organizations rescue thousands of ill-treated or unwanted animals — and destroy many. Perhaps ignorance is a factor, as is sometimes claimed; more likely, cruelty in, say, slaughterhouses, has to do with desensitization (which may be necessary to do the job) and the need of the people doing it to suppress their own ambivalence.

Despite the training that discourages the expression of concern, however, scientists are often as ambivalent in their beliefs about animals as anyone else. Outside of the laboratory, they may treat some animals as having moral claims (their own domestic pets, for instance). Yet inside the laboratory they may seem to behave as if the animals used in their experiments had few, or at any rate fewer, moral claims. Scientists using animals do, of course, largely accept that animals have less ethical value than humans; that is how research on animals must be justified in the first place. But less ethical value does not mean none, and many people working with laboratory animals do find ways of expressing concern over ethics. While there is no doubt truth in the images of terrified beagles, and of uncaring people force-feeding them, many other people in laboratories seek to ensure the animals' welfare. Welfare, of course, is nowhere enough for those advocating animal rights – and caring for laboratory animals must be justified by those workers by reference to beliefs that using animals is permissible in the first place.

In their public pronouncements – in scientific journals, or in public defences of their research – scientists may seem to present a united front. The ethical issues emphasized in pro-research pronouncements from, say, the Research Defence Society, inevitably focus on the medical (and veterinary) benefits resulting from previous research. The discovery in the 1920s that insulin treatment could alleviate diabetes could not, they urge, have occurred without research on dogs, but has been of inestimable value to millions of human diabetics. Thus a publicity video produced by the Research Defence Society, "What About People?," refers to the early research on diabetes and insulin, accompanied by footage of a diabetic man. He tells us how his life has been saved by regular insulin injections, as he pats his dog.

At other times, however, scientists may be more uncertain. They may express their ambivalence in speech, as conversation allows more scope for uncertainty or for referring to "what can go wrong." On one hand, scientists may use language clearly reminiscent of the "air of bravado." So what if an animal dies, "there's more where that came from" I was once told, when an animal died on the operating table. That masculine bravado, not appearing to be affected by the death of the animal, is part of what the fledgling scientist must learn if she or he is to survive. Learning it meant that I had to learn to write in that "objective," distancing style so characteristic of science; I had to learn to make claims about the relevance or importance (in scientific terms) of what I was doing. By contrast, when I worked with animals at home, training or living with them, I spoke a different language, a language rich with emotion and metaphor; even in the lab I would use that language to talk about the animals I worked with. One rat might be "cheeky" for instance, another "friendly." But those descriptions did not find their way into the scientific papers. Only in writing do scientists routinely distance themselves.

SOCIAL RELATIONS IN THE LAB: SCIENTISTS, ANIMALS AND TECHNICIANS

Scientists (myself included) have been trained in laboratories for so long that the places are taken for granted; what we were trained to do were experiments that would test hypotheses and (in time) generate "facts." Recent work in sociology of science, however, tends to tell a different story. Bruno Latour asks, for example, what it is that makes laboratories a source of political strength, helping to give science such power and authority. The answer, he suggests, lies in part in their reliance on "inscription devices," the various machines and technology of scientific experiments (Latour 1983, 161). It does not matter what is being studied, all laboratories rely on devices that churn out written traces: graphs, tables of numbers, abstract symbols. It is these that create "data," the facts of the scientific experiment, and help to create an air of authority about those data.

An important result of all these traces is that they position the observer (whether that is an observer of laboratory work, or a reader of the resulting written texts); no longer is the observer observing a scientist observing nature, but he or she must now watch numbers, and believe that these machine products represent raw nature. Once that is done, the observer is less able to contest the output; after all, the printed results are there for all to see.

The purchasing and use of these instruments shapes the social relations of the lab. Once bought, they must be used and their products (graphs, lists of numbers, and so on) must be incorporated into a written product, the scientific paper. Producing this is one of the central acts of science (Latour and Woolgar 1979). For my purposes here, an important point is that they also inevitably shape the relationship between humans and nonhumans, and thus the knowledge about animals that can be gained. They structure the space in which the work is carried out, and the work must be fitted into the demands of the technology. In interviews with animal technicians, for example, one told me that she had been expected to "cull" all rats below a certain size (which included virtually all the females); only males over a certain size would fit the stereotaxic apparatus used to hold the head still during surgery for neuroscience experiments. The results, of course, are likely to be written up in such a way that they seem to apply to all rats, irrespective of sex.

Another example of how apparatus helps to construct (and limit) what we know about animals comes from studies of the sexual behaviour of rats. Until fairly recently, the literature was full of accounts of the passive receptivity of the female, who would be mounted actively by a male. One obvious reason why the active behaviour of female rats (who solicit males, choose between them, and help to "pace" male activity; McClintock and Adler 1979) was ignored was prevailing ideology, the image of recumbent female sexuality. But another important reason was simply the apparatus; scientists had put the animals in heterosexual pairs in tiny enclosures to watch the sex. In larger enclosures, in groups as they would be in the wild, a very different picture emerges.

Physical space matters in another sense, too. It may seem a trivial point, but most "laboratory animals" used for research do not generally live in laboratories. They live in specially-built animal houses, cared for by specialist animal technicians. Many animals never go near a lab; they are kept as breeding stock, fed and watered regularly. The design of animal houses and cages has come under increasing scrutiny in recent years in the wake of growing public concern and consequent legislative changes. Lab animals, then, live in cages in animal houses. What this means is that there is a spatial separation between the animal house, where the animals live and are cared for, and the laboratories in which many procedures are carried out. In part, this separation has evolved to ensure the health of the animals and their quality, but it also ensures that at least some laboratory personnel rarely, if ever, come into direct contact with the animals (or their caretakers) in their daily lives.

It is, of course, not only the physical space of the laboratory and its apparatuses that contribute to the construction of what we know about animals. It is also the people who work in them; at a general level it is "scientists" who are doing the experimental procedures on animals that the anti-vivisectionists abhor. They are scientists in that they are involved in a process called science. But so are the animal technicians, whom we do not usually call scientists. In practice, there are many people who are involved in "doing science," from the lab director and the researchers at the lab bench to the technicians, as well as the secretaries and cleaners (not to mention the women whose domestic work reproduces the scientists themselves, as Hilary Rose has pointed out; 1983, 1994). Many of these people are not thought of as "doing science," even if they are essential to it; others are doing it, but are not labelled as scientists (Latour 1987).

There may be others who are involved in the negotiations concerning what happens to lab animals. In Britain, for example, the use of animals in research is regulated by law, and managed through the Home Office and a system of inspectors. The law requires licences (for the institution the researcher and the particular project); it also requires that there is a named vet associated with the institution. So the inspector is likely to be consulted as part of the process of obtaining licences.

Within this division of labour, there are different relationships to laboratory animals. Some scientists may have little to do with the animal house, the place where the animals are kept; instead, they might request that an animal is delivered to the lab for an experiment. Depending on the research, the animal may be killed first, or it may be sent to the lab alive and never allowed to wake up from the anaesthetic. Some may undergo surgical procedures (usually in an operating theatre) so that scientists can study the subsequent effects. For these scientists, the animal merely appears at a predestined time and place, as part of the apparatus. It has no meaning *as* a living animal, only as an exemplar of particular physiological systems or biochemical processes.

Some scientists, by contrast, do their work in the animal house itself. They may prefer to give animals injections rather than to ask a technician, for example. Others work on topics that involve observations of the animals. My own background, for instance, is in animal behaviour. I conducted research by observing animals in the animal house where they lived. The meaning of the animal for those scientists who do so is likely to be different from the meaning of the animal if it simply appears in the lab. Watching animals daily going about their behavioural routines meant that I could not easily see them as bits of apparatus. Like many technicians who work with animals, I would often go into the rat room in the morning and greet them all with a cheery hello. You don't say "hi" to your ultracentrifuge.

Animal technicians must care for stock animals, deliver animals to the labs, and care for animals recovering from surgery. They must set up breeding programmes, and may also take part in some of the research (if their involvement is permissible under the laws or guidelines of the country in which they work). They must also cull animals that are too old, or if there is overstocking.

The technician is thus closer to the animals than most scientists; not surprisingly, many feel therefore that they are "buffers" between the animal and the scientist. They see themselves as caring people, who come into the job because they like animals. Because of that, they may also feel that they are the "best ones for the job" when it comes to the unpleasant task of having to kill their charges; no one else, after all, knows the animals as well as they. One technician told me, for example, that the ferrets she worked with "were her friends"; she knew them best and they trusted her. Paradoxically, this meant that she was the best person to deal with them "when the time came."

Technicians must care for the animals as individuals. They may empathize with the animals, yet must justify the research. But they can do little about these contradictions (even if they find ways of quietly resisting); they lack the power that the research scientists have. Similar questions of power are familiar in feminist writing; what structures the division of labour in the laboratories is, inevitably, gender, class, and race. Technicians are more likely than research scientists to be women or to be black, for example. The relationship of each of these actors to the laboratory animals may be different; but each relationship is situated within a wider public arena, and in different relationships of power. Scientists (and inspectors) have more power than technicians and are more likely to be male. Thus relationships of humans to animals acquire an overlay of gender – though the end result for the animals is, of course, always the same. Laboratory animals are at the bottom of the social pecking order.

Most of those involved in research, not surprisingly, tend publicly to defend it, but few privately are that sanguine. In private, scientists sometimes also express feelings about the animals, and acknowledge the need for empathy and "good handling" (Lynch 1988), even though open discussion of these feelings is not encouraged. Talking publicly about scientists' unease can meet resistance in scientific circles; Arnold

Arluke encountered suggestions, for example, that he change the title of his talk to one that was less "provocative" than one expressing unease. In the end, he called it "untitled" (Arluke 1992b).

Similarly, scientists in conversation may seek to convey an impression of themselves as caring, emphasizing for example ways in which they draw the line at particular techniques, at using particular species, or at the use of animals for testing cosmetics (Birke and Michael 1992a, 1992b). Others may state that while they could justify using rats or mice, they could not bring themselves to work on dogs, cats, or primates (noting as they did so, that they were being hypocritical or contradictory in adopting this position). Using euphemisms, too, is a way of avoiding admitting to the dilemmas caused by using animals. While some animal technicians do use the word "kill," they are far more likely to use "cull" or "sacrifice" or "put down" – even when I had explicitly used the more direct word in posing the question.

Perhaps one reason why scientists often find it easier to work with rodents rather than larger animals is that rodents are relatively standardized. At least to the untrained eye, one white rat looks much like another. They therefore lose individuality (unless singled out in some way for special treatment, when they may cross the boundary and may even become "pets"; Arluke 1988). I well remember one rat in our lab who had problems with his teeth. Rodent incisors keep growing, but his were slightly skewed, so they failed to meet properly and were in danger of circling round and through his jaw. We didn't "cull" him; instead, we regularly trimmed his teeth so that he could eat. Somehow, because of his infirmity, we singled him out, and created a pet; we were upset when he died. Yet we gave none of his sisters and brothers any special treatment. They remained numbers in cages, part of the experimental protocol, each much the same as another. We were not unique in this strange behaviour of creating "pets."

In one visit to an animal house, I was struck by the way that the animal technicians spoke of the need for opaque cages. The reason, they said, was that the research scientists felt "disturbed" by seeing the rats in clear cages, "because they kept looking at you." Once they do so, animals begin to cross the boundary from being "apparatus." In this sense, they become less clearly "other" when they start to watch you – they become individuals, real animals. For these laboratory scientists at least, there are clearly ethical dilemmas – better not to see that they are animals at all.

The relationship of scientists to the animals under investigation is somewhat different when the animals are being studied in the field. In the first place, the animal populations are usually being studied for their own sake, as exemplars of a particular species or as part of a particular ecosystem. Not surprisingly then, field studies cover a much wider range of species, from nematode worms to chimpanzees. Laboratory studies, by contrast, are typically based on cheap and easily bred small mammals such as rodents. In many laboratory-based studies, the animals used are frequently standing as a substitute for humans – the "animal model" of mammalian physiology. They are, furthermore, artifacts of laboratory practice, having only a symbolic relationship to "nature" outside of the laboratory. Animals in the wild, unlike laboratory animals, clearly have a less symbolic relationship to wild nature; they are also more likely to be seen by scientists as whole animals, rather than as suppliers of bits. Second, the ethical dilemmas are different. A scientist (or others) might be concerned about inflicting possible pain or suffering on the animal(s) concerned, in much the same way as someone might be concerned about laboratory animals. This would be the case, for example, if a field study involved capturing an animal and subjecting it to an injection, say, or to minor surgery. There are other ethical dilemmas involved in field studies, however. Should a scientist be allowed to remove one animal from a population that is breeding? What happens to that animal if moved elsewhere? What happens to other animals in the population, including that individual's mate and offspring? And, of course, these problems may be compounded if the species in question is endangered.

A third difference between field work and what goes on in the lab is one of degree rather than kind. The relationship of scientist to animal is, as I have said, embedded in a wider social context of relationships between people which both structure it and give it meaning. Unlike lab studies, which tend to be done most frequently in affluent Western countries, some of the best-known field studies take place in poorer, developing countries. In that case, the researcher enters another culture. In primate studies, for example, Donna Haraway has pointed to the ways in which the research lies at the intersection of politics of gender and race. What we know, scientifically, about chimpanzees or gorillas has been obtained predominantly by white people (significantly, often white women) whose presence in the African countries where the animals live depends upon a long history of Western colonization of those countries. How we think about other apes, in their taxonomic closeness to us, is also part of the politics and negotiation of the meanings given in Western science to "nature" (Haraway 1990).

DEFENDING THE BOUNDARIES: THE ANIMAL EXPERIMENTATION CONTROVERSY

It is, of course, precisely their closeness to us that makes the apes special in our eyes. For that reason, many people are more opposed to using them in laboratory work of any kind than other species of mammals. Not surprisingly, the use of primates has been an important theme in the growing controversy about the use of animals in laboratory research.

Since the mid-1970s, there has been such growth in anti-vivisectionist feeling that we can speak of a new social movement for animal rights (Jasper and Nelkin 1992). Scientists can no longer dismiss the opposition as merely a lunatic fringe; they ignore anti-vivisectionist feeling at their peril. Increasingly, they must act

to protect their laboratories and animal houses (with the high protection described so caustically by animal-rights activists), and they

> must engage in a battle for public opinion, seeking to undermine the animal rights movement by associating it with violence and terrorism, and to improve their own public image by defending the value of their work. And they try to steal back the moral high ground with emotional rhetoric. In effect the scientists have developed a counter-crusade. (Nelkin and Jasper 1992, 38)

Thus in 1990 more than one thousand people signed a declaration on scientists' use of animals organized by the British Association for the Advancement of Science. The subsequent short report (published in 1993) stressed the benefits to medicine of animal research, and included a special section on the importance of using primates for certain areas of research such as vaccines (AIDS is mentioned here) and Alzheimer's disease.

A key strategy of this report is to emphasize that scientists have clear responsibilities in using animals. "If there were a Hippocratic oath for scientists," the report argues,

> it would surely include two primary responsibilities that a research worker must accept when planning animal-based studies. The first ... is to use animals only for research intended to contribute to the advancement of knowledge. The second is to minimize any possible pain or distress that an animal in the scientist's care may experience. Those are two of the key criteria taken into account when deciding the scientific merit of a research project and before a request is made for funds for the research. (BAAS 1993, para. 5)

My main point here is to emphasize this text as part of a counter-strategy on the part of scientists. Note the stress placed in this writing on responsibility and on using animals only for certain purposes and under certain conditions. This rhetoric is designed to reassure waverers in the controversy that animal experiments are not done for trivial reasons (as is often claimed by animal-rights protesters). It will do little of course to mollify the protests. After all, it is quite easy to claim that a research programme is *intended* to contribute to the advancement of knowledge; what self-respecting scientist would claim otherwise, when advancing knowledge is the name of the science game? And minimizing distress is in the scientists' interests as well as the animals', because it helps to keep unwanted variability in the results to a minimum.

The counter-strategy draws us back to the kinds of critique that both feminists and animal-rights protesters have made against science. Thus, while individual scientists may indeed be responsible, collective responsibility is less likely in a system that so subordinates the animals' interests. Appeals to the responsibilities of scientists focus on the individual, removing him or her from the social relationships of the laboratory, and from the economic and political structures in which research is done. In practice, it is not likely to be the research scientists themselves who will oversee the day-to-day welfare of the animal (even though they may be legally obliged to take that responsibility). And no funding agency is likely to give money to a research project that did not appear to be "advancing knowledge."

A less obvious counter-strategy is to defend one's own research in contrast to that done by others. Here, the trick is to admit that "abuses" of animals in research might occur elsewhere while believing that everything "here" is all right. The "here" might be one's own lab, or country, or social group; it is always "others" who perpetrate misdeeds. Given the high profile of the controversy, it is hardly surprising that researchers would be loath to recognize problems in their own lab, while admitting that they may occur elsewhere.

Here, the "other" distinction is not between humans and other animals, but between the scientist him/herself and other people who might, in some contexts, be seen as part of the same social group. These others are ones whose treatment of the animals is held by the speaker to be insufficient or cruel. Thus others might include "foreigners" (explicitly racist or ethnocentric),

that is, scientists from those countries or cultures whose attitudes to animals may not be the same as the speaker's (Birke and Michael 1992b). It might be petkeepers among the lay public, who often fail to live up to standards they expect of scientists. These "others" serve the purpose of marking out ethical boundaries; for the British scientists we interviewed, it was British science that was seen to be better – more ethical, better controlled – than science done elsewhere.

One way of surreptitiously policing the boundaries so that anyone with suspect tendencies toward feminine empathy for animals is excluded is simply to expect everyone within science to adopt an air of bravado, of not asking awkward questions – or not in public, at any rate. Meanwhile, the "sentimentality" (or caring empathy, if you will) of people outside of science is scorned in pronouncements by the research establishment, and people are derogated as being "ignorant" of the benefits of animal-based medical research. Ironically, that establishment is beginning to fight back not on grounds of scientific reason, but of emotionality itself. People in wheelchairs or children saved by the products of research provide emotive images and language that can counter the gruesome pictures of antivivisectionist literature. As the American Medical Association put it in 1989, scientists must fight back using tactics as hard-hitting as their rivals', for "the general public is up for grabs" (Jasper and Nelkin 1992, 132).

It is, of course, precisely appeals to emotions and "feminine sentimentality" that have had currency in feminist writing about the use of animals. Sally Gearhart, writing in the newsletter of Feminists for Animal Rights (Gearhart 1992, 1–4), points out that scientists may not be intentionally cruel, but they have become dehumanized. That dehumanization, that lack of caring compassion, promotes a deep alienation of scientists from the life of the nature they purport to study; that alienation concerns Gearhart, because of its potential links to wider domination. Alienation breeds violence, she implies.

My purpose in this chapter was to explore two themes about the laboratory use of animals that raise feminist questions. One is the social relationships of the lab, not only between people in different occupational positions, but also between people and animals. The meanings of the animals (and the practice of what happens to them) are structured by those relationships, which in turn are deeply gendered.

The other kind of feminist question focuses on the gendered nature of scientific inquiry and practice. Caring empathy is, as Miriam Rothschild noted, "suspiciously unmanly" and weak, while the façade of emotional detachment is one that we must learn if we are to survive in science. Feminists have questioned those stances and the underlying assumption that detachment is more valuable as part of our broad critiques of science. Scientific writing, meanwhile, continues to perpetuate a language devoid of emotional nuance or richness of metaphor – a language, indeed, that is largely devoid of any sense that there are sentient animals in the laboratory at all.

REFERENCES

Arluke, A. (1988) Sacrificial symbolism in animal experimentation: Object or pet? *Anthrozoos*, 2, 97–16.

Arluke, A. (1992a) The ethical culture of primate labs, paper given at Science and the Human-Animal Relationship meeting, Amsterdam, March.

Arluke, A. (1992b) Trapped in a guilt cage, *New Scientist*, 134 (1815), 33–35.

Birke, L. and Michael, M. (1992a) The researchers dilemma, *New Scientist*, 4 April, 25–28.

Birke, L. and Michael, M. (1992b) Views from behind the barricade, *New Scientist*, 4 April, 29–32.

Bleier, R. (1984) *Science and Gender*. Oxford: Pergamon.

British Association for the Advancement of Science (BAAS) (1993) *Animals and the Advancement of Science*. London: BAAS.

Collard, A. (with J. Contrucci) (1988) *The Rape of the Wild*. London: The Women's Press.

Gearhart, Sally (1992) [Editors' note: reference missing in original and cannot be located or verified.]

Guerrini, A. (1989) The ethics of animal experimentation in seventeenth-century England, *Journal of the History of Ideas*, 50, 391–408.

Halpin, Z.T. (1989) Scientific objectivity and the concept of "the other," *Women's Studies International Forum*, 12, 285–94.

Haraway, D. (1990) A manifesto for cyborgs: Science, technology and socialist feminism in the 1980s, in L. Nicholson (ed.) *Feminism/Postmodernism*. London: Routledge, 190–233.

Jasper, J. and Nelkin, D. (1992) *The Animal Rights Crusade*. New York: The Free Press.

Keller, E. F. (1985) *Perspectives on Gender and Science*. New Haven, CT: Yale University Press.

Kite, S. (1990) *Secret Suffering: Inside a British Laboratory*. London: British Union for the Abolition of Vivisection.

Klinkenborg, G. (1993) Barnyard diversity. *Audubon*, 95, 78–88.

Latour. B. (1983) Give me a laboratory and I will raise the world, in K. Knorr Cetina and M. Mulkay (eds) *Science Observed*. London: Sage.

Latour, B. (1987) *Science in Action: How to Follow Engineers in Society*. Milton Keynes: Open University Press.

Latour. B. and Woolgar, S. (1979) *Laboratory Life: The Construction of Scientific Facts*. London: Sage.

LeGuin, U. (1987b) Mazes, in U. LeGuin, *Buffalo Gals and Other Presences*. Santa Barbara: Capra Press.

Lynch, M.E. (1988) Sacrifice and the transformation of the animal body into a scientific object: Laboratory culture and ritual practice in the neurosciences, *Social Studies of Science*, 18, 265–89.

McClintock, M. and Adler, N. (1979) The role of the female during copulation in wild and domestic rats *(Rattus norvegicus)*, *Behaviour*, 67, 67–96.

McGaughey, C.A., Thompson, H.V., and Chitty, D. (1947) The Norway Rat, in A. Worden (ed.) *UFAW Handbook on the Care and Management of Laboratory Animals*. London: Universities Federation for Animal Welfare/Bailliere.

Nelkin, D. and Jasper, J. (1992) The animal rights controversy, in D. Nelkin (ed.) *Controversy: Politics of Technical Decisions*. London: Sage.

Potter, E. (1988) Modeling the gender politics in science, in N. Tuana (ed.) *Feminism and Science*. Bloomington: Indiana University Press.

Rollin, B. (1989) *The Unheeded Cry: Animal Consciousness, Animal Pain and Science*. Oxford: Oxford University Press.

Rose, H. (1983) Hand, brain and heart: A feminist epistemology for the natural sciences, *Signs,* 9, 73–90.

Rose, H. (1994) *Love, Power and Knowledge: Towards a Feminist Transformation of the Sciences.* Cambridge: Polity.

Rothschild, M. (1986) *Animals and Man: The Romanes Lecture 1984–5.* Oxford: Clarendon.

Ryder, R. (1989) *Animal Revolution: Changing Attitudes towards Speciesism.* Oxford: Blackwell.

33

SARAH WHATMORE

Hybrid Geographies: Rethinking the "Human" in Human Geography*

Sarah Whatmore studies environmental geography with a focus on the relationship between nature and culture. She has published on the theoretical and political implications of the relations between people and the living world in scientific practice in a wide variety of areas including agriculture and food, land use, and biotechnology. In Whatmore's work, geography is a study of the places between the real and the ideal, the natural and the social, the objective and the subjective, the human and the nonhuman, and similar to Lynda Birke, she draws heavily on feminist challenges to scientific objectivity. In the extract reproduced here, Whatmore proposes a critical human geography that rejects binary thinking about the "natural" and the "social." She argues for an acknowledgement of the relational conception of social life that includes bonds between people, organisms, machines, and elements in a way that also allows for the recognition of the "creative presence of creatures and devices amongst us." The notion of agency looms large in Whatmore's work. Noting that agency is not equal to intentionality with linguistic competence, she draws on Bruno Latour's actor network theory [often called actant network theory to embrace both human and nonhuman actors], she emphasizes hybridity, collectivity, and corporeality as interlinking processes necessary to reconfigure the "purified spaces" of nature and society as fluid networks. Networks are constituted of a multiplicity of actants (human and nonhuman, technological and textual, organic and mechanic) which hold each other in position. In Whatmore's hybrid geographies, social life is always "in the making through networks of actants-in-relation that are at once local and global, natural and cultural, and always more than human." You will recall that this unique way of thinking about fluidity and affinity relations was brilliantly described in Deleuze and Guattari's concept of becoming-animal [see Section 1], and Whatmore demonstrates the usefulness of these concepts in theorizing about nature, space, and society.

---

* Reprinted from Sarah Whatmore (1999) "Hybrid Geographies: Rethinking the 'Human' in Human Geography." In Doreen Massey, John Allen, and Philip Sarre (eds) *Human Geography Today*. Cambridge: Polity Press, with permission from Polity Press.

This place
we have not seen before
these old woods
your hands
touching knowledge.

Susan Griffin, "Knowledge"

INTRODUCTION

The Enlightenment antinomy between nature and society marks a pervasive tension in the institutional configuration of scientific knowledge and authority including that of geography, not least through the discipline's complicity in the project of empire (Livingstone 1992). But it is Margaret Fitzsimmons's critique of what she calls a "peculiar silence on the question of nature" (1989, 106) which provides the most telling indictment of its implications for the more critical aspirations of contemporary human geography. In the pages of *Antipode*, she called the (then largely Marxist-inspired) community of "radical" geographers to account for theorizing space without nature in all but a few isolated cases.[1] Fitzsimmons identified three contributory factors in their failure to "come to grips with the theoretical problem of Nature" (1989, 107): the institutional separation of human and physical geographies, the ontological separation of nature and space in human geography, and the urban bias of the intellectual culture which shaped "radical" concerns.

Critical human geography has since witnessed a reawakening of debate on "the question of nature." This has been animated by intellectual impulses which have broadened the horizons of "critical" work beyond the compass of Marxism, most significantly through poststructuralist, feminist, post-colonial and environmentalist projects. Wider political and policy imperatives have added further impetus to interest in the environment on the research agendas of the social sciences (and humanities) at large. This mass trespass over the manicured lawns of natural science challenges the categorical cordon that has marked off the "nonhuman world" and the

grounds for understanding it. Yet, even as these energies put the importance of the question of nature for social science beyond dispute, so a new form of enclosure threatens with the proliferation of "environmental" sub-disciplines such as environmental sociology (Hannigan 1995), environmental anthropology (Descola and Palsson 1996), environmental history (Bird 1987), and environmental politics (Dobson and Lucardie 1995).

Across the disciplinary spectrum a tendency to "add nature in" to already entrenched constellations of "critical" social science has produced an equally unhelpful cul-de-sac. This takes the form of a dogged impasse between versions of "social constructionism," in which "Nature" is treated as an artefact of the social imagination, and versions of "natural realism," in which "nature" consists of substantive entities and objective forces (Soper 1995). The first of these positions is broadly associated with modes of critical enquiry labelled postmodern and linked with the so-called cultural turn in the social sciences, in which the question of nature rapidly becomes reformulated as an exclusively epistemological one about the "socially constructed nature of scientific enquiry or technological enterprise" (Robertson et al. 1996, 2). Here, Nature is the always already crafted product of human interpretation. Critical analysis of this inescapably mediated Nature becomes fixed on the social hierarchies and discursive conventions and devices of Nature's inscription by (and in) landscape paintings, TV nature programmes, computer models, and so on. Unsurprisingly, since an important strand of this critical effort has been focused on their story-telling powers and practices, such work has provoked outright hostility amongst the science establishment (Gross and Levitt 1994).

More significantly for those laying claim to a "critical" positionality, such work has been met with deep scepticism amongst environmental (Soulé and Lease 1995) and social (Redclift and Benton 1994) scientists, whose own stakes in this same intellectual territory and in projects of ecological and/or socialist salvation are founded, in different ways, on a "crucial distinction …

between material processes and relations on the one hand and our understandings of, and communications about, those processes on the other" (Dickens 1996, 83). Here, "nature" in the raw can, and must, be recognized as ontologically separate from the "Natures" of social representation in order to sustain the possibility of (and their own pretensions to) a singular analytic-diagnostic truth – an account of society's relationship with nature that uniquely corresponds to a real, objective world. In human geography these battle lines are variously rehearsed and interrogated in recent papers by Demeritt (1996), from a broadly poststructuralist perspective, and Gandy (1996), from a critical realist perspective.

There is undoubtedly a generous measure of caricature in this embattled depiction of the treatment of Nature/nature in social theory which serves primarily to reaffirm intellectual prejudices and identities. Only the most vulgar of "postmodern" accounts (and there are some) suggest that the world is – to borrow Sheets-Johnstone's evocative phrase – "the product of an immaculate linguistic conception" (1992, 46). Accounts that get lumped into the "social constructionist" category are much more diverse than their detractors acknowledge (the textual emphasis of the deconstructionist current as against the performative emphasis of various theories of embodied practice, for example: see Conley 1997). In most cases, some interval between the moments of "reality" and "representation" is sustained; it is just that it is deemed ineluctably opaque. Equally, only the crudest of "natural realist" accounts (and again, there are some) refuse to recognize the contingency of knowledge claims about "real-world" entities and processes. This label eclipses the richness of Marxist-inspired analysis (dialectical materialism, critical realism and political ecology to name a few: see Castree 1995). It is just that such accounts share an inclination to exempt themselves from the representational moment, by variously claiming a privileged correspondence between concept and object, logic and process.

Ironically, this categorical insistence on an either/or, constructionist/realist approach to the question of nature itself echoes the binary mode of thinking that sets up an opposition between "the natural" and "the social" as the absolute and only possibilities in a purified world of black and white. For all their loudly declared enmity, these analytic encampments are similarly premised on the acceptance, however unrecognized, of the *a priori* separation of nature and society. As Bruno Latour has put it:

> Critical explanation always began from the poles and headed toward the middle, which was first the separation point and then the conjunction point for opposing resources ... In this way the middle was simultaneously maintained and abolished, recognized and denied, specified and silenced ... How? ... By conceiving every hybrid as a mixture of two pure forms. (Latour 1993, 77–8)

This same nature/society binary informs more everyday geographical imaginations and environmental sensibilities rehearsed in pervasive distinctions between "built environments" (the social pole) and "natural environments" (the natural pole), with hierarchies of human "settlement" in between marking inverse gradations of social/natural presence and absence. From the conventions of cartographic colour coding to the protocols of land-use planning or of environmental designation, numerous professional and policy practices impress this binary imaginary upon the fabric of the world (Carter 1996). With its celebration of "wild(er)ness," configured as both species and places marked out precisely by their distance from humankind, much environmentalist rhetoric is also complicit in this purification of the spaces of society and nature (Cosgrove 1990). As Tim Ingold has observed, "Something [...] must be wrong somewhere, if the only way to understand our own creative involvement in the world is by taking ourselves out of it" (1995a, 58).

Human geography thus finds itself at an important juncture in its critical engagement with the question of nature, in which neither the "bracketing off" of an environmental sub-field common in other disciplines, nor the threadbare promise of a reintegration of physical and human geography, will suffice. Nor, in my view, does recourse to variants of dialectical reasoning centred on the ways in which nature and society interact provide a radical enough basis for critical enquiry (see, for example, Harvey 1996). Far from challenging this *a priori* categorization of the things of the world, dialectics can be seen to raise its binary logic to the level of a contradiction and engine of history.[2] Rather, any critical engagement with the "question of nature" must begin, as Donna Haraway argues, by building theories whose "geometries, paradigms and logics break out of binaries ... and nature/ culture modes of any kind" (1991, 129). This, of course, is more easily said than done.

Geographers have already taken up the challenge of exploring what Taussig has called the "desperate places" in between the "real" and the "ideal," the "natural" and the "social," the "objective" and the "subjective," the "human" and the "non-human" (1993, xvii). Examples range from studies of urban wildlife (Wolch et al. 1995) and technological "subjects" (Bingham 1996) to computer-simulated environments (Light 1997) and domestication (Anderson 1997). These forays share, I suggest, a concern to re-cognize the "human" in "human geography" and thereby to signal a rather different agenda for critical geographical thinking about the question of nature, which, in various ways, seeks "to accommodate the nonhumans in the fabric of our society" (Latour, in Crawford 1993, 262). This "hybrid" geographical enterprise, as I have called it in the chapter title, is concerned with studying the *living* rather than abstract spaces of social life, configured by numerous, interconnected agents – variously composed of biological, mechanical, and habitual properties and collective capacities – within which people are differently and plurally articulated.

Such an agenda attunes geography to a broader chorus of "critical" voices in the social sciences searching for ways out of the impasse between "constructionist" and "realist" accounts of "nature." The kinds of hybrid space being opened up include the "virtual ecologies" of computer simulation (Wark 1994), the "artefactual nature" of Oncomouse (Haraway 1997) and the "quasi-objects" which bring socio-technologies to life (Serres and Latour 1995). These efforts are tentative and uncoordinated but can be traced through a broad spectrum of contemporary social theory, ranging from feminist challenges to scientific objectivity (such as Haraway 1991) to rethinking the importance of embodiment amongst cognitive scientists (such as Varela et al. 1991). Amidst these unsteady glimmerings, Katherine Hayles suggests that "it is possible to glimpse ... the shape of an answer ... [in] a common emphasis on interaction and positionality" (Hayles 1995, 43). The opening epigraph offers one such glimpse of a non-binary world that signals many of the themes and ideas that follow, but in language more redolent of the sensory texture of what this might mean than the vernacular of social science seems able to approach. In the next section I sketch out what I see as some key dimensions of a hybrid geography which recognizes agency as a relational achievement, involving the creative presence of organic beings, technological devices and discursive codes, as well as people, in the fabrics of everyday living. I then focus on the spatial implications of this kind of approach, illustrated through a consideration of contemporary (re)configurings of wildlife – a category of "nonhumans" most thoroughly outcast from the conventional compass of social life, social science, and human geography.

FROM SOCIAL ACTORS TO ACTANT NETWORKS

Through exclusively social contracts, we have abandoned the bond that connects us to the world ... What language do the things of the world speak that we might come to an understanding of them contractually? ... In fact, the Earth speaks to us in terms of forces, bonds and interactions ... each of the partners in symbiosis thus owes [...] life to the other, on pain of death.

Michel Serres, *The Natural Contract*

The relational conception of social life that I want to outline here takes up the "common emphases" on positionality and interaction identified by Hayles amongst the disparate theoretical efforts to disrupt the binary terms in which the question of nature has been posed. I take these emphases to imply an epistemological insistence on the situatedness of knowledge and a "modest" ontological stance rooted in the everyday practice or performance of *ordering*, as against some abstract order attributed to a colossal logos outside or above the social fray.[3] At its most basic then, the hybrid geography that I am proposing implies a radically different understanding of *social agency* in the senses both that agency is decentred, a "precarious achievement" (Law 1994, 101) spun between social actors rather than a manifestation of unitary intent, and that it is decoupled from the subject/object binary so that, as Nigel Thrift has put it, "the 'material' and the 'social' intertwine and interact in all manner of promiscuous combinations" (1996, 24).

My elaboration of these themes draws particularly on the work of Michel Callon, Bruno Latour, John Law, Michel Serres and others which goes under the label of actor (or actant) network theory (ANT) and is beginning to make a mark on geography (for a review see Murdoch 1997). It also reflects a strong feminist strand of work on science, technology, and the body which Haraway has recently termed "a lumpy community of modest witnesses" (1997, 268), concerned with "the interactions of humans and non-humans in the distributed networks of technoscience" (1997, 141). I have explored the ethical dimensions of a relational understanding elsewhere (Whatmore 1997). Here I want to emphasize three interwoven aspects of such an understanding – the processes and properties of hybridity, collectivity, and corporeality – and their implications for reconfiguring the purified spaces of "nature" and "society" as fluid sociomaterial networkings.

The concept of hybridity as it is deployed by writers like Latour and Haraway seeks to implode the object/subject binary that underlies the modern antinomy between nature and society and to recognize the agency of "nonhuman" actants – acknowledging their presence in the social fabric and exploring ways of making it register in the vocabularies of social analysis. For ANT the erasure of "nonhuman" agency is an effect of particular, and partial, configurations of social practice and discourse rather than a categorical presumption. This decoupling of human/agency is denoted by the (variable) use of the term "actant," as distinct from the more conventional "actor," signalling a methodological commitment to treating any distributions of authority and intentionality amongst actants as practical achievements to be elucidated (Callon and Law 1995, 490).

Actant networks then mobilize, and are constituted by, a multiplicity of different agents, or "actants," human and nonhuman, technological and textual, organic and (geo)physical, which hold each other in position. This hybridized conception of agency admits states of being which fall somewhere between the passive objects of human will and imagination which litter the social sciences, and the autonomous external forces favoured in natural science accounts. Latour follows Serres in designating these in-between states of being as "quasi-objects," which are as "real as nature, narrated as discourse, collective as society [and] existential as being" (1993, 89). An actant network is thus simultaneously an assemblage of actants, whose activities are constituted in and through their connectivities with heterogeneous others, and a network that performs as a more or less durable (extensive in time) and more or less long (extensive in space) mode of ordering amongst its constituent parts. Crucially, in terms of the modest ontological stance of ANT, such modes of ordering, however extensive their reach, are neither as obdurate as a social "structure" nor as volatile as a social "actor's" change of mind. No more, and no less, than their performance, they represent "patterns or regularities that may be imputed to the particulars that make up the recursive and generative networks of the social. They are nowhere else. They do not drive those networks. They aren't outside them" (Law 1994, 83).

This extension of the compass of social agency beyond the human/subject, through the notion of hybridity, has two immediate corollaries for the elaboration of a relational conception of social life. One concerns the implications of a decentred notion of agency or, in terms of ANT, the inherently collective nature of networking – what Callon and Law (1995) call the "hybrid collectif." The other pursues the implicit break with the logocentric presumption that agency is an exclusively human attribute, predicated on particular cognitive and linguistic competences, a move associated with what Thrift calls "non-representational" theories of the social [...]. Each requires some brief elaboration.

The notion of the hybrid collectif implodes the inside/outside binary which discerns social agency as an internal property of discrete, unitary individuals (including corporate individuals). Agency is reconfigured as a relational effect generated by a network of heterogeneous, interacting components whose activity is constituted in the networks of which they form a part (Law and Mol 1995, 277). "Nonhuman" agents are vital to this conception of a network's collective capacity to act "because they attach us to one another, because they circulate in our hands and define our social bond by their very circulation" (Latour 1993, 89). Not to be confused with the more established notion of a social collectivity (that is, an already existing ensemble of people acting in concert), the whole point of speaking of a "collectif," as Callon and Law (1995) insist, is that it erodes the divisions and distinctions that are taken to reside in the order of things – a world of purified monads and the dualisms that keep them segregated. From this perspective "the inside-and-outside [becomes] an active category, created by the actors themselves not [one] already defined" (Latour in Crawford 1993, 257).

How then is the social "agency" of the hybrid collectif to be understood? The answer provided by Callon and Law is that agency in ANT is an:

effect [...] generated in configurations of different materials ... [that] also ... take the form of attributions ... which localise agency as singularity – usually ... in the form of human bodies. Attributions which endow one part of the configuration with the status of prime mover. Attributions which efface the other entities and relations in the collectif or consign these to a supporting and infrastructural role. (1995, 503)

In other words, the property of collectivity does not preclude inequality (non-equivalence) amongst heterogeneous actants but rather insists that the distribution of power within a network can only be understood as a relational effect, conditioning the performance of any particular actant (including humans). This represents the point of greatest tension between ANT and conventional social theories: a refusal to equate agency (the capacity to act or to have effects) with intentionality, premised on narrow linguistic competences. The agency of the hybrid collectif is a bold attempt to shift the weight of this logocentric bias to recognize other, material, forms of signification, by which the specific capacities and properties of entities from X-rays to viruses make their presence felt. This brings us to the third dimension of relationality which, for the sake of abbreviation, I have referred to as corporeality.

The broader significance of the body in social theory has been associated with the elaboration of various theories of practice which reassert, against the lexical cast of the cultural turn, the corporeal properties that condition the very capacities of cognition and communication that are the hallmark of conventional notions of social (human) agency.[4] In ANT, effort has focused on driving "a wedge between re-presentation and language" (Callon and Law 1995, 501) by extending the register of semiotics beyond its traditional concern with signification as linguistic ordering, to all kinds of un-speakable "message bearers" and material processes of inscription, such as technical devices, instruments and graphics, and bodily capacities, habits, and skills (Serres 1995b). This *materialist semiotics* has two important implications for the kind of relational understanding of social life that I am advancing. On the one hand, it reinforces the hybrid and collective dimensions of this understanding by re-embodying human *being*, recalling our place as organisms and acknowledging our varied and changing embeddedness in the material properties and presences of diverse others (Ingold 1995b). On the other hand, it disrupts the binary construction of "reality" and "representation" which, as I suggested earlier, has dogged discussion of the question of nature.

The privileging of language as a precondition and hallmark of social agency rests on and reproduces a worn-out distinction between language and the world, in which the world is treated as an external referent and language as a medium which represents "it" in a more or less transparent manner (Callon and Law 1995, 499). To admit that the relationship is much more opaque and unruly does *not* mean that there is nothing beyond the text; that nothing else matters. Rather it is to refuse the Cartesian designification of nature which simultaneously denies "animals any linguistic capacities at all and [defines] language strictly as the reflection of the conscious mind" (Senior 1997, 67). Instead of reality, on the one hand, and a representation, on the other, ANT recognizes chains of translation of varying kinds and lengths which weave sound, vision, gesture, and scent through all manner of bodies, elements, instruments, and artefacts – so that the distinction between being present and being represented no longer exhausts, or makes sense of, the compass and possibility of social conduct (Latour 1994).

The relational understanding of social life that I am working toward, as will by now be apparent, involves no small imaginative shift, but rather a series of manoeuvres each of which disconcerts the categorical infrastructure on which the edifice of conventional social theories is built, and which has become insinuated in less formal ways of making sense of "who" (what) constitutes our social worlds. My own sense of the theoretical space opened up by these manoeuvres is at best tentative. And, like Marilyn Strathern (1996), I do not think that one can, or ought to, look to ANT to provide some sort of ready-made compass. None the less, there are useful beginnings here for journeys out of the impoverished wor(l)d of N/nature, which make it possible to explore the ways in which the entities, capacities, and processes conventionally preassigned to the spheres of the "natural" and the "social" are mutually conditioned and constituted in the everyday business of *living* in the world. These manoeuvres do not preclude the analytical possibility of still obtaining nature and society as an outcome of specific modes of ordering (networkings), but they do insist that "there is no longer any reason to limit the ontological varieties that matter to two ... At last the middle kingdom [can be] represented" (Latour 1993, 79).

Theoretical ventures in this vein must confront, and cannot succeed without disrupting, the spatial configurations of the nature/society binary that litter contemporary environmental thinking and practice. These configurations inhere in the boundaries, at once real and imagined, erected to keep the things of "nature" and of "society" in their proper place. Even Latour's metaphor of the "middle kingdom," for example, is haunted by the territorial grammar that pervades these geometric habits of mind. Re-cognizing nature not as "a physical place to which one can go" (Haraway 1992, 66) but as an active, changeable presence that is always already in our midst challenges spatial, as well as, social (pre)dispositions.

GEOGRAPHIES IN/OF MOTION

Wildness (as opposed to wilderness) can be found anywhere: in the seemingly tame fields and woodlots of Massachusetts, in the cracks of a Manhattan sidewalk, even in the cells of our own bodies.

W. Cronon, *Uncommon Ground*

The analytic device of the network, freighted with the hybrid, collective, and corporeal properties that I have outlined, has immense significance for (re)imagining the geographies of social life. Thus far, geographers have focused on its implications for understanding globalization (Thrift 1995; Whatmore and Thorne 1997), economic geographies (Murdoch 1995; Thrift and Olds 1996), and the spaces of socio-technologies (Bingham 1996; Hinchliffe 1996). All these efforts seek to disrupt the geometric configuration of the world as a single grid-like surface – a *tabula rasa* which invites the inscription of general theoretical claims as omnipresent, universal rationalities. In contrast, they elaborate a *topological* spatial imagination, emphasizing the *simultaneity* of multiple and partial space-time configurations of social life, and the *situatedness* of social institutions, processes, and knowledges as always contextual, tentative, and incomplete, however long their reach (Thrift 1995).

This fluid geographical vocabulary betokens a shift in analytical emphasis from reiterating fixed surfaces to tracing points of connection and lines of flow (Mol and Law 1994). This means not ignoring the effects of established contours and boundaries that mark the social landscape but, rather, recognizing that these spatial parameters inhere in a host of socio-technical practices – such as property, sovereignty, and identity – that are always in the making, not in some *a priori* order of things. The significance of this shift is that it unsettles any account which is inclined to render messy, fragile networks as slick, consolidated totalities – like science, capitalism, or the state – and recovers a myriad of life-size orderings overshadowed by their heroics (see Gibson-Graham 1996).

In the above quotation, the environmental historian William Cronon signals some of the implications of this "topological" imaginary for the question of "nature" which I want to take up in this section. Playing on Thoreau's famous dictum "in Wild[er]ness is the preservation of the world," he highlights the significance of geography to discerning the world in binary terms. Just as nature tends to be mapped onto spaces designated "rural" so wildlife, the embodiment of a purified nature, is associated with those most rarefied of spaces designated "wilderness." This co-incidence between "wild" plants and animals (species) and the "wild" spaces they inhabit (habitats) pervades Western environmental sensibilities.

It is powerfully evoked, for example, in the protocols of "global environmental management" which police the place of nature by means of territorial archetypes – like biodiversity reserves – that enact a scientific blueprint of who and what should live there (McNeely et al. 1990). But it is a coincidence that is no less resonant in the political dramatics of radical environmental groups like EarthFirst! or Greenpeace, which reinforce the place of nature by means of iconographic landscapes – like "the rainforest" – that are framed by/as their televised sites of struggle (Foreman 1991). Ignorant of their ephemeral status as "representations," such imagined spaces all too readily become flesh as heterogeneous communities are purified in their name through the sometimes violent removal of people, animals, and plants that find themselves on the wrong side of the wire. The ethnic minority Karen people in southern Burma are even now being forcibly ejected by the military government from their traditional lands to make way for the million-hectare My-Inmoletkat "Biosphere" Reserve.[5] In Britain, the ruddy duck recently found itself the target of a bizarre alliance of ornithological and nature conservation agencies intent on culling (that is, killing) its insurgent population here, in order to preserve the genetic purity and species integrity of the "indigenous" European whiteheaded duck from the ruddy duck's "aggressive" mating habits (Lawson 1997). Accommodating nonhumans in the fabric of social life requires more intimate, lively, and promiscuous geographies than these quarantined fragments of a too precious nature.

The hybrid geographical enterprise that I am proposing unsettles this glib co-incidence of the things/spaces of nature by focusing critical energies closer to home. I cannot imagine, still less claim to know, where all the currents of such geographies of wildlife might lead. But their destination is not, as some would have it, yet another brave new world emerging perfectly formed from the engine of history (or capitalism or modernity) – a "third nature" of "cyborg ecologies" forged in the "machinic totality" of "contemporary global capitalism" in which *everything* is caught up (Luke 1996, 11). Rather, such geographies alert us to a world of commotion in which the sites, tracks, and contours of social life are constantly in the making through networks of actants-in-relation that are at once local and global, natural and cultural, and always more than human.

In contrast to the universal ambitions of "third nature" and its forebears, the hybrid geographies that I have in mind are inescapably situated. Their own part in the networks they describe is to be acknowledged, rather than effaced, in terms both of the imprint of researchers and of the words and instruments that extend their ordering presence in time/space (Law 1994). Refusing any vantage point that purports to take in the world at a glance, they are more modest in the claims they can, and want to, make and, by the same token, are more attendant to the energies of those they make claims about. Conceived of topologically, wildlife is no longer fixed at a distance but emerges within the routine interweavings of people, organisms, elements, and machines as these configure the partial, plural, and sometimes overlapping time/spaces of everyday living. These humdrum spaces include, amongst others, the mutable fabric of embodiment, the ordinary motions of inhabitation, and the mediating devices that make "us" present even in "our" absence.

In place of the rigid contours of the flat maps and species inventories of conservation science, or the objectifying gaze of landscape studies, a topology of wildlife is a much more fluid beast in at least three senses. The first of these senses concerns the *spaces of embodiment*. The mutability of organisms (including humans), in terms of their intrinsic organization and morphological plasticity (Goodwin 1988), has been somewhat overshadowed by the heady talk of their malleability in the socio-technical networks of genetic engineering; organ transplantation and the like. Yet at the very heart of these artefactual worlds we are reminded by the proliferation of changeling viruses, mutant cells (dis)figuring corporeal stability, and the startling appearance of pink and purple frogs in suburban garden ponds that we are not the only agents in their fabrication.

The second sense of fluidity has to do with the *spaces of motion*. Animals (including humans) and, rather less obviously, plants, lead mobile lives – on scales that vary from the Lilliputian travels of a dung beetle to the global navigations of migrating whales and birds. Their mobilities are relational achievements – plant seeds journeying in the bellies of animals; the learning of spatial markers and seasonal routines within creature communities. Moreover, plants and animals have been caught up in socio-technical networks with "humans" for some 30,000 years, before we recognized ourselves as *Homo sapiens* (Ingold 1995b). In other words, the categorical boundaries between the wild and the cultivated that we now insist on were unsettled long before the unravelling of DNA. Efforts like the UN Convention on Biological Diversity to fix their place in the world as "indigenous species" within "natural habitats" are a no less political regulation of mobile lives than the paraphernalia of passports and border controls.

The third sense in which a topological rendition of wildlife is more fluid concerns the *spaces of relation*. "Wild" animals and plants whose designation depends on their being forever somewhere else find their place in the world less than secure. The radio collars and tags which adorn the remotest parts of the animal kingdom, no less than their daily exhibition in the wildlife documentaries that occupy TV screens in millions of homes around the world, disturb the geometry of distance and proximity. In place of a straight line from here to there, or a relation rooted in the same spot, the wild and the domestic get swept up in the volatile eddies and flows of socio-technical networks that bring people, living organisms and machines together in new and particular ways (Clark 1997). Against the technological hyperbole of "third nature," the novelty of these networks is the *ways* in which they reconfigure humans/animals/artefacts, not that they are unprecedented in actively unsettling these categories.

CONCLUSION

> What happens if we begin from the premise not that we know reality because we are separate from it (traditional objectivity), but that we can know the world because we are connected with it? (Hayles 1995, 48)

What happens, I have tried to suggest, is an upheaval in the binary terms in which the question of nature has been posed and a recognition of the intimate, sensible, and hectic bonds through which people, organisms, machines, and elements make and hold their shape in relation to each other in the business of everyday living. This upheaval implicates *geographical* imaginations and practices both in the purifying logic which, like "ethnic cleansing," fragments living fabrics of association and designates the proper places of "nature" and "society," and in the promise of its refusal. That refusal does not lead to a world in which the properties and things ascribed to nature have been comprehensively extinguished by, or absorbed within, the compass of those ascribed to human society. Rather, it requires an acceptance of the world as it is – an always already inhabited achievement of "heterogenous social encounters, where all of the actors are not human and all of the humans are not 'us' however defined" (Haraway 1992, 67).

Working through the relational conception of social life that I am proposing, geographically, means (amongst other things) looking again at the spatial organization and ethical contours of agency and power within hybrid networks. Their conventional attribution, theoretically and methodologically, to a single (and always human) epicentre – the faceless corporation, scientific laboratory, or regulatory authority – has to be destabilized. One aspect of doing this is to re-cognize such "powerhouses" as networks in themselves – fragile achievements of actants-in-relation fraught with daily conflicts, illnesses, misunderstandings, technical glitches, and all manner of breakdowns – whose efficacy depends on a host of more diffuse alignments of practices and properties that are not of their ordering. This strategy at least disperses attention through the simultaneous performances of social competences and affordances at different points in a network, and registers the mass of currents rather than single line of force that give it shape (Whatmore and Thorne 1997). In these terms, the reach and durability of any network performance is less an attribute of an individual's, or organization's, inherent forcefulness than an interactional effect.

As I hope I have made clear, the hybrid geographical enterprise that I have in mind shares little with the totalizing incarnations of a "third nature" which have begun to appear in geographical writing and elsewhere. Hybrid geographies cannot be other than plural and partial, if they are not to repeat the error of trying to roll the life worlds and inhabited spaces of radically different kinds of subject into one, by virtue of some unacknowledged vantage point outside all and any of them. Rather than passing judgement on a nature that is always at a distance, such geographies have to be situated in terms of the hybrid networks which we (their authors) and they (as portable inscriptions of various kinds) participate in. Finally, and this is harder to put into words, such geographies must strive to find ways of exploring and expressing the kinds of sensible and relational knowledge of these hybrid worlds as pungently as the kind of writing quoted at the start of this paper. This is perhaps the greatest challenge for those of us trained as social scientists: to overhaul our repertoire of methods and poetics in ways that admit and register the creative presence of creatures and devices amongst us, and the animal sensibilities of our diverse human being.

ACKNOWLEDGEMENTS

This chapter owes much to shared intellectual adventures with colleagues and friends in the Geography Department at Bristol University – notably Lorraine Thorne, Nigel Thrift, and Nick Bingham – and elsewhere, particularly Jon Murdoch. I am grateful to Doreen Massey and Philip Sarre for their much-needed encouragement with a piece that I have found challenging to write. The wildlife theme which illustrates some of the key points is the subject of a more sustained research effort in a project with Lorraine Thorne on "Spatial formations of wildlife exchange," funded by ESRC (award no. R000222113).

NOTES

1. The key exception identified by Fitzsimmons was the spate of writings on the transition from first to second nature by Marxist geographers in the late 1970s and early 1980s, most notably Neil Smith's *Uneven Development* (1984) and the special issue of *Antipode* on "Natural resources and environment" edited by Dick Walker (1979).
2. For a critique of dialectical analysis see Castree (1996) on Harvey's treatment of nature.
3. The "actant" variant of this "modest" ontology as it is manifest in actor or actant network theory (ANT: see Callon and Latour 1981) is reminiscent of Deleuze and Guattari's (1987) "rhizome" metaphor. Latour comments directly on this link in an interview with Crawford (1993, 262). The description of such ontological stances as "modest" is first, and best, made by John Law (1994).
4. Of course the cognitive and linguistic competences that conventionally define the fully fledged subject and social actor are patriarchal constructs from which various categories of "humans" have been, and are still being, excluded. Moreover, the status of these competences as the distinguishing mark of "humanity" is troubled by the comparable skills of other classes of animals (notably, primates and cetaceous mammals) and broader reassessments of animal cognition (see Ingold 1988; Noske 1989).
5. Leading international conservation agencies, including the WWF-UK, the Wildlife Conservation Society in New York and the Washington-based Smithsonian Institute, lent their scientific expertise and credentials to the designation of the Myinmoletkat Reserve and continue to pursue research and conservation programmes there on "endangered" species like the Sumatran rhinoceros and tiger (*Observer*, 23 March 1997).

REFERENCES

Anderson, K. (1997) "A walk on the wild side: a critical geography of domestication." *Progress In Human Geography*, 21/4, 463–85.

Bingham, N. (1996) "Objections: from technological determinism towards geographies of relations." *Society and Space*, 14/6, 635–57.

Bird, E. (1987) "The social construction of nature: theoretical approaches to the history of environmental problems." *Environmental Review*, 11, 255–64.

Callon, M. and B. Latour (1981) "Unscrewing the big leviathan." In K. Knorr-Cetina and A. Cicourel (eds), *Advances in Social Theory and Methodology*. London, Routledge & Kegan Paul, 83–103.

Callon, M. and J. Law (1995) "Agency and the hybrid collectif." *South Atlantic Quarterly*, 94/2, 481–507.

Carter, P. (1996) *The Lie of the Land*. London, Faber & Faber.

Castree, N. (1995) "The nature of produced nature: materiality and knowledge construction in Marxism." *Antipode*, 27/1, 12–48.

Castree, N. (1996) "Birds, mice and geography: Marxisms and dialectics." *Transactions of the Institute of British Geographers*, 21/2, 342–62.

Clark, N. (1997) "Panic ecology. Nature in the age of superconductivity." *Theory, Culture and Society*, 14/1, 77–96.

Conley, V. (1997) *Ecopolitics: The Environment in Poststructuralist Thought*. London, Routledge.

Cosgrove, D. (1990) "Environmental thought and action: pre-modern and post-modern." *Transactions of the Institute of British Geographers*, 15/3, 344–58.

Crawford, T. (1993) "An interview with Bruno Latour." *Configurations*, 1/2, 247–68.

Cronon, W. (ed.) (1995) *Uncommon Ground: Towards Reinventing Nature*. New York, W.W. Norton.

Deleuze, G. and F. Guattari (1987) (English translation). *A Thousand Plateaus*. London, Athlone Press.

Demeritt, D. (1996) "Social theory and the reconstruction of science and geography." *Transactions of the Institute of British Geographers*, 21/3, 484–503.

Descola, P. and G. Palsson (eds) (1996) *Nature and Society: Anthropological Perspectives*. London, Routledge.

Dickens, P. (1996) *Reconstructing Nature*. London, Routledge.

Dobson, A. and D. Lucardie (eds) (1995) *The Politics of Nature*. London, Routledge.

Fitzsimmons, M. (1989) "The matter of nature." *Antipode*, 21/2, 106–20.

Foreman, D. (1991) *Confessions of an Eco-Warrior*. New York, Harmony Books.

Gandy, M. (1996) "Crumbling land: the postmodernity debate and the analysis of environmental problems." *Progress in Human Geography*, 20/1, 23–40.

Gibson-Graham, J. K. (1996) *The End of Capitalism (As We Knew It)*. Oxford, Blackwell.

Goodwin, B. (1988) "Organisms and minds: the dialectics of the animal–human interface in biology." In T. Ingold (ed.), *What Is an Animal?* London, Allen & Unwin, 100–9.

Griffin, S. (1987) "Knowledge." In *Unremembered Country*. Port Townsend, Copper Canyon, 22–5.

Gross, P. and N. Levitt (1994) *Higher Superstition: The Academic Left and its Quarrels with Science*. Baltimore, Johns Hopkins University Press.

Hannigan, J. (1995) *Environmental Sociology*. London, Routledge.

Haraway, D. (1991) "Situated knowledges: the science question in feminism and the privilege of partial perspective." In *Simians, Cyborgs and Women: The Reinvention of Nature*. San Francisco, Free Association Books, 183–202.

Haraway, D. (1992) "Otherworldly conversations; terran topics; local terms." *Science as Culture*, 3/1, 64–98.

Haraway, D. (1997) *Modest Witness@Second Millennium. FemaleMan meets OncoMouse*. London, Routledge.

Harvey, D. (1996) *Justice, Nature and the Geography of Difference*. Oxford, Blackwell.

Hayles, N. K. (1995) "Searching for common ground." In M. Soulé and G. Lease (eds), *Reinventing nature? Responses to Postmodern Deconstruction*. Washington DC, Island Press, 47–64.

Hinchliffe, S. (1996) "Technology, power and space." *Society and Space*, 14/6, 659–82.

Ingold, T. (1988) "The animal in the study of humanity." In T. Ingold (ed.), *What Is an Animal?* London, Allen & Unwin, 84–99.

Ingold, T. (1995a) "Building, dwelling, living: how animals and people make themselves at home in the world." In M. Strathern (ed.), *Shifting Contexts:* *Transformations in Anthropological Knowledge*. London, Routledge, 57–80.

Ingold, T. (1995b) "'People like us': the concept of the anatomically modern human." *Cultural Dynamics*, 7/2, 187–214.

Latour, B. (1993) *We Have Never Been Modern*. Brighton, Harvester Wheatsheaf.

Latour, B. (1994) "Pragmatologies." *American Behavioural Scientist*, 37/6, 791–808.

Law, J. (1994) *Organising Modernity*. Oxford, Blackwell.

Law, J. and A. Mol (1995) "Notes on materiality and sociality." *Sociological Review*, 42/3, 274–94.

Lawson, T. (1997) "Brent duck." *Ecos*, 17, 27–34.

Light, J. (1997) "The changing nature of nature." *Ecumene*, 4/2, 181–95.

Livingstone, D. (1992) *The Geographical Tradition*. Oxford, Blackwell.

Luke, T. (1996) "Liberal society and cyborg subjectivity: the politics of environments, bodies, and nature." *Alternatives*, 21, 1–30.

McNeely, J., K. Miller, W. Reid, R. Mittermeier, and T. Werner (1990) *Conserving the World's Biodiversity*. Geneva, IUCN.

Mol, A. and J. Law (1994) "Regions, networks and fluids: anaemia and social topology." *Social Studies of Science*, 24, 641–71.

Murdoch, J. (1995) "Actor-networks and the evolution of economic forms: combining description and explanation in theories of regulation, flexible specialisation and networks." *Environment and Planning A*, 27/5, 731–57.

Murdoch, J. (1997) "Towards a geography of heterogenous associations." *Progress in Human Geography*, 21/3, 321–37.

Noske, B. (1989) *Humans and Other Animals: Beyond the Boundaries of Anthropology*. London, Pluto.

Redclift, M. and T. Benton (eds) (1994) *Social Theory and the Global Environment*. London, Routledge.

Robertson, G., M. Mash, L. Tickner, J. Bird, B. Curtis, and T. Putnam (eds) (1996) *Future Natural: Nature, Science, Culture*. London, Routledge.

Senior, M. (1997) "'When the beasts spoke': animal speech and classical reason in Descartes and La Fontaine." In J. Ham and M. Senior (eds), *Animal Acts: Configuring the Human in Western History*. London, Routledge, 61–84.

Serres, M. (1995a) *The Natural Contract* (trans. E. MacArther and W. Paulson). Ann Arbor, University of Michigan Press.

Serres, M. (1995b) *Angels: A Modern Myth*. Paris, Flammarion.

Serres, M. and B. Latour (1995) *Conversations on Science, Culture and Time* (trans. R. Lapidus). Ann Arbor, University of Michigan Press.

Sheets-Johnstone, M. (1992) "Corporeal archetypes and power: preliminary clarifications and considerations of sex." *Hypatia*, 7/3, 39–76.

Smith, N. (1984) *Uneven Development*. Oxford, Blackwell.

Soper, K. (1995) *What is Nature?* Oxford, Blackwell.

Soulé, M. and G. Lease (eds) (1995) *Reinventing Nature? Responses to Postmodern Deconstruction*. Washington DC, Island Press.

Strathern, M. (1996) "Cutting the network." *Journal of the Royal Anthropological Institute* (n.s.), 2, 517–35.

Taussig, M. (1993) *Mimesis and Alterity*. London, Routledge.

Thrift, N. (1995) "A hyperactive world." In R. Johnston, P. Taylor and M. Watts (eds), *Geographies of Global Change*. Oxford, Blackwell, 18–35.

Thrift, N. (1996) *Spatial Formations*. London, Sage.

Thrift, N. and K. Olds (1996) "Refiguring the economic in economic geography." *Progress in Human Geography*, 20/3, 311–37.

Varela, F., E. Thompson, and E. Rosch (1991) *The Embodied Mind*. Cambridge MA, MIT Press.

Walker, R. (ed.) (1979) "Natural resources and environment." Special issue of *Antipode*, 11/2.

Wark, M. (1994) "Third nature." *Cultural Studies*, 8/1, 115–32.

Whatmore, S. (1997) "Dissecting the autonomous self: hybrid cartographies for a relational ethics." *Society and Space*, 15/1, 37–53.

Whatmore, S. and L. Thorne (1997) "Nourishing networks: alternative geographies of food." In D. Goodman and M. Watts (eds), *Globalising Food: Agrarian Questions and Global Restructuring*. London, Routledge, 287–304.

Wolch, J., K. Wesk, and T. Gaines (1995) "Transpecies urban theory." *Society and Space*, 13/4, 735–60.

34

SARAH FRANKLIN

Dolly's Body: Gender, Genetics and the
New Genetic Capital*

Sarah Franklin studies the social aspects of biomedicine, science as a contemporary cultural domain and new reproductive and genetic technologies. She has published widely in the areas of assisted conception, pre-implantation genetic diagnosis, and the changing definitions of life and death in embryo and cloning research. In this extract, Franklin describes the making of Dolly, the first cloned sheep, from the lens of anthropology, feminist theory, and science studies. Written before Dolly was euthanized in 2003 [she had a progressive lung disease typical of sheep kept in confined areas], this article describes Dolly's creation and the embodiment of scientific knowledge. [Because Dolly was cloned from a mammary gland, it is said that the stockmen who helped with her birth named her in honor of Dolly Parton – a striking example of stereotyped gendered embodiment!] Franklin regards Dolly as a commodity species that she calls "breedwealth," a form of genetic capital "in sheep's clothing." Producing Dolly (who was not actually cloned, but rather made from nuclear transfer, or the merger between the cells of two animals) demonstrated the success of producing an exact replica of an animal's nuclear genetic blueprint, thus bypassing her own "inexact" reproductive capacity. She notes that, while animals have always been owned and valued for their reproductive power (as have slaves been so owned and valued), the separation of reproduction from genealogy is particularly evident in cloned animals. Franklin argues that this new form of commodifying genealogy not only has important implications for the meaning of maternity, paternity, gender, and sex, but also raises questions about the meaning of nature in "a post-natural culture." The manipulation of animal genetics is further explored by Haraway in the next reading.

The birth of Dolly, the now-famous cloned Scottish sheep, was first reported on February 23rd, 1997 in the British Sunday paper *The Observer* by its science editor, Robin McKie. Later that week the means of her creation were officially documented in the British science journal *Nature*, in an article by Ian Wilmut and his colleagues entitled "Viable offspring derived

* Reproduced from Sarah Franklin (2002) "Dolly's Body: Gender, Genetics and the New Genetic Capital." *Filozofski Vestnik* 23(2): 119–136, with permission from Zalozba ZRC/ZRC Publishing.

from fetal and adult mammalian cells."[1] Like that other famous British birth, of the world's first test-tube baby, Louise Brown, in June of 1978, Dolly's viability instantly became the subject of world-wide media attention and public debate. Her birth was seen to alter the landscape of future reproductive possibility and once again to raise questions about the ethics of man-made life.

In the first full-length account of the making of Dolly the sheep, *Clone: the road to Dolly and the path ahead*, *New York Times* science journalist Gina Kolata describes the cloning of Dolly from an adult cell as one of the most important scientific accomplishments for which the previous century will come to be known, comparable to the splitting of the atom, the discovery of the double-helix, and the elimination of smallpox (Kalata 1997). According to the most comprehensive account of Dolly's birth, written by the Roslin scientists who created her, Dolly inaugurates a new era, "the age of biological control" (Campbell, Wilmut, and Tudge 2001). Prominent ethicists, philosophers, and scientists have spoken out about cloning, testified before Congress, and published their views in editorials and anthologies. Numerous advisory and legislative bodies worldwide have provided reports and recommendations.[2] Controversy continues to surround the question of whether or not humans should be cloned, and has now been extended to include wide-ranging debates about cloning human tissue via stem cells and the emergent science of what has become known as tissue engineering. A different set of questions about the cloning of Dolly arises from the perspective of anthropology and feminist theory in relation to kinship gender and biology. In this article I explore the notion of "viable offspring" from the perspective of the relationships between kinship, genealogy, and property which shape our and Dolly's futures in the "Age of Biological Control." Using Dolly as a kind of shepherd, I want to follow the implications of her creation in terms of how scientific knowledge comes to be *embodied*, how biology is seen to be authored, and how in turn such acts of creation are protected as forms of property. Dolly's coming into being disrupts the traditional template of genealogy: she was born from a new kind of cellular assemblage, in which donor cytoplasm effectively "reprogrammed" her nuclear DNA to "go back in time" and become newly embryonic. Dolly's biology is as cultural as her ontology is historical, and she is part of a number of new animal kinds, or breeds, which instantiate larger changes in what Foucault denominated "the order of things" connecting life, labour, and language. If Dolly were a sentence, we would need a new syntax to parse her, because her counterfactual existence troubles existing grammars of species, breed, property, and sex.

These troubles are not new – indeed many of them are quite ancient: like other animal forms of livestock, Dolly embodies a commercial purpose written into her flesh. With Dolly, however, genealogy is reconstituted as a unique and unprecedented conduit for the production of biowealth, and she thus requires some altered templates of theoretical explanation to address the significance of her making, her marking, and her marketing as a successful product.[3] Like older breeds, Dolly was created to explore new possibilities of making animal reproduction more efficient. In the process, she has altered the landscape of animal reproduction far more than anyone imagined possible.

"Viable" is an important word to describe Dolly in several senses. She is viable in the biological sense of being capable of life outside the womb, as in a viable new-born. She is also viable in the wider sense of being capable of success, or continuing effectiveness: she is viable in the corporate sense of a viable plan or strategy. Her existence confirms the viability of a particular scientific technique, the technique of cloning by nuclear transfer using fully differentiated adult cells, which was not believed to be biologically possible until she was born. As a viable offspring, Dolly confirms the viability of a merger between corporate sponsorship and research science. It is the successful merging of all of these meanings of "viable" that Dolly both embodies and symbolizes: she represents the viability of a scientific technique, and of a corporate strategy, through her existence as a viable offspring. Her ability to survive, to function normally, and to reproduce naturally guarantees other kinds of viability: the viability of man-made life, for example, and the viability of the stock options of her parent company, PPL therapeutics, who financed her creation. Dolly is live-stock in a very overdetermined sense: she is not only viable as a single animal, but as a *kind* of animal, a new commodity species of what might be described as breedwealth.[4] Above all, she is a newly viable form of genetic capital, in sheep's clothing.[5]

In an era defined by the emergence of biowealth as the ultimate futures market, Dolly's birth is yet further confirmation of the means by which biological reproduction can become an engine of wealth generation and capital accumulation. Cloning and cell fusion have become increasingly significant means of reproduction in an era of polymerize chain reaction, immortal cell line banking, and genomic libraries. Dolly is owned as an individual animal, much as any farmer owns livestock. But she is much more valuable as an animal model for a technique that is owned as intellectual property, by means of a patent which covers the technique of nuclear transfer.[6] In addition, ownership of Dolly involves the production of what might be thought of as new forms of biological enclosure, that is by the refinement of specific biotechnological pathways which reliably deliver certain kinds of functionality. For example the means of reactivating the recombined cells out of which Dolly was made involved identifying the significance of particular stages in the cell cycle, and learning how to manipulate these stages using electricity. The ability to "enclose" distinct components of the emergent biotechnological toolkit as private property thus involves a combination of skill, ingenuity, secrecy, and legal instruments such as patents, in order to create new forms of biowealth. Anthropologically, such alterations in the fungibility of animal genealogy pose questions not only about the production of new forms of genetic capital, but about the very basis for distinguishing among animal kinds – a question

that in turn leads back into familiar questions about the connections between so-called "biological differences," the formal categorizations based on sex, gender, kinship, and descent.

GENETIC CAPITAL

In the past, as today, the profitable reproduction of animals as livestock has depended upon specific technological innovations and market refinements. Writing of the eighteenth-century livestock breeder Robert Bakewell, historian Harriet Ritvo describes an important shift through which this "master breeder" altered the ways in which prized animals came to be valued as individual repositories of genetic capital. It was the development of careful pedigree recording by Bakewell which enabled him to transform the livestock market, so that he could effectively rent out his animals for stud duty. To bring about this shift in how animal reproductive capacity could be bought and sold, Ritvo argues Bakewell needed to transform the entire conceptual basis of livestock breeding. She claims that Bakewell accomplished this transformation through a shift in the definition of the genetic capital from the breed as a whole to the reproductive power of a single animal. She writes that

> Bakewell claimed that when he sold one of his carefully bred animals, or, as in the case of stud fees, when he sold the procreative powers of these animals, he was selling something more specific, more predictable, and more efficacious than mere reproduction. In effect, he was selling a template for the continued production of animals of a special type: that is, the distinction of his rams consisted not only in their constellation of personal virtues, but in their ability to pass this constellation down their family tree. (1995, 416)

The shift here involves a part being enabled to stand for a larger whole. It could be described as metonymic in the sense that the individual comes to be so closely associated with the breed as a whole it can stand in its stead. More specifically, the shift is synechdochic, in the sense that *the substance from which it is made* can stand for an object itself, as in steel for sword. The accomplishment of this change in kind described by Ritvo, whereby a single animal could become a template for an entire type or breed, was accomplished through careful written records – that is, through the establishment of the studbook as a marketing device. The maintenance of such records enabled a differentiation to be drawn between male animals that were "good sires" and those who were not. In turn this differentiation enabled a reduction of the male animal to a template of his kind. It also depended upon the redefinition of the breed, or breeding group, as a lineage. And it was these *conceptual* changes that enabled an exchange – of the stud fee for generations of careful breed selection.[7]

The point of all of this was its profitability. The successful enterprising-up of new property values in animals, and the establishment of a market in which to sell them, enabled Bakewell to increase by four-hundredfold within thirty years the value of his breeding livestock. It is no exaggeration to claim, as Ritvo does, that his approach changed forever how livestock breeding is both practised and conceptualized: "So complete was the conceptual transformation wrought by this redefinition of an animal's worth, that at a remove of two centuries it may be difficult to recover its novelty" (1995, 417). It is also not irrelevant that these eighteenth-century breeding innovations established Britain as "the stud stock farm of the world,"[8] a legacy still manifest in animals such as Dolly.[9]

As Ritvo observes, it is entirely commonsensical today that breeds are the result of careful selection, in-and-in breeding to improve the "line," and the application of breeding principles to the improvement of stock by their owners. It is equally taken for granted that some animals are better breeders than others, and that this is a component of their monetary value. What her analysis reveals most compellingly is how much conceptual apparatus must exist in relation to the animal for its biology to emerge as "obvious" in this way, or indeed for the biology of a prized

ram to emerge at all. A breed is thus a biotechnological assemblage, its very constitution a discursive formation, its genome a manifestation of the breeder's art.

Dolly extends the uses of breeding in some important new directions. The definitive technology through which Dolly emerges as yet another kind of template for the breedline as a whole is the technique of nuclear transfer – the form of cell fusion through which Dolly was cloned.[10] Dolly's viability as an offspring has now authenticated this technique, and its profitability, much as the performance of Bakewell's Dishley rams secured the viability of an earlier form of breedwealth in livestock husbandry, and Louise Brown's viability confirmed the success of IVF (In-Vitro-Fecundation). Like the studbook, nuclear transfer also effects a reduction of the animal to its DNA. But this time, there are several important differences. First, it is the female animal, and not the male, whose DNA serves as a template. And second, it is not the animal herself, but a laboratory technique which provides the means of reproduction. Let us pause to consider what these shifts entail in more detail, for they are, like those described by Ritvo, both technological and conceptual. In the industrial version of breedwealth established by Bakewell, the individual animal provided *both* the template *and* the means of reproduction: its genes *and* its own generative power were the package being sold. In the case of Dolly, *neither* her own genes *nor* her own generative capacity are valuable. The *only* value she embodies is as an animal model for a patent application, providing living (and extensively DNA-tested) proof that Ian Wilmut's technique can be successful. It is the viability of the means of reproduction used to make her, nuclear transfer technology, which is the source of new genetic capital – which is why it is nuclear transfer technology, and not Dolly herself, for which intellectual property rights were sought. In this sense, cloning by nuclear transfer enables genetic capital *to be removed from the animal herself* – and doubly so. This has significant consequences for how both reproduction and genealogy can be owned, marketed, and sold, and also for what they mean, and how they are (dis)embodied.

These shifts have implications for both genealogy and gender. Very much in contrast to Bakewell's Dishley rams, Dolly is at a remove from the source of her reproductive value, which has, in a sense, been seconded to do service for (to establish the viability of) a technique of reproductive biology. Her own ability to reproduce is not an important conduit for the production of other animals, and in fact Dolly's own ability to produce lambs is merely a subordinated sign of her individual viability as a natural-technical product of corporate bioscience. Dolly was a successful trial run.

In sum, she is the cookie, not the cutter. PPL therapeutics is the world leader in transposing human genes into animals, in order to harvest peptides from their milk, in order to make new drugs. The aim of producing Dolly was to demonstrate the viability of a technique that *bypasses* her own reproductive capacity, which is too inexact. Cloning by nuclear transfer is useful because, unlike conventional breeding, it enables exact reproduction of an animal's complete nuclear genetic blueprint. In a sense, nuclear transfer decontaminates mammalian reproduction: we might say it eliminates nuclear waste. This innovation is valuable because it enables a new form of pure reproduction in higher mammals, removed from the genetic "noise" of the rut. The problem with conventional breeding, of course, is that it is very unreliable, inefficient, and thus costly. Every time a breeder mates a prized animal, the recombination of genes that is an unavoidable component of sexual reproduction introduces the equivalent of a genetic lottery: you never know what kind of match, or mismatch, is going to result.

Nuclear transfer removes this genetic gamble: it eliminates the genetic risk of sex, producing an exact replica of the desired genetic traits.[11] Through this means, it is argued by the Roslin team who produced Dolly, the precise genetic composition of prized individual animals be both preserved in perpetuity, and more efficiently reproduced in other animals. The possibilities opened up by nuclear transfer are indeed for any animal, male or female, wild or domesticated, or even extinct, to become a perpetual germline repository, a pure gene bank, because it is no longer only the gametes, the eggs, and the sperm, which are necessary for reproduction to be viable. A single animal can be cloned to produce an entire herd of identical animals, which would otherwise take years to establish. These animals can also be improved with the addition of precise genetic traits, including those from other species. In sum, the value of nuclear transfer is so obvious it had to be invented. While compressing genealogical time, it also offers total nuclear genetic purity, in perpetuity, and under patent.[12]

Nuclear transfer technology thus offers a specific redefinition of breedwealth, or livestock, by introducing new recombinant models of genealogy, species, and reproduction. The principle of nuclear transfer is the exact reverse of Bakewell's contribution, and inverts what we might describe as the modern industrial model of breedwealth into its fragmented, postmodern successor project. If the studbook was a way to transform an animal's genealogy into a source of individual value, nuclear transfer is a way to depart from conventional genealogical spatiality and temporality altogether. Dolly's pedigree is removed from natural time, or the time of genealogical descent. Her mother is genetically her sister, as are her offspring.[13] She was produced from the nucleus of a mammary cell, amplified from a frozen tissue sample taken from a pregnant Finn Dorset ewe who had been dead for six years. This nucleus was inserted into an enucleated "donor" egg cell from a Scottish Blackface sheep. The resulting embryo was gestated by two more sheep, the second of which gave birth to Dolly. Dolly instantiates a new form of commodifying genealogy, *because she establishes a new form of genealogy altogether.*

So what are the implications of this enterprised-up genealogy for other naturalized categories, such as gender, sex, or species — all of which have depended upon the orderly brachiations of the unilinear, bilateral, and unified genealogical descent system Darwin envisaged as the real tree of life's? If Dolly is the product of a fertile union among several females – if she is the offspring of a kind of same-sex tissue merger – does this mean biological sex difference has become obsolete in terms of reproduction? Have we seen the transcendence of not only sexual difference, but reproductive difference as well? One reading of the Dolly episode might lead to the suggestion that maternity has triumphed over paternity, in a kind of recapitulation of the ancient matriarchy theories so influential in early feminism.[14] And how appropriate that sheep are a very matrilineal species, each flock with its wise and woolly head ewe – just like in the film "Babe." But the triumph-of-the-genetrix reading of cloning, which might be celebrated as the ultimate female-defined reproduction, is in tension with another possibility: that paternity has not so much been displaced as dispersed, into acts of scientific creation and principles of legal ownership. It may be the stud has vanished, but there are other father figures.

Dolly's conception raises paradoxical implications for the meanings of maternity, gender, and sex. For although the nuclear transfer technique is designed to produce female sheep from other female sheep, this occurs under the sign of familiar forms of paternity. The best transgenic ewes can be used to create the equivalent of studlines for entire flocks. Because all, or many, of their adult cells can be used for reproduction, they surpass even the much-celebrated heights of male sperm production, with every cell in their body potentially a new ewe. But these ewes are not analogous to super-studs *because their embodiment of a unique genetic template has been separated from their ability to pass it on.* The whole point of a studline derives from the idea of the unique genetic capital of a prized individual combined with that animal's capacity to pass these traits on down the family tree.[15] This was Bakewell's contribution, as outlined by Ritvo, whereby the reproductive power of a specific animal could be sold as a template. Nuclear transfer technology anachronizes this connection in the same stroke

with which it eliminates conventional genealogical time, order, and verticality altogether.[16]

Such observations inevitably lead to questions about paternity and property, to Dolly's "parent" company, and to her "scientific" father. Nuclear transfer is a device for seeding a corporate plan for the production of biowealth in the form of what Roslin describes as "bioreactors." These bioreactors are the sheep that will function as living pharmaceutical producers, by producing valuable proteins in their milk. Dolly's own now-proven reproductive capacity, in the form of her own viable offspring, becomes a kind of publicity stunt for the more important viable offspring known as nuclear transfer. Dolly's lambs provide further "proof" that cloning is a perfectly natural, sound and healthy means of reproduction (and what an attractive advertisement they are, timed perfectly to arrive each year at Easter). Ironically, Dolly's lambs do service for the scientific paternity of her own creation, which lies with Wilmut and his colleagues, who designed the blueprint of the technique that made her a viable offspring to begin with. Dolly's own maternity is as inconsequential in itself as are her healthy eating habits: just one more sign she is a perfectly sound animal. It might be said her maternity is a paradoxical stamp of approval for her thoroughly man-made viability.[17]

The meaning of paternity in the context of Dolly's creation is also evident in relation to the patent application that covers specific uses of nuclear transfer technology. The patent, after all, is a form of intellectual property protection which derives from the institution of copyright, first established by the Statute of Anne in 1710 in England, not far from Bakewell's farm either geographically or historically. As Mark Rose (1993) has suggestively chronicled, the establishment of copyright was explicitly argued by analogy to paternity. An author's original works were an inviolable possession of their creator just as his children belonged to him because he was their procreator. Offspring of the brain and of the loin, argued prominent literary figures such as Daniel Defoe, derive from individual acts of creation, and must be protected as such.

"Plagiarism" derives from the Latin word for kidnapping.

The invisibility of the maternal in such an argument directly anticipates the situation with Dolly. Defoe's argument that authors are essentially the fathers of their texts comprises a fantasy of male-birthing from which the maternal is excluded. It is an exclusion that recalls a phrase in Zora Neale Hurston's ethnography, *Tell My Horse*. Hurston describes the use of the expression "the rooster's egg" to describe children of white fathers and black mothers who were defined as "white" by virtue of their paternity.[18] The subordination of maternity in the attempt to secure racial privilege is mocked by the figure of "the rooster's egg," marking this denial of maternity as an absurdity, a fantasy, and a lie. The invisible, or subordinated, maternal in the context of copyright was directly paralleled on Bakewell's farm, where the female animal was irrelevant, and only the male line "counted" for stud fees. Dolly's subordinated maternity thus repeats this long-standing pattern of maternal erasure, only in her case compounded by the explicit display of her recuperated maternity to confirm the skill of her creator. It is this original creator's skill, as an innovator, which is protected under the patent for nuclear transfer that Dolly authenticates as the viable offspring of pater Wilmut, also her genitor by technological proxy. To be patentable, an invention must be original, of utility, and non-obvious – and nuclear transfer is all of these, although, like much contemporary patented biowealth, it relies closely on designs that are "found in nature," most notably the cell cycle. This form of ownership does not explicitly accrue to Dolly herself, who is but its means of realization, or its proof. Dolly is herself owned under much more conventional arrangements, as personal property, in the manner that any farmer owns his or her sheep. The difference the patent protection secures in Dolly's case, however, is that the capacity for her maternity to be distributed has been enhanced. Her reproduction becomes partible: she is newly profitable because she is multiply divisible, and it is her divisibility which makes her newly fungible. In the same sense Hortense Spillers famously described the distributed maternity of female slaves, whose reproductive capacities their nineteenth-century masters could either sell or use themselves. The production of Dolly similarly conjoins commercial and biological enclosure, by isolating particular reproductive pathways, and creating a market in access to them. What is required in both cases is the separation of reproduction from genealogy – a feat particularly evident in cloned animals that are transgenics.

The popular association of cloning with slavery shares this recognition of the shame and disempowerment that occasions the loss of reproductive power.[19] It might be argued that animals have long been owned in this way, their reproductive power part and parcel of their value. But, as Ritvo shows, this is not quite so simply and self-evidently the case. The capacity to own, to market, and to sell the reproductive powers of animals has changed quite dramatically over time, and has done so in close association with redefinitions of other forms of property, such as intellectual property. Moreover, the reconceptualization of property is itself technologically-assisted, through inventions such as studbooks, pedigrees, and patents. Today, frozen cell lines, molecular biology, and nuclear transfer are part of a wider set of conceptual and technological transformations in the capacity to own, to manipulate, and to profit from the reproductive power of animals, plants, and micro-organisms. There is no other way to describe this than as an intensification of the politics of reproduction, and an enterprising-up of genealogy. And in the same way that capital is changing, so the new biology does not guarantee the same syntax it used to for other domains as well: what does it mean when genealogy can be remade as technique? What happens when the means of reproduction themselves can be owned under a patent? What is Dolly's proper gender, or sex, if instead of being born she was made?

Using the patented transgenic oncomouse as one of her guides, or figures, in *Modest Witness @SecondMillennium*, Donna Haraway describes what she calls a "shift from kind to brand" (1997,

65–6). Borrowing from, and mutating, Marilyn Strathern's work on kinship in *After Nature*, Haraway describes kinship as "a technology for producing the material and semiotic effect of natural relationship, of shared kind" (1997, 53). She describes kinship "in short" as "the question of taxonomy, category and the natural status of artificial entities" adding that "establishing identities is kinship work in action" (1997, 67). In the context of such denaturalized animate entities as oncomouse, Haraway argues that "type has become brand," and that the brand has become a kind of gender. The brand becomes for Haraway a kind of hyper-mark establishing kind and type in a *semantics of propriety* that is explicitly post-natural.

Haraway's shift from kind to brand thus describes the way in which the production of a certain type of animal, such as oncomouse, occurs out from under the sign of natural history and instead beneath its brand name. This interpretation thus literalizes the brand slogan of Dupont, "where better things for better living come to life," which Haraway first brought to her reader's attention in 1992, in the article "When Man™ is on the Menu" in which she claimed that the new cyborg animals of corporate biotechnology "will be literate in quite a different grammar of gender" (1992, 42).

Haraway's 1992 article appeared in the same *Zone* anthology, entitled *Incorporations*, in which Paul Rabinow argued that the new genetics represent the apotheosis of modern rationality, in that "the object to be known – the human genome – will be known in such a way that it can be changed." It was also in this article that Rabinow made the often-requoted prediction that

> In the future, the new genetics will cease to be a biological metaphor for modern society and will become instead a circulation network of identity terms and restriction loci, around which and through which a truly new type of autoproduction will emerge, which I call "biosociality." … In biosociality, nature will be remodelled on culture understood as practice. Nature will be known and remade through technique and will finally become artificial just as culture becomes natural. (1992, 241–2)

For Rabinow, the nature-culture split will disappear in a penultimate collapse of the very distinction out of which modernity emerged as a discursive condition in the first place.[20] For Haraway, nature is not so much displaced as reanimated, acquiring a new capacity to mark a different set of relations in the context of corporate technoscience, in which unnatural relations such as transgenics reappear as naturalized kinds through brands. There is no doubt Dolly is the founder animal for a new species of product, in which family resemblance is at a premium. She is not branded as such, but she secures a patent application through what might as well be her brand slogans: "Made in Scotland, Designed by Roslin, and Brought to You by PPL therapeutics." As the technology for making cloned transgenics improves, so will emerge successor generations of products in a commodity lineage of designer sheep. Global marketing strategies, such as those used by Intel, Nokia, and BMW, borrow from familiar kinship idioms to provide analogies for the ways in which products are "related," but what is more revealing is how these analogies *can also travel back*. In other words, the brands and trademarks connecting products to their "parent company" stand in for shared substance, forming the basis of kin-relatedness as a familiar form of propriety-by-descent. These commodity descent lines are therefore instantiations of a different kind of substantial connection, which is established through trademark or brand as its mark. What is interesting is that, as Strathern argues, such analogies can be reversed: the traffic can make a U-turn. Hence, whereas genitorship has historically been the model for the naturalized propriety of copyright, we might argue that commercial propriety can now engender and naturalize paternity. Possession itself can figure technoscientific fatherhood.

What this suggests is that it is not only nature, but paternity which is "known and remade as technique," to redirect Rabinow's apt phrasing.

Haraway's "shift from kind to brand" also points to this collapse, of the commercial and the paternal. Only now, as distinct from earlier episodes, it is *the means of reproduction itself*, and not merely its offspring, which paternity defines as its own. This made-in-the lab paternity may in fact perfectly instantiate what Rabinow describes as "the truly new form of autoproduction" which is "the apotheosis of modern rationality." Like maternity, nature does not so much disappear as become a kind of trope in the context of late-twentieth century biotechnology (see further in Franklin, Lury, and Stacey 2000). The same can be said for kinship and gender, which become much more like brand in their capacity to signify difference – through relations of enterprise and propriety rather than through relations such as genealogical descent. Now that animals such as Dolly are both born and made, they not only embody "nature remade as technique" but also "the shift from kind to brand" in their corporately owned and redesigned corporeality. In sum, I have argued here that the gender of the new genetic capital is very familiarly paternal, but that this repeat of an ancient tradition has taken a few new turns. For one, the means of reproduction have been removed from the animal, and placed under the sign of patent. For another, Dolly's own maternity does service to the value of nuclear transfer as a means of both producing and protecting genetic capital. And all of this is possible, I suggest, because reproduction has been removed from genealogical time and space, becoming no longer either vertical or bilateral through new technologies. Life after Dolly is, in sum, both differently viable and newly profitable. I also suggest that Dolly shows us some important dimensions of what happens to gender when it is made not born. She helps us to ask what happens to what Monique Wittig calls "the mark of gender" when that marking occurs through branding, as a proprietary relation. In asking how brands are naturalized as what Haraway calls "genders," there are important questions to be asked about how nature comes to signify in a post-natural culture. Does this model of gender simply give us more of them? If gender

becomes a commercial equation is it easier to buy out altogether? Is cloning a form of gender trouble?

In terms of genealogy, the technique of nuclear transfer effects a 90-degree turn, whereby "descent" is no longer the equivalent of genealogical gravity. Instead, enterprised-up genealogy is newly flexible, so that it is more subject to redesign, and freed from the narrow trammels of species-specific reproductive isolation to become newly promiscuous: a mix 'n' match recombinatoria, wistfully like alchemy.

CONCLUSION

Examining Dolly in this way suggests she belongs to what Foucault might have described as a new order of things, in which life, labour, and language have been transformed in their constitutive relations. Never concerned with nature and culture per se, Foucault took from his predecessor Georges Canguilhem a historical and philosophical question about the relation of knowledge production to life forms, and indeed of epistemology to life itself. Always attentive to the constitutive power of knowledge in its many forms (disciplinarity, governmentality, classification, surveillance), and its myriad corresponding objects (prisons, clinics, museums, bodies, sexualities), a main theme of Foucault's writing concerned the transformation of consanguinity into population, and sovereignty into regimes of public health. Dolly perfectly instantiates this same constellation, *and simultaneously inaugurates its transformation*: she is, after all, part of a corporate plan to put human genes into animals in order to be able to derive pharmaceutical products from her milk, for profit. Her coming into being is as a new life form belonging to the future of medical treatment, wired to the human genome on the internet, in which the genetic specificity of the individual will replace the formerly generic model of the human used to develop new drugs in the past. Known and remade as technique, Dolly embodies changes in both knowledge production and governmentality. She is the viable offspring of the epistemological coordinates of the new biology in which it is less important to know what she *is* than what she *does*. Though it is now proven feasible, cloning by nuclear transfer is still poorly understood scientifically. The effects of imprinting in particular remain dimly recognized, despite being of utmost importance to genetic expression. An enormous discrepancy separates the Lego-like logic of molecular biology, its daunting technical language full of noun-verb hybrids for components that allow pieces to be put together and pulled apart, from the self-evident complexity of the relationalities out of which "genetic expression" emerges. The very term "genetic information" is a fiction, like "numeric value"; it makes sense only if you take for granted everything needed to explain it.

What holds Dolly together is consequently not Foucault's order of things connected to the "life itself" he claims is the foundational concept of modern biology, but Lifeitself™, as in the Dupont slogan "where better things for living come to life."[21] The new order of things instantiated through biotechnology has been vastly enabled by a loosening of patent law, which, from the early 1980s onward have increasingly liberally allowed life forms to be patented not only when they are non-obvious inventions, but, increasingly in the age of genomics, simply when they are useful techniques. This mechanism of the nation-state to promote industry, the patent and its officers, and to connect labour and life into a productive force, is precisely aimed to fuel market speculation and encourage venture capital in a market dominated by multinational pharmaceutical giants, to create a situation one journalist has compared to the sixteenth-century competition between France, England, and Spain to claim the New World.[22]

To say such changes have cultural implications seems a self-evident observation. The density and power of the capital resource, Lifeitself™, asks that it be understood as part of a historical transformation of a very distinctive kind. The splicing together of human genes with those of other species into a new *ars recombinatoria* of life forms which no longer belong to natural history or genealogy as we have known it means that none of the naturalized categories hold still in relation to what used to be seen as their given attributes. Is cloning by nuclear transfer sexual reproduction or not? How many parents does Dolly have? Kinship and gender, those serviceable anthropological digging tools, offer one way of thinking about what happens to these categories as kinds of kinds, or as the grammatical categories of a sociality understood to be glued together in some way by relationships established through reproduction and sex. In seeking to understand the recalibration of life itself in the context of biotechnology, the question has to be asked: what happens when we understand genes as themselves the vehicle for cultural expression?

NOTES

1. In fact, Dolly was already more than six months old at the time of her birth announcement: she had come into the world in a shed in a small Scottish village on the fifth of June 1996.

2. A list of several of these reports and anthologies about cloning is provided in the references to this paper, which is part of a larger project on kinship and cloning supported by a fellowship from the Leverhulme Foundation.

3. Although Dolly clearly continues a long tradition of animal breeding for human purposes, and thus is hardly unique for embodying human technical and discursive markers, this paper is less focussed on such continuities, instead seeking to articulate the ways in which cloning comprises a distinctive moment in animal manufacture. Another chapter could be written in which this distinctiveness is not the central focus, and a reverse set of claims about Dolly's links to historical traditions of animal breeding are emphasized.

4. The ability to control animal breeding is one of the main definitions of domestication as applied to livestock such as sheep, cattle, goats, and pigs. Human control over animals, often expressed as dominion, has been linked to wealth generation since the emergence of what are now called breeds, or breedlines. Breedwealth is a term which emphasizes both the commercial motivations of "the breeder's hand," and the intensification of

commercial interest in cellular and molecular biology applied to animal reproduction.

5. Part of Dolly's parent company was purchased in 1999 by the company Geron, who specialize in medical applications of cloning and have developed techniques for stem-cell amplification aimed to provide replacement organ tissue. This application of cloning by nuclear transfer, and its potential use as a form of assisted conception, are the most likely means by which "human cloning" will be inaugurated.

6. Dolly's creation is covered by two patent applications filed by Roslin Institute, PCT/GB96/02099, entitled "Quiescent cell populations for nuclear transfer" and PCT/GB96/02098 entitled "Unactivated oocytes as cytoplast recipients for nuclear transfer." These applications are filed in most countries in the world and cover all animal species, including humans. Roslin Institute's policy is to license its patents by field of use.

7. By definition this is a very brief summary of Ritvo's argument, whose work is of great importance in understanding not only the emergence of animal pedigrees, but of the importance of many domesticated species to Darwin's model of evolution.

8. As Cooper claims in his mid-century evaluation of Bakewell, "there are in fact only two breeds today not of British origin, namely Friesian cattle and Merino sheep, which have a truly international status (1957, 90).

9. The Roslin Institute in Scotland is itself heir to this same lineage, as a direct descendant of the Imperial Bureau of Animal Breeding and Genetics, created in 1929.

10. Dolly is not properly described as a clone and the term "clone" does not appear anywhere in the *Nature* article by Wilmut, et al, announcing her birth. She is the result of a merger between the cells of two animals, not a "clone" in the strict botanical sense of an entity grown from a single cell of its progenitor. ("Cloning" comes from Greek for "twig" and is perhaps most accurately used to describe the way a gardener grows a new hydrangea from a single twig of a parent plant.)

11. The exact genetic traits sought by PPL therapeutics are transgenic. The first cloned transgenic sheep was announced in July 1997, named Polly. Polly was created by "a version" of the technique used to create Dolly, namely the technique used to produce Megan and Morag, the sheep born at Roslin in 1996, using fetal rather than adult cells. The important point about Polly is not only that she carries the targeted human gene, but the marker for it. The Roslin web pages explain that "earlier techniques have been hit-or-miss for mixing animal DNA but cloning should make that process more precise." Clearly there is little efficiency gain until cloning by nuclear transfer is significantly improved.

12. I exaggerate deliberately, only to make the point that the promise of nuclear transfer corresponds with a commercial logic that is, by definition, hyperbolic. It is important to qualify many of the claims made about cloning and stem cells not only in terms of their low success rates and worryingly high levels of pathology, but also because it is likely to take many decades before any widely available therapeutic benefits are derived from this highly publicized area of scientific research.

13. Although it is tempting to use traditional kinship categories to play with Dolly's family tree, it is misleading insofar as these terms assume certain kinds of genetic relationality, at the same time they often depart from them entirely (such is the admirable flexibility of kinship categories in general), Dolly [both has] "her own" DNA and is a genetically-distinct individual, at the same time that the "blueprint" from her genome was inherited from only one "parent."

14. Philip Kitcher (1998), for example, supports cloning-for-families on behalf of stable lesbian couples who would like to have a child, and who could, if one partner donates the egg and the other the nucleus, more closely emulate the heterosexual ideal of conjugal and procreative unity (arguably not the most widely shared aspiration among lesbian couples). This example is only one of many in which we see how readily a technique often described as bringing about "the end of sex" is perfectly easily resituated within very normative family values.

15. As Ritvo explains, Bakewell used progeny tests to chart the performance of his studs to discover their "hidden" qualities. In addition to seeking purity of descent (preserved through in-and-in breeding), he sought what is technically known as "prepotency," which Ritvo defines as "a heritage sufficiently concentrated and powerful to dominate the heritage of potential mates."

(1995, 419). This is only one example of some of the many rather curious ideas about inheritance which continue to influence the breeder's art. For example, even though Bakewell's celebrated Dishley sheep did not prove to have much staying power as a breed, their best-known descendants, the Blue-faced Leicesters, are still primarily used to produce "tups," young rams which are sold to be used for cross-breeding with other sheep.

16. It is tempting to note that the transgenic possibilities opened up through sheep-human combinations create a new kind of ewe-man genome initiative, but to suggest such a merger is to overlook the technical complexities that continue to beset this field of endeavour.

17. Dolly is herself better known for stamps of disapproval, the standard threat gesture of the ewe. From the beginning treated with special care, Dolly is reported to be well aware of her stature, and to respond with an irritated stamp of the hoof to transgressions such as inadequate dinner.

18. This is also the title of a collection of essays by Patricia Williams (1995).

19. Interestingly, the use of the term "clone" to denote loss of reproductive propriety is also evident in the marketplace, where a clone is used to denote an illegitimately copied product, as in a "Gucci clone," or the risk of illegitimate product use to markets, as in mobile-phone fraud. Genetic markers are used by companies such as Monsanto to prevent "cloning" of their agricultural products in both the scientific and commercial sense as a means of protecting their reproductive rights.

20. In contrast, Latour argues this division was only an enabling fiction for modernity to begin with, hence his title claim that *We Have Never Been Modern.*

21. I am borrowing back and remutating the term life itself from Haraway's description of it as "a thing-in-itself where no trope can be admitted," or as "a congeries of entities that are themselves self-referential and autotelic," like Dawkins' selfish gene, in sum, a kind of fetish (1997, 134–5). I would like to argue it is not only the fetishism of life itself as a commodity which is in evidence, but specifically its removal from genealogy, which has consequences for what propriety, enterprise, or commerce can connect.

22. Writing in *Wired*, journalist Michael Gruber suggests that: "The 21st century will be more like the 16th than the 20th, with biology standing in for the New World. The pharmas and the big chemical companies are the great expeditionaries – Cortés, Pizarro, de Soto, Raleigh, and so on. Government regulatory agencies are – what else? – the European imperial powers. The pharmas are after treasure, of course. The regulators want to keep control, which they express as an overarching social good – back then it was Defence of the Realm and Propagation of the Faith: today it's Public Health (1997, 198).

REFERENCES

Campbell, Keith, Ian Wilmut, and Colin Tudge. 2001. *The Second Creation: The Age of Biological Control by the Scientists who Created Dolly.* London: Heineman.

Cooper, M. McG. 1957. "Present Day Evaluation." In *Robert Bakewell: Pioneer Livestock Breeder*, edited by H. Cecil Pawson, 89–95. London: Crosby Lockwood & Son.

Croke, Vicki. 1999. "Tufts-Genzyme Team Cites Cloning Advance." In *The Boston Globe*, 27 April, pp. A1, A13.

Foucault, Michel. 1970. *The Order of Things: An Archaeology of the Human Sciences.* New York: Pantheon.

Gruber, Michael. 1997. "Map the Genome, Hack the Genome." In: *Wired*, October, pp. 153–156, 193–198.

Haraway, Donna. 1992. "When Man is on the Menu." In *Incorporations*, edited by Jonathan Crary and Sanford Kwinter, 38-43. New York: Zone.

Haraway, Donna. 1997. *Modest Witness @SecondMillennium: Female Man© meets OncoMouse.* London and New York: Routledge.

Kitcher, Philip. 1998. "Life after Dolly." In *The Human Cloning Debate*, edited by Glen McGee, 107–124. Berkeley, California: Berkeley Hills Books.

Kalata, Gina. 1997. *Clone: The Road to Dolly and the Path Ahead.* London: Allen Lane.

Rabinow, Paul. 1992. "Artificiality and Enlightenment: From Sociobiology to Biosociality." In *Incorporations*, edited by Jonathan Crary and Sanford Kwinter, 234–252. New York: Zone Books.

Ritvo, Harriet. 1995. "Possessing Mother Nature: Genetic Capital in Eighteenth-Century Britain." In *Early Modern Conceptions of Property*, edited by John Brewer and Susan Staves, 413–426. London and New York: Routledge.

Rose, Mark. 1993. *Authors and Owners: The Invention of Copyright.* Cambridge MA: Harvard University Press.

Spillers, Hortense. 1987. "Mama's Ba Maybe: An American Grammar Book," *D* 17(2): pp. 65–81.

Wilmut, I., A. Schnieke, J. McWhir, A. Kind, an K. Campbell. 1997. "Viable Offspring Derived from Fetal and Adult Mammalian Cells," *Nature* 385: 810–813.

35

DONNA HARAWAY

s to Companion Species: Reconfiguring Kinship in Technoscience*

Donna Haraway is one of the most influential scholars of the twenty-first century. She was trained in the philosophies of evolution, English, zoology, and biology and studied under Evelyn Hutchinson, biologist and author of the classic work on the ecological theater and the evolutionary play. Haraway's work has been central to the development of the social studies of science and technology, feminist theory, the history of animal-human relationships, and "naturecultures." Her recent writing focuses on the emergence of the category "companion species" and other aspects of animal-human relationships in the world of technoscience. In a preamble to the extract reproduced here, Haraway made a distinction between two "cobbled together figures" – her now famous "cyborgs" and her new "companion species." While there are similarities between the two [they are both mergers of the human and nonhuman, the organic and technological, the natural and cultural], a cyborg is a subjective transformative creature constructed from the merger of multiple "outsider identities" [such as Deleuze and Guattari's vampire, an anomalous becoming-animal]. While companion species can consist of artifacts, organisms, technologies, or other humans (Haraway focuses primarily on the human-dog companionship), they are not substitutes for other things, they are not surrogates for theory, they are "not here just to think with" [pace Lévi-Strauss, see Section 5] – they are here to live with. Haraway argues that there is "lots of dog agency in the drama of genetics and co-habitation," and that humans and dogs have been companion species from the very beginning – they co-constitute each other, and their "obligatory, constitutive, protean" relationship as companion species takes shape in interaction. But while the human-dog interaction is reminiscent of the Sanders and Arluke concept of "minded coactors" and their discussion of the positive benefits of anthropomorphism [see Section 2], Haraway values non-anthropomorphic ways to think about actors in interaction. She concludes with a discussion of the Canine Diversity Project's Species Survival Plan (a program that involves "a long list of companion species," such as specialist groups, databases, and the endangered animals themselves) designed to resolve the problem of canine genetic disease. Haraway argues that the breeders' discourse does not match the discourses of genetic diversity, technoscience, and the Species Survival Plan – genetic diversity does not fit well with increased homogenization and standardization.

COMPANION SPECIES

Dramatis Personae

In United States English, "companion animal" is a recent category, linked to the medical and psycho-sociological work done in veterinary schools and related sites from the middle 1970s (Beck and Katcher 1996). This is the research that told us that, except for non-dog-loving New Yorkers who worry to excess about uns-cooped dog shit in the streets, having a dog (or, *in extremis,* a cat or even a hamster) lowers one's blood pressure and ups one's chances of surviving childhood, surgery, and divorce. Certainly, written references in European languages to animals serving as companions, rather than as working or sporting dogs, for example, predates this biomedical, technoscientific literature by centuries. However, "companion animal" enters technoculture through the land-grant academic institutions housing the vet schools. That is, "companion animal" has the pedigree of the mating between technoscientific expertise and late industrial pet-keeping practices, with their democratic masses in love with their domestic partners, or at least with the nonhuman ones. Companion animals can be horses, dogs, cats, or a range of other beings willing to make the leap from pet or lab beast to the biosociality of service dogs, family members, or team members in cross-species sports. Generally speaking, one does not eat one's companion animals (nor get eaten by them); and one has a hard time shaking colonialist, ethnocentric, ahistorical attitudes to those who do.

"Companion species" is a much bigger and more heterogeneous category than companion animal, and not just because one must start including such organic beings as rice, bees, tulips, and intestinal flora, all of whom make life for humans what it is – and vice versa. I want to rewrite the keyword entry for "companion species" to insist on four tones simultaneously resonating in the linguistic, historical voice box that makes uttering this term possible. First, as a dutiful daughter of Darwin, I insist on the tones of the history of evolutionary biology, with its key categories of populations, rates of gene flow, variation, selection, and biological species. All of the debates in the last 150 years about whether the category denotes a real biological entity or merely figures a convenient taxonomic box provide the over- and undertones. Species is about biological kind, and scientific expertise is necessary to that kind of reality. Post-cyborg, what counts as biological kind troubles any previous category of organism. The machinic is internal to the organic and vice versa in irreversible ways. Second, schooled by Thomas Aquinas and other Aristotelians, I remain alert to species as generic philosophical kind and category. Species is about defining difference, rooted in polyvocal fugues of doctrines of cause. Third, with an indelible mark on my soul from a Catholic formation, I hear in species the doctrine of the Real Presence under both species, bread and wine, the transubstantiated signs of the flesh. Species is about the corporeal join of the material and the semiotic in ways unacceptable to the secular Protestant sensibilities of the American academy and to most versions of the human sciences of semiotics. Fourth, converted by Marx and Freud, I hear in species filthy lucre, specie, gold, shit, filth, wealth. In *Love's Body,* Norman O. Brown taught me about the join of Marx and Freud in shit and gold, in specie. I met this join again in modern US dog culture, with its exuberant commodity culture, its vibrant practices of love and desire, its mongrel technologies of purebred subject and object making. Pooper scoopers for me is quite a joke. In sum, "companion species" is about a four-part composition, in which co-constitution, finitude, impurity, and complexity are what is.

WHO'S ON FIRST? AN ACCOUNT OF CO-EVOLUTION[1]

Pleasures and anxieties over beginnings and endings abound in contemporary dog worlds. This should not be surprising when we are awash in millennial discourses. Why shouldn't dogs get in an apocalyptic bark or two? Dog tales demand a serious hearing; they concern the basic *dramatis personae* in the ecological theater and the evolutionary play of rescripted naturecultures in technonatural, biosocial modernity (Hutchinson 1965; Rabinow 1992). This modernity is a living fictional territory; it is always here and now, in the technopresent. With reference to anthropology's late and little-lamented "ethnographic present," the technopresent names the kind of time I experience inside the *New York Times* Science Tuesday section and on the front pages and business pages so attuned to the animation and cessation of NASDAQ. History in the technopresent is Whig time enterprised up (Strathern 1992); i.e., this history is reduced to the vehicle for getting to the technopresent. In the technopresent, beginnings and endings implode, such that the eternal here and now energetically emerges as a gravity well to warp all subjects and objects in its domain. I write this paper suspended in this odd, millennial, American chronicity; but in this dimensionally challenged medium, I sense some code fusions promising another and better story about animals, machines, and people. I sense the emergence of companion species after the departure of possessive individuals and hermetically sealed objects, who will have finally succumbed to their own alien invasion of the earth. In this paper, I want to tell the story of companion species in the context of diversity discourses in US dog worlds.

Evolutionary origin stories are always a good place in US technoscientific worlds to check for the moves of nature and culture on the board game of widely disseminated Western metaphysics and for the players in the current versions of the game. In recent years, the long-running dog-wolf romance has a stirring new series. The origin of dogs might be a humbling chapter in the story of *Homo sapiens,* one that allows for a deeper sense of co-evolution and co-habitation and a reduced exercise of hominid hubris in shaping canine natureculture.

Accounts of the relations of dogs and wolves proliferate, and molecular biologists tell some of the most convincing versions. Robert Wayne and his colleagues at UCLA studied mitochondrial DNA (mtDNA) from 162 North American, European, Asian, and Arabian wolves and from 140 dogs representing 67 breeds, plus a few jackals and coyotes (Vilá et al. 1997). Their analysis of mtDNA control regions concluded that dogs merged uniquely from wolves – and did so much earlier than scenarios based on archaeological data permit. The amount of sequence divergence and the organization of the data into clades support the emergence of dogs more than 100,000 years ago, with very few separate domestication events. Three-quarters of modern dogs belong to one clade; i.e., they belong to a single maternal lineage. The early dates give *Canis familiaris*[2] and *Homo sapiens* roughly the same calendar, so folks walking out of Africa soon met a wolf bitch who would give birth to man's best friends. And, building a genetic trellis – not a tree – as they went, both dogs and people walked back into Africa (Templeton 1999). These have been species more given to multidirectional traveling and consorting than to conquering and replacing, never to return to their old haunts again. No wonder dogs and people share the distinction of being the most well-mixed and globally geographically distributed large-bodied mammals. They shaped each over a long time. Their pedigrees are a proper mess.

Further – in a story familiar from the post-World War II studies of human population gene frequencies that were so important to the early 1950s anti-racist UNESCO statements and to subsequent reforms of physical anthropology and genetics teaching – dog mtDNA haplotypes do not sort out by breed, indicating that breeds have diverse doggish ancestries. "Pure" breeds are an institutional fiction, if one that threatens the health of animals regulated by the story. Variations of many genes and markers within breed exceed variations between populations of dogs and wolves. And, in another lab's study, "greater mtDNA differences appeared within the single breeds of Doberman pinscher or poodle than between dogs and wolves," even while "there is less mtDNA difference between dogs, wolves and coyotes than there is between various ethnic groups of human beings" (Coppinger and Schneider 1995, 33). Genetic difference studies are a high-stakes game, and emphases on similarity or divergence shift with the theoretical bets laid.

Findings from Wayne's lab have been controversial, partly because the mtDNA clock doesn't measure up to the accuracy demanded by Swiss watchmakers. At an International Council for Archaeozoology symposium in 1998 at the University of Victoria, controversy waxed over Wayne's arguments. Relevant to this paper are implications for thinking about agency in dog-human interactions. Wayne argued that to domesticate dogs took a lot of skill, or it would have happened more often. His story bears the scent of the anatomically wolfish hunting dog, and this dog is a man-made hunting tool/weapon. In this version, morphologically differentiated dogs did not show up in the fossil or archaeology record until 12,000–14,000 years ago because their jobs in settled post-hunter-gatherer, paleo-agricultural communities did not develop until then; so they got physically reshaped late in the relationship. People call the shots in both chapters of a story that makes "domestication" a one-sided human "social invention." But archaeozoological expert Susan Crockford, who organized the Victoria symposium, disagreed. She argued that human settlements provided a species-making resource for would-be dogs in the form of garbage middens and – my addition – concentrations of human bodily waste. If wolves could just calm their well-justified fear of *Homo sapiens*, they could feast in ways all too familiar to modern dog people. "Crockford theorizes that in a sense, wild canids domesticated themselves" (Weidensaul 1999, 57; Crockford 2000).

Crockford's argument turns on genes that control rates in early development and on consequent paedomorphogenesis. Both the anatomical and psychological changes in domesticated animals compared to [those of] their wild relatives can be tied to a single potent molecule with stunning effects in early development and in adult life – thyroxine. Those wolves with lower rates of thyroxine production, and so lower titres of the fright/flight adrenaline cocktail regulated by thyroid secretions, could get a good meal near human habitations. If they were really calm, they might even den nearby. The resulting pups who were the most tolerant of their two-legged neighbors might themselves make use of the caloric bonanza and have their own puppies nearby as well. A few generations of this could produce a being remarkably like current dogs, complete with curled tails, a range of jaw types, considerable size variation, doggish coat patterns, floppy ears, and – above all – the capacity to stick around people and forgive almost anything. People would surely figure out how to relate to these handy sanitary engineers and encourage them to join in useful tasks, like herding, hunting, watching kids, and comforting people. In a few decades, wolves-become-dogs would have changed, and that interval is too short for archaeologists to find intermediate forms.

Crockford made use of the 40-year continuing studies of Russian fur foxes, beginning in the 1950s, which have been much in the recent popular science news (Weidensaul 1999; Trut 1999; Belyaev 1969). Unlike domesticated animals, wild farmed foxes vigorously object to their captivity, including their slaughter. In what were originally experiments designed to select tamer foxes for the convenience of the Soviet fur industry, geneticists at the Siberian Institute of Cytology and Genetics found that by breeding the tamest kits from each fox generation – and selecting for nothing else – they quickly got very dog-like animals, complete with non-fox attitudes like preferential affectional bonding with human beings and phenotypes like those of Border Collies.[3] By analogy, wolves on their way to becoming dogs might have selected themselves for tameness. People got in the act when they saw a good thing. With a wink and a nod to problems with my argument, I think it is possible to hybridize Wayne's and Crockford's evolutionary accounts and so shamelessly save my favorite parts of each – an early co-evolution, human-canine accommodation at more than one point in the story, and lots of dog agency in the drama of genetics and co-habitation. First, I imagine that many domestication sequences left no progeny, or offspring blended back into wolf populations outside the range of current scientific sensors. Marginally fearless wolfish dogs could have accompanied hunter-gatherers on their rounds and gotten more than one good meal for their troubles. Denning near seasonally moving humans who follow regular food-getting migration routes seems no odder than denning near year-round settlements. People might have gotten their own fear/aggression endocrine systems to quell murderous impulses toward the nearby canine predators who did garbage detail and refrained from threatening. Paleolithic people stayed in one place longer than wolf litters need to mature, and both humans and wolves reuse their seasonal sites. People might have learned to take things further than the canines bargained for and bring wolf-dog reproduction under considerable human sway. This radical switch in the biopolitics of reproduction might have been in the interests of raising some lineages to accompany humans on group hunts or perform useful tasks for hunter-gatherers besides eating the shit. Paleoagricultural settlement could have been the occasion for much more radical accommodation between the canids and hominids on the questions of tameness, mutual trust, and trainability.

And, above all, on the question of reproduction. It's on this matter that the distinction between dogs and wolves really hinges; molecular genetics may never show enough species-defining DNA differences. Rather, the subtle genetic and developmental biobehavioral changes through which dogs got people to provision their pups might be the heart of the drama of co-habitation. Human baby sitters, not Man-the-Hunter, are the heroes from doggish points of view. Wolves can reproduce independently of humans; dogs cannot. Even Italian feral dogs still need at least a garbage dump (Boitani et al. 1995). As Coppinger and Schneider summarized the case: "In canids with a long maturation period, growth and development are limited by the provisioning capacity of the mother ... Wolves and African hunting dogs solved the pup-feeding problem with packing behavior, in coyotes the male helps, and jackal pairs are assisted by the 'maiden aunt.' The tremendous success of the domestic dog is based on its ability to get people to raise its pups" (1995, 36). People are part of dogs' extended phenotype in their Darwinian, behavioral ecological, reproductive strategies. Pace Richard Dawkins.

Two points emerge from this evolutionary origin story: (1) coevolution makes humans and dogs companion species from "the beginning," but with historically changing and specific sets of interspecies biotechnosocial relations and with agency a mobile and distributed matter; and (2) the fine arts of molecular genetics and hormone biochemistry are indispensable for this account of the agency of nature in the person of dog-wannabe wolves. The latest in sequencing machinery, sampling protocols, and DNA comparison software are crucial to the tale of "nature" making the first moves in a "social" invention. But this nature does not have the shape of the specters from the recent US science and culture wars, where unruly science studies people were accused of arguing that scientists invented nature rather than reported on her in a mood of humble truth-telling. Here, with those worried realist warriors, I am also arguing that hominids did not "invent" nature or culture (wolves become dogs), then or now, but that all of the players emerge in a kind of Whiteheadean concrescence, where none of the actors precede, finished, their interaction. Companion species take shape in interaction. They more than change each other; they co-constitute each other, at least partly. That's the nature of this cat's cradle game. And the ontology of companion species makes room for odd bedfellows – machines; molecules; scientists; hunter-gatherers; garbage dumps; puppies; fox farmers; and randy bitches of all breeds, genders, and species.

I want to use the figure of companion species to do a lot of analytical and associative work. Figures are powerful attractors that collect up the hopes, fears, and interests of collectives. Figures promise to fulfill hopes in a sense related to Christian realism (Auerbach 1953). Companion species are figures of a relational ontology, in which histories matter; i.e., are material, meaningful, processual, emergent, and constitutive. In the past, I have written about cyborgs, and cyborgs are a kind of companion species congeries of organisms and machines located firmly in the Cold War and its offspring. Equally on my mind have been genetically engineered laboratory organisms like OncoMouse™, also companion species tying together many kinds of actors and practices. Dogs and humans as companion species suggest quite different histories and lives, compared to cyborgs and engineered mice, emergent over the whole time of species being for the participants. In much of my own work, I have tried to figure out the consequences for biology and for cultural theory and politics of the implosion of biologics and informatics in post-World War II life sciences. In this implosion, organisms lost their ontological privilege to genomes, those wonderful generators of new wealth, new knowledge, and mutated ways of living and dying. While I take for granted many of the consequences of the implosion of biologics and informatics in shaping ways of being and knowing in the technopresent, I am here attending to a related but different sort of implosion – that of the utterly "natural" and the wholly "technical," where, for example, endangered species in the necessarily managed wilderness wear electronic sensors and live in habitats monitored by satellites as a crucial part of their biological reproductive apparatus. It remains to be seen if this arrangement will be an Evolutionary Stable Strategy (Dawkins 1982), but it has surely become a figure of biosocial modernity. Simply put, biodiversity has become dependent upon high technology in many parts of the world. The physical implosion of the "natural" and the "technical," materially-semiotically speaking, is a normal, everyday, earthly fact in the most biophillic, diversity-committed communities every bit as much as in the most technophillic worlds. And none of it is innocent – or guilty.

Is there a moral to this story? Dogs invented themselves; they are not an invention of humans? Or dogs and people shaped each other in a long and complicated history, where the story of the wannabe dogs taking the first steps

is more convincing than its opposite? If dogs are a human technology, so also is the reverse true, as part of an extended phenotype in a canine sociobiological tale. I like the co-evolution story better than either the version that the dogs did it, or the people did it. It redoes the story of the human place in nature in homely ways that also impact on fortifications between categories of nature and culture.

There are stakes here beyond what we think about dog evolution. The stakes are how we think about liveliness and agency in different worlds. We require a multi-species and a multi-expertise way of doing/thinking worlds and ways of life, and that requires muting the command/communication/control/intelligence idiom of cyborgs.

Companion species are, among other things, a serious feminist matter, right at the heart of the ongoing Western feminist effort to do better than recycling idioms of liberalism and their benefits-maximizing, bounded, and independent selves as archetypes of freedom. Companion species offer a kind of bypass surgery for liberal idioms of both individuals and of diversity. Companion species do this right in the belly of the monster – inside biotechnology and the New World Order, Inc. Genders, breeds, races, lines, species – all the kinds are in play in these narrative morphings, with material-semiotic consequences. This is concrescence from the point of view of the birth of the kennel, in ongoing, relentlessly historical layers of practice, where all the actors and agencies are not human.

BIODIVERSITY GOES TO THE DOGS[4]

Genetic disease is not news to dog people, and perhaps especially purebred dog people. Many breeders and owners – some willingly, some not – have become used to thinking about the genetic difficulties common to their breeds and even about polygenic traits with unknown modes of inheritance and strong environmental and developmental components affecting expression, like canine hip dysplasia. In myriad ways, genetic disease discourse shapes communities of practice for owners, breeders, researchers, dog rescue activists, breed clubs, kennel clubs, journalists, shelter workers, veterinarians, dog sports competitors, and trainers. There is much to say about the fascinating cultures of genetic disease in dogs, but in this paper I want to focus on a much more unsettling topic in purebred dog land: genetic diversity in small populations. First, let us look at why genetic diversity concerns are news – and hard to digest news – for most dog people, in spite of the long history of population genetics and its importance for the modern theory of natural selection and the neo-Darwinian synthesis and its offspring.

Genetic culture for both professionals and non-professionals, especially but not only in the United States, has been strongly shaped by medical genetics. Human genetic disease is the moral, technoscientific, ideological, and financial center of the medical genetic universe. Typological thinking reigns almost unchecked in this universe; and nuanced views of developmental biology, behavioral ecology, and genes as nodes in dynamic and multi-vectorial fields of vital interactions are only some of the crash victims of high-octane medical genetic fuels and gene-jockey racing careers. For my taste, genomes are too much made up of investment opportunities of the "one region-one product" sort, a kind of enterprised-up descendant of the "one gene-one enzyme" principle that proved so fruitful in research. Taken one at a time, genes, especially disease-related genes, induce brain damage in those trying to come to grips with genetic diversity issues and their consequences.

Evolutionary biology, bio-social ecology, population biology, and population genetics (not to mention history of science, political economy, and cultural anthropology) have played a woefully small role in shaping public and professional genetic imaginations, and all too small a role in drawing the big money for genetic research. Considering only dog worlds, my preliminary research turns up millions of dollars in grants going into genetic disease research (even though peanuts compared to dollars for genetic research

in organisms like mice who are conventionally models for human disease; dog genetics gets more money as it is shown that genome homologies across taxonomic divisions make canines ideal for understanding lots of human conditions, e.g., narcolepsy, bleeding disorders, and retinal degeneration), and only a few thousand dollars (and lots of volunteer time from both professionals and lay collaborators) going into canine genetic diversity research.

The emergence since the 1980s of biodiversity discourses, environmentalisms, and sustainability doctrines of every political color on the agendas of myriad NGOs and of First World institutions like the World Bank, the International Union for the Conservation of Nature and Natural Resources (IUCN), and the Organization for Economic Cooperation and Development (OECD), as well as in the Third World, has made a difference in this situation.[5] The notoriously problematic politics and also the compelling naturalcultural complexity of diversity discourses requires a shelf of books, some of which have been written. I think the emergence of genetic diversity concerns in dog worlds only makes sense historically as a wavelet in the set of breakers constituting transnational, globalizing, biological and cultural diversity discourses, in which genes and genomes (and immune systems) are major players. Noticing some of the conditions of emergence of a discourse is not the same thing as reducing its value to ideological stepchild status. Quite the opposite: I am compelled by the irreducible complexity – morally, politically, culturally, and scientifically – of diversity discourses, including those leashed to the genomes and gene pools of purebred dogs and their canine relatives in and out of "nature."

The last few paragraphs are preparation for logging onto the Canine Diversity Project website, www.magma.ca/~kaitlin/diverse.html, owned by Dr. John Armstrong, a lover of Standard and Miniature Poodles and a faculty member in the Department of Biology at the University of Ottawa until his death in the summer of 2001. Armstrong wrote and distributed as widely as possible his analyses of the effects of a popular sire and a particular kennel in Standard Poodles. Also the owner of CANGEN-L, Armstrong conducted collaborative research with dog health and genetics activists to study whether longevity is correlated to the degree of inbreeding. Aiming in its introductory sentence to draw the attention of dog breeders to "the dangers of inbreeding and the overuse of popular sires," the Diversity Project website started in 1997. Used by at least several hundred dog people of several nationalities, in the first three and half months of 2000, the site registered 4,500 logons. I have myself learned a tremendous amount from this website; I appreciate the quality of information, the controversies engaged, the evident care for dogs and people, the range of material, and the commitments to issues I am concerned with. I am also professionally acutely alert to the semiotics – the meaning-making machinery – of the Canine Diversity Project website.

Animated by a mission, the site draws its users into its reform agenda at every turn.[6] Some of the rhetorical devices are classical American tropes rooted in old popular self help practices and evangelical Protestant witness, devices so ingrained in US culture that few users would be conscious of their history. For example, right after the introductory paragraph with the initial link terms, the Diversity Project website leads its users into a section called, "How You Can Help." The question the visitor confronts is like that used in advertising and in preaching – Have you been saved? Have you taken the Immune Power pledge? (slogan from an ad for a vitamin formulation in the 1980s). Or, as the Diversity Project puts the query, "Ask the Question – Do you need a *Breed Survival Plan?*" This is the stuff of subject-reconstituting, conversion and conviction discourse (Harding 1999).

The first four highlighted linkage words in the opening paragraphs of the website are "popular sires," a common term for many years in purebred dog talk about the overuse of certain stud dogs and the consequent spreading of genetic disease; "Species Survival Plans," a term that makes a new link for dog breeders to zoos and the preservation of endangered species; "wild

cousins," which places dogs with their taxonomic kin and reinforces considering purebreds within the family of natural (in the sense of "wild"), and frequently endangered, species; and "inherited disease," firmly in last place on the list and of concern primarily because a high incidence of double autosomal recessives for particular diseases is an index of lots of homozygosity in purebred dog genomes. Such high incidences of double recessives are certainly related to excessive in- and line breeding, which are diversity-depleting practices. But, as I read it, the soul of the website is the value of diversity for itself in the semiotic framework of evolutionary biology, biodiversity, and biophilia (Wilson 1988; 1992), not diversity as an instrument for solving the problem of genetic disease. Of course, these two values are not mutually exclusive; indeed, they are complementary. But priority matters. In that sense, "breeds" become like endangered species, inviting all the wonderful apparatus we have become familiar with in wildlife biology at the turn of the millennium.

The web site is constructed as a teaching instrument; it constructs its principal audience as engaged lay breeders and other committed dog people. These are the subjects invited to declare for a breed survival plan. Secondarily, scientists of whatever specialty might learn from using the site, but scientists are more teachers here than they are researchers or students. Nonetheless, there are plenty of trading zones and boundary objects linking lay and professional communities of practice in this very inviting site. Further, the nature of a website, as opposed to many other writing technologies (King forthcoming), resists reduction to single purposes and dominating tropes. Links lead many places, and these paths are explored by users, within the webs initially spun by designers, to be sure, but rapidly spiraling out of the control of any designer, no matter how broad minded. The Internet is hardly infinitely open, but its degrees of semiotic freedom are many.

"Popular sires" is sufficiently recognized that the linking term would appeal to the tender-footed neophyte thinking about genetic diversity.

For one thing, the link stays with dogs as the principal focus of attention, and does not launch the user into a universe of marvelous creatures in exotic habitats whose utility as models for dogs is hard to swallow for many breeders, even those interested in such non-dog organisms and ecologies in other contexts. "Species Survival Plans," on the other hand, open up controversial metaphoric and practical universes for breeders of purebred dogs and, if taken seriously, would require major changes in ways of thinking and acting.[7] The first obvious point is that "survival plans" connote that something is endangered. The line between a secular crisis and a sacred apocalypse is a very thin one in US American discourse, where millennial matters are written into the fabric of the national imagination from the first Puritan City on a Hill to *Star Trek* and its sequelae. The second obvious point is that the prominent role given to species survival plans on the Canine Diversity Project website invites a reproductive tie between natural species and purebred dogs. This is one of those ties where the natural and the technical keep close company, semitotically and materially.

To illustrate this point, I will dwell on the material on my screen after I click on "Species Survival Plan" and follow up with a click on "Introduction to a Species Survival Plan." I am teleported to the website for the Tiger Information Center; and, appreciating a face-front photo of two imposing tigers crossing a stream, I am presented with a paper on "Regional and Global Management of Tigers," by R. Tilson, K. Taylor-Holzer, and G. Brady. Now, I know lots of dog people love cats, contrary to popular stereotypes about folks being either canine or feline in their affections. But tigers in zoos around the world and in shrunken "forest patches spread from India across China to the Russian Far East and south to Indonesia" is a leap out of the kennel and the show ring or herding trials. I learn that three of the eight recognized subspecies of tigers are already extinct, a fourth on the brink, and all the wild populations stressed. Ideally, the goal of a SSP masterplan for an endangered species is, out of existing animals in zoos and some new

"founders" brought in from "nature," to create viable, managed, captive populations to maintain as much of the genetic diversity for all the extant taxa of the species as possible. The purpose is to provide a genetic reservoir for the reinforcement or reconstitution of wild populations where necessary and possible. A practical SSP, "because of space limitations generally targets 90% of genetic diversity of the wild populations for 100–200 years as a reasonable goal." I am in love with the hopefulness of that kind of reasonableness. The "Zoo Ark" for the tigers, lamentably, has to be more modest because the resources are too few and the needs too great. An SSP is a complex, cooperative management program of the American Zoo and Aquarium Association (AZA).

What does developing and implementing a SSP involve? The short answer is – a long list of companion species of organic, organizational, and technological kinds. A minimum account of such companion species must include: the World Conservation Union's specialist groups who make assessments of endangerment; member zoos, with their scientists, keepers, and boards of governors; a small Management Group under the AZA; a database maintained as a Regional Studbook, using specialized software like SPARKS (Single Population and Records Keeping System) and its companion programs for demographic and genetic analysis, produced by the International Species Information System; funders; national governments; international bodies; and, hardly least, the animals in danger. Crucial operations within a SSP are measurements of diversity and relatedness. One wants to know Founder Importance Coefficients (FIC) as a tool for equalizing relative founder contributions and minimizing inbreeding. Full and accurate pedigrees are precious objects for an SSP. Mean Kinship (MK) and Kinship Values (KV) rule mate choice in this sociobiological system. "Reinforcing" wild species requires a global apparatus of technoscientific production, where the natural and the technical have very high coefficients of semiotic and practical inbreeding.[8]

Purebred dog breeders also value deep pedigrees, and they are accustomed to evaluating matings with regard to breed standards, which is a complex, non-formulaic art. Inbreeding is not a new concern. So what is so challenging about a SSP as a universe of reference? The definition of populations and founders is perhaps first. Discussions among engaged breeders on CANGEN – i.e., people sufficiently interested in questions of genetic diversity to sign on and post to a specialized Internet mailing list – show that dog people's "lines" and "breeds" are not equivalent terms to wildlife biologists' and geneticists' "populations." The behavior properly associated with these different words is quite different. A dog breeder educated in the traditional mentoring practices of the fancy will attempt through line breeding, with variable frequencies of outcrosses, to maximize the genetic/blood contribution of the truly "great dogs," who are rare and special. The great dogs are the individuals who best embody the type of the breed. The type is not a fixed thing, but a living, imaginative hope and memory. Kennels often are recognized for the distinctiveness of their dogs, and breeders point proudly to their kennel's own founders, and breed club documents to the breed's founders. The notion of working to equalize the contribution of all of the founders in the population geneticists' sense is truly odd in traditional dog breeders' discourse. Of course, a SSP, unlike nature and unlike dog breeders, is not operating with adaptational selectional criteria; the point of a SSP is to preserve diversity as such as a reservoir. Small populations are subject to intense extinction pressures – loss of habitat, fragmented subpopulations no longer able to exchange genetic material, loss of genes through the random process called genetic drift, crisis events causing population crashes like famines or diseases, and on and on.

The SSP is a conservation management plan, not nature, however conceptualized, and not a breed's written standard or an individual breeder's interpretation of that standard. Like a SSP, a breed standard is also a kind of large-scale action blueprint, but for other purposes. Some breeders

talk of those purposes in capital letters, as the Original Purpose of a given breed. Others are not typological in that sense and are attuned to dynamic histories and evolving goals within a partly shared sense of breed history, structure, and function. These breeders are keenly aware of the need for selection on the basis of many criteria as holistically as possible to maintain and improve a breed's overall quality and to achieve the rare special dogs. They take these responsibilities very seriously; and they are not virgins to controversy, contradiction, and failure. They are not against learning about genetic diversity in the context of the problems they know or suspect their dogs face. Some breeders – a very few, I think – embrace genetic diversity discourse and population genetics. They worry that the foundation of their breeds might be too narrow and getting narrower. But the breeder's art does not easily entertain adopting the heavily mathematical and software-driven mating systems of a SSP. I witness in my research several courageous breeders insisting on deeper pedigrees and regular calculations of coefficients of inbreeding, with efforts to hold them down where possible. But the breeders I overhear are loathe to cede decisions to anything like a master plan. In my judgment, they do not see their own dogs or their breed primarily as biological populations. The dominance of specialists over local and lay communities in the SSP world does not escape dog breeders' attention. Most of the breeders whom I overhear squirm if the discussion stays on a theoretical population genetics level and if few if any of the data come from dogs, rather than, say, a Malagasy lemur population or lab-bound mouse strain. In short, breeders' discourse and genetic diversity discourse do not hybridize smoothly, at least in the F1 generation. This mating is what I hear breeders call a "cold outcross" that they worry risks importing as many problems as it solves.

There is much more to the Canine Diversity Project website than the SSP links, and if I had the space to examine the rich texture of the whole web site, many more sorts of openings, repulsions, inclusions, attractions, and possibilities would be evident for seeing the ways dog breeders, health activists, veterinarians, and geneticists relate to the question of diversity. At the very least, the serious visitor to the website could get a decent elementary education in genetics, including Mendelian, medical, and population genetics. Fascinating collaborations between individual scientists and breed club health and genetics activists would emerge. The differences within dog people's ways of thinking about genetic diversity and inbreeding would be inescapable, as the apocalyptic and controversial Jeffrey Bragg's "evolving breeds" and Seppala Siberian Sled Dogs meet John Armstrong's more modest Standard Poodles (and his more moderate action plan, "Genetics for Breeders: How to Produce Healthier Dogs") or Leos Kraal's and C. A. Sharp's ways of working in Australian Shepherd worlds. Links would take the visitor to the extraordinary Code of Ethics of the Coton de Tulear Club of America and this breed's alpha-male geneticist activist, Robert Jay Russell, as well as to the online documents with which the Border Collie website teaches genetics relevant to that fascinating breed. The visitor could follow links to the molecular evolution of the dog family, updated lists of current DNA gene tests in dogs, discussions of wolf conservation and wolf taxonomic debates, accounts of a cross-breeding (to a Pointer) and backcross project in Dalmatians to eliminate a common genetic disease and of importing new African stock in Basenjis to deal with genetic dilemmas. One could click one's way to discussions of infertility, stress, and herpes infections, or follow links to endocrine disrupter discourse for thinking about how environmental degradation might be affecting dogs, as well as frogs and people, globally. Right in the middle of the Diversity Project website is a bold-type invitation to join the mailing list Armstrong ran until his death, the Canine Genetics Discussion Group (CANGEN-L), where a sometimes rough and tumble exchange among heterogeneous lay and professional dog people stirred up the pedagogical order of the website.

So dogs, not tigers – and breeds, not endangered species – actually dominate on the Canine Diversity Project website. But the metaphoric, political, and practical possibilities of those first links to Species Survival Plans attach themselves like well positioned ticks on a nice blade of grass, waiting for a passing visitor from purebred dog land. Frontline defenses are not always enough.[9] We are in the fiercely local and linked global zones of technobiopolitics, where few species are more than a click away. Naturalcultural survival is the prize.

NOTES

1. The dog-human co-evolution story below is slightly revised from "For the Love of a Good Dog: Webs of Action in the World of Dog Genetics," Haraway 2003a.

2. Recent taxonomic revisions make dogs into a subspecies of wolves, *Canis lupens familiaris,* rather than into a species of their own, *Canis familiaris.* This technical issue has multiple consequences beyond the scope of this paper. See Coppinger and Coppinger 2001, 273–282. For a critique of Vilá et al.'s dating of dog evolution from mtDNA data, see Coppinger and Coppinger 2001, 283–294.

3. Like much in the former USSR, this trickster drama of worker safety, industrial efficiency, and evolutionary theory and genetics in the far north devolved in the post-Cold-War economic order. Since the salaries of the scientists at the Genetics Institute have not been paid, much of the breeding stock of tame foxes has been destroyed. The scientists scramble to save the rest – and fund their research – by marketing them in the West as pets with characteristics between dogs and cats. A sad irony is that if the geneticists and their foxes succeed in surviving in this enterprise culture, the population of remaining animals bred for the international pet trade will have been genetically depleted by the slaughter necessitated by the rigors of post-Soviet capitalism and commercializing the animals not for fur coats but as pets. Note also the tones of the Lysenko affair in the story of the evolution of tame Soviet foxes.

4. The section on biodiversity in dogland below is drawn from an earlier version of parts of "Cloning Mutts, Saving Tigers: Ethical Emergents in Technocultural Dogland," in Franklin and Lock, 2003.

5. See for example *World Conservation Strategy,* IUCN, 1980; the Bruntland Report, *Our Common Future,* WECD, 1987; Agenda 21; Convention on Biodiversity, 1992; Guiding Principles on Forests; *Valuing Nature's Services,* WorldWatch Institute Report of Progress toward a Sustainable Society, 1997; *Investing in Biological Diversity,* Cairns Conference. OECD, 1997; *Saving Biological Diversity: Economic Incentives,* OECD, 1996.

6. I am using a version of the website online in 2000.

7. The Rare Breed Survival Trust in the UK (mainly for poultry, sheep, pigs, cattle, and other "farm livestock heritage" animals not usually thought of as either companion animal – especially not as "pets" – or wild animals, including the working collie dogs that the Trust attends to), and its journal *The Ark,* would repay close attention in relation to action in dog worlds. Thanks to Sarah Franklin and Thelma Rowell for handing me into *The Ark.*

8. SSP is a North American term. Europeans have European Endangered Species Programs (EESPs); Australasians have Australasian Species Management Programs, and China, Japan, India, Thailand, Malaysia, and Indonesia all have their own equivalents. This is global science of indigenous species.

9. Information for those whose lives are not ruled by real ticks and real dogs: Frontline™ is a new-generation tick and flea control product that has made dogs' and dog people's lives much less irritable.

REFERENCES

Auerbach, Eric. 1953. *Mimesis: The Representation of Reality in Western Literature.* Princeton, NJ: Princeton University Press.

Beck, Alan, and Aaron Katcher. 1996. *Between Pets and People: The Importance of Animal Companionship.* 2nd edn. West Lafayette, Ind.: Purdue University Press.

Belyaev, D.K. 1969. "Domestication of Animals," *Science Journal,* UK 5, 47–52.

Boitani, L., F. Francisci, P. Ciucci, and G. Andreoli. 1995. "Population Biology and Ecology of Feral Dogs in Central Italy." In Serpell, ed., 217–244.

Brown, Norman O. 1966. *Love's Body.* New York: Random House.

Coppinger, Raymond, and Lorna Coppinger. 2001. *Dogs: A Startling New Understanding of Canine Origin, Behavior, and Evolution.* New York: Scribner.

Coppinger, Raymond, and Richard Schneider. 1995. "Evolution of Working Dogs." In Serpell, 21–47.

Crockford, Susan J. 2000. "Dog Evolution: A Role for Thyroid Hormone Physiology in Domestication Changes." In *Dogs through Time: An Archaeological Perspective,* edited by S. Crockford, 11–20. Oxford: BAR International Series 889.

Dawkins, Richard. 1982. *The Extended Phenotype: The Gene as a Unit of Selection.* London: Oxford University Press.

Franklin, Sarah and Margaret Lock, eds. 2003. *Remaking Life and Death.* Santa Fe, NM: SAR Press.

Haraway, Donna. 2003a. "For the Love of a Good Dog: Webs of Action in the World of Dog Genetics." In *Race, Nature, and the Politics of Difference,* edited by Donald Moore. Durham, NC: Duke University Press, 254–295.

Haraway, Donna. 2003b. "Cloning Mutts, Saving Tigers: Ethical Emergents in Technocultural Dogland." In Franklin and Lock.

Harding, Susan. 1999. *The Book of Jerry Falwell.* Princeton, NJ: Princeton University Press.

Hutchinson, George Evelyn. 1965. *The Ecological Theater and the Evolutionary Play.* New Haven: Yale University Press.

King, Katie. forthcoming. *Feminism and Writing Technologies.* Manuscript, University of Maryland at College Park.

Rabinow, Paul. 1992. "Artificiality and Enlightenment: From Sociobiology to Biosociality." In *Incorporations,* edited by J. Crary and S. Kwinter, 234–252. New York: Zone Books.

Serpell, James, ed. 1995. *The Domestic Dog: Its Evolution, Behaviour, and Interactions with People.* Cambridge: Cambridge University Press.

Strathern, Marilyn. 1992. *Reproducing the Future: Anthropology, Kinship, and the New Reproductive Technologies.* New York: Routledge.

Templeton, Alan. 1999. "Human Race in the Context of Human Evolution: A Molecular Perspective." Paper for the Wenner Gren Foundation Conference on Anthropology in the Age of Genetics, June 11–19, Teresopolis, Brazil.

Trut, Lyudamila N. 1999. March/April. "Early Canid Domestication: The Fox-Farm Experiment." *American Scientist* 87 (March/April), 160–169.

Vilá, Carles, Peter Savolainen, Jesús E. Maldonado, Isabel R. Amorim, John E. Rice, Rodney L. Honeycutt, Keith A. Crandall, Joakim Lundeberg, and Robert K. Wayne. 1997. "Multiple and Ancient Origins of the Domestic Dog," *Science* 276 (June 13), 1687–1689.

Weidensaul, Scott. 1999. "Tracking America's First Dogs," *Smithsonian Magazine,* March 1, 44–57.

Whitehead, Alfred North. 1948. *Science and the Modern World.* New York: Mentor; orig. 1925.

Whitehead, Alfred North. 1969. *Process and Reality.* New York: Free Press; orig. 1929.

Wilson, E. O. 1992. *The Diversity of Life.* New York and London: W. W. Norton.

Wilson, E. O. ed. 1988. *Biodiversity.* Washington, DC: National Academy Press.

FURTHER READING IN ANIMALS AS SCIENTIFIC OBJECTS

Gordon, Andrew H. and Calvin Schwabe. 2004. *The Quick and the Dead: Biomedical Theory in Ancient Egypt*. Leiden: Brill.Styx.

Greek, C. Ray and Jean Swingle Greek. 2004. *Sacred Cows and Golden Geese: The Human Cost of Experiments on Animals*. Continuum International Publishing Group.

Green, Alan. 1999. *Animal Underworld: Inside America's Black Market for Rare and Exotic Species*. New York: Public Affairs/Perseus Book Group.

Guerrini, Anita. 2003. *Experimenting with Humans and Animals: From Galen to Animal Rights*. Johns Hopkins Introductory Studies in the History of Science. Baltimore, MD: Johns Hopkins University Press.

Haraway, Donna. 1989. *Primate Visions: Gender, Race, and Nature in the World of Modern Science*. New York: Routledge.

Haraway, Donna J. 1997. *Modest_Witness@Second_ Millennium.FemaleMan©_Meets_OncoMouse™* . New York: Routledge.

Haraway, Donna. 2003. *The Companion Species Manifesto: Dogs, People, and Significant Otherness*. Chicago: Prickly Paradigm Press.

Isenberg, Andrew C. 2000. *The Destruction of the Bison: An Environmental History, 1750–1920*. New York: Cambridge University Press.

Kellert, Stephen R. 1996. *The Value of Life: Biological Diversity and Human Society*. Washington, DC: Island Press.

LaFollette, Hugh and Niall Shanks. 1996. *Brute Science: Dilemmas of Animal Experimentation*. Oxford: Routledge.

Lynch, Michael. 1988. Sacrifice and the Transformation of the Animal Body into a Scientific Object: Laboratory Culture and Ritual Practice in the Neurosciences. *Social Studies of Science* 18: 265–289.

Michael, Mike. 1996. *Constructing Identities: The Social, the Nonhuman, and Change*. London: Sage.

Philo, Chris and Chris Wilbert (eds.). 2000. *Animal Spaces, Beastly Places: New Geographies of Human-Animal Relations*. London: Routledge.

Rollin, Bernard E. 1995. *The Frankenstein Syndrome: Ethical and Social Issues in the Genetic Engineering of Animals*. Cambridge: Cambridge University Press.

Rupke, N. (ed.) 1987. *Vivisection in Historical Perspective*. New York: Croom Helm.

Scarce, Rik. 1999. *Fishy Business: Salmon, Biology and the Social Construction of Nature*. Philadelphia: Temple University Press.

Shapiro, Kenneth. 1998. *Animal Models of Human Psychology*. Cambridge, MA: Hogrefe & Huber.

Thompson, Paul B. 1997. Ethics and Genetic Engineering of Food Animals. *Journal of Agricultural and Environmental Ethics* 10(1), 1–23.

Wolch, Jennifer and Jody Emel (eds.). 1998. *Animal Geographies: Place, Politics, and Identity in the Nature-Culture Borderlands*. London: Verso

INDEX